Taming the Megabanks

Taming the Megabanks

Why We Need a New Glass-Steagall Act

Arthur E. Wilmarth, Jr.

OXFORD
UNIVERSITY PRESS

OXFORD
UNIVERSITY PRESS

Oxford University Press is a department of the University of Oxford. It furthers the University's objective of excellence in research, scholarship, and education by publishing worldwide. Oxford is a registered trade mark of Oxford University Press in the UK and certain other countries.

Published in the United States of America by Oxford University Press
198 Madison Avenue, New York, NY 10016, United States of America.

© Oxford University Press 2020

Library of Congress Cataloging-in-Publication Data
Names: Wilmarth, Arthur E., 1951– author.
Title: Taming the megabanks : why we we need a new Glass-Steagall Act /
Arthur E. Wilmarth, Jr.
Description: New York : Oxford University Press, 2020. |
Includes bibliographical references and index.
Identifiers: LCCN 2020007759 (print) | LCCN 2020007760 (ebook) |
ISBN 9780190260705 (hardback) | ISBN 9780190260729 (epub)
Subjects: LCSH: Universal banks. | Banks and banking, International. |
Banking law. | Securities. | Organizational change.
Classification: LCC HG1601 .W465 2020 (print) |
LCC HG1601 (ebook) | DDC 332.1—dc23
LC record available at https://lccn.loc.gov/2020007759
LC ebook record available at https://lccn.loc.gov/2020007760

3 5 7 9 8 6 4 2

Printed by Sheridan Books, Inc., United States of America

Contents

Acknowledgments and Note on Statistics

I first became interested in the Glass-Steagall Act as a young banking lawyer in the early 1980s. Big banks had recently launched a legislative campaign to repeal Glass-Steagall, as described in Chapter 8. To find out more about Glass-Steagall, I read the U.S. Supreme Court's landmark decision in *Investment Company Institute v. Camp*, 401 U.S. 617 (1971). That decision (discussed in Chapter 7) struck down a federal agency's attempt to open a loophole in the Glass-Steagall Act. The Supreme Court's detailed analysis of Glass-Steagall's historical background and underlying purposes made a great deal of sense to me. I concluded that the big banks' campaign to repeal Glass-Steagall was contrary to prudent banking standards and sound economic policies. My study of the financial industry and its regulation over the past four decades has affirmed and strengthened that conclusion.

I am deeply indebted to many people who generously supported and encouraged my work on this book. The following friends and colleagues read substantial portions of the manuscript and provided very helpful comments: Lawrence Baxter, Bill Black, Brooks Bowen, Naomi Cahn, June Carbone, Don Clarke, Ryan Clements, Peter Conti-Brown, John Crawford, Mark Extein, Erik Gerding, Bruce Grohsgal, Tom Hoenig, Kate Judge, Dennis Kelleher, Jeremy Kress, Paul Mahoney, Lev Menand, Jeremy Pam, Chris Peterson, Morgan Ricks, Dick Ruffin, David Schroeder, Sunil Sharma, Ganesh Sitaraman, Marcus Stanley, John Sturc, Jennifer Taub, Andrew Tuch, Tom Weil, and Bob Wingert. I received highly valuable feedback from participants in conferences and workshops at the Law Schools of George Washington, Tulane, and Vanderbilt Universities and the Association of American Law Schools, as well as my students in a reading group course that reviewed the manuscript. Pat McCoy, Bob Tuttle, and two anonymous reviewers very generously read the final manuscript and shared wonderful insights that helped me to improve the clarity, organization, and persuasiveness of the book.

Morgan Ricks (and his book *The Money Problem*) provided the intellectual foundation for this book's proposal to prohibit nonbanks from issuing short-term financial claims that function as deposit substitutes (shadow deposits). That proposal—which would fulfill the original purpose of Section 21 of the Glass-Steagall Act—would greatly shrink the shadow banking system and prevent nonbanks from gaining unfair competitive advantages over regulated banks. It would also enable the Federal Reserve System to regain effective control over our nation's monetary policy, as explained in the Conclusion.

GW Law School generously provided summer research grants that supported my work on this book. Germaine Leahy, the Head of Reference for the Jacob Burns Law Library, provided outstanding research assistance. I also received excellent help from my student research assistants over the past three decades. Their assistance is acknowledged individually in my articles included in the list of references. I am deeply grateful to my editors at Oxford University Press—James Cook, Macey Fairchild, and Scott Parris—for their many contributions to the book. I am very thankful to Narayanan Srinivisan, the project manager for this book, and Susan Warga, the copy editor, whose skill and diligence corrected a number of technical errors in the manuscript.

I owe a very special debt of gratitude to my wife, Ellen, and my daughter, Megan, for their love, support, and encouragement. This book is dedicated to them—and also to the memory of my parents, who instilled in me a love of learning, provided me a wonderful education, and showed me what it means to live a life of love, integrity, and service to others.

Unless otherwise indicated, this book includes developments through January 31, 2020. Most of the statistics in the book are presented on a nominal (non-inflation-adjusted) basis. It is not an easy matter to determine how "inflation" should be measured for statistics related to banks and financial markets. If inflation is based simply on the rise in the Consumer Price Index, $1 in 1930 would be equal to about $2.20 in 1970, $5 in 1980, $8 in 1990, $10 in 2000, $13 in 2010, and $15 in 2019.[1]

The results are very different if one considers the growth of total U.S. private sector and public sector debts as a more realistic measure of "inflation" in U.S. financial markets. That approach seems plausible, as most private and public debts are funded through financial intermediaries. I therefore believe that the growth of domestic private and public debts provides a reasonably good proxy for "inflation" in U.S. financial markets. Under that approach, $1 in 1930 would be equal to about $8.60 in 1970, $25 in 1980, $75 in 1990, $150 in 2000, $290 in 2010, and $390 in 2019.[2] In my view, those figures provide a more accurate reflection of the stunning—and many would say disturbing—growth of the U.S. financial industry during the past four decades.

Introduction

Those who cannot remember the past are condemned to repeat it.

George Santayana[1]

The financial crisis of 2007–09 caused the Great Recession, the most severe global economic downturn since the Great Depression. The financial crisis began with the collapse of the subprime mortgage market in the U.S. in 2007 and spread to financial markets around the world. Similarly, the financial disasters that led to the Great Depression began with the crash of October 1929 on Wall Street and swept through the U.S. and much of the rest of the world during the early 1930s.[2]

This book demonstrates that universal banks played leading roles in causing the financial crises that led to the Great Depression and the Great Recession. Universal banks are large financial conglomerates that engage in a broad range of businesses.[3] Those businesses include traditional banking activities (such as deposit-taking and lending) and nontraditional capital markets activities (such as securities underwriting and trading).[4]

As described in Chapter 1, universal banks emerged in the U.S. during the late nineteenth century. Large commercial banks took advantage of new opportunities to expand into securities underwriting and trading—businesses that were previously controlled by private investment banks (securities firms). Several leading commercial banks formed universal banking organizations and became important participants in U.S. securities markets by 1910. Universal banks were highly successful in selling war bonds during World War I, and they greatly expanded their securities activities after the war.

During the 1920s, as explained in Chapters 2 and 3, universal banks competed aggressively with private investment banks in arranging risky domestic and foreign loans. Universal and investment banks packaged those loans into bonds, which they sold to investors in America and around the world. Universal and investment banks also competed in underwriting and selling speculative stocks to American and overseas investors. The intense rivalry between universal and investment banks during the 1920s produced an unsustainable credit boom and a hazardous stock market bubble.

Universal and investment banks assumed large risk exposures in the securities and real estate markets by making investments and loans that supported their securities underwriting and trading operations. As discussed in Chapter 4, U.S. securities and real estate markets collapsed after the crash of October 1929, inflicting grievous losses on heavily indebted borrowers, highly leveraged investors, and overly aggressive banks. The plummeting values of securities and real estate after 1929 triggered widespread loan defaults, caused steep drops in consumption by households and investment by businesses, and destroyed millions of jobs, thereby paving the way for the Great Depression.

As described in Chapter 5, financial upheavals in the U.S. quickly spread to Europe and Latin America, where many governments and businesses depended on loans from American banks. Universal and investment banks financed those loans by selling foreign bonds to American and overseas investors during the 1920s. Large-scale transfers of credit from U.S. banks and investors to European and Latin American borrowers ended when the foreign bond market shut down in 1930.

The sudden cutoff of credit flows from U.S. banks and investors triggered systemic banking crises in Austria, Germany, and other European nations. Universal banks dominated the financial systems of most European countries, and failures of universal banks precipitated the worst European crises. Similarly, a dozen leading U.S. universal banks either failed or received bailouts during a series of crises that devastated the U.S. banking system between November 1930 and March 1933. Universal banks in the U.S. and Europe were highly vulnerable to systemic crises because problems in securities markets and the general economy quickly spilled over into the investment and loan portfolios of universal banks.

In contrast, the United Kingdom (U.K.) and Canada did not experience systemic banking crises during the Great Depression. The structural separation of commercial banks from securities markets in Britain and Canada was a major factor that helped to explain why the banking systems of both countries were far more resilient during the Great Depression.[5]

As described in Chapter 6, Congress responded to the Great Depression by passing the Glass-Steagall Banking Act of 1933. The Glass-Steagall Act broke up universal banks to prevent a recurrence of the speculative boom-and-bust cycle that led to the Great Depression. Banks were forced to divest their securities activities, and nonbanks were prohibited from accepting deposits. The Glass-Steagall Act also established a new federal deposit insurance system, which greatly reduced the threat of bank failures due to depositor runs.

The Glass-Steagall Act made the U.S. financial system more stable and less vulnerable to contagion because it protected bank deposits and divided the financial system into separate sectors with clearly defined legal boundaries. The statute also sought to eliminate the destructive conflicts of interest and perverse incentives for excessive risk-taking that universal banks displayed during the 1920s, when they sold risky bonds and speculative stocks to unsophisticated, poorly informed investors. Glass-Steagall's supporters believed that banks could not act as prudent, objective lenders or as impartial investment advisers if they were allowed to underwrite and trade in securities (except for government bonds).

The Glass-Steagall Act and related statutes created a decentralized U.S. financial system consisting of three separate, independent, and culturally distinct sectors. Commercial banks accepted deposits, made loans, and provided trust (wealth management) services to consumers and businesses. Securities firms underwrote debt and equity securities, which provided longer-term financing to business enterprises. Insurance companies protected consumers and businesses from various types of risks in exchange for the payment of premiums.

Glass-Steagall's system of segmented financial sectors prospered from the end of World War II through the 1970s, as explained in Chapter 7. During that period, no major financial crisis occurred, even though the financial system faced significant challenges from rising inflation rates. An important reason for that era's financial stability was that problems occurring in one sector of the financial system were much less likely to have contagious spillover effects on other sectors. Regulators could address financial disruptions with targeted responses that did not require massive bailouts of the entire financial system. In addition, regulators could mobilize financial institutions in one sector to help troubled institutions in another sector.[6]

Despite Glass-Steagall's successful record, the largest U.S. banks and their supporters waged a determined campaign to break down the legal barriers that prevented banks from engaging in securities and insurance activities. During the 1980s and 1990s, as described in Chapter 7, federal agencies and courts issued rulings that opened loopholes in Glass-Steagall's barriers. Large U.S. banks used those rulings to conduct a widening array of securities and insurance activities. Conversely, the biggest securities firms became "shadow banks," as regulators allowed them to offer short-term financial instruments, including money market mutual funds and securities repurchase agreements (repos). As a practical matter, those financial instruments allowed holders to obtain repayment at par (100% of the amount invested) on demand and thus functioned as deposit substitutes.

As discussed in Chapter 8, the largest U.S. banks persuaded Congress to repeal Glass-Steagall's core provisions in 1999. The repeal of Glass-Steagall allowed banks to establish full-scale affiliations with securities firms and insurance companies. Big U.S. banks quickly reorganized themselves as universal banks. The U.K and the European Union (EU) also deregulated their financial sectors during the 1980s and 1990s. By 2000, universal banks dominated financial markets in the U.S., U.K., and EU.

As explained in Chapters 9 and 10, universal banks played leading roles in the toxic subprime lending boom, which occurred on both sides of the Atlantic and led to the financial crisis of 2007–09. Universal banks packaged trillions of dollars of high-risk mortgages into mortgage-backed securities, which were sold as purportedly "safe" investments to investors around the world. The five largest U.S. securities firms were also major participants in the surge of subprime lending and securitization. Big securities firms became de facto universal banks as they relied on short-term deposit substitutes to fund a growing share of their activities.

The subprime lending and securitization boom of the 2000s displayed many of the conflicts of interest and excessive risk-taking that characterized the credit boom and stock market bubble of the 1920s. The "assembly line" that packaged subprime mortgages into mortgage-backed securities included multiple participants, such as loan brokers, lending institutions, loan servicers, securities underwriters, credit ratings agencies, and issuers of financial guarantees. All of those participants received lucrative fees, which encouraged them to disregard the long-term risks of subprime mortgages and related securities. Universal banks displayed the most pervasive conflicts of interest because they vertically integrated the subprime assembly line to create a unified "soup-to-nuts" process. That highly integrated process allowed universal banks to fulfill multiple roles in the subprime assembly line and to generate the highest possible revenues.

Universal banks paid large fees to induce credit ratings agencies and financial guarantors to ignore their customary standards for evaluating risk. The subprime assembly line created a system of "Ponzi finance" that relied on a continuing stream of credit from lenders and investors to finance ever-growing volumes of subprime mortgages. In turn, that flow of credit depended on the deeply flawed assumption that U.S. housing prices would keep rising, thereby allowing subprime borrowers to refinance their mortgages and avoid defaults.

The flow of credit into subprime mortgages shut down in 2007, when U.S. housing prices began to fall. As described in Chapter 10, the collapse of the subprime mortgage market triggered a wave of defaults by subprime borrowers. Those defaults inflicted huge losses on universal banks, securities firms, and other financial institutions that held large exposures to subprime mortgages and related securities. The demise of the subprime mortgage market precipitated systemic financial and economic crises on both sides of the Atlantic. The boom-and-bust cycle of the 2000s bore a striking and disturbing resemblance to the destructive cycle of the 1920s and early 1930s. Universal banks played leading roles in both cycles, and they were at the epicenter of the calamities that followed.

As explained in Chapter 11, the U.S., U.K., and EU adopted enormous bailout programs to prevent the Great Recession from becoming a second Great Depression. Those nations provided more than $12 trillion of capital infusions, financial guarantees, and emergency loans to stabilize financial markets. They rescued universal banks and large shadow banks, with the prominent exception of Lehman Brothers. They protected holders of short-term financial instruments issued by shadow banks, even though shadow banks were not regulated as banks and the deposit substitutes they issued were not protected by deposit insurance. The U.S., U.K., and EU wrapped their financial safety nets around their entire financial systems, going far beyond their traditional practice of protecting banks and bank depositors.[7]

Governments on both sides of the Atlantic accumulated very heavy debt burdens to rescue their financial sectors and to implement fiscal stimulus programs that mitigated the economic and social effects of the Great Recession. By 2017, ratios of government debt to gross domestic profit (GDP) reached 103% in the U.S., 83% in the U.K., and 88% in the EU. The EU—with the help of the International Monetary Fund (IMF)—barely managed to contain sovereign debt crises in Greece, Ireland, Portugal, and Spain, and to stave off a potential crisis in Italy. Meanwhile, tens of thousands of businesses failed, millions of workers lost their jobs, and millions of families lost their homes.

Central banks cut short-term interest rates to zero and below. Central banks also adopted quantitative easing (QE) programs, which purchased huge amounts of longer-term bonds to push down interest rates, provide relief to debtors, and facilitate the issuance of government bonds with lower yields (and lower costs). The central banks of the U.S., U.K., EU, and Japan expanded their balance sheets from $4 trillion to $15 trillion between 2007 and 2018 by purchasing government bonds, mortgage-backed securities, and other financial assets. The unprecedented scope and impact of unconventional monetary policies triggered widespread concerns that central banks were exceeding their mandates and risking their legitimacy and political independence.[8]

Unlike the Great Depression, the Great Recession did not result in fundamental changes to the financial systems of most developed nations. In 2009, as described in Chapter 12, the U.S. and other members of the Group of 20 (G20) nations agreed on a reform agenda that largely preserved the status quo.[9] Instead of proposing changes to the structure of financial institutions and markets, the G20's agenda recommended technical reforms to improve the effectiveness of financial regulation. Those reforms included higher capital and liquidity requirements for banks and better procedures for handling failures of systemically important financial institutions (including shadow banks).

Congress adopted most of the G20's recommended reforms when it passed the Dodd-Frank Wall Street Reform and Consumer Protection Act of 2010 (Dodd-Frank). The Obama administration and most members of Congress rejected proposals to break up universal banks, and they did not try to bring back the Glass-Steagall Act. The Obama administration opposed "structural" solutions to the problems that caused the financial crisis and instead opted for "technocratic" reforms.[10]

As discussed in Chapter 12, the Obama administration failed to implement several of Dodd-Frank's key mandates before its second term came to an end in January 2017. In addition, the financial industry persuaded Congress and the Trump administration to repeal or weaken a number of Dodd-Frank's reforms by the end of 2019. If President Trump is reelected in 2020, the trend toward deregulation will undoubtedly continue in the U.S.

Similarly, financial reforms in the U.K. and the Eurozone lost most of their momentum after 2017. In October 2018, the IMF stated that "reform fatigue and rollback pressures" were "already visible ... [a]s memories of the global financial crisis fade." A year later, Germany's top bank regulator warned that policymakers were being "pushed into a new cycle of downward regulation," which was "planting the seeds for the next financial crisis."[11]

Universal banks are inherently dangerous because their business model promotes dangerous boom-and-bust cycles. That is true for four reasons. First, universal banks use cheap, government-subsidized deposits to fund risky loans. Second, universal banks package risky loans into asset-backed securities, which are sold as purportedly "safe" investments to poorly informed buyers. The ability to earn lucrative, up-front fees from securitizing risky loans encourages universal banks to pursue reckless lending and securitization strategies.

Third, the combination of deposit-taking, lending, securities underwriting, and trading creates pervasive and toxic conflicts of interest within universal banks. Universal banks have powerful financial incentives to sell—and trade for their own account in—asset-backed securities and other investments that their capital markets units underwrite. Universal banks also have strong reasons to make loans that support their underwriting and trading activities. Those incentives destroy the ability of universal banks to act as objective, prudent lenders and impartial investment advisers.

Fourth, the investment banking units of universal banks almost always produce the banks' dominant culture. The incentive compensation policies of investment banks (securities firms) create a speculative, bonus-driven culture, which encourages universal banks to take excessive risks to produce higher short-term returns.

Thus, conflicts of interest and incentives for excessive risk-taking in universal banks push them to pursue aggressive lending, securities underwriting, and trading strategies. Those strategies are likely to produce highly-leveraged credit booms in financial systems dominated by universal banks.[12] Credit booms are dangerous because they frequently lead to severe busts and prolonged economic recessions. Governments are usually compelled to pay a very high price to contain such busts.[13]

The experiences of the U.S. and U.K. during the Great Depression and the Great Recession illustrate the strong tendency toward destructive boom-and-bust cycles in financial systems dominated by universal banks. Figures 0.1 and 0.2 display the impact of the Great Depression and the Great Recession in the U.S. and the U.K. The left-hand panel of Figure 0.1 shows that the U.S. economy performed badly during the Great Recession and much worse during the Great Depression. U.S. GDP did not return to its pre-Recession (2007) level until four years later, while GDP did not return to its pre-Depression (1929) level until a decade later. Despite the faster recovery from the Great Recession, U.S. GDP remained more than 10% below its pre-Recession trend line in 2016, confirming that the Great Recession had severe and long-lasting effects on the U.S. economy.

The left-hand panel of Figure 0.2 shows the much more aggressive fiscal response of the U.S. government to the Great Recession compared with the Great Depression. The ratio of U.S. government debt to GDP rose at a significantly faster rate after 2007 than it did after 1929, reflecting the massive bailout and stimulus legislation that Congress adopted to limit the financial, economic, and social fallout from the Great Recession. Those emergency measures helped the U.S. to avoid a second Great Depression.

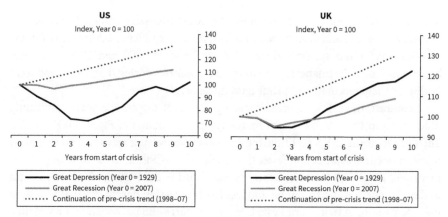

Figure 0.1 Changes in U.S. and U.K. GDP During the Great Depression and Great Recession

Source: Aikman et al. (2018: 40) (chart 1)

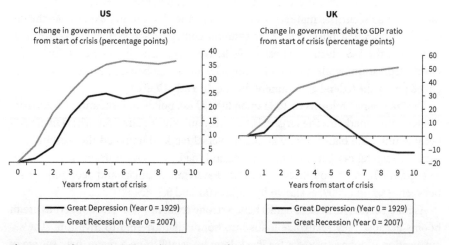

Figure 0.2 Changes in U.S. and U.K. Ratios of Government Debt to GDP During the Great Depression and Great Recession

Source: Aikman et al. (2018: 41) (chart 2)

However, the huge budget deficits that the U.S. accrued after 2007 imposed a very heavy debt burden on current and future U.S. taxpayers.

The right-hand panel of Figure 0.1 shows that the U.K. experienced a somewhat larger decline in GDP during the Great Recession than the U.S. did. The U.K.'s GDP also recovered more slowly, as it did not return to its 2007 level until 2013 (two years later than in the U.S.). The right-hand panel of Figure 0.2 indicates that the U.K.'s ratio of government debt to GDP increased at a rate similar to the U.S. ratio during the Great Recession, as both governments ran enormous budget deficits to stabilize their financial systems and economies. Thus, the Great Recession inflicted comparable injuries on the U.S. and U.K. because both countries experienced destructive boom-and-bust cycles and systemic financial crises between 2000 and 2009. Universal banks dominated the financial systems of both countries during that period and were leading participants in the subprime lending boom.[14]

In contrast, the U.K.'s experience during the Great Depression was significantly different from the U.S., as shown by the right-hand panels of Figures 0.1 and 0.2. The decline in the U.K.'s GDP during the Great Depression was less severe and its recovery occurred earlier and faster than in the U.S. In addition, the ratio of government debt to GDP did not rise nearly as much during the 1930s in the U.K. as it did in the U.S. The U.K. had a milder and less costly recession during the 1930s because the U.K. banking system—unlike its U.S. counterpart—did not experience a systemic crisis during that period.[15]

As discussed in Chapters 5 and 6, an important factor that helps to explain the very different experiences of the U.S. and the U.K. during the Great Depression was that large universal banks played leading roles in the U.S. banking and securities markets during the 1920s, while the U.K.'s major commercial banks were structurally separated from its securities markets. Consequently, the U.K. did not experience the destructive boom-and-bust cycle or the systemic contagion across financial sectors that devastated the U.S. during the early 1930s. No major U.K. banks failed during the Great Depression, while a dozen leading U.S. universal banks either failed or were bailed out by the federal government during the early 1930s.

The "Big Bang" reforms of 1986 ended the U.K.'s policy of separating banks from the securities markets. The largest U.K. banks quickly acquired securities firms and became universal banks. By 2000, big universal banks dominated the banking systems and capital markets of both the U.S. and the U.K. That common element helps to explain why both countries experienced systemic financial and economic crises between 2007 and 2009, as shown by Figures 0.1 and 0.2.[16]

As noted earlier, universal banks have a strong tendency to create dangerous credit booms because they securitize loans into bonds that are sold to investors. The securitization of loans creates a feedback loop by establishing a major new source of funding (bond investors) to support the expansion of lending. The resulting spiral of loan origination and securitization frequently leads to high-risk lending, asset bubbles, excessive loan volumes, widespread loan defaults, severe losses on asset-backed securities, and a systemic bust.[17]

The credit booms that U.S. universal banks produced during the 1920s and 2000s are shown in the bottom panel of Figure 0.3. The first credit boom occurred during the 1920s and caused total U.S. private sector debts to reach 250% of GDP in 1930–31. The second boom began in the mid-1980s as large banks and federal regulators pursued a long campaign to undermine and repeal the Glass-Steagall Act. U.S. private sector debts reached a second peak of more than 280% of GDP in 2007, on the eve of the financial crisis.

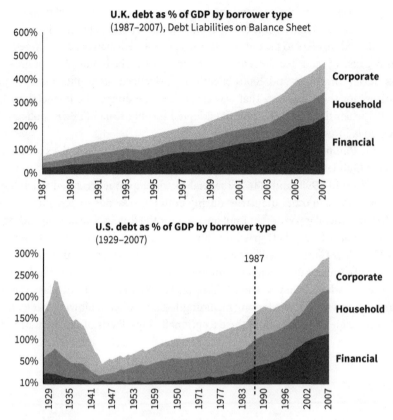

Figure 0.3 Changes in U.S. and U.K. Ratios of Total Debt to GDP During the Credit Booms Leading to the Great Depression and Great Recession
Source: FSA (2009: 18) (exhibit 1.10)

The top panel of Figure 0.3 shows a comparable credit boom in the U.K. following the "Big Bang" reforms of 1986, which allowed U.K. banks to acquire securities firms and become universal banks. Private-sector debts rose rapidly in the U.K. after the mid-1980s and peaked in 2007. Thus, the destructive credit booms that occurred in the U.S. and the U.K. between the mid-1980s and 2007 coincided with the growth and increasing dominance of universal banks in both countries.[18]

––––––

As discussed previously, the risk-taking culture of investment banking usually becomes the dominant culture within universal banks. Most universal banks therefore adopt aggressive bonus plans that resemble the incentive compensation policies of securities firms. Those bonus plans encourage executives and other key insiders to pursue risky strategies that produce higher short-term profits for shareholders and bigger bonuses for themselves. The bonus plans of most universal banks during the 1920s and 2000s had asymmetric payoff structures ("heads I win, tails you lose"), which allowed insiders to keep their bonuses even if their banks later suffered large losses because of their decisions to take outsized risks. The bonus plans of universal banks during the 1920s and 2000s effectively "privatized the profits and socialized the losses" for their insiders. That was especially true during the financial crisis of 2007–09, when the U.S., U.K., and EU adopted too-big-to-fail (TBTF) policies that prevented failures of universal banks.[19]

Thomas Philippon and Ariell Reshef found that the U.S. financial sector paid remarkably high levels of compensation to its employees during the 1920s and again between the mid-1990s and 2007. Financial sector employees received much higher pay than workers in other industries during both periods, due to deregulatory policies that the federal government implemented for the financial sector (including the removal of Glass-Steagall's restrictions during the 1990s). In contrast, between 1945 and 1980, when Glass-Steagall's restrictions were enforced, financial sector employees received compensation that was similar to the pay of workers in other industries.[20]

Figure 0.4, which is drawn from Philippon and Reshef's study, displays the close connection between deregulation (including federal policies allowing banks to engage in securities activities) and the exceptionally high levels of compensation that

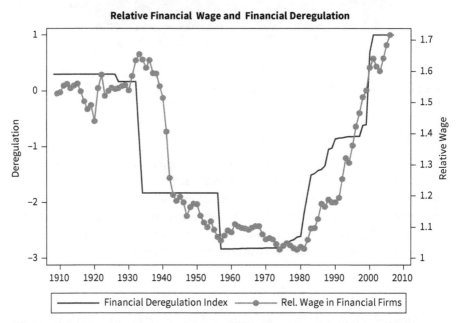

Figure 0.4 The Impact of Financial Deregulation on Compensation in the Financial Industry Compared with Other U.S. Industries, 1910–2008

Note: The "relative wage" is the ratio of the average wage in finance to the average wage in the nonfarm private sector (excluding finance).

Source: Philippon & Reshef (2012: 1578) (figure VIII C)

U.S. financial sector employees received during the 1920s and again between the mid-1990s and 2007.[21] The dominance of universal banks during both periods reinforced those high levels of compensation.

Philippon and Reshef also highlighted the extraordinarily generous compensation that upper-level financial executives received during the 1990s and 2000s, as the Glass-Steagall Act was eroded and ultimately repealed. Chief executive officers (CEOs) in the financial sector received a 250% premium on their earnings between 1995 and 2005 compared with CEO earnings in other sectors. Similarly, the gap in compensation levels between top financial executives and senior financial regulators widened from 10:1 in 1980 to more than 60:1 in 2005.[22]

Rising compensation levels for financial sector employees mirrored the growing economic power of the financial industry after 1980. Total compensation paid by the financial sector doubled as a share of U.S. gross national income between 1980 and 2007. During the same period, the financial sector's share of all corporate pretax profits rose from 13% to 27%. Stock prices for financial firms included in the Standard & Poor's (S&P) 500 index had the highest aggregate market value of any industry group for all but three years between 1995 and 2007.[23]

The financial sector wielded much greater political influence as its economic importance grew. The largest U.S. banks accomplished their most important political goal in 1999, when they joined forces with big securities firms and insurance companies to convince Congress to repeal the Glass-Steagall Act. The political alliance among the largest banks, securities firms, and insurance companies gave the financial industry unrivaled political clout, and it also ended a long period of internecine warfare among those three industry sectors. The financial industry achieved an unbroken string of legislative and regulatory triumphs from 1999 until the outbreak of the financial crisis in 2007. Those victories enabled universal banks to unleash the toxic subprime lending and securitization boom of the 2000s.[24]

The 1920s were another period in U.S. history when the largest U.S. financial institutions enjoyed commanding political influence.[25] As shown by the experience of the 1920s and 2000s, a legal regime that authorizes universal banking is likely to produce highly concentrated financial markets that are dominated by large financial conglomerates. The TBTF status of universal banks insulates them from effective market discipline by investors and creditors, and it also shields them from effective oversight by financial regulators.[26]

Seventeen global financial conglomerates—including the four biggest U.S. banks, the five largest U.S. securities firms, and eight U.K. and European universal banks—dominated global financial markets during the 2000s. Those conglomerates were leaders in financing the subprime credit boom. Thirteen successor firms—including six U.S. universal banks and seven U.K. and European universal banks—continue to dominate global financial markets today.[27]

———

More than a decade has gone by since the G20 issued its agenda for post-crisis reforms in early 2009. As explained in Chapter 12 and the Conclusion, those reforms left in place a dangerously unstable financial system dominated by universal banks and shadow banks. That is the same system that brought us the financial crisis of 2007–09. Post-crisis reforms have perpetuated what I call a "global doom loop," in which (1) governments and central banks provide TBTF guarantees to universal banks and large shadow banks and frequently intervene to maintain the stability of financial markets, (2) universal banks and large shadow banks finance rapidly rising levels of public sector and private sector debts, with support from the easy-money policies of central banks, and (3) investors and creditors take outsized risks because they expect that governments and central banks will take all necessary actions to stabilize financial markets and prevent failures of universal banks and large shadow banks.

The global doom loop creates a hazardous web of mutual dependence among governments, central banks, universal banks, shadow banks, and financial markets. In view of that dependence, our financial markets are not truly markets. Instead, they are a form of crony capitalism, which is supported and subsidized by explicit and implicit government guarantees.[28]

Central banks have played a key role in the doom loop by implementing QE and other unconventional monetary policies since 2008. Those policies have suppressed interest rates and injected trillions of dollars into global financial markets, thereby enabling universal banks and shadow banks to underwrite record levels of debt for corporations, households, and governments. Worldwide private sector and public sector debts increased by 50% between 2007 and 2019. In 2019, the ratio of global sovereign debts to global GDP reached its highest level since World War II.[29]

Governments and central banks have found it impossible to move past "crisis containment" and restore "normal market functioning."[30] The U.S. Federal Reserve Board (Fed) has repeatedly tried—and failed—to accomplish the "delicate task of normalizing monetary policy."[31] For example, the Fed increased short-term interest rates seven times in 2017 and 2018 and reduced the size of its balance sheet from $4.5 trillion to less than $4 trillion. Other central banks also tried to return to more "normal" monetary policies. However, the concerted efforts of central banks to abandon QE and move toward a policy of "quantitative tightening" (QT) frightened investors and led to a sharp sell-off in global financial markets during the fourth quarter of 2018. That market turbulence revealed the extreme dependence of global investors on prolonged easy-money policies from central banks, with their implicit assurance of abundant liquidity.[32]

In January 2019, the Fed made a "dramatic U-turn" away from QT and said it would be "patient" before making any further increases in short-term interest rates. The Fed intensified that U-turn between June and October, when it approved three reductions in short-term interest rates. When the repo market experienced a sudden shortage of liquidity in September 2019, the Fed injected almost $500 billion of new liquidity into financial markets by providing repo loans and buying short-term Treasury bills. Other leading central banks followed the Fed's actions by adopting their own dovish monetary policy measures. In September the European Central Bank (ECB) cut its short-term interest rate to an all-time low of −0.5% and restored its QE bond-buying program.[33]

Thus, central banks were "forced to abandon [their] hopes of normalising monetary policies" in 2019, and the global doom loop remains in place.[34] As discussed in Chapter 12 and the Conclusion, that doom loop turns governments and central banks into hostages of universal banks and large shadow banks. Bankers and other financial market participants assume that governments and central banks will quickly act to contain market disruptions, as they did in 2019, thereby ensuring the survival of universal banks and shadow banks. That widely shared assumption creates an asymmetric risk curve and encourages moral hazard. Bankers and other creditors and investors believe they can make highly-leveraged bets on risky assets because governments and central banks will always intervene to create a floor under financial markets if the threat of a serious disruption appears.

Leading experts are deeply concerned about the fragility of our current financial system, and their concerns implicitly acknowledge the existence of a global doom loop. The three principal architects of the response to the last financial crisis—Ben Bernanke, Tim Geithner, and Hank Paulson—have issued strong warnings about the risk of another systemic financial crisis.[35] They fear that governments and central banks might not be able to give the same open-ended support to universal banks and large shadow banks (through capital infusions, financial guarantees, and emergency loans) that they provided during the Great Recession. They argue that such open-ended support is essential to prevent a future crisis from turning into a second Great Depression. Other experts agree that governments and central banks must be prepared to act as guarantors of last resort for all systemically important financial institutions and markets during any future crisis.[36]

Advocates for guarantor-of-last-resort policies have not explained where governments and central banks would find the resources needed to fulfill such far-reaching financial commitments. In view of the staggering debt burdens that many nations shouldered during the Great Recession, it is doubtful whether they could authorize comparable amounts of deficit spending to combat a future crisis without triggering sovereign debt crises. Similarly, most leading central banks have little or no room to reduce interest rates. They would also find it challenging to undertake massive new bond-buying programs, given their already bloated balance sheets. Additional large-scale purchases of government bonds could strain the credibility of some central banks as well as the currencies they oversee.[37]

Thus, many governments and central banks might lack the necessary financial resources to act as guarantors of last resort when the next major crisis erupts. Large financial institutions could fail, and such failures could unleash a global financial panic. A global panic could lead to another Great Depression.

The Conclusion argues that we must take a different approach to avoid such a disastrous outcome. We must abolish universal banks and shadow banks to break the doom loop that links them to governments and central banks. Congress must adopt a new Glass-Steagall Act to establish a clear structural separation between banks and the capital markets. Banks must be prohibited from engaging in capital markets activities (except for underwriting and investing in government bonds). Shadow banks and other nonbanks must be barred from issuing short-term financial claims that function as deposit substitutes. To accomplish that outcome, nonbanks must be prevented from issuing any financial instruments with a maturity of ninety days or less that are payable in practice at par (100% of the amount invested). The shadow banking system (which hardly existed before 1975) would largely disappear if Congress prohibited nonbanks from issuing such short-term financial claims.

A new Glass-Steagall Act would create a more resilient and stable financial system, as well as a more diverse, competitive, and productive economy. It would prevent banks from exploiting government subsidies to support speculative capital markets activities. It would create clear structural boundaries between financial sectors, thereby reducing the risk of contagion across those sectors. It would promote more effective regulatory and market discipline by reducing the size, scope, and complexity of financial institutions. It would greatly reduce the influence wielded by large financial institutions over our political and regulatory policies. It would allow the Fed to fulfill its traditional role as lender of last resort for the banking system without providing open-ended guarantees to the entire financial system. It would improve the effectiveness of monetary policy by enabling the Fed to regulate the reserves of banks without worrying that depositors could transfer short-term funds to shadow banks.

We urgently need a new Glass-Steagall Act to break up universal banks and shadow banks, thereby preventing them from continuing to generate destructive boom-and-bust cycles. A new Glass-Steagall Act would restore sanity and stability to our banking system and our capital markets. It would greatly reduce conflicts of interest and incentives for excessive risk-taking within our financial institutions. It would promote a more prudent and sustainable allocation of credit and capital investments. It would end our current system of crony capitalism, which exploits massive government subsidies and severely distorts our financial markets. It would return banks and other financial institutions to their proper roles as servants—not masters—of nonfinancial business firms and consumers.

In 2016, both the Democratic and Republican Party platforms called for a return to Glass-Steagall's fundamental policy of separating banks from the capital markets. In 2013 and 2017, Senator Elizabeth Warren (D-MA) and three other Senators introduced bills to enact a "21st Century Glass-Steagall Act."[38] It is long past time to make those proposals a reality.

1
Origins

The Emergence of Universal Banks in Early Twentieth-Century America

Commercial banks in the U.S. began to explore the possibility of becoming universal banks during the last two decades of the nineteenth century. Prior to 1880, commercial banks engaged in a narrow range of businesses that included accepting deposits, handling foreign exchange, discounting negotiable instruments, and making loans.[1] The National Bank Act of 1864 did not allow national banks to buy or sell securities except for federal, state, and local government bonds. Most state laws imposed similar restrictions on state-chartered banks.[2] As a result, private investment banks controlled the business of underwriting and trading in corporate stocks and bonds between 1840 and 1880.[3]

Beginning in the 1880s, a group of large commercial banks in New York, Boston, and Chicago participated in underwriting syndicates for corporate stocks and bonds. Those syndicates were organized by private investment banks such as J. P. Morgan & Co. and Kuhn, Loeb & Co. Private investment banks organized underwriting syndicates to provide financing for business formations, mergers, acquisitions, and reorganizations involving railroads, shipping lines, and enterprises that produced oil, steel, electricity, and other commercial and consumer goods. Private investment banks invited leading commercial banks to join their underwriting syndicates in order to expand their syndicates' ability to sell large volumes of securities to the public. Commercial banks participated in underwriting syndicates by selling securities to their correspondent banks and customers, and by providing loans to syndicate members and their associated brokers.[4]

During the 1880s and 1890s, the First National Bank of New York participated in many of the underwriting syndicates organized by J. P. Morgan & Co., while National City Bank joined a number of underwriting syndicates headed by Kuhn, Loeb. After 1900, National City Bank also became a regular member of J. P. Morgan's underwriting syndicates. In addition, National City Bank formed its own syndicates with smaller investment banks to underwrite bonds for electric and gas utilities.[5]

By 1910, First National Bank and National City Bank were members of the top tier of U.S. investment banks, along with J. P. Morgan and Kuhn, Loeb, as well as the two largest investment banks in Boston (Lee, Higginson and Kidder, Peabody). The three largest commercial banks in Chicago—First National Bank of Chicago, Illinois Trust & Savings Bank, and Continental and Commercial National Bank—also engaged in securities activities and worked closely with the leading New York and Boston investment and commercial banks.[6]

The National Bank Act of 1864 authorized national banks to buy and sell federal, state, and local government bonds. However, it did not specifically allow other types of securities activities. National banks relied on their unspecified "incidental powers" to underwrite and trade in corporate securities during the 1880s and 1890s, with the tacit permission of their regulator, the Comptroller of the Currency.[7] The Comptroller suddenly reversed course in 1902 and ruled that national banks did not have authority to invest in corporate stocks or to sell corporate debt or equity securities to public investors. The Comptroller's ruling was based on a series of court decisions, which held that national banks did not have authority to engage in securities underwriting or trading, except for buying and selling government bonds.[8]

In contrast to the limited authority granted by Congress to national banks, a number of state legislatures in the late nineteenth century gave broader securities powers to state-chartered banks and trust companies. National banks therefore faced a significant disadvantage in competing with state-chartered institutions.[9]

Large national banks sought to evade the Comptroller of the Currency's 1902 ruling and to take advantage of more lenient state laws by organizing state-chartered affiliates to conduct their securities underwriting and trading businesses. Some national banks established or acquired state-chartered trust companies. Most national banks, however, chose to organize their securities affiliates as nonbank companies under general state corporation laws. Nonbank companies offered greater flexibility and little regulatory oversight because they were not subject to state banking laws and were not supervised by state banking departments.[10] In addition, the attractiveness of trust company affiliates diminished after more than a dozen trust companies failed during the Panic of 1907.[11] The advantages of trust company affiliates declined further after Congress granted trust powers to national banks in 1913 and expanded those powers in 1918.[12]

Accordingly, after 1907 most commercial banks that wanted to engage in a full-service securities business established nonbank securities affiliates.[13] The First National Bank of New York organized the first nonbank securities affiliate in 1908, followed by National City Bank in 1911 and Chase National Bank in 1917. Those three affiliates "served as models for other banks." More than 130 national banks and state banks established securities affiliates by 1929.[14]

Sponsoring banks used a variety of mechanisms, including voting trusts and shared stock certificates, to exercise control over their securities affiliates. Those control devices guaranteed (1) that the sponsoring bank's management would retain control of both the bank and its affiliate and (2) that shares of the sponsoring bank's stock could not be bought, sold, or transferred unless the transaction also included the corresponding shares of the affiliate's stock. In addition, some securities affiliates organized during the 1920s were established as nonbank subsidiaries of bank holding companies that also controlled commercial banks.[15]

Some public officials strongly opposed the establishment and growth of bank securities affiliates. When National City Bank organized National City Company (NCC) as its securities affiliate in 1911, Attorney General Charles Wickersham promptly challenged NCC's legality. Wickersham was an "ardent trustbuster" who wanted to break up concentrations of economic and financial power.[16]

At President Taft's request, Wickersham asked Solicitor General Frederick Lehmann to prepare a legal opinion addressing National City Bank's authority to establish NCC as a securities affiliate. Lehmann's opinion—which Wickersham endorsed—determined that National City's affiliation with NCC violated the National Bank Act by involving the bank "in business and ventures beyond its corporate powers." Lehmann therefore concluded that National City's creation of NCC represented a "usurpation of Federal authority."[17]

Lehmann's opinion emphasized the complete control that National City's officers and directors exercised over NCC. Lehmann also pointed out that NCC owned large blocks of shares in fifteen U.S. banks and one foreign bank. In Lehmann's view, NCC's ownership of those bank stocks was unlawful under an 1899 Supreme Court decision, which held that a national bank could not own the stock of any other bank.[18] Lehmann also argued that NCC's ownership of controlling interests in bank stocks enabled National City to engage in "nationwide chain banking." Lehmann believed that NCC's control over a chain of banks contravened the National Bank Act's prohibition against the establishment of branch offices by national banks. Lehmann's analysis focused on the practical and substantive effects of National City's affiliation with NCC, rather than the legal formalities of their relationship.[19]

Lehmann expressed additional concerns about the financial risks created by National City Bank's affiliation with NCC. He warned that securities affiliates would create a "temptation to the speculative use of the funds of the [sponsoring] banks" that would be "irresistible." The close connections between banks and their securities affiliates would allow "many enterprises and many banks [to be] brought and bound together," with the consequence that "the failure of one may involve all in a common disaster."[20] Lehmann's warnings were prescient, as they anticipated the debacles that occurred at National City Bank, Chase National Bank, and other large banks with securities affiliates during the Great Depression.[21]

Secretary of the Treasury Franklin MacVeigh and Secretary of State Philander Knox strongly disagreed with the views of Wickersham and Lehmann. MacVeigh wanted to expand the powers of national banks, which the Treasury Department indirectly supervised through the Office of the Comptroller of the Currency. MacVeigh endorsed securities affiliates because they were not specifically prohibited by the National Bank Act and allowed national banks to compete with the broader securities powers of state-chartered commercial banks and trust companies. According to MacVeigh, securities affiliates were useful devices that helped to keep "a large part of the banking system within [Treasury's] jurisdiction" by creating a more level playing field between national banks and their state-chartered competitors.[22]

After considering the conflicting opinions presented by the Justice, Treasury, and State Departments, President Taft decided not to challenge National City's affiliation with NCC. As an apparent quid pro quo for Taft's nonintervention, National City caused NCC to divest its portfolio of domestic bank stocks. NCC thereafter focused on underwriting and investing in bonds and stocks issued by governments and non-bank companies.[23]

While Taft allowed NCC to remain in operation, other political leaders challenged the legality and desirability of NCC and other securities affiliates. Congressman Charles A. Lindbergh, Sr. (R-MN) denounced National City's creation of NCC and called for a congressional investigation of the "Money Trust" on Wall Street. Lindbergh attacked the Money Trust as a powerful and dangerous financial combination that resembled the great industrial trusts. In April 1912, the House Committee on Banking and Currency established a subcommittee to "investigate the concentration of money and credit" in the U.S. Representative Arsène Pujo (D-LA) chaired that subcommittee, which became known as the Pujo Committee. After a lengthy series of hearings, the Pujo Committee issued its final report in February 1913.[24]

The Pujo Committee's report determined that a group of six financial institutions—J. P. Morgan & Co., First National Bank of New York, National City Bank, Kuhn, Loeb & Co., and two Boston investment banks (Lee, Higginson and Kidder, Peabody)—were "the most active agents in forwarding and bringing about the concentration of control of money and credit" in the U.S. The committee's report also identified two leading New York trust companies (Guaranty Trust and Bankers Trust) and Chicago's three largest commercial banks as important allies of the six leading institutions. The report described those institutions as "the principal banking agencies through which the greater corporate enterprises of the United States obtain capital for their operations."[25]

Thus, the Pujo Committee's investigation revealed that a close-knit group of Wall Street investment and commercial banks and their associates in Boston and Chicago controlled the market for financing "the great interstate corporations." The committee warned that the group's collective influence over leading business firms created a "situation ... fraught with too great peril to our institutions to be tolerated." Many Americans shared the Pujo Committee's concerns with the "centralization of financial power" on Wall Street and "the absence of any public control over it."[26]

The Pujo Committee's attacks on the Money Trust reached a broad public audience through Louis Brandeis' popular book *Other People's Money* (1914), which summarized the committee's work.[27] Among other topics, Brandeis highlighted "the revolutionary change in the conduct of our leading banking institutions" that resulted from the "invasion by the banks into the realm of the investment banker." According to Brandeis, the expansion of commercial banks into securities activities marked "a departure from the legitimate sphere of the banking business, which is the making of temporary loans to business concerns." Brandeis warned that the opportunity to make "large profits from promotions, underwritings and security purchases" created a "temptation" that was "irresistible" to commercial bankers.[28]

Brandeis alleged that the most important commercial banks had formed a strategic "alliance" with leading investment banks "to control the business of the country, and to 'divide the spoils.'" The Pujo Committee found that directors of J. P. Morgan, National City, and First National collectively held 341 directorships in 112 corporations, with total assets exceeding $22 billion. Based on his own research, Brandeis concluded that the Pujo Committee's figures significantly "understate[d]" the full extent of business and financial influence wielded by "the inner group of the Money Trust."[29]

Brandeis described the Money Trust as a "financial oligarchy" that possessed unchallenged power to "bestride as masters America's business world."[30] He maintained that the top commercial and investment banks reigned supreme within America's most important business and financial centers. J. P. Morgan, National City, and First National "dominated America's financial center, New York," as well as Philadelphia. Lee, Higginson and Kidder, Peabody, along with the three largest Boston commercial banks (National Shawmut, First National, and Old Colony Trust), controlled Boston's business and financial markets. The three biggest Chicago banks (First National, Illinois Trust & Savings, and Continental and Commercial) dictated business and financial affairs in Chicago, and the Chicago banks also participated in underwriting syndicates organized by investment banks from New York and Boston.[31]

The Pujo Committee recommended that national banks should be prohibited from underwriting and trading in securities (except for government bonds), from owning bank stocks, and from affiliating with companies engaged in securities activities. The committee also recommended that private investment banks should be barred from accepting deposits. However, Congress did not adopt any of those recommendations. As a result, commercial banks remained free to operate securities affiliates and to establish holding companies that owned bank stocks, while investment banks continued to accept deposits.[32]

Due to the popularity of *Other People's Money*, "the Pujo Committee's findings long outlived the Wilson Administration" and influenced the Senate's investigation of Wall Street in 1933.[33] *Other People's Money* was republished in 1933, and its editor stated, "The fatalities following 1929 came to a large extent from the failure to act on the principles sharply drawn in *Other People's Money*."[34]

———

In the absence of any restraining legislation from Congress, First National Bank of New York, National City Bank, and other large commercial banks rapidly expanded their activities in the securities markets. World War I provided attractive new opportunities for that expansion. Between 1915 and 1917, commercial banks joined with investment banks in forming nationwide syndicates that sold $2.5 billion of bonds issued by the Allied powers (primarily Great Britain and France).[35]

Success in selling Allied war bonds convinced National City's leaders—chairman James Stillman and president Frank Vanderlip—that the bank should significantly expand its capacity to distribute securities to the public. Stillman and Vanderlip wanted to make National City "the foremost financing house in America," and they knew National City needed "broader distribution" capabilities to achieve that goal. In August 1916, National City Company acquired N. W. Halsey & Co., a prominent securities firm with retail brokerage offices located in major cities across the U.S. At the same time, National City Bank transferred its bond department to NCC. Those transactions centralized all of National City's securities underwriting and trading activities within NCC.[36] NCC publicly announced that its acquisitions of the Halsey firm and National City's bond department would enable NCC to offer "a superior investment service" and satisfy "the requirements of investors throughout the country."[37]

National City appointed Charles E. Mitchell as president of NCC to lead its newly expanded operations. Mitchell was a physically powerful and imposing man with boundless self-confidence. When his Amherst College classmates voted him "the greatest" member of his graduating class, Mitchell replied, "I am." Prior to becoming president of NCC, Mitchell traveled throughout Europe to study how European banks sold securities to the public, and he founded and managed a successful bond trading firm. Frank Vanderlip said that Mitchell had "an astonishing capacity to create energy," and a newspaper profile described him as "a human power plant."[38]

After the U.S. entered World War I in 1917, the U.S. Treasury Department assumed responsibility for providing loans to help the Allies. The Treasury Department called on American commercial and investment banks to help raise funds from the public to finance the U.S. government's war effort. Treasury commissioned four Liberty Loans in 1917 and 1918, followed by a Victory Loan in 1919 to "finish the job" and "bring the boys home."[39] To fund those loans, Treasury worked with commercial and investment banks to sell $21.5 billion of Liberty bonds to the public. The federal government organized elaborate campaigns to persuade ordinary citizens to buy Liberty bonds. Those campaigns featured patriotic rallies, parades, and speeches by bankers, business leaders, and celebrities (including prominent actors such as Charlie Chaplin, Douglas Fairbanks, and Mary Pickford).[40]

Government officials and bankers encouraged ordinary citizens to buy Liberty bonds on the installment plan or to buy war savings stamps (for 25¢ each), which could be bundled together to purchase a $50 bond. More than twenty million Americans bought Liberty bonds, and sales of war savings stamps accounted for over half of all Liberty bond sales.[41] The experience of owning Liberty bonds persuaded many Americans that "money could be made by the simple process of holding paper securities until they went up in value."[42] As Harvard professor Edwin Gray observed in 1932, the Liberty bond campaigns "placed government bonds in the hands of millions of people who never before had possessed such instruments ... The basis was thus laid for the vast and credulous post-war market for credit which culminated in the portentous speculation of 1928 and 1929."[43]

Commercial and investment bankers played leading roles in planning and implementing the Liberty bond drives. Commercial banks sold more than half of the Liberty bonds issued between 1917 and 1919, and they provided installment loans that enabled retail investors to buy many of those bonds.[44] Banks received no commissions or other compensation from the federal government, but they became familiar with "the use of high-pressure selling techniques" and were introduced to "a tremendous number of new potential buyers of securities." Most importantly, banks "won [the] confidence" of ordinary investors because the Liberty bonds that banks sold had "unquestioned soundness."[45]

The great success of the Liberty bond campaigns caused many commercial banks to expand their bond underwriting activities. Charles Mitchell recognized that National City Company's prominent role in selling Liberty bonds would enable NCC to sell many other types of bonds to ordinary investors after the war ended. In 1917, Mitchell declared that the nationwide sale of Liberty bonds was creating "a large, new army of investors in this country who have never heretofore known what it means to own a coupon bond and who may in the future be developed into savers and bond buyers."[46]

In 1919, Mitchell told a class of National City Bank and NCC trainees that "if we could bring the investment banking house to the people in such a way that they would look upon it as a part and parcel of their everyday life; if we could spread the gospel of thrift and saving and investment; ... we could then ... lift this investment banking business to a level it had never reached before." By 1919, NCC was operating branch offices in more than fifty U.S. cities. Mitchell assured his recruits that NCC's branches "are already working to make connections with the great new bond-buying public ... and are preparing to serve the public on a straightforward basis, just as it is served by the United Cigar Stores or Child's Restaurants."[47]

―――――

After the U.S. entered the World War I in 1917, the U.S. Treasury Department and the Federal Reserve Board encouraged investment banks and commercial banks to focus on selling Liberty bonds, and to refrain from underwriting corporate securities that competed with the federal government's war financing efforts. The Fed created a Capital Issues Committee (CIC) to review proposed new issues of corporate stocks and bonds, and the CIC "strongly restricted private financing" by business firms.[48]

Commercial banks took advantage of the dormant private securities markets by expanding their loans to corporations.[49] Lending by banks to business firms continued to grow rapidly during the postwar boom in 1919 and the first half of 1920. During that period, the Fed kept short-term interest rates low (1) to allow Treasury to sell massive volumes of Liberty bonds with relatively low yields (resulting in lower war financing costs for the U.S. government) and (2) to support the market values of Liberty bonds after the war ended. Treasury also issued large amounts of short-term government debt certificates and encouraged banks to buy those certificates to help the war effort. The Fed supported Treasury's war financing efforts by providing discount window loans to commercial banks at preferred rates if banks posted short-term government debt certificates as collateral. National City Bank and other commercial banks earned handsome profits by purchasing government debt certificates, posting them as collateral for cheap loans from the Fed, and using the Fed's loans to finance higher-yielding business loans.[50]

The Fed's low-interest-rate policy and its easy terms for discount window credit led to a surge in bank lending and rising inflation during the postwar boom. However, Treasury completed its war financing program by the end of 1919, and inflation fears caused the Fed to raise its discount rates sharply during the first half of 1920. Rising interest rates ended the postwar boom and triggered a severe recession during the second half of 1920. Businesses cut back on their production of goods and liquidated their surplus inventories, while banks dramatically reduced their commercial lending. The severe recession that began in mid-1920 continued through most of 1921.[51]

———

The postwar recession left National City Bank holding a large volume of nonperforming loans. The bank also was buffeted by crises in Russia and Cuba. During World War I, National City greatly expanded its operations in Russia under Frank Vanderlip's leadership. National City opened several branches in Russian cities and made large investments in Russian government bonds and other assets. Following the Bolshevik Revolution in November 1917, the new Soviet government defaulted on debts incurred by the czarist regime and seized the assets of domestic and foreign banks. Those measures inflicted severe losses on National City, and the bank's board of directors demanded Vanderlip's resignation in June 1919. Meanwhile, the bank's chairman, James Stillman, had died in 1918.[52]

National City's directors elected Stillman's son to replace Vanderlip. However, National City continued to pursue Vanderlip's policy of expanding its operations in Cuba. Cuban sugar prices skyrocketed during World War I and its immediate aftermath, due to the disruption of beet sugar production in Europe and wartime price controls on U.S. sugar. Cuba's sugar boom attracted the attention of National City and several other big New York banks, including Chase National Bank and Guaranty Trust. National City opened more than twenty branches in Cuban cities and provided $80 million of loans to Cuban sugar producers. By 1921, National City held almost a fifth of all bank loans in Cuba, and National City's exposure to Cuban loans equaled four-fifths of the bank's capital.[53]

The removal of wartime price controls led to higher production of U.S. sugar, and European beet sugar producers were back in operation by 1920. Increased competition from U.S. and European sugar caused the market price for Cuban sugar to collapse between 1920 and 1921.[54] Many Cuban sugar producers defaulted on their loans, and National City's Cuban branches were left with over $60 million of non-performing loans. At the same time, "National City's debt to the Federal Reserve stood at $144 million, three times its required reserves, and many domestic loans were under water or threatened." Stillman's son resigned under pressure in May 1921, and National City's board of directors elected Charles Mitchell as the bank's new president.[55]

National City's directors gave Mitchell a sweeping mandate to overhaul the bank and repair the damage inflicted by its Russian and Cuban misadventures and the postwar recession. Mitchell centralized National City's management and assumed complete control of the bank: "He made his presence felt throughout the organization. People in the bank began to refer to their new boss as the Chief."[56] Mitchell toured Cuba in January 1922 and restructured National City's Cuban operations. National City organized General Sugar Corporation to take ownership of and attempt to revive National City's foreclosed Cuban properties (including sugar plantations, sugar mills, and railroads). The price of Cuban sugar rose slightly between 1922 and 1923, but it soon fell again and General Sugar suffered mounting losses after 1925. In 1927, National City still held more than $30 million of nonperforming Cuban loans on its books.[57]

Despite the continuing problems in Cuba, Mitchell was relentlessly optimistic about the future of National City as well as the American economy.[58] In November 1922, Mitchell gave a pep talk to National City's employees. Mitchell assured them that "National City Bank's future is brighter, I believe, than it has ever been. We have been going through a period of readjustment and a time of rebuilding. We are getting ready now to go ahead full speed."[59] Mitchell was determined to make National City a "financial department store," which would "bring to each customer all things financial." Mitchell pursued that universal banking strategy during the 1920s and built National City into the largest U.S. bank and the world's largest distributor of securities. Other commercial banks followed National City's lead.[60]

———

Before National City Bank and other large commercial banks could fully implement their universal banking strategy, they had to overcome one final regulatory challenge. John Skelton Williams was a tough-minded regulator who joined the Wilson administration as Assistant Secretary of the Treasury in 1913 and was appointed Comptroller of the Currency (the chief regulator of national banks) the following year. Williams also served as an ex officio member of the Federal Reserve Board.[61]

Before entering government service, Williams was a highly successful businessman and banker in Virginia. In 1900, he organized and became president of the Seaboard Air Line Railway, which established the first railroad link between New York City and Florida. He later became president of the Bank of Richmond.[62]

Williams lost control of Seaboard in 1904, after a bitter struggle with Thomas Fortune Ryan, a prominent Wall Street speculator. Williams orchestrated a publicity campaign against Ryan's management, and he was vindicated when Seaboard collapsed into bankruptcy during the Panic of 1907. However, Williams was excluded from the group of investors who brought Seaboard out of bankruptcy in 1912. The new ownership group was headed by leading New York bankers, including Frank Vanderlip of National City Bank, Albert Wiggin of Chase National Bank, and Benjamin Strong of Bankers Trust.[63]

Williams' battles for control of Seaboard left him with a deep-seated hostility toward Wall Street's commercial and investment bankers. In May 1914, Williams gave a speech to a group of North Carolina bankers in which he praised the recently enacted Federal Reserve Act of 1913. Williams commended the statute for freeing the nation's money supply from Wall Street's control. He leveled a broadside against Wall Street that clearly reflected his Seaboard experience as well as the attacks on the Money Trust by Louis Brandeis and the Pujo Committee:

> New York has become the commercial capital of the country, the great citadel of the money power, the reservoir of money supply. It is the walled city from which the barons have levied tribute on a territory and population vaster than any Lord or King of the Middle Ages dreamed of, yet sometimes using methods as ruthless and savage as those of the fiercest of the robber nobles. . . .
>
> No sudden sweep by a feudal magnate on his peaceful neighbors was a more cruel or shameless plundering than some of the transactions which have been brought to light by which the shareholders of railways and other great enterprises . . . were despoiled. Their property and money were taken from them by the might of masses of money working stealthily.[64]

Williams warned his audience that "no group of men at any centre ... can be intrusted safely with the unlimited and unrestrained control" of the nation's supply of credit. According to Williams, the Federal Reserve Act provided a much-needed opportunity "to change the relation of New York to the country generally from an attitude of dominating ownership to friendly partnership."[65]

When Williams and other Wilson appointees entered the Treasury Department in 1913, they discovered that National City Bank and Riggs National Bank of Washington, D.C., had arranged for a jointly employed clerk to work at a desk in the Office of the Comptroller of the Currency. For several years, that clerk reported to National City and Riggs on the financial condition of national banks as soon as the banks filed their periodic "call reports" with the comptroller. Treasury Secretary William McAdoo stopped the practice and denounced it as "improper and irregular" because it gave National City and Riggs "an undue advantage, in the way of advance information, over all other banks in the country."[66]

National City and Riggs tried unsuccessfully to block Williams' confirmation as Comptroller of the Currency in 1914. After a lengthy hearing before the Senate

Banking Committee, the Senate confirmed Williams with only one dissenting vote.[67] In his first annual report as Comptroller, Williams stated that National City Bank would no longer receive the "special favors and privileges" it had enjoyed "under previous administrations."[68]

Thomas Kane, a career bank regulator who served as Deputy Comptroller of the Currency from 1899 to 1923, published a narrative history of the Office of the Comptroller of the Currency in 1922. According to Kane, Williams' tenure as Comptroller was

> distinguished at the outset by a rigid enforcement of the banking laws, and much good was accomplished by him in compelling the banks to observe the law and to respect the requirements of the Comptroller's office.... [H]is administration was considered by many of the banks [as] the most radical and exacting of any in history.[69]

Kane described Williams as "courageous, blunt and outspoken," with "unimpeachable integrity and honesty." In Kane's opinion, Williams was "one of the ablest officials, and without doubt the most forceful Comptroller of the Currency who ever occupied the office." Kane acknowledged, however, that Williams was "relentless toward those with whom he had business or personal differences."[70] Williams publicly criticized National City and other New York banks for charging interest rates that he viewed as usurious.[71] He engaged in a lengthy court battle with Representative Louis McFadden (R-PA), a senior member of the House Banking Committee, over McFadden's alleged mismanagement of a Pennsylvania bank.[72]

During his service as an ex officio member of the Federal Reserve Board, Williams engaged in private and public debates with William P. G. Harding, Governor of the Federal Reserve System, and Benjamin Strong, Governor of the Federal Reserve Bank of New York.[73] At first Williams supported the Fed's efforts to restrain the inflation triggered by the postwar boom after World War I. He agreed with the Fed's decision to raise the discount rate from 4.75% to 6% in January 1920. However, he opposed the Fed's decision to hike the discount rate to 7% in June 1920. As the recession of 1920–21 deepened, Williams publicly urged Harding and Strong to cut interest rates and provide relief to struggling farmers and other distressed borrowers. Williams' vocal opposition to the deflationary policies of Harding and Strong made him "*persona non grata* at the Federal Reserve Board" by the time his term as Comptroller of the Currency expired in March 1921.[74]

In July 1921, Williams delivered a speech at a Georgia bankers' conference, in which he criticized the Fed for pursuing a "stubbornly unwise course" that produced a "drastic shrinkage and deflation of values," resulting in "losses and ruin" for many farmers and business owners.[75] In response to attacks from Williams and other public officials (including members of Congress), the Fed abandoned its tight-money policy and reduced the discount rate during the summer of 1921. The Fed's interest rate reductions, along with a large inflow of gold from Europe, prompted a strong recovery of the U.S. economy by 1922.[76]

―――

During his tenure as Comptroller of the Currency, Williams rigorously exercised his authority to supervise and examine national banks as well as state banks that chose to become members of the Federal Reserve System. The National Bank Act required banks under the Comptroller's supervision to submit at least five reports of their financial condition each year, and the Comptroller had discretion to demand additional reports. In 1915, Williams instructed national banks and state member banks to file six reports each year rather than five. He also significantly expanded the amount of information required by call reports.[77]

Williams' call report policies and his agency's strict examinations triggered a wave of complaints from national banks and state member banks. Many state banks refused to join the Federal Reserve System because of their opposition to Williams' demanding supervision. In response to the uproar among bankers over Williams' policies, Congress amended the Federal Reserve Act in 1917. The 1917 amendments transferred authority to examine state member banks from the Office of the Comptroller of the Currency to the regional Federal Reserve Banks, and the minimum number of call reports for state member banks was set at only three. In addition, the 1917 amendments reduced reserve requirements for both national and state member banks. The 1917 provisions made membership in the Federal Reserve System more attractive for larger state banks, and 1,600 state banks joined the system between 1917 and 1922.[78] By 1922, most large U.S. banks were either national banks or state member banks.[79]

Williams took a special supervisory interest in National City Bank and National City Company. In 1916, he tried to examine NCC based on its status as an affiliate of National City. However, National City successfully blocked Williams' attempt, and the bank thereafter followed a "fixed policy" of refusing to allow the Comptroller of the Currency to examine NCC.[80] The National Bank Act did not specifically refer to affiliates of national banks until Congress enacted the Glass-Steagall Act in 1933. The Comptroller therefore lacked explicit authority to supervise such affiliates during Williams' tenure. In addition, Congress' amendments to the Federal Reserve Act in 1917 were widely viewed as a repudiation of Williams' tough supervisory policies. Those amendments undoubtedly weakened his ability to obtain NCC's voluntary compliance.

Despite his inability to supervise NCC, Williams continued to challenge National City Bank. In a meeting with officers of National City Bank in February 1921, Williams severely criticized the bank for its reckless lending policies, which resulted in large amounts of nonperforming loans in the U.S., Europe, and Cuba. Williams also rebuked the bank for failing to maintain adequate liquidity reserves and for borrowing $144 million from the New York Fed—an amount that substantially exceeded the bank's capital.[81]

Williams also cast a disapproving eye on Chase National Bank. In December 1920, Williams wrote to Federal Reserve Board Governor William P. G. Harding to criticize Chase for providing $40 million of loans to insiders and their related interests, including $10 million of loans extended to its president, Albert Wiggin, and his family. Williams pointed out that Chase's insider loans were substantially larger than the bank's capital and left Chase in a vulnerable position.[82]

Williams also stated, in the same letter to Harding and a subsequent newspaper article, that the New York Fed's loans to the five largest New York City banks exceeded the *total* amount of discount window loans that *five* regional Federal Reserve Banks had extended to *all* of the banks in their regions. Williams denounced the "inequalities and injustice in the distribution of [discount window] loans" within the Federal Reserve System, and he also criticized the New York Fed for allowing its "big favored banks" to use discount window loans to finance "call money" loans that supported "stock gambling."[83]

In December 1920, Williams issued his final annual report as Comptroller of the Currency. That report strongly condemned securities affiliates of national banks. Williams may have received support for that condemnation from Carter Glass, who served as Treasury Secretary from 1918 to 1920 and was Williams' nominal superior. Glass was a Virginian like Williams, and Glass shared Williams' firm opposition to efforts by Wall Street to exercise centralized control over the nation's banking system and financial markets. Glass played a leading role in drafting the Federal Reserve Act of 1913 as a member of the House Banking Committee, and he helped to defeat efforts by Republicans and Wall Street bankers to establish a single, banker-owned and banker-managed central bank in New York. Glass insisted on a decentralized Federal Reserve System consisting of regional Federal Reserve Banks that were supervised by a Presidentially appointed Federal Reserve Board. Glass was determined to "curb financial power by fragmenting that power."[84]

Glass also strongly opposed the use of bank credit to support "speculation" in securities. Glass adhered to a theory of commercial and central banking that later became known as the "real bills doctrine." He believed that the Fed should "discount" (provide credit against) short-term bills of exchange and other negotiable instruments resulting from commercial transactions in the "real" economy, such as sales, imports, and exports of goods. Glass therefore strongly opposed the use of discount window credit to finance "call money" loans to brokers and other loans that supported "speculation" in the securities markets.[85] As a U.S. Senator in the 1930s, Glass argued that securities affiliates of national banks were unlawful, and he led the campaign to outlaw those affiliates in the Glass-Steagall Act of 1933.[86]

In his final annual report as Comptroller, Williams declared that "securities companies" should operate "separate and apart from the national banks" and should not be allowed to share officers and directors.[87] Williams warned that securities affiliates were "an element of increasing peril to the banks with which they are associated." According to Williams, securities affiliates had become

> instruments of speculation, and headquarters for promotions of all kinds of financial schemes ... Many of the flotations promoted by the "securities companies" which are operated as adjuncts to national banks have proven disastrous to their subscribers, and ... in some cases have damaged the credit and reputations of national banks with which the "securities companies" are allied.[88]

Williams argued that securities affiliates were incompatible with the business of commercial banks because "it would be difficult, if not impossible, for the same set of officers to conduct safely, soundly, and successfully the conservative business of the national bank and at the same time direct and manage the speculative ventures and promotions of the ancillary institutions." Securities affiliates received extensive financial support from their sponsoring banks and thereby exposed the banks' depositors to serious losses. In addition, national banks frequently invested funds from their customers' trust accounts to support risky ventures promoted by their securities affiliates. Williams maintained that securities affiliates enabled their bank sponsors to engage "indirectly" in "speculation and ... dealings in bonds and stocks" that the banks could "neither safely nor lawfully do directly."[89]

Williams' final report did not provide specific examples of banks that engaged in the "disastrous" securities practices he condemned. However, he probably had in mind Guaranty Trust, the second-largest bank in New York City and a state-chartered member of the Federal Reserve System. In May 1920, an examination of Guaranty Trust by New York state officials revealed that the bank held more than $43 million of slow, doubtful, and impaired assets, equal to two-thirds of its capital. Those unsound assets included millions of dollars of depreciated or unmarketable securities.[90]

Williams reviewed the examination report for Guaranty Trust as a member of the Federal Reserve Board, and he wrote a blistering critique to Governor Harding in February 1921. Williams declared that Guaranty Trust "HAD BECOME AN ENORMOUS ENGINE OF SPECULATION" by "investing their own funds in the stocks of highly speculative corporations" and by participating in "all kinds of speculative [underwriting] syndicates" for newly issued securities. Williams charged that the New York Fed accommodated Guaranty Trust's hazardous activities by providing more than $120 million of discount window loans to the bank. A few months after Williams wrote his letter, J. P. Morgan & Co. organized a group of banks that provided a $180 million emergency loan to save Guaranty Trust from failure.[91]

The Republicans recaptured control of the Senate in the midterm elections of 1918. At the urging of Representative Louis McFadden, the Republican members of the Senate Banking Committee blocked efforts by the Wilson administration to appoint

Williams for a second term as Comptroller of the Currency. Williams was therefore obliged to leave office when Wilson's term as President ended in March 1921.[92]

In contrast to Williams, his successors under Republican Presidents Warren G. Harding and Calvin Coolidge pursued deregulatory policies that pleased large national banks. Daniel Crissinger, an Ohio banker and lifelong friend of President Harding, replaced Williams in March 1921. Crissinger immediately removed a large number of items that Williams had added to the call reports submitted by national banks.[93]

In 1922, Crissinger adopted a new policy that allowed national banks to open branch offices in the same cities where their main offices were located. The National Bank Act did not expressly permit national banks to establish branches, and Crissinger's predecessors had interpreted the statute's silence as an implied prohibition against branching.[94] In 1924, the U.S. Supreme Court held that Crissinger's pro-branching policy violated the National Bank Act.[95]

Henry Dawes succeeded Crissinger as Comptroller of the Currency in May 1923,[96] and Joseph McIntosh followed Dawes in December 1924.[97] Dawes and McIntosh lobbied Congress to expand the real estate lending and securities powers of national banks and to allow national banks to open branch offices. The deregulatory policies of Crissinger, Dawes, and McIntosh mirrored the pro-business, pro-bank, and pro–Wall Street policies of Harding and Coolidge.[98] President Coolidge was especially popular on Wall Street, where bankers and traders referred to the stock market boom as "the Coolidge market." When Coolidge announced his decision not to run for reelection in 1928, Charles Mitchell and other leading bankers and business leaders publicly urged him to reconsider.[99]

Henry Dawes commissioned a survey of bankers, bank examiners, and other banking experts. Dawes' survey asked the recipients to recommend changes in federal banking laws that would improve the competitive position of national banks and "would be in the interests of the country's business and of banking in general." The stated purposes of Dawes' survey did not include any reference to the interests of consumers, and consumers were not invited to participate in the survey.[100]

After reviewing the responses to his survey, Dawes presented a list of recommended statutory amendments to Congress. Joseph McIntosh continued to lobby for those changes after he succeeded Dawes in December 1924. Both Comptrollers urged Congress to expand the powers of national banks in the areas of branching, real estate lending, and securities trading and underwriting. House Banking Committee chairman Louis McFadden incorporated most of Dawes' and McIntosh's recommendations in the McFadden Act, which Congress passed in February 1927.[101]

The McFadden Act expanded the real estate lending powers of national banks and allowed them to establish branch offices in their home cities if competing state-chartered banks could do so under state law. The McFadden Act also authorized national banks to buy and sell "investment securities" that were deemed "marketable" by the Comptroller of the Currency. The "investment securities" permitted under the statute included "marketable" bonds and other debt securities but excluded equity stocks. However, Dawes and McIntosh allowed securities affiliates of national banks to underwrite and trade in equity stocks as well as bonds. Thus, unlike John Skelton Williams, Dawes and McIntosh strongly supported broader securities powers for national banks, and they tacitly approved securities affiliates that conducted a full range of securities activities.[102]

Crissinger, Dawes, and McIntosh also adopted supervisory policies that were far more lenient than those followed by Williams. Crissinger significantly reduced the amount of information that national banks were required to provide in their call reports. The number of call reports required each year by the Comptroller dropped from six in 1921 to five in 1922, four from 1923 through 1925, and only three in 1926. The total amount spent by the Office of the Comptroller of the Currency on bank examinations declined from $3.8 million in 1922 to less than $2.3 million in each year from 1923 through 1926. Meanwhile, the total assets of national banks grew from $20.6 billion in 1922 to $25.2 billion in 1926. Dawes and McIntosh also followed a much more liberal policy for chartering new national banks, compared with Williams' strict requirements.[103]

The deregulatory policies approved by Congress and followed by the Comptrollers of the Currency during the Harding and Coolidge administrations had fateful consequences. Those policies enabled national banks to greatly expand their real estate lending and securities activities during the 1920s.[104] As discussed in Chapter 2, the rapid expansion of real estate lending and securities offerings during the Roaring Twenties produced an unsustainable boom in the U.S. economy, which led to a severe bust and the Great Depression.

The dialectic interplay between the banking industry and the Office of the Comptroller of the Currency between 1915 and 1927 provides a striking example of "regulatory compliance rot," as described by Erik Gerding in his "regulatory instability" hypothesis.[105] The regulatory cycle between 1915 and 1927 included (1) John Skelton Williams' implementation of rigorous supervisory and examination policies, (2) the industry's vehement pushback against those policies, (3) the industry's success in persuading Congress to pass deregulatory legislation in 1917 and 1927, and (4) the industry's ability to obtain much more accommodating policies from Daniel Crissinger, Henry Dawes, and Joseph McIntosh. The "compliance rot" of the 1920s encouraged the rapid growth of first-generation universal banks as well as their aggressive expansion into speculative real estate and securities activities between 1921 and 1930.

2
Frenzy

Universal Banks Helped to Promote an Unsustainable Boom in the U.S. Economy During the 1920s

From 1922 to 1929, the U.S. experienced a long economic expansion that Frederick Lewis Allen called "the seven fat years."[1] The U.S. economy grew steadily during those years, except for mild recessions during 1923–24 and 1926–27. The Federal Reserve System responded to both recessions with interest rate cuts and open-market purchases of government securities that stimulated quick recoveries and prolonged the boom. By 1929, the nation's real gross national product (GNP) was 22% above its level in 1923 and 62% higher than its level in 1914. The seven-year boom created widespread confidence among politicians, business leaders, bankers, and the general public that the U.S. had entered a "new era" of permanent prosperity.[2] The Fed's success in ending the brief recessions of 1923–24 and 1926–27 led many investors to believe that the Fed could control "the whole problem of booms, slumps, and panics."[3]

Large commercial banks and investment banks aggressively competed to provide the financing that drove the seven-year boom. Commercial banks greatly expanded their loans collateralized by securities as well as their investments in securities, and they also increased their real estate loans and consumer loans. Commercial and investment banks attracted legions of new customers to purchase their offerings of domestic and foreign securities.[4] Top executives of commercial and investment banks became "celebrities" during the boom, and many investors relied on their advice. As Allen explained in 1935, "For seven years the public distrust of Wall Street steadily diminished, until by 1928 and 1929, the big financiers, like the big industrialists, had become objects of a general veneration."[5]

As enacted in 1864, the National Bank Act prohibited national banks from making loans secured by real estate, exercising trust powers, trading in or underwriting securities (other than federal and state government bonds), and opening branch offices. As explained in Chapter 1, Congress relaxed those constraints by passing a series of liberalizing statutes between 1913 and 1927, culminating in the McFadden Act. Those laws broadened the powers of national banks in all four areas so that they could compete more effectively with state-chartered banks and trust companies. By 1927, national banks could provide real estate loans with five-year terms in amounts up to half the value of mortgaged properties. National banks could exercise trust powers equal to those of state-chartered institutions in their home states. National banks could underwrite and trade in government and corporate bonds that were deemed "marketable" by the Comptroller of the Currency. National banks could not underwrite or trade in corporate stocks, but they could engage indirectly in those activities through their securities affiliates.[6] Finally, national banks could open branches in their home cities if competing state-chartered banks were allowed to do so under state law.[7]

National banks took full advantage of their expanded powers during the 1920s. Real estate loans made by national and state-chartered banks (including commercial banks, savings banks, and trust companies) more than doubled between 1921 and 1929, rising from $4.7 billion to $10.4 billion.[8] The surge in real estate financing by banks and other lenders during the 1920s supported large booms in residential and commercial real estate markets.

Banks, along with finance companies and manufacturers and retailers of consumer goods, produced comparable growth in consumer loans. Outstanding consumer non-mortgage loans more than doubled during the 1920s, rising from $3.2 billion to $7.6 billion (including an increase in consumer installment debts from $2.1 billion to $4.9 billion). The rapid growth of consumer credit enabled Americans to buy vast quantities of cars, radios, phonographs, household appliances (such as refrigerators and washing machines), furniture, jewelry, and other durable consumer goods. Purchases of durable goods accounted for 9% of consumer spending during the 1920s, and consumer credit financed nearly half of those purchases. Car registrations increased from 11 million to 26 million between 1921 and 1929, and automobile loans were the single largest source of consumer installment credit. Sales of refrigerators rose from 11,000 in 1922 to 630,000 in 1929, while sales of radios skyrocketed from 100,000 to more than 4 million during the same period. By 1926, consumers bought two-thirds of their new cars and three-quarters of their new radios and refrigerators on credit.[9]

In contrast to other types of bank credit, commercial lending did not grow significantly during the 1920s. Many corporations experienced great hardships during the severe recession of 1920–21, when banks cut back dramatically on their lending. As the economy recovered, larger corporations reduced their reliance on bank loans and satisfied a growing share of their funding needs by selling debt and equity securities to institutional and individual investors. Bank loans to large corporations showed very little growth after 1921.[10]

Given the stagnant demand for corporate loans, commercial banks shifted their focus from lending to the securities markets. The number of commercial banks engaged in securities activities, either directly through bond departments or indirectly through securities affiliates, rose from 277 in 1922 to 591 in 1929. During the same period, the number of banks with securities affiliates shot up from 18 to 132 (and rose further to 180 in 1930).[11]

Commercial banks expanded their securities activities in three major ways. First, they more than doubled their "loans on securities" (loans collateralized by securities) from $5.7 billion to $13 billion between 1921 and 1930. Loans on securities included "call money" loans (loans to securities brokers that were repayable on demand and secured by pledges of securities) as well as margin loans (loans to bank customers that were also secured by pledges of securities). Banks provided more than 85% of all loans on securities during the 1920s, and the share of total bank credit represented by loans on securities rose from 24% to 38% during that period.[12]

Second, banks increased their direct investments in securities from $8.4 billion to $13.7 billion between 1921 and 1930. Four-fifths of that growth represented investments in higher-risk securities, including state and municipal bonds, corporate bonds, and foreign securities. In contrast, bank holdings of low-risk federal government bonds fell from 35% to 26% of bank investments during the 1920s.[13]

Third, and most significantly, commercial banks greatly expanded their share of the securities underwriting business, especially after the McFadden Act enlarged the securities powers of national banks in February 1927. The share of U.S. bond offerings for which banks and their affiliates acted as lead underwriters rose from 22% in 1927 to more than 45% in 1929 and 1930. In addition, the share of U.S. bond offerings for which banks or their affiliates participated in underwriting syndicates led by other institutions grew from 37% in 1927 to 51% in 1929 and 61% in 1930.[14]

By the end of the 1920s, "commercial banks and their affiliates were equal in importance to all [private] investment banks in the distribution of long-term capital and in the facilities and values of their business." The leading roles played by commercial banks and their affiliates in distributing securities to investors throughout the country "made commercial banks by far the most important element in the investment banking business."[15]

Large commercial banks and their affiliates possessed significant competitive advantages over private investment banks in marketing and distributing securities to investors. Commercial banks and their affiliates maintained significantly larger networks of branches and representative offices. Commercial banks and their affiliates could obtain large amounts of low-cost funding through deposits and could also draw on a broader client base that included depositors, borrowers, trust customers, and recipients of cash management services (such as corporations and insurance companies).[16] Most importantly, the largest commercial banks enjoyed a higher degree of "good will" in selling securities, due to the public's greater "confidence" in their soundness and stability.[17]

The largest commercial banks also benefited from their ability to attract deposits from correspondent banks and to provide investment advice and sell securities to those banks. During the 1920s, an intricate network of correspondent banking relationships existed among "money center banks" in New York and Chicago, "reserve city banks" in regional financial centers (such as Atlanta, Cleveland, Detroit, Philadelphia, San Francisco, and St. Louis), and "country banks" located in smaller cities and rural areas. Country banks typically established correspondent relationships with reserve city banks (where they deposited surplus funds and received check-clearing services and lines of credit) and also with money center banks (where they deposited surplus funds and received foreign exchange and investment services, such as the ability to invest in the New York call loan market or the Chicago market for short-term loans to commodity traders). Reserve city banks kept deposits with, and received correspondent services from, money center banks.[18]

Deposits from correspondent banks accounted for about a quarter of all deposits held by reserve city banks and money center banks. Money center banks held almost half of the nation's interbank deposits, with New York banks holding 37% and Chicago banks holding 9%. Money center banks and reserve city banks relied on those interbank deposits as a major funding source for their investments in securities and loans backed by securities.[19] Money center banks and reserve city banks also provided investment advice and encouraged correspondent banks to buy the securities they offered for sale through their bond departments and securities affiliates.[20]

———

The intense rivalry between commercial banks and investment banks during the 1920s produced a dramatic increase in the number of firms and offices devoted to the public sale of securities. The number of securities dealers in the U.S. (including affiliates of commercial banks) rose from 250 in 1914 to 6,500 in 1929. Securities dealers operated offices in seven hundred U.S. cities in 1929. More than thirty of those cities were served by at least fifteen securities dealers.[21] Securities firms operated 2,500 offices in New York City and almost 600 offices in Chicago.[22]

Favorable economic conditions and aggressive competition between commercial and investment banks fueled an explosion of new securities issues in the U.S. Domestic corporations issued $54 billion of debt and equity securities between 1919 and 1930.[23] During the same period, state and local governments issued almost $15 billion of bonds,[24] while foreign governments and foreign corporations sold $12 billion of debt and equity securities in the U.S.[25] Thus, more than $80 billion of securities were issued in the U.S. between the end of World War I and the onset of the Great Depression.

Contemporary observers agreed that the tremendous surge in new securities issues could not have occurred without the active participation of large commercial banks. During a 1931 Senate hearing, Allan Pope, a prominent banker, explained that securities affiliates of commercial banks created "large sales organizations" that made it possible to "successfully distribute" large issues of securities. If banks had not established securities affiliates, Pope said, "private capital probably could not have been found in sufficient volume ... to develop private investment houses to a point where they would have been in a position to handle [the] enormous increase in underwriting and distribution" during the 1920s. In Pope's view, securities affiliates of commercial banks provided significant benefits to "industry and trade" by creating a "vast mechanism of underwriting and distributing of both domestic and foreign securities."[26]

During a Senate debate on the Glass-Steagall Act in 1932, Senator Frederick Walcott (R-CT) and Senator Carter Glass (D-VA) agreed with Pope's factual premises but not his optimistic conclusion. Walcott maintained that the "phenomenal" growth of securities affiliates produced a "flood tide of speculation," which relied on the credit and distribution facilities of large commercial banks. Walcott argued that private investment banks, such as J. P. Morgan & Co. and Kuhn, Loeb & Co., did not have sufficient financial capital or physical facilities to handle the massive public offerings of domestic and foreign securities that occurred during the 1920s. Those offerings required nationwide distribution networks and "very expansive credit, which, of course, brought in the banks."[27] Similarly, Glass alleged that securities affiliates of commercial banks "were perhaps the greatest contributors to the riot of credit inflation in 1928–29, with the result that the country is now almost in an irreparable condition."[28]

Thus, commercial banks played a crucial role in promoting the great boom in securities offerings during the 1920s. In contrast to private investment banks (except for J. P. Morgan & Co.), the biggest commercial banks and their securities affiliates could draw on much larger pools of deposits and reservoirs of capital to finance their securities operations.[29] The largest commercial banks and their affiliates could also mobilize their extensive networks of branch offices, which gave them a clear advantage in distributing securities to institutional and retail investors.[30]

Private investment banks worried about the competitive threat posed by commercial banks, and they expanded their own operations to meet that threat. One leading strategy used by investment banks was to organize investment trusts (the forerunner of today's mutual funds). Commercial banks responded by forming their own investment trusts toward the end of the 1920s. A large number of investment trusts organized by investment and commercial banks collapsed after the crash of 1929 and inflicted heavy losses on investors.[31]

Commercial and investment banks engaged in "a veritable orgy of competition" by offering a wide range of domestic and foreign securities to U.S. investors during the 1920s. Intense competition resulted in "a marked decline in banking judgment and ethics and unscrupulous exploitation of public gullibility and avarice." Both commercial and investment bankers "scrambled to win new offerings" due to "the speculative fever of the times and the opportunities for quick, easy profits which it promised."[32]

———

Under Charles Mitchell's leadership, National City Bank exemplified the universal banking strategy that many large U.S. commercial banks pursued during the 1920s. After becoming president of National City Bank in May 1921, Mitchell vigorously pursued the strategy of his predecessors (James Stillman and Frank Vanderlip) to build National City into a "global, all-purpose financial intermediary."[33] In December 1921, Mitchell announced that National City would be a "financial department store" offering a comprehensive set of "savings, commercial and investment banking, and trust [services]" to satisfy its customers' financial needs "from the cradle to the grave."[34] To implement his universal banking strategy, Mitchell expanded National City's operations across a wide range of financial services, including deposit-taking, commercial and consumer lending, cash management, trust services, and securities underwriting and trading.[35]

National City Bank acquired three other New York City banks during the 1920s and operated thirty-seven branch offices throughout the city. National City Bank also enlarged its international branching network and maintained ninety-eight branches in twenty-three countries by 1930. The New York City branches served more than 230,000 depositors, while the international branches served an additional 160,000 depositors.[36]

National City Bank's domestic and foreign branches offered lending, fiduciary, and investment services to both individuals and companies. In addition, National City was the first major commercial bank to make substantial volumes of unsecured consumer loans. The bank provided deposit, cash management, and investment services to more than six thousand domestic corporations and correspondent banks. It was the leading provider of trust services in New York City by 1929. Its deposits, loans, and total assets more than doubled between 1921 and 1929.[37]

National City's most spectacular growth occurred in its securities business. National City Bank more than quadrupled the amount of its broker call loans between 1923 and 1929. Like other large New York banks, National City Bank encouraged its corporate customers and correspondent banks to transfer funds from their deposit accounts at National City to the broker call loan market, where they could earn higher rates of interest.[38]

National City Bank also made extensive loans to support the activities of its securities affiliate, National City Company. NCC frequently borrowed amounts up to National City Bank's legal lending limit (about $30 million) to meet NCC's short-term funding needs.[39] National City Bank also provided loans to many of NCC's customers. In 1930 and 1931, National City Bank held more than $80 million of "bridge" loans, which it had extended to NCC's customers in anticipation of securities offerings that NCC could not complete after the stock market crashed in October 1929.[40]

In 1929, Mitchell installed his trusted subordinates, Gordon Rentschler and Hugh Baker, as presidents of National City Bank and NCC. Mitchell served as chairman of both organizations and retained "ultimate authority" over all aspects of their operations.[41] During Senate committee hearings in 1933, Mitchell acknowledged that the bank and NCC were "inseparably interwoven" and that the two companies acted together as "one institutional entity." Baker similarly admitted that the bank and NCC helped each other "all the time."[42] Ferdinand Pecora, who led the Senate committee's investigation of National City as chief counsel, remarked that "the Bank and the Company were treated, quite simply, as two departments of a single organization."[43]

Mitchell established lucrative bonus plans for the senior executives of National City Bank and NCC. Senior officers of both firms received fixed salaries, typically $25,000 per year. Under Mitchell's bonus plans, the first 8% of each firm's annual net earnings were retained for the benefit of shareholders, and one-fifth of all net earnings above the 8% level were paid into a "management fund." The management fund for each firm then distributed bonuses to qualifying senior executives. Mitchell received about 40% of the bonuses paid by National City Bank's fund and about 30% of the bonuses paid by NCC's fund. Mitchell received $3.5 million in salary and bonuses from 1927 through 1929, while Baker received total compensation of $750,000 during the same period.[44]

National City's executive committee approved the management bonus plans, but those plans were not disclosed to National City's shareholders. In addition, National City arranged for the bonus payments to be distributed to its executives by two other New York banks so that National City's staff would not be aware of the bonuses. Examiners in the Office of the Comptroller of the Currency discovered the bonus payments in 1925 but did not object to them. During the Senate committee's investigation of National City in 1933, Ferdinand Pecora revealed the very large bonuses paid to Mitchell and his colleagues. That revelation triggered widespread public outrage.[45]

National City's and NCC's bonus plans created perverse incentives that encouraged Mitchell and other senior executives to assume greater risks in their pursuit of higher profits. As Pecora explained, the bonus plans made it "quite easy to understand the reckless, anything-for-a-profit mood in which the National City was operating. The officers had nothing to gain, and everything to lose, individually, by a conservative policy." Top executives at each company knew they would receive only their salaries, without any bonuses, if their company produced net profits of less than 8% per year, because all of those earnings would go to the shareholders. In contrast, senior managers would collect one-fifth of any "superprofits" above 8% per year. Moreover, there were no clawback provisions requiring them to return their bonuses if their company subsequently suffered losses. In Pecora's view, National City Bank and NCC gave their leaders "a gigantic, foolproof device for gambling freely with the stockholders' money, taking huge profits when the gambles won, and risking not one penny of their own money if they lost."[46]

During the Senate committee's hearings in 1933, Mitchell tried to defend NCC's bonus plan. He argued that the bonus plan created "an esprit de corps" among NCC's top officers by giving them a personal "interest" in the efforts of their colleagues. He also contended that the bonus plan was necessary to "meet the competition of private [investment banking] partnerships" in attracting top executives. According to Mitchell, NCC's leaders were "the equivalent of partners in a private banking or investment firm," and it was therefore appropriate for them to receive "some share in the profits that they should make."[47]

Mitchell's testimony reflected the intense rivalry between securities affiliates of commercial banks and private investment banks, as well as the high-risk, high-reward culture that characterized both types of institutions during the 1920s. Mitchell admitted that he could "readily see" why outsiders might believe that NCC's bonus plan "must have some influence" in encouraging aggressive risk-taking by NCC's top executives. However, he said, "I do not recall seeing it operate that way." Senator James Couzens (R-MI) responded to Mitchell by commenting, "You would not see it. Only the customers would see it after they had gotten the securities" sold by NCC.[48]

During the 1920s, Mitchell built NCC into "the largest agency in the world for the distribution of securities to the public."[49] By 1929, NCC employed almost two thousand people and operated sixty-nine branch offices in fifty-eight cities across the U.S. NCC's branches were linked by more than 11,000 miles of private telegraph lines. NCC also offered investment services through National City Bank's branches in New York City as well as the bank's foreign branches around the world.[50]

NCC did not locate its sales offices on the upper floors of office buildings. Instead, NCC catered to the growing middle class by opening its offices "on the street level where people walked by." According to a 1923 magazine article, Mitchell instructed his sales agents that ordinary investors "were just waiting for someone to come and tell them what to do with their savings ... [Now] go down and tell them." The article summarized Mitchell's marketing philosophy as follows:

> Instead of waiting for investors to come, [Mitchell] took young men and women, gave them a training course in the sale of securities, and sent them out to *find* the investors. Such methods, pursued with such vigor and on such a scale, were revolutionary.[51]

Frederick Lewis Allen described Mitchell as a man with "inexhaustible energy ... There flowed from him the sort of vital personal force which enables a military commander to rally his men for a successful assault—a force [that he] directed into rallying bond salesmen."[52] Under Mitchell's leadership, NCC sold $20 billion of securities to the public between 1922 and 1932, either as the lead underwriter or as a participant in underwriting syndicates led by other firms.[53] The securities sold by NCC included more than a fifth of all domestic and foreign bonds issued in the U.S. between 1921 and 1929. NCC also sold common stocks to the public beginning in 1927.[54]

With $20 billion of sales, NCC was by far the largest distributor of securities to the public between World War I and the Great Depression. Chase National Bank's securities affiliate and J. P. Morgan & Co. each sold about $6 billion of securities, Dillon, Read & Co. sold about $4 billion of securities, and Kuhn, Loeb & Co. sold a similar amount.[55] In Ferdinand Pecora's view, NCC's preeminence as a seller of securities was "a gigantic monument to Mr. Mitchell's supersalesmanship, his limitless energy, and driving genius."[56] Edmund Wilson similarly described Mitchell as "the banker of bankers, the salesman of salesmen, the genius of the New Economic Era," a man who "blazed like the great central source of the energy and heat of the boom."

Mitchell's unfailing belief in the continued success of National City and the American economy earned him the nickname "Sunshine Charley."[57] When National City announced its decision to begin selling common stocks in February 1927, Mitchell declared that it was time for the American public to "invest in progress instead of merely in static wealth" offered by bonds. According to Mitchell, National City's "new policy" of selling common stocks reflected the bank's "faith in the future, faith in the reliability of conservative financial analysis, faith in progress and faith in America and the continued and steady advance of modern civilization."[58]

Mitchell recognized that National City's success depended on maintaining the trust of unsophisticated investors, including middle-income families, professionals, smaller business firms and nonprofits, and small correspondent banks.[59] In his lecture to a class of trainees in March 1919, Mitchell stressed the importance of building on the customer goodwill that National City Bank and NCC established through their sales of Liberty bonds. Mitchell told the trainees that ordinary investors could not be expected to evaluate the risks of corporate and foreign bonds. Accordingly, to "fulfill our trust" and maintain the "confidence" of customers, National City Bank and NCC must sell investments that were suitable for their needs:

> We have gained the confidence of the investor and we are building our institution upon that confidence. We want the public to feel safe with us. We are going to make more exacting our yard-stick, because the small investor who buys from us today a thousand or a five hundred dollar bond is not in a position to know whether that security is good or not and must rely on us. . . . [W]e recognize that as between ourselves and this small investor, the law of *caveat emptor* cannot apply, and that if we are to fulfill our trust, we must supply that which means safety and a reasonable return to him.[60]

NCC used mass marketing techniques that Mitchell had perfected during the Liberty bond drives. NCC's sales literature sought to win the trust and confidence of investors. NCC's advertising "assured prospective investors that if they saved, it would advise them how to invest," and NCC would only sell them securities that received NCC's "seal of approval" after careful study by its research staff.[61] One NCC advertisement stated that investors "should not try to decide alone" and instead should rely on "the considered opinion of a world-wide investment organization . . . National City['s] judgment as to which bonds are best for you is based on both strict investigation of the security and analysis of your own requirements."[62]

Another NCC advertisement stated, "Only when the facts indicate sound values are we willing to say, 'This bond meets our standard—we recommend it.' "[63] A third advertisement assured investors, "When you buy a bond recommended by [NCC], you may be sure that all the essential facts which justify [NCC's] confidence in the investment are available to you."[64]

However, NCC's single-minded drive to become the largest global seller of securities resulted in a marked departure from Mitchell's avowed principles of trust, suitability, and full disclosure. Under the direction of Mitchell and Hugh Baker, NCC sent out a steady stream of sales "flashes" to its branch offices over NCC's network of private wires. Those "flashes" recommended securities currently being offered for sale by NCC and promised cash rewards and other incentives to sales agents who met their goals. From 1927 to 1929, the "new sales department" of NCC furnished the names of more than 220,000 prospective customers to its sales agents, and many of those names were drawn from tax lists and automobile registration lists. Employees of National City Bank routinely referred depositors to NCC's sales agents if the depositors asked about investments.[65]

Julian Sherrod, who worked for NCC as a sales representative during the 1920s, later described the relentless pressure that NCC's managers imposed on him and his colleagues:

> All day long the message was the same—hurry up, hurry up, hurry up—send some orders.... When things slowed up a little, some genius would hatch up a contest of some kind and then we would be under extra pressure from every direction sometimes for weeks.

Sherrod admitted that his typical customer "did not know what he was buying, and I did not know what I was selling. I was just merchandising."[66]

Sales agents who failed to meet their goals were shamed or fired. In a telegram sent to NCC's sales force, Mitchell warned:

> I should hate to think there is any man in our *sales crowd* who would confess to his inability to sell at least some of any issue of either bonds or preferred stocks that we think good enough to offer. In fact, this would be an impossible situation and, in the interest of all concerned, one that we would not permit to continue.[67]

———

Mitchell did not adhere to his professed standards of trust and suitability even when he dealt with National City's shareholders and employees. Mitchell arranged a series of transactions that misled shareholders and inflicted grievous losses on many of them. The first transaction arose out of National City's continuing struggles with its legacy of defaulted Cuban sugar loans. As described in Chapter 1, National City held more than $30 million of nonperforming Cuban loans on its books in early 1927. Examiners in the Office of the Comptroller of the Currency repeatedly criticized those loans. To address the Cuban loan problem, National City Bank sold $50 million of newly issued stock to its shareholders in February 1927. Half of those funds were added to the bank's capital, and the other half were added to NCC's capital. NCC immediately invested its $25 million of new capital in General Sugar Corporation, an affiliate of NCC that owned National City Bank's Cuban sugar properties. General Sugar promptly paid $21 million in cash and issued $11 million in promissory notes to acquire National City Bank's portfolio of delinquent Cuban loans, thereby transferring the loans from the bank's books to NCC's accounts. However, NCC and General Sugar could not resolve the Cuban loan problem. At the end of 1931, NCC wrote down its entire investment in General Sugar to $1, thereby creating a large loss for National City's shareholders.[68]

As Michael Perino observed, the General Sugar transaction "neatly excised the Cuban debt from [National City Bank's] books and placed it in [NCC], with the bank's shareholders picking up the tab." Shareholders who bought the $50 million of newly issued National City Bank shares in 1927 were not told that half of their investment would be used to finance NCC's investment in General Sugar as well as General Sugar's acquisition of the nonperforming Cuban loans. When Ferdinand Pecora pressed Mitchell on that issue, Mitchell responded, "I hardly think there was any necessity" for such disclosure.[69] As Perino explained, Mitchell had a powerful motive for hiding the General Sugar deal from National City's shareholders:

> Mitchell was clearly using [NCC] to obscure [National City Bank's] mistakes, both to outsiders and to the bank's own shareholders. As Mitchell confided to one of his bond salesmen, "We wash our dirty linen on the back porch rather than the front porch."[70]

After National City Bank and NCC transferred the troubled Cuban loans to General Sugar, they launched a vigorous campaign to pump up the bank's stock price and attract new investors. In January 1928, National City Bank delisted its stock from the New York Stock Exchange (NYSE) and moved its stock to the "curb exchange" (an alternative market operated by securities brokers). The curb exchange had more lenient rules and allowed NCC to exercise greater control over trading operations in National City's stock.[71] NCC promptly began a massive trading program in National City's stock to raise its market price and recruit a larger group of shareholders. NCC bought shares of National City stock on the curb exchange, either directly or through brokers, and resold those shares to other investors. By the end of 1930, NCC had purchased and resold almost two million shares of National City stock, for which investors paid about $650 million. In addition, National City Bank and NCC increased their capital by selling $140 million of newly issued National City shares in 1928 and 1929. The number of National City shareholders increased from fewer than 16,000 in 1927 to almost 80,000 at the end of 1930.[72]

National City Bank and NCC wanted to attract more shareholders to create "more business opportunities" and "more prospective customers" for the financial services they offered. In February 1929, National City Bank arranged a 5-for-1 stock split, in which five new shares of National City stock were issued in exchange for each existing share. The stock split was designed to reduce the market price of National City's stock so that it would be "within the reach of the smaller investor." Depositors who asked employees of National City Bank or NCC for investment advice were frequently encouraged to buy National City stock. NCC also urged many of its customers to sell other securities from their portfolios and invest the proceeds in National City stock. NCC offered special commissions to reward sales representatives who sold National City stock. National City Bank supported NCC's trading program by providing short-term loans to NCC and associated brokers who purchased NCC's shares.[73]

NCC's trading campaign helped to boost National City's stock price from $780 per share in January 1928 to $2,900 per share in the fall of 1929 (adjusted for the 5-for-1 stock split). At that point, National City's stock price was equal to 120 times its annual earnings and 13 times its book value. Following the stock market's crash in October 1929, National City's stock price plummeted by more than 90% to $200 per share in early 1933.[74] The Senate committee investigating National City in 1933 received many letters from individuals who suffered heavy losses from their investments in National City stock. One woman wrote that NCC's sales representatives persuaded her to sell her entire portfolio of government bonds and reinvest all of the proceeds in National City stock. After the stock price collapsed, she wrote to Mitchell to complain. He replied that he was "sorry" for her loss, but she "shouldn't have gambled."[75]

National City Bank created a stock purchase plan for its high-ranking officers in February 1927, after it addressed the Cuban loan problem and before NCC began its massive campaign to pump up the bank's stock price. National City Bank also established a stock purchase plan for its ordinary employees in December 1929, after the stock market crashed and after National City's stock price had already declined by more than half from its peak. Employees bought 60,000 shares of National City stock under the program at prices ranging from $1,000 to $1,100. Many employees purchased their shares under a four-year installment plan, which deducted monthly payments (with 5% interest) from their paychecks. The difference in timing between the two programs showed that National City wanted to offer its senior executives an extraordinary opportunity to make profits during NCC's upcoming trading campaign, while it later encouraged its employees to buy stock in a vain effort to prop up the bank's falling stock price.[76]

After the stock market crashed, National City Bank provided $2.4 million of interest-free "morale" loans to its high-ranking officers to enable them to hold on to their bank shares despite the plunging stock price and margin calls. Those executives ultimately paid off only 5% of their morale loans. National City Bank transferred the unpaid morale loans to NCC in December 1930, and NCC either wrote the loans off or did not try to collect them.[77]

In stark contrast, National City Bank rigorously enforced the installment stock purchase contracts signed by its ordinary employees in December 1929. Many employees were still paying off their loans (with interest) in 1933, and the remaining obligations for most employees were much larger than the value of their shares. Ferdinand Pecora remarked, "Mr. Mitchell and his colleagues seem at times to have been no more concerned about protecting the interests of the rank-and-file employees than they were to protect the interests of the rank-and-file stockholders or the public." One newspaper commented that National City's forgiveness of its morale loans for senior executives stood "in ugly contrast with the manner in which the same officials are still compelling their lower-caste employees to repay loans for similar purposes ... There can be no sympathy with men who do such things."[78]

———

Chase National Bank and its securities affiliate, Chase Securities Corporation (CSC), represented the second most important U.S. universal bank during the 1920s. Albert Wiggin was the "active head and guiding spirit" of both units, and he "dominated [Chase] as overwhelmingly as Mitchell dominated the National City."[79] Like Mitchell, Wiggin achieved personal success through exceptional ambition and enterprise. After working for several other banks, Wiggin joined Chase National Bank as a vice president and director in 1904. He became president of the bank in 1911 and chairman of the bank in 1918.[80]

In 1929, examiners from the Office of the Comptroller of the Currency called Wiggin "the most popular banker in Wall Street." Like Mitchell, Wiggin received extensive press coverage, and the public viewed both men as preeminent Wall Street leaders. Both men "radiated an air of confidence," and Pecora described them as "shrewd, aggressive men intent on pursuing success with as few distractions as possible."[81]

Wiggin was determined to build Chase into a full-service financial giant that could compete on equal terms with National City.[82] He pursued a growth and diversification plan for Chase that mirrored Mitchell's strategy for National City. By 1920, Chase offered a full range of financial services to its business and retail customers.[83] Chase acquired six other New York City banks during the 1920s, and its assets doubled from $560 million in 1919 to $1.12 billion in 1929. In 1930, Chase entered into a megamerger with the Equitable Trust Company. That merger created a $2.65 billion institution that surpassed National City Bank as the largest U.S. bank.[84]

Following National City's example, Chase National Bank organized CSC as a securities affiliate in 1917 to expand Chase's capacity to underwrite and trade in securities. At first, CSC distributed securities on a wholesale basis to correspondent banks, securities dealers, and other institutional investors. In 1927, Wiggin diversified CSC's operations to include retail sales of securities to individual customers. CSC quickly built a network of domestic and foreign branch offices that rivaled NCC's far-flung system of branches. In 1930, CSC acquired the Harris Forbes securities firm and thereafter operated more than fifty domestic sales offices as well as several foreign offices. CSC sold more than $6 billion of securities, with most of those sales occurring between 1927 and 1930.[85]

Chase also imitated National City by conducting a massive trading program to pump up its stock price. Like National City, Chase delisted its stock from the NYSE in January 1928 and moved its stock to the curb exchange so that CSC and another affiliate (Metopan Securities Corp.) could more easily manage their trading campaign in Chase's stock. Like National City, Chase arranged a 5-for-1 stock split to reduce the market price of its shares and encourage a "wider distribution" of its stock to small investors.[86]

CSC organized eight trading pools, which bought and resold $860 million of Chase National Bank stock between 1927 and 1931. Chase National Bank provided loans to CSC and Metopan to support their purchases of Chase stock on the curb exchange. As a result of CSC's and Metopan's trading campaigns, the number of Chase's shareholders grew to 89,000, and the market price for Chase stock rose from $575 per share in 1927 to $1,125 per share in 1929 (adjusted for the 5-for-1 stock split). At that point, Chase's stock price was equal to sixty-two times its annual earnings and more than four times its book value. After the stock market crashed, the price of Chase stock fell by more than 90% to $89 per share in 1933.[87] Thus, Chase shareholders who bought their stock at the peak of the stock market boom in 1929 suffered investment losses similar to their National City peers. According to Barrie Wigmore, the common stocks of National City and Chase were "probably the most overvalued stocks in the market" in 1929.[88]

At the end of 1927, Chase National Bank and CSC created a stock purchase program that gave their ordinary employees the opportunity to buy Chase stock and pay for their purchases under a five-year installment plan. However, participating employees purchased their stock at an unfavorable price that was, $100 per share *above* the existing market price for Chase stock. Like National City and NCC, Chase and CSC rigorously enforced their ordinary employees' installment purchase contracts. Many Chase and CSC employees were still paying off their installment obligations with interest in 1933, even though the value of their Chase stock had fallen far below their original purchase price.[89] The extent to which National City and Chase followed parallel policies that took unfair advantage of their shareholders and ordinary employees was both remarkable and chilling.

———

NCC and CSC also engaged in speculative trading in the stocks of numerous client companies, and they sold large blocks of shares in those companies to the public. NCC's and CSC's trading and selling operations produced handsome profits for them, their top executives, and key insiders of their client companies, but inflicted significant losses on many public investors.

In late 1928 and early 1929, NCC participated in three syndicates that traded in the stocks of a subsidiary of Anaconda Mining and two other copper mining companies that Anaconda wanted to acquire. Anaconda's two top executives participated in those trading syndicates. The syndicates completed their operations in early 1929, producing substantial profits for all participants (including NCC, Charles Mitchell, and other senior executives of NCC). Shortly thereafter, Anaconda acquired the other two mining companies, and Mitchell joined Anaconda's board of directors.[90]

In August 1929, NCC launched an aggressive campaign to sell Anaconda shares to the public. During the next two months, NCC sold more than 1.3 million shares of Anaconda stock to public investors at an average price of $120 per share. NCC pursued its public sales of Anaconda shares at a time when NCC knew (but did not disclose) that the market price for copper had recently fallen from 24¢ per pound to 18¢ per pound. When questioned by Ferdinand Pecora about why NCC sold the public so many shares of Anaconda stock, Mitchell replied, "It became our duty, or so we conceived it, so long as our customers viewed that stock as an investment stock, to buy in the market and to sell additional shares to them." In other words, NCC kept selling as long as its customers were willing to buy Anaconda stock at prices that were favorable to NCC. NCC ultimately made a profit of more than $20 million on its purchases and resales of Anaconda stock. After the stock market crashed, Anaconda's stock price fell by more than 90%, to $7 per share in 1933. NCC's campaign to market and sell Anaconda stock was similar to other sales campaigns managed by NCC.[91]

Similarly, CSC organized two trading syndicates for the stock of Sinclair Oil in 1928. One of Albert Wiggin's family corporations and several of Sinclair's senior officers and directors participated in those syndicates. The two syndicates bought and sold nearly 2.5 million shares of Sinclair stock and earned almost $13 million of profits for CSC and the other participants. Chase National Bank supported the acquisition of Sinclair stock by providing a short-term loan of $12 million to the two syndicates. The syndicates sold Sinclair stock to the public at an average price of $38 per share. By 1933, the market price of Sinclair stock had fallen by more than two-thirds, to $12 per share.[92] CSC participated in more than thirty other trading syndicates between 1928 and 1932. In Pecora's view, CSC's trading syndicates were "raiding expeditions in the market in the spirit of the times," which indicated CSC's willingness to exploit "the speculative frenzy ... for its own profit."[93]

———

National City Bank and Chase National Bank were the preeminent American universal banks of the 1920s. They served as models for other large urban banks, which also grew rapidly during the 1920s by acquiring other banks, opening branches, and establishing securities affiliates.[94] After completing major acquisitions in 1929, the two biggest Chicago banks (Continental Illinois and First National Bank of Chicago) ranked among the nation's ten largest banks. They "towered over the Chicago money market like giants" and accounted for "about half the banking business transacted in the city."[95]

Many large urban banks established securities affiliates that sold securities (including the stocks of their affiliated banks) to institutional and retail investors. In addition to National City, Chase, and the two biggest Chicago banks, the most important metropolitan banks with securities affiliates were the two largest New York trust companies (Guaranty Trust Company and Bankers Trust Company), the First National Bank of Boston (which acquired the Old Colony Trust Company and its securities affiliate in 1930), and Bank of America. Bank of America operated the largest network of branches in California, and it also controlled a commercial and investment banking organization in New York City between 1928 and 1931.[96]

To circumvent restrictions on bank branching under federal and state laws, bank executives organized bank holding companies as well as banking chains (groups of banks owned by the same shareholder or group of shareholders). The resulting banking groups dominated several regional financial centers in the U.S., including Cleveland and Detroit. At the end of 1929, 330 bank holding companies controlled more than 2,000 banks.[97] Many of the largest bank holding companies established securities affiliates to provide investment banking services to customers of their subsidiary banks. Those securities affiliates frequently sold stock of the parent holding companies to the public to finance the holding companies' acquisitions of additional banks.[98]

The investment banking firm of Caldwell and Company in Nashville, Tennessee, controlled the largest chain of southern banks. Caldwell and Company was called "the Morgan of the South," and it was the leading underwriter of municipal, real estate, and industrial bonds in the South during the 1920s.[99] As described in Chapter 5, losses from securities activities played a significant role in the failures or near-failures of Caldwell and Company and several other large banking organizations with securities affiliates during the Great Depression.

————

The securities underwritten during the 1920s by investment banks and securities affiliates of commercial banks included $4 billion of real estate bonds. Real estate bonds represented an early form of securitized commercial real estate debt. Special-purpose corporations issued real estate bonds that investment and commercial banks sold to investors to finance the construction or renovation of apartment buildings, office buildings, hotels, retail stores, and other commercial properties. Each bond was backed by mortgages on a single commercial property or a small group of properties. Real estate bonds were sold in denominations ranging from $100 to $1,000, and unsophisticated investors purchased most of those bonds.[100]

Buildings in New York City and Chicago accounted for half of the real estate bonds issued in the U.S., while Detroit (with its boom in automobile production) had the third-largest number of buildings financed by real estate bonds. Many prospectuses for real estate bonds contained false or misleading information, including inflated appraisals of property values and unrealistic projections of future rental income. The quality and performance of real estate bonds steadily declined as the commercial real estate boom reached its peak between 1924 and 1928. More than two-thirds of all real estate bonds defaulted by 1931, and 95% of those bonds defaulted by 1936.[101] Banks and other investors who held substantial amounts of real estate bonds suffered heavy losses during the Great Depression.[102]

The real estate bonds and debentures underwritten by Chase Securities Corporation for the Lincoln Forty-Second Street Corporation (LFSSC) provided typical examples of the poor quality and disastrous performance of most real estate bonds sold during the late 1920s. LFSSC was organized in early 1928 to build a new fifty-three-story office building on 42nd Street in New York City. An underwriting group led by CSC sold more than $17 million of LFSSC's bonds and debentures to the public in May 1928. CSC's prospectuses stated that the new building would be "one of the tallest and most imposing structures in the city" and "one of the finest office buildings in the country." The prospectuses assured investors that "demand for high grade office building space and for shops and stores in this very accessible location has been definitely established." The prospectuses also said that projected rental revenues would easily cover the required annual debt service payments on the bonds and debentures.[103]

CSC's prospectuses did not disclose that two of Chase National Bank's directors opposed CSC's involvement in the project and that a Chase officer questioned the project's viability. Due to falling demand for office space in New York City after the stock market crash, the new building signed leases for only half of its offices. LFSSC defaulted on its bonds and debentures in 1931. At the foreclosure sale in July 1933, CSC made the highest bid and purchased the building for $4.75 million, less than a fifth of its original appraised value. LFSSC's bondholders recovered less than 40% of their investments, and LFSSC's debenture holders lost all of their investments.[104]

———

The issuance of real estate bonds accounted for about one-fifth of the tremendous surge in real estate debt after World War I. The total amount of urban nonfarm mortgages (including commercial real estate loans) more than tripled from $10 billion in 1919 to $32 billion in 1930. Commercial banks, savings banks, building and loan associations, and life insurance companies greatly expanded their real estate lending and held about $24 billion of urban nonfarm mortgages in 1930.[105]

The remaining $8 billion of mortgages were held by (or for the benefit of) individual investors, including investors who bought real estate bonds and mortgage guarantee participation certificates.[106] Like real estate bonds, mortgage guarantee participation certificates were an early form of securitized real estate debt. Most of those certificates defaulted along with real estate bonds during the 1930s.[107] Thus, securitized real estate investments sold by private issuers in the 1920s were as disastrous for investors as the private-label securitizations of residential mortgages proved to be during the financial crisis of 2007–09.[108]

The dramatic growth of real estate lending during the 1920s was spurred by a sharp rise in demand by individuals and families for homes and apartments, by travelers for hotel rooms, and by business firms for offices and production facilities. The feedback loop between growing demand and the surge in real estate loans fueled a large boom in residential and commercial real estate. More than $100 billion was spent on private and public construction projects between 1919 and 1929, including $40 billion for building more than seven million housing units. Construction of one-to-four-family homes peaked in 1925 and declined thereafter. In contrast, real estate owners and developers continued to build new apartment buildings, hotels, office buildings, and manufacturing facilities at a rapid pace until 1929.[109]

Between 1922 and 1931, developers constructed 235 buildings taller than 70 meters in New York City, a higher number than in "any other ten-year period before or since." The scramble by developers to build skyscrapers responded to investors' enthusiastic demand for real estate bonds. As one study observed, "Investors' appetite for real estate securities ... created an incentive for developers to build big."[110] In late 1928, John J. Raskob, the Democratic Party's national chairman, announced his plan to build the Empire State Building as a "monument" to "the American way of life that allowed a poor boy to make his fortune on Wall Street."[111] In early 1931, when the Empire State Building was completed, "there were apple salesmen shivering on the curbstone below. Yet it was none the less a monument to the abounding confidence of the days in which it was conceived."[112]

Chicago enjoyed a comparable real estate boom, financed in part by the issuance of $800 million of real estate bonds. During the mid-1920s, "new office buildings soared upwards to the sky" in Chicago, and "there was a rapid increase in the number of apartment houses."[113] Developers constructed more than 85,000 new buildings in Chicago during the six-year period ending in 1927.[114]

The real estate financing boom reached its peak in most areas of the country by 1927 or 1928, lost steam in 1929, and collapsed thereafter.[115] The financing boom of the 1920s produced an oversupply of housing units and commercial buildings in many large cities as well as suburban areas and towns.[116] A contemporary observer reported that Chicago's suburbs were scarred by "unfinished buildings [that] towered gaunt against the skyline ... while the grass-covered streets of [unfinished] real-estate developments ... were even more numerous."[117] Writing in 1931, Frederick Lewis Allen commented:

> Many suburbs were plainly overbuilt; as one drove out along the highways, one began to notice houses that must have stood long untenanted, shops with staring vacant windows, districts blighted with half-finished and abandoned "improvements"; one heard of suburban apartment houses which had changed hands again and again as mortgages were foreclosed, or of householders in uncompleted subdivisions who were groaning under a naively unexpected burden of taxes and assessments.[118]

In 1933, the Senate Banking Committee determined that an "immense increase in the volumes of real-estate bond issues and of real-estate mortgages in banks and [other] financial institutions" produced many "overbuilt" real estate markets by 1929.[119] Modern scholars have agreed with that assessment.[120]

———

The real estate financing boom and the rapid growth in consumer credit during the Roaring Twenties left many American households in a highly vulnerable position at the end of the decade. The ratio of mortgage debt to household wealth for nonfarm families nearly tripled, rising from 10% to almost 30% between 1920 and 1930.[121] Most home mortgages—including those made by banks—carried a significant risk of default because they had relatively short terms (typically five years or less), provided for payment of only a small percentage of the principal during their terms, and required a large balloon payment of principal upon maturity. More than half of homeowners with first mortgages also took out second mortgages to finance their down payments. Second mortgages usually had short terms of one to three years and required borrowers to pay high interest rates. Homeowners who could not repay or refinance their first or second mortgages when they came due during the Depression were faced with the unenviable choice of selling their homes into a falling market or defaulting.[122]

Many households took on large amounts of installment debt and other consumer credit to finance purchases of automobiles, appliances, radios, and home furnishings during the 1920s. The ratio of consumer nonmortgage debt to total household income nearly doubled between 1920 and 1930, growing from 4.7% to 9.3%.[123] Total U.S. household debt equaled almost 100% of annual U.S. output in the early 1930s, a level not surpassed until the eve of the global financial crisis of 2007–09.[124]

The U.S. business sector was also vulnerable in 1930, after firms assumed large debt obligations during the credit boom of the 1920s. Corporate debt rose by 68% between 1919 and 1929, a growth rate comparable to the 64% increase in individual and noncorporate debt during the same period. At the end of 1929, total private sector debt equaled nearly 160% of U.S. gross national product (GNP), compared with 116% of GNP in 1919.[125]

The federal government's outstanding debt declined during the 1920s, as Andrew Mellon (Secretary of the Treasury under Harding and Coolidge) focused on paying off the nation's wartime loans.[126] However, state and local government debt more than doubled in amount and rose from 6.5% to 13.2% of GNP between 1919 and 1929.[127] As a result of massive increases in private sector debt and state and local obligations during the 1920s, the U.S. faced an annual debt service ratio equal to 9% of GNP in 1929. In contrast, Canada's annual debt service ratio in 1929 was only 3.9% of GNP.[128]

Thus, a credit boom of historic proportions financed the prolonged expansion of the U.S. economy during the 1920s. That credit boom was fueled in substantial part by large commercial banks, which greatly expanded their loans collateralized by real estate and securities, and also competed vigorously with investment banks to underwrite debt securities for corporations and state and local governments.[129] The enormous expansion of U.S. domestic credit during the 1920s became a "credit boom gone wrong" when financial conditions deteriorated rapidly following the stock market crash in October 1929.[130]

3

Foreign Affairs

Sales of Risky Foreign Bonds by Universal Banks Produced a Hazardous Foreign Lending Boom

During the financial euphoria of the 1920s, American commercial and investment banks aggressively competed to sell foreign bonds to U.S. and overseas investors. Commercial and investment banks sold more than $12 billion of foreign bonds between 1919 and 1930, with the U.S. government's strong encouragement. The Harding and Coolidge administrations believed that foreign bond offerings by U.S. banks would support postwar recovery in Europe and promote economic development in Asia and Latin America. Federal officials hoped that economic growth in all three regions would improve international political stability and stimulate greater demand for U.S. agricultural products and manufactured goods.[1]

U.S. commercial and investment banks arranged successful offerings of foreign bonds in the early 1920s and greatly expanded their sales of foreign bonds between 1924 and 1928.[2] In February 1924, J. P. Morgan & Co., Kuhn, Loeb & Co., National City Bank, and First National Bank of New York promoted a public offering of $150 million of Japanese government bonds to American investors. The U.S. government publicly expressed its strong support for the offering. At the same time, Morgan Grenfell and other British merchant banks marketed a smaller amount of Japanese government bonds in London. The *New York Herald Tribune* hailed the New York offering of Japanese bonds as "the largest long-term foreign bond issue ever floated in the United States." According to the *Herald Tribune,* the offering of Japanese government bonds demonstrated "America's newly acquired position of banker for the world." In contrast, "London for the first time on record definitely takes a secondary position to New York."[3] The Japanese bond offering was a harbinger of the great onrush of foreign bond sales that occurred between 1924 and 1928.[4]

The U.S. could act as "banker for the world" during the 1920s because it emerged from World War I as the largest creditor nation and the strongest economic power on the globe. U.S. armed forces suffered relatively low casualties during the war, and America's labor force was essentially intact when the war ended. U.S. industrial and agricultural output expanded steadily between 1914 and 1919 to satisfy enormous demands for wartime supplies, first from Allied nations and then from U.S. military forces. At the war's outbreak in 1914, U.S. annual GDP was about the same as the combined GDPs of Britain, France, and Germany. By 1919, the U.S. economy had grown 50% larger than the combined economies of those three nations.[5]

The U.S. economy's impressive growth and America's status as a safe haven from the European war zone attracted large inflows of gold. Gold reserves were a leading indicator of national economic strength under the international gold standard that most developed nations adhered to prior to World War I. The gold standard determined currency exchange rates among member nations based largely on their comparative gold reserves. Countries that were members of the gold standard club were obliged to convert their currencies into gold based on internationally agreed exchange rates. Member countries could not unilaterally decide to devalue their currencies. The central banks of member nations worked cooperatively to maintain the stability of exchange rates or to make mutually agreed adjustments to those rates.[6]

In 1914, the U.S. held $2 billion of gold, compared with $3 billion held collectively by Britain, France, and Germany. Britain, France, and Germany suspended the gold standard during World War I because of their need to issue massive volumes of government bonds to finance their huge wartime budget deficits. In contrast, the U.S. decided to remain on the gold standard during the war, and that decision encouraged European investors to move gold and other assets to the U.S. By 1923, the U.S. held more than $4 billion of gold reserves, while the combined gold reserves of Britain, France, and Germany dropped to less than $2 billion.[7]

Millions of British, French, and German soldiers died or were disabled during the war, and the economies of all three countries suffered major disruptions. After the war, Britain, France, and Germany struggled to cope with wartime debts that collectively topped $90 billion. The U.S. government lent $12 billion to the Allied powers during the war, including $5 billion to Britain and $4 billion to France. Private American investors bought over $2 billion of British and French war bonds. Both the U.S. government and private investors expected the Allies to repay those debts after the war ended.[8]

The daunting challenges posed by Allied and German war debts were compounded by Germany's obligation to pay war reparations. The Treaty of Versailles required Germany to pay reparations to the Allies in the same way that France paid reparations to the victors after the defeat of Napoleon in 1815 and after the Franco-Prussian War in 1871. The U.S. did not seek reparations from Germany, but it refused to forgive its loans to the Allies or to accept payments of German reparations in satisfaction of those loans.

The Allies insisted on collecting German reparations to finance their debt payments to the U.S., while Germany strongly opposed the Allies' demands. Germany's opposition to reparations was a significant motivating factor behind its government's decision to allow rapid inflation during the early 1920s. Hyperinflation resulted in a massive depreciation of Germany's currency, which destroyed Germany's ability to pay reparations. In response to Germany's nonpayment of reparations, French and Belgian troops occupied the Ruhr in January 1923.[9]

Hyperinflation severely damaged German industry and commerce, and the French and Belgians gained little from occupying the Ruhr. Germany and the Allies were therefore willing to address the twin problems of hyperinflation and reparations by the autumn of 1923. Germany introduced a credible new currency (the Rentenmark) in November, which ended its inflationary spiral. Soon thereafter, the Allies and Germany agreed to meet in Paris to discuss reparations.[10]

The Harding and Coolidge administrations followed a policy of ostensible "neutrality" with respect to Europe's postwar problems. Accordingly, the U.S. sent a delegation to the Paris conference that included prominent business executives and bankers rather than government officials. The U.S. delegation was led by Charles Dawes (a well-known Chicago banker) and Owen Young (the president of General Electric). Dawes and Young received unofficial support and encouragement for their efforts from President Coolidge and Secretary of State Charles Evan Hughes.[11]

Dawes and Young proposed a temporary fix rather than a permanent solution to the reparations problem. Under the "Dawes Plan," as adopted in 1924, the Allies and Germany established an interim five-year schedule for reparations payments. During that time, Germany's annual payments would gradually rise from $250 million to $600 million. In return, France and Belgium agreed to withdraw their troops from the Ruhr. To monitor Germany's compliance, the Allies appointed S. Parker Gilbert, a senior U.S. Treasury official, to act as "agent general" in overseeing the German government's collection of revenues and payment of reparations. Gilbert became the de facto "economic czar" of Germany, and he supervised Germany's payment of almost $2 billion in reparations between 1924 and 1929.[12]

The Dawes Plan included a $200 million loan to Germany, which helped to finance Germany's first payment of reparations under the plan. The British and French governments extended the loan in partnership with U.S. banks. As security for the loan's repayment, Germany gave the lenders a first lien on specified government revenues, including income from Germany's state railways. A syndicate of American banks, led by J. P. Morgan & Co. and National City Bank, agreed to underwrite $110 million of the Dawes Plan loan.[13]

The American banks launched an ambitious bond marketing campaign to finance their portion of the Dawes Plan loan. The Dawes Plan bonds carried an effective yield of 7.6%, which was substantially higher than the yields available on medium-grade U.S. corporate, state, and municipal bonds. The syndicate's campaign included a speech by President Coolidge, who urged Americans to buy Dawes Plan bonds to support Germany's economic recovery and increase German demand for American goods. The Dawes Plan campaign resembled the wartime Liberty bond drives, and American investors eagerly purchased the Dawes Plan bonds.[14]

The Dawes Plan provided that Germany's debt service payments on the Dawes Plan loan would receive priority over other German foreign obligations, including reparations payments. That provision—known as "transfer protection"—created a widely shared (but mistaken) assumption that the same priority would also apply to other foreign loans to Germany. The success of the Dawes Plan loan, and the assumption that subsequent loans to Germany would also receive priority treatment, encouraged an inflow of $3 billion of credit into Germany from New York, London, and other financial centers between 1924 and 1928. U.S. and British officials hoped that the large infusion of foreign credit would boost Germany's economy and generate the necessary tax revenues to cover German reparations.[15]

German officials welcomed the influx of foreign loans, but for a very different reason. German leaders believed that foreign lenders would eventually become "hostages" to Germany's ability to pay its foreign debts, and foreign lenders would therefore join Germany in pressing the Allies to reduce or eliminate Germany's reparations burden.[16] Thus, the Dawes Plan's short-term success was more apparent than real. The plan did not soften Germany's vehement opposition against the Allies' demands for reparations.[17]

———

The Dawes Plan did not solve the reparations problem, but it did enable Germany to return to the gold standard in 1924. Political leaders and central bankers in the U.S., Britain, France, Germany, and many other countries wanted to restore some version of the international gold standard that most developed countries had followed before 1914. During World War I, the need to finance huge wartime budget deficits drove many nations off the gold standard. In 1919, only the U.S. and four small countries (whose economies were closely tied to the U.S.) remained on gold.[18]

More than forty nations joined a new gold exchange standard that was established during the 1920s. Supporters of the new standard wanted to impose fiscal discipline on the governments of member countries, stabilize exchange rates, and promote capital transfers and trade among member countries, as the prewar gold standard had done. Severe inflationary episodes damaged the economies of Austria, Germany, France, Poland, and other countries after World War I. The painful legacy of hyperinflation produced a strong consensus among public officials, business owners, and bankers in favor of adopting a new international gold standard.[19]

After Germany joined the new gold exchange standard in 1924, leaders in the U.S. and the U.K. worked to bring Britain back onto gold. Despite opposition from John Maynard Keynes and a few other experts, most British politicians, business leaders, and bankers wanted the British pound to return to gold at its prewar exchange rate (£1 for $4.86). They believed that a restoration of the pound's prewar gold exchange value would strengthen Britain's status as a preeminent global power and maintain London's position as the world's top financial center. In addition, the Parliamentary statute that suspended the gold standard during World War I was scheduled to expire in 1925. A failure to return to the gold standard at the prewar exchange rate would have embarrassed the Conservative government that took office in late 1924.[20]

Montagu Norman, Governor of the Bank of England, was a leading champion of the campaign to restore the gold standard in Britain. Norman was convinced that Britain's return to gold was essential to improve global economic stability and maintain the Bank of England's preeminence among the world's central banks. Norman formed a close friendship and working partnership with Benjamin Strong, Governor of the Federal Reserve Bank of New York. Strong shared Norman's enthusiasm for rebuilding an international gold standard, and Strong also agreed that the British pound should return to gold at its prewar exchange rate.[21]

Strong orchestrated a significant easing of monetary policy by the Federal Reserve in 1924. The Fed cut its discount rate from 4.5% to 3% and bought $500 million of Treasury bonds in the open market to increase the U.S. money supply. The Fed's actions produced a significant decline in U.S. interest rates and created a large gap between lower interest rates in New York and higher interest rates in London. That gap encouraged investment capital to flow from New York to London and supported a rise in the pound's exchange value versus the dollar. The increased value of the pound enabled Britain to rejoin the gold standard in 1925 at the pound's prewar exchange rate. The Federal Reserve Bank of New York and J. P. Morgan & Co. supported Britain's return to gold by providing $300 million in standby lines of credit to the Bank of England and the British Treasury. The Fed's easing of monetary policy in 1924 also had a domestic motivation, as Strong wanted to counteract a domestic recession that had begun in 1923.[22]

Under the newly-established gold exchange standard, member countries were obliged to hold reserves against their outstanding currency liabilities in the form of either gold or foreign exchange reserves (i.e., financial assets denominated in the currencies of member nations).[23] As Britain and the U.S. were the world's two leading financial centers, the pound and the dollar became the dominant currencies in which other member nations maintained their foreign exchange reserves. In 1929, the pound and the dollar accounted for 97% of all foreign exchange reserves, and the dollar represented a majority of those reserves.[24]

Britain and the U.S. shared global financial leadership under the gold exchange standard during the second half of the 1920s. However, the status of the pound and the dollar as primary reserve currencies created significant vulnerabilities for both countries. If other nations and private investors began to fear that Britain or the U.S. might stop converting their currencies into gold, those nations and investors would have strong incentives to "run" on the pound or the dollar by converting their sterling- or dollar-denominated assets into gold or other currencies.[25]

———

The first major challenge to the viability of the gold exchange standard occurred in 1927. Britain's decision to restore the pound's prewar exchange rate in 1925 proved to be a costly mistake, as that rate substantially overvalued the pound. In contrast, France returned to gold in 1926 at an exchange rate that significantly undervalued the franc. As a result, French goods enjoyed a substantial pricing advantage over British goods in international trade, and investment capital flowed from London to Paris. Britain's gold reserves declined substantially, and the Bank of England came under great pressure to raise interest rates to attract gold back to London. In the spring of 1927, Britain's economy was struggling, and British workers engaged in widespread strikes. Montagu Norman warned his American, French, and German counterparts that he could not risk a political crisis by increasing the Bank of England's benchmark interest rate.[26]

Strong and the Fed again intervened to help Britain. In July 1927, Strong convened an emergency meeting in New York that included Norman and representatives of the French and German central banks. Strong agreed that the Fed would cut interest rates to encourage the movement of capital from New York to London, thereby relieving exchange rate pressures on the Bank of England. Strong persuaded his Fed colleagues to reduce the Fed's discount rate to 3.5% and to buy more than $200 million of government securities, despite adamant opposition from the Presidents of four regional Federal Reserve Banks. Strong defended his monetary easing plan by arguing that it would provide domestic benefits by mitigating the impact of the mild U.S. recession that had begun in late 1926. However, Strong's desire to prevent a breakdown of the interwar gold exchange standard was at least an equally important factor in the Fed's decision to relax its monetary policy in 1927.[27]

Thus, the Fed's reductions in short-term interest rates in 1924 and 1927 served both domestic and international purposes.[28] The Fed's actions also had significant domestic and international consequences. At home, the Fed's low-interest policies encouraged the credit boom that inflated the values of real estate and securities investments between 1924 and 1929.[29] Strong admitted that his rate cut in 1927 would give a "petit coup of whiskey" to the stock market, and his critics went much further. Two members of the Federal Reserve Board (Adolph Miller and Charles Hamlin) condemned Strong's policies, as did Secretary of Commerce Herbert Hoover. All three men accused Strong of pursuing measures that served the interests of European nations while promoting dangerous speculation at home.[30]

Since 1923, Hoover had repeatedly warned his colleagues in the Harding and Coolidge administrations that the Fed's lenient credit policies were promoting unhealthy speculation. In 1925, Hoover privately urged members of the Federal Reserve Board to increase the Fed's discount rates to reduce the flow of bank credit into securities, real estate, and other risky investments. In January 1927, Hoover published an article in the *New York Evening Post* warning that the unbridled growth of credit was likely to produce an unsustainable economic boom followed by a severe slump. Hoover believed that Montagu Norman and other European central bankers exerted too much influence over the New York Fed's policy decisions. Hoover criticized Benjamin Strong for being a "mental annex to Europe."[31]

In August 1927, after the Fed approved Strong's rate cut, Hoover urged President Coolidge to ask the Federal Reserve Board to rescind the cut. Coolidge declined to do so. Hoover also sent a strongly worded memorandum to the Federal Reserve Board. In his memorandum, Hoover argued that "inflation of credit is not the answer to European difficulties," and he warned that the resulting "speculation . . . can only land us on the shores of depression."[32]

In March 1929, Russell Leffingwell, a leading partner in J. P. Morgan & Co., made a similarly dire prediction in a private letter to his colleague, Thomas Lamont. Leffingwell warned Lamont that "Monty [Norman] and Ben [Strong] sowed the wind. I expect that we shall all have to reap the whirlwind.... I think we are going to have a world credit crisis."[33]

Several modern scholars have agreed that the Fed's interest rate cuts in 1924 and 1927 "poured fuel on the fire" in domestic markets by promoting speculative investments in U.S. real estate and corporate bonds and stocks.[34] The Fed's lax monetary policies also encouraged a boom in the sale of foreign bonds to American investors between 1924 and 1928. The Fed's low interest rates caused many Americans to turn away from U.S. government and corporate bonds in favor of higher-yielding foreign securities. Commercial and investment banks found it easy to persuade American investors to buy foreign bonds with their attractive yields.[35]

The interwar gold exchange standard provided additional support for the growth of the foreign bond market during the 1920s. Bond investors had greater confidence in the soundness of bonds issued by countries that adhered to the gold standard, with its built-in fiscal discipline. In addition, many foreign governments and corporations sold dollar-denominated bonds to attract American investors. Investors believed that dollar-denominated bonds would protect them against the risks of exchange rate devaluations by foreign governments.[36]

———

The successful marketing of the Dawes Plan bonds for Germany and the completion of loans to Austria and Hungary from the League of Nations appeared to stabilize Europe's political and economic situation in 1924. The Coolidge administration encouraged American banks to take advantage of the improved international outlook by expanding their sales of foreign bonds. U.S. officials hoped that foreign bond sales would promote international economic development and increase demand for exports of American goods.[37]

American bankers shared the administration's hopes and goals. Melvin Traylor, president of the First National Bank of Chicago, later testified that

> American lenders [after the Dawes Plan] not only felt that it was their duty to furnish rehabilitation capital to Europe but that, first of all, they were perfectly safe in so doing, and, second, that there was no better way to serve American industry and American agriculture and American labor than to follow that course.[38]

The Harding and Coolidge administrations established an informal review procedure for foreign bonds in the early 1920s. That lenient process reflected the probanker policies of both administrations and disregarded Commerce Secretary Hoover's prescient warnings about the dangers of foreign bonds. In 1921, Hoover proposed a formal approval plan to prevent U.S. banks from underwriting foreign bonds that posed excessive risks to American investors. Hoover advised President Harding that American bankers were underwriting hazardous, high-yielding foreign bonds that paid large up-front fees to the bankers but were likely to default. Hoover's proposed plan would have allowed banks to underwrite only sound foreign bonds that seemed likely to "bless both the borrower and the lender."[39]

New York bankers strongly opposed Hoover's plan, and it was not adopted. Instead, Secretary of State Charles Evans Hughes and Treasury Secretary Andrew Mellon developed an informal review procedure that was much less demanding. Under the Hughes-Mellon program, the State Department reviewed foreign bond offerings to determine whether they were consistent with "national policy."[40] A major goal of this informal review program was to stop American banks from providing loans to Allied nations that had not agreed with the U.S. on a schedule for repaying their U.S. war debts. Another objective was to prevent American banks from financing overseas monopolies in commodities. The State Department's informal review process gave the department a "de facto veto power over foreign bond issues in the United States."[41]

The State Department did not consider either the soundness of foreign loans or the suitability of foreign bonds as investments for American purchasers. State Department reviews of foreign bonds typically included a disclaimer, which stated that the department did not "pass upon the merits of foreign loans ... nor assume any responsibility whatever in connection with loan transactions."[42] Nevertheless, the State Department's reviews encouraged many American investors to buy foreign bonds "under the impression ... that the [U.S.] Government had approved the issue or it could not have been made."[43] The State Department's tacit endorsement of foreign bonds led American investors to believe that "a government safety net was in place," which would protect bondholders if defaults occurred. Such "wishful thinking" encouraged bankers to sell—and investors to buy—"a dizzying array of foreign bonds" during the 1920s.[44]

Hoover and his Commerce Department colleagues continued to voice serious concerns about the risks posed by foreign bonds. In 1924, Commerce Department officials warned the State and Treasury Departments about the dangers of selling large volumes of German bonds to American investors. However, State and Treasury officials rejected the Commerce Department's attempts to place tighter restrictions on loans to Germany. In August 1925, Arthur Young of the State Department said that any initiative to warn American investors about the hazards of German bonds would be counterproductive because it "would tend to injure the market value of the loans already floated." Treasury Secretary Andrew Mellon rebuffed proposals to stop U.S. banks from making loans to German state and local governments because Mellon did not want British banks to take that business away from American banks. In October 1925, Hoover admitted that the Commerce Department had failed in its efforts to restrict sales of German bonds to American investors.[45]

Two years later, S. Parker Gilbert, the U.S. official monitoring Germany's compliance with the Dawes Plan, issued a public report that echoed Hoover's concerns. Gilbert warned that foreign bankers were making unsound loans to German state and local governments to finance extravagant and unproductive public works proj-ects. According to Gilbert, "If present tendencies are allowed to continue unchecked, the consequence is almost certain to be serious economic reaction and depression, and a severe shock to German credit, at home and abroad."[46]

Despite Hoover's and Gilbert's admonitions, Andrew Mellon's belief in the be-nign nature of foreign bonds prevailed. In the Treasury Department's 1926 annual report, Mellon stated that "so long as credit facilities [in the U.S.] are ample, no harm is done to the American fiscal system" by selling foreign bonds to "an intelligent and widespread body of our citizenship."[47] Mellon "believed deeply in the laissez-faire ap-proach to foreign lending—that the market knew best."[48] Mellon's faith in the wisdom of bankers and markets reflected the prevailing zeitgeist of the Roaring Twenties, much as the pro-deregulation views of Alan Greenspan, Robert Rubin, and Lawrence Summers embodied the "Washington Consensus" of the 1990s and early 2000s.[49]

———

U.S. commercial and investment banks sold $12 billion of foreign government and corporate bonds between 1919 and 1930. European nations accounted for almost half of the foreign government bonds that were sold in the U.S. after World War I, and Latin American countries accounted for another quarter.[50]

American bankers engaged in a frenzied scramble to secure underwriting man-dates from foreign bond issuers. In 1933, Max Winkler, a leading bond analyst, described the "senseless competition among underwriting houses whose represent-atives were crowding hotels and inns, pleading with [foreign] governments, states and cities, as well as with [foreign] corporations, to borrow American money."[51] Otto Kahn, the leader of Kuhn, Loeb & Co., similarly observed:

> 15 American bankers sat in Belgrade, Yugoslavia, making bids, and a dozen American bankers sat in half a dozen South and Central American States, or in the Balkan States . . . one outbidding the other foolishly, recklessly, to the detriment of the public, compelling him to force bonds upon the public at a price which is not determined by the value of that security so much as his eagerness to get it.[52]

Thomas Lamont, a leading partner in J. P. Morgan & Co., warned in 1927 that "American bankers and firms [are] competing on almost a violent scale" to win bond underwriting deals. Lamont said it was not unusual for "European governments to find a horde of American bankers sitting on their doorsteps offering them money.... That sort of competition tends to insecurity and unsound practice." In the same year, a U.S. diplomat stationed in Peru described the "general promotion atmosphere" cre-ated by American bankers who pursued bond deals with the Peruvian government and provided lavish "entertainment" to Peruvian officials.[53]

In 1931 a senior German official reported that "German authorities had been virtu-ally flooded with loan offers" by American bankers during the 1920s. In a well-known example, the mayor of a small Bavarian town applied for a $125,000 loan to improve the town's power plant. American bankers persuaded the mayor to approve a $3 million bond issue, which financed a number of other projects, including a gymnasium and swimming pool. The bankers promptly sold the Bavarian town's bond issue to U.S. investors even though the town had little prospect of repaying the loan.[54]

Feverish competition for foreign bond issues was driven by the large fees that bankers could charge for underwriting those bonds.[55] The underwriting fees of U.S. banks for foreign bond issues often exceeded 4% and sometimes topped 10%, compared with typical underwriting fees of 2–3% for domestic bonds.[56] National City Bank and Chase National Bank earned average fees of nearly 5% on the foreign government bond issues for which they acted as lead underwriters during the 1920s.[57]

National City Bank's securities affiliate was the lead underwriter or a participating underwriter in syndicates that sold more than $4.3 billion of foreign bonds between 1919 and 1930. National City's underwriting syndicates accounted for over a third of all foreign bonds sold in the U.S. during that period.[58] National City's foreign bond business was highly lucrative and produced $25 million in net profits.[59] Chase National Bank's securities affiliate was the lead or participating underwriter in numerous offerings of foreign bonds during the 1920s. National City and Chase each ranked among the top ten U.S. underwriters of Latin American bonds in terms of bonds issued and gross profits.[60]

Underwriting standards for foreign bonds declined after 1923 in response to investor enthusiasm for buying higher-yielding securities. During that period, "the strong demand for bonds made foreign lending a very attractive business as the issuing banker knew that selling them at a profit would be easy."[61] The high fees that banks received for underwriting foreign bonds produced a situation in which "eagerness for profits warped the judgments of bankers," resulting in "a marked decline in banking judgment and ethics and unscrupulous exploitation of public gullibility and avarice."[62]

Thus, Wall Street's underwriting standards for foreign bonds "declined sharply during the 1920s," along with the creditworthiness of newly issued bonds. Long-term default rates for foreign bonds rose steadily for bonds issued after 1923, and the highest default rates were recorded for foreign bonds issued between 1927 and 1929.[63] More conservative underwriters—including J. P. Morgan & Co. and Kuhn, Loeb & Co.—cut back on their underwriting of foreign bonds as the foreign lending boom intensified. In contrast, more aggressive banks expanded their underwriting of foreign bonds, and their bonds defaulted at much higher rates.[64]

Many American investors who bought foreign bonds during the 1920s were unsophisticated and inexperienced. Purchasers of foreign bonds included middle-class households, churches, other nonprofit organizations, small insurance companies, and local banks. Wall Street banks focused much of their bond selling efforts on the rapidly growing class of professional and white-collar workers, including "school teachers and army officers and country doctors and stenographers and clerks." Many investors in foreign bonds had earned favorable returns by purchasing Liberty bonds from the same banks during World War I.[65] A 1924 magazine article that analyzed the marketing of foreign bonds emphasized the vital role played by ordinary investors who purchased such bonds: "We are living in the day of the small investor, and the small investor is the real owner of Wall Street."[66] National City regularly published advertisements touting the benefits of bond investing in "popular magazines like *Harper's* and *Atlantic Monthly*."[67]

Enticed by Wall Street's marketing campaigns, unsophisticated investors eagerly bought foreign bonds. In 1927, Dwight Morrow, a leading partner in J. P. Morgan & Co., published a study of the sale of several foreign government bond issues between 1923 and 1925. Morrow determined that over 85% of the buyers—accounting for about half of the bonds purchased—were small investors who bought bonds in amounts of $5,000 or less.[68] A 1935 report from the bondholders' committee for defaulted Peruvian bonds stated that the average bondholder held about $800 of bonds. The holders of defaulted Chilean bonds included many individuals and trust funds, as well as smaller banks and nonprofit organizations. Charles Mitchell estimated that more than 1.5 million American investors owned foreign bonds in 1932.[69]

Smaller banks from rural communities were among the most active buyers of foreign bonds. As described in Chapter 2, those country banks relied on money center banks, like National City and Chase, for a wide range of correspondent banking services, including investment advice and purchases of investment securities. Money center banks encouraged their correspondent country banks to improve the yields on their investment portfolios by selling lower-yielding U.S. government securities and reinvesting the proceeds in higher-yielding foreign bonds. Many of those foreign bonds were underwritten by securities affiliates of the same money center banks. When the Great Depression began, country banks held much greater exposures to foreign bonds (as a percentage of their capital) compared with large urban banks.[70]

During Senate debates on the Glass-Steagall Act in 1932, Senator Carter Glass charged that "the great banks in the money centers choked the portfolios of their correspondent banks from Maine to California with utterly worthless investment securities, nearly eight billions of them being the investment securities of tottering South American republics and other foreign countries." Glass alleged that the securities affiliates of major banks "sent out their high-pressure salesman and literally filled the bank portfolios of this country with these investment securities."[71]

During a Senate committee hearing in 1932, Senator Smith Brookhart (R-IA) claimed that securities affiliates of New York City banks caused the failures of many country banks by selling them unsuitable, high-risk bonds. Comptroller of the Currency J. W. Pole did not dispute Brookhart's claim, and Pole acknowledged, "A great many banks have been affected through the depreciation in bonds."[72] During the Senate's investigation of abusive securities practices in 1933, Senator Thomas Gore (D-OK) condemned the "practice on the part of the affiliates of these big banks and these big [securities] underwriting houses of unloading foreign bonds on other banks throughout the country.... The little banks took the word of the big banks that these securities were good."[73]

————

Leaders of major commercial and investment banks recognized that middle-class individuals and other unsophisticated investors relied on bank underwriters to identify sound foreign bonds that were suitable for investment. In his 1927 article, Dwight Morrow commented:

> How is the investor to form an intelligent judgment as to the safety of his investment? ... [H]e would put in the very forefront of his reasons for making the investment that he had confidence in the banker who offered him the investment. After all, the people who buy bonds must rely largely on the judgment of the offering houses. They must believe that their investment banker would not offer them the bonds unless the banker believed them to be safe.[74]

During Senate committee hearings on the sale of foreign bonds in 1931–32, Charles Mitchell of National City acknowledged that "faith in the banker was the only measuring rod for the investor," and that investors purchased foreign bonds "entirely on the faith of the house issuing them in New York."[75] Other Wall Street leaders agreed during those hearings that investment bankers had a duty to underwrite only "good" foreign bonds.[76]

In view of the strong reliance of unsophisticated investors on the advice they received from bankers, Dwight Morrow concluded that "the responsibility rests heavily upon the investment banker in recommending investments. The banker must never be lured, either by the desire for profit or by the desire for reputation, to recommend an investment that he does not believe to be good."[77] Morrow defined a standard of "responsibility" for investment bankers that was similar to the duty of "trust" and "safety" that Charles Mitchell articulated in his lecture to National City's trainees in 1919.[78]

Despite the public assurances given by Wall Street's leaders, the sales practices of commercial and investment banks fell woefully short of any concept of "responsibility" or "trust." Bankers used the same high-pressure sales techniques and nationwide promotional campaigns to sell foreign bonds that they employed to sell other types of risky securities to unsophisticated investors during the 1920s.[79] Commercial and investment banks used misleading prospectuses and other deceptive practices to persuade inexperienced investors to buy hazardous foreign bonds.[80] A contemporary observer charged that Wall Street bankers pursued their bond customers

> through hosts of young salesmen, carefully schooled in "high pressure" methods of breaking down "sales resistance." The keynote was pressure—all down the line.

The home office kept the branch-offices "on their toes" by a stream of phone-calls, "flashes," "pep-wires," and so forth. The branch managers kept the young salesmen all "burned up" with "pep-talks," bonuses, and threats of getting fired. Everybody in authority demanded "results"; which meant, more sales. Every salesman must sell his "quota." What he sold, how he sold it, and whom he sold it to, did not much matter. Verily, business had got into banking; or, rather, "banking," in the old sense of the word, had been kicked out of doors by business.[81]

———

Many of the foreign bonds that were sold by the securities affiliates of National City Bank and Chase National Bank proved to be disastrous investments for their customers. Defaults occurred on three-fifths of the foreign bond issues for which National City and Chase acted as lead underwriters during the 1920s.[82] The default rates for foreign and domestic bonds underwritten by National City and Chase were (1) significantly higher than default rates for bonds underwritten by J. P. Morgan & Co. and Kuhn Loeb & Co., (2) about the same as default rates for bonds underwritten by other private investment banks, and (3) somewhat higher than default rates for bonds underwritten by securities affiliates of other commercial banks.[83]

The Senate's investigation of securities abuses in 1933 included detailed studies of several foreign bond issues underwritten by National City and Chase. That inquiry revealed that National City and Chase knowingly or recklessly engaged in deceptive practices in marketing and selling those bonds. As shown in the following analysis, National City's and Chase's officers either knew or should have known that their offering materials did not disclose the bonds' very high risks.

National City's bond offerings for Peru: National City Company (the securities affiliate of National City Bank) joined with a private investment bank, J. W. Seligman & Co., to underwrite three issues of Peruvian government bonds (totaling $90 million), which were sold to American investors between March 1927 and October 1928.[84] Before it sold those bonds, National City received a series of highly critical reports from its officers about Peru's economic and political conditions. In December 1921, a National City official warned that the country's finances were "positively distressing" and that "the Government treasury is flat on its back and gasping for breath."[85] In July 1923, another National City executive advised that "Peru has been careless in the fulfillment of her contractual obligations."[86] In December 1925, a third National City employee cautioned that "the internal debt of Peru has not yet been placed on a satisfactory footing."[87] A National City vice president wrote an internal memorandum highlighting Peru's "bad-debt record," its "adverse moral and political risk," and its "bad internal-debt situation."[88] Nevertheless, National City participated in the first offering of Peruvian bonds in March 1927.

Four months after the first offering, J. H. Durrell, a senior executive in National City's overseas operations, sent a report to Charles Mitchell about Peru's ongoing challenges. Durrell described Peru's "uncertain" political situation as well as "factors that will long retard the economic importance of Peru." Durrell stated that he had "no great faith in any material betterment of Peru's economic condition in the near future."[89] A March 1928 report from another National City executive advised that Peru's "whole taxation system is a hodge-podge."[90] An October 1928 report from a third bank official cautioned that "economic conditions in the country leave considerable to be desired" and that "local banks are still badly over-extended." He also warned that the Peruvian government's "budget is not balanced and in fact the floating debt is larger than ever."[91] Despite all those warnings, National City participated in the second and third offerings of Peruvian bonds in 1928.

Lawrence Dennis, a consultant for J. W. Seligman & Co., was equally critical of the Peruvian bonds. After conducting a study of Peru's economic situation in 1928, Dennis recommended against making the second bond offering. However, the Seligman firm's partners rejected his advice. In 1932, Dennis gave the following testimony before the Senate Finance Committee:

> I took the very strong view that [the second Peruvian loan] was not sound, and I immediately became involved in a long debate. . . . [The Seligman partners] said I was pessimistic, and that these things would work themselves out. I took the position that in the face of the statistics of commerce, production and trade of the country, the government could not go on borrowing at that rate and remain solvent.[92]

The offering prospectuses distributed to American investors by J. W. Seligman & Co. and National City did not contain any references to Peru's past defaults on its debts, or Peru's ongoing economic problems, or the very weak condition of Peru's government finances. Peru defaulted on all three issues of bonds in 1931. By 1933, the market value of those bonds had fallen more than 90% since the dates of their issuance.[93]

National City's Brazilian bond offerings: In March 1928 and September 1929, National City Company underwrote two offerings of bonds (totaling $16.5 million) issued by the Brazilian state of Minas Gerais.[94] National City sold the Minas Gerais bonds to American investors after receiving very negative reports about the state's creditworthiness. In June 1927, George Train, a National City officer who worked on the bond issues, wrote that "the laxness of the State authorities borders on the fantastic." Train also warned about "the complete ignorance, carelessness and negligence of the former State officials in respect to external long-term borrowing."[95] In April 1928, following the completion of the first bond offering, Train reported that "there is a considerable uneasiness on the part of all concerned over the question of the State's willingness to meet its obligations."[96]

In spite of Train's misgivings, National City's offering materials for both bond issues assured investors that "prudent and careful management of the State's finances has been characteristic of successive administrations in Minas Gerais." National City published that false assurance even though another National City executive warned that the statement would expose National City to "criticism" in view of "the extremely loose way in which the external debt of the State was managed."[97] Train subsequently admitted—under questioning by Ferdinand Pecora (chief counsel for the Senate investigating committee)—that Train supported the Minas Gerais bond offerings because he was "a little overenthusiastic with respect to the merits of the particular credit I was investigating."[98]

The offering prospectus for the second Minas Gerais bond issue did not disclose that almost half of the $8 million of sales proceeds would be used to pay off short-term loans, which National City and its co-underwriters extended to Minas Gerais after the first bond offering. National City's underwriting group provided those loans to keep Minas Gerais from transferring its future bond business to Kuhn, Loeb & Co. and other underwriters.[99] The second prospectus assured investors that "the proceeds of this loan will be utilized for purposes designed to increase the economic productivity of the State" in accordance with Peru's "law No. 1061 of August 16, 1929."[100] The prospectus did not disclose that National City's Brazilian counsel drafted Law No. 1061 for the specific purpose of allowing the underwriting group to recoup their short-term loans from the bond proceeds.[101]

National City understood that the second offering of Minas Gerais bonds would be "hard to sell." In July 1929, a senior executive in New York wrote to a member of National City's Brazilian team, asking for additional "selling arguments" to bolster National City's "educational campaign" for the bonds.[102] National City was not able to sell the entire second issue of Minas Gerais bonds when the offering began on September 16, 1929. Eleven days later, National City Company sent out a "sales flash" to its U.S. sales offices, announcing "one of the greatest sales contests" it had ever conducted. The contest offered "liberal cash prizes" to reward sales agents who were successful in selling National City's inventories of unsold securities, including Minas Gerais bonds.[103]

Minas Gerais defaulted on both bond issues in early 1932. By 1933, the market value of those bonds had fallen by more than three-quarters.[104]

National City's bond offering for Lautaro Nitrate of Chile: In June 1929, National City Company led an underwriting group that sold $32 million of convertible bonds issued by Lautaro Nitrate Co. (LNC), the largest producer of sodium nitrate fertilizer in Chile.[105] Before the bonds were issued, National City sent Sterling Bunnell, a professional engineer, to study Chile's sodium nitrate industry. Bunnell reported that Chilean nitrate was vulnerable to growing competition from synthetic nitrate produced by European and U.S. companies. In addition, the Chilean government imposed a high export duty that impeded the sale of Chilean nitrate to foreign buyers.[106] In evaluating the prospects for Chilean nitrate, Bunnell warned that the "unknown factor is obsolescence" and that "it is impossible to prophesy the conditions which may exist in the Chilean nitrate industry within the 25-year term of the [projected] financing." Bunnell concluded that the highly uncertain future for Chilean nitrate made the proposed bond offering "speculative" from "the banking standpoint."[107]

National City's prospectus for LNC's bonds did not refer to Bunnell's study or his reservations about LNC's prospects. The prospectus also did not disclose that National City underwrote $30 million of bonds issued by American I.G. Chemical Co. (AIGC) a few months before its LNC bond offering. One of AIGC's subsidiaries was I.G. Farbenindustrie, the largest German producer of synthetic nitrate, which competed directly with the nitrate produced by LNC. Thus, National City had an undisclosed conflict of interest when it sold the LNC bonds.[108]

National City encountered significant problems in selling the LNC bonds. National City's "sales contest" in September 1929 offered "liberal cash prizes" to encourage its sales force to find buyers for National City's unsold inventory of LNC bonds as well as the unsold Minas Gerais bonds. After the stock market crashed in October 1929, National City bought $1 million of LNC bonds on the open market to support the market value of the bonds. National City resold those LNC bonds to public investors when market conditions temporarily improved in early 1930. By March 1933, the LNC bonds had defaulted and their market value had fallen by more than 95%.[109]

Chase's sale of Cuban bonds: Chase National Bank and its securities affiliate, Chase Securities Corporation, arranged a series of bank loans and bond offerings for Cuba between 1927 and 1930 to finance Cuba's new public works program. In February 1927, Chase and Blair & Co. provided $10 million of loans to Cuba to jump-start the program.[110] In June 1928, Chase, Blair, and two other banks extended $30 million of additional loans to Cuba. At the same time, a Chase-led underwriting group sold $20 million of Cuban bonds to the public.[111]

In early 1930, Chase's underwriting group made a second public offering of $40 million of Cuban bonds, and Chase's banking group provided $20 million of new loans to Cuba. Cuba agreed that the proceeds of the second bond offering would be used to pay off the $40 million of existing loans that Chase's banking group had previously extended to Cuba.[112] As a practical matter, the Chase banking group used the 1930 Cuban bond offering to shift $40 million of sovereign credit risk from the banking group to public investors.[113]

To attract and retain Cuba's business, the Chase group paid large amounts of purported fees and also provided substantial loans to President Gerardo Machado and his business firms as well as his friends, associates, and other key Cuban officials.[114] Chase's Havana branch office employed José Obregón, the son-in-law of President Machado, even though Chase officials admitted that, "from any business standpoint," Obregón was "perfectly useless."[115] The prospectuses for the 1928 and 1930 Cuban bond offerings did not disclose the extensive benefits that Chase provided to President Machado and other influential Cubans.[116]

The prospectuses for the Cuban bond offerings stated that Cuba's government had produced significant budget surpluses for several years when, in fact, the government had run net deficits.[117] The prospectuses also misled investors by stating that Cuba deposited designated revenues into a "special account" each year to ensure repayment of the bonds. Cuba established an "accounting fund" for the designated revenues, but

Chase learned in 1929 that Cuba was using those revenues to meet its general operating expenses and was commingling those revenues with other funds.[118]

The prospectus for the 1930 bond offering did not disclose that Cuba ran a budget deficit of more than $7 million during its previous fiscal year.[119] The prospectus also did not reveal that the bond proceeds would be used to repay the $40 million of outstanding loans owed by Cuba to Chase's banking group. The prospectus created the misleading impression that the 1930 bond offering would reduce Cuba's "total funded debt" by $40 million. In fact, Cuba's "funded debt" remained the same because the new bonds simply replaced the bank loans.[120]

After receiving a series of short-term advances from Chase's banking group, Cuba managed to pay off its 1928 bond issue. However, Cuba defaulted on its 1930 bond issue in 1933, and Cuba also failed to pay the $20 million loan that Chase's banking group provided as part of the 1930 financing package.[121]

———

National City and Chase were not the only underwriters who sold hazardous foreign bonds to unsophisticated investors. A Senate committee investigation in 1933 uncovered similar abuses in underwritings of high-risk foreign bonds by private investment banks, including $186 million of Brazilian bonds offered by Dillon, Read & Co. and $90 million of Chilean bonds underwritten by Kuhn, Loeb & Co. Those bonds also defaulted in the early 1930s.[122] Ferdinand Pecora, the Senate committee's chief counsel, directed his strongest criticism at National City and Chase because they exploited their sterling reputations as the nation's leading commercial banks to win the trust of unsuspecting depositors and other poorly informed investors. Pecora condemned National City's record in the following passage from his 1939 memoir:

> From coast to coast, literally from house to house, sales were pushed in every possible manner. In 1928, the head office of [National City] sent out the names of 122,332 "prospects" ... who were lured into disaster by similar means.... A bank was supposed to occupy a fiduciary relationship and to protect its clients, not to lead them into dubious ventures; to offer sound, conservative financial advice, not a salesman's puffing patter.
>
> But the introduction and growth of the investment affiliate had corrupted the very heart of these old-fashioned banking ethics. Because it had wares of its own to sell, the National City was no longer an impartial adviser. It did not scruple to use its own depositors, who came ... seeking investment advice, as "prospects" for the busy salesmen of the Company [who were] clothed with all the authority and prestige of the magic name "National City."[123]

Pecora charged that Chase, "behind its imposing façade of unassailable might and rectitude, was not a whit better than the National City Bank itself." According to

Pecora, "Most of the characteristic evils which beset the National City organization flourished [at Chase] in equally glaring fashion."[124]

Bankers sought to justify their massive sales of foreign bonds by claiming that they simply responded to the public's demand for high-yielding investments. Frederick J. Lisman (of F. J. Lisman & Co.) stated that bankers competed to sell foreign bonds in order to "satisfy the public demand for securities."[125] Henry C. Breck (of J. W. Seligman & Co.) said the "appetite on the part of the American public to buy foreign bonds" was the main reason for the "extraordinarily keen competition among international bankers for South American loans."[126] However, as Barbara Stallings pointed out, U.S. bankers were responsible for "feeding that 'appetite' by withholding information on the true risk involved" in the Latin American bonds they sold to investors.[127]

Charles Mitchell presented the same basic justification, with some caveats, when he testified at a Senate committee hearing in December 1931. Mitchell acknowledged that banks were "too ready to loan, too ready to meet the competition of neighbors, too willing to cut down their margins to a point of encouraging excessive borrowing" during the 1920s.[128] Nevertheless, Mitchell assigned primary responsibility for the unsustainable credit boom to the issuers and buyers of securities. Mitchell claimed that issuers aggressively sold securities because they saw "the possibility of changing their capital structure to their advantage" by responding to "the public's interest in and fever and fervor for investments and speculation." Mitchell said the "investment banking community" was merely "one of the tools by which the demands of each side operated to satisfy their requirements."[129] In Mitchell's view, bankers should have been more careful, but they acted largely as passive agents who followed their clients' instructions. Thus, Mitchell tried to shift most of the blame for the speculative frenzy of the 1920s to the issuers of securities and public investors.[130]

Attempts by Wall Street bankers to disclaim their responsibility for the crash failed to insulate them from public condemnation. By 1931, the aggregate market value of Latin American bonds sold to American investors had fallen to 26% of their face value. By 1936, more than three-quarters of Latin American bonds were in default.[131] By 1938, more than half of all foreign bonds held by American investors had defaulted.[132] The devastating impact of foreign bond defaults during the 1930s created widespread anger among investors, who believed that Wall Street had betrayed their trust.[133]

———

American investors purchased almost two-thirds of the foreign bonds that were issued by Central and Eastern European nations and Latin American countries between 1924 and 1928. By the end of that period, the economies of many countries depended on a continued flow of credit from banks and investors in the U.S. as well as Britain, France, Holland, Sweden, and Switzerland.[134]

Foreign bond sales in the U.S. leveled off in 1928 and declined sharply in 1929, due to domestic and foreign developments. At home, the booming U.S. stock market caused many American investors to switch their focus from foreign bonds to domestic stocks in 1928 and 1929. The stock market boom (during which many investors used margin loans to finance their stock purchases) resulted in higher demand for credit by U.S. investors. Consequently, interest rates rose sharply on short-term call money loans and margin loans. The New York Fed and other regional Federal Reserve Banks responded to the stock market boom by hiking their discount rates from 3.5% to 5% during the first half of 1928. Rising U.S. interest rates reduced the yield gap between foreign bonds and domestic debt securities. As the yield advantage of foreign bonds declined, so did demand from American investors.[135]

Abroad, a recurrence of economic and political problems in Germany produced new concerns about Germany's political stability and the creditworthiness of German bonds. Germany received $3 billion of foreign credit between 1924 and 1928, with about half of that amount coming from the U.S. Germany relied on foreign loans to finance its payment of almost $2 billion of reparations, and Allied governments used Germany's reparations payments to fund about $1 billion of payments on their U.S. war debts. Thus, foreign loans to Germany created a fragile cycle of payments, which enabled Germany to pay reparations and the Allies to pay war debts. However, new loans by foreign creditors to Germany declined sharply in 1928, and Germany was obliged to pay $625 million of reparations in 1929 under the Dawes Plan. As the 1929 payment date approached, Germany expressed growing doubts about its ability to continue paying reparations.[136]

Faced with the threat of a second default by Germany, the Allies convened another conference in Paris in early 1929 to develop a long-term solution to the reparations problem. That conference was chaired by Owen Young, who had worked with Charles Dawes on the Dawes Plan. After a year of difficult negotiations, the Allies and Germany agreed on the Young Plan in March 1930. The Young Plan required Germany to pay reparations over a period of fifty-nine years but significantly reduced the annual amounts of those payments.[137]

To oversee Germany's reparations payments, the Young Plan established a new Bank for International Settlements in Basel, Switzerland, to replace the unpopular agent general under the Dawes Plan. The Young Plan also promised $300 million of new loans to help Germany meet its next reparations payment. The British and French governments and U.S. banks jointly provided the Young Plan loans. However, unlike the Dawes Plan, the Young Plan made clear that foreign lenders would no longer enjoy any priority over reparations creditors in receiving future payments from Germany.[138]

The terms of the Young Plan were generally more favorable to Germany than those of the Dawes Plan, and the Young Plan also produced new loans for Germany from Britain, France, U.S. banks, and the infamous Swedish financier Ivar Kreuger. However, the removal of priority treatment for foreign lenders effectively destroyed international demand for long-term German bonds after the Young Plan loans were completed. Without the assumption of preferential treatment, most U.S. and European investors were not willing to buy any more German bonds. The resulting collapse of foreign credit flows into Germany and a severe recession in the German economy placed Germany on the brink of economic crisis in early 1931.[139]

J. P. Morgan & Co. and National City Bank led the syndicate of U.S. banks that sold $98.5 million of Germany's Young Plan bonds in June 1930. The Young Plan syndicate resembled the syndicate that successfully sold $110 million of Dawes Plan bonds in 1924. However, U.S. investors showed little enthusiasm for the Young Plan bonds. Members of the bank syndicate therefore conducted a "particularly intense" campaign to "encourage investors" to purchase the bonds. It took several weeks for the banks to complete the offering.[140]

The Morgan–National City syndicate found it very difficult to sell the Young Plan bonds at the stated offering price of $90 per bond. The syndicate therefore decided to "peg" (support) that price by purchasing $9.2 million of the bonds at a "steady price" of $90 per bond during a three-week period. The syndicate members stopped supporting the market price after they sold all of their Young Plan bonds, and the market price dropped sharply. A contemporary observer argued that the syndicate's pegging campaign raised "a serious issue of business ethics," because the syndicate did not disclose to the public that it was buying Young Plan bonds on the open market to prop up their market price during the offering.[141]

Despite the great difficulties that the bank syndicate encountered in selling Young Plan bonds, National City remained a bullish promoter of the offering. On the third day of the Young Plan offering, National City distributed a circular to its sales force and customers, assuring them that "it is reasonable to believe that the new loan ... marks the beginning of a widening demand for German bonds, both in this country and abroad. And the present, therefore, would seem to be an opportune time for their purchase."[142]

National City's optimistic sales pitch proved to be a completely erroneous forecast of future events. The Young Plan offering marked the end of the boom for foreign bonds in America. Only about $200 million of non-Canadian foreign bonds were sold in the U.S. between the completion of the Young Plan offering in July 1930 and the end of 1931, when the U.S. market for foreign bonds shut down completely.[143] Purchasers of the Young Plan bonds, like investors in many other foreign bonds, became casualties of the catastrophic wave of defaults that swept through the foreign bond market during the early 1930s as the global economy collapsed into the Great Depression.[144]

4
Crash

Universal Banks Played Central Roles in the Stock Market Boom and Crash and the Onset of the Great Depression

Beginning in 1924, the U.S. stock market experienced a bull market of unprecedented length and magnitude. The price index for common stocks traded on the New York Stock Exchange (NYSE) rose by 70% between 1924 and 1927. Annual trading volumes for NYSE-listed stocks doubled during that period. The Dow Jones Industrial Index also doubled, rising from 100 in early 1924 to 200 in December 1927.[1] The Fed's easing of monetary policy in 1924 and 1927 helped stock market prices and business profits to maintain their upward trajectory despite brief recessions in both years.[2]

The stock market boom attracted the attention of many investors who had never previously owned stocks. As the bull market continued to gain momentum, commercial and investment banks encouraged ordinary investors to buy common stocks instead of bonds. In February 1927, Charles Mitchell announced that National City Company would begin to sell "selected common stocks" that were "sound investments" for its customers.[3]

A month later, Mitchell intensified his sales pitch for common stocks. Mitchell said that he saw "no reason why the man who has faith in the continued growth of these United States need bury all of his capital in the security strong box of gilt-edged bonds." According to Mitchell, "even the conservative investor" should invest in "progress instead of merely in static wealth." Mitchell declared that National City's "new policy" of selling common stocks reflected its "faith in the future, faith in the reliability of conservative financial analysis, faith in progress and faith in America, and the continued and steady advance of modern civilization."[4] Other commercial and investment banks similarly urged the public to buy common stocks, as did corporations that were soliciting new investors for their stocks.[5]

The great bull market of the 1920s entered its final, frenzied stage in early 1928. The Dow Jones Industrial Index rose from 200 in December 1927 to 300 a year later and finally peaked at 381 on September 3, 1929. Many scholars have concluded that a speculative bubble occurred in the stock market between the spring of 1928 and the fall of 1929.[6] Stock prices rose at about the same rate as corporate profits and dividends from 1924 through 1927. In contrast, stock prices increased much faster than either corporate earnings or dividends during 1928 and 1929. The widening gap between stock prices and corporate earnings and dividends indicated the presence of a speculative bubble during those two years.[7]

Rapid increases in trading volumes also indicated the presence of a bubble during 1928 and 1929. Annual trading volumes for NYSE-listed common stocks nearly doubled between 1927 and 1929.[8] Yearly trading volumes for common stocks listed on the alternative "curb exchange" almost quadrupled between 1927 and 1929.[9]

Many investors took out margin loans from their brokers to finance a large portion of their stock purchases, and they offered securities held in their brokerage accounts as collateral for those loans. Brokers funded their loans to customers by taking out short-term call loans, and brokers provided collateral for their call loans by pledging securities held in their proprietary trading accounts or their customers' margin accounts. Accordingly, a sharp decline in stock prices could quickly become a panic if investors and brokers were forced to sell large amounts of stock to pay off their loans.[10]

The outstanding volume of call loans to NYSE brokers increased from $3.3 billion at the end of 1926 to $4.4 billion at the close of 1927. Call loans then rose at an even faster pace to reach $6.4 billion at the end of 1928 and $8.5 billion on October 1, 1929.[11] Banks held about half of the outstanding call loans in December 1928, but banks held only 30% of those loans in October 1929. Due to strong pressure from the Fed (discussed later in this chapter), banks chose not to increase their call loans significantly during 1929. Consequently, nonbank lenders—including insurance companies, business corporations, wealthy individuals, and foreign investors—became the primary source of new call loans to brokers in 1929.[12] Nonbank lenders in the call loan market effectively functioned as the "shadow banks" of the late 1920s.[13]

Prominent speculators—including Walter Chrysler, Arthur Cutten, William Crapo Durant, the Fisher brothers, and John J. Raskob—organized hundreds of trading pools in 1928 and 1929 to boost the prices of targeted stocks. Trading pools conducted purchasing and selling campaigns to increase the trading volumes and market prices of featured stocks, especially "glamour stocks" such as Radio Corporation of America. Pool operators expected that larger trading volumes would boost the prices of targeted stocks and encourage public investors to buy those stocks. Pool operators could then reap handsome profits by selling their shares back into the market.[14] National City Bank, Chase National Bank, and other large banks financed and participated in many of those trading pools.[15]

National City and Chase also conducted aggressive trading programs to increase the prices of their own stocks.[16] The shares of both banks were among the stocks "most affected by speculation," as they traded at price-earnings multiples that were significantly higher than other bank stocks and the overall stock market. In 1929, National City's stock traded at 120 times annual earnings, and Chase's stock traded at 62 times annual earnings. In contrast, the stocks of five other large banks traded at price-earnings multiples ranging from 31 to 41, while 142 well-known, publicly traded stocks had an average price-earnings multiple of 30.[17]

The rapid growth of investment trusts—the forerunners of mutual funds—added further momentum to the relentless rise of stock prices after 1926. Investment trusts sold equity and debt securities to investors and used the proceeds to buy stocks and bonds issued by other companies and governments. Sponsors (primarily investment banks) established nearly six hundred investment trusts between 1927 and 1929, and those trusts controlled $6 billion of stocks and bonds. New issues of investment trust shares accounted for more than a fifth of all new stock issues in 1928 and 1929.

Most investment trusts sold their shares to investors at prices that were substantially higher than the aggregate market values of investments held by the trusts. The willingness of investors to pay large premiums for shares of investment trusts reflected investors' confidence in the presumed expertise of the trusts' sponsors and managers. In addition, the trusts boosted their returns to investors by borrowing heavily to increase their leverage. Consequently, shares of investment trusts represented highly leveraged bets on the long-term success of the companies in which the trusts invested. Public demand for shares of investment trusts collapsed after the stock market crashed in October 1929, and many investment trust shares lost all or most of their value by 1932.[18]

———

No institution was more heavily committed to the stock market boom of the 1920s than National City. National City's chairman, Charles Mitchell, repeatedly urged the public to put its faith in the continued success of the stock market and the U.S. economy. In October 1928, Mitchell declared, "We are enjoying enormous prosperity in America and I am convinced that nothing can impede the progress we are making." He saw "no cause for alarm" from rising stock prices or the growing volume of brokers' call loans as long as the Fed took appropriate measures to "guard against inflation."[19] Mitchell's assurances echoed the comforting resolutions adopted at the 1928 annual convention of the American Bankers Association (ABA). The ABA's resolutions stated that "the credit situation would correct itself [and] the situation would find a solution of its own problem before it reached the danger stage."[20]

On New Year's Day in 1929, Mitchell's public letter to National City's shareholders stated that "business is entering the new year upon a high level of activity." Mitchell attributed the continued increase in stock prices "largely to prevailing confidence that American business is destined to grow rapidly in volume and that the leading corporations will enjoy increasing prosperity."[21]

The Coolidge administration expressed similar optimism about the stock market and the economy. In early 1928, President Coolidge publicly stated that he did not consider brokers' call loans to be too high, and he privately ignored Commerce Secretary Herbert Hoover's advice that measures should be taken to deflate the stock market boom. In September 1928, Treasury Secretary Andrew Mellon told Americans, "There is no cause for worry. The high tide of prosperity will continue."[22]

In his last annual message to Congress in December 1928, Coolidge said, "In the domestic field, there is tranquility and contentment ... and the highest record of years of prosperity." Coolidge told Congress and the nation that they could "regard the present with satisfaction and anticipate the future with confidence." In February

1929, shortly before leaving office, Coolidge opined that stocks were "cheap at current prices" and economic conditions were "absolutely sound."[23]

In contrast to Coolidge and Mellon, the Fed was deeply concerned in early 1928 about the stock market boom and the accelerating growth of brokers' call loans and total bank credit. Bank credit increased 8% during 1927, and bank loans on securities showed the most rapid growth. The Federal Reserve Board supported decisions by regional Federal Reserve Banks to raise their discount window rates from 3.5% to 5% in early 1928, thereby reversing the interest rate cuts arranged by Benjamin Strong in 1927. However, the Fed did not raise interest rates further in 1928, due to concerns about the potentially disruptive impact of higher rates on agriculture and business as well as the Presidential election in November.[24]

Despite the Fed's higher discount rates, total bank credit and call loans continued to expand during 1928. Credit extended by Federal Reserve Banks to their member banks reached $900 million at the end of 1928—double the amount at year-end 1927—and much of that additional credit went into the call loan market, where annual interest rates on call loans rose to 9%. During the 1920s, the Fed preferred to extend credit to member banks by discounting bills of acceptance and exchange resulting from imports, exports, and other commercial transactions. The Fed's prevailing discount rate for those types of bills during the second half of 1928 was 4.5%, lower than the general discount window rate of 5%. Under either rate, member banks could make handsome profits by borrowing from the Fed and making call loans to brokers.[25]

In early 1929, the Fed viewed the continued rise of stock market prices and call loans with great alarm. Both the Dow Jones Industrial Index and the volume of call loans increased by almost half during 1928, and total bank credit rose by 8%, while the nation's economic output grew by only 3%. The Federal Reserve Board and regional Federal Reserve Banks agreed that the stock market boom and the rapid growth in loans on securities posed a serious potential threat to U.S. economic stability. However, they could not reach a consensus on the appropriate policy response.

The Federal Reserve Board and a majority of regional Federal Reserve Banks preferred a policy of "direct pressure," under which the regional Banks would refuse to provide credit to banks if they planned to use that credit to make loans that financed trading in securities. In contrast, the New York Fed and some other regional Banks argued that direct pressure was impractical, and they wanted to raise discount window rates to restrain the growth of credit. The Federal Reserve Board and its allies responded that higher interest rates would inflict collateral damage by restricting the availability of credit for the "legitimate needs" of agriculture and business. Supporters of direct pressure also did not want to expose the Fed to political attacks like those the Fed endured after its high-interest-rate policy triggered a sharp recession during 1920 and 1921.[26]

The Board and its allies prevailed and implemented their strategy of direct pressure. The Board rejected repeated requests by the New York Fed to raise its discount window rate to 6% during the first half of 1929. The Board also issued a policy statement on February 6, 1929, which expressed the Board's great concern about "the excessive amount of the country's credit absorbed in speculative security loans." The Board declared that it felt "a grave responsibility" to take action "whenever there is evidence that member banks are maintaining speculative security loans with the aid of Federal Reserve credit."[27]

In response to the Federal Reserve Board's policy of direct pressure, Fed member banks increased their call loans by only 3% between January and October 1929. However, the Board's policy did not stop nonbank lenders from expanding their loans to brokers, and nonbank lenders held 70% of call loans when the stock market crashed.[28] Thus, the Fed's attempt to deflate the stock market bubble in early 1929 ultimately failed because its "regulatory perimeter" did not reach beyond member banks. A similar lack of regulatory authority over securities firms, insurance companies, and other "shadow banks" undermined the effectiveness of the Fed's responses during the early stages of the global financial crisis in 2007 and 2008.[29]

———

Despite its shortcomings, the Federal Reserve Board's policy of direct pressure came close to bursting the stock market bubble in March 1929. On March 25 and 26, a "wave of fear swept the market" and heavy selling occurred, due to widespread concerns that the Board (which was then meeting in Washington) would take further steps to deflate the stock market boom.[30] Call loan rates rose from 12% to 20% during the early afternoon of March 26, and the situation looked grim. As John Kenneth Galbraith later explained, "March 26, 1929, could have been the end. Money could have remained tight.... The panic might have continued."[31] According to contemporary journalist Elliott Bell, "At 1:30 o'clock, it seemed inevitable that the session was going down in history as the blackest on record, more dismal to the bulls even than any deflation any panic year could offer."[32]

The bull market did not end on March 26, "and if any man can be credited with this, the credit belongs to Charles E. Mitchell."[33] Early that afternoon, in the midst of the market's panic, Mitchell announced that National City Bank had "an obligation, which is paramount to any Federal Reserve warning, or anything else, to avert, so far as lies within our power, any dangerous crisis in the money market." Mitchell pledged that National City would provide $25 million of new call loans at rates ranging from 15% to 20%. Mitchell's pledge effectively capped the interest rate for call loans at 15%, and it also assured market participants that credit for call loans would be available.[34]

Mitchell's intervention worked "like magic," and the stock market rallied.[35] Call loan rates declined to 8% within a few days.[36] As Elliott Bell reported, "From the nadir of despair, the emotions of the financial district moved up to a level of hopefulness for the future.... [Brokerage] room occupants wore the air of one who discovers that he has a friend after all."[37] National City's monthly bulletin of April 1, 1929, included a message from Mitchell, who acknowledged "the dangers of overspeculation." However, Mitchell argued that the bank's intervention on March 26 was necessary "to avoid a general collapse of the securities market such as would have a disastrous effect on business."[38] Other New York bankers agreed with Mitchell that "the great banks of the city would not stand aside and see a credit crisis develop."[39]

Mitchell served as a Class A director of the New York Fed in 1929, after being elected to a three-year term by the member banks of that district. George Harrison, Governor of the New York Fed, gave "tacit approval" for National City's intervention in the call loan market on March 26. (Harrison succeeded Benjamin Strong as Governor following Strong's death in October 1928).[40] In contrast, Senator Carter Glass strongly condemned Mitchell's actions. Glass was a staunch supporter of the Federal Reserve Board's policy of direct pressure, and he alleged that Mitchell violated his oath as a Class A director when he defied the Board's policy:

> [A] Class A director of a Federal reserve bank, himself president of a great banking institution, vigorously slaps the [Federal Reserve Board] in the face and treats its policy with contempt.... He avows his superior obligation to a frantic stock market over against his oath as a director of the New York Federal Reserve Bank, under the supervisory authority of the Federal Reserve Board.[41]

Glass called on the New York Fed to demand Mitchell's resignation. The New York Fed did not do so, and Mitchell continued to serve as a Class A director until his term expired in December 1931.[42] Mitchell's intervention in the call loan market, with the implicit backing of the New York Fed, reflected the ongoing policy disagreements among the New York Fed, other regional Federal Reserve Banks, and the Federal Reserve Board. The Fed's internal conflicts became even more heated after the stock market crashed, as described in Chapter 5, and those conflicts undermined the Fed's ability to respond effectively to the Great Depression. Congress amended the Federal Reserve Act in 1935 by changing the Fed's structure in ways that established the Federal Reserve Board's supremacy over the regional Banks.[43]

After Mitchell's intervention stabilized the stock market, the Federal Reserve Board toned down its policy of direct pressure and largely abandoned that policy after July 1929. In August, the Board agreed that the New York Fed could raise its discount window rate to 6%. That rate increase proved to be largely symbolic. Other regional Federal Reserve Banks decided not to increase their discount window rates above 5%, and the New York Fed mitigated the impact of its discount window rate hike by reducing its discount rate for bankers' acceptances. The New York Fed's actions therefore had relatively little short-term impact on the stock market, and the boom continued. In John Kenneth Galbraith's view, the Fed's indecisive actions after March 1929 indicated the Fed's reluctance to take measures that could trigger a stock market crash, as well as the "mastery" that Mitchell and other Wall Street bankers enjoyed during the stock market boom.[44] Frederick Allen agreed that "Reserve authorities were beaten" by Mitchell's intervention in March 1929, and that defeat provided renewed momentum for the bull market.[45]

The stock market enjoyed a final spectacular surge during the summer of 1929. The *New York Times* industrial index increased by almost 30% during June, July, and August.[46] As Frederick Allen recounted in 1931, investor confidence rose in tandem with the market's relentless advance. Market participants "were comforted by the fact that every crash of the past few years had been followed by a recovery, and that every recovery had ultimately brought [stock] prices to a new high point."[47]

A few commentators warned of impending disaster, but most business and financial leaders, journalists, and economists dismissed those warnings. On March 8, 1929, Paul Warburg, a distinguished banker and one of the architects of the Federal Reserve System, warned that the ongoing "orgies of unrestrained speculation" would ultimately lead to a collapse of the stock market and "a general depression involving the entire country." Wall Street spokesmen attacked Warburg for "sandbagging American prosperity," and some alleged that he was trying to short the market.[48]

Warburg's admonition was quickly forgotten as the stock market boom accelerated during the summer of 1929. Bernard Baruch, a well-known speculator, said in June that "the economic condition of the world seems on the verge of a great forward movement." In August, another prominent speculator, John J. Raskob, published an article entitled "Everyone Ought to Be Rich" in the *Ladies' Home Journal*. Raskob, who was Chairman of the Democratic National Committee, claimed that anyone who invested $15 each month in the stock market and reinvested dividends would build a fortune of $80,000 within twenty years.[49]

Joseph Lawrence, a young economics professor at Princeton, published a book entitled *Wall Street and Washington* in 1929. Lawrence's book expressed unlimited faith in the accuracy of the stock market's judgments. In support of his claim that "stocks are not at present over-valued," Lawrence pointed to "the consensus of judgment of the millions whose valuations function on that admirable market, the Stock Exchange." Lawrence challenged critics who questioned the sustainability of the stock market boom by asking, "Where is that group of men with the all-embracing wisdom which will entitle them to veto the judgment of this intelligent multitude?"[50]

Charles Amos Dice, a professor of business organization at Ohio State, published a similarly optimistic book in 1929, entitled *New Levels in the Stock Market*. Dice's book described "a mighty revolution in industry, in trade, and in finance," and he argued that rising stock prices were simply "registering the tremendous changes that were in progress." Dice enthused that "the Coolidge [stock] market had gone forward like the phalanxes of Cyrus."[51] Much like the politicians, regulators, bankers, and real estate investors who embraced the housing market bubble during the mid-2000s, believers in the stock market boom of 1929 scoffed at anyone who pointed to the storm clouds on the horizon.

The great bull market of the late 1920s peaked on September 3, 1929, when the Dow Jones Industrial Index closed at 381. Two days later, the market suffered a sharp loss. On the same day, Roger Babson, a business statistician who had predicted a market crash since 1927, forecast that "sooner or later, a crash is coming ... and it may be terrific." He warned that "the result will be a serious business depression."[52]

Irving Fisher, a prominent Yale economist, promptly rebutted Babson's dire prediction. Responding to an inquiry from the *New York Times,* Fisher declared, "Stock prices are not too high, and Wall Street will not experience anything in the nature of a crash." The stock market rallied on September 6, and Wall Street journalists mocked Babson as a "prophet of loss" who suffered from "Babsonmindedness."[53]

President Hoover had deep and long-standing concerns about the stock market boom. In March, he urged Richard Whitney, the NYSE's vice president, to adopt measures to discourage excessive speculation. In October, Hoover sent his close friend Harry Robinson, a Los Angeles banker, to discuss the situation on Wall Street with leading New York bankers. On both occasions, Wall Street's leaders assured Hoover that the stock market was in fine shape. On October 19—less than a week before the Great Crash—Thomas Lamont, a leading partner in J. P. Morgan & Co., told Hoover in a letter, "There is a great deal of exaggeration in current gossip about speculation.... Since the war the country has embarked on a remarkable period of healthy prosperity.... The future appears brilliant."[54]

Despite the unwavering optimism of Wall Street bankers, the stock market could not sustain any upward movement during September and October, and stock prices began to slip. After a sharp drop on October 21, the market had lost most of its gains since the spring of 1929.[55] In response to the weakening market, Wall Street's leaders assured the public that the stock market and the economy remained strong. On October 13, the annual convention of the Investment Bankers Association (IBA)—an organization representing investment banks and commercial banks with securities operations—declared that "the securities business would continue to prosper and that stock prices would climb to new highs." The convention's proceedings "made no mention of the fact that the stock market had already suffered serious declines ... since September 5." Instead, the IBA's members said they "look forward to 1930 with the greatest of confidence."[56]

Charles Mitchell expressed similarly bullish sentiments on October 15 as he boarded an ocean liner in Germany for his return voyage to New York. Mitchell opined, "The markets generally are now in a healthy condition [and] values have a sound basis in the general prosperity of our country."[57] On October 22, after Mitchell arrived in New York, he told journalists that declines in stock prices had gone "too far," and he assured them that economic conditions were "fundamentally sound." He argued that the public was "suffering from 'brokers loanitis' " because the press placed too much emphasis on the unprecedented volume of brokers' call loans.[58]

Irving Fisher of Yale supported the bankers' optimism. On October 15, Fisher proclaimed, "Stock prices have reached what looks like a permanently high plateau.... I expect to see the stock market a good deal higher than it is today within a few months."[59] On October 21, Fisher downplayed the significance of the market's sharp decline that day. In his view, the market decline was "only shaking out the lunatic fringe."[60]

———

Despite the many assurances given by Wall Street's leaders and advocates, investor confidence vanished and the Great Crash occurred during the last week of October. On October 23, the stock market experienced "a sudden avalanche of sell orders" and "a perfect Niagara of liquidation." The *New York Times* industrial average "dropped from 415 to 384, giving up all of its gains since the end of the previous June."[61] Following the market's severe losses on October 23, brokers made widespread margin calls on their customers, and many speculators decided it was time to get out of the market.[62]

When trading began on October 24—Black Thursday—a "tidal wave of panic" swept through the stock market. The ticker tape was more than ninety minutes late by 1 p.m., and closing prices for stocks were not reported until about four hours after the NYSE closed at 3:30 p.m.[63] During the morning session on Black Thursday, stock prices fell "with an altogether unprecedented and amazing violence." As the ticker ran further and further behind actual trading, "uncertainty led more and more people to try to sell." In describing Black Thursday two years later, Frederick Allen recalled, "It is the unknown which causes real panic."[64]

On the afternoon of Black Thursday, Wall Street's chieftains tried to rescue the stock market as J. P. Morgan, Sr. had saved New York City's banking system during the Panic of 1907.[65] Six leading bankers—Charles Mitchell of National City, Albert Wiggin of Chase, William Potter of Guaranty Trust, Seward Prosser of Bankers Trust, and George Baker of First National Bank—went to the offices of J. P. Morgan & Co. shortly after noon. Following a brief meeting, Thomas Lamont of Morgan met with reporters. Showing a "sangfroid" that was "legendary," Lamont commented, "There has been a little distress selling on the Stock Exchange ... due to a technical condition of the market." Lamont assured the assembled journalists that market conditions were "susceptible to betterment."[66]

At 1:30 p.m., Richard Whitney, the NYSE's vice president, went to the NYSE's trading floor and placed bids for more than a dozen leading stocks, starting with United States Steel. Market participants understood that Whitney was acting for the bankers' group, since he was the House of Morgan's regular broker. Whitney placed his bids at levels equal to the last reported sale price for each stock, thereby sending a clear signal that the bankers' group intended to stabilize market prices. As Frederick Allen explained, "The desperate remedy worked. The semblance of confidence returned." Although prices began to slide again during the final hour of trading, "the bankers' pool had prevented for the moment an utter collapse."[67]

The bankers' group purchased about $130 million of stocks during their collective efforts to stabilize the market between Black Thursday and November 11. News headlines on October 25 and October 26 praised the bankers for their timely intervention.[68] The *New York Times* reported that Wall Street felt "secure in the knowledge that the most powerful banks in the country stood ready to prevent a recurrence" of panic selling. After a meeting on the evening of Black Thursday, representatives of thirty-five securities brokerage firms told the press that the stock market was "fundamentally sound" and "technically in better condition than it has been in months." Charles Mitchell similarly maintained that the panicked selling on Black Thursday was due to "purely technical" factors, and "fundamentals remained unimpaired."[69]

Prices remained relatively stable on the stock market during the Friday and Saturday trading sessions that followed Black Thursday. On Friday, October 25, President Hoover assured the nation that "the fundamental business of the country, that is production and distribution of commodities, is on a sound and prosperous basis." The bankers' group asked Hoover to endorse the soundness of the stock market, but he declined. Wall Street bankers and brokers quickly stepped into the breach by organizing a "concerted advertising campaign," which urged the public to buy stocks. One advertisement stated, "We believe that the investor who purchases securities at this time with the discrimination that is always a condition of prudent investing may do so with utmost confidence."[70]

Despite all the assurances from Wall Street after Black Thursday, a "second hurricane of liquidation" occurred on Monday, October 28. Declines in stock prices were "far more severe" than on Black Thursday, and the Dow Jones Industrial Index fell by 38 points to 260, "the largest drop on record." There was no sign of any intervention by the bankers' group, and prices did not recover during the afternoon. Trading volume was exceptionally heavy, and the ticker tape was almost three hours late when trading ended on the NYSE. "Margin calls over the weekend were a substantial factor in the decline. Foreigners were also heavy sellers ... because the end of the U.S. boom was clearer to foreign investors."[71]

The bankers' group held a two-hour meeting after the stock market closed on October 28. Thomas Lamont emerged from the meeting and told the press that the market had "hopeful features." Lamont said the bankers' group would continue "to offer certain support and to act as far as possible as a stabilizing factor." However, he cautioned that the group did not intend "to maintain prices as such, but to insure a free and open market."[72]

Lamont's statement had a "chilling" effect on investor confidence. On Black Thursday, the bankers' group "had supported prices and protected profits—or stopped losses." In contrast, Lamont's statement on the evening of October 28 made clear that "prices were to be allowed to fall." As a result, "no one any longer could feel secure" that the banks would intervene to maintain the current level of stock prices.[73]

The next day—"Tragic Tuesday"—was "the most devastating day in the history of the New York stock market." Trading volume on October 29 was "immensely greater than on Black Thursday," and "great blocks of stock were offered for what they would bring." Efforts by the bankers' group to stabilize the market were "swept violently aside" as sell orders "deluged the market." Total losses for the day on NYSE-listed stocks exceeded $8 billion.[74]

After Tragic Tuesday, public opinion turned against Wall Street. The bankers' group was "blamed for having failed to prevent the crash," and rumors spread that banks were selling the market short. Lamont met with the press again that evening, and he denied that any members of the bankers' group were selling stocks.[75] (In fact, as described in Chapter 6, the Senate's 1933 investigation of Wall Street revealed that Albert Wiggin of Chase National Bank made large profits from short sales of Chase's stock during the crash.)

As John Kenneth Galbraith observed, "Few men ever lost position so rapidly as did the New York bankers in the five days from October 24 to October 29."[76] Similarly, Vincent Carosso concluded:

> The events of the crash made a mockery of the investment bankers' much touted expertise and overoptimistic forecasts. The crash demonstrated how powerless they were in the face of disaster. Public confidence in financiers generally and in Wall Street bankers particularly was shattered entirely as the stock market belied their every statement.[77]

———

The New York Fed helped to prevent a complete breakdown of New York's financial markets during the Great Crash. During the last week of October, nonbank lenders demanded repayment of over $2 billion of brokers' call loans. Those demands threatened to cause widespread defaults among brokers and could have triggered a general collapse of the call loan market. To prevent that outcome, the New York Fed provided extensive liquidity support to its member banks by purchasing $160 million of government securities and by offering to provide discount window loans on request to all member banks. The New York Fed's assistance allowed New York banks to acquire more than $1 billion of call loans from brokers, thereby avoiding the liquidation of those loans by nonbank lenders. While the call loan market shrank, it did not collapse, and most brokers survived the crash.[78]

The stock market continued to spiral downward until November 13, 1929. The Dow Jones Industrial Index declined to 198 on that day, marking a fall of 48% from its peak on September 3, and wiping out all of the gains of the past two years.[79] The market finally stabilized on November 14, and stock prices rose modestly during the rest of 1929. The Dow Jones Industrial Index climbed back to 248 by year's end, still 35% below its peak. The combined value of all NYSE-listed common and preferred stocks dropped by $25 billion, or 28%, between September 1 and the end of 1929.[80]

The Fed's internal debates continued, but the Fed ultimately agreed on measures that helped to stabilize financial markets during November and December. The Federal Reserve Board and some regional Federal Reserve Banks criticized the New York Fed for acting unilaterally in buying $160 million of government securities during the last week of October. After prolonged discussions, the Board agreed with the New York Fed's plan to purchase up to $200 million of additional government securities during December. The Board also approved requests by the New York Fed to cut its discount window rate in two steps from 6% to 4.5%. In return, the New York Fed agreed not to make additional open-market purchases of government securities without the Board's prior consent, except in emergencies. Thus, at the end of 1929, the Federal Reserve Board and the regional Banks reached a temporary consensus on how the Fed should respond to the crash.[81]

The Fed's easing of monetary policy after the crash reversed much of the tightening that the Fed had imposed during 1928 and the first half of 1929. Short-term interest rates for prime commercial paper, bankers' acceptances, and brokers' call loans dropped significantly between September and December 1929. As a result, short-term rates in the money market returned to levels close to those of mid-1928.[82]

President Hoover responded to the Great Crash with a series of measures designed to support the economy. In November 1929, Hoover held a series of meetings with business and labor leaders. Business leaders promised not to dismiss workers or cut wages, based on reciprocal pledges from labor leaders not to demand higher wages or call strikes. In December, Hoover persuaded Congress to approve a $160 million reduction in income tax rates. At Hoover's urging, federal government agencies approved $250 million of new public works projects for 1930, and some state and local governments implemented similar public works programs. Hoover also encouraged public utilities and railroads to accelerate their plans for new construction, and those industries increased their construction projects by about $1 billion during 1930.[83]

During the first half of 1930, the Fed took further steps to ease monetary policy. The New York Fed reduced its discount window rate in four steps to 2.5% (with the Federal Reserve Board's approval), and the New York Fed also reduced its discount rate for bankers' acceptances to 1.875%. Short-term interest rates for commercial paper and call loans continued to decline during the first half of 1930. In addition, the amount of outstanding commercial paper doubled to more than $550 million during the first half of 1930. Conditions in the money market appeared to be relatively favorable during the early months of 1930.[84]

At the beginning of 1930, many politicians, business leaders, and investors believed that the worst effects of the crash had dissipated, and they expected economic conditions to improve.[85] The huge inflow of money into the stock market from domestic and international investors during 1928 and 1929 had created tight money conditions as well as higher interest rates in the U.S., Britain, and Europe. Many observers hoped that the end of the stock market boom would lead to more favorable credit conditions and greater economic stability. The volume of brokers' call loans in New York dropped from $8.5 billion in October 1929 to $4.0 billion in January 1930. Many foreign investors withdrew their funds from the call loan market and returned those funds to Britain and Europe. As they did so, exchange rate pressures on foreign central banks eased. The Bank of England and many European central banks reduced their lending rates in early 1930 in concert with the Fed.[86]

Foreign bond markets temporarily revived after the crash, as investors in the U.S., Britain, and Europe shifted from stocks to foreign bonds. During the first half of 1930, substantial new offerings of foreign bonds occurred in New York, London, and West European financial centers. The Young Plan's authorization of new loans for Germany created additional grounds for optimism that 1930 would be a year of economic stability and growth on both sides of the Atlantic.[87]

The Hoover administration and business leaders assured the American public that the U.S. economy would soon recover, just as it had done in 1922, 1924, and 1927.[88] Charles Mitchell and Albert Wiggin played prominent roles in those confidence-building efforts. When Mitchell addressed National City's annual meeting of shareholders in January 1930, he reported that "industry and trade are more adequately financed than at any time in the past," and he hailed the positive effects of declining interest rates. According to Mitchell, "A general feeling of confidence exists throughout the country.... It does not appear probable that business will remain below the normal stage of activity for any protracted period."[89]

Wiggin similarly professed that "business morale is good" in his annual report to Chase's shareholders in January 1930. Wiggin praised President Hoover and the Fed for their timely responses to the crash, and he argued that "Wall Street remained a disciplined army in the face of the shock." Wiggin therefore concluded, "We are thoroughly justified in saying 'business as usual.' "[90]

———

In response to all of the hopeful signals from political and business leaders, the U.S. stock market staged an encouraging rally during the early months of 1930. The Dow Jones Industrial Index rose to 294 on April 17, nearly matching its level at the end of 1928 and marking a strong recovery from its low point of 198 in November 1929.[91]

The U.S. bond market also rallied in early 1930. Domestic and foreign corporations and governments issued more than $3 billion of bonds during the first five months of 1930.[92] Commercial and investment banks took advantage of that window of opportunity to underwrite a number of risky bond issues that subsequently performed very poorly. Widespread defaults on those bonds indicated that underwriters were eager to resume their strategy of selling speculative securities to the public—a strategy that provided handsome fees and profits for underwriters but inflicted disastrous losses on investors.

In January 1930, Halsey, Stuart & Co., a prominent Chicago investment bank, and its syndicate partners sold $60 million of convertible debentures issued by Insull Utility Investments, Inc. (IUI). Halsey, Stuart's syndicate included securities affiliates of several large Chicago banks, including Continental Illinois, National Republic, and the Foreman State group. IUI was one of two giant holding companies that sat on top of Samuel Insull's complex pyramid of utility companies. Insull's multi-tiered utility empire produced more than 10% of all electric power in the U.S. and served more than five thousand communities in thirty-two states.[93]

During World War I, Insull helped to organize highly successful Liberty bond drives in Illinois. Like Charles Mitchell of National City, Insull used his Liberty bond experiences to perfect "high-pressure sales tactics" for marketing securities issued by his utility companies. Insull strongly encouraged customers of his utility companies to buy stocks and bonds issued by those companies. Insull believed that he could maintain effective control over his empire if customers were the primary owners of his utility companies.[94]

Insull worked closely with Halsey, Stuart to organize the sale of Insull utility securities to retail investors. For example, Halsey, Stuart sponsored a series of radio programs in which a University of Chicago professor—known as the "Old Counselor"—provided advice on "principles of sound investment to millions of listeners." Reading from scripts prepared by Halsey, Stuart, the "Old Counselor" encouraged the public to buy Insull utility securities as well as other securities underwritten by Halsey, Stuart.[95]

Halsey, Stuart's underwriting syndicates for Insull utility securities used the sales pitch "If the light shines, you know your money is safe." When Halsey, Stuart offered securities issued by Insull companies, it did not disclose that it held significant ownership stakes in those companies. Halsey, Stuart "tried to disguise its ownership interest in Insull by placing its holdings in the name of a midlevel corporate executive." The public eagerly purchased Insull securities because "the name of Insull was magic." More than a million investors held stock or bonds in Insull's companies when his empire collapsed in 1932.[96]

Beginning in 1928, Samuel Insull conducted a two-year campaign to block a hostile takeover attempt by Cyrus Eaton, a Cleveland financier. In 1929, Insull created two top-tier holding companies—IUI and Corporation Securities Co. (CSC)—to centralize his control over his empire. IUI and CSC issued more than $250 million of securities in 1929 and 1930 in public offerings underwritten by Halsey, Stuart's syndicates. Those financings included IUI's offering of $60 million of debentures in January 1930, and CSC's contemporaneous offering of $30 million of debt securities. Middle West Utilities Co., an intermediate-level holding company, issued $50 million of new bonds in early 1930.[97]

The audacity and success of Insull's financings in 1930 "set Chicago observers gaping."[98] The public had great faith in Insull and viewed his securities as "blue chip" investments. It was therefore relatively easy for Halsey, Stuart's syndicates to sell the 1930 bond issues. However, Insull's empire was so structurally complex—with multiple layers of holding companies stacked on top of dozens of operating companies—that it was impossible for investors to evaluate the actual risks of the Insull bond offerings in 1930.[99]

In June 1930, Insull increased the vulnerability of his highly leveraged empire when IUI and CSC purchased Cyrus Eaton's holdings of Insull securities for $56 million. To finance that buyout, IUI and CSC took out $48 million of short-term loans from banks in Chicago and New York, and Insull pledged his personal holdings of CSC and IUI stock as collateral for those loans. When Insull's utility empire collapsed in 1932, the holders of equity and debt securities issued by CSC, IUI, and Middle West lost most of their investments.[100]

Commercial and investment banks sold other high-risk securities to the public during the bond market rally in early 1930. In February, Chase Securities Corp., the securities affiliate of Chase National Bank, led an underwriting group that sold $40 million of Cuban government bonds to the American public. As described in Chapter 3, the offering prospectus did not disclose that all of the 1930 bond proceeds would be used to pay off $40 million of loans that Cuba had previously received from Chase and other members of its banking group. Thus, investors did not know that the 1930 bond offering had the practical effect of transferring $40 million of Cuban sovereign debt risk from Chase's banking group to public investors. Cuba defaulted on those bonds in 1933.[101]

In April 1930, Chase arranged an equally hazardous public offering of $30 million of ten-year debentures issued by General Theatres Equipment, Inc. (GTE). Chase and its syndicate partners received an "unusually high underwriting fee" of 9.5% for that offering.[102] The GTE debentures were part of a complex financing scheme that enabled GTE to acquire control of Fox Film Corp. (Fox), which owned a chain of theaters and a motion picture studio.

Fox had encountered serious financial problems in late 1929, after Fox took on large amounts of debt in an unsuccessful attempt to acquire Loew's Inc. (the owner of a competing chain of theaters and a rival movie studio, Metro-Goldwyn-Mayer). In early 1930, Chase and Halsey, Stuart financed GTE's hostile takeover of Fox. Chase provided a $15 million loan to GTE and served as lead underwriter for GTE's ten-year debentures. Another syndicate organized by Chase and Halsey, Stuart sold $65 million of one-year notes issued by GTE and its subsidiary Westco. GTE's takeover of Fox proved to be calamitous for Chase, for Halsey, Stuart, and for the investors who bought GTE securities. GTE filed for bankruptcy in 1932.[103]

In April 1930, National City underwrote an offering of $25 million of Chilean bonds to American investors. National City had good reason to know that Chile was a high-risk debtor. In 1929, as described in Chapter 3, National City performed extensive research on Chile's economic situation and encountered significant problems in selling bonds issued by Lautaro Nitrate, a Chilean company. Chile's economy depended heavily on exports of copper and nitrate, and prices for those commodities plunged after early 1929. In 1931, Chile defaulted on all of its outstanding bonds, including the bonds sold by National City in 1930.[104]

In May 1930, Hallgarten & Co., a private investment bank, led a similarly ill-fated offering of $17.6 million of Uruguayan bonds to American investors. Uruguay defaulted on those bonds in 1931.[105]

In June 1930, J. P. Morgan & Co. and National City led a syndicate of American commercial and investment banks that underwrote $98.5 million of Young Plan bonds issued by Germany. As discussed in Chapter 3, the Morgan–National City syndicate experienced great difficulties in completing that offering, due to a lack of investor enthusiasm for the Young Plan bonds. By 1932, the market value of those bonds had fallen by almost two-thirds. In 1934, the Nazi regime defaulted on all bonds held by American investors.[106]

Relatively few non-Canadian foreign bonds were issued in the U.S. after the Young Plan offering, and the foreign bond market shut down completely in 1931. Offerings of domestic corporate bonds also declined sharply in mid-1930 due to deteriorating business conditions and the slumping stock market. Municipal bonds continued to be issued at a relatively steady pace until October 1930, but the municipal bond market became dormant thereafter as serious banking problems emerged.[107]

———

The short-lived rallies in the stock and bond markets ended during the early summer of 1930, as it became clear that the U.S. economy had entered a severe recession.[108] Prices for most commodities declined steadily after the spring of 1929. Industrial production peaked in July 1929, declined modestly during the early fall, and dropped more rapidly after the Great Crash. By December 1929, auto production and machine tool orders had fallen to about half their levels for the previous year. There was a temporary revival of industrial production in early 1930, but output fell sharply thereafter. In December 1930, total industrial output was 37% below its peak in July 1929.[109]

The primary reason for the economy's rapid deterioration in 1930 was "a collapse in domestic consumption spending."[110] Consumer demand declined sharply for durable and semidurable goods, including automobiles, appliances, radios, furniture, other home furnishings, clothing, and shoes. Those were the same categories of consumer goods for which demand and output had expanded most rapidly during the 1920s. The nation's output of durable goods fell by a third in 1930, and output of semidurable goods declined by a fifth.[111] Passenger car production fell by almost 40%, leading to steep drops in output for steel, plate glass, and tires.[112]

Consumers also stopped buying new homes, and the value of new home construction fell by almost half in 1930. As consumer demand weakened across many economic sectors, manufacturers canceled plans to build new plants and stopped buying new equipment. Many real estate developers abandoned projects for building new apartments, hotels, offices, and stores. The total value of new private sector construction declined by more than a quarter in 1930, despite increases in construction by railroads and public utilities. Investments in production equipment fell by more than a fifth.[113]

Rapid declines in private sector consumption and most types of fixed investments led to a sharp decline in national output during 1930. Falling consumption accounted for almost half of the 9.3% drop in U.S. GNP during 1930, while reductions in fixed investments were the second-most-important factor. Government spending rose during 1930, due in large part to President Hoover's public works initiatives, but that increase was far too small to offset the steep drops in private sector consumption and output.[114] Corporate profits in 1930 fell more than two-thirds below their level in

1929. More than twenty-six thousand commercial and industrial firms filed for bankruptcy in 1930.[115]

There were several reasons for the dramatic decline in consumption during 1930. Rising unemployment and falling incomes forced many households to cut back on discretionary purchases of nonessential goods. The number of unemployed workers nearly tripled in 1930, as 2.8 million people lost their jobs and the national unemployment rate reached almost 9%. Producers of durable goods cut their employment rolls by 20%. Widespread layoffs and shorter workweeks caused total personal income to fall by more than 10% during 1930.[116]

As discussed in Chapter 2, many consumers carried heavy debt burdens from real estate mortgages and installment loans they had taken on during the economic boom of the 1920s. Consumers made deep cuts in discretionary spending as they tried to avoid losing homes, cars, appliances, and other goods they had purchased on credit.[117]

Many affluent households—who were most likely to buy new homes, automobiles, and other expensive goods—suffered heavy losses during the Great Crash and faced severe financial stress due to continued declines in their investment portfolios and their need to pay off margin loans. The top 5% of U.S. households accounted for a third of total private incomes, and their reductions in big-ticket purchases contributed significantly to the fall in demand for housing and durable goods.[118] British journalist Francis Hirst, who visited the U.S. in late 1929, reported that "the first result [of the crash] has been a heavy decline in luxury buying of all sorts and also a large amount of selling of such things as motor cars and fur coats." Hirst commented that "the favored health resorts have suffered enormously ... a very great number of servants, including butlers and chauffeurs, have been dismissed."[119]

The Great Crash and its aftermath dealt a powerful psychological blow to the confidence that the long boom of the 1920s had instilled in American consumers and business firms. In November 1929, *The Magazine of Wall Street* reported that the crash had "an unfavorable influence on general trade both by curtailing purchasing power and by impairing the confidence of consumers and businessmen alike." The same article noted an emerging "tendency to reduce or postpone projected commitments." In December 1929, *Moody's Investors Service* stated that "the stock market break ... undermined general confidence," and "almost everyone held his plans in abeyance and waited for the horizon to clear." Six months later, *The Magazine of Wall Street* commented that "uncertainty and confused price trends have been the order of the day."[120]

Writing in June 1931, Frederick Allen highlighted the "profound psychological reactions from the exuberance of 1929" that Americans experienced after the crash. According to Allen, "There was hardly a man or woman in the country whose attitude toward life had not been affected by [the stock market boom] in some degree and was not now affected by the sudden and brutal shattering of hope." The economic boom of the 1920s had resulted in "overproduction of capital; overambitious expansion of business concerns; [and] overproduction of commodities under the stimulus of installment buying and buying with stock-market profits." In 1931, Americans found "themselves living in an altered world which called for new adjustments."[121] Given the widespread loss of confidence and the highly uncertain economic conditions that followed the Great Crash, many consumers and business firms decided that the most prudent course of action was to reduce their spending and pay down their debts.[122]

U.S. banks system faced their own significant problems after the crash. During the 1920s, banks greatly expanded their holdings of higher-risk, illiquid assets, including real estate loans and securities-based loans and investments, as explained in Chapter 2. Many of the securities that banks held as investments or as collateral for loans were equity stocks or lower-quality debt securities, such as municipal bonds, corporate bonds, foreign bonds, and real estate bonds.[123]

As discussed in Chapter 2, most real estate mortgages held by banks had terms of five years or less. Those mortgages typically provided for little or no payment of principal during their terms and required borrowers to make large balloon payments of principal on maturity. In addition, more than half of homeowners with first mortgages had taken out second mortgages, typically with terms of one to three years. Many homeowners therefore faced high default risks on their mortgages after the Depression began. Thus, banks held large amounts of risky assets in 1930 that were vulnerable to defaults by struggling households and heavily indebted business firms.[124]

The Fed failed to take effective measures to counteract the sharp economic downturn that occurred during 1930. George Harrison, Governor of the New York Fed, proposed further steps to ease monetary policy during the late spring and early summer of 1930. The Federal Reserve Board permitted the New York Fed to purchase $50 million of government securities in June 1930. However, the Board (with support from the Governors of several regional Federal Reserve Banks) refused to allow the New York Fed to buy additional government securities or to reduce its discount rate during the summer of 1930. Harrison's opponents argued that short-term rates in the money market were already quite low in mid-1930, indicating that credit was "easy." Opponents also warned that additional purchases of government securities could unleash a new wave of unhealthy speculation in the stock and bond markets.[125]

Even Harrison stopped pushing for a more liberal policy after the largest New York banks significantly reduced their borrowings from the New York Fed and increased their liquidity reserves. Harrison sent a letter to other Fed Governors in July 1930, stating that "conditions in the money market" did not require further easing because major banks were "substantially out of debt" and had "some surplus funds available" for lending to the private sector.[126] In September, Harrison strongly opposed a proposal for further easing made by Adolph Miller, a member of the Federal Reserve Board. Miller argued that the Fed should purchase additional government securities to stimulate the "stagnant" economy. Harrison and most of the other Fed Governors and Board members rejected Miller's proposal. Harrison contended that Miller's call for a "heavy dose of easy credit" would be "fraught with a great many dangers," as it could encourage a renewed bout of speculation as well as an outflow of gold to Europe.[127]

Beginning with Milton Friedman and Anna Schwartz in the 1960s, economic historians have strongly criticized the Fed for not adopting additional monetary stimulus measures in 1930.[128] Given the severity of the nation's economic slump in 1930, the Fed's fears about encouraging a new speculative episode were clearly overstated. However, the Fed's worries were not entirely irrational in light of its recent experience with the stock market boom, its inability to counteract that boom, and the flurry of high-risk bond offerings that banks quickly arranged when market conditions temporarily improved in early 1930.

Most Fed policymakers did not see any reason to provide further monetary stimulus in the late summer and autumn of 1930 because they thought monetary policy was already "easy" and most private sector borrowers were not seeking new loans. In a November 1930 speech, Charles Hamlin of the Federal Reserve Board commented that banks "have ample reserves and stand ready to finance a growing volume of business as soon as signs of recovery express themselves in an increasing demand for credit."[129] The Fed failed to recognize that money center banks had become "gun-shy" and were not eager to make new loans. Large banks reduced their borrowings from the Fed, trimmed their loan portfolios, and built "larger cash reserves as a precaution against further disasters."[130]

In addition, the Fed's focus on the low level of interest rates for short-term loans in the money market was mistaken because the Fed "failed to distinguish between real and nominal interest rates." Consumer and wholesale prices fell by 14–15% between September 1929 and September 1930. As a result, even though the New York Fed cut its discount and bill acceptance rates after the crash by more than 3%, real short-term interest rates (adjusted for deflation) were actually "more than ten percentage points above the level of the earlier year." Because the Fed failed to account for price deflation, its monetary policy in the fall of 1930 was therefore much tighter than Fed policymakers realized.[131]

The Hoover administration also failed to respond effectively as the economy deteriorated during 1930. President Hoover believed that state and local governments and private charities should continue to take primary responsibility for helping poor and hungry people. He strongly encouraged relief efforts by local communities and charities, but he viewed direct, large-scale federal aid programs as an unprecedented and undesirable approach that should be used only as a last resort. Hoover did propose additional federal public works projects to boost employment and consumption. However, his desire to avoid large federal budget deficits and his disagreements with congressional leaders limited the size and economic impact of any new federal projects.[132]

The U.S. economy continued to spiral downward during the autumn of 1930, and the speculative risks that commercial and investment banks assumed during the boom years of the 1920s caused severe problems as the nation encountered its first major banking crisis since the Panic of 1907. That crisis began in November 1930, as described in Chapter 5, and it proved to be the first of a series of banking crises that plunged the U.S. and Europe into the Great Depression.

5
Nemesis

The Universal Banking Model Failed During the Banking
Crises of the Great Depression

A series of banking crises erupted in the U.S. and Europe from the fall of 1930 through the spring of 1933. Those banking crises caused recessions on both sides of the Atlantic to become the global Great Depression. Universal banks were at the epicenter of each major banking crisis.

Countries with banking systems dominated by universal banks were more likely to experience systemic banking crises during the Great Depression, compared with nations in which banks were separated from securities markets.[1] Universal banks suffered heavy losses from securities investments and loans related to their securities underwriting and trading activities. As a result of those securities-related losses, "relatively minor shocks on the securities markets could produce crisis and stagnation for the entire economy." Universal banks also incurred significant losses from their long-term equity investments in business clients. Those ownership interests "ensured that a recession in manufacturing would ripple rapidly through the banking system and the economy as a whole."[2]

Thus, nations with banking systems dominated by universal banks experienced contagious spillovers of risks and losses during the 1930s. In contrast, neither Britain nor Canada experienced a systemic banking crisis. While additional factors contributed to the greater resilience of British and Canadian banks, it was very significant that commercial banks were separated from securities markets in both countries.

———

The first major banking crisis of the Great Depression occurred in the U.S. in late 1930. That crisis was triggered by the collapse of two universal banks—Caldwell and Company and Bank of United States.

Caldwell and Company was a large financial-industrial conglomerate founded by Rogers Caldwell and headquartered in Nashville, Tennessee. Caldwell and Company was the leading underwriter in the South for municipal bonds, drainage bonds, and real estate bonds for hotels and apartment buildings. Caldwell and Company also purchased controlling equity interests in a chain of banks and several insurance companies. The firm required its bond underwriting customers to deposit the proceeds of their bond issues in Caldwell-controlled banks. Caldwell's insurance companies also kept large deposits in those banks. Caldwell and Company used its affiliated banks and insurance companies as dumping grounds (purchasers of last resort) for bonds that the firm could not sell to the public.[3]

Caldwell and Company gained control of two dozen industrial and commercial enterprises, including textile mills, clothing manufacturers, department stores, newspapers, and Nashville's minor league baseball team, as well as producers and distributors of asphalt, cement, coal, petroleum, and dairy products. Caldwell and Company underwrote bonds for those companies, and the companies maintained large deposits in Caldwell-controlled banks. Caldwell and Company also created an investment trust, known as Shares-in-the-South, which sold more than sixty thousand shares to the public. Shares-in-the-South bought two-thirds of its portfolio of investment securities from Caldwell and Company.[4]

In 1929, Caldwell and Company was "the dominant investment banker of the South" as well as "the largest financial conglomerate in the South."[5] The enterprises controlled by Caldwell and Company had more than $500 million of assets.[6] Caldwell and Company promoted the firm's political interests through the three newspapers it controlled. Rogers Caldwell and his partner, Luke Lea, built a political machine that helped to elect Henry Horton as Governor of Tennessee in 1928. Horton told state officials to award contracts to Caldwell and Company for underwriting state agency bonds and paving roads. Horton also directed state agencies to deposit large sums in Bank of Tennessee, Caldwell's primary bank.[7]

Caldwell and Company faced severe problems after the Great Crash in October 1929. The firm suffered large losses from the declining value of its securities portfolio as well as its failed efforts to support the market price of Shares-in-the-South. At the end of 1929, more than four-fifths of the securities held by Caldwell and Company were defaulted bonds, securities issued by its controlled companies, and other illiquid securities that the firm could not sell to the public. More than half of Caldwell and Company's liabilities were due on demand, and those demand liabilities were nine times as large as its liquid assets.[8] Caldwell and Company operated with dangerously low capital, and its assets-to-equity ratio rose to 21:1 at the end of 1929.[9]

Bank of Tennessee (Caldwell and Company's primary bank) was also in a gravely weakened state. The bank relied heavily on deposits of state government funds, and most of the bank's assets were illiquid securities that Caldwell and Company had dumped on it.[10] In a last-ditch effort to save his empire, Rogers Caldwell arranged a merger in June 1930 between Caldwell and Company and BancoKentucky Company. BancoKentucky controlled National Bank of Kentucky in Louisville and several other banks in Kentucky and Ohio. National Bank of Kentucky provided a $2.4 million loan that gave temporary relief to Caldwell and Company. However, BancoKentucky was plagued by its own serious problems.[11]

Caldwell and Company's position became untenable as economic conditions deteriorated during the second half of 1930, due in part to a severe drought that afflicted much of the Midwest and South. The Tennessee superintendent of banks closed Bank of Tennessee on November 7, 1930, and Caldwell and Company was placed in receivership six days later. News of Caldwell and Company's collapse precipitated a severe regional banking panic, which spread throughout the Federal Reserve Districts of St. Louis, Atlanta, and Richmond. Depositor runs led to the failures of National Bank of Kentucky and more than a hundred other banks that either were controlled by Caldwell and Company or were correspondent banks of Caldwell affiliates. The widespread failures of Caldwell-connected banks in Arkansas, Kentucky, North Carolina, and Tennessee triggered depositor runs that closed dozens of other vulnerable banks in southern Illinois, Iowa, Missouri, and Mississippi.[12]

Many of the Caldwell-controlled insurance companies and industrial firms failed, and most of the industrial and real estate bonds underwritten by Caldwell and Company defaulted. Caldwell and Company's demise "resulted in tremendous losses to investors, depositors, and policyholders, and ... brought about an impairment of resources in the South and certain sections of the Mid-West sufficient to cause an intensification of the depression in those regions."[13]

———

Bank of United States (BUS) was the second large universal bank that failed during the first U.S. banking crisis in late 1930. BUS was the twenty-eighth-largest bank in the U.S. and a state-chartered member bank of the Federal Reserve System. BUS operated almost sixty branches in the New York City metropolitan area and held $315 million of assets and $240 million of deposits. The bank was founded in 1913 by Joseph Marcus, and its primary customers were garment firms, garment workers, and Jewish families in New York City. In 1929, BUS had 440,000 depositors, more than any other bank in the nation.[14]

Joseph Marcus operated BUS in a prudent manner until he died in July 1927. After Joseph's death, his son Bernard and friend Saul Singer assumed control of the bank. Bernard and Saul quickly embarked on an aggressive growth and diversification program that resembled Rogers Caldwell's empire-building spree. BUS created two securities affiliates, and the shares of one of those affiliates (Bankus Corporation) were combined with the shares of BUS to create stock "units." BUS's securities affiliates actively traded in the units of BUS-Bankus stock to boost their market price, in the same way that National City Corporation and Chase Securities Corporation traded in the stocks of their bank affiliates to increase their market values. The second securities affiliate of BUS (City Financial) managed a portfolio of more than $30 million of securities. BUS made large loans to its securities affiliates to support their operations.[15]

In 1928 and 1929, BUS acquired five banks and extended its branch network into all of New York City's boroughs. To accomplish the last and largest of those mergers, BUS issued a large number of stock units to directors and principal shareholders of the acquired bank.[16] BUS also established more than thirty real estate affiliates, which received loans from BUS and sold real estate bonds to finance the construction of apartment buildings.[17]

The price of BUS-Bankus stock units declined during the summer of 1929, as shareholders of the most recently acquired bank sold their units into the market.

BUS's securities affiliates and a trading syndicate organized by Marcus and Singer bought large numbers of those units in the market to support their price. BUS extended almost $12 million of loans to its securities affiliates and provided additional loans to the Marcus-Singer syndicate to finance those purchases. Marcus and Singer also launched a high-pressure sales campaign that persuaded thirty thousand of BUS's depositors to buy $6 million of its stock units. After the stock market crashed in October, BUS extended loans to its employees to help them meet margin calls and hold on to their units.[18]

By early 1930, BUS faced severe financial problems. To improve BUS's liquidity, Marcus and Singer launched a drive to attract new depositors. BUS offered generous prizes to branch employees who signed up new customers. BUS's deposit drive recruited eighty thousand new depositors during the spring of 1930.[19] However, bank examiners from New York State and the New York Fed determined in September 1930 that BUS was in a highly precarious position. BUS had suffered $16 million of losses related to investments in its stock units, and BUS held more than $23 million of troubled loans, including $7 million of nonperforming loans to its real estate affiliates.[20]

New York superintendent of banks Joseph Broderick and New York Fed officials tried to save BUS by arranging a merger between BUS and three other New York City banks. Those merger efforts failed after the New York Clearing House and the largest New York banks refused to contribute $30 million to support the merger. Broderick and New York Lieutenant Governor Herbert Lehman made last-minute appeals for help, but the leaders of New York's major banks again refused to save BUS. When the public learned about the failed merger negotiations, a depositor run began, and Broderick closed BUS on December 11, 1930.[21] The New York Fed had provided $18 million of discount window loans to BUS during 1929. However, the New York Fed declined to provide additional help to BUS in late 1930, apparently because it viewed BUS as insolvent and therefore ineligible for further loans.[22]

Like Caldwell and Company, BUS collapsed as a result of high-risk securities and real estate activities, pervasive conflicts of interest, and extensive self-dealing by its insiders. When BUS failed, the bank and its affiliates held $32 million of BUS's stock units, $11 million of loans secured by stock units, $7.7 million of real estate bonds issued by BUS's real estate affiliates, and $10.2 million of loans made by BUS to those affiliates. BUS's affiliates had $38 million of liabilities and almost no assets.[23]

The failure of BUS triggered depositor runs on three smaller New York City banks with connections to BUS, including two of the banks that participated in the failed merger negotiations. The smallest of those three banks failed, but the New York Clearing House rescued the other two banks. Seventeen banks failed in the Federal Reserve Districts of New York and Philadelphia during December 1930 and January 1931.[24]

BUS's failure received extensive coverage in domestic and international newspapers, due to its name and its status as a Fed member bank in the nation's leading financial center. The New York Fed's failure to arrange a rescue of BUS created widespread doubts about the Fed's ability to prevent failures of other large banks. In August 1931,

Owen Young, a director of the New York Fed, told his colleagues that BUS's failure "had shaken confidence in the Federal Reserve System more than any other occurrence in recent years."[25]

The first U.S. banking crisis lasted from November 1930 through January 1931 and resulted in failures of more than eight hundred banks, which held more than $600 million of deposits.[26] The Federal Reserve Bank of Atlanta and the New York Fed tried to mitigate the effects of failures within their districts. The Atlanta Fed provided emergency liquidity assistance to threatened Fed member banks in Tennessee and Mississippi, thereby mitigating the impact of Caldwell and Company's collapse within its Federal Reserve District. In contrast, the Federal Reserve Bank of St. Louis did not provide liquidity assistance to member banks in its district. Consequently, a higher percentage of banks failed in the St. Louis District, and the economic impact of Caldwell and Company's demise was significantly more severe in that district.[27]

None of the regional Federal Reserve Banks acted as lender of last resort for vulnerable state banks that were not members of the Federal Reserve System.[28] The Fed's refusal to help state nonmember banks during the banking crisis of 1930 mirrored the Fed's policy during the previous decade. More than 5,700 banks failed during the 1920s, and most of them were small state nonmember banks located in rural farming areas. The Fed followed a hands-off policy toward state nonmember banks because they were not subject to Fed oversight with its generally stricter standards. The Fed also did not believe that small bank failures could undermine the stability of the U.S. banking system.[29] The Fed did not realize that a prolonged wave of bank failures could eventually destroy public confidence in banks generally and trigger widespread depositor runs.[30]

In response to BUS's failure, the New York Fed injected funds into the New York money market by purchasing government securities and discounting bankers' acceptances.[31] However, the New York Fed did not take further action after conditions in the New York money market improved in January 1931. Most Fed policymakers opposed any further measures to stimulate the U.S. economy because they did not want to encourage a new round of speculation in the securities markets. They also concluded that most banks and business firms did not want to borrow additional funds for "legitimate" commercial transactions. Money center banks were holding larger than normal excess reserves in early 1931, and relatively few creditworthy borrowers wanted new loans.

Adolph Miller of the Federal Reserve Board told his colleagues that they were misinterpreting economic and financial trends. In Miller's view, the wave of bank failures during 1930 caused bankers to hold extra reserves due to their "excessive caution and excessive desire for liquidity." The Fed ignored Miller's warning and did not approve any additional significant measures to increase liquidity in the financial markets during 1931.[32]

In late 1930 and early 1931, as shown in Figures 5.1 and 5.2, four negative trends showed that the nation's economic recession intensified during the first banking crisis. First, the crisis caused many depositors to withdraw funds from banks and hoard cash. The volume of bank deposits declined during the last two months of 1930, and the amount of currency (cash) in circulation increased. Most of the additional currency held by the public did not return to banks after December 1930, reflecting a reduced level of public confidence in the banking system after the crisis ended.

Second, the nation's money supply declined during late 1930, reversing a long-term trend in which the money supply increased from 1922 to 1927 and remained essentially unchanged from 1928 through the first nine months of 1930. Third, the interest rate spread between higher-risk (Baa-rated) corporate bonds and federal government bonds widened sharply during the last two months of 1930, after having remained

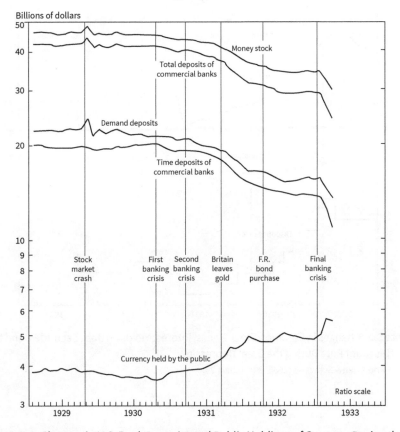

Figure 5.1 Changes in U.S. Bank Deposits and Public Holdings of Currency During the Great Depression

Source: Friedman & Schwartz (1963: 302) (chart 27)

Common Stock Prices, Interest Yields; and Discount Rates or Federal Reserve Bank of New York, Monthly, 1929–March 1933

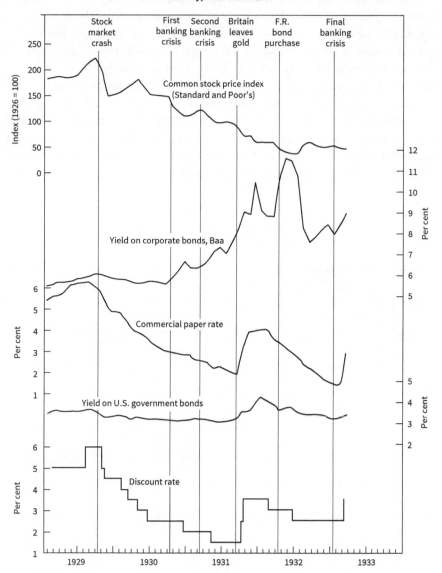

Figure 5.2 Changes in Common Stock Prices, Interest Yields on Debt Securities, and the Fed's Discount Rate During the Great Depression

Source: Friedman & Schwartz (1963: 304) (chart 29)

steady during the previous two years. Fourth, banks reduced their outstanding loans during late 1930 and early 1931 and built excess reserves by purchasing government securities.[33]

The widening credit spreads for higher-risk bonds and the decline in bank loans indicated that investors and banks had growing concerns about the viability of business firms, except for the largest and safest "blue chip" companies. Smaller and riskier firms faced a significantly higher cost of credit (if they could obtain credit at all) after the first banking crisis ended in January 1931.[34]

———

After the first U.S. banking crisis ended, the U.S. economy seemed to make a positive upturn during the first few months of 1931. Industrial production rose modestly during the first quarter of 1931, and the stock market staged a brief rally. Those temporary gains may have resulted in part from an influx of capital into the U.S. from Germany, where investors withdrew funds in response to an alarming deterioration in Germany's political and economic situation.[35]

The hopeful mood among U.S. investors ended during the late spring and early summer of 1931, as banking and currency crises erupted in Austria and Germany. Those crises swept through Europe and caused a deepening of the Great Depression on both sides of the Atlantic. Troubled universal banks were at the center of the disasters that occurred in Austria, Germany, and other European nations.

The Austrian and German crises resulted in part from the unresolved problems of German reparations and Allied war debts. As described in Chapter 3, those problems had plagued Europe since the early 1920s. The Young Plan of 1930 and its accompanying new loans for Germany provided only a temporary respite. The Young Plan ended the implicit understanding that long-term foreign loans to Germany would receive priority over Germany's payments of reparations. As a result, foreign banks and investors stopped making long-term loans to Germany after the Young Plan loans were completed. German banks and business firms therefore relied more heavily on short-term deposits and short-term loans from foreign banks and other creditors. By the beginning of 1931, German financial institutions and businesses were highly vulnerable to sudden withdrawals of short-term funding by foreign depositors and creditors.[36]

Germany's stock market had crashed in July 1927, and that crash caused a sharp reduction in equity investments in German companies.[37] The country's economy stopped expanding in 1928 and entered a deep recession in 1929. Germany's economic downturn between 1929 and 1932 was at least as severe as the economic slump in the U.S.[38]

Germany's politics became increasingly volatile as its economy slumped. Heinrich Brüning became Chancellor of Germany in 1930, after the previous coalition government collapsed due to fundamental disagreements over economic policy and reparations. Brüning adopted a policy of strict austerity, which produced a significant rise in unemployment. Economic hardship generated popular support for the Nazi Party and other nationalist groups that called for an end to reparations payments.

Brüning called a snap election in September 1930 to strengthen his mandate. Instead, the election produced large gains for the Communists and Nazis and left Brüning in a weak position. The election results and rising levels of political violence created widespread fears among domestic and foreign investors about Germany's willingness to continue paying its foreign obligations. Those fears triggered a large-scale flight of capital from Germany.[39]

Brüning tried to improve his political standing by appealing to German nationalism. In March 1931, he agreed with Austria's leaders on a plan for an Austro-German customs union. The proposed customs union was widely viewed as a first step toward a political union between Germany and Austria.

Austria's economy was even weaker than Germany's, and Austria was equally dependent on short-term foreign credit. Universal banks dominated the financial systems of both nations. Universal banks in both countries underwrote and traded in securities, and they also maintained close connections to industrial firms by holding long-term equity stakes and appointing bankers as directors of their client companies. As a result, problems that arose in either the banking or commercial sector were likely to spread across the entire economy.[40]

The proposed Austro-German customs union provoked intense opposition from France and Czechoslovakia, which feared a revival of German economic and military power. France and Czechoslovakia threatened to launch a trade war against Austria and Germany unless they abandoned the customs union. In the midst of this diplomatic imbroglio, Austria's leading bank, Creditanstalt, appealed to the Austrian government for emergency assistance in May 1931.[41]

Creditanstalt was the largest bank in Austria and held more than half of the country's banking assets. Austria experienced chronic banking problems during the 1920s, and the government arranged several mergers between large banks and smaller, weaker institutions. The most ambitious merger occurred in 1929, when the Austrian government persuaded Creditanstalt to acquire Bodencreditanstalt, the country's second-largest bank. Austria's central bank (Nationalbank) and the Bank of England provided secret financial support for that merger, which represented a last-ditch effort to avoid a collapse of Austria's banking system.[42]

Creditanstalt held large equity investments in a wide range of business firms, and its acquisition of Bodencreditanstalt intensified its exposures to Austria's industrial and commercial sectors. Creditanstalt's capital had eroded significantly during the 1920s, due to losses from Austria's postwar hyperinflation and the bank's speculative trading in securities. The bank concealed its problems by inflating the reported value of its securities portfolio and postponing write-offs of nonperforming loans. Like the big German banks, Creditanstalt relied heavily on short-term funding from foreign sources. Foreign banks and investors held a third of Creditanstalt's deposits in 1931.[43]

On May 11, 1931, the Austrian government announced a rescue plan for Creditanstalt. However, that plan failed to restore confidence in either Creditanstalt or Austria. Many depositors and investors concluded that Austria could not save Creditanstalt without abandoning the gold exchange standard and devaluing its currency. Depositors and investors therefore ran on both Creditanstalt and Austria's currency. Austria appealed for loans from Britain, France, and the U.S. The French refused to help unless Austria repudiated its proposed customs union with Germany.

The Bank of England and the Bank for International Settlements provided loans, but they were too small to enable Austria to remain on the gold standard. Austria decided to nationalize Creditanstalt to prevent its collapse. Austria also departed from the gold exchange standard by imposing exchange controls and arranging a standstill agreement with foreign creditors. To placate the French, Austria abandoned the proposed customs union in September 1931.[44]

Creditanstalt's collapse led to a larger and more devastating crisis in Germany. German banks did not have large exposures to Austrian banks or businesses. However, many depositors and investors believed that Germany and its major banks were exposed to the same problems that undermined Austria and Creditanstalt. Germany, like Austria, amassed huge foreign debts during the 1920s. By 1931, Germany had about $6 billion of outstanding foreign debts, in addition to its reparations obligations under the Young Plan. More than half of Germany's foreign debts were bank deposits and short-term loans owed to foreign creditors.[45]

The six largest German banks (the "Berlin great banks") were universal banks, and their weaknesses were similar to those of Creditanstalt. Four of the great banks (Deutsche Bank, Danatbank, Dresdner Bank, and Commerzbank) maintained extensive networks of branches, while the other two great banks (BHG and RKG) were wholesale banks and did not operate branches. The great banks doubled their share of Germany's banking assets between 1914 and 1928 by acquiring more than two hundred smaller banks. The great banks relied heavily on foreign deposits, and over 40% of their deposits were held by foreign individuals and institutions in 1930.[46]

The great banks underwrote stocks and bonds issued by commercial and industrial firms, and they maintained equity stakes and directorships in their client companies. The great banks enjoyed preferential access to the discount window of the Reichsbank (Germany's central bank), which provided short-term loans secured by the banks' commercial bills of exchange. The privileged access of the great banks to the Reichsbank's discount window allowed them to operate with liquidity ratios significantly below those of smaller German banks. The great banks also operated with relatively low capital ratios after they suffered heavy losses during Germany's hyperinflation of the early 1920s and Germany's stock market crash in July 1927. Isabel Schnabel concluded that the great banks engaged in "excessive risk-taking" during the 1920s because of their "implicit Reichsbank guarantee."[47]

The great banks suffered additional losses from declines in the values of their securities portfolios after the crash of October 1929 on Wall Street. German banks purchased their own stock in a vain effort to boost their stock prices and maintain public confidence in their solvency. As Schnabel explained, "The extreme case was Danatbank, which had bought up more than 50% of its own shares by the middle of 1931." As a result of their extensive stock buybacks, the actual levels of equity capital at the great banks were substantially below their publicly reported figures.[48]

The strong similarities between Creditanstalt and Germany's great banks caused foreign depositors to withdraw large sums from the great banks (especially Danatbank and Dresdner Bank) in May 1931. On June 5 and 6, Chancellor Brüning announced a new series of austerity measures, and he also declared that Germany would no longer pay reparations under the Young Plan. Brüning's statement created widespread concerns that Germany would default on its foreign debts as well as its reparations obligations.

Foreign depositors fled from the great banks, and the banks turned to the Reichsbank for help. The Reichsbank provided massive loans to the great banks secured by their pledges of bills, including bills that were not ordinarily eligible as collateral for Reichsbank loans. The Reichsbank's gold and foreign exchange reserves plummeted as depositors and investors continued to withdraw funds from German banks and business firms.[49]

On June 20, 1931, President Hoover responded to the German crisis by proposing a one-year moratorium on payments of German reparations and Allied war debts. A few days later, the Bank of England, Bank of France, Bank for International Settlements, and Federal Reserve Bank of New York provided a joint $100 million stabilization loan to the Reichsbank. Many investors hoped that the U.S., Britain, and France would arrange a third rescue package for Germany, similar to the Dawes and Young Plans. However, that optimism vanished after France strongly objected to President Hoover's proposed moratorium on reparations payments. After difficult negotiations, the French finally agreed to the moratorium on July 7. By that time, however, Germany's banking crisis had spiraled out of control.[50]

During the first week of July, a large-scale depositor run occurred at Danatbank. Danatbank had made extensive loans to Nordwolle, a textile firm that collapsed in late June after gambling that wool prices would rise. When the magnitude of Danatbank's exposure to Nordwolle became publicly known, the run on Danatbank intensified and spread to the other great banks in Berlin. Gold also fled Germany. The Reichsbank requested an additional $1 billion loan from other central banks and the Bank for International Settlements. That request was denied, and the Reichsbank imposed tight restrictions on loans to all German banks (including the great banks) on July 10.[51]

Danatbank failed to open for business on July 13. To prevent a complete breakdown of its banking system, Germany guaranteed Danatbank's deposits and declared a two-day bank holiday. When the banks reopened, Germany abandoned the gold exchange standard and imposed exchange controls, including restrictions on withdrawals by foreign depositors. In late July, Germany entered into a preliminary standstill agreement with its largest short-term foreign creditors (including U.S. and British banks).

Under that agreement (which was ratified in September 1931 and lasted until 1939), short-term foreign creditors agreed to maintain and renew (roll over) their loans in exchange for stipulated payments of interest.[52]

Germany allowed some of its smaller banks to fail, but the government ensured the survival of big universal banks by providing liquidity assistance, capital infusions, and other support (including financial assistance for an emergency merger between Danatbank and Dresdner Bank). Thus, Germany—like Austria—followed a too-big-to-fail policy and rescued its largest universal banks after they were threatened with failure. Both countries abandoned the gold exchange standard as the price of those rescues.[53]

In addition to the upheavals in Austria and Germany, there were systemic banking crises in several other European countries with universal banking systems, including Italy and Belgium. The largest universal banks in Italy behaved similarly to those in Austria and Germany during the 1920s. They expanded aggressively, acquired large equity stakes in their client business firms, provided those firms with generous loans, enjoyed privileged access to liquidity support from the Bank of Italy (Italy's central bank), operated with below-average ratios of capital and liquidity, and bought their own stock to hide their problems. By 1929, Italy's leading banks and industrial companies were closely linked through cross-ownership stakes, extensive bank loans, and large corporate deposits.

Italy's universal banks and their client firms suffered devastating losses during the Great Depression. During a prolonged banking crisis that lasted from 1930 to 1934, Benito Mussolini's regime quietly arranged secret bailouts for Italy's five largest universal banks. The Italian government effectively nationalized all five banks, and the banks transferred their ownership stakes in industrial firms to a state-owned holding company.[54]

Belgium's universal banks followed the general European pattern of providing extensive loans to industrial enterprises and making large equity investments in their client companies. Belgian banks had very low levels of liquidity in 1930, and their assets included large concentrations of nonperforming business loans and unmarketable equity interests in client firms. The Belgian government rescued several failing universal banks during 1934 and 1935.[55]

The widespread failures of universal banks in Italy and Belgium completely discredited the universal banking model in both countries. Italy and Belgium enacted laws in the mid-1930s that prohibited banks from holding ownership interests in nonfinancial firms.[56]

———

The German crisis of July 1931 had a highly negative impact on Britain. As discussed in Chapter 3, Britain struggled after 1926 to remain on the gold exchange standard with an overvalued pound. The British economy recorded sluggish growth after 1926, and its unemployment rate remained high. The Bank of England did not want to raise its discount rate to defend the pound's exchange rate, due to concerns that higher interest rates would stifle economic growth, increase unemployment, and cause political instability.[57]

Germany's departure from the gold exchange standard and its standstill agreement with short-term foreign creditors imposed severe exchange rate pressures on Britain. British financial institutions were heavily exposed to both Central Europe and Latin America. By the end of July 1931, British creditors held large amounts of short-term loans to Austrian, German, and Hungarian debtors that were frozen by standstill arrangements. In addition, Bolivia, Peru, and Chile defaulted on their foreign debts, including large debts owed to British banks, by the summer of 1931. British banks relied heavily on funding from foreign depositors, and the Bank of England had relatively low reserves of gold and foreign exchange. Accordingly, British banks were vulnerable to runs by foreign depositors, and the Bank of England's ability to defend the pound was doubtful.[58]

The Macmillan Report, published on July 13, 1931, revealed that the Bank of England's gold and foreign exchange reserves were much smaller than the total volume of foreign deposits and other short-term liabilities at British banks. The Macmillan Report led many investors to conclude that Britain would soon be forced to follow Germany in abandoning the gold exchange standard. During the last two weeks of July, depositors and investors withdrew large sums from British banks and converted large amounts of British pounds into foreign currencies with stronger gold backing. The Bank of England's gold and exchange reserves fell by £250 million during that period.[59]

Unlike Austrian and German universal banks, British banks were highly specialized institutions. Britain's five largest commercial banks (known as "clearing banks") maintained extensive branch networks, accepted deposits, cleared checks and other payments, and provided short-term loans to businesses. Britain's banking system was highly concentrated, as the five largest banks held about 80% of the country's deposits. British commercial banks did not underwrite or trade in securities and were therefore separated from London's securities markets.[60]

Britain's merchant banks were a separate class of financial institutions and were similar to American private investment banks. Merchant banks underwrote new issues of securities, traded in securities, and financed international commercial transactions through trade acceptances. Trade acceptances were a form of credit guarantee. When a bank "accepted" a bill of exchange, the bank guaranteed that the bill's obligor (typically an importer of goods) would pay the bill when it became due. Banks received fees for their acceptances and assumed that they would have to honor only a small fraction of the acceptances they issued. Discount houses (bill brokers) purchased and sold bills of exchange. They also presented acceptances for payment by the accepting banks if the obligors defaulted on the underlying bills. The big clearing banks provided credit to both merchant banks and discount houses. The Bank of England ensured the liquidity of the British banking system by acting as lender of last resort.[61]

The standstill agreements negotiated by Germany, Austria, and Hungary with for-eign creditors threatened the solvency of many British merchant banks. Those agree-ments prevented accepting banks from enforcing bills of exchange issued by debtors residing in the three nations. However, the accepting banks were still exposed to claims by the bills' creditors for performance (payment) of their acceptances. Twelve of the twenty largest U.K. merchant banks had outstanding acceptances for frozen bills of exchange that exceeded their capital and liquidity reserves in 1931. The big British clearing banks held much smaller amounts of trade acceptances (relative to their capital), but they did have substantial credit exposures to merchant banks and discount houses. If defaults on trade acceptances had resulted in widespread failures among merchant banks and discount houses, the clearing banks would have suffered significant losses.[62]

In July 1931, depositors withdrew large sums from British merchant banks that were most exposed to debtors in Central European nations. The merchant banks turned to the Bank of England for help. The Bank of England provided discount window loans secured by the merchant banks' frozen bills of exchange, even though those bills did not satisfy the Bank's ordinary standards. The Bank of England's loans to merchant banks enabled their depositors to withdraw their funds and also resulted in a steady erosion of the Bank of England's gold and foreign exchange reserves. Given its weak reserve position, the Bank of England (like the Reichsbank) was caught in a dilemma where it could support its banking system or its currency but not both.[63]

On August 1, the New York Fed and the Bank of France provided $250 million of loans to the Bank of England. However, on the same day the May Committee released a report stating that the British government would run a large budget deficit during the following year. The May Committee proposed a series of austerity measures to reduce the deficit, but its prediction of a large deficit triggered a renewed run on the pound.[64]

Britain's Labour government could not agree on the proposed austerity measures and collapsed. A new coalition government took office on August 24. The coalition government quickly agreed on an austerity plan that included severe pay cuts for public sector workers and reductions in welfare payments. In reliance on that plan, banks from the U.S. and France provided $400 million of additional loans to Britain. However, the run on the pound accelerated after Labour members of Parliament denounced the austerity plan, violent demonstrations broke out in London, and British sailors mutinied at Invergordon. Those events caused many foreign inves-tors to lose confidence in the coalition government's ability to implement its aus-terity plan. Britain abandoned the gold exchange standard on September 21, and the pound's value fell by 30% by the end of 1931. More than two dozen countries (in-cluding Canada) followed Britain off gold.[65]

In contrast to Austria and Germany, Britain's departure from the gold standard did not occur in tandem with a systemic banking crisis, and Britain did not have to bail out its leading banks with equity infusions.[66] No major commercial banks failed in Britain during the 1930s. Moreover, Britain's big clearing banks were able to provide loans to assist troubled merchant banks in conjunction with liquidity support provided by the Bank of England. As a result of the joint rescue program carried out by the Bank of England and the clearing banks, most merchant banks survived the 1930s, even though the Austro-German standstill agreements with British creditors collapsed when World War II broke out in 1939.[67]

In addition to Britain's success in avoiding a systemic banking crisis, the British economy performed significantly better than the German and U.S. economies during the Great Depression. Industrial output declined at a much lower rate in Britain during the early 1930s, compared with Germany and the U.S. Similarly, the drop in Britain's GDP was substantially smaller and did not last nearly as long as the fall in U.S. GDP during the Great Depression.[68]

Britain's economy performed better because its specialized commercial banks were much more resilient during the Depression, compared with universal banks in Austria, Belgium, Germany, Italy, and the U.S. Countries with banking systems dominated by universal banks were more vulnerable to systemic financial and economic crises during the 1930s, as many universal banks were crippled by large holdings of depreciated, unmarketable securities as well as illiquid, nonperforming loans to business and securities clients. Nations with large universal banks faced much higher risks of contagious and destructive spillovers of losses among their banking systems, their securities markets, and their nonfinancial business sectors.[69]

During the Senate's debates on an early version of the Glass-Steagall Act in 1932, Senator Robert Bulkley (D-OH) highlighted the greater resilience of England's specialized commercial banks, compared with Germany's universal banks:

> The English banks of deposit have kept themselves strictly clear of the investment-security business, while the big German banks, on the other hand, have not hesitated to make substantial investments of their own funds in promotions and refinancings with a view to public distribution at such time as might be convenient. In banking literature there are arguments both ways. It seems, however, that the English banking situation has been maintained in a more satisfactory and creditable manner than the German, and that whatever we may learn from comparison of English and German banking should lead us to prefer the English practice, under which commercial banking is strictly segregated from the origination and underwriting of capital issues.[70]

The performance of Canada's banking system during the Great Depression paralleled Britain's experience. In Canada, as in Britain, a small group of large banks with extensive branch networks dominated the banking system. There were only eleven Canadian banks in 1929, and the smallest bank was acquired by a larger bank in 1931. The three largest banks controlled 75% of Canada's banking assets. Canada's banks followed the same specialized business model as Britain's big clearing banks. Canadian banks engaged primarily in deposit-taking and short-term commercial lending. Canadian banks did not underwrite securities, as that activity was reserved to Canada's securities dealers. Canadian banks also did not make real estate loans, as authority to make mortgage loans was assigned to Canada's mortgage lending and trust companies.[71]

Some commentators contend that the British and Canadian banking systems performed better during the Depression primarily because of their highly concentration and geographic diversification.[72] However, other factors were probably more important in explaining the greater resilience of British and Canadian banks. One reason for questioning whether nationwide branching was the most important factor behind the survival of Canada's banks is that diversified branching would have shielded those banks against local and regional problems but not against the nationwide economic shocks that struck Canada during the Great Depression.[73]

British and Canadian banks possessed four important advantages that were not directly linked to branching. First, unlike large U.S. banks, British and Canadian banks conducted a specialized commercial banking business and were separated from their countries' securities markets. Second, Britain and Canada abandoned the gold exchange standard and devalued their currencies in the fall of 1931. (In 1929, even before it left the gold standard, Canada imposed restrictions that made it difficult for investors to convert Canadian financial assets into gold.) In contrast, the U.S. remained firmly committed to the gold standard until March 1933. The U.S. thereby experienced a longer period of deflation and exposed its banks to damaging runs by foreign depositors between the fall of 1931 and the spring of 1933.[74]

Third, British and Canadian banks had much more effective lenders of last resort, compared with U.S. banks. The Bank of England provided short-term liquidity assistance and long-term loans that prevented the failures of more than a dozen merchant banks and overseas banks during the late 1920s and early 1930s.[75] Canada did not have a central bank until 1935. However, the Canadian Treasury Board acted as lender of last resort and prevented bank failures by issuing Dominion Notes to Canadian banks in exchange for their pledges of assets. Thus, British and Canadian banks received financial assistance that was far more generous than the very limited help given by the Fed and the Reconstruction Finance Corporation to U.S. banks prior to the New Deal.[76]

Fourth, Britain and Canada provided implicit guarantees to their leading banks by arranging emergency acquisitions of troubled banks and granting forbearance.[77] Canada's federal and provincial governments gave vital support to Canadian banks by (1) providing government guarantees to prevent the collapse of cooperative "wheat pools" in the western provinces, which owed large sums to Canadian banks, and (2) allowing Canadian banks (as well as broker-dealers and insurance companies) to defer investment losses by continuing to report their holdings of securities based on inflated pre-1930 values.[78] As a result of implicit government guarantees and supervisory forbearance, Canada did not experience a systemic banking crisis during the 1930s.[79]

Canada's blanket support for its banking system did not eliminate the Great Depression's adverse effects on Canadian banks. Canada's banks closed more than 10% of their four thousand branches, and their total assets fell by 22% between 1929 and 1933.[80] However, no Canadian banks failed, and their deposits declined by only 17%. Canada's money supply fell by only 13%.[81]

The Depression's impact on the U.S. banking system and monetary supply was far worse. More than a third of U.S. banks failed between 1929 and 1933, and the assets of U.S. banks dropped by 29%.[82] Widespread bank failures triggered massive depositor runs and currency hoarding. Deposits of U.S. banks dropped by 28% between 1929 and 1933, and the U.S. money supply plummeted by a third during those years.[83]

U.S. banks sharply reduced their lending and greatly expanded their holdings of government securities and cash during the Great Depression. Total loans held by U.S. banks fell by almost half between 1929 and 1933, while their combined holdings of securities and cash rose from 36.7% to 50.5% of their assets.[84] The absence of a reliable lender of last resort caused U.S. banks to call in loans, terminate lines of credit, and build abnormally large reserves of cash and government securities to improve their chances of survival. This was true for small rural banks (which were threatened by depositor runs) as well as regional and money center banks (which were subject to large-scale withdrawals of interbank deposits by correspondent banks). Canadian banks, which were backed by implicit government guarantees and a strong lender of last resort, increased their liquidity reserves to a much lesser extent than U.S. banks.[85]

The very different performances of the Canadian and U.S. banking systems are noteworthy, given the similarity in underlying economic trends in both countries during the Depression. Canada's declines in national output and industrial production were almost as severe as those recorded by the U.S.[86] Canada suffered greatly from the collapse of foreign trade and the shutdown of foreign capital flows during the Depression, as the Canadian economy relied heavily on exports, foreign loans, and foreign direct investments.[87] Even so, the U.S. economy was even more vulnerable to the Depression because American universal banks and investment banks financed a huge credit boom during the 1920s. That credit boom left American consumers and business firms with much heavier debt burdens in 1929, compared to their Canadian counterparts. America's ratio of total debt service to gross national product was 9% in 1929 and rose to 19.8% in 1933, compared with ratios of only 3.5% and 6.4% for Canada in the same years.[88]

In sum, the presence or absence of universal banks was a very important factor that helped to explain the very poor performance of the U.S. banking system and the superior performance of the British and Canadian banking systems.[89] That conclusion is strengthened by the disastrous performance of universal banks in Austria, Belgium, Germany, and Italy.[90]

The Austrian, German, and British crises of 1931 had devastating effects on the confidence of American business leaders, bankers, investors, and ordinary citizens. The convulsions in Europe destroyed any hope that the U.S. economy could sustain the modest upturn that occurred during the early months of 1931.[91] As Barrie Wigmore explained, "Prior to the Sterling Crisis, there was a sense that the nation would be able to cope with the problems at hand…. After the Sterling Crisis, a heavy sense of despair invaded affairs, and the ability of governments or businesses to cope seemed lost."[92]

U.S. stock and bond markets declined sharply after April 1931, in response to the series of shocks that began with the Creditanstalt crisis in May. The Dow Jones Industrial Index fell from 151 at the end of April to 78 at the end of December. The index's year-end value for 1931 represented a cumulative decline of 80% from the stock market's peak in September 1929.[93]

U.S. bond prices also dropped significantly after the outbreak of the European crises.[94] The most devastating losses occurred on low-grade domestic bonds and foreign bonds. As shown in Figure 5.2, yield spreads between corporate bonds with lower (Baa) credit ratings and U.S. Treasury securities widened dramatically during the second half of 1931. As yield spreads widened, the values of low-grade domestic and foreign bonds declined rapidly. Most Latin American bonds became virtually worthless by the end of 1931, due to defaults by several Latin American countries on their foreign debts. Prices for most other foreign bonds fell by at least 20% during 1931. Depositor runs on troubled banks produced further downward pressures on bond prices as weak banks liquidated their bond portfolios in a desperate effort to raise cash for depositor withdrawals.[95]

Britain's abrupt departure from the gold exchange standard triggered a massive withdrawal of gold from the U.S. The central banks of Belgium, France, Holland, and Switzerland withdrew large amounts of gold from the U.S. shortly after Britain left the gold standard. Many foreign investors withdrew their funds from U.S. banks and converted their dollars into other gold-backed currencies. The Fed lost more than $700 million of its gold reserves during October 1931.[96]

U.S. bank deposits fell by more than $2.5 billion between August and October 1931. Widespread bank failures caused domestic depositors to pull their funds out of banks and hoard currency, while foreign depositors converted their dollar-denominated deposits into other gold-backed currencies. The combined impact of runs on banks and the run on the dollar caused the U.S. money supply to shrink by more than 10% during the second half of 1931.[97] Figure 5.1 shows the sharp decline in deposits and the public's increased hoarding of currency during the second half of 1931.

In response to the huge outflow of gold that followed Britain's departure from the gold standard, the Fed tightened monetary policy and raised its discount rate from 1.5% to 3.5% in October 1931. The Fed did not make open-market purchases of government securities to soften the impact of its interest rate hikes because its overriding concerns were to defend the dollar, to discourage further outflows of gold, and to keep the U.S. on the gold standard. The Fed discounted trade acceptances for member banks to offset their loss of deposits in late 1931. However, the Fed did not provide any comparable liquidity assistance to nonmember banks.[98]

———

The number of U.S. bank failures increased steadily between June and December 1931. More than 400 banks, with total deposits exceeding $400 million, failed between June and August. More than 1,350 banks, with aggregate deposits exceeding $1 billion, failed from September through December.[99]

The close correspondence in time between the crises in Austria, Germany, and Britain and the rising rate of U.S. bank failures indicated that the European crises had a highly negative impact on confidence in U.S. banks and the U.S. economy.[100] Albrecht Ritschl and Samad Sarferaz determined that the German banking and currency crisis transmitted a high degree of financial stress to the U.S. economy and banking system.[101] Gary Richardson concluded that Britain's decision to leave the gold standard and the Fed's decision to tighten monetary policy "weakened the financial position of [U.S.] banks" and caused depositors to become "increasingly apprehensive about the health of depository institutions."[102]

The first major U.S. banking panic of 1931 occurred in Chicago. The Chicago metropolitan area experienced a spectacular real estate boom during the 1920s, and many Chicago banks held large portfolios of residential and commercial mortgage loans and real estate bonds. The securities affiliates of leading Chicago banks sold large amounts of real estate bonds during the 1920s and promised investors that their affiliated banks would repurchase those bonds on demand.[103]

Illinois law prohibited banks from opening branches, but the most important Chicago banks evaded that prohibition by establishing chains of puppet banks. The two largest Chicago banks—Continental Illinois and the First National Bank of Chicago (First Chicago)—each controlled several smaller banks. The Bain group, the Foreman State group, Central Trust Company, and National Bank of the Republic operated their own chains of banks in the Chicago metropolitan area.[104]

In the spring of 1931, Continental Illinois and First Chicago responded to sharp declines in real estate values by announcing that they would no longer repurchase real estate bonds sold by their securities affiliates. Those announcements alarmed depositors and investors and undermined public confidence in weaker Chicago banks with large real estate exposures (including the Bain and Foreman State banking chains and National Republic). On June 7, First Chicago agreed to acquire Foreman State Bank (the largest Foreman bank) and its affiliated trust company, with support provided by the Chicago Clearing House. Central Trust agreed to merge with National Republic at the same time. Those mergers protected the acquired banks against failure. However, the Bain group of twelve banks collapsed in late June 1931, along with several smaller members of the Foreman group and more than a dozen other Chicago-area banks.[105]

Another local banking panic occurred in August, when several banks failed in Toledo, Ohio.[106]

A more severe and widespread banking crisis broke out in September 1931, after Britain left the gold standard. During that crisis, local panics occurred in Chicago, Philadelphia, and Pittsburgh, as well as several cities in Indiana, Ohio, and West Virginia. Of the 2,300 banks that failed during 1931, more than 1,700 were state non-member banks. The Fed did not take any steps to prevent bank failures in 1931, except for providing loans to individual Fed member banks that could pledge eligible acceptances and other commercial bills of exchange. The Fed was apparently unconcerned by bank failures as long as they did not threaten the survival of the leading money center banks. The largest banks to fail in 1931 were a Pittsburgh bank and a Boston bank, each with less than $60 million of deposits.[107]

Hundreds of smaller banks failed during 1931 and 1932 because of losses connected to their real estate loans and securities portfolios. Failed banks frequently held large amounts of delinquent mortgages and illiquid real estate bonds that were secured by residential and commercial properties with heavily depreciated market values. In addition, the securities portfolios of many smaller banks held large concentrations of lower-grade domestic and foreign bonds, with similarly eroded market values.[108]

At the end of 1930, country banks (banks in small towns and rural areas) held foreign bonds equal to 17% of their equity capital, compared with only 7% for member banks in New York City, Chicago, and large regional cities. Similarly, country banks held railroad bonds equal to 23% of their equity capital, compared with 12% or less for member banks in larger cities. The market values of foreign bonds and railroad bonds plunged in 1931 and 1932, and many of those bond issues defaulted.[109]

The securities affiliates of money center banks in New York and Chicago had aggressively sold foreign bonds and lower-grade corporate bonds to smaller banks during the 1920s. Securities affiliates focused their selling efforts on country banks that maintained correspondent relationships with their affiliated money center banks.[110] Sales representatives from securities affiliates encouraged country banks to sell their lower-yielding U.S. government securities and invest in higher-yielding foreign bonds and lower-grade corporate bonds, which the affiliates underwrote. During the hearings and debates that led to the Glass-Steagall Act, Senator Carter Glass and other members of Congress blamed securities affiliates of large commercial banks for selling unsuitable, high-risk securities that caused the failures of many country banks.[111]

———

In response to the Fed's hands-off policy toward bank failures, banks in several large cities launched their own efforts to rescue important banks during 1931. In Chicago, as noted earlier, the largest banks organized emergency mergers that saved the Foreman State Bank and National Bank of the Republic. In Baltimore, a consortium of

New York banks and Baltimore business firms rescued the Baltimore Trust Company. In Philadelphia, several leading banks joined forces to save the Integrity Trust Company. In New York City, Manufacturers Trust acquired Chatham Phenix Bank, a troubled $230 million bank that had lost more than $60 million of its deposits during 1931.[112]

In addition, National City Bank purchased more than $300 million of assets—including thirty-two branches and a securities affiliate—from Bank of America's subsidiary bank in New York City. Bank of America's New York operation had suffered crippling losses from hazardous stock investments and nonperforming loans. With the encouragement of J. P. Morgan & Co., National City acquired most of Bank of America's New York assets to resolve the problems created by that "sick" unit.[113]

The limited scope of such self-help measures became clear in October 1931, when President Hoover asked the nation's largest banks to create a credit pool to offer emergency loans to threatened banks. At Hoover's urging, a group of large Fed member banks organized the National Credit Corporation (NCC) and promised to contribute $500 million for Hoover's requested credit pool. The participating banks appointed local lending committees to make loans to threatened banks, based on pledges of securities and other assets that were not eligible to be used as collateral for the Fed's discount window loans.[114]

Large banks agreed to Hoover's proposal with great reluctance. They were primarily concerned with their own survival and did not want to share their financial resources with weaker banks. Hoover assured the banks that he would recommend a new government funding agency if the NCC could not resolve the banking industry's problems. The NCC's local committees followed extremely conservative lending policies, and the NCC approved only $10 million of loans to troubled banks by the end of November 1931.[115]

The NCC's reluctance to provide loans to struggling banks convinced Hoover that the banking industry could not save itself. In December 1931, Hoover called on Congress to create a new government agency, the Reconstruction Finance Corporation (RFC), which could provide emergency loans to financial institutions and railroads. Hoover modeled the RFC on the War Finance Board, which Congress created in 1918 to finance the production of military supplies during World War I. In January 1932, Congress established the RFC and authorized it to provide up to $2 billion of loans to financial institutions and railroads.[116]

Hoover also persuaded Congress to expand the Fed's authority to assist threatened banks by adopting the first Glass-Steagall Act in February 1932. The 1932 statute broadened the categories of assets that the Fed could accept as collateral for discount window loans beyond commercial bills of exchange. Under the 1932 law, the Fed could provide member banks with loans that were collateralized by U.S. government securities and a wider range of commercial paper. In addition, the 1932 statute allowed each Federal Reserve Bank to use its portfolio of U.S. government securities to satisfy the non-gold (60%) share of its required reserves for the Federal Reserve notes it issued. The 1932 law enabled the Fed to buy government securities and expand the nation's money supply without undermining the Fed's ability to maintain the non-gold reserves required by the Federal Reserve Act.[117]

The Fed made $1 billion of open-market purchases of government securities between February and August 1932. Fed policymakers approved those purchases because they feared that Congress might adopt more aggressive inflationary measures if the Fed did not use its expanded authority under the first Glass-Steagall Act. The New York Fed strongly supported the open-market purchase program and made more than half of the Fed's total purchases. However, even the New York Fed stopped making open-market purchases in August 1932, after (1) its gold reserve ratio fell below 50% of its outstanding notes, (2) the Federal Reserve Banks of Boston and Chicago refused to make their proportionate share of open-market purchases and insisted on maintaining much higher levels of gold reserves, and (3) Congress adjourned in July for the upcoming fall elections, thereby removing the threat of more inflationary legislation for several months.

The Fed's open-market purchase program had modestly favorable effects on the U.S. economy. However, those positive effects quickly dissipated after the Fed ended the program. The Fed did not take any additional measures to stimulate the economy during the last four months of 1932.[118]

———

In contrast to the Fed, the RFC provided $950 million of loans to several thousand banks and trust companies during 1932.[119] The RFC focused on ensuring the survival of banks that were important regional or national institutions. It therefore provided more than a third of its loans to 26 large banks, which ranked among the nation's 210 biggest banks.[120] The two largest recipients of RFC loans in 1932 were Bank of America and Central Republic Bank. Both institutions were universal banks and were among the leading financial institutions in their respective geographic areas.

Bank of America was founded by A. P. Giannini, who opened a small bank in San Francisco in 1904 and expanded that bank throughout California. By 1930, Bank of America owned $1.2 billion of assets, operated more than four hundred branches in California, and controlled more than 30% of the state's deposits. In 1928, Giannini acquired a bank in New York City with $400 million of assets and more than thirty branches. In the same year, Giannini acquired a large New York securities firm (Blair and Company) with offices in twenty-seven U.S. cities and five foreign countries. Giannini established a top-tier holding company (Transamerica) to centralize his control over Bank of America's banks and their securities affiliate (renamed Bancamerica-Blair Corporation). Transamerica also owned two insurance companies, several real estate mortgage and investment companies, and other nonbanking subsidiaries.[121]

Giannini suffered serious health problems in early 1930, and he delegated day-to-day management of Transamerica to Elisha Walker, the former head of Bancamerica-Blair. Walker quickly encountered severe problems. Transamerica's stock price dropped sharply after the crash of 1929, and Transamerica lost $70 million after buying its own shares in a vain effort to support their market price. Transamerica and Bancamerica-Blair suffered additional losses from aggressive trading in other securities. Meanwhile, Bank of America's California and New York operations were plagued by nonperforming real estate loans and frozen loans to Germany. Large withdrawals of deposits from Bank of America's branches in California and New York forced the bank to borrow $40 million from a consortium of New York banks and the National Credit Corporation (NCC).

Walker developed an emergency plan to reduce the size and scope of Transamerica's operations. The first step in his plan was to sell Bank of America's New York City branches and Bancamerica-Blair to National City Bank. Walker completed that sale to National City in October 1931 despite vehement protests from Giannini, who had long dreamed of building a nationwide banking empire.[122]

Giannini launched a successful proxy contest and regained control of Transamerica in February 1932. The RFC approved $65 million of loans to Transamerica to help Giannini deal with Bank of America's problems in California. The RFC viewed Bank of America's survival as essential to maintain the stability of the U.S. banking system and restore California's economy.[123]

In June 1932, another banking panic occurred in Chicago. By the summer of 1932, borrowers in Chicago had defaulted on over $1 billion of residential mortgages, and Chicago's city government faced a financial crisis. Samuel Insull's heavily leveraged utility empire collapsed in April 1932, and his principal holding companies were placed in receiverships. The Insull disaster wiped out the savings of many Chicago-area residents and threatened the solvency of leading Chicago banks. Chicago banks had extended $150 million of loans to Insull's companies or to borrowers who pledged Insull securities as collateral.[124] The securities affiliates of the three largest Chicago banks underwrote bond offerings for Insull's companies, and those banks held over $90 million of Insull-related loans. Insull-related loans equaled 40% or more of the capital of all three banks.[125]

In June 1932, public confidence in Chicago banks was further shaken when the city's newspapers carried sensational accounts of John Bain's trial for bank fraud. The trial revealed that Bain and his associates had engaged in self-dealing and fraud before his group of banks collapsed during the summer of 1931. A generalized run on Chicago banks began on June 15, 1932, and thirty-six banks failed by the end of that month.[126]

On Friday, June 24, and Saturday, June 25, depositor runs occurred at Continental Illinois and First Chicago. On the morning of June 25, Melvin Traylor, First Chicago's charismatic chairman, climbed onto a pillar in the bank's main lobby and urged a nervous crowd of depositors to remain calm. He assured them that First Chicago was "sound" and their deposits were safe. The crowd applauded Traylor's remarks, and the runs on First Chicago and Continental Illinois tapered off during the afternoon of June 25.[127]

In contrast, Central Republic (Chicago's third-largest bank) experienced escalating deposit withdrawals and was in a very weak position by the close of business
on June 25. On the morning of Sunday, June 26, Charles G. Dawes, Central Republic's
chairman (as well as the author of the Dawes Plan and Vice President under Coolidge),
informed Chicago's top bankers and RFC officials that his bank would not reopen
the following day. Dawes was not willing to allow Central Republic to stay open unless the RFC approved a rescue plan that would protect all of the bank's remaining
depositors. Central Republic's assets included large loans to Insull companies as well
as German bonds with substantially depreciated values.[128]

Melvin Traylor and other leading Chicago bankers held emergency conferences
with RFC officials and spoke by telephone with President Hoover throughout the day
on June 26 and during the early morning on Monday, June 27. The Chicago bankers
and the RFC's directors agreed (with Hoover's concurrence) that Central Republic
must be saved to prevent a complete collapse of Chicago's banks and a potential nationwide banking panic. The RFC approved a $90 million loan to Central Republic,
and Chicago's leading banks agreed to provide $5 million of additional loans. The
RFC effectively treated Central Republic—like Bank of America—as too big to fail.
The size of both banks, their locations in key financial centers, and their close connections with other money center banks convinced the RFC that the failure of either
bank would have catastrophic effects.[129]

The RFC's rescues of Bank of America and Central Republic provided a brief re-
prieve for the U.S. banking system. However, those rescues revealed some very un-
pleasant truths about America's banking system in mid-1932. The crises at Bank of
America and Central Republic confirmed the dangers of combining banking, real
estate, and securities operations—the same combination of activities that doomed
Caldwell and Company and Bank of United States. In addition, as shown by the
NCC's ineffectiveness and the RFC's dominant role in saving Bank of America and
Central Republic, the largest U.S. banks were no longer able to prevent banking panics through collective self-help measures. Given the Fed's unwillingness to stop bank
failures, the RFC was the only possible bulwark against a complete collapse of the
nation's banking system.[130]

The RFC's stringent lending terms provided only stopgap relief for many troubled
banks, and the RFC could not solve fundamental problems of insolvency or long-
term shortages of liquidity. Most RFC loans during 1932 had six-month terms and
required frequent renewals. The RFC charged interest rates that were substantially
higher than the Fed's discount rates and therefore imposed a significant penalty on
banks that borrowed from the RFC. The RFC accepted collateral that was not eligible
for discounting by the Fed, but the RFC demanded collateral that would fully secure
the RFC against any risk of loss. "In practice, therefore, the RFC often took a bank's
most liquid assets as security for loans, increasing the risk of default on remaining
bank debt and undermining the stabilizing effect of assistance."[131]

As shown by Central Republic's ultimate fate, the RFC did not provide effective long-term assistance to seriously troubled banks. Central Republic pledged

all $118 million of its remaining assets to secure the RFC's $90 million loan. The RFC charged an interest rate of 5.5%, which was substantially higher than Central Republic's average return on assets (4.625%), thereby making it impossible for the bank to earn a profit. Four months after its rescue, Central Republic transferred all of its deposits to a newly organized bank (City National Bank and Trust Co.) and went into voluntary liquidation. The demise of Central Republic and many other banks that borrowed from the RFC showed that RFC loans could not resolve the nation's banking problems.[132]

———

The Fed's open-market purchase program for government securities and the RFC's loans did reduce the number of bank failures and the amount of deposits in failed banks in 1932, compared with the figures for 1931. In addition, as shown in Figure 5.1, the amount of currency held by the public did not increase significantly during 1932, and the nation's money supply declined only modestly.[133]

Nevertheless, the RFC's loans did not convince the public to put more of their savings in banks, and banks were not persuaded to increase their lending.[134] Deposits and loans in open banks declined during 1932 at an even faster rate than they had fallen in 1931.[135] The occurrence of more than fourteen hundred bank failures in 1932 undermined local and regional economies by (1) destroying or freezing the savings held by depositors in closed banks, (2) disrupting lending relationships between closed banks and their borrowers, (3) causing open banks to cut back on lending and buy government securities to boost their liquidity reserves, and (4) triggering bankruptcies and liquidations of bank-dependent businesses (especially small and mid-sized firms) that could not find alternative sources of credit after their banks closed or called in their loans.[136]

The Great Depression therefore deepened as the U.S. banking system continued its downward spiral. On a real (inflation-adjusted) basis, GNP fell by almost 30% between 1929 and 1932.[137] The economy experienced severe deflation, as prices for farm and industrial commodities plunged by over 60% and wholesale and retail prices fell by more than a third between 1929 and 1932.[138]

The number of unemployed workers and the nation's unemployment rate increased almost eightfold between 1929 and 1932. Nearly a quarter of the nation's workers were without jobs at the end of 1932.[139] Industrial output fell by almost half between 1929 and 1932, while auto production fell by three-quarters and building contracts declined by four-fifths.[140] Investors suffered staggering losses, as shown by (1) a decline of $74.1 billion (83%) in the total value of all NYSE-listed stocks between the stock market's high point in September 1929 and its low point in July 1932 and (2) a reduction of $18.7 billion (38%) in the total value of all NYSE-listed bonds between the bond market's high point in September 1930 and its low point in April 1933.[141]

By 1932, even the largest U.S. banks faced severe problems. That was especially true for Chase National Bank and National City Bank, the two biggest and most aggressive universal banks. The stocks of both banks traded in 1932 at less than 10% of their market highs in 1929. Each bank held about $90 million of frozen short-term loans to German borrowers after U.S. and U.K. banks signed the standstill agreement with Germany in 1931.[142] As noted in Chapter 4, Chase and its securities affiliate suffered heavy losses after GTE defaulted on loans and securities that Chase and its affiliate underwrote to finance GTE's takeover of Fox Films in 1930. Chase and its affiliate established reserves for losses that reduced their capital by $180 million between 1929 and 1932, and Chase cut its annual dividend from $4 per share to $2.25 per share.[143]

National City's problems were comparable to those of Chase. National City wrote off almost $90 million of defaulted loans between 1930 and 1932, and the bank still carried twice that amount of nonperforming assets on its books at the end of 1932. National City's securities affiliate reduced its capital by more than $100 million due to trading and investment losses between 1929 and 1932.[144] The two largest banks in Chicago—Continental Illinois and First Chicago—also recorded large write-downs in their assets and cut their dividends as they grappled with challenges similar to those faced by Chase and National City.[145]

New York and Chicago banks sharply reduced their lending and greatly expanded their liquidity reserves to cope with the Depression. New York banks increased their reserves by $400 million during 1932, while Chicago banks increased their reserves by $100 million. The largest New York and Chicago banks built additional liquidity buffers as they attracted funds from business firms and other large depositors, who sought greater safety by moving their deposits from smaller banks to money center banks.[146] The large excess reserves established by money center banks and their steep cuts in lending contributed to the Fed's decision to stop purchasing government securities after August 1932. Most Fed policymakers concluded that additional open-market purchases would not convince banks to make new loans and therefore would not produce any meaningful benefits for the broader economy.[147]

The intertwined problems of German reparations and Allied war debts reappeared on President Hoover's agenda in the summer of 1932. In June, German and Allied representatives met at a conference in Lausanne to address both problems. Hoover did not send a delegation to the conference, but he encouraged its deliberations. In July, the conferees proposed to terminate Germany's payment of reparations in exchange for Germany's transfer of $750 million of bonds to the Allies. The proposed agreement was implicitly conditioned on U.S. forgiveness of Allied war debts, and ratification was delayed until the U.S. agreed to cancel those debts. The Lausanne conference did not produce a binding agreement, but it effectively ended Germany's payment of reparations.[148]

Hoover said that the U.S. would not consider any cancellation of Allied war debts until after the November 1932 elections. Hoover did offer to extend the existing U.S. moratorium on repayment of Allied war debts for an additional year (until

December 1933), if Congress agreed. However, Congress rejected Hoover's proposed extension, and the American public overwhelmingly opposed any forgiveness of Allied war debts.

When the existing U.S. moratorium expired in December 1932, France and several other Allied nations repudiated their U.S. war debts. Britain paid the installment due in December 1932, but its willingness to keep paying its war debts was highly doubtful. The nonpayment of Allied war debts further damaged public confidence, as it threatened to wipe out $11 billion of foreign obligations owed to the U.S. government. In addition, the breakdown of cooperation between the U.S. and its former allies provided stunning evidence of their inability to agree on any new plan to improve the world's economic situation.[149]

Congress created further problems for the U.S. banking system when it published the names of banks that received RFC loans. On July 21, 1932, Congress passed a statute that expanded the RFC's lending authority. Over Hoover's strenuous objections, that statute required the RFC to send monthly reports to Congress describing the RFC's loans to banks, including the names of the recipients. Congressional leaders assured Hoover that the RFC's reports would not be published without formal approval by Congress.[150]

Congress included the reporting requirement in the 1932 statute because of intense controversy surrounding two RFC loans. In March 1932, the RFC lent $13 million to the Missouri Pacific Railroad, which was controlled by the Van Sweringen brothers. That loan was strongly criticized after the Van Sweringens used almost half of the loan proceeds to pay outstanding debts to Wall Street firms, including J. P. Morgan & Co., Kuhn, Loeb & Co., and Guaranty Trust Company of New York. In April 1932, Franklin Roosevelt delivered his "Forgotten Man" speech, in which he alleged that the Hoover administration was ignoring "the forgotten man at the bottom of the pyramid" and placing the RFC's "two billion dollar fund . . . at the disposal of big banks, the railroads, and the corporations."[151]

In June 1932, the RFC's $90 million loan to Central Republic Bank provoked even greater criticism because Charles Dawes, the bank's chairman, had served as Coolidge's Vice President and later as the RFC's first president. Many Democrats and commentators echoed Roosevelt's charges that the Hoover administration was using the RFC to support big banks, Wall Street interests, and Republican leaders while denying assistance to smaller banks and struggling communities.[152]

In August 1932, Speaker of the House John Nance Garner instructed the clerk of the House of Representatives to publish the monthly lists of bank loans that the RFC submitted after July 20, 1932. The Democratic Party's convention had recently nominated Garner as Roosevelt's running mate, and Garner evidently viewed the RFC's loan lists as political weapons to be used against Hoover and the Republican Party. On January 4, 1933, the House approved Garner's proposal to publish more names of banks that received RFC loans.[153]

Publishing the RFC loan lists stigmatized the banks named on those lists and damaged the banking system in general. Publication deterred banks from applying for

RFC assistance until they were dangerously close to failure, and it also encouraged depositors to pull their money out of banks that appeared on the published lists of RFC loans.[154] Banks on the published lists suffered significant losses of deposits and were more likely to fail, compared with other recipients of RFC loans whose names were not published.[155]

More than 350 banks failed during the last quarter of 1932, including 140 banks that had previously received RFC loans.[156] The Wingfield chain of banks, which controlled two-thirds of the deposits and three-quarters of the loans in Nevada, collapsed in December 1932. The RFC had loaned $5 million to the Wingfield chain in mid-1932, but it refused to make a second loan in December. Nevada's Governor declared a bank holiday to prevent a complete breakdown of the state's financial system.[157]

The Wingfield banking disaster "contributed to a loss of depositor confidence on a national level" because it produced the Depression's first statewide bank holiday and revealed "the complete ineffectiveness of the Federal Reserve and the RFC in coping with financial breakdown at the regional level."[158] On January 20, 1933, Iowa's Governor declared a statewide bank holiday after several Iowa banks failed. During the last week of January and the first week of February, the RFC provided loans to prop up three large banks in Memphis, Kansas City, and New Orleans. However, many other banks failed after the RFC denied their requests for loans. More than 240 banks closed their doors in January 1933, the highest number of failures in any month since the RFC began operating in February 1932. The growing list of bank failures, and bank holidays damaged the RFC's prestige and created widespread doubts about the solvency of the entire U.S. banking system.[159]

———

In February 1933, the collapse of two large universal banks in Detroit precipitated a nationwide banking panic. Detroit's auto industry had enjoyed a spectacular boom during the 1920s, as the annual production of new American cars tripled from 1.5 million to 4.5 million between 1921 and 1929.[160] Two large Detroit bank holding companies expanded throughout the state of Michigan during the boom and controlled about three-fifths of the city's and state's banking assets in 1930. Those two holding companies—Guardian Detroit Union Group (Guardian) and Detroit Bankers Company (DBC)—each owned more than twenty banks as well as several securities and real estate affiliates. Guardian, with $370 million of assets, was controlled by Henry Ford's family and was known as "Ford's bank." Henry's son, Edsel, was Guardian's largest investor and served on Guardian's board of directors, while Edsel's brother-in-law, Ernest Kanzler, was chairman of the board.

DBC, with $560 million of assets, was controlled by a group of twelve Detroit business leaders, who jointly acted as voting trustees for DBC's stock. Real estate investments and loans accounted for more than a third of the assets of both holding companies. The securities affiliates of each holding company traded in their parent company's stock and invested in a wide range of other securities.[161]

Guardian and DBC encountered severe problems after the car-based economy of Detroit and Michigan collapsed during the Depression. U.S. automobile production plummeted by three-quarters from its peak in 1929 to its low point of 1.1 million new cars built in 1932. Property values in the Detroit area fell by more than 40%, and Detroit's city government teetered on the brink of default in January 1933.[162]

Guardian acquired more than $14 million of depreciated securities and non-performing real estate assets from its securities and banking subsidiaries to improve their reported financial position. Guardian's largest subsidiary bank provided $6 million of loans to its securities affiliate, backed by the affiliate's pledges of illiquid securities. Guardian told its subsidiary banks to transfer to the parent holding company dividends in amounts that exceeded their profits, so that the holding company could pay high dividends to its shareholders between 1930 and 1932. Guardian also directed its subsidiary banks to make large loans to insiders to finance their purchases of the holding company's stock. By mid-1932, Guardian's banks held loans collateralized by 150,000 shares of the holding company's stock, which had fallen in value by over 90% since 1929. Guardian provided false and deceptive reports to regulators and shareholders that concealed its rapidly deteriorating financial position.[163]

DBC followed a similar pattern of risky and manipulative practices. DBC acquired more than $7 million of depreciated stocks from its securities subsidiary in 1930. DBC promised a 17% annual dividend to its shareholders and extracted large dividends from its subsidiary banks to maintain that dividend between 1930 and 1932. DBC's subsidiary banks made loans to insiders to finance their purchases of 250,000 shares of the parent's stock. Like Guardian, DBC issued deceptive reports to regulators and shareholders to hide its mounting losses. DBC's securities affiliate sold risky real estate bonds and mortgage participation certificates to DBC's trust customers after the affiliate could not sell those securities in public offerings. Many of those securities defaulted by 1934.[164]

The RFC loaned $16 million to Guardian in 1932. On January 25, 1933, Guardian requested an additional loan of $43.5 million "to relieve the burdens of its illiquid securities and real estate investments and rapidly declining deposits."[165] The RFC offered to lend $37.2 million after reviewing Guardian's financial condition and available collateral. However, the RFC insisted that the Ford family must subordinate $7.5 million of their deposits in Guardian's banks and also contribute $4 million of new capital to Guardian. Henry Ford rejected the RFC's demands. The Fords had previously provided $16 million of loans and guarantees to Guardian, and Henry Ford was unwilling to do more. He was confident that the RFC would bail out Guardian for the same reasons that it rescued Central Republic in 1932.[166]

The Hoover administration and the RFC recognized that Guardian's failure would probably force all banks in Michigan to close and might well trigger a nationwide banking crisis. President Hoover telephoned Henry Ford (a personal friend and supporter) and urged him to reconsider. Hoover also sent Treasury Undersecretary Arthur Ballantine and Commerce Secretary Roy Chapin to meet with Ford in Detroit.

Despite Ballantine's and Chapin's appeals, Ford refused to change his mind, especially after he learned that his old business rival, Senator James Couzens, opposed the RFC's loan to Guardian.

Couzens argued that the RFC had exceeded its authority by lending $90 million to Central Republic without sufficient collateral. He similarly maintained that Guardian could not provide enough good collateral to justify the RFC's proposed loan. Couzens warned Hoover and the RFC that he would "denounce the proposed loan from the housetops unless the loan was secured to the last dime." After hearing about Couzens' threat, Henry Ford said, "There isn't any reason why I should tie up several million to keep Senator Couzens from shouting from the housetops."[167]

Ford told Ballantine and Chapin that he "could not believe that the government would let the banks of Detroit close for lack of the aid asked of him." Ballantine and Chapin responded that Ford's assistance was crucial because the RFC could not "supply new capital" or provide loans beyond the $37 million appraised value of Guardian's collateral. Ford warned that he and his family members and companies would immediately withdraw $25 million of deposits they held in DBC's banks if the RFC allowed Guardian to fail. Ballantine and Chapin replied that Ford's threatened withdrawal would doom DBC and trigger a statewide banking crisis that would "paralyze business in Michigan" and "probably extend throughout the country."[168] Ford said he would allow a systemic crisis to occur before he would accept an unfair deal. When Senator Couzens publicly stated that all the weak banks in the country should be closed, Ford responded, "For once in his life, Jim Couzens is right."[169]

After Ford threatened to withdraw his family and corporate deposits, DBC appealed to the RFC for a $100 million loan. The RFC denied the loan because it saw no purpose in funding Ford's withdrawal. Faced with the imminent collapse of both Guardian and DBC, federal and state regulators closed all of Guardian's and DBC's banks, and Michigan's Governor declared a statewide bank holiday on February 14, 1933.[170]

As Barry Eichengreen pointed out, the RFC's loan to Central Republic in June 1932 resembled the Fed's rescue of Bear Stearns in March 2008, while the federal government's decision to let Guardian and DBC fail in February 1933 was comparable to its decision to let Lehman Brothers fail in September 2008. The rescues of Central Republic and Bear Stearns postponed the full onset of the financial crises of the Great Depression and the Great Recession. In contrast, the refusals to save the Detroit banks and Lehman Brothers precipitated the most virulent phases of both crises.[171]

In 1933, federal officials decided not to rescue the big Detroit banks because they had received so much public criticism from saving Central Republic. (Similarly, as described in Chapter 11, public condemnations of the Bear Stearns bailout contributed to the federal government's decision not to save Lehman Brothers.) The RFC's loan to Central Republic had triggered widespread attacks on the RFC and the Hoover administration, and many commentators who attacked the "Dawes loan" also opposed any loan to "Ford's bank." Given the drumbeat of criticism from public figures such as Senator Couzens, Father Charles Coughlin, and John T. Flynn of *Harper's Magazine*, the Hoover administration and the RFC were not willing to approve any rescue of Guardian that looked like a bailout of Henry Ford.[172] Even so, their decision to let Guardian and DBC fail remains surprising because they clearly understood that Guardian's and DBC's failures would probably cause a nationwide banking panic.

6
Reckoning

Universal Banks Were Discredited by the Pecora Investigation and Abolished by the Glass-Steagall Act

The failures of the two largest Detroit banks and Michigan's bank holiday on February 14, 1933 precipitated a nationwide panic that led to "the collapse, during the next three weeks, of the nation's entire financial system."[1] Most of the nation's banks were closed or subject to severe restrictions on deposit withdrawals when Franklin Roosevelt became president on March 4, 1933. The nationwide banking crisis set the stage for the Glass-Steagall Act, which ended America's first experiment with universal banking.

Herbert Hoover spent the last three weeks of his presidency trying to contain the panic that spread across the country after Michigan declared its bank holiday.[2] On February 18, Hoover wrote to President-elect Roosevelt, warning that "a steadily degenerating confidence in the future … has reached the height of general alarm." Hoover argued that the panic represented a lack of confidence in the dollar as well as a run on banks. He cited widespread speculation that Roosevelt would abandon the gold standard, as Britain had done in September 1931. Hoover urged Roosevelt to restore confidence in the dollar by declaring publicly that his administration would keep the U.S. on gold and work toward a balanced budget.[3]

Roosevelt did not share Hoover's commitment to the gold standard. Roosevelt ran for president on a Democratic Party platform that included promises to balance the budget and preserve a "sound currency … at all hazards." However, Roosevelt carefully avoided making any promises about budget issues or the gold standard after his landslide victory in November. During the four-month interregnum between Roosevelt's election and his inauguration, some of his advisers and several Democratic members of Congress publicly called for the U.S. to abandon gold and devalue the dollar to halt the continuing slide in prices for agricultural and manufactured goods. Roosevelt neither endorsed nor rejected those proposals.[4]

Roosevelt replied to Hoover in a letter dated February 20, but the letter did not reach the White House until March 1 (a delay that Roosevelt blamed on his secretary's oversight). In his letter, Roosevelt declined to make the public commitments requested by Hoover. Roosevelt said he recognized "the gravity of the present banking situation, but my thought is that it is so very deep-seated that the fire is bound to spread in spite of anything that can be done by way of mere statement."[5] Raymond Moley, a key Roosevelt adviser, was amazed by Roosevelt's calmness in the midst of rapidly deteriorating economic conditions and by his "complete confidence in his own ability to deal with any situation that might arise." According to Moley, Roosevelt believed that "the baby was Hoover's anyhow" until noon on March 4, and Roosevelt "could not take any responsibility for measures over whose execution he would have no control."[6]

After failing to gain Roosevelt's support, Hoover turned to Congress, the Reconstruction Finance Corporation, and the Fed. Hoover instructed federal bank regulators to prepare draft legislation that would authorize the RFC to purchase preferred stock in troubled banks and empower the Office of the Comptroller of the Currency (OCC) to reorganize and reopen closed national banks. In February 1933, Hoover sent both legislative proposals to Senator Carter Glass, the "most influential member" of the Senate Banking Committee. Glass told Hoover that it was not feasible to pass such legislation during Congress's lame-duck session prior to Roosevelt's inauguration. Glass also advised that the lame-duck session would be unlikely to consider any proposal for a federal guarantee of bank deposits.[7]

Hoover also urged the RFC to develop a plan to reopen Detroit's two leading banks (Guardian and DBC) and end Michigan's bank holiday. On February 22, the RFC approved a plan to reopen the two banks that included loans from the RFC and New York City banks, as well as $8.5 million of new capital from Henry Ford (who had changed his mind about helping the RFC). The RFC never implemented its plan for reasons that remain unclear. Some historians have blamed bankers from Detroit and New York for refusing to accept the RFC's proposed terms for reopening the banks.[8]

Barrie Wigmore has blamed Roosevelt. On February 23, Roosevelt's Treasury Secretary-designate, William Woodin, met with the RFC's directors and told them that "the problems now under consideration should be determined by the [RFC] board in accordance with its own views *and on its own responsibility.*" Wigmore interpreted Woodin's statement as a veiled warning to the RFC's directors that their actions might be second-guessed after Roosevelt took office. Wigmore concluded that Roosevelt "scuttled the RFC's efforts to halt the bank crisis" by "creating doubts and then refusing to support a course of action." The RFC took no further steps to stop the nationwide bank panic until after Roosevelt was inaugurated.[9]

Hoover asked the Federal Reserve Board on February 22 for its recommendations on measures to resolve the banking crisis. The Board responded that it "did not desire to make any specific proposals for additional measures or authority." On February 27, Treasury Secretary Mills asked the Fed to buy $100 million of government securities in the open market to ease the monetary strain caused by withdrawals of bank deposits and outflows of gold from the U.S. The Fed declined to make any large-scale purchases of government bonds. The Fed bought relatively few government securities during February 1933, and it raised both its discount and acceptance rates. The Fed believed that it needed to tighten monetary policy (as it had done during the fall of 1931) to discourage the outflow of gold and defend the gold standard.[10]

On February 28, Hoover requested advice from the Federal Reserve Board on whether the federal government should guarantee bank deposits or arrange for the issuance of clearinghouse certificates as a substitute for currency. The Board replied on

March 2, stating that it did not advise either course of action and it did not have any other recommendations to offer.[11]

In the absence of any effective countermeasures, the nationwide bank panic continued to spread and intensify. Almost four hundred banks closed their doors during January and February. Michigan's inability to reopen its largest banks and end its bank holiday convinced many depositors across the country to pull their money out of banks. The amount of currency hoarded by the public increased by almost $1.8 billion during the second half of February and the first week of March. During the same period, a steadily growing number of states declared bank holidays or imposed tight restrictions on deposit withdrawals. By the time Roosevelt took office on March 4, virtually every state had either closed its banks or placed severe constraints on deposit withdrawals.[12]

The run on the dollar escalated during the last week of Hoover's presidency. Massive outflows of gold produced a $700 million decline in the nation's gold reserves during February and the first week of March.[13] The New York Fed was forced to borrow $165 million of gold from the Chicago Fed on March 1 and 2. On March 3, the Chicago Fed refused a request from the New York Fed to borrow an additional $150 million of gold, after Chicago's leading bankers strongly objected to any further transfers of gold to New York. At a meeting on the same day, the New York Fed's directors concluded that "we could not pay out gold and currency much longer at the rate of the past few days."[14]

On the evening of March 2, Hoover's advisers contacted Roosevelt's team and asked whether Roosevelt would join Hoover in declaring either a national bank holiday or an embargo on foreign withdrawals of currency and gold. Roosevelt declined and told Hoover that he should proceed as he thought best. Hoover raised the issue again during a personal meeting with Roosevelt on March 3 (Hoover's last full day in office). Hoover explained that his Attorney General doubted whether the President had authority to declare a national bank holiday under the Trading with the Enemy Act, because that statute arguably expired after World War I. Hoover was therefore willing to declare a bank holiday only if Roosevelt publicly endorsed the measure and agreed to request ratification by the incoming Congress. Roosevelt replied that he thought Hoover had sufficient authority to declare a holiday, and he again said that Hoover must make his own decision.[15]

Hoover refused to declare a national bank holiday without Roosevelt's public endorsement. In the absence of any federal bank holiday, the Governors of New York and Illinois declared bank holidays for their states during the early morning of March 4. The Governors' decisions reflected grave doubts among financial leaders in New York and Chicago whether their commercial banks and their regional Federal Reserve Banks could continue to withstand the runs occurring on bank deposits and the dollar.[16] National City Bank lost a third of its deposits—an outflow of more than $400 million—during February and the first week of March 1933. As a result, National City was forced to borrow almost $120 million from the New York Fed's discount window.[17]

Hoover certainly waited far too long to propose measures that might have prevented or shortened the nationwide banking panic in early 1933. However, other officials shared responsibility for the panic's magnitude and duration. Congress and the Fed declined to support any of Hoover's proposals, evidently because they thought it would be politically risky to cooperate with a defeated and unpopular president. Roosevelt's repeated refusals to endorse any of Hoover's proposals are difficult to explain on policy grounds, as Roosevelt quickly implemented several of Hoover's ideas after he became President. It appears that Roosevelt found it politically expedient to allow the nation's financial system to collapse in March 1933 so that Hoover would bear all of the blame for the collapse and Roosevelt would receive all of the credit for any recovery.[18]

———

During the final weeks of Hoover's presidency, Wall Street faced another challenge that had a decisive impact on the future direction of U.S. financial regulation. On February 15, 1933, a Senate subcommittee launched a new stage of its investigation into securities practices on Wall Street. Ferdinand Pecora, the subcommittee's newly appointed chief counsel, led that investigation.[19]

Pecora began his work by examining the collapse of Samuel Insull's utility empire in 1932. Pecora showed that Charles Dawes' Central Republic Bank and several other Chicago banks made huge loans to Insull's companies that violated the spirit (if not the letter) of applicable lending limits under Illinois law. Pecora also demonstrated that underwriting syndicates led by Halsey, Stuart, a leading Chicago investment bank, used high-pressure marketing and deceptive advertising to sell Insull company securities to hundreds of thousands of utility customers and other unsophisticated investors.[20]

Pecora's next target was National City Bank and its securities affiliate, National City Company. During eight days of hearings between February 21 and March 2, 1933, Pecora destroyed the public reputations of National City and its chairman, Charles Mitchell. Pecora's inquiry stripped away the last "vestiges of the aura of invincibility that surrounded [National City and Mitchell] at the height of the market bubble."[21]

Pecora had only a few days to review National City's records before the hearings began, and National City did its best to hinder Pecora's investigation. Accordingly, Pecora did not try to present a comprehensive overview of National City's securities operations. Instead, he illustrated National City's aggressive and fraudulent sales practices by focusing on several offerings of securities that National City sold to its depositors and other retail investors.[22] Pecora carefully examined National City's trading in its own stock, its sales of Anaconda Copper and Boeing stock, and its marketing of foreign bonds issued by Peru, the Brazilian state of Minas Gerais, and a Chilean nitrate producer (Lautaro Nitrate Co.). Pecora demonstrated that all of those transactions were tainted by conflicts of interest, unethical sales practices, and deceptive offering materials.[23]

Pecora also uncovered evidence of extensive self-dealing by Charles Mitchell and other senior officers. National City and its securities affiliate paid bonuses to their top executives equal to one-fifth of their earnings above a base target of 8% of annual net profits. Mitchell received $3.5 million from National City and its securities affiliate between 1927 and 1929, while Hugh Baker (the affiliate's president) received more than $750,000. In July 1929, National City's senior officers received $1.9 million of "advances" from the bonus plans for the first six months of the year (including $667,000 for Mitchell and $220,000 for Baker), even though losses from the October crash wiped out all bonuses for the full calendar year. National City never recouped those "advances" and forgave them in 1932.

Additionally, National City provided $2.4 million of interest-free "morale" loans that enabled top executives to pay off margin loans on their National City stock after the crash. National City collected only 5% of those morale loans and wrote off the rest. In contrast, National City rigorously enforced installment purchase contracts (bearing 5% interest) that ordinary employees used to buy the bank's stock.[24]

Pecora's revelations of Mitchell's and Baker's bonuses and National City's "morale" loans for senior executives triggered widespread public outrage and angered many members of Congress. The public viewed Mitchell's and Baker's compensation as "astronomical" and unjust at a time when a quarter of the nation's workforce was unemployed and factory workers typically earned less than $1,000 per year. Even Babe Ruth earned only $80,000 in 1930.[25]

Pecora also demonstrated that Mitchell and other National City insiders and clients received large windfalls from National City's offerings of Boeing Air Transport stock. In October 1928, National City sold a large block of Boeing stock to a "preferred list" that included Boeing insiders as well as National City's "officers, key men, directors, and special friends." National City then listed Boeing's stock for trading on the New York curb exchange (the forerunner of the American Stock Exchange) and encouraged public investors to buy the stock. Boeing's stock price rose rapidly after public trading began in November 1928, producing potential profits of at least $1.6 million for members of the preferred list. In January 1929, National City arranged a second public offering of Boeing's stock. Before launching that public offering, National City sold another block of Boeing stock to the same preferred group. The preferred group bought their shares at a heavily discounted price, which enabled them to make substantial trading profits after the public offering began.[26]

The most devastating blow to Mitchell's reputation occurred when Pecora and Senator Smith Brookhart forced Mitchell to admit that he arranged a large tax-avoidance transaction. Mitchell sold 18,300 shares of National City stock to his wife in December 1929 (after the crash) and repurchased the same shares from her at the same price in early 1932. Mitchell relied on that sham sale to claim a $2.87 million tax loss for 1929. He used that tax loss to avoid paying any federal income taxes on his $1.2 million in compensation and $1.6 million of other net income received in 1929. Mitchell's admission created a stunning "portrait of a greedy banker willing to use any artifice to hang on to every cent of his enormous salary."[27]

Mitchell's "reputation was in tatters" after Pecora's inquest, and Mitchell resigned as chairman of National City on February 26, 1933. National City's board of directors accepted Mitchell's resignation after Hoover, Roosevelt, and Eugene Meyer (Governor of the Federal Reserve Board) told the directors that Mitchell should go.[28] A *New York Times* editorial commented, "No banking institution ... could afford even to appear to approve or condone the transactions of which [Mitchell] was a guiding spirit and one of the beneficiaries."[29]

Hoover instructed the Justice Department to investigate Mitchell, and the Roosevelt administration vigorously pursued that investigation. Mitchell was arrested and charged with criminal tax evasion in March 1933. The charges were based on Mitchell's false claim of a huge tax loss from his sham sale of stock to his wife, as well as his failure to declare as income his $667,000 "advance" from National City's bonus plan in mid-1929. After a six-week trial, the jury acquitted Mitchell of tax evasion in June. The commissioner of internal revenue subsequently imposed a civil assessment on Mitchell for unpaid taxes of $728,000, plus a 50% civil penalty for "fraud with intent to evade tax." Mitchell challenged the commissioner's civil assessment, but the Supreme Court upheld the commissioner's decision in 1938.[30]

Roosevelt and his advisers took a keen interest in the Pecora hearings, which provided powerful ammunition for Roosevelt's planned reforms of the financial markets.[31] The hearings on National City coincided with the final collapse of the U.S. banking system and furnished a dramatic context for Roosevelt's inauguration on March 4, 1933. In his inaugural address, Roosevelt denounced Wall Street's "money changers" in stark, Biblical terms:

Practices of the unscrupulous money changers stand indicted in the court of public opinion, rejected by the hearts and minds of men.

... Stripped of the lure of profit by which to induce our people to follow their false leadership, they have resorted to exhortations, pleading tearfully for restored confidence. They know only the rules of a generation of self-seekers. They have no vision, and when there is no vision the people perish.

The money changers have fled from their high seats in the temple of our civilization. We may now restore that temple to the ancient truths. The measure of the restoration lies in the extent to which we apply social values more noble than mere monetary profit.

... [T]here must be an end to a conduct in banking and in business which too often has given to a sacred trust the likeness of callous and selfish wrongdoing.

... [T]here must be a strict supervision of all banking and credits and investments, so that there will be an end to speculation with other people's money.[32]

Roosevelt quickly implemented several measures that Hoover had proposed during his final weeks in office. Roosevelt declared a national bank holiday and prohibited further exports of gold or withdrawals of gold from Federal Reserve Banks. He also convened an emergency session of Congress to address the banking crisis.

Roosevelt's senior financial advisers worked closely with Hoover's top financial regulators to develop legislation that incorporated several of Hoover's ideas. The resulting Emergency Banking Act (1) ratified the national bank holiday and amended the Trading with the Enemy Act to give Roosevelt clear authority to control the nation's gold supply, (2) authorized the OCC to appoint conservators to reorganize and reopen closed national banks, (3) empowered the RFC to buy preferred stock to recapitalize weak banks, and (4) authorized Federal Reserve Banks to provide emergency loans to banks in the form of short-term notes backed by pledges of the banks' holdings of government securities and other qualifying collateral.[33]

The Emergency Banking Act granted the status of legal tender (currency) to the short-term notes that Federal Reserve Banks issued to banks when they reopened after the bank holiday. The Fed's short-term notes "created the expectation that the government would guarantee all depositors [of reopened banks] against loss," as the Fed could issue those notes in amounts equal to most of the assets held by reopened banks.[34] Thus, the Emergency Banking Act enabled federal bank regulators to ensure the viability of reopened banks by providing liquidity through the Fed's notes as well as fresh capital through the RFC's purchases of preferred stock.[35]

Congress passed the Emergency Banking Act during an extraordinary one-day session on March 9, and the Roosevelt administration began to reopen the nation's banks on March 13. More than 12,700 banks reopened by March 15, accounting for about 70% of the banks in existence on March 3. Another 1,300 banks reopened by April 12. However, 4,200 banks remained closed in mid-April. About half of those closed banks were reopened by the end of 1934 (with RFC assistance), while more than 2,000 closed banks went into liquidation.[36]

Bank of America reopened on March 14, 1933, following the intervention of California's two Senators and a heated argument between Treasury Secretary William Woodin and John Calkins, Governor of the Federal Reserve Bank of San Francisco. Fed officials had long maintained a highly adversarial relationship with A. P. Giannini (Bank of America's chairman), and Calkins claimed that Bank of America was "hopelessly insolvent." Woodin and Acting Comptroller of the Currency Francis Awalt disagreed with Calkins' assessment. With strong backing from Senators Hiram Johnson (R-CA) and William McAdoo (D-CA), Woodin persuaded Calkins to reopen the bank.[37]

As in 1932, when Bank of America received the RFC's first loan, Giannini's giant bank was deemed too big to fail. Raymond Moley remarked, "Bank of America had 410 branches. With its one million depositors it was in a very real sense the bank of the common people of California. To keep it closed would shock the state beyond description."[38]

In April 1933, Roosevelt used his authority under the Emergency Banking Act to take the U.S. off the gold exchange standard by prohibiting purchases, sales, exports, or ownership of gold by private parties. During the next nine months, Roosevelt experimented with various measures to devalue the dollar and boost domestic prices for commodities and manufactured goods. In January 1934, Roosevelt exercised newly delegated authority from Congress to establish the official price of gold at \$35 per ounce. That step effectively devalued the dollar by almost 60%. The Treasury Department announced that it would buy gold from foreign central banks and governments at that price.[39]

Roosevelt's devaluation of the dollar, Treasury's willingness to buy foreign gold, and deepening political problems in Europe attracted large inflows of gold and investment capital into the U.S. after 1933. Inflows of foreign gold and capital significantly expanded the U.S. money supply between 1933 and 1935. That expansion was further boosted by almost \$10 billion of new U.S. bank deposits, as many American firms and households returned their hoarded cash to the banking system. These developments ended the severe deflation and monetary contraction that had plagued the U.S. during the Great Depression.[40]

————

The RFC purchased preferred stock in thousands of banks that federal regulators reopened after the national bank holiday. The RFC's preferred stock program helped to restore public confidence in the U.S. banking system, working in conjunction with the Fed's liquidity assistance program under the Emergency Banking Act and the establishment of a new federal deposit insurance program in January 1934.[41] The RFC's purchases of preferred stock played a crucial role because many reopened banks struggled with serious capital shortfalls and not just liquidity problems.[42] Thus, as would also be true in 2008–09, the federal government provided large-scale capital infusions, liquidity support, and financial guarantees to stabilize a banking system that had been severely disrupted by a systemic financial crisis.[43]

At first, many banks were reluctant to participate in the RFC's preferred stock program because of the stigma that recipients of RFC loans suffered when Congress had published their names in 1932 and early 1933. The Roosevelt administration addressed the stigma problem by ending public disclosure of the RFC's assistance to banks. The administration strongly encouraged banks to accept the RFC's capital infusions so that they could make new loans to individuals and businesses. Jesse Jones, the RFC's powerful chairman between 1933 and 1945, spearheaded the administration's campaign. In August 1933, Jones addressed the annual convention of the American Bankers Association. He warned the ABA's members that "more than half the banks represented at the gathering in front of me were insolvent." He urged them to "be smart, for once," and sell preferred stock to the RFC.[44]

In October 1933, the New York Clearing House publicly endorsed the RFC's preferred stock program. Leading New York and Chicago banks soon agreed to sell preferred stock to the RFC. By March 1934, the RFC owned \$362 million of preferred stock in forty of the one hundred largest U.S. banks. The RFC's investments in large banks accounted for a third of the RFC's \$1.1 billion of equity investments in all banks.[45] The RFC ultimately determined that "fewer than twenty" of the 6,139 banks that received capital from the RFC "had no need of it."[46]

The RFC made its largest preferred stock investments in National City Bank, Chase National Bank, and Continental Illinois—the three leading U.S. universal banks. Those three banks operated the largest and most active securities affiliates during the 1920s.[47] The magnitude of the RFC's investments reflected the enormous losses that all three banks suffered during the Great Depression.

In January 1934, National City Bank sold $50 million of preferred stock to the RFC. At the same time, National City Bank recognized $60 million of losses, bringing the bank's total charge-offs since 1929 to $167 million.[48] In addition, the bank's securities affiliate, National City Company, recorded losses that reduced its capital by $115 million between 1929 and 1933. Thus, National City's combined losses between 1930 and 1934 topped $280 million.[49]

In January 1934, Chase National Bank sold $46 million of preferred stock to the RFC and $4 million of preferred stock to its common shareholders.[50] Chase established reserves for losses that reduced its equity capital by $212 million between 1929 and 1933. In addition, its securities affiliate, Chase Securities Corporation, established loss reserves that reduced its capital by $120 million during the same period. Hence, Chase's combined losses during the Great Depression exceeded $330 million.[51]

Continental Illinois established more than $140 million of reserves for losses between 1931 and 1934. Those losses included a write-off of the bank's entire $15 million investment in its securities affiliate. The bank sold $50 million of preferred stock to the RFC in late 1933 and reduced its common equity capital from $75 million to $25 million. Given the bank's gravely impaired financial condition, the RFC insisted on the appointment of Walter Cummings as the bank's new chairman. Cummings played a leading role in organizing the new Federal Deposit Insurance Corporation (FDIC) in the fall of 1933, and he served as the FDIC's chairman until he was appointed as Continental Illinois' new leader in early 1934.[52]

The banking crisis of 1933 required the federal government to provide liquidity assistance, loans, and capital infusions to dozens of large U.S. banks. In addition to the $362 million of preferred stock that the RFC purchased from forty big banks, the RFC provided $312 million of loans to twenty-two large banks during 1933 and 1934. Those loans represented almost half of all loans that the RFC extended to banks during that period.[53] The three leading universal banks—National City, Chase, and Continental Illinois—received the largest RFC bailouts, due in large part to their massive losses from securities activities.[54] By any objective measure, the universal banking business model failed the acid test of the Great Depression in the U.S. as it had in Europe.

————

Unlike Hoover, Roosevelt campaigned in 1932 on a platform that advocated fundamental reforms in the structure and regulation of U.S. financial markets. The Democratic Party's platform proposed federal regulation of securities offerings as well as a strict separation between securities markets and the commercial banking system.[55] Senator Carter Glass drafted the platform plank calling for "the severance of affiliated security companies from and the divorce of the investment banking business from commercial banks." In a campaign speech, Roosevelt declared that the "consolidation and mingling" of commercial and investment banking was "contrary to public policy," and he demanded their "separation."[56]

In late March 1933, Roosevelt sent Congress a draft bill authorizing federal regulation of securities offerings. He also encouraged Ferdinand Pecora and Senator Duncan Fletcher (D-FL), the new chairman of the Senate investigative subcommittee, to choose J. P. Morgan & Co. as the next subject of the Senate subcommittee's inquiry.[57] The House of Morgan initially refused to cooperate with Pecora's requests for information, based on its status as a "private bank." Pecora promptly "waged war against the bank in the press and on Capitol Hill." On April 4, the Senate approved a resolution empowering Pecora's subcommittee to investigate "the business of banking, financing, and extending credit" conducted by any person, partnership, or firm.[58] Armed with that sweeping congressional mandate, Pecora convinced the Morgan firm to cooperate. The subcommittee's hearings on the House of Morgan during late May and early June generated additional public support for reforming the securities and banking industries.[59]

The first witness, J. P. Morgan, Jr., declared that his firm followed "a code of ethics and customs," which ensured that the firm did "only first class business and that in a first class way." Morgan was the firm's senior partner and the son of its founder. He told the subcommittee that the House of Morgan was "a national asset and not a national danger."[60]

Pecora later remarked, "Mr. Morgan was not the first wielder of power to believe profoundly in the invincible rectitude of his own regime." Pecora acknowledged that J. P. Morgan & Co. did not engage in "glaring abuses" similar to those committed by National City, Chase, and some other commercial and investment banks. Pecora concluded, however, that the House of Morgan's conduct exhibited "more subtle dangers," including a "terrific concentration of power."[61]

Pecora pursued four lines of inquiry that turned public opinion decisively against J. P. Morgan & Co. First, Pecora showed that the House of Morgan's twenty partners claimed capital losses from sales of investments that allowed them to pay only $48,000 in income taxes during 1930 and no income taxes at all during 1931 and 1932. The Internal Revenue Service (IRS) did not closely examine the tax returns filed by Morgan partners because it assumed that "any schedule made by that office is correct." Pecora did not document any illegal tax evasion by Morgan partners. However, their collective avoidance of taxes and the complete deference given to them by the IRS were "politically explosive" issues that produced widespread public resentment.[62]

Second, Pecora revealed that J. P. Morgan & Co. provided financial favors to almost five hundred influential "friends" of the firm. The scope and magnitude of the House of Morgan's favors were considerably larger than National City's preferential allocations of Boeing stock. In five securities transactions, the House of Morgan offered large blocks of stock to individuals on "preferred lists" at prices that were heavily discounted from those paid by public investors for buying the same stocks on securities exchanges. The "preferred lists" included leading politicians from both political parties as well as top financiers, business executives, and other public figures. Republican beneficiaries included former President Calvin Coolidge, former Secretary of the Navy Charles Francis Adams, and Charles Hilles, former Chairman of the Republican National Committee. Democratic recipients included former Secretary of War Newton Baker, current Treasury Secretary William Woodin, Senator William McAdoo, and John J. Raskob, a leading speculator and Chairman of the Democratic National Committee. Other favored individuals included Charles Mitchell, Albert Wiggin, Democratic adviser (and prominent financier) Bernard Baruch, General Electric chairman Owen Young, Charles Lindbergh, and General John J. Pershing, as well as the chairmen of U.S. Steel, Standard Oil of New Jersey, and AT&T.[63]

The House of Morgan's partners told individuals on the "preferred lists" that there were "no strings tied to the stock, so you can sell it whenever you wish ... We just want you to know that we were thinking of you in this connection and thought you might like to have a little of the stock at the same price we are paying for it."[64] Albert Wiggin testified that J. P. Morgan & Co. sold him 10,000 Alleghany Corporation shares for $20 per share, when the public trading price was $35 per share. Wiggin said, "I assumed it was a favor, and I was glad to take it."[65]

Some "preferred list" recipients expressed a strong sense of reciprocity for their favorable treatment. John J. Raskob sent a letter to Morgan partner George Whitney in which Raskob stated, "I appreciate the many courtesies shown me by you and your partners, and sincerely hope [that] the future holds opportunities for me to reciprocate."[66] In Pecora's view, Raskob's letter displayed "the silken bonds of gratitude in which [the Morgan firm] skillfully enmeshed the chosen ranks of its 'preferred lists.'"[67]

Third, Pecora returned to a primary theme of the 1913 Pujo hearings when he revealed the House of Morgan's extensive network of relationships with many of the largest and most influential U.S. companies and financial institutions. More than 140 leading corporations maintained large deposits with J. P. Morgan & Co., and Morgan partners held 126 directorships in 89 major financial institutions, railroads, public utilities, and business corporations. The Morgan firm provided loans to 60 officers and directors of other banks, including a multimillion-dollar loan to Charles Mitchell. Pecora concluded that the Morgan firm's influence "was a great stream that was fed by many sources, by its deposits, by its loans, by its promotions, by its directorships, by its pre-eminent position as investment bankers, by its control of holding companies," as well as "the silken bonds of gratitude" created by its preferred lists. Pecora warned that a firm with such far-reaching influence "might be a formidable rival to government itself."[68]

Fourth, Pecora charged that J. P. Morgan & Co. had compromised its professed code of ethics in 1929 when it underwrote the stocks of two giant holding companies, United Corporation and Alleghany Corporation. United Corporation owned public utilities that generated a fifth of the nation's power supply. Alleghany Corporation controlled the huge railroad empire built by the Van Sweringen brothers. Due to the House of Morgan's credibility as an underwriter, the stock prices of both companies rose to dizzying heights before the crash in October 1929 and produced huge profits for Morgan partners as well as individuals on Morgan's preferred lists.[69] The stock prices of both companies plunged after the crash. In 1933, the stocks of both companies were trading at prices that were more than 90% below their 1929 highs, inflicting severe losses on shareholders who did not sell before the crash.[70]

Pecora's inquest of J. P. Morgan & Co. created "extreme disillusionment" among many observers.[71] A *New York Times* editorial commented, "Here was a firm of bankers, perhaps the most famous and powerful in the whole world.... Yet it failed under a test of its pride and prestige.... [I]t sacrificed something intangible, imponderable, that had to do with the very highest repute." According to the *New York World-Telegram*, the House of Morgan did not carry out any "crude crime against the law," but it committed "the far deeper, more dangerous offense of what Lord Bryce well calls 'The submarine warfare which wealth can wage.'"[72]

———

The banking system's collapse and the Pecora committee's hearings on National City and J. P. Morgan & Co. produced widespread public support for the Securities Act of 1933 and the Glass-Steagall Banking Act of 1933.[73] In his memoir, Pecora remarked, "Never before in the history of the United States had so much wealth and power been required to render a public accounting."[74] Joel Seligman later observed that "the First Hundred Days of the Roosevelt administration was that rare period when money talked and nobody listened."[75]

The Securities Act was drafted and passed in only two months. Supporters described it as a "Truth in Securities Act," modeled on the British Companies Act. The statute required issuers and underwriters of securities to file registration statements with federal authorities before making public offerings that crossed state lines or used the mail, the telephone, or other methods of interstate communication. Issuers and underwriters were required to furnish investors with offering documents (prospectuses) containing specified disclosures about the issuer, the securities being offered, and the terms of the offering. Federal regulators could block a public offering if the offering documents were incomplete or misleading in any material respect. Issuers and their senior executives, directors, underwriters, accountants, and other experts were liable for damages if the offering documents contained false or misleading statements of material fact.[76] Under the new Securities Act, "there would be no more skimpy prospectuses like the ones [National] City Bank distributed to its investors."[77]

Roosevelt signed the Securities Act into law on May 27, 1933. The Federal Trade Commission (FTC)—which was given responsibility for administering the new law—stated that it would "prevent further exploitation of the public by the sale of fraudulent and worthless securities through misrepresentation." The FTC estimated that $25 billion of "worthless securities" had been sold to the American public during the previous decade "through misrepresentation and fraud."[78]

In contrast to the Securities Act, the Glass-Steagall Banking Act of 1933 had a long and tortuous journey. Senator Carter Glass held hearings in 1931 and 1932 to consider whether commercial banks should be required to get rid of their securities affiliates. Universal banks, investment banks, and most federal regulators strongly opposed any such requirement. Nevertheless, Glass introduced a bill in January 1932 to mandate divestitures of securities affiliates. Glass' bill made little progress until Roosevelt took office.[79]

During the 1931 hearings, Albert Wiggin, chairman of Chase National Bank, argued that securities affiliates of commercial banks provided "an essential banking service in financing the large corporations of the [nation] and other clients of the banks." National City Bank chairman Charles Mitchell maintained that securities affiliates were "an exceedingly important factor in security distribution," as they participated in underwriting half or more of all U.S. bond issues in 1929 and 1930. Melvin Traylor, chairman of the First National Bank of Chicago, contended that securities affiliates were part of "the well-rounded service that a bank ought to render to a community." Allan Pope, executive vice president of the First National Bank of Boston's securities affiliate, declared, "I do not believe that this country could have developed industrially to the extent it has since [World War I] without the assistance of bank affiliates."[80]

Pope testified again in 1932, while serving as president of the Investment Bankers Association. Pope declared that the IBA's members—including investment banks as well as securities affiliates of commercial banks—opposed the Glass bill "without a single exception." Harry Haas, president of the American Bankers Association, stated that the ABA fervently opposed the Glass bill. Henry Scott, president of the Wilmington Trust Co., argued that the Glass bill would make the Depression worse by forcing banks to close down their securities affiliates and liquidate their investments in securities.[81]

The Hoover administration did not support Glass' bill. Comptroller of the Currency J. W. Pole and New York Fed governor George Harrison stated that they strongly opposed the Glass bill during the 1932 hearings.[82] In contrast, Federal Reserve Board Governor Eugene Meyer acknowledged that "many evils have developed through the operation of affiliates connected with member banks, particularly affiliates dealing in securities." Meyer expressed qualified support for a mandatory divestiture of securities affiliates after a three-year waiting period. Similarly, Meyer's colleague, Board member Charles Hamlin, told Glass in September 1932 that the misconduct of major banks in pressuring small banks to buy risky securities from their affiliates "certainly would seem to justify the clause in your bill requiring member banks to divorce themselves from their affiliates."[83] However, the Hoover administration's lack of support and vehement attacks by universal banks and Wall Street investment banks prevented Glass from advancing his bill to the Senate floor until the lame-duck session of Congress that followed the November 1932 elections.[84]

Despite the strong opposition they encountered, Senator Glass, Representative Henry Steagall (D-AL), and other members of Congress persevered in their efforts to separate commercial banks from the capital markets. They wanted commercial banks to confine their operations to traditional banking activities—accepting deposits, providing payments services (including check clearing and foreign exchange), making loans to consumers and businesses, and providing trust services. They believed that universal banks bore much of the blame for promoting the unsustainable booms that occurred in the bond and stock markets during the 1920s.[85]

Glass contended that securities affiliates of commercial banks "were the largest contributors, next to the gambling on the stock exchange, to the disaster which was precipitated upon the country in 1929." He argued that the speculative activities of securities affiliates helped to precipitate "the financial catastrophe which ... was mainly responsible for the depression under which we have been suffering since."[86] Similarly, Steagall declared:

> Our great banking system was diverted from its original purposes into investment activities, and its service devoted to speculation and international high finance.... Agriculture, commerce, and industry were forgotten. Bank deposits and credit resources were funneled into the speculative centers of the country for investment in stocks [sic] operations and in market speculation. Values were lifted to fictitious levels.[87]

Senator Frederic Walcott (R-CT) maintained that the "gambling fever" and "flood tide of speculation" during the 1920s would not have occurred without the "money, currency [and] very expansive credit" furnished by large commercial banks, as well as the extensive marketing operations of their securities affiliates. In Walcott's view, the "excessive use of bank loans for the purpose of stock speculation" and "the dangerous use of the resources of bank depositors for the purpose of making speculative profits" fueled the destructive boom-and-bust cycle that led to the Great Depression.[88]

Representative Herman Kopplemann (D-CT) agreed that "one of the chief causes of this depression has been the diversion of depositors' moneys into the speculative markets of Wall Street. Instead of keeping the money for the use of the legitimate needs of commerce and agriculture, money has been lent to gamblers to use in buying stocks on margin."[89] According to Representative Hamilton Fish, Sr. (R-NY), securities affiliates of commercial banks were "largely" responsible for "the mass overproduction of stocks, bonds, and other securities," which financed "a mass overproduction of factories, commodities, real estate, and everything else—an enormous inflation that sooner or later had to crash."[90]

Supporters of the Glass bill contended that securities affiliates of commercial banks created toxic conflicts of interest, which destroyed the ability of banks to serve as prudent, objective lenders or as impartial investment advisers. The Pecora hearings revealed that universal banks could "take bad loans, repackage them as bonds, and fob them off on investors, as National City had done with Latin American loans. [Universal banks] could even lend investors the money to buy the bonds."[91]

Senator Robert Bulkley (D-OH) and others emphasized that conflicts of interest at universal banks created powerful incentives (1) to make risky loans and capital investments to support their securities affiliates; (2) to buy unsound securities for their own accounts, or the accounts of their customers, to ensure the success of offerings made by their affiliates; (3) to provide loans to customers who purchased securities underwritten by their affiliates; and (4) to target their depositors and trust customers as potential buyers for securities underwritten by their affiliates. Securities affiliates also carried out aggressive trading operations to boost the stock prices of their affiliated banks.[92]

Bulkley pointed out that securities affiliates of universal banks had "large fixed investments," as they established far-flung branch office networks, expensive marketing programs, and substantial sales forces to be "efficient" in selling securities. Securities affiliates were therefore eager to recoup their "fixed expenses" by underwriting speculative securities for lucrative fees. In Bulkley's view, securities affiliates had strong incentives to recommend and sell risky securities that were not suitable for many customers. Bulkley asked:

> Can any banker ... be a fair and impartial judge as to the necessity and soundness for a new security issue which he knows he can readily distribute through channels which have been expensive to develop but which presently stand ready to absorb the proposed security issue and yield a handsome profit on the transaction?[93]

Bulkley concluded that banks could not provide objective investment advice to their depositors and other customers unless they had "nothing to sell" to their clients.[94] Representative Kopplemann agreed that "in banking, as elsewhere, no man can serve two masters." Bankers could not "judge impartially" the quality of securities when they acted as "promoters and sellers of these securities." Kopplemann stated that, under the Glass bill, banking could become "an honored profession," as bankers would be "public servants charged with a sacred responsibility to administer the funds entrusted to them for the benefit of their depositors and not for the gain of themselves." Kopplemann's colleagues in the House of Representatives applauded his remarks.[95]

The Glass bill bogged down during Congress's lame-duck session, due to heated debates over Glass' proposal to expand the branching powers of national banks, which Glass believed would encourage the creation of larger and more geographically diversified banks. The McFadden Act of 1927 allowed national banks to open branches only within their home cities, and only if state law allowed equivalent branching rights for state banks.[96] Glass' original bill would have allowed each national bank to establish branches anywhere in its home state, and also in other states up to 50 miles from its main office, regardless of state-law restrictions. Defenders of community banks and state-chartered banks attacked Glass' branching proposal, claiming that it would destroy smaller banks and permit large banks to dominate America's financial system.[97]

Senator Huey Long (D-LA) launched a ten-day filibuster against the Glass bill in January 1933. To end Long's filibuster, Glass accepted a compromise provision on branching that allowed national banks to establish branches only in their home states and only to the extent that state laws expressly allowed state banks to open branches. That compromise created the potential for statewide branching by national banks, but it also prevented interstate branching and preserved each state's ability to determine the extent of branching within its borders.[98]

Deposit insurance presented a second major hurdle for the Glass bill. In May 1932, the House of Representatives passed a deposit guarantee bill sponsored by Steagall. Steagall's bill would have established a mutual guarantee program covering deposits held by regulated banks. Steagall's deposit guarantee plan attracted widespread public support as the U.S. banking system collapsed in late 1932 and early 1933.[99]

Steagall and his supporters argued that businesses and consumers would never bring back funds they had withdrawn from the banking system without a strong deposit guarantee. If such a return of deposits did not occur, banks could not provide the credit needed for economic recovery. Glass, Roosevelt, and most large banks strongly opposed Steagall's deposit guarantee plan, arguing that it would give an undesirable subsidy to weaker banks. Glass offered a much more limited proposal for a federal "liquidating corporation," which would use funds contributed by Federal Reserve Banks and Fed member banks to offer partial reimbursements for losses suffered by depositors in closed banks. Glass' proposal would not have applied to open banks, and it therefore would not have helped vulnerable banks to survive.[100]

Public demands for deposit insurance proved to be irresistible, and Glass was again forced to compromise. The Glass-Steagall Act established a new federal deposit insurance program on January 1, 1934, administered by the FDIC. The new program was funded at first by contributions from Federal Reserve Banks and Fed member banks and later by premiums paid by banks that became members of the FDIC. The program provided only partial protection for deposits, instead of the full guarantee proposed by Steagall.

The new deposit insurance program also included substantial federal oversight. National and state member banks were admitted to the program only if they were certified as sound by the Treasury Secretary. State nonmember banks were admitted only if they were certified as sound by state regulators, and those banks were thereafter subject to examination and supervision by the FDIC.[101]

Glass' compromises on limited statewide branching and partial deposit insurance (with federal oversight) paved the way for final agreement on the Glass-Steagall Act. The final terms of the act represented a series of trade-offs between members of

Congress like Glass, who favored larger banks and wanted to establish a more uniform, federalized system of bank regulation, and members of Congress like Steagall,
who supported smaller, local banks and wanted to preserve a decentralized banking
system with a significant regulatory role for the states.[102]

_____

By the time House and Senate leaders reached final compromises on branching and
deposit insurance, resistance to the separation of commercial banks from the securities markets had weakened considerably. On March 7, 1933, James Perkins announced
that National City Bank's board of directors had approved a "policy of working toward
the divorcement of the bank and its securities affiliate." Perkins had become chairman
of National City the previous week, replacing the disgraced Charles Mitchell. Perkins
was a personal friend of President Roosevelt, and he met with Roosevelt on March 6
to discuss National City's plan to divest its securities affiliate.[103]

On March 8, Winthrop Aldrich, chairman of Chase National Bank, "heartily com-
mend[ed] the action of the National City Bank," and he stated that Chase would also
divest its securities affiliate. In Aldrich's view, events during the previous decade had
demonstrated that "intimate connection between commercial banking and investment banking almost inevitably leads to abuses."[104]

Aldrich emphasized that getting rid of securities affiliates would not be sufficient to
separate the banking industry from the securities markets. He called for a prohibition
on deposit-taking by securities dealers and all other firms that were not regulated as
banks. Aldrich also declared that the "spirit of speculation must be eradicated from
the management of commercial banks." He therefore proposed that deposit-taking
banks should be barred from sharing any officers or directors with securities dealers.[105] Aldrich's plan represented a complete repudiation of the policies followed by
his predecessor, Albert Wiggin. When Wiggin retired as Chase's chairman in January
1933, he stated that any effort to abolish bank securities affiliates would be "very
ill-advised."[106]

The decisions by National City and Chase to divest their securities affiliates gave
a significant boost to Glass' proposal to separate commercial banks from the securities markets. National City's and Chase's announcements followed the examples of
several other large banks, which had already closed their securities affiliates after suffering large losses during the Depression. The public's angry response to the Senate
hearings on National City and J. P. Morgan & Co. provided further momentum for
Glass' plan.[107]

A few large financial institutions continued to oppose separation. On March
9, 1933—the day after Aldrich's public statement—William Potter, president of
Guaranty Trust Co., denounced proposals to separate banks from securities dealers
as "drastic" and "destructive." Potter said that Guaranty Trust intended to retain its securities affiliate, and he added, "My conscience is easy."[108]

Guaranty Trust's board of directors included two partners from J. P. Morgan & Co.—Thomas Lamont and George Whitney—and the Morgan firm strenuously opposed the Glass bill. Russell Leffingwell, a prominent Democrat who served as Assistant Secretary of the Treasury under President Wilson, was the House of Morgan's principal emissary to Franklin Roosevelt. In 1932, Leffingwell wrote a personal letter to Roosevelt, arguing that "we cannot cure the present deflation and depression" by adopting the "prohibition and regulation stuff" proposed by Glass. Roosevelt rebuffed Leffingwell's argument, adding, "I wish we could get from the bankers themselves an admission that in the 1927 to 1929 period there were grave abuses." Roosevelt stated that Glass' reforms would benefit the banking industry by preventing a "recurrence" of the abusive practices of the 1920s. After taking office in March 1933, Roosevelt similarly rejected Thomas Lamont's advice that the new administration should "avoid drastic measures" in responding to the banking crisis.[109]

A final attempt to weaken the Glass-Steagall Act occurred during the Senate's debates on the legislation in May 1933. Senator Millard Tydings (D-MD) introduced an amendment that would have exempted private partnerships engaged in securities activities from the prohibition against deposit-taking by nonbanks contained in Section 21 of the statute. Tydings argued that "private investment houses of the better class"—including his constituent Alexander Brown & Sons of Baltimore—performed an important public service in "financing private businesses ... on long-term paper." Tydings contended that without his amendment, the Glass bill would reduce the availability of credit by undermining "the usefulness of bona fide, finely run ... private institutions."[110]

Senators Bulkley and Glass strongly opposed the Tydings amendment. Bulkley declared that an "absolute prohibition" on deposit-taking by securities firms was necessary "to separate investment from commercial banking" and, therefore, was "vital to the principles" of the Glass-Steagall Act. Glass agreed that Section 21's prohibition was a "vital provision" because it would "confine to their proper business activities these large private concerns" and "deny them the right to conduct the deposit bank business." Glass reminded the Senate that private investment banks had "unloaded millions of dollars of worthless investment securities upon the banks of this country." He also pointed out that Section 21's prohibition on deposit-taking would not prevent "large investment houses" from providing longer-term financing for businesses in the same way that merchant banks did in England.[111] Glass noted that officials at Chase National Bank's securities affiliate were already planning to reorganize the affiliate as an independent securities firm. The Senate voted down the Tydings amendment after Bulkley and Glass completed their remarks.[112]

The House and Senate passed the Glass-Steagall Act on June 13, 1933. Large banks "launched a vigorous campaign" to persuade President Roosevelt to veto the legislation. However, Roosevelt signed the act into law on June 16, and he called it the most important federal banking legislation since the Federal Reserve Act.[113]

———

The Glass-Steagall Act sought to prevent a recurrence of the Great Depression by establishing a strict separation between commercial banks and the securities markets. Sections 5(c) and 16 of the act—which still remain in force—prohibit commercial banks from underwriting or trading in securities except for limited types of "bank-eligible" securities (including U.S. government securities and state and local government bonds) that are lawful for underwriting or purchase by national banks.[114] Sections 20 and 32—which Congress repealed in 1999—barred commercial banks from affiliating with firms that were "engaged principally" in underwriting or trading in securities, and from sharing directors, officers, or employees with such firms.[115]

Section 21—the provision targeted by Senator Tydings—also remains in force and prohibits securities firms and other nonbanks from accepting "deposits." Section 21's prohibition applies to all "deposits subject to check or to repayment upon presentation of a passbook, certificate of deposit, *or other evidence of debt*, or upon request of the depositor."[116] The literal terms of Section 21 are broad enough to embrace all short-term debt instruments that are payable by the borrower on demand by the creditor.

The Glass-Steagall Act was designed to prevent the federal government from being compelled "to protect speculators to save depositors." The nationwide banking panic of early 1933 had forced the Fed and the RFC "to stand behind both depositors and speculators" by providing emergency short-term loans and capital infusions to universal banks that controlled securities affiliates. The Glass-Steagall Act instituted federal deposit insurance to support "conservative loan-and-deposit banking." After the Great Depression, "nobody wanted to insure securities affiliates of banks."[117]

Supporters of the Glass-Steagall Act contended that money center banks encouraged the stock market bubble of the late 1920s by paying high interest rates to attract deposits from smaller rural banks and by investing those deposits in margin loans to speculators and call loans to brokers. Accordingly, Section 11(b) of the Glass-Steagall Act barred commercial banks from paying interest on demand deposits and instructed the Fed to issue regulations limiting interest rates payable on time deposits. Glass stated that Section 11(b) would prevent money center banks from offering high interest rates to attract deposits from smaller banks, thereby decreasing the flow of correspondent banking deposits into margin loans and other loans collateralized by securities.[118]

Glass also explained that Section 11(b) would empower the Fed to "put a stop to the competition between banks" that caused many banks to pay "excessive interest on time deposits." Glass believed that interest rate competition during the 1920s had produced destructive consequences by increasing the cost of time deposits and pressuring banks to take excessive risks by investing those deposits in higher-yielding and riskier loans and securities.[119]

Section 11(a) of the Glass-Steagall Act prohibited Fed member banks from acting as "the medium or agent" for investments by nonbank firms or individuals in margin loans made by securities brokers and dealers. Section 11(a) was designed to prevent banks from promoting another massive influx of funds from nonbank investors into call loans and margin loans, similar to the one that occurred during the stock market bubble of 1928–29.[120] The restrictions imposed by Sections 11(a) and (b) contributed to a significant decline in deposits held by smaller banks at money center banks, as well as a substantial reduction in broker call loans and other bank loans collateralized by securities.[121]

The Glass-Steagall Act also tried to prevent the Fed from providing credit to support speculative activities related to securities, commodities, and real estate. Glass claimed that the New York Fed encouraged the unsustainable boom of the 1920s by providing excessive credit to large money center banks on liberal terms, thereby enabling those banks to finance hazardous securities and real estate ventures. To stop the Fed from financing a future boom, Section 3(a) of the statute instructed the Federal Reserve Board to bar Federal Reserve Banks from providing loans to member banks that made "undue use" of Fed credit for "the speculative carrying of or trading in securities, real estate, or commodities." Section 9 called for immediate repayment of Fed loans if member banks used those loans to increase their securities lending or investing activities after the Fed warned them not to do so.[122]

Congress believed that the restrictions imposed on the Fed's lending policies by Sections 3(a) and 9 were of great importance. However, the Fed "rarely" applied those mandates after 1933.[123] It does not appear that the Fed paid any attention to the restrictions in Sections 3(a) and 9 when it provided massive loans to prop up large universal banks and securities firms during the financial crisis of 2007–09.[124]

―――――

The Senate's investigation of abusive practices on Wall Street continued for another year after Congress passed the Glass-Steagall Act. The next subject of Ferdinand Pecora's inquiry was Dillon, Read & Co., a leading New York private investment bank that underwrote $4 billion of securities during the 1920s. Pecora showed that Dillon, Read engaged in "many of the same abuses, violations of fiduciary trust, and selfish profit-seeking that [the] subcommittee had brought to light when Pecora interrogated Mitchell of the National City Co." Like National City, Dillon, Read marketed risky Latin American bonds to American investors based on misleading prospectuses, and most of those bonds defaulted during the early 1930s.[125]

Dillon, Read also sponsored two large investment trusts, the United States & Foreign Securities Corp. and its subsidiary, the United States & International Securities Corp. Dillon, Read made an initial investment of $5.1 million in those trusts and exercised complete control over them. Dillon, Read sold $75 million of shares in the trusts to public investors, and it extracted more than $40 million of profits from the trusts prior to the crash of October 1929, while public investors received much smaller distributions. Investors who retained their shares after the crash suffered large losses.

Pecora and members of the Senate subcommittee challenged Clarence Dillon about the hugely disproportionate investment returns that he and his partners received from the trusts. Dillon replied, "We could have taken 100%. We could have taken all that profit." Senator Ava Adams (D-CO) responded to Dillon's statement by commenting, "Do you remember what Lord Clive said? 'When I consider my opportunities, I marvel at my moderation.'"[126]

After finishing with Dillon, Read, Pecora conducted an extensive investigation of Chase National Bank and its securities affiliate, Chase Securities Corporation. Pecora's inquest produced "a shocking disclosure of low standards in high places," including "most of the characteristic evils which beset the National City organization."[127] Pecora showed that Chase used offering prospectuses containing false and misleading statements to market high-risk bonds for the Cuban government, the builders of a highway tunnel project between Detroit and Windsor, Canada, and the developers of a New York City office building. All of those bonds defaulted by 1933.[128]

Chase also organized trading pools that conducted large-scale trading operations in the bank's stock as well as the stocks of numerous clients. Pecora alleged that Chase's trading pools had no relationship to any "proper functions of the Chase National Bank or any other bank. They were simply raiding expeditions on the market in the spirit of the times."[129]

Chase paid its chairman, Albert Wiggin, $1.3 million in salary and bonuses between 1928 and 1932. Wiggin obtained hundreds of thousands of dollars in additional fees by serving as a director of fifty-nine companies, including many of Chase's banking clients. Chase did not require Wiggin to return any of his bonuses, even though the bank and its securities affiliate suffered more than $330 million of losses during the Great Depression. Chase awarded Wiggin a lifetime pension of $100,000 per year when he retired in December 1932.[130]

Pecora destroyed Wiggin's reputation by revealing that Wiggin engaged in massive self-dealing that enriched him and his family at Chase's expense. Wiggin organized three family corporations to participate in Chase's trading pools for the bank's stock and client stocks. Wiggin's family corporations provided jobs, trading profits, and loans to senior Chase officials, thereby ensuring their acquiescence in Wiggin's self-dealing. Wiggin's family corporations skimmed off more than $12 million of profits from Chase's trading pools between 1928 and 1930, including more than $10 million from trading in Chase National Bank's stock. During the same period, Chase Securities Corporation earned profits of less than $160,000 from trading in the bank's stock. Wiggin avoided federal taxes on most of his family's trading profits by transferring those profits to family-owned Canadian corporations. The Canadian corporations offset those profits against subsequent investment losses.[131]

Under questioning by Pecora, Wiggin admitted that his family corporations had earned $4 million of their trading profits by selling short more than 42,000 shares of Chase National Bank stock between September and December 1929. Wiggin did not inform Chase's board of directors that his family corporations were making large short sales of the bank's stock. Many of those short sales occurred while Chase's securities affiliate was actively buying the bank's stock for the purpose of "stabilizing" its stock price during and after the October crash. Wiggin arranged for the bank to lend

$8 million to his family corporations, which they used to finance their purchases of the bank's stock to cover their short positions. The *New York Herald Tribune* reported that "more than one of Mr. Wiggin's answers left Mr. Pecora and members of the committee momentarily speechless." Pecora's revelations of Wiggin's shocking conflicts of interest and brazen self-dealing caused a "storm of popular disapproval," and "Mr. Wiggin felt constrained to renounce [his] pension."[132]

Pecora's inquests of Dillon, Read and Chase during the autumn of 1933 produced a second wave of public anger against money center banks and Wall Street securities firms. By reinforcing the public's condemnation of Wall Street practices, the Senate's investigation of Dillon, Read and Chase blunted the securities industry's aggressive campaign to repeal the Securities Act of 1933 and defeat the proposed Securities Exchange Act of 1934. Securities firms and their supporters argued that both statutes would destroy the ability of U.S. financial markets to provide the equity capital and long-term credit needed by business firms. Wall Street's determined and well-funded campaign forced the Roosevelt administration to make concessions that weakened both statutes.

Even so, the Securities Act and the Securities Exchange Act—as, respectively, amended and enacted in June 1934—granted broad regulatory authority to the newly established Securities and Exchange Commission over public offerings of securities, disclosures by publicly traded companies, and the activities of securities brokers, dealers, and exchanges. Without the Pecora hearings, it is very doubtful whether the Glass-Steagall Act, the Securities Act, and the Securities Exchange Act would have been enacted at all, or would have been nearly as effective and enduring.[133]

———

The Glass-Steagall Act encountered its first serious challenge in 1935. That challenge came, ironically, from Carter Glass, with the eager support of J. P. Morgan & Co. Glass had a long and cordial relationship with the House of Morgan, due to his close friendships with Thomas Lamont, Russell Leffingwell, and S. Parker Gilbert. As Treasury Secretary, Glass persuaded President Wilson to include Lamont in the U.S. delegation to the Paris Peace Conference in 1919. Leffingwell and Gilbert served as senior deputies and close advisers to Glass during his tenure as Treasury Secretary between 1918 and 1920. Glass publicly criticized Ferdinand Pecora's adversarial questioning of the House of Morgan's partners during the Senate subcommittee hearings in May 1933.[134]

In 1935, Glass charged that securities firms were not underwriting enough new bond offerings for industrial firms. Glass may have been influenced by the "bankers' strike" of late 1933 and early 1934, when securities firms reportedly abstained from underwriting new bond offerings for the purpose of discrediting the Securities Act of 1933 and undermining support for the proposed Securities Exchange Act of 1934.[135] Glass persuaded the Senate Banking Committee to include an amendment to the Glass-Steagall Act in its version of the Banking Act of 1935. Glass' proposed amendment would have allowed Fed member banks to reenter the securities business to a limited extent by underwriting "marketable" corporate bonds for sale to securities brokers and dealers (but not to banks or retail customers). Under Glass' amendment, the OCC would have supervised the bond underwriting activities of member banks.[136]

J. P. Morgan & Co. lobbied aggressively in favor of Glass' amendment. The amendment would have preserved a large portion of the House of Morgan's securities underwriting business, thereby avoiding the need to break up the firm. In addition, Russell Leffingwell urged President Roosevelt to endorse the House of Morgan's efforts to secure repeals of both the Securities Act of 1933 and the Glass-Steagall Act. Leffingwell claimed that both statutes impaired the ability of American companies to raise funds in the capital markets. However, Roosevelt firmly rebuffed Leffingwell's request.[137]

Roosevelt also wrote to Glass to express his strong opposition to Glass' amendment. Roosevelt told Glass, "I have seen more rotten practices among banks in New York City than you have. Regulations and penalties will not stop them if they want to resume speculation." Roosevelt added that "if you had my experience ... you would know that the old abuses would come back if underwriting were restored in any shape, manner or form."[138]

Senator Robert La Follette, Jr. (R-WI)—whose father ran for President as the Progressive Party's candidate in 1924—vigorously opposed Glass' amendment during the Senate debates on the Banking Act of 1935. La Follette warned that Glass' amendment represented "the nose of the camel under the tent" as well as "a first step in the backward track toward the conditions which prevailed" in the securities markets during the 1920s. La Follette reminded the Senate that "the underwriting and the sale of securities by commercial banks" in the 1920s "served to wipe out the reserves and the savings of a lifetime which millions of people in this country had accumulated." In La Follette's view, the "whole experience of the investing public and of the people of the United States during the boom period and the depression proves that [Glass'] proposal is loaded with dynamite as far as the investing public is concerned."[139]

La Follette argued that two years of experience under the Glass-Steagall Act did not provide an adequate test of the wisdom of separating commercial banks from the securities markets. According to La Follette, there was no evidence showing that securities firms were failing to underwrite bonds for creditworthy industrial firms. La Follette said many industrial firms did not want to sell bonds because they did not have enough business to justify expanding their plants and buying new equipment.[140]

La Follette warned that the OCC could not be trusted to establish strict standards for bond underwriting by banks, especially since the OCC tried to insert a provision in Glass' amendment that would have insulated banks from any liability for underwriting bonds. Senator Arthur Vandenberg (R-MI) joined La Follette in opposing Glass' amendment. Vandenberg stated that the Senate Banking Committee's "attempt to surround this limited [underwriting] privilege with boundaries and safety zones and regulations is a confession of the fact that the committee itself believes it is a very dangerous field to invade."[141]

The Senate rejected La Follette's motion to strike Glass' amendment from the Senate's version of the Banking Act of 1935. However, the House bill did not include a similar provision, and Glass' amendment became the subject of further debate by the House-Senate conference committee. The House conferees (led by Henry Steagall) and the Roosevelt administration insisted on removing Glass' amendment from the legislation, and the Senate conferees (led by Glass) acquiesced. Steagall received applause from his House colleagues when he told them that the conference committee had removed Glass' amendment from the final version of the Banking Act of 1935.[142]

———

The defeat of Glass' proposed amendment ensured the long-term survival of the Glass-Steagall Act. J. P. Morgan & Co. broke itself into two separate firms, with the House of Morgan retaining its status as a deposit-taking bank. Three Morgan partners left the firm and established a new partnership, Morgan Stanley & Co., to conduct a securities business "of the character formerly handled" by the old J. P. Morgan & Co.[143] New securities firms also emerged from affiliates that were spun off by commercial banks, including The First Boston Corporation and Brown, Harriman & Co. Several other private investment banks, including Kuhn, Loeb & Co. and Lehman Brothers, gave up their deposit-taking activities and became securities firms.[144]

Markets for corporate securities made an unsteady recovery as the country slowly pulled out of the Great Depression. The volume of new issues of U.S. corporate securities rose from $380 million in 1933 to $4.6 billion in 1936. However, new corporate issues dropped by more than half during the severe recession of 1937–38. Only $2.7 billion of new corporate securities were issued in 1940, compared with $9.4 billion in 1929. Most corporate securities issued after the Depression were bond offerings by large, established corporations with strong financial records. Public offerings of corporate stock almost disappeared, and very few bonds were issued by newly established firms and smaller companies. Issues of new corporate securities did not surpass their 1929 peak until 1952.[145]

Carter Glass criticized securities firms for excessive risk aversion in 1935, but banks behaved in a similar way. Bank deposits grew steadily after 1933 and reached $59.5 billion in 1937, surpassing their 1929 level. However, lending by banks remained severely depressed. Bank loans dropped from $41.9 billion in 1929 to $22.3 billion in 1933 and remained at that very low level through 1940. Bank loans did not exceed their 1929 level until 1948.[146]

During the 1930s, banks shifted much of their assets from loans to U.S. government securities, cash, and other highly liquid financial instruments. National City Bank chairman James Perkins told shareholders in December 1933 that "in these times the obligation of a commercial bank to its depositors, customers and shareholders is to pursue a conservative policy, maintain an adequate degree of liquidity, reduce expenses, and increase reserves." At the end of 1935, National City invested almost 60% of its deposits in government securities and discretionary (excess) reserves, up from 40% two years earlier.[147] Most banks held reserves far in excess of the Fed's required levels because "the past decade had given the banks little confidence that the Fed would act as a [strong] lender of last resort."[148]

The establishment of federal deposit insurance and the RFC's capital assistance program stabilized the banking industry but did not convince banks to adopt more liberal credit policies. Banks continued to hold excess reserves, and they extended credit only to well-established business firms and affluent individuals. In a speech to New York bankers in February 1934, RFC chairman Jesse Jones declared, "The common cry everywhere is that banks are not lending. We get it on every side."[149]

Despite appeals from Jones and other Roosevelt administration officials, most banks refused to provide credit to borrowers with less than sterling credit histories. Banks defended their low levels of lending by arguing that strong borrowers did not want new loans. Many businesses focused on maintaining high levels of capital and liquidity, and they did not want to take on the risk of incurring more debt. In March 1934, Perkins told a colleague, "It is almost impossible to lend money to anybody from whom you have a reasonable chance of getting it back."[150]

Congress passed legislation in June 1934 to increase the availability of credit for business firms. That legislation authorized the Fed and RFC to provide loans directly to businesses. However, the Fed and RFC disbursed less than half of their authorized loans by the end of 1937. Jones and other federal officials were surprised by the lack of strong demand for government loans from creditworthy firms.[151]

The disappointing results of the 1934 lending programs mirrored the Fed's dismal record under Section 13(3) of the Federal Reserve Act. Section 13(3), enacted in July 1932, empowered the Fed to extend credit directly to nonbank firms in "unusual and exigent circumstances" when those firms could not obtain bank loans. The Fed provided only $1.5 million of credit to companies under Section 13(3) between 1932 and 1936.[152]

The severe recession of 1937–38 intensified the conservatism of banks and borrowers in the same way that it increased the risk aversion of securities issuers and underwriters. The recession reinforced the Great Depression's painful lessons about the hazards of borrowing and investing. Risk aversion played an important role in delaying the nation's economic recovery during the late 1930s.[153] In his monthly letter to National City's shareholders in May 1938, Perkins stated that National City Bank would avoid "excessive risk" by making only "loans of good quality and ... high-grade investments." Perkins also reported that National City had achieved only "small success" in finding "good borrowers" for "good loans."[154]

The U.S. economy created seven million new jobs between 1933 and 1940, but eight million people (14.6% of the workforce) remained unemployed in 1940. Real (inflation-adjusted) GDP did not surpass its 1929 level until 1941, a year after the Roosevelt administration significantly increased federal defense spending to prepare for war. Per capita consumption did not equal its pre-Depression level until 1942. Thus, the U.S. economy did not fully emerge from the Depression until the Roosevelt administration substantially boosted spending on military preparedness during 1940 and 1941.[155]

The Great Depression's devastating effects on confidence within financial markets, the business community, and the household sector greatly hindered U.S. economic recovery during the 1930s. The Great Depression—like the financial crisis of 2007–09—severely disrupted markets for loans and investments, bankrupted many business firms and households, and produced much higher levels of risk aversion among creditors, borrowers, investors, and consumers. Consequently, both crises were followed by weak and protracted economic recoveries.[156]

———

During the 1980s and 1990s, several leading economists argued that Congress was mistaken in believing that securities affiliates of commercial banks played a significant role in causing the Great Depression. In 1990, George Benston published a book-length attack on the Glass-Steagall Act. He contended that "the evidence from the pre-Glass-Steagall period is totally inconsistent with the belief that banks' securities activities or investments caused them to fail or caused the financial system to collapse." He also argued that "the record does not support the belief that the pre-Glass-Steagall period was one of abuses and conflicts of interest on the part of banks involved with securities transactions, either directly or through affiliates."[157] This book reaches diametrically opposed conclusions on both points, based on my review of much of the same evidence that Benston considered as well as additional materials published since 1990.

A 1986 study by Eugene White concluded that national banks with securities affiliates or bond departments were more likely to survive the Depression, compared with national banks that did not have such securities units. However, as White recognized, most banks with securities affiliates or bond departments were "far larger than average." White's study did not control for the positive effects of larger size on bank survival. As shown in Chapter 5 and this chapter, large troubled banks (including leading universal banks) received much greater financial support from the RFC, the Fed, and other large banks, compared with struggling small banks. Therefore, White's results should not be viewed as conclusive. In addition, White did not consider the systemic and highly adverse effects of failures involving large banking organizations with securities affiliates, such as Caldwell and Company, Bank of United States, and the two largest Detroit banks.[158]

Four economic studies published during the 1990s found that domestic and foreign bonds underwritten by securities affiliates of commercial banks generally performed as well or better than comparable bonds underwritten by private investment banks. Those studies also determined that J. P. Morgan & Co. and Kuhn, Loeb & Co.—the two most prestigious private investment banks—recorded the best performance among all bond underwriters. In contrast, bonds underwritten by the securities affiliates of National City Bank and Chase National Bank had default records that were much worse than the House of Morgan and Kuhn, Loeb, and also worse than other commercial bank affiliates and some investment banks. Thus, the two commercial banks that operated the largest securities affiliates produced below-average performance records and appropriately received intense scrutiny during the Pecora hearings.[159]

In contrast to those four studies, Congress did not consider the comparative underwriting performance of commercial bank affiliates and private investment banks when it debated and passed the Glass-Steagall Act. Congress did not make such a comparison because it would not have been relevant to the primary policy goals of the Glass-Steagall Act. The statute reflected Congress's judgment that the banking industry should be strictly separated from the securities markets to keep *both* banks *and* nonbanks from using deposits as a funding source for speculation in securities. Congress also concluded that universal banks had powerful incentives to make unsound loans to support their securities operations, thereby increasing the production of risky loans as well as the likelihood of destructive credit booms and busts.

Congress further determined that the involvement of commercial banks in securities activities (1) produced competitive pressures that encouraged *both* banks *and* securities firms to underwrite and sell hazardous, high-risk securities to unsophisticated, poorly informed investors, and (2) created pervasive conflicts of interest that destroyed the ability of banks to act as objective lenders and impartial providers of investment advice. Finally, Congress wanted to promote greater economic and financial stability by establishing strong structural safeguards that would prevent contagious spillovers of risk between the banking system and the capital markets. Thus, Congress almost certainly would have adopted the Glass-Steagall Act even if it believed that securities affiliates of commercial banks had much better underwriting records during the 1920s—which they did not.[160]

7

Resurgence, Part I

Federal Agencies and Courts Opened Loopholes in the
Glass-Steagall Act During the 1980s and 1990s

The Glass-Steagall Act of 1933 contained five major provisions, which were designed
to establish a more stable financial system and prevent a recurrence of the Great
Depression. First, the statute prohibited banks from engaging in securities activities
and confined banks to their traditional business of accepting deposits, providing payments services (including clearing checks and handling foreign exchange), making
loans, providing fiduciary services, and investing in government securities. Second,
the statute barred nonbanks from accepting deposits, thereby preventing nonbanks
from engaging in the banking business.

Third, Glass-Steagall established a new program of federal deposit insurance to
reduce the risk of depositor runs on banks. Fourth, the statute stopped destructive
interest rate competition between banks by (a) prohibiting the payment of interest
on demand deposits (checking accounts) and (b) directing the Fed to impose maximum limits on interest rates paid on time deposits (including certificates of deposit
and savings accounts)—a mandate that the Fed implemented by adopting Regulation
Q. Finally, Glass-Steagall limited the growth of large banks by maintaining the existing ban on interstate branching and by allowing each state to determine the degree
to which local banks could open branches within its borders.[1]

In 1956, Congress passed the Bank Holding Company Act (BHC Act), which reinforced Glass-Steagall's policy of maintaining separate and decentralized financial
markets. The BHC Act required the Fed to approve proposed acquisitions of banks by
bank holding companies, and it authorized the Fed to supervise bank holding companies and regulate their nonbanking activities.[2] The BHC Act also prohibited bank
holding companies from affiliating with securities firms, insurance companies, and
commercial enterprises.[3]

Congress passed the BHC Act in response to the rapid growth and diversification of Transamerica and other large bank holding companies after World War II. In
1956, Transamerica controlled banks in ten states, as well as insurance companies and
commercial enterprises engaged in oil and gas development, fish canning, production of frozen foods, and manufacturing.[4] The Fed strongly opposed Transamerica's
joint control of banks, insurance companies, and commercial firms. The Fed urged
Congress to pass legislation that would limit the growth of bank holding companies
and empower the Fed to regulate their activities.[5]

Section 3(d) of the BHC Act (popularly known as the Douglas Amendment) pro-hibited bank holding companies from acquiring banks across state lines unless such acquisitions were specifically authorized by the laws of the states where the acquired banks were located. The Douglas Amendment was designed to stop the spread of multistate bank holding companies, and it effectively blocked interstate banking until the late 1970s.[6]

Section 4 of the BHC Act allowed bank holding companies, with the Fed's permis-sion, to own nonbank subsidiaries engaged in activities that were "closely related" to banking. The "closely related" standard prevented bank holding companies from owning subsidiaries involved in securities or insurance activities. Section 4 also pro-hibited bank holding companies from controlling, or being controlled by, commercial or industrial firms. Thus, the BHC Act reinforced the prudential structural barriers of the Glass-Steagall Act by separating bank holding companies from enterprises en-gaged in securities, insurance, commercial, or industrial activities.[7] After Congress passed the BHC Act, Transamerica decided to retain ownership of its commercial and insurance operations, and it therefore divested all of its banks.[8]

———

The Glass-Steagall Act and the BHC Act established a financial system consisting of three separate, independent, and culturally distinct sectors. Under that system, (1) "banks accepted deposits and extended loans to businesses and consumers," (2) "securities firms accessed 'at risk' funds of long-term investors to meet the capital needs of commercial and industrial firms," and (3) "the insurance industry collected premiums to underwrite business and individual risks, allocating the funds received to the capital markets."[9] The segmented U.S. financial system ensured that regulated depository institutions were the primary repositories for household savings and short-term funds held by business firms, while securities firms relied on longer-term commitments of invested funds, and insurance companies depended on longer-term streams of premium income. The post–New Deal system of separate financial sectors "generally prospered well into the 1970s." No major financial crisis occurred during that period.[10]

During the 1960s and 1970s, federal courts defended the post–New Deal finan-cial system and struck down attempts by federal bank regulators to undermine that system's structural boundaries. The courts overruled attempts by the Office of the Comptroller of the Currency (OCC) to expand the securities and insurance powers of national banks between 1961 and 1966.[11] The courts and Congress also prevented the Fed from expanding the permissible scope of insurance activities for bank holding companies during the 1970s and early 1980s.[12]

Glass-Steagall and the BHC Act helped to maintain a "golden age of financial stability … [b]etween the end of World War II and the 1970s."[13] The profitability of the banking industry increased from 1950 to 1970 and remained relatively high until 1980.[14] In addition, memories of widespread bank failures during the Great

Depression "traumatized bankers and instilled a deeply ingrained culture of risk-aversion" in many bankers who lived through the Depression. The average annual failure rate for banks was less than 0.1% between 1945 and 1979.[15]

In an article published in 2002, I argued that the Glass-Steagall Act and the BHC Act significantly reduced systemic risks in U.S. financial markets by establishing a clear structural separation between the banking industry and the securities and insurance sectors. As a result of that separation, risks and losses in one sector were less likely to spill over into other sectors, and financial institutions in one sector could support other sectors that were under stress. Regulators could address problems arising in one sector without needing to bail out the entire financial system.[16]

For example, major banks (with supporting loans from the Fed's discount window) provided emergency credit to issuers of commercial paper following Penn Central's default in 1970, to securities broker-dealers after the stock market crash of 1987, and to securities firms and nonfinancial corporations after Russia's debt default in 1998. During those disruptions, large banks did not suffer crippling losses because they were not deeply engaged in capital markets activities. The banking system could therefore serve as a backup source of liquidity for other sectors of the financial industry and for nonfinancial corporations. Similarly, securities firms provided an alternative source of credit to nonfinancial businesses in the early 1990s, when major banks cut back sharply on their lending after suffering severe losses during the previous decade.[17]

Economist Luigi Zingales concluded in 2012 that Glass-Steagall made the U.S. financial system "more resilient" by separating banks from the capital markets. He noted the beneficial impact of Glass-Steagall during the 1987 stock market crash and the 1990–91 banking crisis. He also pointed out that following the repeal of Glass-Steagall, "in 2008 the banking crisis and the stock market crisis infected each other, pulling down the entire economy."[18]

———

Despite the success and stability of the post–New Deal financial system, large U.S. banks greatly resented the limitations imposed by Glass-Steagall and the BHC Act. Accordingly, leaders of major banks and sympathetic regulators probed for weaknesses in both statutes, as shown by the OCC's and the Fed's unsuccessful attempts to open loopholes in the 1960s and 1970s. Securities firms and insurance companies also began to create bank-like products that could compete with the deposits and loans provided by banks.[19]

During the 1980s and 1990s, regulators opened a series of loopholes in the structural barriers established by the Glass-Steagall and BHC Acts. Those loopholes fell into four main areas: (1) removing the interest rate controls on time (non-checking) deposits imposed by the Fed's Regulation Q, (2) allowing nonbanks to offer short-term financial instruments that functioned as deposit substitutes, (3) permitting banks to "securitize" their loans by packaging them into asset-backed securities, and (4) allowing banks to provide over-the-counter derivatives that served as synthetic substitutes for securities and insurance. In combination, those four sets of regulatory loopholes significantly undermined the post–New Deal system of financial regulation.

The demise of Regulation Q: The interest rate ceilings on bank time deposits established by Regulation Q were the first major component of Glass-Steagall to disappear. Regulation Q's interest rate limits became a major problem during an extended period of high and volatile interest rates that lasted from the late 1960s until the early 1980s. Inflationary pressures began to develop during the late 1960s and early 1970s, as the Johnson and Nixon administrations ran large federal budget deficits to finance ambitious domestic spending programs as well as the Vietnam War.[20]

Growing federal budget deficits and trade imbalances weakened the dollar and forced President Nixon to suspend the convertibility of dollars into gold in August 1971. Nixon's suspension of convertibility led to the collapse of the post–World War II regime of relatively stable international currency exchange rates, established under the Bretton Woods agreement of 1944.[21] The demise of Bretton Woods resulted in much greater volatility for both interest rates and currency exchange rates.[22]

OPEC's oil embargo in 1973 caused a dramatic increase in oil prices, and the Iranian Revolution of 1979 triggered a second spike in oil prices. Rising oil prices and growing federal budget deficits helped to push U.S. inflation rates to all-time highs by 1980. Under the leadership of Chairman Paul Volcker, the Fed adopted an aggressive anti-inflation policy that propelled short-term interest rates to unprecedented levels. The short-term federal funds rate rose to 20% in early 1981 and remained as high as 14% in 1982.[23]

The foregoing developments caused short-term interest rates in the financial markets to rise far above the interest rate limits for bank deposits under Regulation Q. In addition, as discussed in the next section, federal agencies allowed nonbank financial firms to offer money market mutual funds and other short-term deposit substitutes that paid market-based interest rates. Accordingly, depositors withdrew large sums from their bank accounts and transferred those funds into higher-yielding investments outside the banking system.

In response to market pressures, large banks looked for ways to offer higher-yielding time deposits that skirted Regulation Q's limits. Walter Wriston of Citibank—the successor to National City Bank—pioneered the issuance of negotiable-rate, large-denomination certificates of deposit (CDs) through Citibank's domestic branches in the 1960s. Citibank also accepted Eurodollar deposits through its overseas branches. Both types of deposits paid interest rates that were higher than Regulation Q's limits. Citibank acted without advance approval from the Fed, but the Fed acquiesced in Citibank's evasion of Regulation Q, and other big banks quickly followed Citibank's example.[24] Negotiable CDs and Eurodollars were the first of many regulatory avoidance techniques that big banks used to break down Glass-Steagall's constraints.

The high inflation rates of the 1970s and early 1980s threatened the survival of the savings and loan (thrift) industry. Savings and loans were specialized depository institutions that accepted savings deposits and made home mortgage loans. Many thrift institutions faced insolvency in the early 1980s, due to a fundamental mismatch between the yields and maturities for their assets and liabilities. Congress phased out Regulation Q's limits on deposit interest rates for banks and thrifts between 1980 and 1986. The repeal of Regulation Q enabled thrifts to attract and retain more deposits. However, it also significantly increased the interest rates (and costs) of deposits at a time when thrifts' primary assets were low-yielding thirty-year fixed-rate mortgages. As a result, many thrifts became unprofitable and suffered large losses.[25]

Congress tried to solve the thrifts' problems by deregulating their powers. In 1982, Congress passed legislation that allowed thrifts and banks to offer adjustable-rate mortgages (ARMs)—mortgages with floating, market-based interest rates. The 1982 statute also authorized thrifts and banks to offer "alternative" mortgages with more flexible and "affordable" financing terms, including (1) mortgages with low "teaser" introductory interest rates for the first two or three years, followed by significantly higher rates, and (2) mortgages with interest-only payments or even lower payments for the first few years, followed by much larger periodic payments or "balloon" payments. Those "innovative" mortgages created a strong risk of "payment shock" for borrowers when their introductory low-payment periods expired.[26]

The 1982 statute preempted state laws that restricted the terms of adjustable-rate or alternative mortgages. Congress and federal courts also preempted state usury laws that imposed maximum limits on the interest rates that thrifts and banks could charge on home mortgages and other consumer loans. The 1982 statute, along with similar deregulatory laws enacted by many states, allowed thrifts to engage in a wide array of nontraditional activities—including loans to developers of residential and commercial real estate projects as well as investments in high-yield debt securities (junk bonds), real estate projects, and other business ventures (such as casinos, hotels, ski resorts, and thoroughbred horse farms). The percentage of thrift assets represented by residential mortgages dropped from 80% to 56% between 1980 and 1986.[27]

Supporters of deregulation claimed that the newly granted powers would enable thrifts to "grow out of their problems." Federal and state thrift regulators also adopted weak accounting standards and provided supervisory forbearance that allowed many insolvent and undercapitalized thrifts to remain in business during the 1980s. Many weak thrifts "gambled for resurrection" by expanding into high-risk nontraditional activities. Hundreds of those thrifts subsequently failed. The federal government spent $160 billion to resolve the thrift crisis, with $132 billion paid by taxpayers and the remainder covered by federal deposit insurance.[28]

The banking industry also suffered from severe problems during the 1980s and early 1990s. The thrift and banking crises were closely connected to a series of regional booms and busts in residential and commercial real estate markets. Boom-and-bust cycles occurred first in the "oil patch" states of Texas and Oklahoma during the early and mid-1980s, followed by Florida, the Mid-Atlantic region, and New England between 1985 and 1991 and by Arizona and California during the early 1990s. The residential and commercial real estate busts of the 1980s and early 1990s were regional in nature, since thrifts and banks were subject to legal restrictions on geographic expansion and a nationwide market for residential and commercial mortgage loans had not yet developed. As a result of those regional real estate crises, home prices "declined nationally by 2.5% from July 1990 to February 1992—the first such fall since the Depression."[29]

Jennifer Taub identified several key components of deregulation during the 1980s that later contributed to the destructive real estate lending boom of the 2000s. Adjustable-rate mortgages, alternative mortgages, investments in high-risk securities, and preemption of state usury laws and other consumer protection laws all played important roles during the 1980s and were equally important during the nonprime mortgage boom of the 2000s. Bailouts and regulatory forbearance for large troubled financial institutions that were considered "too big to fail" were prominent features of the thrift and banking crises of the 1980s, and they became core elements of the federal government's rescues of financial giants during 2007–09.[30]

Nonbank deposit substitutes and the rise of shadow banking: The second major attack on the Glass-Steagall Act was the creation of short-term deposit substitutes, which enabled nonbank financial firms to operate as "shadow banks." In the early 1970s, the securities industry introduced an "innovative" financial concept known as the money market mutual fund (MMMF). MMMFs were short-term mutual funds that offered deposit-like features but were not subject to the interest-rate limits of Regulation Q. Investors who bought shares in MMMFs could redeem their investments at any time, based on a fixed net asset value (NAV) equal to the original purchase price of $1 per share. MMMFs were not regulated or federally insured like bank deposits, but they functioned like deposits in allowing withdrawal on demand at par (100% of the amount invested). The Securities and Exchange Commission (SEC) supervised MMMFs and required them to invest in supposedly safe short-term securities, such as U.S. Treasury bonds, highly rated commercial paper, and bank CDs. Investors expected that institutional sponsors of MMMFs would provide any financial backing needed to ensure redemption of their shares at the fixed NAV of $1 per share.[31]

In 1977, Merrill Lynch, a leading securities firm, created the cash management account (CMA), which allowed investors to write checks against the funds they held in Merrill Lynch's MMMFs. Other securities firms quickly added check-writing features to their own MMMFs. Thus, after 1977 MMMFs offered customers the principal functional attributes of bank checking accounts, including redemption at par on demand and the ability to transfer funds by writing checks. MMMFs were exempt from Regulation Q because they were classified and regulated as mutual funds (equity investments) rather than deposits. MMMFs could pay significantly higher yields because they did not have to pay deposit insurance premiums or to satisfy capital or reserve requirements like those imposed on banks. Business firms and consumers rapidly shifted their short-term funds from bank deposits to MMMFs, and the total volume of MMMFs mushroomed from $3 billion in 1977 to $235 billion in 1982.[32]

As Morgan Ricks explained, the emergence of MMMFs "represented a deliberate end-run around the U.S. deposit banking system," and the SEC "abetted" that evasion by exempting MMMFs from many of the rules governing mutual funds.[33] The most important of those exemptions allowed MMMFs to redeem their shares based on a stable (fixed) NAV of $1 per share, instead of requiring MMMFs, like other mutual funds, to redeem their shares based on the funds' current market values.[34] The fixed NAV, which permitted redemption at par, was crucial because MMMFs "want[ed] investors to view shares in an MMF as close substitutes for savings and time deposits at commercial banks and other depository institutions."[35]

In October 1979, Morris Crawford, who was chairman of the Bowery Savings Bank of New York, sent a letter to the U.S. Department of Justice (DOJ) and the SEC alleging that MMMFs with check-writing privileges were illegal deposits and therefore violated Section 21 of the Glass-Steagall Act.[36] The DOJ rejected Crawford's claim and ruled that an investor in an MMMF was not a "depositor." According to the DOJ, each investor in an MMMF owned an equity interest with "the potential for capital gain or loss on his investment." The DOJ determined that an investor's ability to "transfer his ownership" in an MMMF to other parties by writing checks was "a mere formality" and did not change "the substance of his status as [equity] owner."[37] The DOJ's highly formalistic ruling ignored the practical reality that MMMFs with CMA features were functionally equivalent to checking accounts and were viewed as such by consumers.[38]

The rapid growth of MMMFs—which federal regulators did not try to stop—provided a convenient rationale for abolishing Regulation Q. As indicated earlier, Congress phased out Regulation Q in the early 1980s and allowed banks and thrifts to offer deposit accounts with market-based yields similar to MMMFs.[39] However, MMMFs did not have to pay deposit insurance premiums or comply with bank capital or reserve requirements. Due to their substantially lower regulatory costs, MMMFs could still pay significantly higher yields than comparable bank deposits. The competitive advantages of MMMFs allowed them to keep growing, and their total assets increased from $235 billion in 1982 to $740 billion in 1995, $1.8 trillion in 2000, and $3.8 trillion in 2007.[40]

The continued growth of MMMFs encouraged the expansion of the shadow banking system—a parallel financial system in which securities firms and other nonbank financial companies provided bank-like services. In the shadow banking system, nonbanks obtained short-term funds from investors by offering deposit substitutes, and nonbanks used those funds to provide longer-term loans to consumers and businesses.[41] For example, securities firms established MMMFs to attract large amounts of short-term funds from consumers and businesses. In turn, MMMFs became leading investors in commercial paper and securities repurchase agreements (repos).

Commercial paper is a short-term debt security issued by a business or financial company, usually with a maturity of ninety days or less.[42] A repo is a short-term, secured lending arrangement in which the lender (such as an MMMF) provides a cash loan and the borrower (such as a securities firm) provides collateral in the form of securities acceptable to the lender. The amount of a repo loan is equal to the market value of the collateral minus a "haircut" (discount) based on the lender's assessment of the collateral's risk. A repo typically lasts for one day or a few days. Upon the expiration of a repo's term, the parties either renew (roll over) the repo loan or the lender returns the collateral and the borrower repays the cash loan with interest.[43]

MMMFs were the largest purchasers of commercial paper and among the largest cash lenders for repos during the 1990s and 2000s.[44] As MMMFs grew, so did the commercial paper and repo markets. Commercial paper and repos were two of the most important short-term funding sources for securities firms and other nonbank financial companies. The volume of outstanding U.S. commercial paper increased from less than $50 billion in 1975 to $560 billion in 1990, $1.3 trillion in 2000, and $2 trillion in 2007.[45] The volume of repos entered into by large U.S. securities firms rose from $110 billion in 1981 to $800 billion in 1990, $2.5 trillion in 2002, and $4 trillion in 2007.[46]

MMMFs, commercial paper, and repos functioned as "shadow deposits" and provided short-term funding that allowed shadow banks—securities firms and other nonbank financial companies—to originate or purchase mortgage loans and other longer-term loans.[47] The growth of shadow deposits and shadow banks undermined Glass-Steagall's structural boundaries because it allowed "capital and money markets to amplify and replicate . . . the functions of traditional banks."[48]

In retrospect, it is clear that rising inflation rates during the 1970s did not force policymakers to allow nonbanks to offer deposit substitutes that funded the shadow banking system. Congress and federal bank regulators could have removed or raised Regulation Q's interest rate ceilings, thereby permitting banks to pay higher rates to depositors in an inflationary environment. At the same time, federal regulators could have enforced the prohibition in Section 21 of the Glass-Steagall Act by preventing nonbanks from issuing short-term financial instruments that were functional equivalents of deposits. Thus, policymakers could have remained faithful to Glass-Steagall's vision of a financial system in which banks were the exclusive recipients of short-term funds that were equivalent to "money claims" because they received explicit or implicit government backing. Federal regulators could have invoked Section 21 to stop securities firms and other nonbanks from issuing deposit substitutes like MMMFs, short-term commercial paper, and short-term repos.[49]

Federal regulators never chose the available option of prohibiting deposit substitutes, and they never required nonbanks to finance their operations in a more stable and resilient manner by issuing stock and longer-term debt securities or by accepting loans from banks. For example, it would not have been possible for MMMFs to offer check-writing privileges without clearing their checks through banks. However, the Fed never used its authority to stop banks from clearing checks written on MMMMF accounts.[50]

Instead of restraining the growth of markets for deposit substitutes, federal officials supported and encouraged those markets. In 1970, the Fed stabilized the commercial paper market after Penn Central's default on its commercial paper caused a panic. The Fed provided $600 million of discount window loans to large banks and urged them to extend credit to companies that could not renew their commercial paper. The Fed also injected liquidity into the financial markets by making open-market purchases of Treasury securities. Moreover, the Fed announced that it stood ready to provide credit directly to companies that lost access to the commercial paper market if they could not obtain bank loans. The Fed's full-scale support for the commercial paper market in 1970 led market participants to expect that the Fed would intervene to maintain the stability of that market during subsequent crises.[51]

Similarly, the Fed stabilized the repo market in 1982 after the Lombard-Wall securities firm defaulted on its outstanding repos. To prevent a panic in the repo market, the Fed significantly increased its loans of government securities to primary dealers—financial institutions that purchased and sold Treasury securities in transactions with the New York Fed. The Fed also encouraged Congress to include a repo-friendly provision in the Bankruptcy Amendments Act of 1984.

That 1984 law created an exemption from the "automatic stay" provisions of the Bankruptcy Code for repos that were collateralized by government securities, bank certificates of deposit, or bankers' acceptances. The automatic stay provisions of the Bankruptcy Code generally impose a freeze on claims filed by creditors against a bankrupt debtor until the bankruptcy court determines the debtor's obligation to pay each of those claims. The 1984 exemption for qualifying repos created a "safe harbor," which allowed lenders for those repos to enforce their contract rights and seize their collateral immediately after a borrower defaulted, without any restriction under the bankruptcy laws. The existence of that safe harbor encouraged further expansion of the repo market.[52]

After banks obtained permission from the Fed to establish subsidiaries with limited securities powers in 1987 (as described in the next section of this chapter), those securities subsidiaries obtained funding by issuing their own deposit substitutes in the shadow banking system. Large banks with securities subsidiaries and Wall Street securities firms both attracted huge volumes of short-term funding by selling commercial paper and entering into repos and other short-term securities lending arrangements.[53] The total volume of short-term shadow banking liabilities grew from less than $500 billion in 1980 to approximately $1 trillion in 1990, $6 trillion in 2000, and more than $12 trillion in 2007.[54]

When the shadow banking system reached its apex in 2007, the total volume of deposit substitutes held by securities subsidiaries of large banks and by independent securities firms substantially exceeded the amount of traditional deposits held by FDIC-insured institutions.[55] As Morgan Ricks pointed out, the rapid increase in shadow bank funding "can be understood as an increasing privatization of the broad money supply in the precrisis years."[56]

The growing reliance of major banks and securities firms on short-term deposit substitutes exposed them to severe liquidity problems when investors engaged in panicked runs on MMMFs, commercial paper, and repos during 2007 and 2008.[57]

To prevent the collapse of big banks and securities firms, the Fed, FDIC, and Treasury provided a "360 [degree] backstop" for shadow bank liabilities through an array of "liquidity facilities, large-scale asset purchases and guarantee schemes." Those ad hoc rescue programs served as "modern-day equivalents of deposit insurance."[58] The collapse of shadow banking markets during the financial crisis and the federal government's massive bailout of those markets revealed the enormous costs associated with the decisions by federal authorities *not* to enforce Glass-Steagall's prohibition on deposit-taking by nonbanks.[59]

Securitization of loans: Securitization of loans was the third major line of attack on the structural barriers of the Glass-Steagall and BHC Acts. The financial industry and financial regulators eagerly embraced securitization as a "financial innovation" that helped them to undermine those barriers. Securitization is a process through which loans and other payment obligations (receivables) are packaged and transformed into various categories of asset-backed securities (ABS), such as residential mortgage-backed securities (RMBS). The process of securitization has been extensively analyzed elsewhere, and only a brief summary will be provided here.[60]

The first step in a securitization transaction occurs when the sponsor—usually a large bank or securities firm—originates or purchases loans, pools the loans, and transfers the loan pool to a special-purpose entity (SPE), which is usually organized as a trust. The SPE promises to pay for the loans after it has finished securitizing the loan pool. The SPE then issues ABS, which give investors the right to receive designated streams of income from payments made on the pooled loans. The SPE hires a securities broker-dealer (typically the sponsor or its affiliate) to underwrite the sale of ABS to investors. After the underwriting has been completed, the SPE transfers the proceeds from the sale of ABS to the sponsor to pay for the pooled loans. The SPE manages the loan pool and, in many cases, hires the sponsor (or another of its affiliates) to act as servicing agent for the pooled loans. The sponsor, the SPE, the ABS underwriter, and the servicing agent all receive substantial fees for their roles in the securitization process. If all of those entities are controlled by the same universal bank, that bank generates very large fees by conducting the entire securitization process within its own organization.[61]

Government-sponsored enterprises (GSEs)—including the Federal National Mortgage Association (Fannie Mae), the Federal Home Loan Mortgage Corporation (Freddie Mac), and the Government National Mortgage Association (Ginnie Mae)— began to securitize home mortgages in the late 1960s and early 1970s.[62] At first, GSEs structured their "agency" RMBS as pass-through certificates that gave investors pro rata interests in the pooled mortgages. However, pass-through certificates were not attractive to many investors because they were long-term instruments that were subject to prepayment risk (the risk that mortgages in the securitized pool would be prepaid before they matured) and interest rate risk (the risk that interest rates would rise after the RMBS were issued and reduce their market value).[63]

To attract a broader group of investors for RMBS, Lawrence Fink of First Boston and Lewis Ranieri of Salomon Brothers developed collateralized mortgage obligations

(CMOs) for GSEs in the early 1980s. A CMO is a structured finance vehicle whose securities are divided into multiple tranches. Those tranches offer investors differing rights and priorities for payments of income and principal from the pooled mortgages. Junior tranches of CMOs receive higher payoffs but are exposed to greater risks of losses from prepayments or defaults on the pooled mortgages. In contrast, senior tranches of CMOs receive lower yields but also benefit from greater protection against losses, because junior tranches bear losses before the senior tranches do.[64]

Securities firms fought hard to prevent GSEs from capturing the entire RMBS market. Ranieri helped the Reagan administration to draft legislation that would allow securities firms to underwrite "private-label" RMBS that could compete with the agency RMBS issued by GSEs. In 1984, Congress included many of Ranieri's ideas in the Secondary Mortgage Market Enhancement Act. The 1984 law exempted private-label RMBS from state securities laws and permitted insurance companies and pension funds to invest in private-label RMBS with high credit ratings. Two years later, the Tax Reform Act of 1986 exempted tranches of private-label RMBS from the threat of double taxation.[65] Both statutes encouraged securities firms to underwrite private-label RMBS as well as other ABS backed by a wide variety of obligations, including credit card receivables, automobile loans, boat loans, commercial real estate loans, home equity loans, student loans, and equipment leases.[66]

———

Commercial banks were determined to follow the path blazed by securities firms in securitizing private-label RMBS and ABS. However, two Supreme Court decisions stood in their way. In 1966, Citibank obtained a ruling from the Office of the Comptroller of the Currency (OCC) that allowed the bank to create an investment fund for its customers. Citibank pooled and managed investments made by Citibank's customers, who received participating "units" in the fund. Citibank's fund amounted to "a mutual fund by another name."[67]

In a 1971 decision—*Investment Co. Institute v. Camp*—the Supreme Court struck down the OCC's ruling and held that Citibank's investment fund ran afoul of the Glass-Steagall Act.[68] The Court determined that the "units of participation" offered by Citibank were "securities" within the meaning of the Glass-Steagall Act. Accordingly, Citibank engaged in an unlawful underwriting of securities when it created the fund and sold units to customers.[69]

The Supreme Court identified a number of "subtle hazards" and "financial dangers" that the Glass-Steagall Act was intended to prevent. As explained in Chapter 6, Congress believed that banks would face intolerable conflicts of interest if they had a "salesman's stake" in marketing securities that were underwritten by them or their affiliates. Banks would be tempted to make unsound loans to support the sale of those securities, and banks would also be inclined to provide biased investment advice to persuade their customers to purchase those securities. In addition, Congress feared that banks would lose their "reputation" and "customer good will" if they encouraged customers to buy unsound investments underwritten by them or their affiliates. The Supreme Court concluded that Citibank's investment fund created a clear risk that all of those hazards could occur.[70]

Thirteen years after *ICI v. Camp*, the Supreme Court issued a similar decision in *Bankers Trust I*.[71] That 1984 decision struck down a Fed order that allowed Bankers Trust to sell to investors commercial paper that was issued by Bankers Trust's corporate clients. The Fed argued that commercial paper was not a "security" under Glass-Steagall because it was a debt obligation that resembled a commercial loan. However, the Court adopted a broad definition of "security" in *Bankers Trust I*, as it had done in *ICI v. Camp*, and rejected the Fed's attempt to distinguish commercial paper from other types of debt securities.[72] Quoting *Camp*, the Court explained in *Bankers Trust I* that the Glass-Steagall Act considered "the promotional incentives of investment banking and the investment banker's pecuniary stake" in selling securities as creating unacceptable risks to "prudent and disinterested commercial banking" and "public confidence in the commercial banking system."[73]

Notwithstanding their defeats in *ICI v. Camp* and *Bankers Trust I*, leading banks and federal regulators continued to challenge Glass-Steagall's structural barriers. Following *Bankers Trust I*, the Fed issued a revised order, which allowed Bankers Trust to sell commercial paper under a different legal rationale. Instead of claiming that commercial paper was not a "security," the Fed's revised order stated that Bankers Trust would not engage in a prohibited "underwriting" as long as the bank sold commercial paper only in private placements to sophisticated institutional buyers. The U.S. Court of Appeals for the District of Columbia Circuit upheld the Fed's revised order in *Bankers Trust II*, and the Supreme Court denied further review.[74]

The D.C. Circuit stated that it owed "substantial deference" to the Fed's revised order in light of the Supreme Court's 1984 decision in *Chevron*.[75] *Chevron* held that courts should follow a two-step analysis when they review interpretations of statutes by federal agencies. Under the first step of *Chevron*, a court should determine whether Congress has expressed a clear intent on "the precise question at issue." If so, the court should require the agency to follow that intent.[76] If, however, the statute is "silent or ambiguous" on the relevant issue, the court should apply the second step of *Chevron*. Under the second step, the court should defer to any "reasonable" interpretation by the agency, even if the court would have reached a different conclusion on its own.[77] As a practical matter, *Chevron* deference gives a federal agency very broad discretion to say "yes" when the agency addresses a question about the scope of its authority, as long as Congress has not explicitly said "no" in addressing the same question.[78]

Applying the first step of *Chevron*, the D.C. Circuit stated that Glass-Steagall was "ambiguous" on the question of whether banks could sell commercial paper in private placements to institutional investors.[79] Applying the second step of *Chevron*, the D.C. Circuit deferred to the Fed's "reasonable" determination that Bankers Trust's sales of commercial paper in private placements did not constitute an "underwriting" of securities that would violate Glass-Steagall.[80] The D.C. Circuit concluded that the Fed was reasonable in construing Glass-Steagall as prohibiting banks from making public offerings of securities but *not* private placements.[81]

The D.C. Circuit acknowledged that private placements of commercial paper would involve at least one of the "subtle hazards" identified by the Supreme Court in *Camp* and *Bankers Trust I*—namely, the danger that a bank would lose its "reputation" and the "confidence" of its customers if it sold them unsound securities.[82] However, the D.C. Circuit dismissed the significance of that risk. The court concluded that "an agency's interpretation that impairs one of the statute's purposes but not others may surely nonetheless be reasonable" under *Chevron*.[83] The D.C. Circuit's decision to disregard potential reputational risks from private placements proved to be a very serious error. Leading banks paid large fines and civil settlements after they sold huge volumes of toxic collateralized debt obligations (CDOs) to institutional investors in private placements under the SEC's Rule 144A.[84]

Bankers Trust II provided a blueprint for subsequent federal court decisions, which upheld agency rulings opening numerous additional loopholes in the structural barriers established by the Glass-Steagall and BHC Acts. The courts repeatedly invoked *Chevron* deference as a rationale for affirming agency rulings that relied on highly creative interpretations of ambiguous statutory provisions to circumvent those barriers.[85]

————

In April 1987, the Fed issued its *Citicorp* order, which allowed bank holding companies to establish "Section 20 subsidiaries." The Fed's order allowed Section 20 subsidiaries to underwrite and trade to a limited extent in four designated categories of "bank-ineligible securities," which were *not* lawful for banks to underwrite or trade in directly under the Glass-Steagall Act.[86] Those bank-ineligible securities were municipal revenue bonds, private-label RMBS, ABS backed by consumer loan receivables, and commercial paper. The Fed's *Citicorp* order explained how far Section 20 subsidiaries could go in underwriting and trading those bank-ineligible securities.[87]

The Fed stated that subsidiaries of bank holding companies would not violate Section 20 of the Glass-Steagall Act as long as they were not "engaged principally" in underwriting or trading ineligible securities.[88] Accordingly, Section 20 subsidiaries were required to focus most of their activities on underwriting and investing in bank-eligible government securities. The Fed stated, however, that Section 20 subsidiaries could underwrite or trade the four designated types of bank-ineligible securities as long as those activities did not account for more than 5% of their gross revenues.[89]

The Fed approved its *Citicorp* order by a 3–2 vote, with dissenting statements from Chairman Paul Volcker and Governor Wayne Angell.[90] Volcker and Angell warned that "the interpretation adopted by the majority would appear to make feasible ... the affiliations of banks with some of the principal underwriting firms or investment houses of the country. Such a legal result, we feel, is inconsistent with the intent of Congress in passing the Glass-Steagall Act."[91]

Volcker decided not to seek a third term as Fed chairman, and his failure to block the *Citicorp* order was evidently a factor in his decision.[92] Volcker's dissenting statement in *Citicorp* reflected his opposition to any "rush to deregulation" until Congress approved an "overall blueprint for change" that would preserve "the stability and impartiality" of the banking system and prevent "conflicts of interest and undue concentrations of banking resources."[93] President Reagan appointed Alan Greenspan to succeed Volcker, in part because Greenspan eagerly supported the Reagan administration's agenda for deregulating the financial industry.[94]

The securities industry challenged the *Citicorp* order, but the Second Circuit upheld the order, and the Supreme Court denied further review.[95] The Second Circuit acknowledged that the Fed's order would help to "dismantle the wall of separation installed ... by the Glass-Steagall Act."[96] However, like the D.C. Circuit in *Bankers Trust II*, the Second Circuit determined that *Chevron* required deference to the Fed's "reasonable" interpretation of an "ambiguous" statute.[97]

In view of *Chevron*, the Second Circuit said that it could not judge the wisdom of the Fed's position based on "[George] Santayana's notion that those who will not learn from the past are condemned to repeat it."[98] While the court clearly recognized the applicability of Santayana's warning, it felt compelled to apply *Chevron*'s highly deferential standard of review. The court's reference to Santayana's admonition proved to be tragically prescient.

The Second Circuit stated that Section 20 of Glass-Steagall was ambiguous on the question of whether banks could affiliate with companies that carried on a securities business but were *not* "engaged principally" in underwriting or trading bank-ineligible securities.[99] Given that ambiguity, the court concluded that the Fed was "reasonable" in allowing bank holding companies to establish Section 20 subsidiaries that derived 5% or less of their gross revenues from bank-ineligible securities activities.[100]

Under Alan Greenspan's leadership, the Fed steadily expanded the scope of activities allowed for Section 20 subsidiaries. In 1989, the Fed permitted Section 20 subsidiaries to underwrite and trade all types of debt and equity securities, and the Fed also raised the revenue limit on bank-ineligible securities operations to 10%. The D.C. Circuit upheld the Fed's order, emphasizing the deference the court owed to the Fed's determinations.[101] By 1996, Section 20 subsidiaries controlled a fifth of the U.S. debt underwriting market and 2% of the equity underwriting market.[102]

In 1996, the Fed raised the revenue limit for bank-ineligible securities activities to 25%. Soon thereafter, the Fed removed several firewalls that imposed tight restrictions on cross-marketing and other transactions between bank holding companies and their Section 20 subsidiaries.[103] Large domestic and foreign banks responded to the Fed's liberalized Section 20 orders by acquiring dozens of small and midsized securities firms. By 1998, forty-five bank holding companies—including all twenty-five of the largest U.S. banks—owned Section 20 subsidiaries.[104]

The OCC pursued its own campaign to allow national banks to securitize residential mortgages and other loans directly, instead of relying on their bank holding company affiliates. The OCC's efforts were part of its heated rivalry with Alan Greenspan's Fed for the position of deregulator-in-chief of the banking industry. The OCC and the Fed wanted to win the allegiance of the largest banking organizations by demonstrating that they were "friendly" regulators and dedicated champions of deregulation.[105]

In 1987, the OCC upheld the authority of Security Pacific National Bank to securitize residential mortgages that the bank originated, and to sell private-label RMBS derived from pools of those mortgages. The securities industry sued the OCC, and a federal district court struck down the OCC's order. However, the Second Circuit reversed the district court's decision and reinstated the OCC's order.[106]

The district court determined that Security Pacific's issuance of RMBS to investors was not a "mere sale of assets" and instead constituted a prohibited "underwriting" of "securities" under Section 21 of Glass-Steagall.[107] The district court pointed out that (1) the pooled mortgages held by each securitization SPE trust had "a separate identity" from the bank's assets, and (2) the bank could choose to "relegate to the trust those mortgages which it saw as most likely to be problems."[108] In addition, the bank would have "an interest in the success of the sales" of RMBS, thereby tempting the bank to become an "advocate" in persuading its customers to buy RMBS.[109] After considering the Glass-Steagall Act's purposes, the district court concluded that the OCC's order "does not take sufficient account" of "the benefits that the bank hopes to gain" from selling RMBS.[110]

The Second Circuit overturned the district court's decision and upheld the OCC's ruling. Applying "principles of deferential review" under *Chevron*, the Second Circuit agreed with the OCC that Security Pacific's sale of RMBS fell within the "business of banking" under Section 16 of Glass-Steagall, as either a direct or "incidental" component of the bank's authority to sell mortgages it originated.[111] The Second Circuit also agreed with the OCC that it was "unlikely" Security Pacific would "make unsound loans so as to encourage purchase of the [RMBS]."[112] The Second Circuit further concluded that investors would be adequately protected by "federal securities laws [that] require full disclosure of all material facts concerning the [RMBS]."[113]

The OCC and the Second Circuit were completely mistaken in assuming that (1) bank underwriters of RMBS would *not* have financial incentives to originate or purchase unsound mortgages for securitization and (2) offering materials for RMBS would provide full disclosure to investors. Those mistaken assumptions had massive costs and far-reaching consequences. As the securitization trend gained momentum after 2000, banks and other lenders originated and securitized huge volumes of poorly underwritten, high-risk subprime and Alt-A mortgages. The enormous fees that lenders could earn by originating and selling nonprime mortgages for securitization created perverse incentives, which caused lenders to disregard sound underwriting standards. Banks and other lenders also used misleading and fraudulent offering materials to sell toxic nonprime RMBS and related CDOs to investors. The SEC did not compel underwriters of RMBS and CDOs to provide investors with timely and detailed information about the mortgage pools that backed the RMBS and

CDOs they purchased. As a result, most investors could not protect themselves from the widespread fraud that occurred.[114]

The OCC relied on *Security Pacific* to justify subsequent rulings that allowed national banks to securitize a wide range of consumer and commercial loans. The OCC also permitted national banks to securitize loans that they did not originate but instead purchased from other lenders. In 1996, the OCC authorized national banks to invest in "marketable" private-label RMBS, ABS, CDOs, and commercial mortgage-backed securities (CMBS).[115] Thus, the OCC provided carte blanche for a wide range of securitization activities by national banks, just as the Fed had done for Section 20 subsidiaries of bank holding companies.

The Fed's and OCC's rulings spurred a rapid growth in securitization activities by banking organizations during the 1990s. The total amount of outstanding private-label RMBS and other ABS rose from less than $100 billion in 1990 to $900 billion in 1999, and large banks accounted for a major share of that growth.[116] Securitization offered multiple benefits to banks in the form of reduced capital requirements, new sources of wholesale funding from the capital markets, greatly expanded fee income, and the ability to move credit risks off their balance sheets.[117]

In 1999, Congress passed the Gramm-Leach-Bliley Act, which removed all remaining restrictions on affiliations between banks and securities firms.[118] The largest banks and securities firms quickly established vertically integrated securitization factories. Those factories included every step in the securitization process, from loan origination to the creation and marketing of RMBS, CDOs, and other mortgage-related securities.[119] As that process unfolded, the outstanding volume of private-label, mortgage-related securities expanded from $1.6 trillion in 2001 to $3 trillion in 2004 and more than $6 trillion in 2007.[120]

Over-the-counter derivatives: Over-the-counter (OTC) derivatives were the fourth major field in which large financial institutions and federal regulators used "financial innovation" to break down the structural barriers that separated banks from the securities and insurance industries. Derivatives are financial contracts whose value is determined by reference to some underlying asset, obligation, index, or rate (the "referenced factor"). Widely used referenced factors include equity stocks, equity indexes, debt obligations, commodities, interest rates, and currency exchange rates. Derivatives are typically used either to hedge against particular risks or to speculate about the direction of future changes in the values of referenced factors.[121]

Exchange-traded derivatives are standardized contracts that are publicly traded on futures and options exchanges. In contrast, OTC derivatives are customized contracts that are privately negotiated between "dealers" (large financial institutions that specialize in creating and marketing OTC derivatives) and "end-users," such as commercial and industrial firms and institutional investors.[122] The most widely used categories of derivatives are (1) a forward, in which the buyer is obligated to purchase, and the seller is required to deliver, some type of commodity or other physical asset at a future date, (2) a swap, in which the parties agree to exchange streams of payments based on the future value of the referenced factor, and (3) an option, in which the option seller gives the option buyer the right—but not the duty—to buy or sell the referenced factor at an agreed price on or before a specified future date.[123]

During the 1970s, the volatility of interest rates, currency rates, and commodity prices increased significantly, due to rising inflation rates and the breakdown of the Bretton Woods system of pegged currency exchange rates. In the post–Bretton Woods environment, exchange-traded futures and options based on interest rates, currency exchange rates, and commodity prices became popular vehicles for hedging (risk management) and speculation.[124]

In 1974, Congress established the Commodity Futures Trading Commission (CFTC) to supervise markets for exchange-traded futures and options under the Commodity Exchange Act (CEA). The CEA, as amended in 1974, required that certain types of derivatives must be traded on futures or options exchanges regulated by the CFTC.[125] However, the 1974 legislation also included a clause known as the "Treasury Amendment," which allowed other types of financial contracts to be traded privately in over-the-counter transactions. When OTC derivatives began to emerge in the early 1980s, their status was highly uncertain under the 1974 legislation.[126]

Markets for OTC currency exchange swaps and OTC interest rate swaps grew rapidly during the 1980s. The largest U.S. banks and securities firms captured the lion's share of both markets.[127] In 1992, Congress authorized the CFTC to exempt certain types of OTC swaps from regulation under the CEA. The CFTC responded by issuing a 1993 rule, which exempted OTC swaps from regulation if they were not "standardized," were not traded on any exchange, and were entered into by "eligible swap participants." Eligible swap participants under the 1993 exemption included regulated financial institutions, qualified business firms, state and local governments, institutional investors, and wealthy individuals.[128] However, OTC derivatives dealers and end-users had serious concerns about the precise scope of the 1993 exemption as well as the risk that the CFTC could change its policy and modify or rescind the exemption.[129]

―――――

The OCC allowed national banks to engage in a steadily widening array of derivatives activities during the 1980s and 1990s. Saule Omarova has provided a comprehensive analysis of the OCC's step-by-step campaign to expand the derivatives powers of national banks, and only a brief overview will be provided here.[130]

In 1987 and 1988, the OCC permitted national banks to enter into OTC swaps and exchange-traded derivatives based on interest rates, currency rates, and commodity price indexes for precious metals. The OCC argued that those derivatives were comparable to the traditional powers of national banks to discount promissory notes and trade in foreign currencies and precious metals under the National Bank Act.[131]

The OCC authorized a much broader range of commodity-related derivatives for national banks between 1987 and 1992.[132] The OCC claimed that commodity swaps were "functionally equivalent" to the interest rate swaps and currency swaps that the

OCC had previously approved for national banks. In fact, the risks embodied in commodity swaps were much different from the risks created by interest rate and currency swaps.[133] In the mid-1990s, the OCC developed a "financial intermediation" theory of banking powers, which created a virtually limitless scope for the activities that national banks could conduct. Based on that theory, the OCC claimed that the "business of banking" encompassed "virtually any ... financial activity for customers' account[s] involving exchanges of payments and assumption or transfer of financial risk."[134]

The OCC's step-by-step expansion of derivatives powers was exemplified by a series of rulings that (1) allowed national banks to offer deposits with payoffs based on stock indexes, (2) permitted banks to use equity swaps to hedge their risk exposures from such deposits, and (3) authorized banks to buy equity stocks to hedge their risk exposures from equity swaps. In 1988, the OCC allowed Chase Manhattan National Bank (Chase) to offer certificates of deposit (CDs) that paid "interest" based on the performance of the S&P 500 index. The OCC ruled that Chase's offering of "equity-linked" CDs was a lawful exercise of the bank's authority to accept "deposits," even though Chase was using a stock index to determine the amount of gains that would be paid on those deposits.[135]

The OCC's ruling did not consider the crucial fact that equity-linked CDs created significant stock market risks for Chase. Chase paid CD holders the amount of any increase in the S&P 500 index during the term of their CDs, while Chase bore the risk of loss if the S&P 500 index declined during that period. (To ensure that equity-linked CDs qualified as "deposits," Chase agreed to repay 100% of the holders' originally invested amounts when the CDs matured.) Moreover, the OCC allowed Chase to purchase exchange-traded S&P 500 index futures to hedge the stock market risks created by its equity-linked CDs.[136]

A mutual fund trade association sued the OCC, alleging that Chase's equity-linked CDs and Chase's investments in S&P 500 index futures violated the Glass-Steagall Act. A federal district court dismissed the lawsuit. The court agreed with the OCC that the "plain language" of Glass-Steagall "does not encompass stock index futures" as representing either "stock" or "securities." The district court also concluded that it should defer under *Chevron* to the OCC's interpretation of permissible activities within the "business of banking."[137]

The OCC and the district court adopted extremely narrow and formalistic interpretations of the Glass-Steagall Act. They disregarded evidence showing that Chase was engaged in "stock-trading" in two respects: first, by offering investment contracts whose payoffs were linked to stock prices included in the S&P 500 index, and second, by using S&P 500 index futures to hedge the stock market risks created by those contracts.[138] A functional, risk-based analysis—like the Supreme Court's approach in *ICI v. Camp* and *Bankers Trust I*—would have concluded that Chase's offering of equity-linked CDs represented a prohibited "underwriting" of "securities," while Chase's investments in S&P 500 index futures constituted a forbidden "dealing" in stock under Glass-Steagall.[139]

The rulings of the OCC and the district court concerning equity-linked CDs were typical of the asymmetric approach that federal banking agencies and most federal courts followed during the creeping deregulation of financial markets in the 1980s and 1990s. Federal agencies relied on the concept of "functional equivalency" as a one-way ratchet that expanded—but never limited—the permissible activities of banking organizations. Most court decisions either endorsed the regulators' asymmetric approach or deferred to the regulators' decisions under *Chevron*.[140] The financial industry and federal regulators took full advantage of the fact that "there was no explicit provision in Glass-Steagall against trading in derivatives products."[141]

In 1994, the OCC allowed national banks to enter into OTC equity swaps and equity index swaps to hedge their risk exposures created by equity-linked CDs and stock index futures. The value of an equity swap is determined by referring to the price of an identified equity stock, while the value of an equity index swap is calculated by referring to the price of a specified equity index. The OCC asserted that "equity swaps and equity index swaps are permissible for national banks as a financial intermediation activity" and would benefit banks by "expanding their customer base, and increas[ing] their revenues." The OCC's 1994 order ignored the additional stock market risks posed by OTC equity swaps and equity index swaps and was part of the OCC's campaign to help national banks develop new revenue sources.[142]

In 2000, the OCC permitted several large national banks to buy equity stocks to hedge their risk exposures created by equity swaps and equity index swaps. The OCC's ruling allowed national banks to generate additional revenues and save costs by purchasing equity stocks directly, instead of entering into hedging transactions with their affiliated securities broker-dealers.[143] The OCC's ruling also enabled bank holding companies to finance their purchases of equity stocks by using "the more favorable [borrowing] rate enjoyed by the banks," instead of borrowing at the higher rates paid by nonbank affiliates.[144]

National banks could obtain lower-cost funds from depositors and other creditors because of their access to the federal safety net. That safety net includes (1) federal deposit insurance, (2) liquidity (lending) assistance from the Fed's discount window, and (3) the Fed's guarantees of interbank payments made on Fedwire. The OCC's 2000 ruling deliberately allowed national banks to exploit their safety net subsidies by using their deposits to fund their derivatives activities. The OCC recognized that national banks would have to pay higher costs if they were required to obtain the necessary funding through nonbank affiliates that were not protected by federal deposit insurance, did not have access to the Fed's discount window, and could not process payments through Fedwire.[145]

The OCC's 2000 ruling also ignored the fact that derivatives activities conducted inside FDIC-insured national banks (instead of through nonbank affiliates) would create significantly higher risks of losses for the federal deposit insurance fund and taxpayers.[146] In sum, the OCC's derivatives rulings displayed the OCC's willingness to use intellectual gymnastics to expand the powers and profits of national banks, as well as the OCC's disregard of the "potential systemic risks" that its rulings imposed on the public.[147]

The OCC's derivatives campaign enabled national banks to create OTC derivatives that provided synthetic substitutes for a wide array of capital market instruments, including equity stocks, debt securities, and exchange-traded options and futures.[148] OTC derivatives largely escaped regulation during the 1980s and 1990s because they occupied an "ambiguous position spanning the categories of futures, securities, and loans."[149] OTC derivatives played a very significant role in undermining the Glass-Steagall Act by "blurring the boundary between commercial and investment banking."[150]

———

In the mid-1990s, J. P. Morgan & Co. (JPMC) introduced a new type of OTC derivative, known as the credit default swap (CDS). CDS helped to break down the barriers that separated banks from the insurance business. Federal laws generally prohibited banks from providing guarantees, underwriting insurance, or affiliating with insurance underwriters.[151] In 1995, JPMC persuaded the OCC and the Fed to allow banks to enter into CDS as both dealers and end-users. JPMC also convinced regulators to permit banks to reduce their capital requirements by purchasing CDS protection against the risk of defaults on their loans.[152]

In a CDS transaction, the "protection buyer" purchases protection against specified events of default on a designated bond or other debt instrument, while the "protection seller" provides that protection in return for the buyer's payment of periodic premiums. Thus, CDS contracts "provide guarantees of repayment" for the underlying debt obligations.[153] As Alan Blinder pointed out, "A CDS is an insurance contract posing as a derivative."[154]

Federal officials allowed banks and other financial institutions to enter into CDS without complying with two fundamental principles enshrined in state insurance laws. (Under the McCarran–Ferguson Act of 1945, the business of insurance is regulated primarily by the states rather than the federal government.) First, state insurance laws prohibit the sale of insurance to persons who do not have an "insurable interest" in the subject covered by the insurance (such as a home, a car, or a person's life or health). Second, state laws require insurance companies to establish financial reserves against the risks they insure. Neither of those state law principles applied to CDS because Congress exempted OTC derivatives from state regulation.[155]

Federal regulators allowed financial institutions and investors to purchase CDS protection against defaults on debt obligations when the protection buyers did not have any financial interest in those obligations as borrowers, creditors, or guarantors. Similarly, protection sellers could furnish CDS protection for debt obligations without posting any collateral or maintaining any reserves (except as required by the terms of their CDS contracts). Both departures from state insurance laws enabled buyers and sellers of CDS protection to make enormous speculative bets on the performance of nonprime mortgages, RMBS, and CDOs during the 2000s.[156]

JPMC's innovations did not stop with CDS. In the late 1990s, JPMC created a new and more complex structure known as BISTRO. BISTRO was the first synthetic collateralized debt obligation (synthetic CDO), an instrument that brought together the worlds of derivatives and securitization.

To create BISTRO, JPMC assembled a pool of $9.7 billion of CDS, which provided protection against defaults on loans made by JPMC to more than three hundred companies. JPMC bundled those CDS into a securitized pool managed by a synthetic CDO. The synthetic CDO issued $700 million of CDO securities to investors, while JPMC retained $9 billion of "super-senior" risk if defaults on the pooled CDS exceeded $700 million. JPMC later got rid of its super-senior risk by entering into credit derivatives with AIG Financial Products, a subsidiary of American International Group (AIG), the world's largest insurance company.[157]

The BISTRO deal demonstrated how banks could use securitization and derivatives to avoid taxes and reduce their regulatory capital requirements. JPMC created a "special-purpose vehicle" (SPV) to hold BISTRO's securitized CDS. The SPV was headquartered in an offshore tax haven, which immunized its cash flows from taxation. The Fed and the OCC agreed to reduce JPMC's regulatory capital requirements by 80% for the corporate loans protected by BISTRO's pooled CDS. The Fed and the OCC approved that capital reduction because JPMC obtained credit protection for its super-senior exposures to those CDS from AIG, a triple-A-rated company.[158] As Gillian Tett explained, BISTRO "pulled a dance around the Basel rules [for international bank capital]. The feat was so clever that some bankers started to joke that 'BISTRO' really stood for 'BIS Total Rip Off,' referring to the Bank of International Settlements (BIS), which had overseen the Basel Accord."[159]

BISTRO provided a template for Wall Street's subsequent creation of CDS and synthetic CDOs based on nonprime mortgages and RMBS, instead of corporate loans. The BISTRO concept had a catastrophic impact when it was applied to the nonprime mortgage market. As explained in Chapter 10, CDS and synthetic CDOs enabled financial institutions and other institutional investors to place multiple, overlapping bets on the performance of designated tranches of nonprime RMBS. When borrowers defaulted on the underlying subprime mortgages in 2007, the pyramid of bets created by CDS and CDOs collapsed and greatly magnified the resulting losses.[160]

In 1990, the International Swaps and Derivatives Association (ISDA)—the trade association representing major dealers in OTC derivatives—persuaded Congress to give OTC derivatives a safe harbor under the Bankruptcy Code, similar to the special treatment provided to exchange-traded derivatives in 1982 and certain repos in 1984. The 1990 safe harbor allowed OTC derivatives dealers and end-users to exercise their contract rights and seize their collateral immediately after a counterparty filed for bankruptcy. The 1990 safe harbor encouraged the growth of OTC derivatives by exempting them from the automatic stay provisions and other restrictions imposed on creditors under the Bankruptcy Code.[161]

The derivatives-friendly actions of the OCC, the Fed, and Congress facilitated a tremendous boom in OTC derivatives, just as they had done for shadow banking deposit substitutes and securitization. The aggregate notional values of OTC derivatives in global markets mushroomed from $7 trillion in 1989 to $88 trillion in 1999 and $595 trillion in 2007. The total notional values of CDS grew from only $180 million in 1997 to $1 trillion in 2001 and $58 trillion in 2007.[162]

By 2000, leading U.S. commercial banks controlled almost a third of the global OTC derivatives market,[163] and they received very handsome returns from their derivatives activities.[164] Trading in derivatives produced $46 billion of revenues for U.S. banks between 1996 and 2000 and generated 6% of the total revenues of the seven largest U.S. bank dealers during that period.[165]

———

Thus, federal agencies and federal courts undermined the integrity and effectiveness of the Glass-Steagall and BHC Acts by opening numerous loopholes in both statutes during the 1980s and 1990s. Those loopholes allowed banks to engage in a variety of securities and insurance activities and also permitted nonbank financial institutions to offer bank-like products, including functional substitutes for bank deposits and bank loans. However, the loopholes were subject to significant limitations and uncertainties, and they did not authorize full-scale affiliations among banks, securities firms, and insurance companies.[166] Accordingly, as described in Chapter 8, major banks pursued legislation that would remove all remaining obstacles to their long-held dream of becoming universal banks again.

8

Resurgence, Part II

Congress Enacted Three Statutes That Enabled Big Banks to Build Nationwide Financial Conglomerates

Big banks were not satisfied with their success in opening loopholes in the Glass-Steagall and BHC Acts during the 1980s and 1990s. Large banks needed Congress's help to achieve their long-term goal of establishing nationwide universal banks. Big banks and their political allies therefore waged a twenty-year legislative campaign, which resulted in the passage of three key statutes. Those statutes (1) removed restrictions on interstate banking, (2) authorized the creation of financial holding companies, which could own banks, securities firms, and insurance companies, and (3) exempted over-the-counter derivatives from any substantive regulation by federal or state authorities.[1]

In January 1981, the outgoing Carter administration proposed a plan for the phased removal of restrictions on interstate banking. Big banks eagerly supported President Carter's plan. With one limited exception, Congress did not adopt that plan. However, Carter's plan set the stage for the big-bank lobby's continuing efforts to secure nationwide banking powers.[2]

In March 1981, the American Bankers Association called on the new Reagan administration to remove Glass-Steagall's restrictions on bank involvement in securities activities. The ABA declared that its efforts to repeal Glass-Steagall were "gaining momentum" because of the "political drift toward deregulation." However, securities firms and community banks strongly opposed the ABA's initiative.[3]

In December 1981, Treasury Secretary Donald Regan announced the Reagan administration's plan for a phased repeal of Glass-Steagall. The administration's desire to remove "artificial barriers between commercial banking and investment banking" was part of its broader efforts to eliminate "excessive and outmoded government regulation." As a first step, the administration proposed that nonbank subsidiaries of bank holding companies should be allowed to underwrite state and local revenue bonds and sponsor mutual funds.[4]

Citibank chairman Walter Wriston was the banking industry's "visionary leader" in pushing for comprehensive deregulation until he retired in 1984.[5] Wriston joined Citibank in 1946 and became president in 1967 and chairman in 1970. Wriston intensely disliked government regulation in general and New Deal legislation in particular. A Wall Street analyst remarked that there "was something emotional about [Wriston's] drive [for deregulation] ... I felt Wriston wanted simply to dismantle the financial system as we knew it."[6] In a newspaper interview, Wriston confirmed his "passion for breaking down old restraints on bank operations."[7]

Wriston dreamed of building Citibank (and its holding company, Citicorp) into a "global financial services corporation" that would "change the face of banking."[8] Wriston wanted Citibank to become a "one-stop financial center" for its retail and institutional customers, just as Citibank's predecessor (National City Bank) had been during the 1920s under Charles Mitchell's leadership.[9] Wriston helped to design the negotiable-rate certificates of deposit and Eurodollar deposits that permitted Citibank and other large banks to circumvent Regulation Q's restrictions on deposit interest rates during the 1960s.[10]

Wriston also pioneered floating-rate syndicated loans, which helped Citibank to expand its lending to large corporations and foreign governments. Floating-rate loans provided credit at an agreed-upon spread over the variable cost of Eurodollar funding in London, thereby shifting to borrowers the risk of future changes in interest rates. The syndication process allowed Citibank to play a role similar to that of "a bond underwriter, negotiating the terms of a credit with the borrower and then arranging for the participation of other banks" in the syndicate. By the early 1970s, floating-rate syndicated loans were the dominant form of bank credit to multinational corporations and foreign governments. Cross-border syndicated lending enabled Citibank and other large U.S. banks to fulfill "the same international role that bond financing had played in the 1920s."[11]

Citibank earned lucrative fees for acting as the "lead bank" in arranging international syndicated loans as well as domestic syndicated loans to American enterprises and state and local governments. Syndicated lending brought Citibank and other large U.S. banks closer to the investment banking model, as "the process of loan syndication is similar to the formation of an underwriting syndicate for publicly issued debt securities, and syndicated loans are often viewed by borrowers as a 'substitute' for underwritten bonds."[12]

Citibank and other large money center banks arranged hundreds of billions of dollars of syndicated loans for less-developed countries (LDCs) during the 1970s and early 1980s. Syndicated loans to LDCs helped to "recycle" petrodollars that oil-exporting nations received from LDCs. Oil exporters deposited many of their petrodollars in overseas branches of U.S. money center banks. U.S. banks used those petrodollars to expand their outstanding loans to Latin American countries from less than $50 billion in 1974 to $160 billion in 1978 and more than $320 billion in 1982. Eight money center banks held $55 billion of LDC loans in 1982, an amount equal to more than twice their capital and reserves.[13]

The LDC debt cycle—which broke down in 1982—resembled the unstable merry-go-round of European debt payments during the 1920s. During the 1920s, as described in Chapters 3 and 5, U.S. banks and bond investors made loans to Germany to finance the payment of German reparations, while Germany paid reparations to the Allies, and the Allies used German reparations to fund the payment of their war debts to the U.S. The LDC debt cycle broke down in 1982—as the reparations cycle did in 1931—when American creditors were no longer willing to provide additional loans to heavily indebted sovereign borrowers.[14]

Wriston was "a pioneer and a booster of the new international lending." He maintained that "nations might experience temporary cash-flow problems, but they could never go bankrupt." Wriston's optimism was flatly contradicted by the tidal wave of sovereign defaults that badly damaged U.S. banks, including his own bank, during the 1930s. Wriston ignored that history. As one analyst commented, "The system through which bankers are recruited and promoted, at least in the United States, does not foster an acute historical sensibility. Bankers tend to be present minded."[15]

The Office of the Comptroller of the Currency encouraged the growth of LDC lending by adopting a lenient interpretation of the rule that barred national banks from making loans to a single borrower in excess of 10% of their capital. The OCC stated that different public agencies of a single foreign government could be treated as separate borrowers if each agency used loans for its own activities and could also "service its debt." The OCC allowed national banks to decide on their own whether foreign government agencies qualified as separate borrowers. A Senate committee later criticized the OCC for permitting national banks to "have loans outstanding to 20 different public entities in Brazil," which "taken together may far exceed the [10%] limit."[16]

Beginning in 1982, defaults by Mexico, Brazil, and other LDC borrowers inflicted huge losses on Citibank and other money center banks. By October 1983, twenty-seven nations had defaulted on $239 billion of their debts. "Informal estimates concluded that many of the large U.S. money-center banks would have been insolvent if they had reported all their positions on a mark-to-market basis at the time the LDC crisis unfolded."[17] Federal regulators adopted a policy of prolonged forbearance and did not force large banks to begin writing off their nonperforming LDC loans until 1987.[18]

The risky LDC loans of the 1970s and early 1980s proved to be as disastrous for creditors as the speculative foreign loans and foreign bonds that National City, Chase, and other big U.S. banks and securities firms arranged during the 1920s.[19] The large up-front fees that big banks received for underwriting foreign bonds during the 1920s and for syndicating LDC loans during the 1970s encouraged bankers to disregard longer-term risks during both periods.[20]

Money center banks spread the risks of LDC loans to regional banks that participated in their lending syndicates. The shareholders of money center and regional banks were the ultimate losers. Citibank wrote off almost a third of its LDC loans in 1987, and other money center and regional banks recorded similar charge-offs between 1987 and 1989. In 1989, Treasury Secretary Nicholas Brady issued the Brady Plan, which resolved the LDC loan crisis by restructuring $190 billion of LDC debt. The Brady Plan required U.S. and European banks to write off an additional $60 billion of their LDC loans between 1989 and 1994.[21] The plight of bank shareholders during the late 1980s resembled the misfortune of "individuals who had bought foreign bonds in the 1920s."[22]

Citibank and other U.S. money center and regional banks also arranged domestic syndicated loans during the 1980s for U.S. energy producers, commercial real estate developers, and organizers of leveraged buyouts of corporations. Those loans, too, performed very badly. In 1990, large U.S. banks held several hundred billion dollars of high-risk loans on their balance sheets, and they charged off $140 billion of those loans between 1986 and 1991.[23]

The disastrous performance of syndicated loans during the 1970s and the 1980s provided a clear warning about the likely behavior of money center banks if they were allowed to reenter the securities underwriting business. When U.S. authorities permitted banks to originate and securitize nonprime mortgage loans during the 1990s and 2000s, those banks faced similar destructive, short-term incentives in the form of up-front fees, as explained in Chapters 7 and 10. In 2013, former Fed chairman Paul Volcker pointed out that the LDC lending crisis was "something like . . . the subprime mortgage thing." Volcker explained that during the 1970s, "money was flowing through the big banks to Latin America in a way that arguably looked constructive for a while but was ultimately unsustainable." In his view, the LDC lending frenzy resembled the avalanche of credit that big banks and securities firms poured into the nonprime mortgage market prior to the financial crisis of 2007–09.[24]

———

Wriston also attempted to evade Glass-Steagall's restrictions by building a mutual fund business at Citibank during the 1960s. However, as discussed in Chapter 7, the Supreme Court outlawed Citibank's "commingled investment account" in its 1971 decision in *ICI v. Camp*. Following that setback, Wriston spearheaded the banking industry's campaign to repeal the Glass-Steagall Act. His successors, John Reed and Sanford (Sandy) Weill, continued to lead that fight until Congress passed the Gramm-Leach-Bliley Act (GLBA) in November 1999.[25]

J. P. Morgan & Co. was the second leading participant in the banking industry's assault on Glass-Steagall. After World War II, JPMC built up a large investment banking business in overseas markets, where Glass-Steagall's limitations did not apply.[26] In 1984, JPMC chairman Lewis Preston told his staff to prepare a white paper advocating the repeal of Glass-Steagall. Alan Greenspan was then a director of JPMC, and he was "very instrumental in getting that document out."[27] JPMC joined with Citicorp and Bankers Trust in persuading the Fed to issue its 1987 order approving Section 20 securities subsidiaries of bank holding companies.[28] Preston's successor, Dennis Weatherstone, led JPMC's continued efforts to repeal Glass-Steagall during the 1990s.[29]

Like Wriston, Preston, and Weatherstone, Alan Greenspan was a fervent opponent of Glass-Steagall. Greenspan shared Wriston's visceral dislike of government regulation and the New Deal. Greenspan was an acolyte and close friend of Ayn Rand from the early 1950s until her death in 1981. He shared her libertarian philosophy and her devotion to laissez-faire capitalism.[30] During the 1960s, Greenspan "wrote several essays for the Rand publication, *The Objectivist*," in which he "criticized both con-sumer protection and antitrust laws because they interfered with the free market."[31] Rand stood at Greenspan's side in 1974, when he was sworn in as Chairman of the Council of Economic Advisers for President Ford.[32]

Greenspan remained deeply committed to a laissez-faire philosophy. In 1997 (ten years after his appointment as Fed Chairman), Greenspan received the Adam Smith Award from the Association of Private Enterprise Education. In his acceptance speech, Greenspan said, "I have never lost sight of the fact that government regula-tion can undermine the effectiveness of private market regulation and can itself be ineffective in protecting the public interest." According to Greenspan, "Regulation by government unavoidably involves some element of perverse incentives." He believed that "rapidly changing technology" was making "much government bank regulation irrelevant." Greenspan maintained that "market-stabilizing private regulatory forces should gradually displace many cumbersome, increasingly ineffective government structures."[33]

In an interview with the *New York Times* in June 1987 (shortly before President Reagan appointed him as Fed Chairman), Greenspan called for unrestricted nation-wide banking, the repeal of Glass-Steagall, and the removal of the BHC Act's pro-hibitions on acquisitions of banks by commercial and industrial firms. Greenspan's positions were identical to the Reagan administration's policy agenda, which Treasury Undersecretary George Gould described in the same news article. Greenspan also said that he did not have any concerns about an "undue concentration of banking powers."[34] Greenspan's views stood in sharp contrast to his predecessor, Paul Volcker, who warned that a "rush to deregulation" could produce an "undue concentration of banking resources."[35]

During testimony before the Senate Banking Committee in December 1987, Greenspan strongly endorsed a bill drafted by Senators William Proxmire (D-WI) and Jake Garn (R-UT). The Proxmire-Garn bill would have repealed Glass-Steagall's anti-affiliation provisions and allowed bank holding companies to establish full-service securities subsidiaries. Greenspan praised the Proxmire-Garn bill for addressing "what is perhaps the single most important anomaly that now plagues our financial system—the artificial separation of commercial and investment banking." Greenspan argued that the "repeal of Glass-Steagall would provide significant public benefits consistent with a manageable increase in risk."[36]

Greenspan acknowledged that "securities activities are clearly risky," as demon-strated by "the unprecedented decline in the stock market that occurred on October 19, 1987, and the subsequent market volatility." However, he assured the Senate committee that "potential risks from securities activities can be effectively man-aged." In his view, banks could be "effectively insulated from their securities affiliates through an appropriate structural framework" that included "institutional fire walls." Greenspan pointed out that "one of the most important" firewalls in the Proxmire-Garn bill would prohibit a bank from "being able to lend to, or purchase assets from, its securities affiliate." Greenspan believed that a "straightforward prohibition on lending to securities affiliates" was necessary to "limit the transfer of the risk of the securities activities to the federal safety net."[37]

Greenspan advised the committee that existing limits on dealings between banks and their nonbank affiliates would *not* be adequate to contain the risks posed by securities affiliates. He explained that those limits, "embodied in sections 23A and 23B of the Federal Reserve Act, do not work as effectively as we would like and, because of their complexity, are subject to avoidance by creative interpretation, particularly in times of stress."[38] Greenspan recognized that, without stronger firewalls, Glass-Steagall's repeal would permit banks to transfer their federal safety net subsidies (and their resulting cost-of-funding advantages) to their securities affiliates through extensions of credit and purchases of assets.[39]

Greenspan's support for strong firewalls proved to be short-lived. In May 1990, the ABA and other big-bank trade associations issued a report arguing that legislation to repeal Glass-Steagall should *not* include any additional firewalls between banks and their securities affiliates. The big-bank coalition maintained that existing laws, including Sections 23A and 23B, would be adequate to prevent conflicts of interest and other adverse effects of such affiliations.[40]

Greenspan quickly fell in line with the big-bank lobby. In testimony before the Senate Banking Committee in July 1990, Greenspan said that the Fed was "reevaluating both the efficacy and desirability of substantial fire walls" between banks and securities affiliates. He gave two reasons for the Fed's reassessment. First, the failure in early 1990 of Drexel Burnham, the fifth-largest U.S. securities firm, "raised serious questions about the ability of fire walls to insulate one unit of a holding company from funding problems of another." The insolvency of Drexel's holding company triggered creditor runs on Drexel's broker-dealer subsidiaries and forced those subsidiaries into receiverships. Second, Greenspan expressed concerns that "high and thick fire walls reduce synergies and raise costs for financial institutions, a significant problem in increasingly competitive financial markets."[41]

It was highly ironic that Greenspan cited the Drexel episode—when firewalls *failed*—to argue for *weaker* firewalls between banks and their securities affiliates. Like the big-bank lobby, Greenspan wanted to avoid strong firewalls and increase the value of expected "synergies" between banks and their securities affiliates. In his 1990 testimony, Greenspan said that "more limited fire walls," including Sections 23A and 23B, would be sufficient if Congress allowed federal regulators to impose higher capital requirements and stricter supervisory standards on bank holding companies that owned securities subsidiaries.[42]

The big-bank coalition responded to Greenspan's testimony with great enthusiasm. Bank trade associations hailed Greenspan's statement as "a bold and ingenious stroke" and "a refreshing insight" because he argued that a "strict-firewalls approach" would be an "obstacle to efficiency in product and service integration." Other supporters of big banks agreed that Greenspan's testimony "effectively undermined the firewall concept."[43]

Greenspan's testimony in 1987 and 1990 should be remembered in the context of GLBA's final provisions and the massive bailouts of financial holding companies during 2007–09. Greenspan recognized in 1987 and again in 1990 that banks would have strong incentives to transfer their federal safety net subsidies to their securities affiliates. Greenspan's 1987 testimony highlighted the importance of strong firewalls (including a "no transfer of credit" rule) to prevent the spread of those subsidies. In contrast, his 1990 testimony proposed high levels of capital and stricter supervisory standards as substitutes for strong firewalls. As will be discussed, GLBA relied almost exclusively on Sections 23A and 23B to prevent the spread of safety net subsidies. The Fed granted frequent waivers of Section 23A after 1999 and did *not* impose strict capital requirements or tough regulatory standards on large diversified banks. The weak provisions of GLBA and the Fed's lax regulatory policies produced a massive and costly expansion of the federal safety net during the decade after GLBA's passage.

Congress did not pass the Proxmire-Garn bill in 1987 or 1988, just as it had failed to pass a similar Senate bill sponsored by Senator Garn in 1984. The securities and insurance industries and community banks worked together to defend Glass-Steagall, and they received significant help from influential Democratic members of Congress. One of Glass-Steagall's most determined champions was Representative John Dingell (D-MI), whose father strongly supported the passage of the Glass-Steagall Act as a Michigan congressman in 1933.[44]

After the stock market crashed in October 1987, Glass-Steagall's defenders pointed out that the legislation played a highly beneficial role by preventing a contagious spillover of risks and losses from securities firms to commercial banks.[45] In addition, the big-bank lobby was severely embarrassed when news media reported that Continental Illinois—the recipient of a billion-dollar federal bailout in 1984—extended more than $600 million of loans to rescue its troubled options trading subsidiary (First Options) during the 1987 crash. Continental's emergency loans exceeded the lending limit that the OCC imposed when it allowed Continental to acquire First Options in 1986. Members of Congress strongly criticized Continental, and the First Options fiasco helped to block the banking industry's efforts to repeal Glass-Steagall in 1987 and 1988.[46]

———

Big banks persisted in their campaign to remove geographic and product line barriers to their expansion, and they received enthusiastic support from President George H.W. Bush's administration. In January 1991, the Bush Treasury Department issued a blueprint for comprehensive deregulation, entitled *Modernizing the Financial System*. The Treasury plan and the accompanying report presented the same three legislative proposals that Treasury Undersecretary George Gould had floated in 1987—unrestricted nationwide banking and branching, the repeal of Glass-Steagall, and the removal of barriers to combinations between banks and commercial or industrial firms.[47] Congress adopted the first two proposals in 1994 and 1999, thereby paving the way for the creation of giant financial conglomerates that stretched across the nation and encompassed all sectors of the financial industry.[48]

The campaign to authorize nationwide banking: Treasury's first proposal called upon Congress to authorize unrestricted nationwide banking through interstate acquisitions of banks by bank holding companies as well as interstate branching. In the late 1970s, states began to exercise their right, under Section 3(d) of the BHC Act, to permit out-of-state bank holding companies to acquire banks within their borders. By 1991, thirty-three states allowed acquisitions of local banks by bank holding companies headquartered anywhere in the U.S. (subject to reciprocity requirements in twenty-one states). Thirteen other states allowed entry by out-of-state bank holding companies if their home states were located within a defined geographical region and also offered reciprocal access. The Treasury plan urged Congress to repeal all federal and state limitations on interstate acquisitions of banks by bank holding companies.[49]

The Treasury plan also advocated a new federal law that would allow national banks to establish branches on a nationwide basis, either by merging with banks in other states or by opening de novo branches across state lines. That proposal represented a more radical change to existing law, because in 1991 the McFadden Act prohibited national banks and state member banks from establishing branches across state lines.[50]

The Treasury report argued that nationwide banking and branching would create stronger and safer banks through geographic diversification. The report also contended that nationwide banking and branching would improve the efficiency, competitiveness, and profitability of the banking industry, as well as providing greater convenience to large corporations, residents of multistate urban areas, and travelers.[51] The Treasury plan contemplated "a rapid consolidation of most of the banking industry into a small number of large nationwide banks."[52]

In a 1992 article, I warned that nationwide megabanks would pose significant risks to the U.S. financial system and the broader economy for several reasons. I questioned whether executives could effectively manage, or whether regulators could effectively supervise, the multitude of risks created by complex financial giants. In addition, Treasury's argument that larger banks would be safer banks was contradicted by the woeful performance of many large banks during the 1980s and early 1990s. Eleven of the fifty largest U.S. banks failed or required federal bailouts between 1980 and 1992.[53] The biggest U.S. banks had the lowest capital ratios, the weakest earnings, and the highest percentages of nonperforming loans in 1990.[54]

Several studies published since 1992 support my doubts about the claimed advantages and benefits of nationwide megabanks. A 2010 study concluded that large-scale diversification by banks increases the likelihood of a systemic financial crisis by producing a higher correlation of risk exposures among a smaller number of big banks. In turn, that higher correlation of risk exposures among a concentrated group of megabanks generates a stronger probability of systemic contagion and joint failures.[55] A 2013 study found that U.S. banks that expanded across state lines between 1986 and 2007 had lower market valuations, in part because they increased their lending to insiders (senior managers and large shareholders) and also recorded higher levels of nonperforming loans. Thus, geographic diversification intensified agency problems and encouraged greater risk-taking.[56] Two additional studies concluded that larger and more diversified banks were at least as risky as smaller banks during the 1980s and 1990s because larger banks operated with lower capital ratios and assumed greater risks in their lending operations and other activities.[57] Similarly, two studies of bank failures during the Great Depression found that banks with branches were *more* likely to fail than unit banks because branching banks operated with lower liquidity reserves and took on greater risks during the 1920s.[58]

A 2017 study determined that states experienced more intense boom-and-bust cycles during the 1980s and early 1990s if they authorized interstate banking before 1983. States that were early adopters of interstate banking experienced bigger credit booms (including larger increases in household debt) and faster economic growth during the 1980s. However, the same states produced higher percentages of nonperforming loans and suffered more severe recessions during the early 1990s.[59]

Another 2017 study found that the four biggest U.S. banks—Bank of America (BofA), Citigroup, JPMC, and Wells Fargo—reduced their small business lending to a much greater extent during the financial crisis of 2007–09, compared with other banks. Counties in which the four biggest banks had larger market shares experienced slower employment growth, higher unemployment rates, larger declines in wages, and more unfavorable terms for small business credit, compared with counties in which the top four banks had relatively small market shares. Thus, the four largest banks provided *inferior* services to small business and local communities during the financial crisis, as they instituted the most severe cutbacks in lending to small businesses, and those cutbacks inflicted serious economic damage on the local communities served by those businesses.[60]

My 1992 article also argued that nationwide megabanks would make the too-big-to-fail (TBTF) problem much worse by creating giant banks that posed systemic threats to the U.S. financial system. Federal regulators invoked the TBTF rationale when they bailed out several large regional banks during the banking crisis of the 1980s and early 1990s—including Continental Illinois in 1984, First RepublicBank in 1988, and Bank of New England in 1991. Regulators protected uninsured depositors in large regional banks in order to prevent creditor runs on large money center banks, which faced equally severe problems during that period.[61]

James Barth, Dan Brumbaugh, and Robert Litan concluded that "the largest banks, as a group, pose[d] the greatest risk to the FDIC" in 1990. Several money center banks—including Citicorp, Chase Manhattan, Chemical, and Manufacturers Hanover—had inadequate loan loss reserves and "very thin capital margins."[62] Federal regulators provided extensive forbearance to Citicorp during the 1980s and early 1990s, as Citicorp recorded massive losses from risky loans in multiple sectors (including LDC loans, commercial real estate loans, residential mortgages, and other consumer loans).[63]

The Fed also supported large banks by rapidly cutting short-term interest rates during 1991 and by maintaining very low short-term rates during 1992 and 1993. Large banks took advantage of the resulting gap between long-term and short-term interest rates by investing their low-yielding deposits in higher-yielding Treasury bonds and mortgage-backed securities. The Fed's highly accommodating monetary policy helped Citicorp and other troubled large banks to recover from their severely impaired condition in 1990.[64]

―――

Given the very serious problems that large banks confronted during the 1980s and early 1990s, the 1991 Treasury plan did *not* seek to abolish the TBTF policy. Instead, the Treasury plan recommended that the TBTF policy should be *codified* by enacting a new "systemic risk exception." That exception would give federal officials explicit authority to protect uninsured depositors and other creditors of a failing megabank in order to prevent or mitigate "systemic risk."[65]

In December 1991, Congress passed the Federal Deposit Insurance Corporation Improvement Act (FDICIA), which strengthened the supervisory, enforcement, and resolution powers of federal bank regulators.[66] As the Treasury plan proposed, FDICIA required regulators to take "prompt corrective action" and implement "early resolution" policies when dealing with troubled banks. Those policies mandate that regulators should impose sanctions on undercapitalized banks and should close severely troubled banks before they become insolvent.[67]

FDICIA also established a "least-cost test" for resolving failed banks. That test bars the FDIC from protecting uninsured depositors and other creditors in most failed banks.[68] However, as the Treasury plan recommended, FDICIA included a systemic risk exception to the least-cost test. Under that exception, the Fed, the FDIC, and Treasury can jointly agree to protect uninsured creditors of a failed bank to "avoid or mitigate serious adverse effects on economic conditions or financial stability."[69] Thus, as my 1992 article explained, FDICIA "for the first time provides a clear statutory basis for the 'too big to fail' doctrine" and thereby codified TBTF treatment for megabanks.[70]

FDICIA contained a second very significant expansion of the federal safety net, which greatly benefited securities firms and other nonbanks. Section 473 of FDICIA amended Section 13(3) of the Federal Reserve Act by allowing the Fed to provide emergency loans to nonbanks, secured by pledges of any collateral that the Fed determined to be satisfactory, including securities and other financial instruments. Prior to 1991, the Fed could not accept securities or many other types of private financial obligations as collateral for emergency loans to nonbanks under Section 13(3).

Goldman Sachs and other large securities firms urged Congress to amend Section 13(3) after the Fed allowed Drexel Burnham to fail in 1990. Senator Christopher Dodd (D-CT) explained that the amendment would allow the Fed "to make fully secured loans to securities firms in instances similar to the 1987 stock market crash."[71]

Morgan Ricks concluded—and I agree—that FDICIA's expansion of the Fed's Section 13(3) authority provided strong encouragement for the explosive growth of securities firms and the rapid expansion of their short-term liabilities (including commercial paper and repos) after 1991.[72]

Community banks and consumer groups defeated efforts by the George H. W. Bush administration and the big-bank lobby to include interstate banking provisions in FDICIA.[73] Consequently, the Treasury plan's recommendation for nationwide banking remained on the big-bank agenda when Bill Clinton became president in January 1993.[74]

The Clinton administration worked closely with big banks to secure passage of the Riegle-Neal Interstate Banking and Branching Efficiency Act (Riegle-Neal) in September 1994. Riegle-Neal authorized nationwide banking and branching by 1997, in accordance with the Treasury plan's recommendation.[75] Community banks and consumer groups failed to block the legislation after the insurance industry saw "passage as inevitable" and "dropped its opposition."[76] When President Clinton signed the legislation, he declared, "Our work is far from over," and he promised to push for further deregulation of the financial industry.[77]

TheRiegle-Neal Act accelerated the wave of consolidation that was already sweeping through the banking industry.[78] Bank regulators and the Department of Justice encouraged that consolidation trend by applying very lenient antitrust review standards to bank mergers. Seventy-four megamergers—in which the acquiring and acquired banks each held more than $10 billion of assets—occurred between 1990 and 2005. During the same period, the ten largest U.S. banks increased their share of U.S. banking assets from 25% to 55%. The three largest U.S. banking organizations in 2007—Citigroup, BofA, and JPMC—each owned more than $1.5 trillion of assets at the end of 2007. Wachovia, the fourth-largest bank, had almost $800 billion of assets at the end of 2007.[79] As the largest banks exploded in size, they also acquired unprecedented political clout.[80]

The campaign to repeal the Glass-Steagall Act: The second major proposal in the 1991 Treasury plan was to remove the structural barriers in the Glass-Steagall and BHC Acts that separated banks from securities firms and insurance companies. The Treasury report argued that unrestricted affiliations between banks and other providers of financial services would create "a stronger, more diversified financial system that will provide important benefits to the consumer" and promote "market innovation."[81] The report also contended that U.S. banks needed broader powers to compete with the universal banking powers that European banks would exercise under the European Union's Second Banking Directive, beginning in 1993.[82]

The Treasury report acknowledged that federal agencies had already opened loopholes that permitted banking organizations to engage "in a broad range of securities activities," including securitizing loans and underwriting bank-ineligible securities through Section 20 subsidiaries. However, the report pointed out that those agency-created loopholes contained "numerous restrictions" and imposed undesirable burdens, including "strict 'firewall' requirements." The Treasury report also warned that deregulation based on agency rulings was proceeding in "a piecemeal, inefficient, and often irrational manner."[83]

The Treasury report therefore urged Congress to authorize financial holding companies, which could own full-service banks, securities firms, and insurance companies, "so that natural synergies can be realized." The report stated that businesses and consumers would benefit from "a greater variety of products at competitively lower prices." At the same time, diversified financial holding companies would produce "a more stable stream of income," thereby improving "the overall stability of financial markets."[84] The report further argued that Sections 23A and 23B of the Federal Reserve Act would provide adequate "firewalls" without impairing the "operational, managerial, or marketing synergies between a bank and its financial affiliates."[85]

FDICIA did not include Treasury's financial holding company proposal, due to the joint opposition of the insurance industry, community banks, and consumer groups.[86] After Congress passed the Riegle-Neal Act in 1994, the big-bank lobby renewed its campaign to break down Glass-Steagall's barriers. The political landscape gradually shifted in favor of financial deregulation between 1995 and 1998. The largest securities firms and insurance companies concluded in 1996 that they could not prevent the continuing erosion of the Glass-Steagall and BHC Acts through regulatory loopholes. Accordingly, they decided to join big banks in endorsing the financial holding company concept, which offered a "two-way street" by enabling securities firms and insurance companies to acquire banks. As a result of that shift, insurance agents and community banks were the only major trade groups that still defended Glass-Steagall.[87]

In April 1998, Travelers and Citicorp announced their decision to merge under the name of Citigroup, thereby creating the world's largest financial institution with over $1 trillion of assets. Travelers was a major insurance company that controlled a large securities broker-dealer (Salomon Brothers), while Citicorp was the biggest U.S. bank holding company. The Citigroup merger created the first "universal bank" that could offer comprehensive banking, securities, and insurance services in the U.S. since the 1930s.[88]

Citigroup's co-leaders—Sandy Weill of Travelers and John Reed of Citicorp—declared that Citigroup would offer unparalleled convenience to customers through "one-stop shopping" for a wide range of banking, securities, and insurance services.[89] They argued that Citigroup would have a superior ability to withstand financial shocks by virtue of its broadly diversified activities. Weill proclaimed, "We are creating a model financial institution of the future.... In a world that's changing very rapidly, we will be able to withstand the storms."[90] Thus, Citigroup's founders cited the same expected benefits of universal banking that the 1991 Treasury report had touted. Many academics agreed that universal banking would provide significant benefits.[91]

By approving the Citigroup merger, the Fed "challenge[d] both the statutory letter and regulatory spirit" of the Glass-Steagall and BHC Acts.[92] The only source of statutory authority for the merger was a temporary exemption in the BHC Act, which allowed newly formed bank holding companies to retain nonconforming assets for up to five years.[93] As a banking lawyer explained, that temporary exemption was "intended to provide an orderly mechanism for disposing of impermissible activities, not warehousing them in hopes the law would change so you could keep them."[94]

The Citigroup merger confronted Congress with a Hobson's choice: either Congress could repeal the anti-affiliation rules of the Glass-Steagall and BHC Acts or Citigroup would be forced to divest all of its nonconforming activities within five years.[95] The Citigroup deal effectively put a gun to the head of Congress, and it did so with the blessing of the federal government's leaders. Sandy Weill and John Reed consulted with Fed Chairman Alan Greenspan, Treasury Secretary Robert Rubin, and President Clinton before they announced the Citigroup merger. All three officials endorsed the transaction.[96] Based on those consultations, Reed told the press that Travelers and Citicorp were confident "there wasn't a legal problem" with the merger.[97]

The advance clearance that Travelers and Citicorp received from Clinton, Greenspan, and Rubin was extraordinary and, to my knowledge, unprecedented. The kid-glove treatment that top federal officials provided to Travelers and Citicorp merger demonstrated the enormous influence that the largest banks and Wall Street firms wielded in their dealings with politicians and regulators.[98] The federal government's advance blessing for Citigroup provided "a stark example of the ease with which the powerful on Wall Street got the ear of key policymakers, and also how easily the Fed, through its rulings, could bypass the intentions of Congress."[99]

Weill and Citigroup spearheaded the final assault on Glass-Steagall, with enthusiastic support from the Clinton administration. Big banks, securities firms, and insurance companies joined Citigroup in financing that campaign, which spent more than $300 million on lobbying and political contributions.[100]

Alan Greenspan strongly endorsed the repeal of Glass-Steagall. He told Congress that Glass-Steagall's "archaic statutory barriers" threatened to "undermine the global dominance of American finance" as well as "the continued competitiveness of our financial institutions." He hailed the benefits of "one-stop shopping" that he believed universal banks would provide to businesses and consumers.[101]

Treasury Secretary Robert Rubin advised Congress that Glass-Steagall imposed "unnecessary costs on the financial system" and could "impede safety and soundness by limiting revenue diversification." He agreed with Greenspan that concerns about "firewalls" between banks and their nonbank affiliates were "adequately addressed" by Sections 23A and 23B.[102] Rubin was a former co-CEO of Goldman Sachs, and he maintained a network of close relationships with leaders of major banks and securities firms. Similarly, President Clinton had strong friendships with leading financiers, and he welcomed political contributions from big banks, Wall Street firms, and their trade associations.[103] In May 1996, Clinton was the featured guest at a White House political fundraiser hosted by the Democratic National Committee. Top executives from several of the nation's largest banks attended the event, along with Rubin, other senior Treasury officials, and Comptroller of the Currency Eugene Ludwig (the top regulator of national banks). The fundraiser included a discussion of strategies for repealing Glass-Steagall.[104]

Congress approved GLBA in November 1999, due to the Clinton administration's efforts as well as the unified support of big banks, securities firms, and insurance companies.[105] During the congressional debates, supporters argued that GLBA would (1) eliminate the "inefficient and costly" and potentially "unstable" loopholes created by federal agency rulings and (2) replace those loopholes with a clearly defined legal framework authorizing full-scale affiliations between banks, securities firms, and insurance companies.[106]

At the signing ceremony for GLBA, President Clinton declared, "This is a very good day for the United States.... [W]e have done right by the American people."[107] Treasury Secretary Lawrence Summers—who succeeded Rubin in July 1999—stated, "With this bill, the American financial system takes a major step forward towards the 21st century.... I believe we have found the right framework for America's future financial system."[108] Senator Phil Gramm (D-TX), whose free-market zeal matched Greenspan's, proclaimed that "when Glass-Steagall became law, it was believed that government was the answer.... We are here to repeal Glass-Steagall because we have learned that government is not the answer."[109] A few months after GLBA's passage, Gramm described Wall Street as "the very nerve center of American capitalism ... to me, that's a holy place."[110]

In contrast to the rosy predictions of GLBA's supporters, GLBA's opponents argued that universal banks would create financial risks and speculative excesses similar to those of the 1920s. Opponents warned that regulators would almost certainly give TBTF protection to universal banks, and that the repeal of Glass-Steagall could trigger a financial crisis comparable to the Great Depression.[111] Senator Paul Wellstone (D-MN), a strong opponent of GLBA, stated:

> We seem determined to unlearn the lessons from our past mistakes.... Glass-Steagall was intended to protect our financial system by insulating commercial banking from other forms of risk.... Now Congress is about to repeal that stabilizer without putting any comparable safeguard in its place.[112]

To stop universal banks from transferring their federal safety net subsidies to their securities and insurance affiliates, GLBA relied primarily on "firewalls" created by (1) the separate corporate identities of banks and their nonbank affiliates and (2) Sections 23A and 23B of the Federal Reserve Act.[113] As Joseph Stiglitz pointed out, the "firewall" arguments of GLBA's supporters relied on "an obvious intellectual inconsistency." If FDIC-insured banks and the federal safety net needed to be shielded from the risks posed by securities and insurance affiliates, "what were the benefits of integration?" If, on the other hand, Congress maintained only flimsy and porous buffers to preserve "economies of scope" across financial holding companies, that approach would impose significant risks on the FDIC and taxpayers and allow banks to transfer their safety net subsidies to their affiliates.[114] During the debates over GLBA, Senator Wellstone warned his colleagues that the "firewalls" remaining after the repeal of Glass-Steagall would be "weak" and would almost certainly disappear during a future financial crisis.[115]

In 1995, Paul Volcker warned Congress that regulators would be forced to extend the federal safety net to protect large securities firms if they were allowed to affiliate with large banks. In testimony before the House Banking Committee, Volcker stated:

> It is obvious that if you had a large investment bank allied with a large [commercial] bank, the possibility of a systemic risk arising is evident.... It may be even evident with the investment bank alone. We are trying to keep them out of the so-called safety net now, but certainly you cannot keep them out if they are combined with a banking institution.[116]

Under Section 23A of the Federal Reserve Act, banks may extend credit to, and may purchase assets from, their nonbank affiliates if banks comply with specified quantitative limits, collateral requirements, and qualitative standards. The effectiveness of Section 23A is undercut by a number of statutory exemptions, which provide ample opportunities to avoid Section 23A's restrictions. In addition, the Fed possessed unilateral authority to waive Section 23A's requirements until 2010.[117]

The first acid test of GLBA's firewalls occurred with the terrorist attacks on September 11, 2001. When the attacks threatened to disrupt financial markets on Wall Street, the Fed flooded the markets with liquidity by purchasing $150 billion of government securities and extending more than $45 billion of discount window loans to banks. The Fed also suspended Section 23A's quantitative limits on affiliate transactions so that major banks could make large transfers of funds to their securities affiliates.[118] In 2002, I argued that the Fed's waivers of Section 23A following 9/11 showed that "the [Fed] views the survival of major financial conglomerates as an indispensable element of its broader mission to preserve market stability. Market participants therefore have strong reasons to expect that the TBTF policy will be applied to all important subsidiaries of leading financial holding companies."[119]

After the financial crisis began in mid-2007, the Fed approved very broad waivers of Section 23A, which allowed big banks to make huge transfers of funds to rescue their securities affiliates and money market mutual funds. The Fed also approved waivers of Section 23A that (1) helped Goldman Sachs and Morgan Stanley to survive the crisis by making emergency conversions into bank holding companies and (2) enabled GMAC to finance vehicle sales by General Motors (GM) after the federal government bailed out both GM and GMAC.[120] The Fed's extraordinary waivers after mid-2007 authorized "massive transfers of funds" from large banks to their nonbank affiliates, which "exposed banks to risks associated with their affiliates' nonbanking business and transferred [the] federal subsidy outside the [banking] system."[121]

The Fed's large-scale waivers of Section 23A during the financial crisis were part of a comprehensive series of bailouts for large financial conglomerates in the banking, securities, and insurance sectors. As described in Chapter 11, those bailouts flatly contradicted the repeated promises made by GLBA's supporters that Glass-Steagall's repeal would avoid any extension of the federal safety net beyond traditional banks.[122]

In contrast, GLBA's opponents proved to be absolutely right when they warned that Glass-Steagall's repeal would inevitably lead to TBTF bailouts of large financial holding companies. On the evening the House of Representatives passed GLBA, Congressman John Dingell predicted:

> What we are creating now is a group of institutions which are too big to fail.... Taxpayers are going to be called upon to cure the failures we are creating tonight, and it is going to cost a lot of money, and it is coming. Just be prepared for those events.[123]

In 2002, I similarly warned that GLBA would "extend the scope of the TBTF subsidy to reach nonbank affiliates of large financial holding companies" because federal regulators would likely "conclude that they should protect nonbank affiliates of big financial conglomerates during economic disruptions in order to reduce systemic risk." Accordingly, I predicted that "major segments of the securities and life insurance industry will be brought within the scope of the TBTF doctrine, thereby expanding the scope and cost of federal 'safety net' guarantees."[124] The enormous bailouts that occurred across the entire span of U.S. financial industry during 2007–09 exceeded my worst expectations in 2002.

The campaign to deregulate OTC derivatives: The third major goal of the legislative campaign pursued by financial giants during the 1990s was to insulate over-the-counter derivatives from any substantive regulation by the Commodity Futures Trading Commission or the Securities and Exchange Commission. Markets for OTC derivatives expanded rapidly during the 1990s, and those markets grew much larger than markets for exchange-traded derivatives.[125] The biggest U.S. banks and securities firms controlled about 40% of the global OTC derivatives market in 1998.[126] However, the exemption of OTC derivatives from regulation under the Commodity Exchange Act had a precarious status, as it depended on a 1993 rule issued by the CFTC.[127]

The explosive growth of OTC derivatives was accompanied by numerous warning signs about their potential risks. The first danger signal occurred when "portfolio insurance" collapsed during the stock market crash in October 1987. Portfolio insurance was a derivatives-based hedging strategy that used short sales of exchange-traded stock index futures to offset declines in stock prices. It was the harbinger of a "brave new world of synthetic instruments [based on] dynamic trading strategies."[128]

When the stock market crashed in October 1987, portfolio insurance triggered huge volumes of sell orders for stock index futures, and liquidity quickly disappeared from futures markets. The collapse of prices for stock index futures had a contagious impact that accelerated the plunge in stock market prices.[129] "Many observers, including the Brady Commission, concluded that portfolio insurance increased the severity of the [1987] crash by magnifying selling pressures in both the stock market and the futures markets."[130]

In 1994, the Fed's unexpected decision to increase short-term interest rates significantly inflicted huge losses on institutional investors who had purchased highly leveraged OTC interest rate derivatives. Gibson Greetings, Procter & Gamble, and several other investors sued their dealer, Bankers Trust. They alleged that Bankers Trust sold them complex interest rate derivatives without disclosing the very high risks of those instruments. Bankers Trust paid more than $250 million to settle investor lawsuits as well as enforcement actions filed by the CFTC and SEC.

Similarly, Orange County, California, sued Merrill Lynch after losing $1.6 billion on highly leveraged interest rate derivatives that the county bought from Merrill. Merrill ultimately paid $470 million to settle civil, criminal, and SEC claims related to the Orange County debacle.[131] In 1995, Barings Bank, a prominent U.K. investment bank, collapsed after it lost more than $1.4 billion on speculative derivatives trades made by Nicholas Leeson, the general manager of Barings' Singapore subsidiary.[132]

The U.S. General Accounting Office issued a report in 1994 warning that OTC derivatives posed significant systemic risks as a result of regulatory gaps and the high concentration of OTC derivatives exposures within a small group of large banks and securities firms. Members of Congress introduced four bills calling for stronger supervision of OTC derivatives.[133]

The International Swaps and Derivatives Association responded with a vigorous lobbying campaign to head off the threat of federal regulation. ISDA represented big banks and securities firms that were leading dealers in OTC derivatives, as well as large corporate end-users.[134] ISDA blocked all four bills dealing with OTC derivatives in 1994–95, thereby achieving "one of the most startling triumphs for a Wall Street lobbying campaign in the twentieth century."[135] The Clinton administration and the Fed also strongly opposed any federal regulation of OTC derivatives. Fed Chairman Alan Greenspan urged Congress to reject the proposed bills because they would create "a regulatory regime that is itself ineffective and that diminishes the effectiveness of market discipline."[136]

Derivatives problems persisted, however. Dealers and end-users suffered significant derivatives-related losses during the Mexican and East Asian financial crises of 1995 and 1997. JPMC paid almost $600 million to settle lawsuits brought by Korean banks and securities firms after they incurred large losses on OTC currency swaps sold by JPMC.[137]

In May 1998, another regulatory threat appeared. Under the leadership of Chairman Brooksley Born, the CFTC issued a "Concept Release," which requested public comment on the question of whether the CFTC should issue new rules governing OTC derivatives.[138] The Concept Release noted "the explosive growth in the OTC market in recent years" as well as "the number and size of losses even among large and sophisticated users" of derivatives. The Concept Release stated that the CFTC would consider whether it should modify its 1993 exemption for OTC derivatives "to enhance the fairness, financial integrity, and efficiency of this market."[139]

Robert Rubin, Alan Greenspan, and SEC Chairman Arthur Levitt responded to the Concept Release by expressing their "grave concerns," and they "seriously question[ed] the CFTC's jurisdiction in this area." They strongly criticized the Concept Release for increasing "the legal uncertainty" surrounding OTC derivatives.[140] Born refused to withdraw the Concept Release, and ISDA lobbied Congress to impose a legislative moratorium on the CFTC's authority to regulate OTC derivatives. The Treasury, Fed, and SEC vigorously supported the proposed moratorium.[141]

At a Senate hearing in July 1998, Treasury Deputy Secretary Lawrence Summers stated that the "dramatic growth of the [OTC] market in recent years is testament not merely to the dynamism of modern financial markets but to the benefits that derivatives provide for American businesses." Summers argued that the CFTC's Concept Release "cast the shadow of regulatory uncertainty over an otherwise thriving market" and created "the risk that the U.S. will see its leadership position in derivatives erode" if dealers and end-users moved their derivatives activities to foreign countries. Summers maintained that there was "no clear evidence of a need for additional regulation of the institutional OTC derivatives market." Dealers in OTC derivatives were "largely sophisticated financial institutions" that were "eminently capable of protecting themselves from fraud and counterparty insolvencies and ... are already subject to basic safety and soundness regulation under existing banking and securities laws."[142]

Alan Greenspan echoed Summers' views at the same Senate hearing. He agreed with Summers that, "aside from safety and soundness regulation of derivatives dealers under the banking or securities laws, regulation of derivatives transactions that are privately negotiated by professionals is unnecessary."[143]

Two months later, a major crisis erupted at Long-Term Capital Management (LTCM). That crisis demonstrated that Summers' and Greenspan's faith in the effectiveness of market discipline for OTC derivatives was completely unfounded.

LTCM, a large hedge fund, was founded in 1994 by "a dazzling array of partners," including Nobel laureates Myron Scholes and Robert Merton. Together with Fischer Black, Scholes and Merton developed modern option pricing theories, which provided the intellectual foundation for trading models that were widely used in OTC derivatives market. LTCM's other founders included former Fed Vice Chairman David Mullins and John Meriweather, the leader of Salomon Brothers' legendary bond trading team during the 1980s. Meriweather recruited several members of that team to join LTCM.[144] During a 1999 hearing, Representative Marge Roukema (R-NJ) described LTCM as "the Cadillac of Hedge Funds. It had star quality."[145]

LTCM produced large profits between 1994 and 1997 by using highly leveraged trading strategies that relied heavily on OTC derivatives. LTCM's profits caused the fund's investors, lenders, and counterparties to ask very few questions about the risks inherent in its financial condition and trading strategy. In early 1998, LTCM held about $5 billion of equity capital, while its huge investment portfolio included $125 billion of securities (including large volumes of debt securities borrowed from commercial and investment banks under repurchase agreements) and derivatives with total notional values of $1.25 trillion.[146]

LTCM's primary strategy during 1998 was to make "convergence-arbitrage" trades, which sought to exploit pricing discrepancies between higher-risk private sector debt securities and lower-risk U.S. and foreign government bonds. LTCM believed that global markets would be relatively calm in 1998, due to the favorable effects of support programs provided by the International Monetary Fund, the U.S., and other Western nations to Asian countries in response to the East Asian financial crisis in 1997. LTCM predicted that credit spreads between risky and "safe" bonds would narrow (converge) in 1998. In addition, LTCM aggressively sold equity options because it believed that volatility in global equity markets would decline. LTCM's trading positions were based on "value at risk" (VAR) models derived from Scholes' and Merton's theoretical work. LTCM's risk models assumed that disruptive events like a sovereign bond default or a stock market crash were very unlikely to happen in 1998.[147]

In August 1998, Russia devalued the ruble and defaulted on debts owed to foreign creditors. The IMF did not intervene with a rescue package, as many investors had expected. Russia's devaluation and debt default triggered a global "flight to quality" as investors frantically bought "safe," very liquid securities (especially U.S. Treasury bonds) and unloaded their positions in illiquid, higher-risk securities and related derivatives. Yield spreads between high-risk and low-risk debt securities widened dramatically, and the volatility of equity markets soared. Those events dealt a death blow to LTCM's "convergence" strategy and doomed LTCM. Scholes later admitted that the VAR models used by LTCM and other major financial institutions failed to anticipate the "liquidity risk" that suddenly materialized in August 1998.[148]

By mid-September, LTCM had lost $4.4 billion of its capital and appealed to the Fed for help. The Fed concluded that a default by LTCM could paralyze global financial markets by setting off a "chain reaction" of failures among large derivatives dealers as well as "fire-sale" liquidations of securities and other assets connected to OTC derivatives.[149] Federal regulators also determined that major banks and securities firms had engaged in "herd behavior" by copying LTCM's trades. As a result, those financial giants were exposed to the same types of losses that crippled LTCM. Regulators feared that LTCM's collapse might threaten the survival of some large banks and securities firms.[150]

To prevent a systemic financial crisis, the Fed cut short-term interest rates three times in seven weeks. The Fed also arranged an emergency rescue of LTCM by fourteen of the largest U.S. banks and securities firms. The rescue group injected $3.6 billion of new capital into LTCM in return for 90% of the hedge fund's equity. The LTCM crisis confirmed previous warnings by many commentators about the systemic dangers posed by OTC derivatives.[151] For example, I predicted in 1995 that "the [federal] government would undoubtedly take steps to prevent any future failure of a major OTC dealer from precipitating a systemic crisis."[152]

The 1998 financial crisis inflicted punishing losses on Citigroup, BofA, Bankers Trust, and other U.S. and foreign financial conglomerates. Bankers Trust suffered more than $2 billion of losses from speculative trading bets and soured investments during 1998 and 1999. To prevent Bankers Trust's failure, the Fed approved an expedited sale of that bank to Deutsche Bank in 1999.[153]

The 1998 crisis revealed that regulators and market participants were completely unaware of the magnitude and correlation of risk exposures held by LTCM and major financial institutions in the form of OTC derivatives and other complex, opaque financial instruments.[154] As described in Chapters 10 and 11, the outbreak of the subprime financial crisis in 2007 and the collapse of AIG in 2008 revealed similar failures of risk assessment by both regulators and market participants.

I have previously argued that the global financial crisis of 1998 was "a precursor and dress rehearsal for the global financial crisis of 2007–09."[155] Yet financial conglomerates and policymakers failed to apply the lessons they should have learned from the 1998 crisis, and they did not build adequate defenses to deal with the devastating crisis that occurred in 2007–09. A 2011 study found that the same large banks and securities firms that suffered the greatest declines in stock market values in 1998 also recorded the worst stock market performances in 2007 and 2008. The authors concluded that large financial institutions with severe losses in 1998 failed to "alter the[ir] business model or to become more cautious regarding their risk culture" before the global financial crisis began in mid-2007.[156]

Similarly, the Financial Crisis Inquiry Commission concluded that large financial institutions did not change their speculative risk-taking strategies despite the severe losses they suffered in 1998. In addition, financial regulators did not compel the institutions they supervised to adopt more conservative business policies.[157] The extraordinary measures that the Fed took to support LTCM and stabilize financial markets in 1998 probably caused large banks and securities firms to believe that the Fed would take similar steps to protect major financial firms during a comparable future crisis.[158] In short, the 1998 crisis was the dead canary in the coal mine that advocates of "financial modernization" chose not to see.

The LTCM crisis certainly did not convince the Clinton administration and Congress to withdraw their opposition to Brooksley Born's proposal to adopt new rules for OTC derivatives. Only a few policymakers agreed with Born that the LTCM debacle demonstrated the need for stronger regulation of OTC derivatives. Opponents of stronger regulation denied any connection between LTCM's failure and its enormous positions in OTC derivatives or the lack of regulation for those instruments. Congress adopted a temporary moratorium that blocked the CFTC from adopting any new requirements for OTC derivatives. Born resigned soon thereafter.[159]

———

Congress did ask for reports on the LTCM crisis and OTC derivatives from the President's Working Group on Financial Markets. That working group included the heads of the Treasury Department, Fed, SEC, and CFTC.[160] Before the working group issued its reports, Fed Chairman Alan Greenspan staked out his own position in a

March 1999 speech. In that speech, Greenspan argued that OTC derivatives "enhance the process of wealth creation" by enabling dealers "to differentiate risk and allocate it to those investors most able and willing to take it." He lauded "the profitability of derivative products" for increasing the earnings of major banks and for contributing to "the significant gain in the overall finance industry's share of American corporate output during the past decade."[161]

Greenspan acknowledged that losses from derivatives "rose to record levels in the third quarter of 1998." However, he claimed that derivatives "were bystanders [and] were scarcely the major players" during the 1998 crisis."[162] In his speech, Greenspan never mentioned LTCM or the fact that the Fed orchestrated an emergency rescue of the firm.

Greenspan also admitted that VAR models used by financial institutions and investors did not anticipate the severe losses that occurred during the East Asian and Russian crises of 1997 and 1998. Greenspan noted that VAR models failed to capture "the extreme negative tail that reflects the probability of occurrence of a panic."[163] However, he rejected the view that regulators should "abandon models-based approaches to regulatory capital and return to traditional approaches." He instead called for improvements in internal risk management by OTC derivatives dealers. In his 1999 speech on derivatives, as on so many other occasions, Greenspan endorsed a supervisory approach that relied heavily on market discipline and gave great deference to internal risk models developed by banks.[164]

Like Greenspan, the President's Working Group on Financial Markets minimized the role played by derivatives in LTCM's failure. The working group's first report, issued in April 1999, stated that LTCM's "excessive leverage" was mainly responsible for the firm's "near collapse." That report included only a limited analysis of LTCM's massive positions in OTC and exchange-graded derivatives.[165] The report focused primarily on LTCM's "opaqueness" and the "minimal scrutiny" that LTCM's risk profile and trading strategies received from investors, creditors, and counterparties.[166]

The working group concluded that outside parties did not provide "an effective check on [LTCM's] overall activities." The report also noted that the "risk management weaknesses revealed by the LTCM episode were not unique to LTCM," as they also occurred "to a lesser degree" at large banks and securities firms.[167] Thus, the working group's first report documented that market discipline *failed* to restrain excessive risk-taking by LTCM and also *failed* to stop major banks and securities firms from suffering heavy losses. Nevertheless, the working group declared that market discipline should remain the "primary mechanism that regulates risk-taking by firms in a market economy."[168]

The working group's strong ideological commitment to market discipline—in the face of abundant evidence showing that market discipline *failed* in 1998—explained why its first report did not recommend any new substantive rules for OTC derivatives.[169] The first report also rejected any new "constraints on leverage" for dealers or end-users of OTC derivatives. Instead, like Greenspan's speech, the report recommended that financial institutions should improve their internal risk management procedures.[170]

The working group's second report, issued in November 1999, called on Congress to adopt legislation exempting OTC derivatives from regulation under the Commodity Exchange Act. The working group praised OTC derivatives for "fostering more precise ways of understanding, quantifying, and managing risk." The working group also warned that "innovation and growth" in OTC derivatives markets and "U.S. leadership" of those markets would be threatened unless Congress promptly removed the "cloud of legal uncertainty" surrounding OTC derivatives.[171] The working group proposed that "sophisticated counterparties" should be allowed to enter into OTC derivatives free from any substantive regulation by the CFTC. The Working Group argued that deregulation was essential to provide "a permanent clarification of the legal status" of OTC derivatives.[172]

Echoing Summers' and Greenspan's views, the working group's second report contended that "sophisticated counterparties" in OTC derivatives transactions did not need any regulatory oversight because most dealers were already subject to adequate supervision by bank regulators, the SEC, or the CFTC. The report also maintained that "most OTC derivatives are not susceptible to manipulation" because their payoffs were based on an underlying "rate or price determined by a separate highly liquid market."[173] The working group's claims that OTC derivatives did not need to be regulated and could not be used for manipulative purposes ignored the actual behavior of derivatives markets during the 1998 crisis as well as previous market disruptions. Those erroneous claims had catastrophic consequences during the following decade.[174]

The working group's second report reiterated that regulators should rely on "private counterparty discipline" as the "primary mechanism" for avoiding "systemic risk." Despite the first report's conclusion that market discipline *failed* to restrain highly leveraged and speculative risk-taking by LTCM and other financial institutions, the second report claimed that "private counterparty credit risk management has been employed effectively by both regulated and unregulated dealers of OTC derivatives, and the tools required by federal regulators [to supplement market discipline] already exist."[175] Except for two brief references, the working group's second report did not mention LTCM and did not contain any discussion of lessons learned from the 1998 crisis.[176] It appeared that members of the working group had already expunged the LTCM fiasco from their collective memories.[177]

Armed with the working group's recommendations, the derivatives industry and its political allies mounted a successful campaign to enact the Commodity Futures Modernization Act (CFMA).[178] The only real question was how broad the scope of deregulation would be for OTC derivatives. Senator Phil Gramm put an extended hold on the legislation until congressional leaders and the Clinton administration agreed on a final bill that was acceptable to him. As enacted in December 2000, CFMA exempted OTC derivatives from substantive regulation under both federal and state laws—including state insurance and gambling laws—as long as the counterparties to those instruments were financial institutions, corporate end-users, institutional investors, or wealthy individuals. The CFTC and SEC retained only a very limited authority to bring enforcement actions for fraud or manipulation on a case-by-case basis.[179]

The President's Working Group on Financial Markets endorsed the final version of CFMA as crafted by Senator Gramm. The working group praised CFMA for preserving the "competitive position" of major U.S. financial institutions in OTC derivatives markets, and for "providing legal certainty and promoting innovation, transparency and efficiency in our financial markets."[180] Gramm declared that CFMA "completes the work of [GLBA]" by providing "legal certainty" for OTC derivatives and by "protect[ing] financial institutions from over-regulation." Gramm predicted that GLBA and CFMA would be viewed as "a watershed, where we turned away from the outmoded Depression-era approach to financial regulation and adopted a framework that will position our financial services industries to be world leaders into the new century."[181]

———

Riegle-Neal, GLBA, and CFMA were highly consequential laws. They enabled banks to become much bigger and more complex, and to undertake a much wider array of activities. They transformed the U.S. financial industry from a decentralized system of independent financial sectors into a highly consolidated industry dominated by a small group of huge financial conglomerates. The big-bank lobby and its political allies secured passage of all three laws through carefully planned and well-funded campaigns. All three laws were justified by an ideology of comprehensive deregulation, and they provided a blueprint for light-touch supervision that relied on the wisdom and self-regulating capacity of untrammeled financial markets.[182]

The ideology of deregulation that produced Riegle-Neal, GLBA, and CFMA was not consistent, and it was arguably disingenuous. Some policymakers and industry leaders acknowledged that large financial conglomerates were likely to benefit from transfers of federal safety net subsidies from banks to their securities and insurance affiliates, as well as implicit TBTF subsidies. Nevertheless, whenever Congress or federal regulators faced a choice between limiting the spread of public subsidies and providing more profit-making opportunities to big banks, the big-bank lobby usually prevailed. Congress's decision to approve GLBA while relying on Section 23A's very weak firewall to limit the spread of public subsidies provides a striking example of that policy choice.[183]

Deregulation served the interests of the largest financial institutions, and their power and influence grew in response to all three statutes. Riegle-Neal allowed the largest banks to expand throughout the nation, thereby increasing their political influence at the expense of smaller banks as well as securities firms and insurance companies. Leading securities firms and insurance companies joined big banks in pushing for GLBA when they realized they could not stop banks from expanding into securities and insurance markets. All three financial groups supported CFMA because it allowed the largest financial institutions to engage in OTC derivatives activities free from any substantive regulation. The enactment of GLBA and CFMA in consecutive years showed just how powerful the biggest financial conglomerates had become.[184]

Some scholars have argued that GLBA and CFMA did not play any substantial role in promoting the reckless credit boom that led to the financial crisis. Those scholars contend that GLBA and CFMA merely ratified what federal regulators and courts had already done by opening loopholes in Glass-Steagall and the BHC Act during the 1980s and 1990s.[185]

I strongly disagree. As described in Chapter 7, the loopholes created by regulators and courts contained many restrictions and relied on highly contestable legal interpretations, which could have been reversed by either regulators or the courts. As shown in this chapter, the drafters of the 1991 Treasury plan and proponents of GLBA and CFMA repeatedly argued that those loopholes were incomplete, burdensome, and inefficient. Supporters of GLBA and CFMA declared that both statutes were urgently needed to provide "legal certainty" so that universal banks could offer a comprehensive suite of financial services through a highly integrated, "one-stop shopping" platform.[186]

It is very unlikely that the largest financial institutions and their trade associations would have chosen to pursue a twenty-year legislative campaign, costing hundreds of millions of dollars in lobbying expenses and political contributions, if they had viewed GLBA and CFMA as insignificant laws. Big banks and Wall Street securities firms clearly viewed GLBA and CFMA as essential components of their strategy to establish giant financial conglomerates that could dominate domestic and global financial markets while exploiting TBTF subsidies.[187]

One very tangible way to measure GLBA's and CFMA's significance is to notice how quickly the financial industry changed in response to those statutes. GLBA's first major dividend was to validate Citigroup's universal banking strategy. Without GLBA, Citigroup would have been forced to divest many of its nonbanking activities within five years, and other banks could not have copied Citigroup's business model. After GLBA was enacted, leading banks quickly followed Citigroup's lead. During 2000, two big European banks—Credit Suisse and UBS—acquired large U.S. securities firms (Donaldson, Lufkin & Jenrette and Paine Webber). In addition, Chase merged with JPMC to form a commercial and investment banking giant.[188]

GLBA created a second immediate benefit for big banks by allowing them to convert their limited Section 20 securities subsidiaries into full-service securities broker-dealers. As a federal regulator commented in 2000, "Loopholes cost money.... A top bank told me [GLBA] was a major boost to their bottom line."[189] GLBA enabled banking organizations to triple their share of the U.S. corporate debt underwriting market, from 25% in 1998 to 75% in 2003. The number of banking organizations that ranked among the top five underwriters of U.S. corporate debt rose from zero in 1996 to four in 2003.[190]

Another indicator of GLBA's and CFMA's importance was the explosive growth that occurred in markets for shadow bank deposits, securitization, and OTC derivatives after 2000. The volume of outstanding money market mutual funds increased from $1.8 trillion to $3.8 trillion between 2000 and 2007, while the commercial paper market grew from $1.3 trillion to $2 trillion.[191] Outstanding securities repurchase agreements (repos) at securities broker-dealers—including securities affiliates of universal banks—rose from $2.5 trillion in 2002 to $4 trillion in 2007, while outstanding structured finance securities produced by private-label securitizations grew from $1.6 trillion in 2001 to more than $5 trillion in 2007.[192] Most dramatically, the aggregate notional values of OTC derivatives in global markets exploded from $95 trillion in 2000 to $673 trillion in mid-2008, with U.S. financial institutions holding about two-fifths of those exposures.[193] It seems highly unlikely that such dramatic growth could have occurred in all of those markets without the comprehensive deregulation authorized by GLBA and CFMA.[194]

Leading securities firms responded to the emergence of universal banks with their own consolidation and diversification campaigns. Morgan Stanley acquired Dean Witter in 1997, and the other four big securities firms—Merrill Lynch, Goldman Sachs, Lehman Brothers, and Bear Stearns—also expanded rapidly during the late 1990s and early 2000s. By 2004, the five largest securities firms held combined assets of $2.5 trillion, compared with $4.7 trillion of assets held by the five largest U.S. banks.[195]

The four largest securities firms (all except Bear Stearns) supplemented their securities activities by acquiring FDIC-insured depository institutions. Securities firms could own two types of FDIC-insured depository institutions—thrift institutions and industrial banks—because those institutions were not treated as "banks" under the BHC Act. By 2006, the four biggest securities firms owned thrifts and industrial banks that held almost $160 billion of FDIC-insured deposits. In addition, all five leading securities firms generated large volumes of shadow bank deposits by sponsoring money market mutual funds and by issuing short-term repos and commercial paper. Thus, the Big Five securities firms had become "de facto universal banks" by the early 2000s.[196]

A similar process of deregulation, consolidation, and conglomeration occurred in the U.K. and EU. The U.K.'s "Big Bang" reforms of 1986 allowed British banks to become universal banks, and the EU's Second Banking Directive authorized European universal banks to do business across the EU with a "single passport" beginning in 1993.[197] Those events paved the way for more than two thousand bank mergers in the U.K. and the Eurozone between 1990 and 2006. Those deals included three giant mergers among UK banks (HSBC-Midland, Lloyds-TSB, and RBS-NatWest), two big combinations among four leading French banks (BNP-Paribas and Credit Agricole–Credit Lyonnais), and a union of two major Swiss banks that produced UBS. In addition, large U.S., U.K., and European banks acquired virtually all of Britain's leading merchant (investment) banks after 1986. The "Big Bang" cemented London's status as a center for international finance and global investment banking that rivaled New York.[198]

By 2007, a group of seventeen U.S. and foreign financial conglomerates dominated global markets for securities underwriting, securitizations, structured financial products, and OTC derivatives. That group—which I call the "Big Seventeen"—included the four largest U.S. banks (BofA, Citigroup, JPMC, and Wachovia), the five largest U.S. securities firms, and eight big foreign universal banks (Barclays, BNP Paribas, Credit Suisse, Deutsche Bank, HSBC, RBS, Société Générale, and UBS). In addition, the giant U.S. insurance company American International Group played a leading role in the credit default swap market.[199]

The nine American members of the Big Seventeen could never have achieved their size and scope in 2007 without the enactment of at least one of the three statutes (Riegle-Neal, GLBA, and CFMA) discussed in this chapter. Similarly, the eight foreign universal banks greatly expanded their size and scope in the U.S., U.K., and EU in response to deregulation that occurred in all three regions.[200] As Barry Eichengreen explained, "The result of [Riegle-Neal, GLBA, and CFMA] was a massive increase in the size, complexity, and leverage of US financial institutions.... And what was true of banks in the United States was similarly true of banks elsewhere, notably in Europe."[201]

9

See No Evil

Policymakers and Regulators Allowed Financial Conglomerates to Inflate a Toxic Credit Bubble on Both Sides of the Atlantic During the "Roaring 2000s"

From 2000 through 2007, U.S. and European financial conglomerates produced a massive credit boom, whose magnitude surpassed the spectacular credit surge of the 1920s. The credit boom of the "Roaring 2000s"—like that of the Roaring Twenties—began in the U.S. and spread to Europe. Universal banks securitized trillions of dollars of high-risk loans and sold the resulting asset-backed securities to investors around the world.[1] By August 2007, the economies of the U.S., U.K., and many European countries depended on the performance of unstable pyramids of risky debts. A transatlantic financial crisis was certain to occur as soon as widespread defaults occurred on those debts.

The Roaring 2000s witnessed massive growth in all types of private sector debts on both sides of the Atlantic. The total volume of outstanding U.S. private sector debts doubled from $20.4 trillion to $41.6 trillion between December 1999 and December 2007. During that period, U.S. household debts increased by $7.6 trillion, nonfinancial business obligations expanded by $4.1 trillion, and financial sector liabilities grew by $9.5 trillion. As reflected in the bottom panel of Figure 0.3 in the Introduction, the ratio of U.S. private sector debts to GDP rose from 212% in 1999 to 288% in 2007. The 2007 peak exceeded the previous high point of 250%, recorded in the early 1930s after the credit boom of the 1920s.[2]

Credit surges of comparable magnitudes occurred in several European nations during the Roaring 2000s, including the U.K., Ireland, Portugal, and Spain.[3] The U.K.'s ratio of private sector debts to GDP doubled from 200% to over 400% between 1999 and 2007. By 2008, the ratio of private sector debts to GDP exceeded 200% in Ireland and Spain and 175% in Portugal.[4]

The Big Seventeen financial conglomerates (discussed in Chapter 8) played leading roles in promoting the credit boom of the 2000s.[5] They dominated U.S. and global markets for underwriting corporate debt and equity securities, dealing in over-the-counter derivatives, and making syndicated loans to businesses.[6] They were also the top underwriters for more than $9 trillion of structured finance securities issued in the U.S. between January 2000 and December 2007. Those securities included $3.5 trillion of "private label" residential mortgage-backed securities (RMBS), $720 billion of commercial mortgage-backed securities (CMBS), $3.6 trillion of asset-backed securities (ABS), $630 billion of collateralized debt obligations (CDOs), and $600 billion of collateralized loan obligations (CLOs). ABS were securitized pools of home equity loans, credit card loans, auto loans, and other consumer loans. CDOs were securitized pools of debt obligations that included RMBS and other loans, while CLOs were securitized pools of leveraged syndicated corporate loans.[7]

Fifteen members of the Big Seventeen were the largest underwriters of structured finance securities. Citigroup was the top-ranked underwriter, followed closely by JPMorgan Chase (JPMC), Bank of America (BofA), Credit Suisse, and Deutsche Bank. Next in line were the Big Five U.S. securities firms (Lehman Brothers, Bear Stearns, Morgan Stanley, Merrill Lynch, and Goldman Sachs), followed by Barclays, UBS, Wachovia, BNP Paribas, and HSBC. The two remaining members, Royal Bank of Scotland (RBS) and Société Générale, were also significant underwriters of structured finance securities.[8] In addition to the Big Seventeen conglomerates, American International Group (AIG), the largest U.S. insurance company, played an important role by issuing credit default swaps that provided financial guarantees (and produced AAA ratings) for super-senior tranches of many CDOs.[9] Large universal banks dominated securitization markets in the U.K. and Europe as they did in the U.S.[10]

As discussed in the next part of this chapter, the credit boom of the Roaring 2000s followed a large bubble in the U.S. stock market that occurred began in 1995 and burst in 2000–02. Thus, stock market and real estate booms and busts led up to the financial crisis of 2007–09, just as similar booms and busts during the 1920s preceded the Great Depression. The sequence of the booms in the two eras was different, as the real estate boom of the mid-1920s occurred *before* the stock market bubble of 1927–29, while the real estate boom of the 2000s came *after* the stock market bubble of 1995–2000. Nevertheless, the four booms that expanded and burst during the Roaring Twenties and the Roaring 2000s all contributed to the excessively leveraged and highly vulnerable position of households, investors, and financial institutions on the brink of the Great Depression and on the eve of the Great Recession.[11]

The stock market bubble of the late 1990s (like its predecessor of the late 1920s) focused on "new economy" firms that seemed likely to benefit from recent technological advances. The hottest stocks in the late 1990s were issued by firms with business plans linked to the Internet (dotcoms) and by companies that were expanding aggressively in the recently deregulated telecommunications industry (telecoms).[12]

The boom in dotcoms and telecoms produced an explosion of securities offerings. The annual volume of new issues of corporate debt and equity securities rose from $600 billion in 1994 to $2.2 trillion in 2001. As their predecessors had done during the late 1920s, many securities analysts, underwriters, investors, and journalists proclaimed a "new era" of seemingly permanent prosperity during the late 1990s. Market "experts" assured investors that emerging dotcom and telecom firms would generate huge profits by providing Internet services to the public through high-speed communications networks. Investor enthusiasm produced a stock market bubble during the late 1990s that resembled the great bull market of the late 1920s.[13]

The stock market boom of the late 1990s was followed by the most severe stock market slump since the early 1930s. The total value of publicly traded U.S. stocks dropped by 45% between March 2000 and the end of 2002, wiping out almost $8 trillion of investor wealth. The stock market's plunge accelerated between December 2001 and October 2002, as massive accounting frauds and insider abuses were revealed at more than a dozen corporations that had been considered "stars" during the boom. Large financial conglomerates were embroiled in several of those scandals.[14]

The sudden collapses of Enron in late 2001 and WorldCom in mid-2002 were particularly shocking to investors. Enron was one of the most glamorous and admired companies during the dotcom–telecom boom. Its reported revenues grew from less than $10 billion in 1995 to $40 billion in 1999 and $100 billion in 2000. Enron's management (led by Ken Lay, Jeff Skilling, and Andrew Fastow) transformed Enron from a conventional energy pipeline company into an aggressive provider of broadband network services as well as a huge trader in energy commodities and derivatives. Enron persuaded Wall Street analysts that its stock deserved an "Internet-style valuation," which was far higher than Enron could have achieved as an energy company.[15]

Many of Enron's ventures outside the energy industry failed to produce profits. Enron therefore relied on banks to structure complex financial transactions that were designed to conceal shortfalls in its revenues and profits. Enron wanted to avoid issuing new stock that would dilute its reported earnings per share. The company also wanted to avoid issuing new debt securities that would threaten its investment-grade credit rating. In addition, Enron needed to remove loss-producing ventures from its financial statements. With the help of large financial institutions, Enron arranged convoluted and opaque transactions, which created fictitious revenues and earnings, provided disguised loans, and moved poorly performing assets off Enron's balance sheet. In October 2001, when Enron finally began to reveal its accounting manipulations, the company quickly lost the confidence of investors, creditors, and trading counterparties. Enron collapsed into bankruptcy in December 2001.[16]

Large financial conglomerates acted as "Enron's enablers," since "Enron's financial shenanigans would simply not have been possible" without their participation.[17] Enron persuaded leading global financial institutions (including several members of the Big Seventeen) to become its partners in structuring deceptive transactions. Financial institutions worked closely with Enron, even though it was a notoriously difficult client. As one banker said, "It was hell doing business with them, but you had to because they were so big."[18]

Citigroup, BofA, JPMC, Barclays, Credit Suisse, Deutsche Bank, Merrill Lynch, and RBS arranged deals, such as prepaid commodity swaps, that provided disguised loans and allowed Enron to account for the proceeds as operating revenues. Banks also helped Enron to make sham sales of unprofitable assets to off-balance-sheet special-purpose entities (SPEs) that were controlled by Enron's officers. Those SPE deals enabled Enron to exaggerate its operating revenues and conceal many of its bad assets and debts. By the time Enron filed for bankruptcy, it had accumulated $38 billion of debts but reported only $13 billion of those obligations on its balance sheet.[19]

Bankers recognized the deceptive nature of Enron's transactions, but they wanted the generous fees that Enron paid them. A Credit Suisse officer described one SPE transaction as "a vehicle enabling Enron to raise disguised debt which appears as equity on Enron's balance sheet" while providing an "off balance sheet parking lot" for unwanted assets." RBS officials described similar SPE deals as "21st Century Alchemy." After reviewing an SPE transaction, a senior Citigroup officer told his colleagues, "Sounds like we made a lot of exceptions to our standard policies. I am sure we have gone out of our way to let them know that we are bending over backwards for them.... [L]et's remember to collect this iou when it really counts."[20]

WorldCom, with $103 billion of assets, was the largest company to declare bankruptcy until Lehman Brothers collapsed in September 2008. Like Enron, WorldCom became a leading "new economy" firm and a Wall Street favorite during the late 1990s. WorldCom depended on large banks to fund its aggressive growth strategy, which included acquisitions of more than seventy companies between 1985 and 2001. WorldCom experienced deepening financial problems after 1999, as its poorly-managed growth and intensifying competition from other telecoms resulted in declining profit margins, excess capacity, and a crushing debt burden. WorldCom followed Enron's example by using fraudulent accounting techniques to conceal its mounting problems.[21]

Universal banks did not participate directly in WorldCom's accounting frauds. However, Citigroup, JPMC, BofA, Deutsche Bank, and other banks underwrote a risky public offering of $12 billion of WorldCom's bonds in 2001. In their script for the bond offering's "road show," the underwriters said, "We are excited about the WorldCom credit story and this debt offering. WorldCom's financial position gives it the strongest credit profile of any of the largest broadband providers." The prospectus and the road show script did not disclose that several bank underwriters had previously downgraded WorldCom in their internal credit ratings and reduced their exposures to WorldCom by entering into credit default swaps and other hedging transactions.[22]

Citigroup, JPMC, and BofA provided personal loans and other individual financial benefits to Bernie Ebbers, WorldCom's CEO, to solidify their positions as WorldCom's most-favored bankers. Citigroup's star telecom analyst, Jack Grubman, formed a close friendship with Ebbers and became the principal adviser to Ebbers and WorldCom's board of directors. Grubman's status as the king of telecom analysts helped Citigroup to become the leading underwriter for WorldCom as well as Global Crossing and other telecom firms. Citigroup received $1.2 billion in fees for underwriting $190 billion of debt and equity securities for telecom firms between 1996 and 2002. Citigroup paid Grubman almost $70 million between 1999 and 2002.[23]

Grubman saw no conflict of interest between his position as a securities analyst recommending stocks to investors and his role as a key business adviser to WorldCom, Global Crossing, and other telecom firms. In a May 2000 interview, Grubman declared, "What used to be a conflict is now a synergy." He claimed to be creating a "virtuous circle" by using "feedback from institutions and CEOs" to provide the best possible advice to investors and telecom clients. According to Grubman, an "objective" analyst would be "uninformed" and of little value to customers.[24]

In 1998, Grubman proclaimed that "the demand for bandwidth is basically insatiable," and "no matter how much bandwidth is available, it will get used." Grubman's advice matched WorldCom's assertions that Internet traffic was doubling every one hundred days. WorldCom, Global Crossing, and Grubman's other telecom clients built competing fiber-optic networks across the country and around the world to gain a competitive advantage in satisfying projected customer demand.[25]

Grubman touted WorldCom more than any other firm in his research reports. He described WorldCom as "our favorite stock" in August 1997 and as a "must-own" stock in November 1998. He urged investors to "load up the truck" with WorldCom stock in August 1999, and he encouraged investors to buy WorldCom's shares at their "dirt cheap" price in early 2001. Grubman maintained positive ratings on WorldCom longer than most other research analysts. He assigned a "buy" rating to WorldCom stock until shortly before Ebbers resigned as CEO in April 2002, and he did not give WorldCom stock an "underperform" rating until a month before the company filed for bankruptcy in July 2002.[26]

By 2002, many industry observers dismissed Grubman's claims of unlimited demand for bandwidth as "wildly hyped." Instead of doubling every one hundred days, Internet traffic doubled every year. Moreover, technological advances increased the transmission capacity of fiber-optic lines by a factor of one thousand between 1995 and 2002. As a result, the frenzied installation of broadband networks by Grubman's telecom clients and their rivals produced a massive glut of transmission overcapacity. By September 2002, only 3% of installed bandwidth capacity was actually being used, and many of Grubman's clients—including WorldCom, Global Crossing, Metromedia Fiber Networks, Winstar, and XO Communications—had filed for bankruptcy.[27]

––––––

Universal banks pressured their securities analysts to issue biased and misleading research reports, and they also engaged in deceptive practices related to initial public offerings (IPOs) of dotcom and telecom stocks.[28] Universal banks told their securities analysts that much of their compensation depended on their success in helping investment banking colleagues to generate new business. In January 2001—ten months after the stock market boom ended—Citigroup's research analysts did not maintain a single "sell" rating, and they posted only one "underperform" rating, for a list that included almost twelve hundred stocks. Citigroup's head of global equity research privately described those ratings as "ridiculous on face," and he acknowledged the "basic inherent conflict between IB [investment banking] and retail [investment sales]." Despite that officer's understanding of the clear linkage between analysts' conflicts of interest and their inflated ratings, Citigroup's analysts still posted no "sell" ratings at the end of 2001, and they maintained only fifteen "underperform" ratings for a list of more than a thousand stocks.[29]

Securities analysts at other universal banks faced similar conflicts of interest and produced similarly biased ratings. At Credit Suisse, Frank Quattrone—the "Prince of Silicon Valley"—and other bankers in his technology group put intense pressure on Credit Suisse's analysts to issue "buy" ratings for all of the group's clients. In May 2001, an analyst confessed to Credit Suisse's top research executives, "I have 'learned' to adapt to a set of rules that have been imposed by Tech Group banking so as to keep our corporate clients appeased. I believe that these unwritten rules have clearly hindered my ability to be an effective analyst."[30]

In mid-2001, analysts at Wall Street firms maintained only twenty-nine "sell" ratings on more than eight thousand stocks. In October 2001—only two months before Enron's bankruptcy—every research analyst employed by a universal bank assigned a "buy" rating to Enron stock, and most rated Enron a "strong buy."[31] Henry Blodget—Merrill Lynch's leading dotcom analyst—did not issue a single "sell" rating during his three years at the firm, even though he privately described some of Merrill's clients as "crap" or worse.[32]

Analysts who published critical reports about existing or potential clients were frequently fired or punished. Citigroup, Merrill Lynch, BNP Paribas, and UBS fired in-house research analysts after they published negative reports about Enron. Credit Suisse persuaded an in-house analyst *not* to publish a critical report about Enron in November 2001. However, Credit Suisse reduced its own exposure to Enron after reviewing the analyst's findings.[33]

The most widely publicized example of analyst corruption occurred at Citigroup. In late 1999, Sandy Weill, co-CEO of Citigroup, persuaded Jack Grubman to upgrade his rating of AT&T from "neutral" to "buy," even though Grubman had a highly negative view of AT&T. Weill needed Grubman's upgrade to persuade AT&T to hire Citigroup as a co-lead underwriter for AT&T's public offering of $11 billion of stock. In addition, Grubman's upgrade helped Weill to enlist the support of AT&T's chairman, C. Martin Armstrong (a director of Citigroup), in Weill's successful campaign to oust John Reed as Citigroup's co-CEO in early 2000.

As a reward for Grubman's upgrade, Weill arranged for Grubman's two children to be admitted to the 92nd Street Y's highly selective preschool. To ensure that the 92nd Street Y accepted Grubman's children, Weill contacted a close friend who served on the Y's board, and Weill also directed the Citigroup Foundation to make a $1 million donation to the Y.[34]

Universal banks displayed similar conflicts of interest when they underwrote IPOs for dotcoms and telecoms. Bankers made preferential allocations of stocks in hot IPOs—a practice known as "spinning"—to top executives of current or prospective clients. Bankers also made preferred allocations of stocks to institutional investors in return for more trading business and larger brokerage fees. Citigroup provided allocations of hot IPO stocks that resulted in $40 million of trading profits for senior executives of WorldCom (including Bernie Ebbers) and four other telecom firms.

Frank Quattrone organized a "Friends of Frank" program, in which Credit Suisse traded allocations of hot IPO stocks to favored clients in exchange for investment banking deals or higher brokerage fees. Credit Suisse earned almost $800 million in dotcom underwriting fees and paid Quattrone $100 million between 1998 and 2000. One Credit Suisse banker admitted, "The only culture here is greed."[35]

The pervasive misconduct at universal banks during the dotcom–telecom boom resembled the conflicts of interest and abusive practices that tarnished the reputations of their predecessors during the Roaring Twenties. The biased research reports issued by bank securities analysts during the dotcom and telecom boom resembled the hyped "news flashes" that National City sent to its offices to promote the sale of risky stocks and foreign bonds during the Roaring Twenties. The spinning by universal banks during the dotcom–telecom boom mirrored the "preferred lists" that National City and J. P. Morgan & Co. used to allocate hot stocks to favored clients and influential public figures during the Roaring Twenties.[36] In 2003, Joseph Stiglitz commented that abuses by universal banks during the dotcom–telecom boom was "a story of conflicts of interest gone out of control." Stiglitz pointed out that the repeal of Glass-Steagall in 1999 greatly increased the opportunities for conflicts of interest within the banking system.[37]

The collapse of the dotcom–telecom boom triggered federal and state investigations and private lawsuits that revealed serious misconduct at many large financial conglomerates. Federal and state agencies issued enforcement orders and imposed civil penalties on eleven of the Big Seventeen financial conglomerates (as well as other large banks) related to the scandals involving Enron, biased research analysts, and IPO spinning. Large financial institutions paid more than $17 billion to settle Enron- and WorldCom-related claims filed by the SEC, investors, and Enron's bankruptcy estate. Leading financial institutions also paid $1.5 billion in civil penalties to settle federal and state enforcement actions related to biased research analysts and IPO spinning.[38] Two bank analysts—Jack Grubman and Henry Blodget—were fined and banned for life from the securities industry for issuing research reports that were contrary to their actual beliefs. However, government agencies did not issue enforcement orders or assess civil penalties against any of the CEOs of the banks that were involved in the foregoing abuses.[39]

Congress responded to the Enron and WorldCom scandals by passing the Sarbanes-Oxley Act in July 2002. Sarbanes-Oxley established stronger audit, disclosure, and governance requirements for publicly traded companies, as well as increased penalties for issuing fraudulent corporate financial statements. The statute also created a new government oversight board for accounting firms. Sarbanes-Oxley did not directly address the conflicts of interest and manipulative practices that occurred at universal banks. However, the SEC and the New York Attorney General's office negotiated a "global settlement" in 2003, which required eleven financial conglomerates to stop engaging in IPO spinning and to establish internal safeguards to shield their research analysts from influence by investment bankers.[40]

The Senate Permanent Subcommittee on Investigations called on the Federal Reserve Board, the Office of the Comptroller of the Currency, and the SEC to stop large financial institutions from arranging deceptive "complex structured finance transactions" (CSFTs) similar to Enron's manipulative deals. In May 2004, the three agencies issued proposed guidelines to prevent abusive CSFTs. Big banks and their trade associations strongly opposed the proposed guidelines. Due to the financial industry's aggressive lobbying, the final guidelines issued in early 2007 represented a "considerable retreat" from the agencies' original proposals. The final guidelines exempted RMBS and CDOs as well as "hedging-type transactions that used 'plain-vanilla' derivatives." The final guidelines also stated that they did not establish any "legally enforceable requirements or obligations."[41] Thus, efforts to stop Enron-style abuses by major financial institutions had minimal impact.

The scandals of the early 2000s should have alerted policymakers to the growing risks posed by universal banks. In a 2006 paper, I argued that the Enron and WorldCom scandals demonstrated that the regulatory framework for universal banks under the Gramm-Leach-Bliley Act was "not adequate to control the promotional pressures, conflicts of interest and risk-taking incentives that are generated by the commingling of commercial and investment banking."[42]

Several economic studies published between 2001 and 2006 determined that "consolidation and conglomeration in the U.S. and European banking industries generated higher levels of systemic risk on both sides of the Atlantic." Those studies found that the "increased reliance by U.S. banking organizations on nontraditional, fee-based lines of business (including securitization and other investment banking activities) increased the volatility of their earnings and increased their exposure to the risk of insolvency." In addition, the "growing convergence among the activities of banks, securities firms and insurance companies [after] the early 1990s intensified the risk that losses in one sector of the financial services industry would spill over into other sectors and produce a systemic financial crisis." Despite the abundant warning signs, policymakers and regulators did not take any meaningful steps to control excessive risk-taking by large financial conglomerates during the 2000s, just as they failed to take appropriate action after the LTCM crisis of 1998.[43]

———

The Fed's aggressive easing of monetary policy represented the federal government's most significant response to the bursting of the dotcom–telecom bubble. Chairman Alan Greenspan and his colleagues had serious concerns about the destruction of almost $8 trillion of investor wealth and the economic recession that followed the dotcom–telecom bust. The terrorist attacks on September 11, 2001, further disrupted U.S. financial markets and aggravated the stock market's slump. The Fed injected $200 billion of liquidity into the financial markets after the attacks, and the Fed reduced its target for short-term interest rates eleven times, from 6.5% in January 2001 to 1.75% after 9/11. During late 2002 and early 2003, Greenspan, Fed Vice Chairman

Roger Ferguson, and Fed Governor Ben Bernanke worried that the lingering economic slump might trigger a deflationary episode similar to those that occurred in the U.S. during the early 1930s and in Japan during the 1990s (after large bubbles burst in both Japan's stock market and its real estate market).[44]

The Fed reduced its target for short-term interest rates to 1% in June 2003—the lowest level since 1954—and the Fed held short-term rates at that level for a year.[45] Economist John Taylor, who developed the "Taylor rule" for determining a stable, noninflationary monetary policy, argued in 2007 that the Fed's "extra-easy policy [during the early 2000s] accelerated the housing boom and thereby ultimately led to the housing bust." According to Taylor's calculations, the Fed's target for short-term rates fell below the levels implied by the Taylor rule in 2002 and were 2–3% below Taylor-implied levels during 2003 and 2004. The Fed's target for short-term rates did not return to the level of Taylor-implied rates until the Fed raised its target to 5.25% in 2006.[46]

Other observers agreed that the Fed's monetary policy was "too expansionary for too long" during the early and mid-2000s. They concurred with Taylor's view that the Fed's ultra-low interest rates helped to promote an unsustainable housing boom.[47] William Fleckenstein maintained that Greenspan and the Fed "bailed out the world's largest equity bubble with the world's largest real estate bubble."[48]

As shown in Figure 9.1, average U.S. home sale prices rose about 5% per year between 1994 and 2001. Home prices increased at an a significantly faster rate after 2001, as the housing boom became much stronger. By January 2007, average U.S. home sale prices were 55% higher than they had been in 2001 and more than double their level in 1994. The annual rate of new home construction rose by 26% between 2001 and 2006, compared with an 11% increase between 1996 and 2001.[49] The substantially higher rates of growth in home prices and new home construction after 2001 indicate that the Fed's ultra-low interest rates played a substantial role in promoting the housing boom.

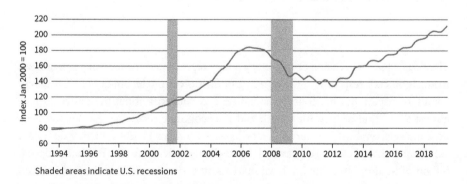

Shaded areas indicate U.S. recessions

Figure 9.1 Changes in U.S. Housing Prices, 1994–2018
Source: Federal Reserve Bank of St. Louis; S&P Dow Jones Indices LLC

Alan Greenspan confirmed the link between the Fed's ultra-low interest rate policy and housing prices during his testimony before Congress in 2002 and 2003. Greenspan told Congress that the Fed reduced interest rates for the specific purpose of stimulating home mortgage lending (by making mortgages more affordable) and boosting housing prices. Greenspan stated that the Fed's ultra-low interest rates increased home values and also enabled homeowners to "extract" more than $850 billion of equity from their homes by refinancing their mortgages and taking out home equity loans. Greenspan told Congress that the large-scale extraction of home equity increased household spending and served as a "powerful stabilizing force" that reduced the adverse effects of the dotcom–telecom bust.[50]

The Fed's ultra-low interest rate policy after 2000 was part of a long-term pattern of interventions orchestrated by Greenspan to stabilize financial markets after the bursting of asset price bubbles and other serious disruptions. In October 1987, the Fed responded to a severe stock market crash by providing emergency infusions of liquidity into the financial markets and cutting interest rates aggressively. In the early 1990s, the Fed sharply reduced interest rates to support large troubled banks that were struggling with nonperforming loans. In 1998, the Fed responded to the Russian debt default crisis by making rapid interest rate cuts, arranging the rescue of LTCM, and approving an expedited sale of Bankers Trust to Deutsche Bank.[51] In mid-December 2000, the financial markets anticipated that the Fed would again intervene to mitigate the impact of the dotcom–telecom bust. A leading financial magazine reported, "The 'Greenspan put' is once again the talk of Wall Street.... The idea is that the Federal Reserve can be relied upon in times of crisis to come to the rescue, cutting interest rates and pumping in liquidity, thus providing a floor for equity prices." The Fed began to cut interest rates less than three weeks later, on January 3, 2001, at Greenspan's urging.[52]

In a series of speeches between 2002 and 2004, Greenspan, Bernanke, Ferguson, and Fed Governor Donald Kohn confirmed that the "Greenspan put" was part of the Fed's emergency toolkit. They argued that it was not feasible or desirable for the Fed or other central banks to "lean against" suspected asset bubbles. In their view, central banks did not have timely and reliable information to determine whether a bubble—a large disparity between asset prices and "fundamental" values—actually existed. In addition, hiking interest rates in an effort to control suspected bubbles could inflict serious harm on the general economy. Greenspan and his three Fed colleagues therefore maintained that the correct approach was to "mitigate the fallout [of a bursting bubble] when it occurs and, hopefully, ease the transition to the next expansion."[53]

In 2005, former Fed Vice Chairman Alan Blinder and economist Ricardo Reis explained that "Greenspan's preferred approach to bubbles is to let them burst of their own accord and then use monetary policy (and other instruments), as necessary, to protect the banking system and the economy from the fallout." Blinder and Reis concluded that Greenspan's " 'mop up after' strategy" achieved good results in the early 2000s, "when the biggest bubble in history imploded, vaporizing $8 *trillion* of wealth in the process," as the Fed's aggressive easing of monetary policy avoided a severe recession.[54]

In contrast, others argued that the "Greenspan put" and the too-big-to-fail (TBTF) policy for large banks created a dangerous, asymmetric risk curve for Wall Street during the 1990s and 2000s. Bankers and investors expected that the Fed would *not* intervene to stop asset price bubbles from inflating but *would* intervene vigorously to establish a "floor" to mitigate the adverse effects of a collapsing bubble, while also preventing failures of major banks. Wall Street's belief that the Fed's policies followed an asymmetric risk curve encouraged bankers and investors to pursue higher-yielding, higher-risk strategies during the 2000s.[55]

In 1999, Alan Greenspan was celebrated in *Time* magazine—along with Robert Rubin and Lawrence Summers—as the "Committee to Save the World," in recognition of their successful responses to global disruptions, from Mexico's "Tequila Crisis" of 1995 to the Russian debt default crisis of 1998. Greenspan's Fed was also lauded for establishing (along with other major central banks) a period of economic and price stability known as the "Great Moderation." The apparent ability of the Fed and other central banks to manage financial crises and maintain economic stability promoted widespread confidence and complacency among bankers and investors. As during the 1920s—when market participants similarly believed in the Fed's ability to stabilize the economy—that confidence and complacency encouraged greater risk-taking.[56] As former Fed Governor Lawrence Lindsey remarked in 2010, "How should any rational investor respond to a less risky world? They should lay on more risk."[57]

———

Other central banks followed the Fed's lead in maintaining very low short-term interest rates during the early and mid-2000s. The Bank of England (BoE) "eased [its monetary policy] significantly" and reduced short-term interest rates in response to the "bursting of the tech bubble" in 2000.[58] The BoE maintained "historically low levels" of short-term interest rates between 2002 and 2007, and its monetary policy "stimulated the demand for credit, particularly for residential mortgages," thereby promoting "a boom in the U.K. housing market." The BoE's policy of maintaining low interest rates encouraged British investors to buy higher-yielding securities, including RMBS and other structured finance bonds. Thus, the effects of the BoE's monetary policy on British lenders, borrowers, and investors were very similar to the impact of the Fed's policy in the U.S.[59]

The European Central Bank established short-term interest rates that were well below Taylor-implied levels between 2002 and 2006.[60] The ECB's prolonged period of low short-term rates produced a softening of lending standards for consumer and business loans in the Eurozone during the mid-2000s.[61] The ECB's low interest rates—which were uniform throughout the Eurozone—facilitated credit booms in Eurozone countries where economic conditions would have called for much higher interest rates under the Taylor rule. For example, the ECB's policy rates created large deviations from the Taylor rule for Spain and Ireland, and both nations experienced intense and destructive real estate bubbles during the 2000s.[62]

Central banks in the U.S., U.K., and Eurozone were able to maintain unusually low interest rates during the 2000s due to very large inflows of investment capital from China, Japan, South Korea, and other Asian countries with balance-of-trade surpluses. Asian countries made massive investments in government bonds issued by the U.S. and other Western nations for two reasons. First, they wanted to increase the competitiveness of their exports by maintaining artificially low exchange rates for their currencies. Investing in Western government bonds boosted the values of Western currencies, thereby supporting favorable exchange rates for Asian currencies. Second, Asian countries built large reserves of Western government bonds to protect their economies from the risk of exchange rate crises and forced devaluations, as they were determined to avoid the very damaging episodes that occurred in East Asia during 1997 and 1998. Oil-producing nations also invested their current account surpluses in Western government bonds.

Inflows of foreign imports and foreign investment funds benefited Western consumers by supporting lower prices as well as lower interest rates, thereby encouraging consumers to spend more on housing and other goods. Asian countries and other foreign investors also purchased large amounts of agency RMBS and other debt securities issued by Fannie Mae and Freddie Mac—the two government-sponsored enterprises that maintained a secondary market for "prime" (highly rated) home mortgages in the U.S. The GSEs' debt securities carried an implicit guarantee from the U.S. government and were therefore viewed as "safe" (and higher-yielding) alternatives to Treasury bonds. Foreign investments in GSE debt securities helped to keep mortgage interest rates low and provided significant additional funding for the U.S. housing boom. As described in Chapter 10, European banks also supported the nonprime mortgage bubble in the U.S. by making large investments in private-label RMBS and other structured finance securities related to nonprime mortgages (including CDOs).

Thus, as was true during the Roaring Twenties—when investors in the U.S. and Western Europe purchased foreign bonds that supported investment and consumption in Central Europe and South America—economic prosperity during the 2000s depended in large part on loans from international investors to borrowers whose economies were assuming rapidly growing debt burdens. In the 2000s, the heavily indebted countries were the U.S., U.K., and several Eurozone nations. Some analysts warned that it was extremely dangerous for Western nations to depend on foreign investors to finance their housing and consumption booms as well as their balance-of-trade deficits. However, Western policymakers and central banks did not take any meaningful steps to reduce the dependence of their economies on continued inflows of foreign funds. The U.S. and U.K. were especially vulnerable, as their economic recoveries relied heavily on continued growth in their housing and financial sectors.[63]

———

The Fed's ultra-low interest rates stimulated a massive refinancing of U.S. mortgages between 2001 and 2003. The annual volume of mortgage refinancing surged from $460 billion in 2000 to $2.8 trillion in 2003 and accounted for more than 70% of all originations of mortgage loans in 2003. "Conforming" or "prime" mortgages—which satisfied underwriting standards established by Fannie Mae and Freddie Mac—represented 62% of the mortgages issued in 2003. "Jumbo" mortgages—loans made to borrowers with prime credit records but in amounts larger than the limits for conforming loans established by Congress for Fannie and Freddie—represented 17% of the mortgages made in 2003. Federally insured mortgages approved by the Federal Housing Authority and Veterans Administration accounted for about 6% of all 2003 mortgages. The remaining 15% of 2003 mortgages were higher-risk loans, such as subprime or Alt-A mortgages or second mortgages. Subprime and Alt-A mortgages were collectively referred to as "nonprime" loans.[64]

Refinancing of prime mortgages fell sharply after 2003. Long-term interest rates began to rise in late 2003, as investors anticipated that the Fed would soon begin to raise short-term rates. The Fed steadily increased its target for short-term rates from 1% to 5.25% between mid-2004 and early 2006.[65] The sudden drop in demand for refinancing prime mortgages created serious problems for mortgage lenders and Wall Street securities firms, as they had made big investments in building extensive mortgage operations. Many of those institutions shifted to nonprime mortgages to keep their mortgage factories running.[66]

Nonprime mortgage lending increased after the early 1990s, but it remained a relatively small share of the overall mortgage market until 2003. Specialized nonprime lenders (both nonbanks and smaller banks) depended on warehouse lines of credit provided by Wall Street securities firms and large banks. Securities firms and large banks with securities affiliates purchased most of the nonprime mortgages originated by specialized lenders and packaged those mortgages into private-label, "nonagency" RMBS. Citigroup created its own nonprime lending unit in the late 1990s.[67]

Many specialized nonprime lenders experienced severe problems when defaults on nonprime mortgages increased and investor demand for private-label RMBS declined during the Russian debt default crisis in 1998, and again during the dotcom–telecom bust of 2000–02. Several FDIC-insured banks that were heavily engaged in originating and securitizing nonprime mortgages and other nonprime consumer loans failed between 1997 and 2002. Two large regional banks (Bank One and First Union) reported large losses from their nonprime consumer lending operations. Conseco, a large insurance company, failed after its nonprime mortgage unit suffered devastating losses. Dozens of specialized nonprime lenders were forced to sell their mortgage operations and shut down after losing their lines of credit.[68]

Major banks and Wall Street securities firms decided to take advantage of disruptions in the nonprime mortgage market and expand their lending operations by acquiring distressed nonprime lenders. In 1999, Washington Mutual (WaMu), the largest U.S. thrift, bought Long Beach Mortgage, while National City, a large Cleveland-based regional bank, purchased First Franklin. Citigroup bought Associates First

Capital in 2000, and JPMC acquired Advanta in 2001. Bear Stearns and Lehman Brothers bought several nonprime lenders, while HSBC purchased Household in 2002. Countrywide, the nation's largest mortgage lender, became a bank holding company in 2001 and rapidly expanded its nonprime lending operations.[69]

Citigroup and HSBC completed their acquisitions of Associates and Household even though Associates faced charges of predatory lending by federal and state agencies and Household had recently paid almost $500 million to settle similar charges. Citigroup ultimately paid $240 million to resolve the charges against Associates in 2002.[70]

In mid-2000, the Department of Housing and Urban Development (HUD) and the Treasury Department issued a joint report that documented widespread predatory practices in the subprime mortgage market. Those practices included frequent refinancing of subprime loans ("flipping"), which resulted in a steady loss of home equity ("equity stripping") through assessments of prepayment penalties and high closing costs for each refinancing. Subprime lending abuses also included high-pressure sales tactics, exploitation of unsophisticated borrowers, lending without regard to the borrower's ability to repay, falsification of the borrower's income or assets, inflated appraisals, and aggressive foreclosure policies.[71] After the HUD-Treasury study was issued, Senator Paul Sarbanes (D-MD) introduced federal legislation to prohibit predatory lending. However, Senator Phil Gramm (R-TX) and other supporters of nonprime mortgage lenders successfully blocked Sarbanes' bill.[72]

Consumer advocates, state and local officials, and some members of Congress urged the Fed to exercise its authority—under the Home Ownership and Equity Protection Act of 1994 (HOEPA)—to issue regulations that would prohibit "unfair" and "deceptive" mortgage lending practices by federally chartered and state-licensed lenders. However, the Fed under Alan Greenspan's leadership issued only one very limited rule in late 2001. The 2001 rule slightly expanded the range of mortgages covered by HOEPA, but it applied to "only about 1% of subprime loans" and was easily avoided by nonprime lenders. Fed Governor Edward Gramlich privately advised Greenspan that the Fed should adopt stronger rules to deter predatory lending. However, the Fed did not take any further action under HOEPA until 2008, when it adopted rules (under Chairman Ben Bernanke's leadership) prohibiting unfair and deceptive practices for a substantially broader category of "high-priced" mortgage loans. The Fed's 2008 rules were issued "a year after the subprime market had shut down," and they were far too late to stop the predatory lending practices that led to the financial crisis.[73]

As the nonprime mortgage boom expanded, federal regulators missed many other opportunities to issue strong rules that could have stopped banks and their subsidiaries from making unsound and predatory nonprime loans. Federal regulators issued several statements of "supervisory guidance" between 1999 and 2003, which warned banks to avoid "abusive practices" in nonprime lending. However, those statements did not impose any binding standards on banks or their subsidiaries.[74]

The Office of Thrift Supervision (OTS) did not issue any formal regulations to address predatory lending by federal thrifts. The OCC adopted two rules, which generally prohibited unfair and deceptive practices by national banks and barred them from making mortgage loans without regard to the borrower's ability to repay. However, the OCC implemented both rules in a weak and ineffective manner. When it issued the first rule, the OCC said that it lacked authority to identify any *specific* practices, such as loan flipping or equity stripping, as being "unfair or deceptive." When it issued the second rule, the OCC told national banks they could use "any reasonable method to determine a borrower's ability to repay, including ... credit history, or other relevant factors."[75] That lenient standard allowed national banks to use "such dubious practices as qualifying borrowers solely based on their credit scores" for loans that required little or no documentation of income.[76]

In 2005, federal regulators conducted an interagency review of two types of "nontraditional" mortgage loans made by six leading banks.[77] The first widely used nontraditional mortgage was the "hybrid" adjustable-rate mortgage (ARM). A hybrid ARM allowed the borrower to pay a low teaser rate during the first two or three years of the mortgage. After the introductory teaser rate period expired, the mortgage's interest rate reset to a much higher level that required the borrower to repay the remaining balance of the mortgage on a fully amortized basis with significantly higher payments.[78]

The second widely used nontraditional mortgage was the "option ARM" ("pick-a-pay") mortgage. An option ARM gave the borrower several payment choices during an initial period of three to five years. Those payment choices included the ability to make interest-only payments or to make even lower payments that did not cover all of the accrued interest (in which case the unpaid interest was added to the mortgage's principal balance). Most borrowers who received option ARMs chose to make either interest-only payments or the lowest possible payments. As a result, the required payments on their mortgages jumped dramatically after the initial period expired. Thus, both hybrid ARMs and option ARMs inflicted substantial payment shock on borrowers after their initial payment periods expired. Hybrid ARMs were usually given to subprime borrowers, while option ARMs were typically provided to Alt-A borrowers, who had slightly better credit records.[79]

The 2005 interagency review by federal regulators determined that during the previous year, nontraditional mortgages accounted for 59% of all mortgage originations at Countrywide, 58% at Wells Fargo, 51% at National City, 31% at WaMu, 26.5% at Citigroup, and 18.3% at Bank of America. The interagency review also found that two-thirds of the nontraditional mortgages made by those banks were low-documentation (low-doc) or no-documentation (no-doc) loans, which did not require verification of the borrower's income or assets. Low-doc and no-doc loans were frequently referred to as "liar's loans" because they encouraged deception by borrowers or lenders (or both). After completing the interagency review, the Fed, FDIC, OCC, and OTS issued proposed guidance and then debated for several months before adopting final guidance in 2006. The final guidance was limited to option ARMs and warned banks about the dangers of making "unsound" option ARMs. However, that guidance was relatively weak and did not impose any binding limits on low-doc and no-doc mortgages.[80]

In July 2007, federal regulators issued similar guidance covering hybrid subprime ARMs. The 2007 guidance stated that mortgage lenders (1) should underwrite hybrid ARMs based on the fully amortized rate instead of the introductory teaser rate and (2) should verify the borrower's ability to repay the loan from sources other than the home's foreclosure value. The 2006 and 2007 statements of guidance did not establish mandatory rules. They "were presented merely as advice on best practices, were not directly enforceable by the agencies, and did not give borrowers any right to file lawsuits if lenders failed to follow the guidance."[81] When the 2006 guidance was issued, Comptroller of the Currency John Dugan told a meeting of bankers that the guidance "is *not* a ban on the use of nontraditional mortgage products" and "does *not* impose a limit on the number of nontraditional mortgages an institution may hold."[82]

Trade associations representing banks and nonbank mortgage lenders strongly opposed both statements of guidance, and they were successful in delaying and weakening those statements.[83] The mortgage industry's determined efforts to block even watered-down, nonbinding guidance showed how far lending standards had fallen by 2006. A Countrywide executive admitted at a congressional hearing in March 2008 that "about 60%" of borrowers who received hybrid subprime ARMs could not pay "the fully indexed rate" after their teaser rate periods expired.[84] As that admission revealed—and as the 2007 guidance implicitly acknowledged—banks and nonbank mortgage lenders had extended millions of nonprime ARMs to borrowers who could not afford to make fully amortized payments over the life of their loans. A massive wave of defaults was therefore certain to occur if home prices stopped rising and began to fall. Under those conditions, borrowers could not refinance their nontraditional mortgages or sell their homes before their teaser rate periods expired.[85]

———

Federal regulators adopted light-touch supervisory and enforcement policies that were as ineffective as their weak rules and guidance. Between 1998 and 2007, the Fed did not examine mortgage lending subsidiaries of bank holding companies for consumer law violations, even though the Fed possessed direct supervisory authority over those subsidiaries. The Fed maintained its no-supervision policy despite critical reports issued by the Government Accountability Office (GAO) in 1999 and 2004 and growing evidence of predatory lending. The Fed chose not to examine mortgage lending subsidiaries even at large bank holding companies that were heavily involved in originating and securitizing nonprime mortgages, such as Citigroup, Countrywide, HSBC, JPMC, National City, and Wachovia.[86]

In the early 2000s, Greenspan rejected Governor Gramlich's proposal to establish a pilot program for determining whether predatory lending abuses were occurring at large bank holding companies. Greenspan worried that the Fed "lacked sufficient resources" to supervise nonbank subsidiaries of bank holding companies. According to Saundra Braunstein, an official in the Fed's Consumer and Community Affairs Division, Greenspan and other Fed officials were also concerned that creating an oversight program could create an "uneven playing field" between bank holding company subsidiaries and independent nonbank mortgage lenders (which the Fed did not regulate).[87]

Thus, Greenspan played a decisive role in the Fed's failure to adopt effective regulations under HOEPA as well as the Fed's refusal to supervise mortgage lending subsidiaries of bank holding companies. As explained in Chapters 7 and 8, Greenspan argued that government regulation was counterproductive. In contrast, he expressed great confidence in the effectiveness of market discipline and private risk management. Greenspan's preference for light-touch regulation reflected a broader mindset at the Fed, which favored deregulatory policies during the decade leading up to the financial crisis. As Fed General Counsel Scott Alvarez explained in 2010, "The mindset was that there should be no regulation; that the market should take care of policing, unless there is already an identified problem."[88]

During a hearing before the House Oversight Committee in October 2008, Greenspan expressed "shocked disbelief" that "the self-interest of lending institutions" had failed to prevent systemic recklessness and fraud in the nonprime mortgage market. Greenspan said he was "shocked because I'd been going for 40 years or so with considerable evidence" that the market's ability to self-correct "was working exceptionally well."[89]

Greenspan's claim of "shocked disbelief" was contradicted by his own testimony six years earlier about pervasive fraud at Enron, WorldCom, and other bankrupt dotcom and telecom firms. During a congressional hearing in July 2002, Greenspan acknowledged that private sector gatekeepers—including corporate directors, auditors, lawyers, Wall Street securities analysts, and credit ratings agencies—"all failed for one reason or another to detect and blow the whistle on those who breached the level of trust essential to well-functioning markets." Greenspan also admitted that "an infectious greed seemed to grip much of our business community."[90] In view of his "infectious greed" testimony, Greenspan's claim of "shocked disbelief" about the collapse of the nonprime mortgage market resembled Captain Renault's professed shock about gambling (while collecting his winnings) at Rick's Café Americain in *Casablanca*.

During the late 1990s and early 2000s, consumer advocates and local and state officials repeatedly warned Greenspan and other Fed Governors and staff members about widespread abuses in the nonprime mortgage market. Except for Gramlich, senior Fed officials dismissed those warnings as "anecdotal." At a meeting of the Fed's Consumer Advisory Council in 2005, one consumer lawyer asked, "How many tens [of] thousands of anecdotes will it take to convince you that this is a trend?"[91]

Greenspan favored nonprime mortgages because they "facilitated the national policy of making homeownership more broadly available." As Bernanke subsequently pointed out, many political leaders and regulators agreed with Greenspan that nonprime mortgages were "a key part of the democratization of credit," which increased homeownership among "African-Americans and Hispanics, and people with low incomes."[92] Bill Clinton's and George W. Bush's administrations strongly advocated policies promoting wider homeownership among lower-income and minority households. Unfortunately, their pro-home-ownership policies provided convenient political cover for predatory nonprime lenders offering complex and opaque mortgages with abusive terms that took advantage of unsophisticated borrowers.[93] FDIC Chairman Sheila Bair condemned hybrid subprime ARMs as a "noxious product" that did not "expand credit" in any positive way. In her view, those mortgages were "purposefully designed to be unaffordable, [and] to force borrowers into a series of refinancings and the fat fees that went along with them."[94]

Greenspan said that he strongly opposed governmental intervention in the nonprime mortgage market except in demonstrated cases of fraud. Even in those cases, Greenspan argued that fraud should be addressed by traditional law enforcement authorities rather than bank regulators. Greenspan's outlook explained why the Fed did so little during his tenure to enforce the consumer protection laws within its jurisdiction.[95]

In 2004, the Fed issued a consent order against Citigroup for predatory lending practices that continued after Citigroup acquired Associates (even though Citigroup had pledged to stop those practices). The Fed assessed a $70 million fine against Citigroup, but it did not impose sanctions on any officers or employees who were responsible for the abusive practices. The Citigroup order was the only public enforcement action that the Fed pursued against any major bank for consumer lending violations between 2000 and 2007. The Fed's other public enforcement actions on mortgage issues were directed at small community banks, which had a negligible presence in the nonprime market.[96]

Senior officials at the Office of the Comptroller of the Currency shared the deregulatory mindset of Greenspan's Fed during the period leading up to the financial crisis. In the mid-1990s, the Fed and the OCC adopted a policy of "risk-focused supervision" under the leadership of Greenspan and Comptroller of the Currency Eugene Ludwig. Greenspan believed that traditional methods of bank supervision—including detailed reviews of loan files and other forms of "transaction-testing"—were "unduly intrusive" for large, complex banking organizations. Ludwig agreed with Greenspan that "a lighter hand at regulation was the appropriate way to regulate" those institutions.[97]

The Fed and the OCC applied their policy of risk-focused supervision to the largest banks from the mid-1990s until the financial crisis began, and they never abandoned that policy despite its manifest failures. The Fed's and the OCC's examiners stopped investigating, in any detailed manner, the actual transactions and activities of megabanks. Instead, they reviewed internal governance procedures, internal risk controls, and internal risk management policies of large, complex banking organizations. Risk-focused supervision encouraged highly deferential evaluations of the internal policies and procedures at megabanks. The OCC's handbook for large bank supervision stated that "examiners do not attempt to restrict risk-taking but rather determine whether banks identify, understand, and control the risks they assume."[98]

The Fed and the OCC continued their light-touch supervisory program despite criticism from the Government Accountability Office in 2000. The GAO warned that the agencies' risk-focused policy "may result in some bank operations receiving minimal scrutiny," and "some risks may not be appropriately identified." The GAO's concerns proved to be well founded. For example, the Fed and the OCC apparently did not perform any rigorous analysis of the risks posed by CDOs to megabanks prior to the outbreak of the financial crisis in August 2007. In addition, the Fed and OCC did not know until the fall of 2007 that Citigroup and other megabanks had transferred more than $1.3 trillion of high-risk, illiquid assets to off-balance-sheet vehicles in transactions that resembled Enron's manipulative shell games.[99]

Eugene Ludwig's successors continued the OCC's light-touch regulatory approach. In a 2005 speech, Acting Comptroller of the Currency Julie Williams told a group of bankers that the OCC's leaders were "advocates on the national stage [for] measures designed to make regulation more efficient, *and* less costly, less intrusive, less complex, and less demanding on [bankers] and [their] resources." In 2007, Comptroller of the Currency John Dugan told Congress that the OCC strongly opposed legislative or regulatory constraints on financial "innovations" because "sorting out which ones are the most positive and somewhat less positive is generally not something that the Federal Government is good at doing." The OCC, like the Fed, was eager to encourage "innovations" by the financial industry, but it was much less interested in determining whether any of those "innovations" were harmful strategies designed to evade regulation and exploit consumers.[100]

In the 1990s, U.K. bank regulators developed a new supervisory program that closely resembled the risk-focused policy of the Fed and OCC. The U.K.'s new supervisory program adopted "a myopic focus on [internal] risk management and control systems" and was "over-reliant on banks' self-assessments of their own risk." U.K. bank regulators, like their U.S. counterparts, stopped "using their [own] judgement about the riskiness of a bank's overall position."[101]

The OTS was the most extreme example of the deregulatory trend. In 2004, OTS Director James Gilleran declared that his goal was "to allow thrifts to operate with a wide breadth of freedom from regulatory intervention." John Reich, who succeeded Gilleran as OTS Director in 2005, described regulatory relief as his "favorite topic" and "something near and dear to my heart." In 2003, Gilleran and Reich (who was then serving as the FDIC's Vice Chairman) posed for a photo with leaders of three bank trade associations. The photo was staged to demonstrate Gilleran's and Reich's commitment to "Cutting Red Tape" by displaying their eagerness to demolish a pile of paper regulations. Reich wielded a pair of garden shears, while Gilleran brandished a chain saw.[102]

The OTS brought only "five to six" public enforcement actions against federal thrifts for "unfair and deceptive practices" between 2000 and 2008. The OCC's record was only marginally better, as it issued just thirteen public enforcement orders against national banks for violations of consumer protection laws between 1995 and 2007. The OCC issued most of those orders against small national banks, and not a single order was entered against any of the eight largest national banks. The largest banks, however, were the subject of a disproportionate majority of complaints filed by consumers with the OCC.[103]

———

In the absence of any effective action by federal regulators, many states tried to stop unfair and deceptive practices by nonprime mortgage lenders. North Carolina was the first state to enact an anti-predatory-lending (APL) law in 1999. Other states quickly passed similar laws. By the end of 2007, thirty states and the District of Columbia had adopted APL laws to combat mortgage lending abuses. State APL laws varied widely in their terms and practical impact. Some state laws, such as those in North Carolina, New Mexico, and New York, established strong protections for subprime borrowers. Other state laws, including those in California, Florida, and Nevada, were relatively weak.[104] Two studies found that strong state APL laws significantly decreased the percentages of subprime mortgages with prepayment penalties and other abusive terms, reduced the rate of defaults on subprime mortgages, and prohibited lenders from "steering" borrowers into subprime mortgages when they qualified for prime mortgages.[105]

State officials brought thousands of enforcement proceedings to stop predatory lending during the nonprime mortgage boom, including more than 4,000 actions in 2003 and more than 3,600 actions in 2006. State attorneys general forced several large nonbank mortgage lenders to enter into multi-state settlements and pay substantial penalties, including a $484 million settlement with Household in 2002, a $60 million settlement with First Alliance in 2002, and a $325 million settlement with Ameriquest in 2006.[106]

The OTS and OCC quickly moved to block the states from enforcing state consumer protection laws against federally chartered depository institutions and their affiliates. The OTS and OCC issued orders and regulations that preempted the application of state APL laws to federal thrifts, national banks, and their subsidiaries and agents. The OTS and OCC also participated in lawsuits to stop state enforcement proceedings against federal thrifts, national banks, and their subsidiaries and agents.[107] The OTS and OCC enabled many nonprime lenders to escape state regulation by transferring their operations to federal thrifts and national banks. Federal preemption made it much more difficult for states to enact APL laws or to enforce those laws against state-licensed lenders, because state-licensed lenders insisted on "competitive parity" with federally chartered lenders.[108]

Thus, the OTS and OCC "hamstrung" the efforts of many states to stop predatory nonprime lending.[109] Three studies found that the OCC's preemption rules had highly adverse economic effects because (1) national banks and their subsidiaries significantly increased the volume and risks of their subprime mortgage lending activities in states with strong APL laws *after* January 2004, when the OCC issued its rules to override those state laws, (2) subprime mortgages made *after* January 2004 in states with strong APL laws had substantially higher default rates, compared with pre-2004 loans, and (3) states with strong APL laws experienced more intense boom-and-bust cycles in home prices and employment *after* January 2004, when those laws were no longer enforceable against national banks and their subsidiaries.[110]

The OCC and the OTS had powerful financial incentives to use preemption and lax regulation to attract depository institutions to their chartering and regulatory regimes. Both agencies funded their operations by making assessments on the institutions they regulated, and the biggest institutions paid the largest assessments. Thus, each new national bank charter increased the OCC's budget, and every new federal thrift charter boosted the OTS's budget. In 2002, Comptroller of the Currency John D. Hawke, Jr. stated that preemption was "one of the advantages of the national charter, and I'm not the least bit ashamed to promote it."[111] Three large multi-state banks converted from state to national charters after the OCC issued its sweeping preemption rules in January 2004, and the OCC's budget increased by 15% in 2005.[112]

The OTS's aggressive preemption of state laws and its ultra-light-touch regulation helped to convince most state-chartered thrifts to convert to federal thrift charters by the early 2000s. In May 2007, OTS Director John Reich described WaMu—the biggest thrift institution, whose fees funded more than 12% of the OTS's budget—as "my largest constituent." In the same year, the OTS persuaded Countrywide to convert from a national bank to a federal thrift by promising to give Countrywide even more lenient treatment than it was receiving from the OCC and the Fed.[113]

———

The international bank capital accords issued by the Basel Committee on Bank Supervision provided strong incentives for banks in the U.S., U.K., and Europe to engage in mortgage lending and securitization. Under the Basel I accord (issued in 1988), banks calculated their risk-based capital requirements by dividing the amount of their qualifying capital by the amount of their risk-weighted assets. Basel I established several categories of risk weights for assets, ranging from 0% for the safest assets (such as U.S. Treasury bonds) to 100% for the riskiest assets (including most types of consumer loans and all commercial loans). Mortgages for one-to-four-family residences received a special risk weight of 50% and therefore required only half as much capital as other types of consumer loans.

A 1996 amendment to Basel I allowed the largest banks to use their own internal risk models to calculate their capital requirements for "market risk" created by trading activities in securities, derivatives and other financial instruments. The Basel II accord (issued in 2004) permitted the biggest banks to use internal risk models to establish their capital requirements for credit risk as well as market risk. In the U.S., banks had to satisfy a separate U.S. leverage capital standard, equal to about 4% of their total (unweighted) assets. The U.S. leverage standard did not apply to foreign banks, and most foreign nations did not impose a leverage requirement.[114]

The Basel accords allowed banks to reduce their capital requirements either by moving their loans (through securitization) to off-balance-sheet conduits or by obtaining financial guarantees from AAA- or AA-rated companies.[115] Basel II's reliance on internal risk models created strong incentives for big banks to reduce their capital requirements by constructing models that minimized their reported exposures to credit risk and market risk. The internal risk models created by major banks were highly complex, and regulators often lacked sufficient expertise and logistical resources to evaluate the accuracy of those models.[116]

Richard Spillenkothen, who served as the Fed's Director of Bank Supervision from 1991 to 2006, later criticized regulatory agencies for accepting the premises of Basel II. Spillenkothen explained that Basel II's flawed assumptions included an "excessive faith in internal bank risk models, an infatuation with the specious accuracy of complex quantitative risk measurement techniques, and a willingness ... to tolerate a reduction in regulatory capital in return for the prospect of better risk management and greater risk-sensitivity."[117]

Large global banks used their internal Basel II risk models to decrease their risk-weighted assets—their assets as adjusted (reduced) based on risk modeling. Reducing risk-weighted assets allowed big banks to decrease the denominator for their risk-based capital ratios and thereby diminish their capital requirements. Between 1994 and 2008, a group of fifteen systemically important banks in the U.S., U.K., and Europe effectively cut their risk-based capital requirements in half by reducing the average ratio of their risk-weighted assets to their total (unweighted) assets from 65% to 33%.[118] Between 2001 and 2006, the nine largest U.K. banks cut the average ratio of their risk-weighted assets to their total assets from 50% to 41%. Northern Rock achieved the most dramatic reduction, as it slashed its capital requirements by more than 40% and increased its dividend by over 30% after adopting new internal risk models under Basel II.[119]

In April 2004, the SEC established consolidated capital requirements for the Big Five securities firms. The SEC's requirements incorporated Basel II's risk-based capital rules along with Basel II's reliance on internal models. However, the SEC's capital requirements for the Big Five did not include any leverage capital standard. All five securities firms increased their leverage substantially between 2004 and 2007. In 2007, the leverage ratio for Goldman Sachs reached 26:1, while the leverage ratios for the other four big securities firms topped 30:1.[120]

In 2007 several major U.K. and European universal banks posted leverage ratios higher than 30:1—including ratios that exceeded 50:1 at Deutsche Bank and UBS—because those banks did not have to satisfy a leverage capital requirement. The absence of a leverage requirement in the U.K. and Europe encouraged large banks in those regions to maintain very low levels of equity capital and to expand their balance sheets by acquiring assets (including mortgage loans and RMBS) that carried relatively low risk weights under Basel II.[121] The U.S. leverage capital standard for banks was better than nothing, but it did not ensure a high level of capitalization for the biggest U.S. banks. The leverage ratios for BofA and Citigroup were almost 21:1 and 25:1, respectively, on the eve of the financial crisis in 2007.[122]

———

U.S. bank regulators implemented the Basel accords with relatively weak capital rules that allowed the largest banks to establish highly leveraged nonprime mortgage factories. The federal agencies issued a joint capital rule in 2001, which was purportedly designed to strengthen capital requirements for securitizations. However, it produced the opposite result. The 2001 rule required banks to hold much higher levels of capital if they retained equity tranches (the lowest or "first loss" tranches) from securitizations of mortgages or other loans.[123] Large banks avoided those higher capital charges by selling equity tranches of their nonprime RMBS and CDOs to hedge funds and other investors with a high risk tolerance. In many cases, bank underwriters of nonprime RMBS and CDOs provided loans to finance the purchases of equity tranches by hedge funds. By providing such loans, bank underwriters avoided capital charges for equity tranches but retained much of the underlying credit risk of those tranches.[124]

The 2001 joint capital rule also contained a major weakness that helped to inflate the nonprime lending boom. The rule stated that tranches of private-label RMBS and CDOs would qualify for a 20% risk weight (instead of 50% or 100%) under regulatory capital rules if the tranches were rated AAA or AA by credit rating agencies, or if the tranches were backed by financial guarantees issued by companies rated AAA or AA. The 2001 rule allowed banks to hold highly rated tranches of private-label RMBS or CDOs with the same 1.6% capital charge that applied to agency RMBS issued by Fannie Mae and Freddie Mac. The 2001 rule ignored the fact that private-label RMBS and CDOs were backed by pools of risky nonprime mortgages, while agency RMBS were backed by much safer pools of prime mortgages that conformed to Fannie's and Freddie's underwriting standards.[125]

Federal regulators approved the 1.6% capital charge for highly rated or guaranteed tranches of private-label RMBS and CDOs even though experts warned that conflicts of interest at credit rating agencies would produce inflated ratings. Banks that underwrote private-label RMBS and CDOs paid fees to credit rating agencies for their ratings, and banks paid extra fees to the same agencies for consulting services. Conflicts of interest at credit rating agencies resulted in highly inflated and erroneous ratings for nonprime RMBS and CDOs.[126]

The 2001 joint capital rule encouraged bank underwriters to obtain financial guarantees for RMBS or CDO tranches from AAA-rated or AA-rated companies. The most widely used financial guarantees were (1) credit default swaps issued by AIG and (2) bond insurance issued by monoline insurers, such as Ambac and MBIA. Financial guarantees allowed banks to secure AAA ratings for the RMBS and CDO tranches they underwrote, and they could retain highly rated tranches on their balance sheets while satisfying low capital requirements. Financial guarantees also established extensive financial linkages between large insurance companies and major banks. Those connections produced devastating concentrations and spillovers of systemic risk in 2007 and 2008.[127]

In 2004, federal regulators issued another joint capital rule, which allowed banks to add even more leverage to their nonprime mortgage factories. The 2004 rule also permitted big banks to blunt the impact of an initiative by the Financial Accounting Standards Board (FASB), which was designed to stop abusive transactions similar to Enron's fraudulent use of off-balance-sheet SPEs. In 2003, FASB issued Interpretations 46 and 46R, which required banks and other publicly owned companies to include assets held by sponsored SPEs on their consolidated balance sheets if they provided financial guarantees to investors who purchased securities from the SPEs.

Large, publicly owned banks were required to follow Interpretations 46 and 46R in preparing their audited financial statements. However, big banks feared that Interpretations 46 and 46R would compel them to include securitized assets held by sponsored SPEs in calculating their regulatory capital requirements. Big banks had established hundreds of off-balance-sheet SPEs to hold securitized assets, and banks frequently provided guarantees to investors who purchased securities issued by those SPEs.

After extensive lobbying by big banks and their trade associations, federal regulators issued a joint rule in July 2004. The 2004 rule established a special 10% risk weight for lines of credit and other guarantees that banks provided to support the sale of securities by their off-balance-sheet SPEs if the guarantees had a term of less than one year. Thus, banks had to maintain only 0.8% of capital for the short-term guarantees they provided to their off-balance-sheet SPEs, and banks could repeatedly renew those guarantees. In addition, banks did not have to satisfy *any* capital charge if they provided only implicit (reputational) support to their off-balance-sheet SPEs.

The 2004 joint capital rule allowed U.S. banks to maintain their extensive networks of off-balance-sheet SPEs for securitized assets while holding minimal levels of regulatory capital against their exposures to those SPEs. Thus, the big-bank lobby persuaded federal bank regulators *not* to support FASB's efforts to stop banks from abusing off-balance-sheet SPEs as Enron had done. Federal regulators allowed the largest banks—including several that helped to structure Enron's fraudulent SPEs—to continue using off-balance-sheet SPEs for the purpose of avoiding higher capital requirements. Many European countries provided similarly lenient capital treatment to banks that transferred securitized assets to off-balance-sheet SPEs.[128]

By 2007, U.S. and foreign banks sponsored and provided financial guarantees to more than three hundred off-balance-sheet conduits. Those conduits held securitized assets and issued more than $900 billion of asset-backed commercial paper (ABCP) to investors. In addition, U.S. and foreign banks established dozens of off-balance-sheet structured investment vehicles (SIVs), a different category of SPEs. SIVs held about $400 billion of securitized assets and sold both ABCP and medium-term notes to investors. Unlike conduits, SIVs usually did not rely on explicit guarantees from their sponsoring banks and instead depended on the banks' implicit (reputational) support.[129]

———

Congress provided a further boost to the nonprime mortgage market by passing the Bankruptcy Abuse Prevention and Consumer Protection Act of 2005 (BAPCPA). BAPCPA expanded the safe harbors for derivatives and securities repurchase agreements (repos) under the Bankruptcy Code. As discussed in Chapter 7, those safe harbors exempt holders of derivatives and repos from the Code's automatic stay provisions that freeze the rights of creditors when a debtor files for bankruptcy. Accordingly, safe harbors permit holders of derivatives and repos to take the following actions *immediately* after a counterparty files for bankruptcy: (1) terminating their contracts with that counterparty, (2) setting off (deducting) their claims against any amounts they owe to that counterparty, and (3) seizing and selling any collateral posted by that counterparty.

Prior to BAPCPA, the safe harbor for repos was limited to repos that were secured by U.S. Treasury securities, qualifying bank certificates of deposit, or debt securities issued by government-sponsored enterprises, including Fannie Mae and Freddie Mac. BAPCPA enlarged that safe harbor to include repos secured by a wide range of mortgage-related assets, including nonprime mortgages, private-label RMBS, and CDOs. BAPCPA greatly expanded the use of repo funding for nonprime mortgages and thereby produced a further expansion of the nonprime mortgage market.[130]

Big banks and securities firms conducted a multi-year lobbying campaign to obtain BAPCPA's passage. As the largest holders of derivatives and repos, they were the primary beneficiaries of BAPCPA's expanded safe harbors. In response to BAPCPA, the volume of repos held by securities broker-dealers (including independent securities firms and securities affiliates of banks) grew from $2.5 trillion in 2005 to more than $3.5 trillion in 2007. BAPCPA weakened market discipline and encouraged excessive risk-taking by large banks and securities firms because the legislation gave them confidence that they would suffer relatively few losses if their counterparties defaulted on derivatives or repos.[131]

———

In 2011, OCC staff economist Douglas Robertson reviewed an interagency statement of guidance on subprime mortgages, which federal regulators issued in 1999. Robertson noted that the 1999 guidance contained detailed warnings about the dangers of subprime lending and "reads like the prophecy of Cassandra." He concluded that "regulators knew the risks of subprime well and accurately," and he therefore asked, "How could the subprime crisis happen?"[132]

Robertson's question becomes even harder to answer when one considers similar warnings contained in the joint statements of guidance on option ARMs and hybrid subprime ARMs that regulators issued in 2006 and 2007. By that time, the annual volume of nonprime mortgage originations had exploded from $200 billion in 2001 to $740 billion in 2004, $940 billion in 2005, and $1 trillion in 2006. Option ARMs and hybrid subprime ARMs accounted for a majority of new nonprime mortgages in 2004, 2005, and 2006.[133]

As explained in Chapter 10, underwriting standards for nonprime mortgages declined steadily as the housing bubble expanded. Federal regulators understood that nonprime mortgages had become riskier by 2005. They also knew that many borrowers with hybrid subprime ARMs and option ARMs would default if housing prices started to decline because they would no longer be able to refinance their mortgages before their introductory teaser rate periods expired. Nevertheless, federal regulators failed to take any meaningful steps to stop the growth of nonprime lending before the financial crisis began in August 2007.[134] Why not?

Economic, political, and ideological factors help to explain why policymakers and regulators on both sides of the Atlantic did not respond to the reckless proliferation of nonprime mortgages and the toxic buildup of high-risk private sector debts. The financial sector became a much more important part of many national economies as the financial industry experienced rapid growth and massive consolidation in the U.S., U.K., and Europe after 1990. Total U.S. financial sector assets (including assets under management) rose from 254% to 420% of U.S. GDP between 1991 and 2006. U.S. financial sector profits increased from 13% to 27% of total pretax domestic profits between 1980 and 2007. Stocks of financial firms included in the S&P 500 index held the highest aggregate value of any industry sector from 1995 to 1998 and again from 2002 to 2007. The percentage of U.S. banking assets held by the three largest banks quadrupled from 10% to 40% between 1990 and 2008.[135]

Total assets held by U.K. banks grew from less than 50% to more than 500% of U.K. GDP between 1970 and 2007. The three largest U.K. banks held more than half of the U.K. banking industry's assets in 2007. Gross profits of U.K. financial companies rose from 8% to 15% of all U.K. corporate profits between the mid-1980s and 2007. In both the U.S. and the U.K., the financial sector's total contribution to GDP increased from about 5% to 8% between the 1970s and 2007.[136]

The rising economic significance and profitability of the financial sector, and the emergence of dominant financial giants, produced a dramatic increase in the financial industry's political influence. This was particularly true after legal changes in the U.S. and the U.K. during the 1980s and 1990s brought together the banking, securities, and insurance industries. The U.S. financial sector has been "far and away the largest source of campaign contributions to federal candidates and parties" since 1998, and it is also the third-ranked sector for lobbying expenditures.[137] The U.S. financial sector provided almost $2.4 billion of political contributions between 1990 and 2008, and it also spent $3.4 billion on lobbying between 1998 and 2008.[138] The U.S. financial sector accounted for 15% of all lobbying expenditures between 1999 and 2006, and it employed three thousand lobbyists in 2007. Many of those lobbyists were former executive branch officials, former members of Congress, and former senior financial regulators.[139]

The U.S. financial industry's increased economic importance, profitability, and political clout made it very difficult for regulators to restrain the industry's risk-taking, especially as the largest financial institutions seemed to be prospering. Roger Cole, the Fed's Director of Bank Supervision between 2006 and 2009, stated that regulators encountered strong pushback whenever they urged big banks to follow more conservative risk management policies. As Cole pointed out, "a lot of that pushback was given credence" by the fact that the largest banks were reporting profits of "$4 to $5 billion per quarter."[140] FDIC Chairman Sheila Bair agreed that it was "difficult to rein in profitable legal financial activities without hard evidence that the activities were creating unwarranted risk."[141]

Ben Bernanke acknowledged that industry lobbying and "political pressure" created serious problems for federal bank regulators whenever they tried to impose more stringent standards on the financial industry during the 2000s.[142] Former U.K. Chancellor of the Exchequer Gordon Brown admitted that the financial industry exerted "a huge amount of pressure" to obtain light-touch regulatory policies from the U.K. Financial Services Authority (FSA) during the pre-crisis period. Howard Davies, who served as the FSA's Chairman during the early 2000s, later conceded that "the political climate in which U.K. regulators were operating ... was highly unfavourable to tight regulation" before the financial crisis began in 2007. As Davies explained, "The City of London was seen as the golden goose that lays golden eggs, which should on no account be frightened into flapping its wings and flying away."[143]

The enhanced influence and prestige of the largest financial firms and the extraordinary rise in financial sector compensation after 1980 encouraged much more frequent use of the "revolving door" between senior government posts and highly compensated positions at top financial firms and their elite service providers (e.g., Wall Street law firms and financial consulting firms). Wall Street securities firms and big banks were eager to place their senior executives in top government posts to gain more favorable regulatory treatment. The rapidly growing gap between financial industry compensation and government pay caused many senior financial regulators to leave government service and work for the financial industry. The ratio between average compensation levels for top financial executives and senior financial regulators widened dramatically from 10:1 in 1980 to 60:1 in 2005.[144]

The careers of former Treasury Secretaries Robert Rubin and Henry Paulson illustrated how the revolving door worked during the 1990s and 2000s. Rubin served as co-chairman of Goldman Sachs before he became Treasury Secretary in 1995, and he joined Citigroup as chairman of its executive committee in 1999, soon after leaving government service. Paulson stepped down as Goldman's chairman in 2006 and served as Treasury Secretary during the remainder of George W. Bush's administration. There were many similar examples, including three senior executives of Goldman who became leading central bankers (Mark Carney, William Dudley, and Mario Draghi), two leading central bankers who subsequently became senior executives of

Goldman and Merrill Lynch (Gerald Corrigan and William McDonough), and three prominent lawyers who served as Comptrollers of the Currency before returning to consulting or law firms (Eugene Ludwig, John D. Hawke, Jr., and John C. Dugan).[145]

The foregoing developments encouraged financial regulators to develop a "confluence of perspectives and opinions" with financial industry leaders, thereby creating a consensus in which "Wall Street's positions became the conventional wisdom in Washington."[146] The revolving door between Washington and Wall Street, in combination with extensive social connections between regulators and industry leaders, promoted a form of "cultural" or "cognitive" capture, in which regulators deferred to the views of industry leaders regarding the best ways to draft, interpret, and implement financial regulations.[147] As former Treasury Secretary and New York Fed President Timothy Geithner later acknowledged, "My jobs mostly exposed me to talented senior bankers, and selection bias probably gave me an impression that the U.S. financial sector was more capable and ethical than it really was." Geithner became president of the private equity firm Warburg Pincus after he left government service in 2013.[148]

As the financial industry became "more complicated and central to the economy, the federal government became more dependent" on industry insiders not only as candidates for regulatory posts but also as sources of information and expertise about financial institutions and markets. Regulators gave great weight to the views of financial industry leaders, and they dismissed the arguments of consumer advocates and other "outsiders" who criticized the deregulatory trend. Many regulators viewed such critics as "people who simply did not understand the bright new world of modern finance."[149]

After becoming President of the New York Fed in 2003, Geithner "recruited some prominent financiers" to join the New York Fed's board of directors to create "an elite roster of the local financial establishment." The new directors included JPMC chairman Jamie Dimon, Lehman Brothers CEO Richard Fuld, former Goldman Sachs chairman Stephen Friedman, and General Electric chairman Jeffrey Immelt. As Geithner later recounted, former Fed Chairman Paul Volcker "presciently warned me that I was exposing the Fed to 'too much reputational risk.'" Geithner admitted that the changes he made to the New York Fed's board contributed to "perceptions of capture [of the New York Fed] by the big banks."[150]

Domestic and international competition among financial agencies encouraged regulators on both sides of the Atlantic to adopt deregulatory policies. As described earlier, federal banking agencies actively competed to enhance their prestige and increase their budgets by attracting more large banks to their chartering and regulatory regimes. Similarly, the globalization of finance after 1980 produced an intense competition between top international financial centers and encouraged a race to the bottom among the regulators of those centers.

The U.K.'s desire to promote London as the world's leading financial center persuaded U.K. regulators to adopt a light-touch philosophy. In May 2005, Gordon Brown declared that he wanted *"not just a light touch but a limited touch"* from the

FSA to improve "London's competitive position" as well as "the competitiveness of the U.K. financial services sector." In June 2007, Brown reaffirmed his commitment to light-touch regulation, and he congratulated London's bankers for helping to create "an era that history will record as the beginning of a new Golden Age." In October 2006, Margaret Cole, the FSA's Director of Enforcement, told an audience in New York City that "London's philosophy of 'light touch' regulation has helped it in becoming the world's leading centre for mobile capital." She added, "The FSA is firmly of the view that regulators must be very wary of the damaging effects they can have on creativity, innovation and competition."[151]

American officials responded vigorously to the U.K.'s challenge. On November 1, 2006—two weeks after Cole's speech—New York Mayor Michael Bloomberg and Senator Charles Schumer (D-NY) published a joint op-ed in the *Wall Street Journal*. They called for an end to "overregulation" and "frivolous litigation" in the U.S. to help New York maintain its "pre-eminence in the global financial-services sector." Bloomberg and Schumer criticized U.S. regulators for "often competing to be the toughest cop on the street," and they praised the FSA for being "more collaborative and solutions-oriented." Three weeks later, Treasury Secretary Henry Paulson delivered a speech at the Economic Club of New York. Paulson said that Bloomberg's and Schumer's op-ed was "right on target," and he declared that America's "broken tort system is an Achilles heel for our economy." Paulson also argued that the U.S. approach to financial regulation and enforcement was "confusing and threatening" to U.S. financial institutions and other business firms.[152]

Bloomberg and Schumer commissioned a report from McKinsey & Company, published in January 2007. McKinsey's report recommended that U.S. financial regulators should adopt a "measured approach to enforcement" similar to the FSA's policies. The report quoted top U.S. financial executives, who praised the FSA as "easier to deal with" and "more responsive to their business needs." The report also argued that U.S. bank regulators should get rid of their leverage capital requirement—which was *not* included in Basel II—to give U.S. banks "an equal footing with their international competitors." Bloomberg's and Schumer's initiative—and the strong support they received from Paulson—illustrated the intense political pressures on U.S. financial regulators to embrace the FSA's light-touch policies and accept Basel II's more lenient capital standards.[153]

———

During the 1990s and 2000s, the conventional wisdom on both sides of the Atlantic was that "deregulation, … financial innovation and self-correcting markets" produced better results than government regulation and supervision.[154] Fed chairman Alan Greenspan exemplified that ideology. In a September 2005 speech, Greenspan argued that "heavy regulation … imped[ed] efficiency and competitiveness" until the federal government adopted a policy of deregulation in the late 1970s. Greenspan contended that deregulation, advances in information technology, and financial innovations created "a far more flexible, efficient, and hence resilient financial system than the one that existed [in 1980]." He praised securitization and over-the-counter derivatives for "enabl[ing] the largest and most sophisticated banks, in their credit-granting role, to divest themselves of much credit risk by passing it to institutions with far less leverage." Greenspan's 2005 speech echoed his earlier comments in October 2004, when he complimented major banks for using credit derivatives to reduce their credit exposures to Enron, WorldCom, and other distressed corporate borrowers during the early 2000s.[155]

In a May 2007 speech, New York Fed President Tim Geithner echoed Greenspan's praise for financial innovation and market discipline, as well as Greenspan's deep skepticism about the effectiveness of regulation.[156] Geithner stated that "changes in financial markets ... have improved the efficiency of financial intermediation and improved our confidence in the ability of markets to absorb stress." Geithner agreed with Greenspan that "financial innovation has improved the capacity to measure and manage risk" and to "spread [risk] more broadly across countries and institutions."[157]

Geithner repeated Greenspan's earlier warning that a prolonged period of economic stability—like the "Great Moderation"—could lead to complacency and excessive risk-taking in financial markets.[158] However, both Geithner and Greenspan were fundamentally optimistic about the future of the financial industry. According to Geithner, "The larger global financial institutions are generally stronger in terms of capital relative to risk. Technology and innovation in financial institutions has made it easier to manage risk. Risk is less concentrated within the banking system ... and [is] spread more broadly across a diversity of institutions."[159] Geithner's assessment in May 2007 proved to be profoundly mistaken only a few months later.

The pro-deregulation ideology of Greenspan, Geithner, and other U.S. regulators was fully shared by policymakers in the U.K. and at the International Monetary Fund (IMF). In 2009 the U.K. Financial Services Authority issued a post-mortem report on the financial crisis that found serious flaws in the "intellectual assumptions on which previous regulatory approaches have been largely built." Those flaws included misplaced confidence in "market discipline ... as an effective tool in constraining harmful risk-taking," as well as a mistaken belief that "financial innovation can [always] be assumed to be beneficial since market competition would winnow out any innovations which did not deliver value added."[160]

The U.K. Treasury's Permanent Secretary, Nick Macpherson, admitted in 2016 that "a monumental collective intellectual error" occurred among central bankers, regulators, and policymakers in the U.K. and U.S. during the credit boom of the 2000s. Officials in both countries "failed to see the crisis coming" and "failed to spot the build-up of risk." Similarly, BoE governor Mervyn King stated in 2012 that "we should have shouted from the rooftops that a system had been built in which banks were too important to fail, that banks had grown too quickly and borrowed too much, and that so-called 'light-touch' regulation hadn't prevented any of this."[161]

The IMF reached similar conclusions in a 2011 post-mortem study of the financial crisis. That study concluded:

> The IMF's ability to correctly identify the mounting risks [of a global financial crisis] was hindered by a high degree of groupthink, intellectual capture, [and] a general mindset that a major financial crisis in large advanced economies was unlikely.... [IMF officials believed that] market discipline and self-regulation would be sufficient to stave off serious problems in financial institutions ... [and] "sophisticated" financial markets could thrive safely with minimal regulation.[162]

The "groupthink" cited by the IMF caused U.S. regulators to ignore repeated warnings about the dangers of the nonprime mortgage boom and the risks of a systemic financial crisis from economists and legal academics who were outside the mainstream.[163] For example, Yale economist Robert Shiller told a 2004 meeting of the New York Fed's Economic Advisory Panel that the housing boom had entered a "bubble" phase. He estimated that home values were "inflated by 30 to 50%," based on his analysis of historical trends in mortgage payments and rents. Shiller later recalled feeling that he was "violating groupthink" during his presentation. New York Fed President Tim Geithner "ignored Shiller's warning and summarily removed him from the [advisory] board."[164]

On two other occasions, Fed Governors and their supporters attacked presentations by economists who questioned the Washington–Wall Street consensus in favor of market-driven deregulation. In August 2003, Claudio Borio and William White, senior economists at the Bank for International Settlements, presented a paper at the Kansas City Fed's annual Economic Policy Symposium in Jackson Hole, Wyoming. Borio and White pointed out that "episodes of severe financial distress" had occurred with increasing frequency after 1980, as many countries adopted a new policy regime that emphasized "financial liberalization." They argued that the new regime's "relaxation of financial and monetary constraints" had caused global financial markets to become more "procyclical," with faster credit growth and more pronounced asset price bubbles. As a result, financial systems and economies had become "more vulnerable to boom and bust cycles."[165]

Borio and White recommended stronger "macroprudential" safeguards—including higher capital requirements—to prevent buildups of "financial imbalances." They warned that the "substantial monetary easing" by central banks after 2000 had produced "unusually buoyant" housing prices as well as rising levels of household debt in many developed countries. They cautioned that a sudden collapse of housing booms would create serious financial and economic challenges. They urged central banks to "lean against the buildup of financial imbalances by tightening policy, when necessary, even if near-term inflationary pressures were not apparent."[166]

Borio and White's proposal for a monetary policy that would counteract asset booms clashed with the Greenspan Fed's policy of allowing asset bubbles to expand and then intervening only *after* a bust to stabilize the financial system. Borio and White's paper also emphasized the housing-related risks of the ultra-low interest rate policies that the Fed and other major central banks adopted after 2000. A few participants at the Jackson Hole conference agreed with Borio and White. However, most participants—including Greenspan, Bernanke, and Fed Vice Chairman Roger Ferguson—strongly criticized the policy proposals presented by Borio and White.[167]

Two years later, at the same conference, University of Chicago economist Raghuram Rajan presented a paper entitled "Has Financial Development Made the World Riskier?" Rajan warned that deregulation, securitization, derivatives, and the globalization of financial markets were creating larger concentrations and correlations of risk that were not well understood by either regulators or investors. He highlighted the risks of bonus plans and stock option plans adopted by most large financial institutions, which heavily rewarded short-term profits and encouraged excessive risk-taking by managers and traders. Rajan also described the growing connections and interdependence between large banks and the capital markets. He cautioned that during a future financial crisis, the banking system might not be able to provide liquidity to the capital markets and business firms as it had done in 1998 during the Russian debt crisis. He agreed with Borio and White that the Greenspan Fed's hands-off policy toward asset bubbles and its repeated interventions to protect financial markets against asset busts had created a "procyclical" financial system as well as "moral hazard" among bankers and investors.[168]

Rajan's presentation provoked a very hostile response, probably because the main focus of the 2005 Jackson Hole conference was to celebrate the completion of Greenspan's nineteen-year tenure as Fed Chairman.[169] Fed Governor Donald Kohn rejected Rajan's arguments and vigorously defended what Kohn called the "Greenspan doctrine"—namely, that "private interest and technological change, interacting in a stable macroeconomic environment, will advance the general economic welfare." Kohn argued that "actions by private parties to protect themselves—what Chairman Greenspan has called private regulation—are generally quite effective." In contrast, "government regulation risks undermining private regulation and financial stability by distorting incentives through moral hazard and by promising a more effective role in promoting financial stability than it can deliver."[170]

Former Treasury Secretary Lawrence Summers maintained that the "the slightly Luddite premise" of Rajan's paper was "largely misguided." According to Summers, "the tendency toward restriction that runs through the tone of [Rajan's] presentation" would "support a wide variety of misguided policy impulses in many countries." Rajan later commented that he "felt like an early Christian who had wandered into a convention of half-starved lions."[171]

The highly adversarial responses of Fed policymakers to the critiques presented by Shiller, Borio, White, and Rajan illustrated the Greenspan Fed's unyielding commitment to a light-touch regulatory regime that relied mainly on private risk management and market discipline. The Greenspan Fed zealously defended the "financial innovations"—including securitization and derivatives—that were key components of the universal banking regime established by the Gramm-Leach-Bliley Act of 1999 and the Commodity Futures Modernization Act of 2000.[172] The Fed's ideological blinders—which other U.S., U.K., and European regulators shared—help to explain why federal regulators did not take any effective measures to restrain the explosive

growth of nonprime mortgages, despite widespread evidence of reckless and predatory lending.[173]

———

Another important motive for regulatory inaction was that many policymakers
viewed continued growth in mortgage debt and other types of consumer credit as
essential to support housing construction, household consumption, and economic
growth. The growth of the nonprime mortgage market was part of a rapid buildup
of household debt in the U.S. after 1990. Residential mortgage debt quadrupled between 1991 and 2007, and most of that growth occurred after 2000. Consumer nonmortgage debt—including auto loans, credit card loans, and student loans—tripled
between 1991 and 2007. Total household debt rose from $3.5 trillion in 1991 to $13.2
trillion in 2007. The ratio of household indebtedness to disposable personal income
increased from 80% in 1990 to more than 130% in 2007.[174]

The growing debt burdens of lower- and middle-income U.S. households reflected
their stagnant incomes and their need to rely more heavily on credit to cover their
living expenses. Total after-tax incomes (including public and private benefits) more
than tripled between 1979 and 2006 for U.S. households with the top 1% of incomes.
Total after-tax incomes rose by more than 50% during the same period for households with incomes between the 80th and 99th percentiles. In contrast, total after-tax
incomes grew much more slowly for households below the 80th percentile.[175] Lower-
and middle-income households therefore took on much greater debt burdens after
1980 to finance their living expenses. By 2004, household debt burdens equaled 400%
of disposable income for the lowest income quintile, almost 250% of disposable income for the second-lowest income quintile, and about 200% of disposable income
for third-lowest income quintile.[176]

The Greenspan Fed was well aware of those trends, and it viewed continued credit
expansion as necessary to support economic growth after the dotcom–telecom bust
inflicted almost $8 trillion of losses on investors between 2000 and 2002. Greenspan
told Congress in 2002 and 2003 that the Fed's ultra-low interest rate policy boosted
housing prices and allowed homeowners to extract large amounts of equity through
home equity loans and cash-out refinancings of their mortgages. Greenspan explained
that home equity extraction provided "a significant support to consumption during
a period when other assets were declining sharply." He advised Congress that "economic activity would have been notably weaker" without the mortgage boom that the
Fed produced with its loose monetary policy.[177]

In March 2007, Greenspan co-authored a Fed staff study that analyzed the economic effects of home equity extraction. The study estimated that homeowners
withdrew almost $2.6 trillion of equity from their homes between 1991 and 2005.
Homeowners used those funds to pay off $600 billion of nonmortgage debts (in-
cluding credit card loans) and to cover more than $1.8 trillion of home improve-
ments and other personal expenses. Greenspan's co-authored study also found that

(1) mortgage debt grew faster than home values after 1990, (2) the personal savings rate of consumers declined, especially after 1998, and (3) home equity withdrawals financed a much larger share of nonmortgage debt payments and personal consumption after 2000.[178]

Thus, the Greenspan Fed clearly recognized that homeowners were becoming more deeply indebted, were relying more heavily on housing credit to meet their living expenses, and were facing greater risks of defaulting on their debts and losing their homes. The Greenspan Fed accepted—and prolonged—those trends because the housing industry and household consumption were the primary engines supporting growth in an otherwise challenging economic environment. In 2015, Bernanke stated that the Fed paid

> close attention to developments in the housing and mortgage markets [after 2001], but we saw pluses as well as minuses. Housing construction helped bolster otherwise sluggish economic growth, and rising house prices supported consumer confidence. Chairman Greenspan often noted that homeowners' borrowing against the equity in their homes was an important source of consumer spending.[179]

Similar patterns of sluggish income growth, growing social inequality, booming home prices, and rising household debt burdens occurred in the U.K., Ireland, Spain, Portugal, and other European countries. Like their U.S. counterparts, European policymakers did not try to alter those patterns. Instead, European officials allowed large European universal banks to finance large-scale credit booms in the U.K., Spain, Ireland, Portugal, and other EU countries. Consequently, the "great mortgaging"—described by Òscar Jordà, Moritz Schularick, and Alan Taylor—unfolded on both sides of the Atlantic during the 2000s.[180] The results were devastating, as shown in Chapters 10 and 11.

10
Déjà Vu

Reckless Lending and Securitization by Financial Conglomerates Triggered a Global Financial Crisis in 2007

The credit surge that occurred on both sides of the Atlantic during the 2000s produced a massive buildup of risky debts, especially in the housing sector. The securitization of risky debts by universal banks played a central role in inflating that toxic credit bubble. The credit bubble of the 2000s unleashed a devastating global financial crisis in 2007–09, just as the credit boom of the 1920s had done during the early 1930s.

Residential mortgage lending expanded rapidly after 2000 in the U.S., U.K., and several European countries, in response to lax monetary policies, light-touch regulation, and the increasing use of securitization to finance mortgages.[1] In the U.S., annual originations of nonprime mortgages rose from $250 billion in 2001 to a peak of $1 trillion in 2006, after which nonprime originations declined to less than $450 billion in 2007 and virtually disappeared thereafter. Lenders provided more than $4 trillion of nonprime mortgages to U.S. borrowers between 2001 and 2007. The share of new U.S. mortgage loans represented by nonprime mortgages jumped from 12% in 2001 to 35% during 2004–06.[2]

Securitization financed most of the nonprime mortgage boom in the U.S. Investors bought more than $3 trillion of private-label residential mortgage-backed securities, backed by pools of nonprime U.S. mortgages, between 2001 and 2007. The percentage of nonprime mortgages securitized into private-label RMBS rose from 39% in 2001 to 62% during 2002–03 and over 75% during 2004–07. Nonprime RMBS represented a rapidly growing share of all securitized mortgages, rising from 8% in 2001 to 37% during 2004–06.[3] Urban housing markets in which lenders relied more heavily on funding from nonprime RMBS experienced the most dramatic booms between 2003 and 2006, as well as the most severe busts between 2007 and 2010.[4]

The four largest U.S. universal banks, the five largest U.S. securities firms, and eight big foreign universal banks were leading underwriters for private-label RMBS, collateralized debt obligations, and other types of structured finance securities based on nonprime mortgages. Countrywide and Washington Mutual were also major underwriters of private-label RMBS, due to their status as top nonprime lenders.[5] The leading underwriters of nonprime RMBS originated nonprime mortgages through their own organizations and also purchased nonprime loans from specialized nonbank lenders like Ameriquest, New Century, and Option One. Specialized nonbank lenders obtained most of their funding from warehouse lines of credit and repurchase agreements provided by the big RMBS underwriters.[6]

The process of originating and securitizing nonprime mortgages to create non-prime RMBS produced large streams of fee income for mortgage brokers, mortgage lenders, underwriters of private-label RMBS, and servicing agents for mortgages held in securitized loan pools. The desire to earn more fees drove each member of the se-curitization assembly line to complete more deals, regardless of the risks embedded in nonprime mortgages. Underwriters of nonprime RMBS paid origination fees to nonprime lenders that were several times higher than the fees that Fannie Mae and Freddie Mac paid to originators of prime (conforming) mortgages.

Nonprime lenders also paid much larger commissions to mortgage brokers and loan officers for completing nonprime mortgage deals, as lenders wanted to capture the higher fees offered by underwriters of nonprime RMBS. Consequently, mortgage brokers and loan officers frequently "steered" borrowers into nonprime mortgages when the borrowers could have qualified for prime mortgages. Many nonprime mort-gages were high-risk loans that created significant payment shock for borrowers after their introductory teaser rates expired. As explained in Chapters 7 and 9, those high-risk loans included hybrid subprime adjustable-rate mortgages and option ARMs.[7]

The incentives for generating nonprime RMBS were especially strong at vertically integrated universal banks, which produced multiple fees by performing every step of the lending, securitization, and servicing process. Universal banks and Wall Street securities firms needed a constant stream of nonprime mortgages to feed their se-curitization factories. Accordingly, big banks and Wall Street firms pressured non-prime lenders, brokers, and loan officers to produce greater volumes of nonprime mortgages.[8] Charles Prince, who was Citigroup's CEO from 2003 to 2007, later acknowledged:

> Securitization could be seen as a factory line.... As more and more and more of these subprime mortgages were created as raw material for the securitization process, not surprisingly in hindsight, more and more of it was of lower and lower quality. And at the end of that process, the raw material going into it was actually bad quality, it was toxic quality.[9]

Citigroup exemplified the decline in lending standards described by Prince. Citigroup steadily lowered its criteria for originating and purchasing nonprime mort-gages between 2005 and 2007. Clayton Holdings—the leading provider of due dili-gence services to underwriters of nonprime RMBS—rejected 42% of the subprime mortgages it reviewed for Citigroup between January 2006 and June 2007, after de-termining that the rejected mortgages did not satisfy Citigroup's established under-writing standards. However, Citigroup "waived in" 31% of the mortgages rejected by Clayton and included those mortgages in its securitized pools.[10]

Richard Bowen and Sherry Hunt were internal quality control officers who reviewed Citigroup's purchases of nonprime mortgages. In 2006 and 2007, Bowen and Hunt repeatedly warned their supervisors that—over their objections—Citigroup's managers were ignoring the bank's underwriting standards and were purchasing large volumes of nonprime mortgages with forged signatures and other indicators of fraud. Citigroup demoted Bowen and forced him to resign. Citigroup's harsh treatment of Hunt caused her to file a successful whistleblower lawsuit.[11] Employees who tried to stop excessive risk-taking and fraud at other RMBS underwriters received the same kind of punitive treatment that Bowen and Hunt endured.[12]

Clayton Holdings rejected between 20% and 35% of the nonprime mortgages it reviewed for eight other leading underwriters of private-label RMBS. Like Citigroup, those eight underwriters waived in and securitized between 29% and 51% of the mortgages that Clayton rejected.[13] Two additional underwriters—Nomura (a big Japanese bank) and RBS—also waived in and securitized a high percentage of mortgages that Clayton rejected from their nonprime mortgage pools.[14] Federal courts determined that Nomura and RBS "systematically disregarded" their underwriting criteria, as 45% or more of the nonprime mortgages they securitized were "materially defective, with underwriting defects that substantially increased the credit risk of the loan."[15]

RBS's chief U.S. credit officer described the origination of nonprime mortgages for securitization as "quasi organized crime." In his view, nonprime lenders produced mortgages that were "f***ing garbage," with "fraud [that] was so rampant" and loan files that were "all disguised to, you know, look okay kind of . . . in a data file." Despite its awareness of systematic fraud in nonprime lending, RBS did not intensify its due diligence efforts to remove fraudulent loans from its securitized pools. On the contrary, RBS did "the least amount of diligence," and one employee referred to RBS' due diligence procedures as "just a bunch of bullsh**."[16]

UBS's head of mortgage trading described a pool of Countrywide mortgages that UBS securitized as "a bag of sh[*]t." Another UBS employee confessed, "When you do business with [Countrywide], you dance with the devil and sell your soul." A UBS trader referred to Fremont loans securitized by UBS as "cr*p." A UBS due diligence manager described a pool of New Century mortgages securitized by UBS as "horrific." Another UBS trader admitted that "our crack due diligence effort is a joke."[17]

Angelo Mozilo, the CEO of Countrywide—one of the top originators of nonprime mortgages and underwriters of nonprime RMBS—was fully aware of the extreme risks his bank was assuming with nonprime mortgages. In August 2005, Mozilo told the head of Countrywide's mortgage division:

> I am becoming increasingly concerned about the environment surrounding the borrowers who are utilizing the pay option loan and the price level of real estate in general. . . . [T]he simple reason is that when the loan resets in five years there will be enormous payment shock and if the borrower is not sufficiently sophisticated to truly understand the consequences then the bank will be dealing with foreclosure in a deflated real estate market. That would be both a financial and reputational catastrophe.

Mozilo also told Countrywide's mortgage chief that Countrywide should not keep option ARMs on its balance sheet unless the properties were owner-occupied and the borrowers had relatively high credit scores. Mozilo said that Countywide should place "less attractive loans in the secondary market" through mortgage sales and securitization. Mozilo's subordinate cautioned that such an approach was problematic because "we need to analyze what [risk] remains if the bank is only cherry picking and what remains to be securitized/sold is overly concentrated with higher risk loans."[18]

In March 2006, Mozilo described his bank's "80/20" subprime mortgage—a no-down-payment deal that included an 80% subprime first mortgage and a 20% subprime second-lien loan—as "the most dangerous product in existence and there can be nothing more toxic." In April 2006, he called second-lien subprime loans "poison." In September 2006, Mozilo admitted that Countrywide had "no way, with any reasonable certainty, to assess the real risk of holding [option ARMs] on our balance sheet ... [W]e are flying blind on how those loans will perform in a stressed environment of higher unemployment, reduced values and slowing home sales." Mozilo urged his subordinates "to sell all newly originated pay options and begin rolling off the bank balance sheet, in an orderly manner, pay options currently [in the portfolio]."[19]

Default rates for nonprime mortgages increased every year after 2003, reflecting a steady decline in the quality of mortgages originated by nonprime lenders.[20] Four indicators of increased risk confirmed the deterioration in nonprime lending standards between 2003 and 2006. First, the share of nonprime mortgages with second-lien ("piggyback") loans nearly quadrupled during those years. Piggyback loans allowed borrowers to obtain financing up to—and in many cases beyond—the full appraised value of their home, *without* buying private mortgage insurance. The percentage of nonprime mortgages with combined loan-to-value ratios above 100% rose from about 5% in 2000 to 25% in 2006.[21]

Second, the percentage of nonprime mortgages originated with less than full documentation of the borrower's income and assets increased substantially between 2003 and 2006. Many applications for low-doc and no-doc mortgages greatly inflated the borrower's income and assets, often with the lender's encouragement and active participation.[22] Third, more than 75% of subprime mortgages provided between 2003 and 2006 were hybrid subprime ARMs with short introductory teaser rate periods (typically two or three years). Similarly, the percentage of nonprime Alt-A mortgages with interest-only payments or option ARM payments during the initial teaser rate period jumped from 18% in 2003 to 70% in 2006. Hybrid subprime ARMs and option ARMs experienced much higher default rates because of the severe payment shock that borrowers experienced after their initial teaser rate periods expired.[23]

Fourth, subprime lenders disproportionately targeted vulnerable borrowers in lower-income neighborhoods. Atif Mian and Amir Sufi found that subprime lending expanded most rapidly between 2002 and 2005 in zip codes populated by borrowers with low credit scores. Low-credit-score zip codes recorded almost no income growth during those years, indicating that lenders weakened their credit standards to originate larger volumes of subprime mortgages. Housing prices collapsed in low-credit-score zip codes after 2006, and the availability of mortgage credit plummeted. The volume of mortgage loans provided in low-credit-score zip codes was lower in 2011 than it was in 1999.[24]

Mian and Sufi also documented that growth rates for household debt between 2000 and 2007 were *highest* in households with the *lowest* 20% of incomes. In addition, growth rates for household debt were much higher in households with incomes in the 20th to 60th percentiles, compared with more affluent households. Default rates on household debt followed the same pattern. The *highest* default rate occurred in households with the *lowest* 20% of incomes, and households in the 20th to 60th percentiles defaulted at rates that were significantly higher than rates for more affluent households. Thus, the nonprime credit boom of the 2000s was an exceptional period when lenders blanketed lower-income neighborhoods with unsustainable subprime mortgages and other high-risk consumer loans, with catastrophic results. The nonprime credit boom depended on the ability of nonprime lenders to securitize their loans into private-label RMBS. The bubble therefore collapsed as soon as the private-label securitization market shut down in 2007.[25]

Nonprime lenders persuaded many lower-income homeowners to replace their existing fixed-rate mortgages with hybrid subprime ARMs or option ARMs, which offered lower teaser rate payments as well as opportunities for cash withdrawals. Many lower-income homeowners did not understand the highly complex terms of hybrid subprime ARMs and option ARMs, including the payment shock that would occur when their teaser rate periods expired. If homeowners expressed concerns about their ability to make higher payments after their teaser rate periods expired, nonprime lenders assured them that they could refinance their homes *before* their introductory periods ran out. However, each refinancing resulted in equity stripping, as lenders assessed prepayment penalties and charged high closing costs, and homeowners often withdrew cash from their remaining equity. Refinancings accounted for three-fifths of all nonprime mortgage loans between 2000 and 2007, and the great majority of those loans were cash-out refinancings.[26]

———

The nonprime mortgage market depended on investors who were willing to buy private-label RMBS, since sales of RMBS were the most important source of funding for additional nonprime lending. It was relatively easy to find investors for the highest (AAA-rated) tranches of nonprime RMBS. Many domestic and foreign institutional investors (including banks, insurance companies, and pension funds) were allowed to buy debt securities only if they carried AAA or AA credit ratings. Many investors considered AAA-rated tranches of nonprime RMBS to be very attractive because they paid interest rates that were significantly higher than yields on other AAA-rated bonds, such as agency RMBS issued by Fannie Mae and Freddie Mac or U.S. Treasury bonds. The higher yields for AAA-rated nonprime RMBS supposedly compensated investors for the higher risks of the nonprime mortgage pools underlying those RMBS. However, investors did not understand how massive those risks actually were.[27]

European banks held more than $2 trillion of U.S. private-label RMBS, ABS, CDOs, and other structured finance securities by 2007. European banks financed most of those investments by entering into interbank loans or by issuing certificates of deposit, asset-backed commercial paper, and repos to U.S. money market mutual funds. Consequently, many European banks were heavily exposed to the U.S. non-prime mortgage market in 2007, and many U.S. MMMFs had large risk exposures to European banks.[28]

Most institutional investors who purchased private-label RMBS relied heavily on the credit ratings provided by Moody's, Standard & Poor's, and Fitch. The SEC designated those three firms as "nationally recognized statistical rating organizations." Investors relied on their credit ratings because it was very difficult to obtain timely and detailed information about the mortgage pools underlying nonprime RMBS. In October 2008, a former managing director of Moody's told Congress, "Subprime [RMBS] and their offshoots offer little transparency around composition and characteristics of the loan collateral.... Loan-by-loan data, the highest level of detail, is generally not available to investors."

Underwriters of nonprime RMBS usually did not give investors final offering documents—which contained general descriptions of the underlying nonprime mortgage pools—until *after* investors purchased RMBS. Those generic descriptions did not provide a detailed accounting of the underlying mortgages, and the SEC typically did not review the final offering documents to evaluate the adequacy of their disclosures. In addition, nonprime RMBS deals were marketed and sold at a rapid pace during the housing boom, allowing very limited time for due diligence by investors. As a result, most investors relied mainly on credit ratings.[29]

AAA-rated tranches typically represented 80% or more of tranches included in a nonprime RMBS deal. Hedge funds were the leading investors for the lowest (unrated) equity tranches, which generally represented 5% or less of the total tranches. As described in Chapter 9, RMBS underwriters frequently provided loans to hedge funds to finance their purchases of the equity tranches.

It was very difficult to find investors for the "mezzanine" tranches of nonprime RMBS. Mezzanine tranches—which ranked above the equity tranches and below the senior tranches—carried A or BBB credit ratings and typically accounted for 15% or less of the total tranches. Many institutional investors did not have legal authority to buy debt securities with credit ratings as low as A or BBB. Other investors did not want to buy mezzanine tranches because they did not consider their interest rates (yields) to be high enough to justify their additional risks.[30]

To overcome the lack of demand for mezzanine tranches, major banks and big Wall Street securities firms "created the investor" by constructing cash flow CDOs—also known as asset-backed securities CDOs. CDO underwriters assembled large pools of unsold mezzanine tranches of nonprime RMBS, pooled those tranches with other debt obligations, and securitized the pools to create cash flow CDOs. In most cash flow CDOs, 80% or more of the tranches received AAA ratings, while mezzanine tranches received A or BBB ratings, and the equity (lowest) tranches were unrated. Cash flow CDOs became the dominant buyers of mezzanine tranches of nonprime RMBS after 2003, thereby providing an artificially created source of investor "demand" that kept the nonprime securitization factories running.[31]

CDO underwriters also repackaged and securitized unsold mezzanine tranches of CDOs to create third-level securitization structures, called "CDOs-squared." Some underwriters created "CDOs-cubed" by repackaging and securitizing unsold mezzanine tranches of CDOs-squared. Thus, CDOs became the principal buyers for unsold mezzanine tranches of RMBS and other CDOs. The Financial Crisis Inquiry Commission found that "by 2005, CDO underwriters were selling most of the mezzanine tranches [of CDOs] ... to other CDO managers, to be packaged into other CDOs." In 2007, CDOs purchased almost 90% of the mezzanine tranches issued by other CDOs. According to SEC attorneys, "Heading into 2007 there was a Streetwide agreement: you buy my BBB tranche and I'll buy yours."[32]

As Jake Bernstein and Jesse Eisinger reported, "In the last years of the boom, CDOs had become the dominant purchaser of key, risky parts of other CDOs, largely replacing real investors like pension funds. By 2007, 67% of those slices were bought by CDOs, up from 36% just three years earlier." Bernstein and Eisinger concluded that CDO underwriters created "fake demand" by purchasing mezzanine tranches of other CDOs, thereby "maintain[ing] the value of mortgage bonds at a time when the lack of buyers should have driven their prices down." In 2006 and 2007, Citigroup, Merrill Lynch, and other top CDO underwriters created new CDOs to serve as buyers of last resort (dumping grounds) for unsold tranches of their previous CDOs.[33]

A study by Sergey Chernenko found that CDO underwriters sent additional deals and paid larger upfront fees to "cooperative" CDO managers. Those CDO managers agreed to buy CDO securities that the underwriters "were unable to sell to anyone else." Thus, cooperative CDO managers profited by acting as "front men for the investment bankers underwriting the CDOs."[34]

In short, major banks and big Wall Street securities firms used cash flow CDOs to perform a kind of "alchemy," in which (1) pools of high-risk nonprime mortgages were packaged into nonprime RMBS, of which 80% or more tranches received AAA ratings, (2) pools of unsold mezzanine tranches of RMBS were repackaged to create cash flow CDOs, of which 80% or more tranches received AAA ratings, and (3) pools of unsold mezzanine tranches of CDOs were repackaged to create CDOs-squared, of which 80% or more tranches received AAA ratings.[35] For a graphic presentation of Wall Street's alchemy, see Figure 10.1.

Bethany McLean and Joe Nocera provided the following summary of the "alchemy" created by CDOs:

> Once the CDO machinery *itself* became the buyer of the triple-Bs [mezzanine tranches], there were suddenly no limits as to how big the [nonprime mortgage] business could get. CDOs could absorb an infinite supply of triple-B-rated bonds

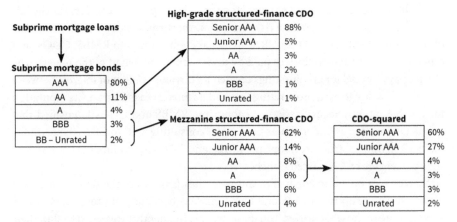

Figure 10.1 Constructing CDO and CDO-Squared Securities
Note: CDO = collateralized debt obligation.
Source: IMF-GFS (2008: 60) (box 2.2)

and then repackage them into triple-A securities. Which everybody could then buy—banks and pension funds included. It really *was* alchemy, though of a deeply perverse sort.[36]

Two types of institutions played crucial supporting roles in converting risky non-prime mortgages and CDOs into AAA-rated securities. First, insurance companies—including American International Group, Ambac, and MBIA—provided credit default swaps and other financial guarantees that protected super-senior tranches of CDOs against default, thereby justifying their AAA credit ratings. AIG's London subsidiary, AIG Financial Products (AIGFP), issued $80 billion of CDS to protect AAA-rated tranches of CDOs. As explained in Chapter 8, the Commodity Futures Modernization Act of 2000 (CFMA) exempted CDS from substantive regulation under federal law or state insurance laws. AIGFP therefore did not have to maintain any financial reserves against its potential liabilities under CDS deals. Those CDS deals provided a steady stream of fee income (and large profits) to AIGFP as long as their collateral and payment requirements were not triggered. AIGFP and its advisers "predicted with 99.85% confidence that there would be no realized economic loss" on their CDS contracts. For AIGFP's executives, issuing CDS to protect AAA-rated CDO tranches "felt like free money." In 2005, AIGFP generated $4.4 billion of profits (including AIGFP's income from CDS), which represented 29% of AIG's total profits.[37]

AIGFP stopped writing CDS contracts for CDO tranches in early 2006, after its top executives began to worry about the performance of nonprime mortgages. CDO underwriters responded by obtaining similar guarantees from Ambac, MBIA, and other monoline bond insurers. Like AIGFP, the monoline insurers welcomed the income produced by their guarantees and assumed they "never would have to take a loss" on the protection they provided for AAA-rated tranches of CDOs.[38]

Credit ratings agencies (CRAs) were the second group of key enablers for the "alchemy" that transformed pools of risky nonprime mortgages into AAA-rated tranches of nonprime RMBS and CDOs. CRAs assigned credit ratings to RMBS, CDOs, and other securities in return for fees paid by underwriters on behalf of the issuers. The "issuer pays" model for credit ratings created an obvious conflict of interest between each CRA's desire to earn more rating fees and its interest in preserving its reputation for reliable ratings. Securitizations of nonprime RMBS and CDOs intensified that conflict of interest, as underwriters paid extra "consulting fees" to CRAs in return for "advice" on how to structure nonprime RMBS and CDOs to produce the highest possible percentage of AAA-rated tranches.

Moreover, a dozen major banks and securities firms were the dominant repeat players in the nonprime RMBS and CDO markets because that group underwrote 80% or more of those securities. Top underwriters frequently threatened to shift their business among the three major CRAs—Moody's, Standard & Poor's, and Fitch—if they did not receive the ratings they wanted from a particular CRA.[39]

CRAs derived a steadily growing share of their revenues from their credit ratings for nonprime RMBS and CDOs. Moody's revenues from rating RMBS and CDOs rose from 33% to 44% of its total revenues between 2000 and 2007. The CRAs' conflicts of interest and fee incentives caused them to issue inflated credit ratings that greatly understated the risks embedded in structured finance securities. One CRA analyst complained that her firm's risk model did not capture "half" of the actual risk of a structured-finance deal. She also admitted that the deal "could be structured by cows and we would rate it." Another analyst warned that inflated credit ratings were creating "an even bigger monster—the CDO market. Let's hope we are all wealthy and retired by the time this house of cards falters."[40]

John Griffin and Dragon Tang concluded that CRAs systematically inflated their credit ratings for CDO tranches. Griffin and Tang found that CRAs repeatedly made "positive adjustments" for their CDO ratings that were not justified by their credit risk models.[41] A former Moody's managing director told the Financial Crisis Inquiry Commission that Moody's "allow[ed] itself to be bullied" by RMBS and CDO underwriters and "traded the firm's reputation for short-term profits."[42]

As Tim Geithner pointed out, "Standard & Poor's estimated a mere 0.12% chance that one of its AAA-rated CDOs would fail to pay out over five years.... [T]he actual default rate for AAA-rated tranches of CDOs would be 28%, more than two hundred times higher than S&P had predicted." Geithner observed that AAA ratings for CDOs "rested on all kinds of flawed assumptions, starting with the assumption that housing prices would never fall simultaneously across the country."[43] The credit risk models used by CRAs—like those of most large financial institutions—did not include the possibility of a significant downturn in housing prices across the nation. As Michael Lewis observed, the nonprime mortgage boom represented a massive "bet" by CRAs, nonprime mortgage lenders, underwriters, and guarantors that "housing prices would never fall."[44]

The assumption of ever-increasing home prices was a fatal error, especially when CRAs assigned AAA ratings to cash flow CDOs, whose underlying asset pools contained mostly mezzanine (BBB-rated) tranches of nonprime RMBS. In October 2006, financial analyst James Grant warned that (1) AAA-rated tranches of CDOs would suffer significant losses if home prices fell by 4% on a nationwide basis, and (2) CDO tranches that were rated A or below would be completely wiped out if national home prices fell by 10%. Grant's warning reflected the fact that (1) mezzanine tranches of nonprime RMBS typically began to incur losses if defaults occurred on more than 3% of the underlying mortgages (thereby wiping out the equity tranches of RMBS), and (2) losses on mezzanine tranches of RMBS would quickly spread to CDOs whose payoffs were based on pools of the same tranches.[45]

CRAs made further crucial errors in evaluating the risks of nonprime RMBS and CDOs. CRAs did not perform their own due diligence on nonprime mortgages held in securitized pools, relying instead on reports from due diligence agencies hired by the underwriters. CRAs therefore did not realize that nonprime mortgage pools became systematically riskier as mortgage lending standards deteriorated between 2003 and 2007, or that underwriters were waiving in large numbers of nonprime mortgages that due diligence agencies rejected. CRAs also overestimated the diversification benefits produced by pooling nonprime mortgages. They were not aware that many securitized pools contained dangerous concentrations of nonprime mortgages from high-risk housing markets in Arizona, California, Florida, and Nevada. Nor did CRAs understand the degree to which (1) housing risks had become highly correlated across the U.S. as a result of nationwide lending programs established by big banks and large nonbank lenders, and (2) housing risks were intensified by reckless, fraudulent, and predatory lending.[46]

Universal banks and Wall Street securities firms further amplified the risks of nonprime mortgages by creating synthetic CDOs. Synthetic CDOs paid financial returns to investors based on payoffs from pools of CDS. The pooled CDS generated payments based on the performance of designated tranches of nonprime RMBS or cash flow CDOs. "Long" investors in synthetic CDOs wagered that the designated tranches would perform well, while "short" investors bet that the tranches would default. Underwriters could provide betting opportunities to investors by pooling CDS contracts and constructing synthetic CDOs from those pools—thereby avoiding the need to buy the designated tranches of nonprime RMBS or cash flow CDOs. Synthetic CDOs multiplied the risks of the nonprime mortgage market because they created additional bets on the performance of designated tranches of nonprime RMBS or cash flow CDOs. In some cases, the bets made by investors in synthetic CDOs were several times as large as the size of the referenced tranches of nonprime RMBS or cash flow CDOs.[47]

Synthetic CDOs created major conflicts of interest for CDO underwriters. The CDS contracts underlying synthetic CDOs were effectively zero-sum games, as losses suffered by either long or short investors would result in corresponding gains for the other side. An underwriter could structure a synthetic CDO to favor either long or short investors by creating CDS with references to tranches of RMBS or cash flow CDOs that were either less or more likely to default. The underwriter could also solicit deal fees from the favored side, while being well aware that the disfavored side would probably suffer large losses. During 2006 and early 2007, several hedge fund managers decided that the nonprime mortgage market was about to collapse, and they realized that synthetic CDOs provided attractive vehicles for betting against that market. John Paulson's hedge fund (Paulson & Co.) and the Magnetar Capital hedge fund were among the funds that worked with underwriters to design synthetic CDOs that favored their short bets.[48]

The most well-known example was a synthetic CDO called Abacus 2007-AC1 (Abacus). Goldman Sachs created Abacus in early 2007, at Paulson's request. Goldman told the long investors in Abacus—IKB, a German regional bank, and ACA Capital (whose obligations were guaranteed by ABN Amro, a large Dutch bank)—that an independent CDO manager was selecting the referenced portfolio of subprime mortgage-related assets. Goldman misled the long investors because it did not disclose that Paulson & Co. had persuaded the CDO manager to choose a portfolio of high-risk subprime assets that Paulson expected to default in the near future.

Goldman also misled the CDO manager by indicating that Paulson would take a long position in the CDO by purchasing the equity (first loss) tranche. In fact, Paulson did not buy the equity tranche, and Paulson shorted the entire referenced portfolio by entering into CDS arranged by Goldman. Goldman did not tell the CDO manager about Paulson's short position, and the manager reportedly did not know that Paulson's interests were directly opposed to those of the long investors. By early 2008, virtually all of the assets in the referenced portfolio had defaulted, and the long investors lost $1 billion. Paulson collected most of that $1 billion under its short bets, while Goldman received a CDO structuring fee of $15–20 million.

In April 2010, the SEC brought a civil enforcement action against Goldman. The SEC alleged that Goldman's misleading disclosures to the CDO manager and the long investors violated federal securities laws. Goldman settled the SEC's enforcement action by paying $550 million in restitution and civil penalties.[49] The SEC subsequently brought similar enforcement actions against JPMorgan Chase and Citigroup for misleading "long" investors in two synthetic CDOs they arranged. Both banks agreed to pay substantial civil penalties to settle those actions.[50]

Universal banks displayed similar conflicts of interest and misconduct when they underwrote nonprime RMBS, the building blocks for CDOs. Empirical studies and litigation revealed that universal banks made systematic misrepresentations about the nonprime RMBS they sold to investors. John Griffin and Gonzalo Maturana analyzed three million nonprime mortgages that were securitized into nonprime RMBS between 2002 and 2007. They found that 30% of those mortgages had unreported

second liens, were incorrectly listed as owner-occupied, or relied on property appraisals that were inflated by more than 20%. The misrepresented mortgages defaulted at
much higher rates than accurately described mortgages. Griffin and Maturana found
that the eighteen largest underwriters of nonprime RMBS (including fourteen of the
Big Seventeen financial conglomerates) had misrepresentation rates for securitized
mortgages ranging from 24% for WaMu to more than 40% for Barclays and JPMC.[51]
Griffin and Maturana concluded that "all large banks in our sample ... had large levels
of apparent fraud, [and] the ten banks with the most misreporting with our indicators
are Barclays, JP Morgan, Morgan Stanley, Merrill Lynch, Lehman Brothers, HSBC,
Deutsche Bank, Nomura Securities, Goldman Sachs, and Bank of America."[52]

Tomasz Piskorski, Amit Seru, and James Witkin obtained similar results from their
review of 1.9 million nonprime mortgages that were securitized into nonprime RMBS
between 2005 and 2007. They determined that 7–14% of the nonprime mortgages
had unreported second liens, and over 6% of the mortgages had absentee owners
even though they were listed as owner-occupied. Nonprime mortgages with unreported second liens or absentee owners defaulted at a rate that was 60–70% higher
than accurately described mortgages.[53]

Piskorski, Seru, and Witkin found that seventeen large RMBS underwriters (including all of the underwriters studied by Griffin and Maturana except GMAC) had
substantial rates of unreported second liens for their securitized mortgage pools.
Lehman Brothers had the worst record, but "a significant degree of misrepresentation exists across *all* underwriters involved with the sale of [nonprime] mortgage securities." Piskorski, Seru, and Witkin also determined that large commercial banks
frequently originated and sold nonprime mortgages to their affiliated broker-dealers
for underwriting, while also providing unreported second-lien loans to the same borrowers. Since "the lender and the underwriter [were] the *same* institution" for those
loans, the underwriters should have known about the unreported second liens.[54]

John Griffin, Richard Lowery, and Alessio Saretto reviewed the performance of
RMBS, asset-backed securities, and CDOs sold by underwriters between 2000 and
2010. They determined that RMBS, ABS, and CDOs sold by underwriters with "high
reputations"—including the largest U.S. and European universal banks and the Big
Five securities firms—had default rates that were much higher than comparable securities sold by smaller underwriters.[55] Similarly, Larry Cordell, Yilin Huang, and
Meredith Williams found that CDOs arranged by the largest underwriters experienced loss rates that were significantly worse than CDOs assembled by smaller
underwriters.[56]

Griffin, Lowery, and Saretto concluded that the poor performance of high-
reputation underwriters resulted from their "strategic" decisions to take advantage of
uninformed investors. High-reputation underwriters knew that most investors could
not evaluate the actual risks embedded in complex structured finance securities, and
investors therefore relied heavily on the underwriters' reputations as well as credit
ratings. Moreover, high-reputation underwriters continued to sell large volumes of

risky RMBS and CDOs during 2007, when they knew that default rates on nonprime mortgages were already rising rapidly.[57]

For example, RBS made two offerings of RMBS during the fall of 2007, backed by pools of nonprime mortgages originated by Option One, a specialized nonprime lender. RBS knew that a high percentage of Option One's mortgages had material defects and violated RBS's underwriting standards. However, RBS had extended a $3 billion warehouse line of credit to Option One, and RBS was "very nervous" that Option One might soon collapse. RBS decided to securitize Option One's mortgages so that Option One could use the proceeds to pay off RBS's line of credit. A senior RBS employee commented that RBS's relationship with Option One was a "good run while it lasted," as it represented a "[r]edistribution of wealth to [Wall S]treet."[58]

Federal agencies filed dozens of lawsuits against leading underwriters of nonprime RMBS, including all of the Big Seventeen financial conglomerates (or their successors, in the cases of Bear Stearns, Lehman Brothers, Merrill Lynch, and Wachovia). Federal agencies alleged that the underwriters violated numerous federal laws when they sold nonprime RMBS to Fannie Mae, Freddie Mac, Federal Home Loan Banks, and federally insured depository institutions that later failed and were placed in receiverships.

The Justice Department provided the most detailed public allegations of misconduct in a 200-page complaint filed against Barclays in December 2016. That complaint alleged that Barclays "systematically and intentionally misrepresented key characteristics of the loans included in [its] RMBS deals." The complaint also alleged that "more than half of the underlying residential mortgages defaulted, resulting in billions of dollars in losses to investors."[59] Federal agencies settled most of their lawsuits and recovered more than $100 billion from underwriters of nonprime RMBS. Statements of facts accompanying those settlements provided "detailed evidence" showing that "misreporting [of mortgage information] was widespread and widely known by mortgage employees within the banks."[60]

In one case that was fully litigated, the Federal Housing Finance Authority won an $800 million judgment against Nomura and RBS for violating federal and state securities laws when they sold $2 billion of nonprime RMBS to Fannie and Freddie. A federal district court determined that Nomura and RBS made material misrepresentations in their RMBS offerings by stating that the underlying mortgages "generally" conformed to their approved underwriting guidelines. In fact, Nomura and RBS "systematically disregarded" their underwriting guidelines, and at least 45% of the underlying mortgages were "materially defective." The district court concluded that the "magnitude of falsity" in Nomura's and RBS's offering documents was "enormous."[61] The Second Circuit endorsed the district court's findings and affirmed the district court's judgment.[62]

―――

A few federal officials realized that mortgage fraud and reckless lending practices had become serious problems by 2004. However, those officials could not persuade their colleagues to take strong measures to stop fraudulent and high-risk lending. During testimony before Congress and at press conferences in 2004 and 2005, FBI Assistant Director Chris Swecker warned that mortgage fraud had become an "epidemic" and "could have as much impact as the S&L crisis." Despite Swecker's warnings, Congress and the FBI did not devote additional resources to prevent mortgage fraud because their primary concern after 9/11 was to stop "terrorist threats."[63]

During a meeting with federal financial regulators in late 2004 or early 2005, Treasury Secretary John Snow "urge[d] regulators to address the proliferation of poor lending practices." However, regulators did not share Snow's concerns. They told him that they did not "see any real big problem" because the institutions they supervised were "very well capitalized" and had "very low delinquencies."[64]

In 2006, Lawrence Lindsey, former Director of the National Economic Council, visited the White House and warned his former colleagues that reckless mortgage lending practices were inflating housing prices and posed a grave threat to the U.S. economy. White House officials dismissed his views as overly pessimistic. Lindsey concluded that "no one wanted to stop [the housing] bubble." Indeed, the housing boom was the main engine driving the economy, as it had been since the Fed adopted its ultra-low interest rate policy in the early 2000s.[65]

In contrast to Swecker, Snow, and Lindsey, most senior financial regulators and economic policymakers expressed few concerns about the rapid growth in nonprime mortgage lending and the corresponding spike in home prices. During testimony before Congress in July 2005, Fed Chairman Greenspan noted the presence of "speculative fervor" and "apparent froth in housing markets." He acknowledged that "declines in home prices ... likely would be accompanied by some economic stress." However, Greenspan advised Congress that "the macroeconomic implications need not be substantial." He believed that the U.S. economy "has remained on a firm footing, and ... the prospects are favorable for a continuation of those trends."[66]

Ben Bernanke gave a similarly reassuring report to Congress in October 2005, while serving as President George W. Bush's chief economic adviser. Bernanke informed Congress that home prices had risen by 25% during the prior two years, and "speculative activity has increased in some areas." However, he said, "at a national level these price increases largely reflect strong economic fundamentals."[67]

During a CNBC interview in July 2005, Bernanke said, "We've never had a [housing price] decline on a nationwide basis." He predicted that "house prices will slow, maybe stabilize, might slow consumption spending a bit." However, he did not think a correction in home prices would "drive the economy too far from its full employment path." Bernanke's "never had" statement was very surprising in view of his pathbreaking research on the Great Depression, when housing prices collapsed across the nation.[68] Bernanke's belief that home prices would not decline substantially on a nationwide basis was generally shared by the Fed's leadership and staff in 2005.[69]

In the absence of any meaningful action by federal regulators, universal banks and Wall Street securities firms continued to churn out RMBS, CDOs, and other structured finance securities. Their underwriting frenzy continued even after housing prices peaked in 2006 and began to decline thereafter in a number of major metropol-itan markets. As housing prices softened, delinquency rates for nonprime mortgages rose sharply. The ABX index—introduced in early 2006 to track the performance of tranches of nonprime RMBS—declined by 4% during the fourth quarter of 2006 for BBB-rated tranches and fell more rapidly during the first quarter of 2007.[70]

Investor demand for nonprime RMBS and CDOs began to weaken during the second half of 2006. However, most major banks and securities firms did not throttle back on their securitization assembly lines. Instead, they continued to underwrite nonprime RMBS and CDOs, and they transferred unsold tranches to two types of off-balance-sheet dumping grounds. First, banks created off-balance-sheet conduits, which sold short-term, asset-backed commercial paper (ABCP) to investors and used the proceeds to buy RMBS, CDOs, and other securities underwritten by their spon-soring banks. Banks provided liquidity "puts" (guarantees) to investors who bought the ABCP issued by their conduits.

Second, banks established off-balance-sheet structured investment vehicles, which also bought securities underwritten by their bank sponsors. SIVs funded those pur-chases by issuing ABCP and medium-term notes to investors. SIVs relied on implicit (reputational) guarantees from their bank sponsors instead of explicit liquidity puts. By January 2007, U.S. and foreign banks had organized conduits that issued more than $900 billion of ABCP, as well as SIVs that held $400 billion of assets. Citigroup was the largest global sponsor of off-balance-sheet entities, as its ABCP conduits and SIVs held $150 billion of assets.[71]

Citigroup transferred $25 billion of unsold super-senior CDO tranches to its ABCP conduits with accompanying liquidity guarantees. After Citigroup's treasury department refused to approve any more liquidity guarantees, Citigroup's CDO trading desk kept growing amounts of AAA-rated CDO tranches in Citigroup's in-vestment portfolio (and thus on Citigroup's balance sheet) as the trading desk com-pleted more CDO deals to earn more fees. By September 2007, Citigroup had $55 billion of nonprime exposures, including $25 billion of CDO tranches parked in its ABCP conduits, $18 billion of CDO tranches held on its balance sheet, and $12 bil-lion of subprime mortgages and RMBS tranches held in its CDO "warehouse."[72]

Citigroup was not the only institution that ate its own toxic cooking. Merrill Lynch surpassed Citigroup to become the top-ranked underwriter of CDOs in 2006, and Merrill accumulated over $55 billion of exposures to CDOs and nonprime RMBS by the fall of 2007. UBS was one of the two most active European banks in the CDO market, and it held more than $50 billion of AAA-rated CDO tranches on its balance sheet in early 2007.[73] Viral Acharya and Philipp Schnabl estimated that in mid-2008, leading underwriters of nonprime ABS, RMBS, and CDOs retained risk exposures to about half of the outstanding AAA-rated tranches of those instruments through on-balance-sheet and off-balance-sheet positions.[74]

Most regulators believed in 2007 that nonprime mortgages, RMBS, and CDOs did not pose serious risks to the largest financial institutions. They assumed (incorrectly) that financial conglomerates were pursuing an "originate-to-distribute" business strategy and were therefore using securitization and credit derivatives to transfer their credit risks to a wide range of institutional investors.[75] As Gillian Tett explained, "By 2007, ... the dominant creed at the Washington Fed and the US Treasury was that credit risk had been so widely dispersed, via credit derivatives and CDOs, that any blows would be absorbed" by institutional investors.[76] In fact, as Acharya and Schnabl showed, many leading financial institutions pursued an "originate to *not really* distribute" strategy. Those institutions retained large risk exposures to nonprime RMBS, ABS, and CDOs that they could not sell to investors because they wanted to keep producing fees from their securitization factories.[77]

The nonprime mortgage market slumped badly during the first half of 2007. Housing prices declined, and many heavily indebted borrowers could not refinance their nonprime mortgages before their teaser rate periods expired. As a result, default rates on nonprime mortgages soared. Large banks and securities firms stopped providing repo funding to specialized nonbank lenders and cut off their warehouse lines of credit. Specialized lenders could not survive without such funding. New Century and three other specialized lenders filed for bankruptcy between December 2006 and July 2007. Other nonbank lenders put their businesses up for sale. Countrywide—the top U.S. nonprime mortgage lender—disclosed in early August 2007 that it was in deep financial trouble.[78]

Instead of retrenching, several of the largest financial conglomerates acquired troubled lenders to expand their nonprime lending and securitization factories. Citigroup acquired the remaining assets of Ameriquest, Deutsche Bank purchased Mortgage IT, Merrill Lynch bought First Franklin, Morgan Stanley bought Saxon Mortgage, and Bear Stearns purchased Encore Credit. Bank of America made the biggest bet of all by purchasing a 16% stake in Countrywide in late August 2007. BofA agreed to acquire all of Countrywide's assets in January 2008. The Fed approved a similar wager in September 2006 when it allowed Wachovia, the fourth-largest U.S. bank, to acquire Golden West, a large option ARM lender in California.[79]

The acquiring institutions believed they could generate higher profits as soon as the nonprime mortgage market recovered from its problems, just as it had done after its previous downturn between 1998 and 2001. When Citigroup announced its acquisition of Ameriquest's assets in September 2007, a senior Citigroup executive declared, "We're big believers in the whole vertical integration of this part of the capital markets." He praised the deal for allowing Citigroup to expand its nonprime lending and securitization capabilities. Similarly, Merrill Lynch acquired First Franklin to enlarge its nonprime lending and securitization operations.[80]

Big financial conglomerates increased their risk-taking in other areas as well. Universal banks and Wall Street securities firms made $1.2 trillion of commercial real estate loans between 2003 and 2007, and they packaged about half of those loans into commercial mortgage-backed securities. As was true with nonprime RMBS, the terms of CMBS became significantly riskier between 2005 and 2007.[81]

Banks and securities firms also arranged $5 trillion of leveraged corporate loans and underwrote $800 billion of high-yield ("junk") bonds between 2003 and 2007. Many of those loans and bonds financed leveraged buyouts of companies. Banks and securities firms pooled more than $500 billion of leveraged loans to create collateralized loan obligations, which sold tranched securities to investors. As the leveraged buyout boom reached its peak in 2006 and early 2007, Citigroup and other major banks arranged leveraged loans that contained interest-only, payment-in-kind, and "covenant lite" terms, all of which imposed greater risks on lenders as well as CLO investors. The risky features of leveraged loans during the later stages of the buyout boom resembled the interest-only, negative amortization, and low-doc or no-doc terms of nonprime mortgages the big lenders issued during the housing bubble.[82]

Citigroup was the third-ranked arranger of leveraged loans in 2007, and it wanted to participate in all of the "mega deals" to "maintain its market leadership."[83] In late June 2007, credit markets were shaken by news that two hedge funds owned by Bear Stearns might collapse. Those hedge funds had invested heavily in nonprime mortgage-related assets, including risky CDOs. Analysts viewed the hedge funds' problems as "emblematic of the widening fallout from the nation's housing downturn," and investors began to wonder "how much longer the era of easy corporate credit can last."[84]

To address those concerns, Citigroup chairman Chuck Prince gave an interview to the *Financial Times* in July 2007. Prince denied rumors that Citigroup was "pulling back" from leveraged lending. He affirmed Citigroup's commitment to leveraged lending by making the most-quoted statement from the credit boom: "When the music stops, in terms of liquidity, things will be complicated. But as long as the music is playing, you've got to get up and dance. We're still dancing."

Prince pointed out that "big Wall Street banks" were acquiring "troubled subprime lenders," a development that showed "how 'liquidity rushes in' to fill the gap as others spot a buying opportunity." Thus, Prince viewed Citigroup's continued funding for leveraged buyouts as a market "opportunity" that resembled Citigroup's acquisition of Ameriquest's subprime lending operations soon thereafter.[85]

In early August, Prince reiterated Citigroup's commitment to leveraged lending in an interview with the *New York Times*. Prince stated, "We see a lot of people on the Street who are scared.... We are not scared. We are not panicked. Our team has been through this before." He added—in a remark that echoed his "still dancing" comment—"I think our performance is going to last much longer than the market turbulence does."[86]

In private, Prince was much less confident. Treasury Secretary Hank Paulson attended a private dinner at the New York Fed on June 26, 2007. Leaders of major New York banks were also present at that dinner. Paulson later recalled:

All [of the bankers] were concerned with excessive risk taking in the markets and appalled by the erosion of underwriting standards. The bankers complained about all the covenant-lite loans and bridge loans they felt compelled by competitive pressure to make.[87]

JPMC chairman Jamie Dimon and Goldman Sachs CEO Lloyd Blankfein told Paulson that their institutions did not plan to make additional leveraged buyout loans. In contrast, Prince asked Paulson, "Isn't there something you can do to order us not to take all of these risks?"[88] Prince's question indicated that Citigroup's leaders felt obliged to keep "dancing"—even though they were greatly concerned about the risks of doing so—as long as some of their top competitors were still on the dance floor.

Prince's attitude reflected the mindset of top executives at many other large U.S. and European financial institutions during the credit boom.[89] Prince and other CEOs had powerful incentives to boost their banks' revenues and returns on equity each quarter and every year. Executives who raised their companies' stock prices by meeting or exceeding Wall Street's profit targets received enormous financial rewards in the form of annual bonuses and stock option grants. Incentive compensation plans at most universal banks and big securities firms did not take account of the longer-term risks of speculative activities that produced higher short-term profits. Very few plans provided for clawbacks of bonuses or option grants if the institution later suffered losses due to excessive risk-taking.[90]

The Financial Crisis Inquiry Commission determined that a leading cause of the failures and bailouts of major financial institutions in 2008 was that "executive and employee compensation systems disproportionately rewarded short-term risk taking" and did not include "proper consideration of long-term consequences."[91] A study by Sugato Bhattacharyya and Amiyatosh Purnanandam found that large U.S. banks reporting higher earnings per share paid substantially larger amounts of compensation (including bonuses) to their CEOs during the 2000s. The same banks produced significantly higher levels of systematic risk and also experienced much worse mortgage default rates in 2007.[92]

According to Sanjai Bhagat and Brian Bolton, the CEOs of the fourteen largest U.S. financial institutions—eight big banks, five big securities firms, and AIG—received total cash compensation (from salaries, bonuses, and sales of stock) of $2.7 billion between 2000 and 2008. Those CEOs suffered paper investment losses of $2 billion in 2008, but they still held equity interests with an estimated total value of $940 million at the end of 2008. The same fourteen financial giants assumed much higher levels of risk, wrote off substantially larger percentages of their assets, and produced far worse returns for their shareholders during 2008 and 2009, compared with a group of thirty-seven midsized banks that did not receive capital assistance from the federal government. Thus, the CEOs of the fourteen largest U.S. financial institutions received very large net gains from aggressive, risk-oriented compensation policies, even though their institutions performed very poorly as a group during the financial crisis.[93] Similarly, Robert DeYoung, Emma Peng, and Meng Yan found that the largest

U.S. banks adopted incentive compensation policies during the 2000s that encouraged their CEOs to take greater risks, particularly at banks that engaged heavily in nontraditional, fee-based activities such as securitizing nonprime mortgages.[94]

The extravagant compensation awarded to CEOs of big banks during the 2000s rivaled the gaudy bonuses that National City Bank and Chase National Bank had paid to Charles Mitchell and Albert Wiggin during the 1920s. Sandy Weill received over $900 million in cash and stock awards from Travelers and Citigroup between 1997 and 2006. Citigroup paid Chuck Prince $158 million in cash and stock awards between 2003 and 2007, while Robert Rubin (chairman of Citigroup's executive committee) received $125 million between 1999 and 2009.[95] Merrill Lynch paid Stan O'Neal $50 million of total compensation in 2006, when the firm reported record profits, and he received a severance package of $160 million when he resigned in 2007. UBS paid its chairman, Marcel Ospel, more than $100 million between 2000 and 2007.[96] Countrywide's CEO, Angelo Mozilo, garnered $520 million from compensation and stock sales between 2000 and 2008, while WaMu's CEO, Kerry Killinger, received $88 million during the same period.[97]

In 2006, as shown in Figure 0.4 in the Introduction, the gap between the average pay of financial sector employees and the average pay of employees in other economic sectors reached its highest level since 1930. Investment banking units of U.S. financial institutions increased their total payouts to employees from 31% to 60% of their gross revenues between 2002 and 2007.[98] In 2006, Citigroup paid $55 million to the two highest-ranking executives in its investment banking division as well as $15 million to the two co-heads of its CDO unit. Merrill Lynch paid $70 million in the same year to the two top executives in its investment bank.[99] AIG paid more than $300 million to Joe Cassano during his tenure at AIG Financial Products.[100]

CEOs who failed to meet Wall Street's revenue and profit targets faced a substantial risk of losing their jobs.[101] In view of that risk, Chuck Prince and most of his peers chose to follow the herd. Tim Geithner later commented, "A financial CEO who was unusually cautious about leverage during the boom [of the 2000s] probably would have been fired before the bust. Many financial executives didn't even want to think about truly extreme events."[102]

Some leaders of big financial conglomerates suffered from "Goldman envy" during the credit boom, and they tried desperately to match the huge profits produced by Goldman Sachs' legendary trading operation and its trend-setting CDO unit.[103] In 2003 and 2004, Goldman paid $100 million to CEO Hank Paulson and president Lloyd Blankfein. In 2006, Goldman set a new record for profits and paid over $200 million to CEO Blankfein, former CEO Paulson, and two co-presidents.[104] Robert Rubin (a former Goldman co-chairman who joined Citigroup in 1999) encouraged Citigroup to follow Goldman's lead by emphasizing proprietary trading and CDO underwriting. Similarly, Merrill Lynch CEO Stan O'Neal and UBS chairman Marcel Ospel pushed their firms to take greater risks in trading and CDO underwriting to match Goldman's performance.[105]

In December 2006, Goldman reversed course as the nonprime mortgage market showed serious signs of weakness. Goldman's top executives decided to get rid of the firm's long positions related to nonprime mortgages. The head of Goldman's fixed income, currency, and commodity trading division instructed his traders and sales representatives to target Goldman's holdings of nonprime mortgage-related securities and "move them out." Goldman's chief financial officer reinforced that directive, stating, "Let's be aggressive distributing things."[106]

At the end of January 2007, the manager of Goldman's mortgage department told Tom Montag, Goldman's head of global securities, that his team had "structured like mad and traveled the world and worked their tails off to make some lemonade from some big old lemons." Two weeks later, CEO Lloyd Blankfein asked Montag, "Could/ should we have cleaned up these books before and are we doing enough right now to sell off cats and dogs in other books throughout the division?"[107]

The Financial Crisis Inquiry Commission determined that "the answer [to Blankfein's question] was yes, they had cleaned up pretty well." Goldman created and sold $17 billion of synthetic CDOs and $8 billion of cash flow CDOs between December 2006 and August 2007. The FCIC found that Goldman "used the cash [flow] CDOs to unload much of its own remaining inventory of other CDO securities and mortgage-backed securities." Goldman also took short positions against some of the securities it sold as well as some of the buyers of those securities. Goldman was later "criticized—and sued—for selling its subprime mortgage securities to clients while simultaneously betting against those securities."[108]

A few other large banks, including JPMC and PNC, also reduced their exposures to nonprime mortgage-related assets in late 2006 and early 2007. However, most big banks did not follow their example. Greg Lippman, the leader of Deutsche Bank's mortgage trading desk, was probably the only trader at a major bank who matched Goldman's aggressiveness in shorting the nonprime mortgage market. The other short sellers were primarily hedge funds, including Cornwall Capital, Magnetar Capital, Paulson & Co., and funds managed by Kyle Bass, Michael Burry, Steve Eisman, and Andrew Redleaf.[109]

———

In 2007, more than $2.7 trillion of subprime and Alt-A mortgages and jumbo ARMs were outstanding in the U.S., of which $2 trillion were held in securitized pools backing private-label RMBS.[110] Other potentially risky debts and structured-finance securities included (1) more than $600 billion of cash flow and synthetic CDOs, (2) $2.5 trillion of home equity, auto, and credit card loans, of which a third were securitized into ABS, (3) $3.3 trillion of commercial mortgages, of which a quarter were securitized into CMBS, (4) $600 billion of leveraged loans, most of which were securitized into CLOs, and (5) almost $1.1 trillion of junk bonds.[111] In sum, about $10 trillion of higher-risk U.S. private sector debts were outstanding in 2007, and over half of those debts had been securitized or resecuritized to create $5 trillion of private-label structured finance securities and over $1 trillion of junk bonds.[112] A majority of those securitized debts carried AAA credit ratings and were sold as purportedly "safe" investments to banks, insurance companies, mutual funds, pension funds, and other investors. The securitization of risky debts and the marketing of the resulting securities as safe investments by large financial conglomerates during the 2000s bore a striking and disturbing resemblance to the packaging and marketing of high-risk corporate bonds and foreign bonds by universal banks during the 1920s.[113]

In addition to the $10 trillion of risky debts that were outstanding in the U.S. in 2007, an unknown volume of CDS contracts represented additional bets on the performance of designated tranches of nonprime RMBS and CDOs. AIG and monoline insurance companies issued more than $800 billion of CDS that protected holders of AAA-rated tranches of CDOs against default.[114] One financial analyst estimated that a third of the $45 trillion of outstanding CDS in 2007 represented bets on the performance of nonprime-related securities or indexes.[115] Thus, U.S. credit markets in 2007 resembled an "inverted pyramid of risk," in which "multiple layers of financial bets" depended on the performance of speculative loans held in securitized pools. When the underlying loans began to default in large numbers, the highly leveraged bets in the pyramid collapsed and inflicted devastating losses on banks and investors. Those losses proved to be much larger than the face amounts of the defaulted loans.[116]

Moreover, financial conglomerates financed many of their loans and trading bets by issuing short-term debt instruments that were subject to significant liquidity (roll-over) risks. As discussed earlier in this chapter, major financial institutions created off-balance-sheet conduits and SIVs as dumping grounds for their unsold tranches of nonprime RMBS and CDOs. Those off-balance-sheet units issued $1.3 trillion of short-term, asset-backed commercial paper and medium-term notes, which were explicitly or implicitly guaranteed by their bank sponsors. In addition, the Big Five Wall Street securities firms and securities affiliates of universal banks obtained $3.5 trillion of funding from repo loans, most of which were renewed on a daily or weekly basis. Large financial institutions sold more than $500 billion of unsecured, short-term commercial paper, primarily to money market mutual funds. Universal banks raised additional short-term funding by accepting uninsured deposits and entering into interbank loans. Thus, the largest banks and securities firms faced enormous liquidity risks if they could not renew their short-term loans from wholesale creditors, or if their secured creditors demanded additional collateral for their loans.[117]

Financial conglomerates essentially followed a Ponzi finance strategy—an approach similar to homeowners who entered into teaser rate hybrid subprime ARMs or option ARMs based on the assumption that they could satisfy their debts by refinancing their mortgages or selling their homes. The economist Hyman Minsky described Ponzi finance as a situation in which debtors cannot meet their debt service obligations without refinancing (rolling over) their loans or selling their assets. Minsky's financial instability hypothesis predicted that the use of Ponzi finance would expand during the euphoric phase of an economic boom, when debtors and creditors were confident that they could easily refinance their debts or sell their assets at a profit. In

2006, Minsky's hypothesis became a tragic reality. The largest financial institutions and millions of U.S. homeowners were linked together in a massive Ponzi finance scheme, which was doomed to fail as soon as home prices dropped significantly.[118]

As shown in Figure 9.1 in Chapter 9, average national home sale prices declined by 5% during 2007 and dropped by an additional 16% between January 2008 and September 2009. The fall in home prices was much more severe in metropolitan areas where larger housing booms had occurred and where nonprime mortgage lenders relied more heavily on funding from sales of private-label RMBS. Mian and Sufi determined that housing prices plummeted by 46% between 2006 and 2010 in twenty "bubble" metropolitan areas in the West and Southeast, while home prices in non-bubble urban areas fell by 12%.[119]

The Ponzi finance pyramid of risk in the U.S. collapsed during the second half of 2007, as housing prices dropped across the nation. Underwriting markets for nonprime RMBS, CDOs, CLOs, and CMBS shut down by the end of 2007. Lenders refused to refinance mortgages held by millions of "underwater" homeowners, whose houses were worth less than their outstanding debts. Large numbers of distressed homeowners could not sell their houses and defaulted on their mortgages. As mortgage defaults rose, wholesale lenders refused to renew their short-term loans to large financial institutions. Similar downward spirals occurred in markets for commercial real estate loans and leveraged loans.[120]

As the nonprime mortgage market experienced severe problems during the first half of 2007, the Fed and Treasury did not seem greatly concerned. On March 28, 2007, Fed chairman Ben Bernanke informed Congress's Joint Economic Committee that the housing market was experiencing a "substantial correction" as subprime mortgage delinquency rates "climbed sharply." Bernanke added, however, that "the impact on the broader economy and financial markets of the problems in the subprime market seems likely to be contained." In a speech on June 5, Bernanke stated that "troubles in the subprime sector seem unlikely to seriously spill over to the broader economy or the financial sector."[121]

In mid-April, Treasury Secretary Hank Paulson told a group of New York business leaders that the subprime mortgage market's problems were "largely contained" and were not a "serious problem." He also opined that the housing market's correction was "at or near its bottom." Paulson reiterated that optimistic assessment during an interview with Bloomberg on July 26, stating, "I don't think [the subprime mortgage market] poses any threat to the overall economy."[122]

Bernanke's and Paulson's optimistic assessments reflected a general consensus within the Fed and the Treasury Department. Bernanke, Geithner, and Paulson were all reasonably confident in mid-2007 that losses in the subprime mortgage market would not undermine the financial system or the broader economy. Bernanke said his views were "widely shared within the Fed" during the first half of 2007. Geithner confirmed that the Fed's staff "didn't flag subprime as a major systemic risk" during that period.[123]

According to Phillip Swagel, who served as Assistant Secretary of the Treasury for Economic Policy from 2006 to 2009, Treasury's economists were "well aware of the looming problems in housing, especially among subprime borrowers as foreclosure rates increased." However, Treasury's economists predicted in May 2007 that "the foreclosure problem would subside after a peak in 2008." As Swagel later acknowledged, Treasury's forecast failed to give adequate weight to a report from the FDIC, which warned that "the situation in housing was bad and getting worse and would have important implications for the banking system and the broader economy."[124]

The Fed's and Treasury's failures to comprehend the magnitude of housing-related financial problems in mid-2007 resulted from several crucial misjudgments. The Fed and Treasury did not recognize the extent to which the largest commercial banks had become deeply intertwined with the capital markets through extensive securities operations that relied heavily on funding from short-term shadow deposits, including repos and commercial paper. The Fed and Treasury did not appreciate the degree to which Wall Street securities firms had become de facto universal banks through their accumulation of shadow deposits and their acquisitions of FDIC-insured thrifts and industrial loan companies. The Fed and Treasury did not realize that both types of financial conglomerates had become highly leveraged and deeply exposed to losses from nonprime RMBS and CDOs by retaining on-balance-sheet risk exposures and by creating off-balance-sheet risk exposures through conduits and SIVs. The Fed and Treasury were not aware of the magnitude of the pyramid of risks created by securitization, over-the-counter derivatives, and other financial "innovations." Indeed, the Fed's and Treasury's leaders generally viewed those "innovations" as positive because they seemed to promote greater "efficiency" in financial transactions.[125]

In 2015, Bernanke stated, "In truth, in the years just before the crisis, neither banks nor their regulators adequately understood the full extent of banks' exposures to dicey mortgages and other risky credit." In 2009, Bernanke conceded that the Fed failed to "understand the interconnections to off-balance-sheet vehicles and complex credit derivatives."[126] Geithner similarly admitted in 2014:

> We didn't appreciate the extent to which nonbanks were funding themselves in runnable short-term ways, or how vulnerable the banking system would be to distress in the nonbanks.... We also failed to anticipate the savage depth of the Great Recession, or the debilitating feedback loop between problems in the financial system and problems in the broader economy.[127]

The Fed's and Treasury's views reflected a broader consensus among global financial regulators. For example, the International Monetary Fund was "sanguine" about the "presumed ability of [securitization and other] financial innovations to remove risks off banks' balance sheets." The IMF did not recognize the risks of a severe financial crisis until October 2007, and as late as the summer of 2008 the IMF still believed that the crisis could be "contained."[128]

In 2018, Bernanke and former Fed Vice Chairman Donald Kohn identified an important reason why the Fed and other central banks failed to anticipate the financial crisis and "significantly underestimated its ultimate impact on the real economy." As Bernanke explained, "Models used by central banks for forecasting and policy analysis ... did not include much role for credit factors [and] provided little guidance to the staff on how to think about the likely economic effects of the crisis." Kohn acknowledged that the Fed's economic models "did not contain enough detail about the financial sector to capture many critical aspects of the disruption to credit intermediation and market functioning."[129]

In a previous lecture in 2013, Bernanke admitted that forecasting models used by the Fed and other central banks were incomplete and flawed. Those models reflected the belief of "macroeconomists ... inside and outside central banks" that "detailed modeling of the financial sector may not be central for understanding private sector decisions or the effects of monetary policy." Central bank models relied on a number of "restrictive assumptions," including "no bankruptcy costs, no agency problems, and no asymmetric information." Based on those highly unrealistic assumptions, "many monetary economists and central bankers concluded that the details of the structure of the financial system could be largely ignored when analyzing the behavior of the broader economy."[130]

Due to the severe limitations of their forecasting models, the Fed and other central banks did not consider the central importance of bank-centered and "shadow bank" financial conglomerates, which created complex, far-reaching, and fragile connections between the banking system and capital markets. Moreover, central bank models did not comprehend the potential risks of "complex financial structures" like CDOs, CDS, and SIVs.[131]

As Joseph Stiglitz pointed out, the forecasting models used by the Fed and other central banks did not include either "a well-specified financial sector" or a foundational role for banks. The Fed's models did not consider the "systemic risk" that could arise if financial shocks spread across a wide range of financial markets and spilled over to the general economy. Stiglitz noted that the risks of "contagion" had become much greater by 2007, due to the financial conglomerates and "capital market integration" that the U.S., U.K., and EU authorized after the mid-1980s. Central bank models also failed to consider "financial frictions"—including "bankruptcy costs" and "credit constraints"—that could turn credit disruptions into systemic crises. Stiglitz concluded that the Fed's forecasting model "ignored issues that turned out to be key to the 2008 crisis; not surprisingly, the model neither predicted [the crisis] *not provided good guidance as to the appropriate policy responses.*"[132]

In sum, the Fed and other central banks failed to predict the financial crisis or anticipate its severity because their decisions were based on theoretical economic models that included *almost no consideration of the actual workings of the financial system as it existed in 2007.* Their forecasting models mirrored their light-touch regulatory regimes, which relied on market discipline as well as the risk management policies and procedures of major banks. As a result, central bank forecasts and supervisory policies ignored the opaque and highly complex transactions, pervasive conflicts of interest, and widespread abuses that were actually occurring at large financial conglomerates. Central bank models also disregarded the high probability of systemic risk, caused by contagion between the banking industry and the capital markets, due to the formation of huge bank-centered and shadow bank financial conglomerates. Yet those were the same financial giants that central banks and other policymakers had eagerly championed since the 1980s.

———

Beginning in July 2007, events began to reveal how poorly the Fed, the Treasury, and their European counterparts understood the immense risks lurking in global housing markets and the international financial system. On July 10, credit ratings agencies began to downgrade thousands of tranches of nonprime ABS, RMBS, and CDOs. By the end of 2007, credit ratings agencies had downgraded 54% of ABS tranches backed by second-lien home equity loans, 13% of CDO tranches, and 17% of nonprime RMBS tranches.[133]

On July 31, 2007, the two troubled hedge funds owned by Bear Stearns filed for bankruptcy after suffering crippling losses from their investments in nonprime RMBS and CDOs. The previous day, IKB (a German regional bank) accepted a bailout from its largest shareholder. IKB had established an off-balance-sheet conduit, Rhineland, which held $19 billion of CDOs, CLOs, and other risky assets. By mid-July, Rhineland's investments—including its purchase of $150 million of securities from Goldman's Abacus CDO—had suffered devastating losses. Purchasers of Rhineland's asset-backed commercial paper refused to renew their investments, and Rhineland called upon IKB to honor $11 billion of guarantees (liquidity puts) that supported Rhineland's commercial paper. IKB's largest shareholder stepped in to provide the necessary funding, and IKB honored its guarantees on August 7.[134]

A more devastating shock to investor confidence occurred on August 9. BNP Paribas—the largest French bank and one of the Big Seventeen financial conglomerates—suspended redemptions by investors in three of its hedge funds after the value of mortgage-related assets owned by those funds dropped by 20% in less than two weeks. BNP defended its suspension of redemptions by stating that it could not calculate a "fair value" for the three funds. BNP stated, "The complete evaporation of liquidity in certain market segments of the US securitization market has made it impossible to value certain assets fairly regardless of their quality or credit rating."[135]

Most experts agree that BNP's suspension of redemptions marked the beginning of the financial crisis of 2007–09.[136] As Tim Geithner explained, "Saying the bank had no idea what its subprime assets were worth was much worse than saying the values had declined by 20 or 30%. It intensified uncertainty about subprime, as well as other U.S. mortgage-backed securities, and helped to create the larger liquidity crunch."[137]

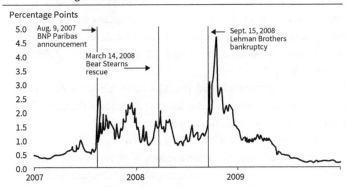

The line tracks the TED spread, a measure of distress in credit markets. It is the difference between the rate paid on three-month interbank loans as represented by the London Interbank Offered Rate (LIBOR) and the interest rate paid on three-month Treasury bills. The TED spread showed that credit risk increased sharply at key points in the crisis.

Figure 10.2 The Cost of Interbank Borrowing Soared During the Crisis

Source: Bernanke (2015: 405) (Figure 1). © 2015 by Ben S. Bernanke. Used by permission of W.W. Norton & Company, Inc.

The global interbank lending market began to freeze up as banks became increasingly concerned about the solvency of their peers. As shown in Figure 10.2, the "TED spread"—the difference between interest rates on three-month interbank loans and risk-free yields on three-month Treasury bills—spiked in August 2007. The rapid widening of the TED spread reflected a general perception that short-term loans between banks had become much riskier.[138] The European Central Bank injected more than $200 billion of cash into the European banking system and declared that it stood ready to provide "unlimited" liquidity assistance to any bank in the Eurozone. The Fed supported the ECB by purchasing over $60 billion of Treasury securities to increase liquidity in U.S. financial markets.[139]

On August 15, Countrywide—a $200 billion financial holding company and a top U.S. nonprime mortgage lender—asked the New York Fed for an emergency loan. Much of Countrywide's funding came from wholesale, nondeposit creditors. Countrywide experienced a liquidity crisis in mid-August, when many commercial paper investors refused to renew their loans. Bank of New York Mellon (BNY Mellon) also threatened to stop clearing (and providing intraday credit for) Countrywide's $45 billion portfolio of triparty repo loans. A failure by BNY Mellon to clear Countrywide's repos would have caused severe problems for money market mutual funds that were lenders on those repos. Those funds would have been forced to take possession of nonprime mortgage-related collateral posted by Countrywide, and the funds could have been required (under SEC rules) to sell that collateral quickly in "fire sales," thereby driving down the value of nonprime mortgage-related assets.[140]

Geithner persuaded BNY Mellon to continue clearing Countrywide's triparty repos. In return, Countrywide agreed to draw down $11.5 billion lines of credit with several banks so that it could provide higher-quality collateral for its repos. Geithner's arrangement was only a stopgap measure. To avoid failure, Countrywide sold a 16% stock interest to Bank of America on August 22, and in January 2008 it agreed to sell all of its assets to BofA.[141]

As Geithner subsequently explained, the "Countrywide episode foreshadowed much of what came later in the crisis. It ... revealed how dependent the entire financial system had become on fragile short-term funding arrangements."[142] Countrywide's emergency exposed stunning gaps in the Fed's knowledge and oversight of conditions in the nation's financial markets. According to Geithner, the New York Fed "had spent a lot of time worrying about the risks in tri-party repo, which had expanded tenfold in a decade, but we hadn't made progress on its worst vulnerabilities." In addition, the Fed "had paid even less attention to the asset-backed commercial paper market, which had nearly doubled during my Fed tenure [since 2003], to $1.2 trillion." As a result of Countrywide's near-failure, Geithner discovered that the ABCP market was "under pressure" because "many of the assets backing the commercial paper were linked to housing."[143]

Geithner also admitted that prior to Countrywide's threatened collapse, he had "spent very little time familiarizing myself with the risks posed by money market funds, which accumulated more than $3 trillion in assets, and in many ways functioned like banks." He did not think money market mutual funds were "much of a danger to the system before the crisis, even though Paul Volcker and others did." He learned from Countrywide's emergency that "money market funds had provided much of the financing for [investment banks and] other sources of systemic risk" by purchasing commercial paper and providing repo loans.[144]

According to Geithner's account, the New York Fed did not appreciate until August 2007 the systemic risks posed by the commercial paper and triparty repo markets, or the potential threats to financial stability posed by money market mutual funds, which were key financial intermediaries in the shadow banking system. The New York Fed also did not recognize until Countrywide's emergency the hazards created by the use of nonprime RMBS and CDOs as collateral for repos, even though repo lenders greatly expanded their reliance on such collateral after Congress expanded the bankruptcy safe harbor for repo collateral in 2005.

The New York Fed had direct supervisory authority over JPMC and BNY Mellon—the two major clearing banks for triparty repos—and could have required both banks to provide more extensive and detailed information about potential risks and vulnerabilities in the repo market. After reading Geithner's account of Countrywide's near-collapse in August 2007, it is very difficult to understand why the Fed was so poorly prepared to deal with the crises at Bear Stearns and Lehman Brothers in 2008. Both crises arose from similar problems of illiquidity and creditor runs connected to repos, commercial paper, and money market mutual funds.[145]

On August 16, 2007, the Fed reduced the rate it charged banks for discount window loans by 0.50%. The Fed also extended the length of its discount window loans from overnight to thirty days. The Fed wanted to encourage banks to borrow from the discount window if they needed additional liquidity. However, most banks declined to do so, due to the stigma associated with borrowing from the Fed (which many market participants interpreted as a sign of weakness). Banks that needed liquidity turned instead to the Federal Home Loan Banks, which provided $235 billion of advances to their member institutions during the second half of 2007. Two-thirds of those advances went to ten big financial conglomerates, including six that later failed, or were acquired in emergency mergers, or received "exceptional assistance" from the federal government in 2008.[146]

On September 13, the financial crisis became headline news on the other side of the Atlantic. Northern Rock, a $200 billion building society and the seventh-largest U.K. depository institution, asked the Bank of England for an emergency loan. Like Countrywide, Northern Rock had aggressively expanded into higher-risk mortgage lending (including making 125% loan-to-value mortgages), and it relied on wholesale lenders for three-quarters of its funding. Northern Rock turned to BoE when wholesale creditors refused to renew their short-term loans. On September 14, BoE agreed to provide the requested loan. Nevertheless, a run by Northern Rock's depositors began after they learned that the U.K.'s deposit insurance scheme provided only partial coverage, was unfunded, and might take several months to reimburse depositors for their losses. The U.K. Treasury stopped the run by guaranteeing all of Northern Rock's deposits on September 17, and the U.K. government nationalized Northern Rock in February 2008. The Northern Rock crisis provided a dress rehearsal for the panic runs and bailouts that occurred in the U.K. and Europe during the fall of 2008.[147]

Credit ratings agencies downgraded thousands of tranches of nonprime RMBS and CDOs during the fall of 2007, and the value of those securities fell sharply, increasing the pressure on banks, securities firms, and investors.[148] Commercial paper investors and other short-term lenders refused to renew their loans to many institutional borrowers. The volume of outstanding asset-backed commercial paper dropped by a third—from $1.2 trillion to $800 billion—between August and December 2007. The interbank lending market showed signs of continued stress, as reflected in elevated levels of the TED spread (see Figure 10.2). At meetings of the Federal Open Market Committee (FOMC) in September and October, the Fed reduced its target for short-term interest rates from 5.25% to 4.5%.[149] The Fed moved slowly, however, as it did not yet recognize the likelihood of a systemic financial crisis. Some members of the FOMC were concerned that an overly lenient monetary policy could trigger a dangerous bout of inflation—a concern that was supported by rising oil prices.[150]

In October 2007, the U.S. Treasury tried to convince the largest banks to join together in filling the void created by the disappearance of investor funding for off-balance-sheet SIVs. The Treasury urged the largest U.S. banks to organize a collective investment fund (a "Super SIV"), which would purchase illiquid assets from bank-sponsored SIVs. The Super SIV would serve as a "buy-and-hold investment vehicle" until financial markets stabilized, thereby avoiding "panic selling" of illiquid assets at "fire-sale prices."[151]

Treasury's proposal failed because the strongest megabanks were not willing to help their weaker peers. Consequently, each bank made its own decision about whether to rescue its SIVs.[152] Citigroup decided to bring $83 billion of assets back onto its balance sheet from its conduits and SIVs, a move that greatly strained its already weak capital position. Other big banks arranged similar rescues of their SIVs, but some sponsors allowed their SIVs to fail.[153]

The failure of Treasury's Super SIV proposal resembled President Hoover's unsuccessful effort in 1931 to create a bank-funded National Credit Corporation that could make emergency loans to struggling banks. In October 2007—as had been true seventy-six years earlier—most large banks confronted serious problems that undermined their ability and willingness to act collectively to support the financial system.[154]

Even after the Super SIV initiative collapsed, most federal regulators believed that "conventional tools of monetary policy and moderate regulatory discretion" would be sufficient to solve the problems faced by the housing and financial markets. According to Phillip Swagel, "In late 2007, policymakers did not believe extraordinary action was required."[155] On October 17, 2007, "things seemed calm enough" to Tim Geithner, and he "referred to the crisis in the past tense" during a private seminar with international financial officials. Geithner assured his international colleagues that "in important respects, the system worked.... The capital cushions at the largest banks proved strong enough to withstand the shock." Geithner believed that the world "had survived a major financial explosion."[156]

––––

The optimism of regulators was quickly proven wrong again, as big problems erupted at Merrill Lynch and Citigroup. Merrill Lynch reported a $7.9 billion loss on October 24, and Citigroup announced an $11.4 billion loss on November 4. Each institution disclosed that it held $55 billion of risk exposures to CDOs and other nonprime-related assets. The CEOs of both institutions—Stan O'Neal and Chuck Prince—resigned shortly thereafter.[157]

A group of senior U.S. and foreign regulators examined Citigroup and found systematic failures in Citigroup's risk management and serious weaknesses in its financial condition. Citigroup's risk managers did not have sufficient independence to challenge excessive risk-taking by business managers and instead acted as enablers for business units. Risk managers relied primarily on AAA credit ratings as a basis for approving Citigroup's retention of super-senior tranches of CDOs. They did not consider the possibility of a nationwide downturn in housing prices. They also did not consider the risk that Citigroup might be unable to sell its CDO tranches or leveraged loan commitments, or that Citigroup might be compelled to honor its guarantees for off-balance-sheet conduits. Due to Citigroup's complex and highly fragmented structure, its senior management team did not have a consolidated, firm-wide view of the bank's risks and did not know that Citigroup had accumulated $55 billion of exposures to nonprime mortgage-related assets. Citigroup was more thinly capitalized, and much more exposed to risky nonprime mortgage-related assets, than regulators believed.[158]

Geithner acknowledged in 2014 that "Citi wasn't as well capitalized as we thought" and that Citigroup's balance sheet was "much riskier than it looked." Regulators did not know that "Citi had stashed another $1.2 trillion in assets off its balance sheet in ways that allowed it to hold virtually no capital against losses in those assets." Regulators also did not realize the magnitude of Citigroup's "dramatic exposure to an increase in mortgage defaults and even more dramatic declines in the price of mortgage securities." The Fed "hadn't required Citi to hold enough capital because we hadn't fully understood the extent of the risks it was taking." Geithner also conceded that Citigroup's weak capital position was a symptom of a much broader problem: "We hadn't pushed banks to raise more capital in good times, because they were comfortably above the required capital ratios."[159]

Robert Rubin—Geithner's former mentor during his service in the Clinton Treasury Department—was chairman of Citigroup's executive committee. Geithner admitted that "Rubin's presence at Citi surely tempered my skepticism … [H]e probably gave Citi an undeserved aura of competence in my mind."[160]

In January 2008, Citigroup and Merrill Lynch reported combined losses of $50 billion for the previous year, primarily due to their heavy exposures to CDOs and other nonprime mortgage-related assets. Morgan Stanley and Bank of America disclosed combined losses of $20 billion, while JPMC reported losses of $5 billion.[161] When the FOMC met at the end of January, New York Fed Executive Vice President William Dudley stated that large U.S. banks had reported more than $100 billion of losses from asset write-downs during the second half of 2007. The five largest banks experienced "significant erosion of their capital ratios," although Dudley said they were still "well-capitalized" under federal regulatory standards.[162]

At the same FOMC meeting, the Fed's staff presented the results of a horizontal review of risk management practices at eleven major U.S. banks and securities firms conducted by a group of senior U.S. and foreign financial supervisors.[163] Those supervisors found "massive deficiencies in the risk management systems of some major financial institutions" (including Citigroup), while others performed better.[164]

Following the staff's presentation, Boston Fed President Eric Rosengren described a horizontal "stress test" that the Fed conducted on the mortgage operations of BofA, Citigroup, JPMC, and Wachovia in 2006. All four megabanks told the Fed that a 10–20% downturn in national housing prices "would affect earnings but wouldn't affect capital." Rosengren commented that "in retrospect, that doesn't seem to have been a good forecast." He urged the Fed's staff to revisit the 2006 stress test and find out why it did not produce more reliable predictions. He also recommended that the Fed should conduct additional stress tests.[165] Kansas City Fed President Tom Hoenig agreed with Rosengren that the Fed should examine the "lessons we've learned about more-effective institutions and less-effective institutions during the horizontal review so that we can be more proactive."[166] Despite the recommendations from Rosengren and Hoenig, the Fed evidently did *not* perform any additional horizontal "stress tests" on the largest U.S. banks until February 2009, *after* enormous bailouts had already occurred.[167]

Geithner gave his FOMC colleagues a surprisingly upbeat assessment of the condition of the largest U.S. financial institutions, in spite of the enormous problems already discovered at Citigroup and Merrill Lynch. Geithner stated that a "process of repair" had begun through "de-leveraging" and "equity raising by major firms," as well as a "pretty substantial improvement of market functioning; and easing of liquidity pressure." Geithner conceded that there was "a huge amount of uncertainty about the size and the location of remaining credit losses across the system." However, he thought "the capital positions of the major U.S. institutions coming into this look pretty good relative to how they did in the early 1990s."[168]

Fed Governor Kevin Warsh offered a far more guarded assessment. In Warsh's view, "The repair process that President Geithner referenced among financial institutions strikes me as very fragile and quite incomplete." He pointed out that large banks continued to struggle with "falling profits" and "balance sheet weakness." In addition, the largest institutions had designed their business models for "a low volatility, high liquidity world, and what they found is the exact opposite." Warsh warned that many large U.K. and European banks were even more vulnerable than their U.S. peers.[169]

Dudley reported to the FOMC on the severe problems faced by Ambac, MBIA, and other monoline bond insurers. Monoline insurers had provided $780 billion of CDS and other guarantees for CDOs and other structured finance securities, and those insurers had total "claims-paying resources" of only $50 billion. Dudley explained that there was "not much transparency" concerning the specific counterparty exposures of the monoline insurers. He cautioned that leading banks and securities firms could suffer big losses if monoline insurers defaulted on their guarantees.[170] Geithner added that the New York Superintendent of Insurance had "very little information" about the detailed risk exposures of monoline insurers.[171]

Neither Dudley nor Geithner mentioned AIG and its $80 billion portfolio of CDS protecting AAA-rated tranches of CDOs. The Fed's apparent lack of awareness about AIG's vulnerability was surprising, given contemporaneous press reports about AIG's discussion of its CDS portfolio during three calls with investors and analysts between August and December 2007. During those calls, AIG executives were peppered with tough questions about AIG's potential exposures to losses and collateral calls on those CDS.[172]

As Kate Judge pointed out, the FOMC's discussion of problems with monoline insurers in late January 2008 "brought to the fore many of the dynamics that contributed to AIG's near failure," including "the magnitude of the interconnections between banks and insurance companies" created by CDS and other guarantees for structured finance securities. The FOMC's discussion also "alerted the Fed" to the fact that federal and state regulators had very little information about "the risk exposures of insurance companies."[173]

On February 11, 2008, AIG publicly disclosed that its auditors had identified a "material weakness" in AIG's financial reports, and AIG reported a $3.6 billion loss from its CDS portfolio. On February 28, AIG published a more alarming set of disclosures, including a net loss of $5.3 billion for its previous fiscal year, due to $11.1 billion of losses from its CDS portfolio and $2.6 billion of losses from its securities lending operation. However, the New York Fed did not attempt to obtain more detailed information about AIG until August 2008. Geithner later admitted that he "went into [Lehman] weekend" in September 2008 with "very little knowledge" about AIG.[174]

The Fed also did not pay close attention to Bear Stearns, even though news coverage of Bear was consistently negative after its two hedge funds with large subprime exposures filed for bankruptcy on July 31, 2007. For unknown reasons, the Fed did not include Bear Stearns in its horizontal review of risk management practices at eleven major banks and securities firms in late 2007.[175]

Many investors stopped buying Bear's commercial paper during the fall of 2007. By the end of December, Bear's commercial paper funding had fallen from $21 billion to $4 billion, while its reliance on repo funding rose from $69 billion to $102 billion. Many of Bear's repo loans were overnight loans that had to be renewed daily.[176]

The Fed and Treasury knew that Bear had become increasingly dependent on short-term repo loans and that Bear offered illiquid, private-label RMBS and CDOs as collateral for many of those loans. However, the Fed and Treasury received comforting assurances from SEC chairman Christopher Cox and his staff that Bear satisfied the SEC's capital and liquidity requirements. The Fed and the Treasury did not insist on detailed information to support the SEC's assurances, which were contrary to the views of most analysts and investors.[177] As Charles Gasparino commented, "What is striking about Cox's inaction, and for that matter Paulson's, Bernanke's, and Geithner's, is that Bear's actual unraveling was a slow-moving event, beginning in earnest [in 2007]." Gasparino stated that "Paulson, Geithner, and Cox had time to react, yet they failed to do so, beyond engaging in a few conference calls" with Bear's senior executives.[178]

Thus, the Fed and Treasury missed multiple warning signs between August 2007 and March 2008 that should have caused them (and other federal regulators) to intensify their monitoring and increase their understanding of the massive risks concentrated at major U.S. banks as well as AIG, Bear Stearns, and other systemically important financial institutions.[179] The Fed's and Treasury's failure to take more proactive measures is difficult to understand, given the liquidity problems and large losses that had already occurred at Bear Stearns, Countrywide, Citigroup, Merrill Lynch, and Morgan Stanley. The most likely explanation for the Fed's and Treasury's passivity is that they were ideologically committed to light-touch, highly deferential policies for supervising large financial institutions. The Fed's and Treasury's lack of detailed, timely, and reliable information about the financial condition and vulnerability of leading financial institutions continued to undermine the effectiveness of their decision during 2008.

———

The Fed responded to deteriorating conditions in the housing market and the financial sector by cutting its target for short-term interest rates from 4.50% to 3% at three FOMC meetings in December 2007 and January 2008. The Fed also established two programs to improve the liquidity of domestic and foreign banks. First, the Term Auction Facility (TAF) allowed banks—including foreign banks operating in the U.S.—to bid at regular auctions for loans from the Fed based on criteria similar to discount window loans. TAF's auction-based procedures allowed banks to get funding from the Fed without incurring the stigma associated with loans from the discount window. Second, the Fed established international dollar swap lines with foreign central banks. Those swap lines allowed foreign central banks to exchange their currencies for U.S. dollars and then lend those dollars to foreign banks with dollar-denominated debt obligations. European banks obtained large amounts of funding from both TAF and the currency swap lines.[180]

The FOMC's consensus prediction at the end of January 2008 was that the U.S. economy would grow slowly during 2008 and somewhat faster during 2009. However, several FOMC members (including Chairman Bernanke) noted "downside risks" from potential adverse developments in the housing and financial sectors.[181] During testimony before the Senate Banking Committee on February 14, Bernanke stated that the Fed's "baseline outlook involves a period of sluggish growth, followed by a somewhat stronger pace of growth starting later this year." Bernanke added that the Fed's "baseline outlook envisions an improving picture." He cautioned that "downside risks to growth remain," including the possibility of more serious problems in the housing and credit markets.[182]

While carefully hedged, Bernanke's testimony presented a generally benign view of the economy's prospects. Bernanke later remarked that the Fed's leaders "had been feeling a bit better about the prospects for the economy and financial system" in February 2008. The Fed's recent interest rate cuts and Congress's passage of a $150 billion fiscal stimulus package in early February provided reasons to believe that the economy would improve.[183]

During the same Senate committee hearing, Treasury Secretary Hank Paulson stated that the U.S. economy was "undergoing a significant and necessary housing correction" but was "fundamentally strong, diverse and resilient." Senator Charles Schumer (D-NY) expressed his concern that Bernanke and Paulson were "underestimating" the "severity of the problem in the credit markets." Bernanke and Paulson admitted that the U.S. economy faced significant challenges, but they did not think a recession would occur. Bernanke said he was "not worried about bank failures" because "banks entered the current downturn with sufficient capital and have been able to raise additional funds."[184]

Bernanke's and Paulson's statements were far too optimistic. The Fed and Treasury did not yet appreciate the magnitude of the problems facing the U.S. economy and the financial system in early 2008. U.S. industrial production declined steadily after the end of 2007, and the housing market continued to spiral downward, as it had done since 2006. The total number of employed workers began to fall in February 2008. The National Bureau of Economic Research ultimately determined that the Great Recession began in December 2007.[185]

In mid-February 2008, a crisis occurred in the $330 billion auction-rate securities market. Auction-rate securities were long-term bonds issued by state government agencies, hospitals, and other nonprofits, which were backed by guarantees from monoline insurers. Banks and securities firms underwrote the long-term bonds and marketed them as safe short-term investments. Underwriters told investors that they would buy any bonds that investors offered but could not sell during scheduled weekly auctions. On February 14 (the date of Bernanke's and Paulson's testimony), four-fifths of the weekly auctions failed, and two-thirds of the auctions failed the following week. Investor demand for auction-rate securities evaporated due to the failed auctions and growing doubts about the solvency of monoline insurers. Contrary to their earlier assurances, underwriters refused to buy bonds that investors could not sell during auctions. The market for auction-rate securities collapsed, and investors holding frozen bonds filed hundreds of claims against underwriters.[186]

The unresolved crisis in the auction-rate securities market triggered further declines in the value of AAA-rated tranches of CDOs and other securities guaranteed by monoline insurers. By March 2008, many investors had lost confidence in the safety of shadow bank instruments like commercial paper and repos. Securities firms and universal banks that relied on funding from shadow bank instruments became vulnerable to liquidity crises like those that had crippled Countrywide and Northern Rock.[187]

Paul McCulley, a managing director at Pimco (a leading bond fund manager), coined the term "shadow banking" during a discussion at the Kansas City Fed's Jackson Hole conference in August 2007.[188] In a blog post the following month, McCulley warned that disruptions occurring in the financial markets were early signs of "a run on what I've dubbed the 'shadow banking system.'" McCulley explained that "unlike regulated real banks, who fund themselves with insured deposits, backstopped by access to the Fed's discount window, unregulated shadow banks fund themselves with un-insured commercial paper.... Thus, the shadow banking system is particularly vulnerable to runs."[189]

The run on shadow bank liabilities caused enormous problems for the Big Five securities firms and universal banks in 2008. In a November 2008 blog post, McCulley pointed out that investors ran on shadow bank liabilities as soon as they were no longer viewed as safe:

Shadow Banks use funding instruments that are *not* just as good as old-fashioned sovereign-protected deposits. But it was a great gig so long as the public bought the notion that such funding instruments were "just as good" as bank deposits—more leverage, less regulation and more asset freedom were a path to (much) higher returns on equity in Shadow Banks than conventional banks.

As McCulley also observed, the belief that shadow bank liabilities were "just as good" as bank deposits was "aided and abetted by both the sovereign and the sovereign-blessed rating agencies."[190]

McCulley stated an essential truth. Shadow bank deposit substitutes—including commercial paper, repos, and money market mutual funds—existed in 2007 because Congress and federal regulators ignored Section 21 of the Glass-Steagall Act. Beginning in the 1970s, as explained in Chapter 7, federal regulators allowed securities firms and asset managers to issue short-term liabilities that functioned as substitutes for bank deposits. Congress and federal regulators encouraged the growth of deposit substitutes by giving them an illusion of safety—including a fixed redemption value of $1 per share for money funds, bankruptcy safe harbors for derivatives and repos, and repeated interventions by the Fed to stabilize the commercial paper and repo markets.[191]

Wall Street and Washington promoted the growth of shadow deposits because they seemed to offer the benefits of bank-like intermediation and maturity transformation (borrowing short to lend long) without the costs of prudential supervision, deposit insurance, and capital requirements. In 2008, as described in Chapter 11, shadow bank instruments turned on their creators with devastating runs that threatened a new Great Depression.

11
Bailouts Without End

Governments Provided Massive Bailouts to Rescue Universal Banks and Shadow Banks During the Financial Crisis

Beginning in March 2008, the financial crisis forced governments on both sides of the Atlantic to confront the same questions their predecessors had faced during the early 1930s. Should governments rescue systemically important financial institutions that were on the brink of failure? What expenditures would such bailouts require? What consequences would follow if governments did *not* bail out those institutions? Would bailouts—even if successful—lead to strong economic recoveries? In addition, would successful bailouts distort market incentives and intensify moral hazard among investors and creditors in the financial markets?

During the first week of March, three investment funds and a nonbank mortgage company (Thornburg Mortgage) collapsed after they could not meet margin calls (demands for increased collateral) from repo lenders and other short-term creditors. Lehman Brothers CEO Dick Fuld and Goldman Sachs CEO Lloyd Blankfein urged the Fed to create a new liquidity facility to help the Big Five securities firms withstand similar threats.[1] On March 10, Fed Chairman Ben Bernanke held a conference call with the Federal Open Market Committee (FOMC) to consider two proposals. The first would expand the currency swap lines granted by the Fed to European central banks in December 2007. The second would authorize the Fed to provide emergency loans to the Big Five securities firms through a new program called the Term Securities Lending Facility (TSLF).[2]

New York Fed Executive Vice President William Dudley told the FOMC that the failures of the three investment funds and Thornburg Mortgage increased the risk of further margin calls by repo lenders. Widespread margin calls could trigger "fire sales" of mortgage-related securities by securities broker-dealers and produce a full-blown liquidity crisis. Dudley reported that "there were rumors today that Bear Stearns was having funding difficulties," and Bear's stock price dropped by over 10%. Dudley explained that the proposed TSLF would provide liquidity assistance to all "primary dealers"—including the five largest securities firms—with whom the New York Fed traded Treasury securities. The TSLF would lend Treasury securities to primary dealers for up to twenty-eight days in exchange for qualifying collateral, including agency residential mortgage-backed securities (RMBS) issued by Fannie Mae and Freddie Mac as well as AAA-rated private-label RMBS. Thus, the TSLF would allow primary dealers to transfer illiquid, mortgage-related securities to the Fed (at a discount) in exchange for highly liquid Treasury securities, which dealers could then offer as collateral for repo loans.[3]

The Big Five securities firms were not banks. Accordingly, the Fed could not provide credit to them unless it invoked its emergency powers under Section 13(3) of the Federal Reserve Act, as amended in 1991. Section 13(3) authorized the Fed, in "unusual and exigent circumstances," to provide loans to nonbanks if the loans were "secured to the satisfaction" of the Fed.[4] By establishing the TSLF, the Fed provided liquidity assistance for the first time in its history to financial institutions that were not banks.[5]

The FOMC's members recognized the TSLF's significance and implications. Kansas City Fed President Tom Hoenig said that the TSLF "opened the safety net to a broader group" of financial institutions and was likely to encourage "moral hazard" among securities firms and other nonbank financial institutions. In Hoenig's view, the TSLF would "create a floor" under private-label RMBS, and the same "logic [could] apply more broadly should [other] markets deteriorate."[6]

Philadelphia Fed President Charles Plosser echoed Hoenig's concerns, and he asked, "Are we going down a path here in which we are going to implicitly provide support for a whole range of potential asset classes?"[7] Hoenig and Plosser did not want the Fed to act as a dealer (market maker) of last resort for broad segments of the financial markets. Richmond Fed President Jeffrey Lacker also opposed such a role for the Fed, and he therefore did not support the TSLF.[8]

Hoenig pointed out that the Fed's willingness to help securities firms showed that the capital markets had become "very integrated" with the largest banks. Fed Vice Chairman Donald Kohn agreed that "the dysfunction in the securities markets and the banking sector were intertwined, and there was just a very vicious spiral going on in many financial markets." At a recent meeting of the Basel Committee on Banking Supervision, European bank regulators told Kohn that their central banks were already providing liquidity support for investment banking activities because most of the largest financial institutions in Europe were universal banks.[9]

Dallas Fed President Richard Fisher asked whether the Fed would exercise any supervisory authority over securities firms that received assistance under the TSLF. Fisher pointed out that neither the Fed nor the SEC applied "safety-and-soundness disciplines" to securities broker-dealers.[10] New York Fed President Tim Geithner replied that the Fed would have to rely on the SEC's oversight because the existing "regulatory framework" did not authorize the Fed to "constrain the risk-taking behavior" of securities firms.[11]

On March 11, the Fed announced that the TSLF would begin lending Treasury securities to primary dealers on March 27. That announcement came too late to save Bear Stearns. On March 12, Bear Stearns' lawyer, Rodgin Cohen, informed Geithner that Bear Stearns was in deep trouble. Hedge funds were pulling their funds out of the firm, and repo lenders were refusing to roll over their loans.[12]

Bear's liquidity reserves plunged from $18 billion on Monday, March 10 to $2 billion at the close of business on Thursday, March 13. To prevent Bear's failure, the Fed invoked its Section 13(3) powers that evening and made an emergency loan of $12.9 billion to JPMorgan Chase, the clearing bank for Bear's triparty repos. JPMC transferred the Fed's loan to Bear to keep it operating on Friday, March 14.[13]

During the weekend of March 15–16, the Fed approved a rescue plan, which supported JPMC's acquisition of Bear at a deeply discounted price. The Fed organized an off-balance-sheet entity called Maiden Lane, and the Fed loaned $29 billion to that entity under Section 13(3). JPMC made a $1 billion loan to Maiden Lane and accepted a "first loss" position on that loan. Maiden Lane used the Fed's and JPMC's loans to acquire $30 billion of Bear's most toxic assets, including nonprime mortgage-related assets. The Fed was exposed to losses if Maiden Lane failed to recover at least $29 billion from Bear's toxic assets. In 2012, Maiden Lane paid off the Fed's loan, after financial markets recovered from the crisis. However, it was very doubtful at the time of Bear's rescue whether Maiden Lane would be able to repay the Fed's loan in full.[14]

Bear Stearns' sudden collapse astonished the Fed and other federal regulators.[15] Rodgin Cohen's call on March 12 came as a surprise to Geithner, since the SEC's staff had told the Fed earlier that day that "Bear had plenty of liquidity." On March 13, Geithner sent a team of New York Fed examiners and JPMC bankers to review Bear's financial condition. According to Geithner, "Bear's books were full of ugly surprises."[16]

The Financial Crisis Inquiry Commission concluded that senior SEC officials "were as stunned as everyone else by the speed of Bear's collapse."[17] Treasury Assistant Secretary Phillip Swagel stated that "regulators thought that Bear was solvent, and yet the firm faced collapse within days." Swagel recalled that one of the "lessons" of the Bear Stearns crisis was that "we had better get to work on contingency plans in case things got worse."[18]

Thus, there were good reasons for Richard Fisher's concern that neither the Fed nor the SEC understood the financial risks faced by the largest securities firms. As Kate Judge pointed out:

> The near-failure of Bear revealed that the Fed lacked access to timely information about the health of at least some systemically important financial institutions. It further revealed massive deficiencies in the oversight regime then in place and cast doubt on the SEC's capacity to understand and respond to risk-taking at the major investment banks.[19]

On March 16, the Fed approved the Bear Stearns rescue plan and established another new liquidity facility—the Primary Dealer Credit Facility (PDCF)—to "shore up confidence in the remaining investment banks."[20] The PDCF offered loans to primary dealers, including the four remaining members of the Big Five (Goldman Sachs, Lehman Brothers, Merrill Lynch, and Morgan Stanley) on terms that were much more generous than the TSLF. The PDCF allowed primary dealers to borrow money (instead of Treasury securities) from the Fed on the same terms, and with the same broader range of collateral, that applied to the Fed's loans to banks through the discount window. The PDCF established the Fed as the lender of last resort for big securities firms. The PDCF provided "a backstop funding source" for repayment of repo loans, thereby encouraging repo lenders not to run on the four remaining major securities firms. The PDCF also encouraged the two clearing banks for triparty repos—JPMC and BNY Mellon—to continue clearing repos for securities firms.[21]

In testimony before Congress and their memoirs, Bernanke, Geithner, and Paulson argued that the Fed's rescue of Bear Stearns was necessary to maintain financial stability. They believed that Bear was "too interconnected to fail," due to its extensive transactions and market linkages with the world's largest financial institutions. Bear had 750,000 derivatives contracts and other trading positions with 5,000 counterparties around the world. Bear had $100 billion of outstanding repo loans, and a third of those loans were collateralized by mortgage-related securities. A default by Bear on its repo loans would have disrupted the triparty repo market and could have forced many repo lenders (including money market mutual funds) to dump their collateral on the market at fire-sale prices. Bernanke said his "greatest fear" was that "the repo market might break down entirely, with disastrous consequences for financial markets and, as credit froze and asset prices plunged, for the entire economy." He also "worried about the broader effects on confidence if [money market mutual] funds, supposedly very safe, began to take losses."[22]

The Fed's rescue of Bear Stearns and its creation of the TSLF and PDCF were highly controversial. As Geithner explained, "The entire Bear episode was a turning point for the Fed, erasing our long-standing lines between commercial banks we considered 'inside the safety net' and the many firms operating outside that net." David Wessel commented that "*after Bear Stearns*, the line between Fed-protected, deposit-taking Main Street banks and less tightly regulated, more leveraged Wall Street investment banks was obliterated."[23] Critics accused the Fed of creating a new form of "moral hazard" by rescuing Bear's creditors and acting as lender of last resort for the other four major securities firms.[24]

In their memoirs, Bernanke and Paulson drew an instructive contrast between the Fed's rescue of Bear Stearns—the fifth-largest U.S. securities firm in 2008—and the Fed's decision to let Drexel Burnham Lambert fail in 1990, when Drexel was the fifth-largest U.S. securities firm. Bernanke stated that "Drexel was far less interconnected than Bear to major firms through derivatives and other financial relationships." Paulson agreed that large financial institutions were not "as entwined" in 1990, and Drexel's counterparties could be "more easily identified."[25]

Bernanke and Paulson did not comment, however, on the major regulatory changes that occurred after Drexel failed in 1990. Those changes encouraged Bear Stearns' rapid growth and the development of complex linkages between Bear and the largest banks. The most important changes included (1) decisions by federal regulators *not* to enforce Section 21 of the Glass-Steagall Act, which enabled nonbank financial institutions to fund their operations with deposit substitutes like repos and short-term commercial paper, and (2) decisions by federal regulators and Congress to tear down Glass-Steagall's barriers that had separated the banking system from the capital markets in 1990. By eliminating those barriers, federal regulators and Congress destroyed the anti-contagion firewalls that allowed Drexel to fail without undermining the banking system.[26]

———

The Fed's rescue of Bear Stearns and its creation of the TSLF and PDCF in the spring of 2008 postponed the onset of a full-fledged financial crisis, in the same way that the Reconstruction Finance Corporation's emergency loan to Central Republic Bank in June 1932 delayed the outbreak of a nationwide banking crisis during the Great Depression.[27] Financial markets maintained an uneasy calm for about four months after the Bear Stearns rescue. As shown in Figure 10.2 in Chapter 10, the TED spread declined after Bear's rescue, indicating a lower degree of perceived risk for interbank loans. Similarly, issuers of credit default swaps charged lower premiums for providing protection against defaults by major financial institutions. During the spring of 2008, the ten biggest U.S. banks raised $100 billion of new capital, and the four largest securities firms raised $40 billion of new capital.[28]

Those positive signs were soon overwhelmed by negative developments. Financial institutions continued to report escalating losses from residential and commercial mortgages, leveraged loans, and related securities. Losses to holders of collateralized debt obligations and other mortgage-related securities reached $400 billion by April 2008. The U.S. economy experienced deepening problems, including drops in auto sales, plummeting home prices, falling home sales, widespread foreclosures, declining payrolls, and a rise in the national unemployment rate from 4.8% to 5.5% between February and May.[29] The FOMC cut the Fed's target for short-term interest rates from 3% to 2% at its meetings in March and April.[30]

At its meeting on June 24–25, 2008, the FOMC reviewed the performance of the TSLF and PDCF as well as the Fed's new monitoring program for Goldman, Lehman, Merrill, and Morgan Stanley.[31] William Dudley stated that all four firms had reduced their leverage. However, they were still experiencing significant financial strains from asset write-downs and falling stock prices. Lehman reported a $2.8 billion second-quarter loss on June 9 and was "under the most stress." Bernanke told his colleagues that the Fed had "considerable concerns about Lehman Brothers."[32]

Art Angulo, the New York Fed's head of banking supervision, explained that the Fed had posted small teams of examiners at the four major securities firms. The Fed was not "conducting examinations," and its monitoring was "narrowly focused on capital, as well as liquidity." The Fed's examiners accepted valuation "inputs" provided by the four firms "at face value" and did not attempt to "validate" that information. Angulo warned that the Fed was exposed to "reputational risk" if it continued to make judgments about the financial condition of the four securities firms without gathering information based on its "traditional bank supervision model." Lehman and Merrill relied heavily on loans from the TSLF, while Barclays, Citigroup, Deutsche Bank, and UBS received large amounts of funding from the TSLF, the PDCF, or both.[33]

Richmond Fed President Jeffrey Lacker argued that the Fed should impose stricter limits on its loans to nonbank financial institutions. He warned that "extending our lending reach to whatever institution that makes itself systemically important just leads us down a path of ever more financial regulation of an ever larger portion of the financial system." He cautioned that the Fed's assistance to nonbanks "entangles us in politics. It risks compromising the independence of our monetary policy." Kansas City Fed President Tom Hoenig strongly endorsed Lacker's views.[34]

Chicago Fed President Gary Stern agreed that it was essential "to limit [the Fed's] involvement in supporting institutions and markets going forward." Stern suggested—with concurrence from Philadelphia Fed President Charles Plosser—that "we may have to be prepared to let one large institution fail" in order to provide "cred-ibility" for the position that there were outer "boundaries" to the Fed's role as lender of last resort.[35]

Bernanke, Geithner, Kohn, and Fed Governor Frederic Mishkin advocated a more flexible and discretionary approach. In their view, it was not feasible for the Fed to identify "bright line" limits on its lender-of-last-resort authority, and the Fed should be prepared to provide liquidity assistance to nonbank financial institutions whose failures might cause "systemic risk."[36] Kohn argued that "the financial markets evolved in such a way that simply having a liquidity backstop for commercial banks was not sufficient to protect the economy from systemic risk." Fed Governor Randall Kroszner pointed out that the policy regimes of the U.S., U.K., and EU encouraged "disintermediation" from banks by promoting "greater reliance on the markets." However, those developments created "exactly the kinds of problems and challenges that we are facing now."[37]

Boston Fed President Eric Rosengren recommended that the Fed should ask Congress for direct supervisory authority over all financial holding companies with potential systemic importance. The Fed was severely hampered by its lack of super-visory powers over large thrift holding companies, like Washington Mutual (WaMu), and the biggest securities firms. Rosengren also cited the risks posed by big foreign banks with extensive U.S. operations. By mid-2008, UBS had reported $37 billion of losses (primarily from its huge CDO portfolio), and its chairman, Marcel Ospel, resigned.[38]

San Francisco Fed President Janet Yellen agreed with Rosengren's supervisory con-cerns. She also expressed serious reservations about the Fed's existing supervisory policies for large bank holding companies. The Fed did not anticipate Countrywide's near-failure in August 2007, even though the Fed supervised Countrywide's holding company until March of that year (when Countrywide converted to a thrift holding company). Yellen explained that the "Fed-lite approach" instituted by Chairman Alan Greenspan during the 1990s was "very focused on process," and involved relatively little "transaction testing." Yellen called for more rigorous oversight of large financial holding companies, including "comprehensive umbrella supervision."[39]

The FOMC's meeting in June 2008 revealed that several FOMC members were deeply troubled by the bailout of Bear Stearns as well as the liquidity support provided to securities firms by the TSLF and PDCF. Some members shared Art Angulo's concern that the Fed was not adequately supervising the four major securities firms after providing extensive loans to them through the TSLF and PDCF. Rosengren and Yellen also had serious reservations about the poor performance of "Fed-lite" policies for supervising large bank holding companies.

On July 10, 2008, Bernanke and Paulson testified before the House Financial Services Committee. They recommended legislation that would empower federal regulators to place large financial holding companies in resolution proceedings similar to FDIC receiverships for banks. Their testimony did not produce a positive response from committee members. Bernanke and Paulson concluded that in an election year Congress was very unlikely to pass legislation that would give significant new powers to federal bank regulators.[40]

The Fed and the SEC conducted stress tests in May and June to evaluate the ability of the four major securities firms to withstand runs by repo lenders and other short-term creditors. The stress tests showed that none of the four firms could survive creditor runs similar to the one that took down Bear Stearns. Goldman and Morgan Stanley survived a less stringent scenario, known as "Bear Stearns Light," but Lehman and Merrill failed that test as well. The stress tests confirmed that Lehman was the weakest firm, while Merrill was also highly vulnerable to a systemic run by wholesale creditors. Top executives at both firms appeared to be "in denial" about the weaknesses in their capital and liquidity positions.[41]

Geithner and Paulson urged all four securities firms—especially Lehman and Merrill—to raise more capital and build stronger liquidity reserves. They told Lehman CEO Richard Fuld that Lehman would have to find a buyer if it couldn't raise enough new capital.[42] However, the Fed did not force either the big securities firms or the largest banks to increase their capital levels significantly. Instead, the Fed and other federal regulators stood by while big banks and securities firms paid out more than $100 billion to their shareholders in dividends and stock buybacks between July 2007 and August 2008.[43]

On September 9, 2008, Patrick Parkinson, a senior Fed official, told Bernanke that "Geithner and [SEC chairman] Cox planned to tell Fuld that, if he didn't raise capital [by September 18], he would have to consider bankruptcy. Their goal was to shock Fuld into action." Parkinson's statement indicates that the Fed and the SEC did not explicitly threaten Fuld with the possibility of bankruptcy until shortly before the final weekend of Lehman's existence (September 13–14).[44]

The Fed also did not increase the intensity of its monitoring of the four big securities firms, despite concerns expressed at the FOMC's meeting in late June and the alarming results of the Fed's joint stress tests with the SEC. The Fed therefore did not have crucial information about the financial vulnerabilities and risk exposures of the four firms prior to Lehman's collapse in September. The Fed also did not adequately evaluate the potential risks that Lehman's failure could pose to "critical markets" and financial stability.[45]

On August 8, Parkinson warned colleagues at the Fed and Treasury that "regulators did not know nearly enough about over-the-counter derivatives activities at Lehman and other investment banks." Parkinson recommended that the Fed should gather detailed information on derivatives exposures at the four securities firms and other major OTC derivatives dealers. He also proposed that regulators and leading derivatives dealers should develop contingency plans for handling the collapse of a large dealer or counterparty. The Fed did not implement Parkinson's proposals before Lehman failed. Fed and Treasury officials were concerned that even asking major derivatives dealers about their exposures could send "a huge negative signal" and "spook the market."[46]

The Fed also did not discover, until *after* Lehman failed, that Lehman used "Repo 105" transactions to move assets off its balance sheet, reduce its reported net leverage, and make its capital position look stronger in two quarterly reports published in June and September 2008. In each "Repo 105" transaction, Lehman sold about $50 billion of assets just before the end of the quarter and then repurchased the same assets a few days thereafter. In addition, Lehman materially overstated the amount of its liquid, unencumbered assets in the same two quarterly reports.[47]

Thus, the Fed adopted a surprisingly lenient policy toward the four remaining major securities firms after Bear Stearns failed, despite the Fed's awareness of serious challenges and information gaps at those firms. As a result, the Fed did not know the true financial condition of those firms, and the Fed was not prepared to deal with the crisis surrounding Lehman Brothers in September 2008.[48]

————

One possible reason for the Fed's and Treasury's failure to intensify their monitoring of securities firms was that both agencies were distracted by other serious financial problems during the summer of 2008. On July 11, IndyMac, a $32 billion thrift with heavy exposures to option adjustable-rate mortgages, collapsed and was placed in an FDIC receivership. IndyMac was the largest FDIC-insured depository institution to fail since Bank of New England in 1991. IndyMac's insured depositors received full protection, but the FDIC paid out only 50% of IndyMac's $1 billion of uninsured deposits. The losses suffered by IndyMac's uninsured depositors caused uninsured depositors at other weakened banks and thrifts to withdraw their funds. Depositors withdrew large amounts from WaMu and Wachovia, as both institutions had large exposures to option ARMs and reported significant second-quarter losses.[49]

The next crisis occurred at Fannie Mae and Freddie Mac, the giant government-sponsored enterprises that bought and guaranteed residential mortgages. Fannie and Freddie were the two largest and most important sources of funding for new mortgages after the private-label RMBS market shut down in mid-2007. In August 2007, Fannie Mae's CEO, Daniel Mudd, asked Fannie Mae's regulator—the Office of Federal Housing Enterprise Oversight (OFHEO)—for relief from a regulatory cap that limited the aggregate size of Fannie Mae's mortgage portfolio and guarantees. Mudd wanted Fannie Mae to buy or guarantee a larger volume of mortgages and thereby increase its profits.[50]

OFHEO was reluctant to allow Fannie and Freddie to expand, particularly when mortgage defaults were rising and housing prices were falling. However, Treasury Secretary Paulson viewed Fannie and Freddie as "the only game in town" after the collapse of the private-label RMBS market. Paulson wanted Fannie and Freddie to increase their purchases and guarantees of mortgages to support the housing market and provide more opportunities for homeowners to refinance their mortgages. In September 2007, OFHEO relaxed its regulatory caps and allowed Fannie and Freddie to expand their mortgage portfolios. During the fourth quarter of 2007, Fannie and Freddie purchased 76% of all newly originated home mortgages, up from 46% in 2006. However, Fannie and Freddie also reported combined losses of nearly $9 billion during the second half of 2007. The stated capital of both companies fell below 2% of their total assets and guarantees at the end of 2007.[51]

In early 2008, Congress and Treasury continued to encourage Fannie and Freddie to fill the void left by the demise of the private-label RMBS market, despite the severely undercapitalized condition of both GSEs. In January, Congress raised the maximum conforming limit for Fannie and Freddie mortgages from $417,000 to $730,000. In March, Fannie and Freddie raised $14 billion of new capital, at Treasury's request. At Treasury's urging, OFHEO removed the remaining regulatory caps on Fannie and Freddie and reduced their required capital surcharges in exchange for their pledges to raise more capital. Fannie sold $7.4 billion of additional preferred stock, but Freddie failed to increase its capital. Fannie and Freddie expanded their mortgage credit exposures by more than $600 billion between June 2007 and June 2008, and their combined mortgage assets and guarantee exposures rose to $5.5 trillion by mid-2008. Fannie's and Freddie's managements made fatal errors by expanding aggressively in the midst of a serious housing crisis and distressed financial markets. However, they did so with the strong encouragement and support of both Congress and Treasury.[52]

Fannie and Freddie reported combined losses of $14 billion during the first half of 2008, and their stated capital levels declined to 1% of their total credit risk exposures. The stock prices of both companies plummeted in early July, following news reports that they would soon need government bailouts. On July 13, Paulson announced a plan to strengthen Fannie and Freddie by (1) increasing their lines of credit with Treasury, (2) giving Treasury unlimited authority to invest in their stock, and (3) establishing a new regulator—the Federal Housing Finance Agency (FHFA)—with stronger oversight powers, including the authority to place Fannie and Freddie in conservatorships or receiverships. Paulson emphasized the urgency of his plan by telling Congress that Fannie and Freddie were "the only functioning secondary mortgage market" in the U.S. Congress approved Paulson's plan in late July, thereby giving him a "bazooka" that he said he did not intend to use. The Fed provided additional support for Fannie and Freddie by giving them access to discount window loans.[53]

After reviewing Fannie's and Freddie's financial condition, the Fed and the Office of the Comptroller of the Currency determined in early August that both companies were probably insolvent. Fannie and Freddie reported big quarterly losses on August 6, and their stock prices fell to eighteen-year lows. Foreign governments and other large investors in Fannie's and Freddie's debt securities and agency RMBS asked the Fed and Treasury for assurances that the GSEs would not default on their debt obligations. On August 26, Paulson obtained President Bush's approval to place Fannie and Freddie in conservatorships and provide bailouts to prevent their failures.[54]

On September 7, Treasury and FHFA announced conservatorships for Fannie and Freddie. Treasury agreed to recapitalize each GSE by purchasing up to $100 billion of its preferred stock (a limit that was later raised to $200 billion for each company). Treasury bought almost $190 billion of Fannie's and Freddie's preferred stock to cover their losses between 2008 and 2011. Treasury received warrants to purchase up to 79.9% of the common stock of both companies, and the existing holders of preferred and common stock were largely wiped out. The terms of the conservatorships stipulated that Fannie and Freddie "would no longer be allowed to lobby the government."[55]

Paulson hoped that the bailouts of Fannie and Freddie would "put a floor under the housing market decline, and provide confidence to the market." Bernanke agreed that the bailouts were "an essential, positive first step toward stabilizing the housing market." The federal government protected Fannie's and Freddie's creditors because of concerns that any default on their debts would cripple many U.S. banks (which held $1 trillion of Fannie's and Freddie's debt securities and agency RMBS) and destroy the U.S. mortgage financing system. In addition, a default on Fannie's and Freddie's debt obligations could have triggered panicked sales by investors (particularly foreign investors) who held U.S. government securities. On November 25, 2008, the Fed provided further support for Fannie and Freddie by announcing that it would buy up to $100 billion of their debt securities and $500 billion of their RMBS.[56]

Paulson believed that the federal government's rescues of Fannie and Freddie would buy time for officials to deal with other pressing problems, including Lehman Brothers. However, Paulson's decision to fire his "bazooka" seriously undermined confidence in the U.S. financial system. The emergency bailouts of Fannie and Freddie caused many investors to conclude that market values of mortgage-related assets would continue to fall and financial institutions with large exposures to those assets were in grave danger.[57]

Gretchen Morgenson, Joshua Rosner, and Peter Wallison have argued that Fannie and Freddie bear primary responsibility for the toxic mortgage boom that caused the financial crisis. In their view, Fannie and Freddie abandoned sound lending practices during the 1990s, due to their cozy relationships with Democratic political leaders as well as the affordable housing goals established for Fannie and Freddie by the Clinton administration. Morgenson, Rosner, and Wallison contend that Fannie's and Freddie's high-risk lending policies encouraged private sector lenders to follow suit and thereby corrupted the entire residential mortgage market.[58]

However, the evidence strongly indicates that Fannie and Freddie were followers— *not* leaders—of the surge into reckless nonprime lending. Fannie's and Freddie's underwriting guidelines for conforming mortgages prevented them from buying or guaranteeing substantial volumes of subprime and Alt-A mortgages prior to 2005. Only 7% of the mortgages purchased by Fannie and 5% of the mortgages bought by Freddie in 2003 had down payments smaller than 10%. As Fannie and Freddie expanded their involvement in nonprime lending, the percentages of their purchased mortgages with low down payments rose to 16% by 2007.[59]

Fannie and Freddie relaxed their underwriting guidelines in mid-2005, after their leaders became alarmed by the rapid growth of nonprime mortgages funded by Wall Street's private-label RMBS. Fannie's and Freddie's combined share of new mortgage business fell from 52% in 2002 to 44% in 2006. The volume of private-label RMBS issued by Wall Street surpassed the output of agency RMBS issued by Fannie and Freddie in both 2005 and 2006. Countrywide sold 72% of its mortgages to Fannie in 2003, when most of Countrywide's mortgages satisfied Fannie's guidelines for conforming mortgages. As Countrywide aggressively expanded into nonprime lending, Countrywide reduced the share of mortgages it sold to Fannie to 45% in 2004 and 32% in 2005. Citigroup, another top nonprime lender, told Fannie's board of directors in 2005 that Fannie would be "marginalized" unless it started buying and guaranteeing more subprime and Alt-A mortgages.[60]

Fannie and Freddie boosted their exposures to nonprime mortgages significantly in 2006. In 2007, after the private-label RMBS market shut down, Fannie and Freddie further expanded their nonprime mortgage portfolios with Treasury's strong encouragement. At the end of 2007, the two GSEs held $340 billion of subprime loans (23% of the subprime mortgage market) and $560 billion of Alt-A loans (58% of the Alt-A market). Thus, the GSEs entered the nonprime mortgage market on a large-scale basis toward the end of the housing boom, and only after they were pressured to do so by intense competition from nonprime lenders and the private-label RMBS market. Large banks and securities firms were the leading underwriters of private-label RMBS, and they were the driving forces behind the nonprime mortgage boom, as shown by the fact that nonprime lending expanded in virtual lockstep with the growth of the private-label RMBS market.[61]

In addition, Fannie and Freddie relaxed their underwriting standards to a much lesser extent compared with nonprime lenders who relied on funding from Wall Street underwriters of private-label RMBS. Nonprime mortgages purchased by Fannie and Freddie posted a record of performance that was much better than nonprime mortgages that were securitized into private-label RMBS. Mortgages purchased by Fannie and Freddie with down payments of less than 10% had an average default rate of 5.7% during 2008 and 2009. Comparable mortgages with low down payments that were securitized into private-label RMBS had an average default rate almost three times higher (15.5%). Alt-A mortgages purchased by Fannie between 2005 and 2007 defaulted at less than half the rate of Alt-A mortgages that were securitized into private-label RMBS. In addition, subprime and Alt-A mortgages purchased by the two GSEs had delinquency rates that were well below the national averages for delinquencies on such mortgages.[62]

Fannie and Freddie also purchased AAA-rated tranches of private-label nonprime RMBS. Those AAA-rated tranches offered attractive yields for purportedly safe securities, and they also helped Fannie and Freddie to meet their affordable housing goals. In 2007, Fannie and Freddie owned about $300 billion of nonprime RMBS, representing about 15% of the private-label RMBS market. Again, Fannie and Freddie were followers—*not* the leaders—when they purchased nonprime RMBS. Large banks and securities firms were the underwriters that sold those private-label RMBS to the GSEs. Fannie and Freddie subsequently sued eighteen leading underwriters of private-label RMBS for negligence and fraud and recovered almost $25 billion in settlements and judgments.[63]

In 2013, Moody's Analytics issued a study of the losses suffered by various participants in the U.S. mortgage market between 2006 and 2012. According to Moody's, Fannie and Freddie suffered mortgage-related losses of $129 billion during that period, representing 2.7% of their $4.82 trillion of mortgage exposures at the end of 2007. The Federal Housing Administration incurred mortgage-related losses of $78 billion, representing 17.3% of its 2007 mortgage exposures of $450 billion. Banks and thrifts suffered $217 billion of mortgage-related losses, representing 5.8% of their 2007 mortgage exposures of $3.73 trillion. Holders of private-label RMBS suffered $450 billion of losses, accounting for 20.3% of the $2.2 trillion of outstanding private-label RMBS in 2007. Thus, the *highest* loss rate occurred on private-label RMBS, indicating that nonprime mortgages securitized into private-label RMBS had the *worst* performance among all categories of mortgages. In contrast, Fannie and Freddie had the *lowest* rate of losses on their mortgage exposures (which included both prime and nonprime loans).[64]

The foregoing evidence strongly indicates that the underwriters of private-label RMBS—big banks and securities firms—were primarily responsible for the nonprime mortgage debacle.[65] That conclusion is reinforced by the woeful performance of CDOs, which were underwritten by most of the same financial conglomerates that were top underwriters of private-label RMBS. As described in Chapter 10, CDOs played an essential role in keeping the subprime securitization factories running, as they were the primary buyers of mezzanine (medium-grade) tranches of private-label RMBS. By February 2009, financial institutions and investors reported $218 billion of losses from their exposures to CDOs, representing a 34% loss rate on the $640 billion of CDOs that were outstanding in 2007. In 2018, losses from CDOs reached $410 billion, constituting an astonishing 65% loss rate.[66]

The crisis at Lehman Brothers erupted two days after Treasury Secretary Paulson announced the bailouts of Fannie and Freddie. Lehman was not able to arrange a sale of the company or a large infusion of new capital during July and August. On September 9, 2008, the Korean Development Bank—widely viewed as the most likely potential investor—announced that it would not invest any funds in Lehman. On

September 10, Lehman released preliminary third-quarter financial results showing $5.6 billion of asset write-downs and $3.9 billion of net losses. With no new investor in sight, the financial markets lost confidence in Lehman's ability to survive.

Lehman's stock price dropped from $14.15 per share on the morning of Tuesday, September 9 to $3.65 per share on the afternoon of Friday, September 12. Money market mutual funds canceled over $20 billion of repo loans to Lehman. JPMC threatened to stop clearing Lehman's triparty repos and forced Lehman to post $8.6 billion of additional collateral. JPMC's collateral demands and withdrawals of funds by creditors caused Lehman's liquidity reserves to drop below $2 billion at the close of business on Friday, September 12. JPMC told Lehman that it would not clear Lehman's repos on Monday, September 15 unless Lehman obtained significant new funding from investors or lenders. Accordingly, Lehman could not reopen for business on September 15 without a rescue.[67]

During the days leading up to "Lehman weekend," Treasury and Fed officials were under intense pressure to reject any bailout for Lehman. Presidential candidates John McCain and Barack Obama issued statements criticizing bailouts. More than a dozen members of Congress—including Senator Christopher Dodd (D-CT)—told Paulson not to bail out Lehman. During a conference call with Bernanke and Geithner on September 10, Paulson said, "I'm being called Mr. Bailout," and "I can't do it again."[68]

On Thursday, September 11, officials from the Fed, Treasury, and SEC held a conference call to prepare for weekend meetings that would determine Lehman's fate. Paulson told the group "there would be no public assistance for a Lehman bailout" and the private sector would have to finance any rescue. The media described Paulson's no-bailout position in reports published the following morning.[69]

On Friday evening, September 12, Paulson and Geithner met with executives of major banks at the New York Fed. Paulson told the bankers, "We did the [rescue of Bear Stearns]. You're doing this one." Geithner confirmed Paulson's position, stating: "There is no political will for a federal bailout."[70] During the weekend, groups of bankers considered whether (1) it would be feasible to spin off Lehman's most toxic assets and finance them with loans from a consortium of banks, assuming a buyer could be found for the rest of Lehman's assets, and (2) whether it would be possible to finance an orderly wind-down if an acquisition of Lehman could not be arranged.[71]

Paulson tried to persuade either Bank of America or Barclays to acquire Lehman. BofA was not interested in buying Lehman. Instead, BofA entered into whirlwind negotiations with Merrill Lynch (the next most vulnerable securities firm), and BofA agreed to acquire Merrill before the weekend ended.

Barclays had a strong interest in acquiring Lehman but did not want $52 billion of Lehman's undesirable assets. Those assets had an estimated value of $27–$30 billion. During the evening of September 13, the assembled bankers agreed in principle to provide $37 billion of loans to support the transfer of Lehman's undesirable assets to a separate asset management company. Paulson and Geithner thought they had a feasible plan to save Lehman.[72]

On Sunday, September 14, Barclays' regulator, the U.K. Financial Services Authority, blocked the transaction. The Fed and Treasury insisted that Barclays must guarantee Lehman's liabilities until Barclays completed the acquisition, in the same way that JPMC guaranteed Bear's liabilities. However, U.K. law required Barclays to obtain approval from its shareholders before providing such a large guarantee, and the FSA refused to waive that requirement. In addition, U.K. authorities had deep misgivings about the transaction. Alistair Darling, the U.K.'s Chancellor of the Exchequer, told Paulson that "he didn't want to import our cancer."[73]

The assembled bankers informed Paulson and Geithner that they did not have sufficient resources to finance an orderly wind-down of Lehman. After the Barclays deal vanished, Paulson, Bernanke, and Geithner decided to send Lehman into bankruptcy while trying to mitigate the consequences. On September 14, Paulson's chief of staff, Jim Wilkinson, sent the following message to a senior JPMC executive: "No way [government] money is coming in.… [J]ust did a call with the [White House] and [U.S. Government] is united behind no money. No way in hell Paulson could blink now."[74] Wilkinson's message indicated the intense pressure on Paulson to refuse any federal bailout for Lehman.

The Fed held an emergency meeting at noon on Sunday and approved measures designed to reduce the impact of Lehman's failure. The Fed expanded the scope of the PDCF by authorizing it to extend credit to primary dealers based on all collateral accepted by the clearing banks for triparty repos (JPMC and BNY Mellon), including speculative-grade securities, corporate stocks, commercial and residential mortgages, and corporate loans. By expanding the PDCF, the Fed effectively became the dealer of last resort for all triparty repos. The Fed also enlarged the scope of the TSLF by authorizing the TSLF to exchange Treasury securities for all types of investment-grade securities (debt securities rated BBB or above), instead of only AAA-rated bonds. The Fed and Treasury hoped that expanding the scope of the PDCF and TSLF would reduce the risk of creditor runs against the two remaining major securities firms—Goldman Sachs and Morgan Stanley—as well as the broker-dealer affiliates of large universal banks.[75]

Lehman asked for broader access to Fed credit based on the PDCF's liberalized collateral terms. The Fed and Treasury allowed the expanded PDCF to provide credit to Lehman's U.S. broker-dealer subsidiary so that it could continue to operate. However, the Fed and Treasury did not permit Lehman's U.S. broker-dealer subsidiary to pledge collateral that was not in its possession at the close of business on Friday, September 12. That restriction prevented Lehman's U.S. broker-dealer subsidiary from using PDCF credit to fund the operations of its parent company and other affiliates, since it could not pledge their collateral. The Fed also refused to provide any credit to Lehman's U.K. broker-dealer subsidiary, thereby ensuring its failure on Monday, September 15.[76]

The Treasury and New York Fed applied heavy pressure to convince Lehman's board of directors to file for bankruptcy before markets opened on Monday. Treasury and Fed officials warned Lehman that the directors of its U.K. broker-dealer subsidiary would face personal liability if that subsidiary opened for business on Monday with knowledge of its near-term insolvency. Lehman's directors reluctantly authorized the company to file for bankruptcy—the largest in U.S. history—late on Sunday evening. When Lehman filed for bankruptcy, it had over $600 billion of assets, more than 200 subsidiaries in 21 countries, $200 billion of outstanding repos, and 900,000 derivatives contracts. Lehman's overseas operations soon became embroiled in 80 insolvency proceedings in 18 countries.[77]

Why did the Fed and Treasury allow Lehman to fail? As shown earlier, the Fed and Treasury were under intense political pressure not to bail out Lehman. The Fed and Treasury also seriously underestimated the consequences of allowing Lehman to fail. On September 23, 2008, Bernanke provided his first congressional testimony concerning Lehman's failure and the Fed's subsequent decision to rescue AIG. Bernanke provided the following explanation to Congress about the decision to let Lehman fail:

> The failure of Lehman posed risks. But the troubles at Lehman had been well known for some time, and investors clearly recognized—as evidenced, for example, by the high cost of insuring Lehman's debt in the market for credit default swaps—that the failure of the firm was a significant possibility. Thus, we judged that investors and counterparties had had time to take precautionary measures.

Bernanke also pointed out that the Fed "took a number of actions to increase liquidity and stabilize markets" after Lehman failed.[78]

Bernanke's testimony on September 23 reflected the Fed's and Treasury's shared belief during Lehman weekend that (1) market participants were generally prepared for the possibility of Lehman's failure, and (2) the expanded PDCF and TSLF would prevent Lehman's collapse from triggering a systemic financial crisis. During a breakfast meeting on Friday, September 12, Bernanke told Paulson, "We can only hope that if Lehman goes, the market will have had a lot of time to prepare for it." Bernanke and Paulson "comforted themselves that, since the Bear Stearns rescue, the Fed had found new ways to lend to other investment houses that might be hurt by a systemic collapse."[79] Treasury Assistant Secretary Phillip Swagel later acknowledged that "the Fed and Treasury did not expect" that "Lehman's failure would spark a panic and play a role in transforming an economic slowdown into the Great Recession."[80]

The same views were reflected in an article in the *New York Times* on September 13, entitled "Tough Love for Lehman." The *Times* reported that "Fed officials as well as Wall Street institutions had months of advance warning about Lehman's problems and far more time than they had with Bear Stearns to assess the potential domino effects, or 'systemic risk' that a collapse might pose." The article also cited "the availability of the Fed's emergency lending authorities for investment banks," which Bear Stearns did not have. Accordingly, "Fed and Treasury officials were convinced that Lehman posed far fewer real risks than Bear Stearns had back in March."[81]

On the morning of September 15, before U.S. financial markets opened, Paulson briefed President Bush on Lehman's collapse. Paulson said "he was cautiously optimistic that investors would be able to accept the news" of Lehman's failure, while noting "there could be further pressure on the financial system." Paulson added that BofA's decision to acquire Merrill Lynch was a sign " 'of strength' in the market that might 'mitigate' the possibility of panic."[82] At a press conference later that day, Paulson said, "I never once considered that it was appropriate to put taxpayer money on the line in resolving Lehman Brothers." In an article covering that press conference, the *New York Times* reported, "Mr. Paulson concluded that the financial system could survive the collapse of Lehman, which has shown signs of weakness for months."[83]

In sharp contrast to the Fed's and Treasury's cautious optimism, several financial experts correctly predicted that Lehman's failure would have disastrous consequences. The *Times* article on September 13 quoted financial analyst Brad Hintz, who said that a Lehman failure "would release an avalanche of unquantifiable systemic risk into the global bond markets." On the morning of September 14, European Central Bank President Jean-Claude Trichet warned Bernanke that Lehman's failure would cause a "total meltdown" of global financial markets.[84]

During the afternoon of September 14, Harvey Miller—Lehman's outside counsel and the dean of New York City's bankruptcy bar—told New York Fed General Counsel Tom Baxter that a bankruptcy filing by Lehman would unleash "Armageddon." Miller warned that forcing Lehman into bankruptcy would destroy "one of the biggest issuers of commercial paper" and "take liquidity out of the market," thereby causing a "collapse" of the financial markets. Baxter responded to Miller's dire warnings by saying that the situation was "under control." Alan Beller, outside counsel to the SEC, added that the Fed and SEC would announce new measures "that we are fairly confident will calm the markets tomorrow."[85]

As former Fed Vice Chairman Alan Blinder observed, "There is close to universal agreement that the demise of Lehman Brothers was the watershed event of the entire financial crisis." He viewed Lehman's failure as a "colossal error" because,

> coming just six months after Bear's rescue, the Lehman decision threw the presumed rulebook out the window. If Bear was too big to fail, how could Lehman, at twice its size, not be? If Bear was too entangled to fail, why was Lehman not? After Lehman went over the cliff, no financial institution felt safe. So lending froze, and the economy sank like a stone.[86]

French Finance Minister Christine Lagarde similarly called the decision to let Lehman fail a "genuine error" because it undermined "the equilibrium of the world financial system."[87] Barry Eichengreen compared Lehman's failure to the decision by federal officials to let Union Guardian Bank of Detroit collapse in February 1933, an event that triggered "the mother of all banking crises." As Eichengreen explained, "Not knowing who might be next, all willingness to lend evaporated [after Lehman failed]. The commercial paper market and the interbank overnight market shut down tight."[88]

Following the announcement of Lehman's bankruptcy on the morning of September 15, the Dow Jones Industrial Average fell by 504 points (4.4%), its largest loss since the first trading day after the terrorist attacks on September 11, 2001. The S&P index for financial stocks dropped by more than 10%, its worst daily loss on record. The stock price of AIG plunged from $12.14 to $4.76, and the stock prices of Citigroup, Goldman Sachs, Morgan Stanley, and WaMu also declined sharply. There was a general flight to safety as investors bought Treasury bonds and dumped higher-risk securities.[89]

A former Goldman colleague called Paulson shortly before noon on September 15 and said, "Hank, you made a big mistake.... This market is too fragile to handle a Lehman Brothers bankruptcy. The system is on the verge of collapse."[90] That evening, Paulson met with General Electric (GE) chairman Jeffrey Immelt. Immelt had informed Paulson a week earlier that GE was having trouble selling commercial paper to finance its day-to-day operations. On September 15, Immelt told Paulson that GE could not sell commercial paper for any term longer than overnight. Paulson replied, "Jeff, we have to put out this fire."[91]

———

AIG—the next focus of the financial crisis—had experienced deepening financial problems during the previous year. The company reported large losses in late 2007 and the first half of 2008, including write-downs and collateral calls on $80 billion of credit default swaps that AIG Financial Products wrote on super-senior tranches of CDOs. In addition, AIG borrowed $75 billion in securities lending transactions and invested those funds in private-label RMBS, CDOs, and other risky securities. As those securities declined in value, AIG's lenders demanded that AIG repay its borrowings or provide additional collateral. By September 12, 2008, AIG had posted over $22 billion of collateral with its derivatives and securities lending counterparties, and it continued to receive demands for more collateral.[92]

In mid-August, a team of New York Fed examiners reviewed AIG's financial condition and advised Geithner that AIG faced "increasing capital and liquidity pressure." On September 9 and 12, AIG executives informed New York Fed officials that AIG urgently needed financial help. At the New York Fed's request, teams of bankers and private equity managers reviewed AIG's books during Lehman weekend to determine whether a private sector rescue was feasible.[93]

On September 12, Hayley Boesky, head of market analysis at the New York Fed, reported, "Now [the market's] focus is on AIG. I am hearing worse than [Lehman]. Every bank and dealer has exposure to them." A few hours later, another New York Fed official, Alejandro LaTorre, warned Geithner and other Fed officials that AIG's "risk exposures are concentrated among the 12 largest international banks (both U.S. and European) across a wide array of product types (bank lines, derivatives, securities lending, etc.) meaning [there] could be significant counterparty losses to those firms in the event of AIG's failure." LaTorre subsequently reported that AIG had

$2.7 trillion of over-the-counter derivatives, and the twelve big international banks were counterparties on $1 trillion of those contracts.[94]

On Sunday evening, September 14, AIG CEO Robert Willumstad told Paulson and Geithner that AIG needed $60 billion of assistance, thereby tripling his request for $20 billion of help the previous day. On September 15, JPMC and Goldman advised Geithner that AIG would need over $80 billion of new funding to survive, an amount that was far too large for private sector lenders to provide. Later that day, the credit rating agencies reduced AIG's rating below AA status, triggering $13 billion of new collateral calls by its derivatives counterparties.[95]

On Tuesday morning, September 16, "all hell broke loose," according to Paulson. Goldman CEO Lloyd Blankfein informed Paulson that the bankruptcy administrator for Lehman's U.K. broker-dealer subsidiary had frozen all of its U.K. assets, including accounts and collateral belonging to hedge funds and other customers. As a result, hedge funds in the U.S. and U.K. were rapidly pulling their funds out of Goldman and Morgan Stanley. Paulson later said that the U.K. administrator's actions were "completely unexpected" by U.S. regulators, a statement confirmed by Phillip Swagel.[96]

During the afternoon of September 16, the Reserve Primary Fund—the oldest U.S. money market mutual fund—announced it was "breaking the buck." The Reserve Primary Fund held $785 million of Lehman's commercial paper, and Lehman's default reduced the fund's net asset value to 97 cents per share. Accordingly, the fund could not continue to redeem its shares at a fixed price of $1 per share. Investors pulled $40 billion out of the Reserve Primary Fund and began running on other MMMFs. Total withdrawals from MMMFs reached $350 billion within a week. Paulson admitted that MMMFs turned out to be "too good to be true" because they promised deposit-like safety without deposit insurance or capital buffers. Consequently, MMMFs functioned as deposit substitutes only as long as "people didn't ask for their money ... [W]hen Lehman failed, people started to ask."[97]

At 1 p.m. on September 16, a Chicago banker advised Paulson that "[t]he commercial paper market is frozen." Neither the Fed nor the Treasury anticipated the run on MMMFs—the largest investors in commercial paper—or the resulting crisis in the commercial paper market. Yet MMMFs and commercial paper had been major sources of Countrywide's liquidity problems in August 2007, as described in Chapter 10. On September 14, as noted earlier, Harvey Miller specifically warned the Fed and SEC about a likely collapse of the commercial paper market if they allowed Lehman to fail. As analyst Joshua Rosner later commented, "Lehman was one of the single largest issuers of commercial paper in the world.... How could you let [Lehman] go bankrupt and not expect the commercial paper market to be completely crushed?"[98]

Given the rapidly deteriorating situation on September 16, Bernanke, Geithner, and Paulson agreed that the Fed must rescue AIG because the nation "couldn't risk another collapse of a systemic institution at a moment of such intense turbulence." The Fed loaned $85 billion to AIG and received warrants to purchase 79.9% of AIG's stock. The Fed appointed Edward Liddy (the former CEO of Allstate Insurance) to replace Robert Willumstad as AIG's CEO. Geithner later remarked that the Fed "had torn down yet another wall between the commercial banking sector and the rest of the financial system." For the first time in its history, the Fed provided financial support to an insurance company. Geithner told reporters that the AIG bailout was necessary because "central banks exist to take out the extreme tail, the catastrophic risk." When Paulson told President George W. Bush that the Fed needed to save AIG, Bush asked the following question—which analysts have struggled to answer since 2008— "How did we get to this point?"[99]

On September 17 (the day after AIG's rescue), the *New York Times* reported, "Asked why Lehman was allowed to fail but A.I.G. was not, a Fed staffer said the markets were more prepared for the failure of an investment bank."[100] That statement matched the government's rationale reported by the *Times* in its "Tough Love for Lehman" article on September 13 and repeated by Bernanke in his congressional testimony on September 23.

The government's explanation suddenly changed a few weeks later. In October, Bernanke and Paulson argued that the Fed did not have legal authority to provide a loan to Lehman under Section 13(3) of the Federal Reserve Act because Lehman was deeply insolvent and could not provide satisfactory collateral. In contrast, they claimed, AIG provided enough security (through its pledge of the stock of its insurance subsidiaries) for the Fed's loan. Bernanke, Geithner, and Paulson have consistently repeated the "no legal authority" argument for letting Lehman fail since that time.[101]

There are several factual problems with the Fed's revised rationale for its disparate treatment of Lehman and AIG. First, according to participants in meetings during Lehman weekend, Paulson and Geithner ruled out a Fed loan to Lehman on policy grounds and never told them that the Fed lacked legal authority to provide a loan.[102] Second, despite repeated requests from the Financial Crisis Inquiry Commission, the Fed never provided any written analysis to support its claim that the Fed lacked legal authority to provide a loan to Lehman under Section 13(3) due to the inadequacy of Lehman's collateral.[103] Third, a recent evaluation of Lehman's assets and liabilities by Laurence Ball and earlier unpublished assessments by New York Fed staff members determined that Lehman was close to insolvency but probably could have provided enough collateral to support a Fed loan in September 2008.[104]

Fourth, the Fed's claim that AIG provided adequate security is very doubtful. As described earlier, AIG's stated needs for financial assistance ballooned from $20 billion on September 12 to $85 billion on September 15, as Wall Street bankers and Fed officials constantly discovered more problems at AIG.[105] AIG's losses continued to escalate after the Fed approved its initial loan. The Fed was forced to give AIG a second loan of $37.8 billion in early October, and Treasury injected $70 billion of capital into AIG in two installments (in November 2008 and March 2009) to ensure its survival. Thus, the federal government more than doubled its original commitment to AIG within six months. Phillip Swagel described AIG as "a black hole for taxpayer money."[106]

Paulson later conceded that "AIG's capital structure was unsustainable" in early November 2008. Treasury made a $40 billion infusion of capital into AIG at that time "to avoid a [credit] rating downgrade that would trigger $42 billion in collateral calls and finish the company off." When Treasury officials informed President Bush of their intention to provide $40 billion of capital to AIG, Bush asked, "Will we ever get the money back?" A senior Treasury official replied, "I don't know, sir."[107] Treasury's emergency capital infusion in early November strongly indicated that AIG was *not* a solvent company with adequate collateral when it was rescued in mid-September.

During subsequent litigation, Geithner admitted that he had serious doubts about AIG's solvency in September 2008. He testified, "I thought we were taking enormous, unprecedented risks and that there was substantial risk that we would lose billions of dollars, if not tens of billions of dollars." The Fed never published a detailed analysis of AIG's collateral to justify its decision to make the $85 billion loan in September 2008.[108] AIG reported total losses of $99 billion in 2008, which exceeded its stated equity of $96 billion at the end of 2007.[109]

Two policy considerations appear to explain the sharp disparity in treatment between Lehman and AIG. First, as discussed earlier, the Fed and Treasury knew during Lehman weekend that big U.S. and European banks were far more exposed to AIG than they were to Lehman. At the end of 2007, AIG had borrowed over $80 billion under securities lending agreements, and AIG had written a comparable volume of credit default swaps on super-senior tranches of CDOs. AIG owed the lion's share of both types of obligations to major U.S. and European financial institutions. In addition, AIG enabled European banks to obtain "regulatory capital relief" under the Basel II accord by providing those banks with $380 billion of CDS protection for their loans. European banks would have been required to increase their capital by $20 billion during extremely difficult market conditions if AIG defaulted on those CDS.[110]

Between November 10 and December 15, 2008, the New York Fed instructed AIG to pay over $100 billion to a group of the largest U.S. and European financial institutions to satisfy AIG's obligations under securities lending deals and CDS contracts. AIG paid the full amount of those claims and did not require its counterparties to accept any losses. The largest recipients of AIG's payments included thirteen of the Big Seventeen financial conglomerates. Goldman Sachs, which received $18.8 billion, was at the top of that list. Critics denounced AIG's payments as "backdoor bailouts" for big U.S. and European banks. The manner in which AIG's financial assistance was quickly converted into payments by AIG to U.S. and European megabanks strongly indicated that the Fed and Treasury rescued AIG to prevent major global banks from suffering punishing losses.[111]

Second, it is at least plausible that the Fed and Treasury allowed Lehman to fail to convince Congress of the urgent need for bailout legislation. At Paulson's direction, Treasury staff prepared a "break the glass" plan for a bailout bill in April 2008. The proposed legislation would authorize Treasury to spend hundreds of billions of dollars either to buy toxic assets from large banks or to recapitalize those banks. Paulson and Bernanke agreed that they had no chance of persuading Congress to approve such legislation without a full-blown financial crisis. Their certainty on that point was reinforced by Congress's very unfriendly response to their proposal in July 2008 for legislation granting federal regulators broader resolution powers.[112]

On September 15, Congressman Barney Frank (D-MA), Chairman of the House Financial Services Committee, told Tim Geithner that Lehman's bankruptcy might "shock the political world into taking the crisis seriously" and "shut up the crazies." Geithner agreed that "there was something liberating" about Lehman's failure because it was "an unwelcome vindication of the case for action. As much as the public hated bailouts, we were pretty sure people would hate the consequences of uncontrolled default even more."[113] On September 17, Paulson told his staff to prepare proposed legislation based on the "break the glass" plan.[114]

On September 18 and 19, Paulson and Bernanke met with President Bush and congressional leaders to discuss their proposal to create a $700 billion Troubled Asset Relief Program (TARP). In his memoir, Paulson said, "For the first time I believed Congress would likely give us what we needed. The extreme severity of the market conditions made it clear that no good alternative existed.... I'd long since learned that you couldn't get anything done in Washington without a crisis." Bernanke similarly recalled, "It seems clear that Congress would never have acted absent the failure of *some* large firm and the associated damage to the system."[115]

Joe Nocera concluded that "Lehman Brothers had to die for the rest of Wall Street to live.... Without the crisis prompted by the Lehman default, it would have been impossible to pass [TARP]."[116] Even after Lehman failed, the House of Representatives voted down the TARP bill on September 29. That rejection triggered the worst drop in stock prices since the stock market crash in October 1987. Chastened by investor panic, the House finally joined the Senate in passing the TARP bill on October 3.[117] In retrospect, the decisions by the Fed and Treasury to rescue AIG and let Lehman fail appear to have served their broader policy goals of (1) supporting the largest U.S. and European banks and (2) persuading Congress to authorize public funding for a comprehensive rescue of the financial system.

After rescuing AIG, Treasury and the Fed bailed out the shadow banking system. To stop the run by investors on MMMFs, Treasury announced on September 19 that it would guarantee all $3.5 trillion held by MMMFs on that date. To fund that guarantee, Treasury relied on its $50 billion Exchange Stabilization Fund (ESF). Treasury's reliance on the ESF (which allowed Treasury to stabilize the dollar's value by purchasing or selling foreign exchange) was "quite a stretch," but the post-Lehman panic called for desperate measures.[118] Treasury collected $1 billion of fees from MMMFs before the guarantee program ended in 2010, representing an average assessment rate of only about 0.03% on MMMFs.[119]

On September 19, the Fed announced that it would provide nonrecourse discount window loans to banks to finance their purchase of asset-backed commercial paper from MMMFs. The nonrecourse terms meant that the Fed would recover its loans solely from the assets that served as collateral for the commercial paper. Accordingly, the Fed would suffer losses if those assets did not have sufficient value to repay the loans. The loan program, which peaked at $150 billion in early October, provided significant relief to MMMFs by enabling them to sell their holdings of asset-backed commercial paper to banks.[120]

On October 7, the Fed announced the Commercial Paper Funding Facility (CPFF), which established a Fed-controlled special-purpose entity to buy three-month commercial paper directly from corporate issuers (primarily large U.S. and European banks and GE Capital). The CPFF "effectively served as a buyer of last resort" for new issues of commercial paper. The Fed's purchases of commercial paper under the CPFF peaked at $350 billion in January 2009, accounting for one-fifth of the commercial paper market at that time.[121]

As described above, the Fed had already given the repo market a full backstop during Lehman weekend by expanding the TSLF and PDCF. By the end of October, the Fed and Treasury provided equally comprehensive support for MMMFs and the commercial paper market. The Treasury's and Fed's programs effectively gave 100% protection to the shadow deposits that funded the shadow banking system.[122] In early 2009, the Fed provided additional support to the shadow banking system by offering loans on highly attractive terms to investors who purchased asset-backed securities.[123]

The Fed's and Treasury's efforts to shore up the shadow banking system did not stabilize the two remaining major securities firms, Goldman Sachs and Morgan Stanley. After Lehman failed, Morgan Stanley experienced the same kind of devastating run by short-term creditors that had taken down Bear and Lehman. By September 18, Morgan Stanley was only a few days away from insolvency. Goldman knew it would face the same situation if Morgan Stanley collapsed. Goldman CEO Blankfein told Paulson, "If they go, we're next."[124]

On Saturday, September 20, Michael Silva of the New York Fed sent an email message to a senior colleague. According to Silva, Morgan Stanley told Tim Geithner "they can not open Monday." Morgan Stanley provided the same information to Goldman Sachs, and Silva reported, "GS is now panicked b/c feel that if MS does not open, then GS is toast."[125] On Sunday, September 21, the Fed approved immediate conversions by Morgan Stanley and Goldman Sachs into bank holding companies. Those emergency conversions strengthened both companies by providing "the Fed's public promise of protection and a permanent source of lending in a crisis." Morgan Stanley CEO John Mack later said that the Fed's approval of immediate bank holding company status sent "a signal that these two firms are going to survive."[126] Thus, the Fed rescued the two largest remaining shadow banks by bringing them inside the banking system, thereby obliterating any remaining distinction between shadow bank financial conglomerates and universal banks.

As the post-Lehman panic continued to intensify, federal regulators struggled to save the banking system. The next domino to fall was WaMu, a $300 billion thrift, which held almost $60 billion of option ARMs on its balance sheet and reported large losses after mid-2007. WaMu suffered a steady erosion of deposits following IndyMac's failure in July 2008. Lehman's collapse on September 15 triggered a devastating run by depositors and creditors on WaMu. The FDIC and the Office of Thrift Supervision closed WaMu ten days later and sold its remaining deposits and assets to JPMC for less than $2 billion. WaMu's holding company filed for bankruptcy, and the FDIC did not protect the holding company's bondholders. FDIC Chairman Sheila Bair determined that the holding company's bondholders and other uninsured creditors did not qualify for protection under the "systemic risk exception" in the FDIC's governing statute. Geithner strongly disagreed with Bair, arguing that "imposing haircuts on bank creditors during a systemic panic is a sure way to accelerate the panic." Geithner urged Bernanke and Paulson to convince Bair to change her mind, but they declined.[127]

After WaMu failed, the panic spread to Wachovia, the fourth-largest U.S. bank, with more than $700 billion of assets. Like WaMu, Wachovia had large holdings of option ARMs and reported growing losses after the summer of 2007. Wachovia also had substantial exposures to risky commercial real estate loans, CDOs, and other toxic securities. Depositors, commercial paper investors, and repo lenders pulled away from Wachovia during 2008, and the run on Wachovia accelerated after WaMu failed. Bernanke, Geithner, and Paulson put intense pressure on Bair to invoke the "systemic risk exception," thereby allowing the FDIC to protect all of Wachovia's creditors. Bair did so with great reluctance. At first, the FDIC planned to sell Wachovia to Citigroup in a transaction that would have required substantial financial assistance from the FDIC. While Citigroup's bid was pending, the Internal Revenue Service issued a ruling that provided much larger tax benefits to banks that acquired failing depository institutions. Those enhanced tax benefits caused Wells Fargo to submit a bid that was more favorable to the FDIC, thereby knocking out Citigroup's bid. Wells Fargo agreed to acquire all of Wachovia's assets and liabilities without any financial assistance from the FDIC.[128]

—————

Wells Fargo's takeover of Wachovia was the last rescue before Congress passed the TARP legislation on October 3, 2008. After TARP, federal regulators adopted a policy of "bailouts without end" to prop up the U.S. financial system.[129] As Geithner explained, the Fed and Treasury "elevated no-haircuts-in-a-panic to the level of doctrine" after Wachovia.[130] Treasury Secretary Paulson and finance ministers from the other Group of Seven nations endorsed that doctrine on October 10. Paulson and his G7 colleagues issued a statement (drafted with Bernanke's help), declaring that their nations would "take decisive action and use all available tools to support systemically important financial institutions and prevent their failure." On October 8, the FOMC reduced the Fed's target for short-term interest rates by 0.50% (to 1.50%) in coordination with similar rate cuts by five other central banks.[131]

Bernanke, Geithner, and Paulson decided in early October that TARP capital infusions would not be large enough to stabilize the banking system, and they agreed to use financial guarantees to accomplish that goal. The Fed and Treasury did not have authority to guarantee bank debts. Accordingly, they asked the FDIC to invoke the "systemic risk exception" in its governing statute as justification for a blanket guarantee protecting all bank liabilities. There were substantial legal doubts about the FDIC's authority to provide a blanket guarantee to the entire banking system, instead of acting on an individualized, bank-by-bank basis. Nevertheless, Paulson, Bernanke, and Geithner urged FDIC chairman Sheila Bair to guarantee all $13 billion of the banking system's liabilities. Bair rejected a blanket guarantee, pointing out that the FDIC's deposit insurance fund had declined to only $35 billion as a result of numerous bank failures.[132]

After extensive negotiations, Bair agreed that the FDIC would guarantee new debts (but not existing liabilities) issued by banks. Bair insisted on establishing a second guarantee program that would protect all transaction (checking) accounts held by banks. That program helped smaller banks to retain large, uninsured business checking accounts, which otherwise would have been likely to migrate to TBTF megabanks. Bair also demanded that banks must pay substantial fees for the FDIC's debt guarantees, instead of the "minimal fees" proposed by Geithner. Financial organizations issued $346 billion of guaranteed debts under the FDIC's program and paid $11 billion in fees. Thus, the FDIC collected a 3% premium for its debt guarantees, compared with the minuscule 0.03% premium charged by Treasury for its MMMF guarantees.[133]

On October 13, 2008, Paulson, Bernanke, Geithner, and Bair met with leaders of the eight largest U.S. banks—BNY Mellon, BofA, Citigroup, Goldman Sachs, JPMC, Morgan Stanley, State Street, and Wells Fargo. The head of Merrill Lynch was also present, due to BofA's pending acquisition of Merrill. Paulson persuaded the eight bank leaders to accept $125 billion of TARP capital investments in the form of preferred stock. Treasury designed the preferred stock investments as "a deal so attractive that banks would be unwise to refuse it." The preferred stock's dividend rate was 5% for five years and 9% thereafter. Treasury received ten-year warrants to buy common stock in each bank equal to 15% of the face amount of its preferred stock. The recipient banks were allowed to pay common stock dividends at their existing rate, and there were no restrictions on lobbying—unlike the lobbying ban imposed on Fannie and Freddie as a condition of their bailouts. Treasury included modest limits on compensation for top executives, and "golden parachutes" were prohibited, while severance payments were limited to three times base salary.[134]

Except for Richard Kovacevich (Wells Fargo's CEO), the big-bank leaders "needed little persuasion" to accept the capital infusions. Citigroup CEO Vikram Pandit described TARP preferred stock as "very cheap capital," and JPMC chairman Jamie Dimon agreed it was "cheap capital."[135] The federal government's terms were much more generous than the conditions Warren Buffett imposed when he agreed to buy $5 billion of Goldman Sachs' preferred stock on September 22. Buffett's preferred stock paid a dividend of 10%, and he received warrants to buy Goldman common stock equal to 100% of the face amount of his preferred stock at a very favorable price.[136] Empirical studies determined that Treasury's TARP capital investments and the FDIC's debt guarantees resulted in very large transfers of wealth from the federal government to shareholders and creditors of the largest U.S. banks.[137]

Why did the federal government offer megabanks such generous terms at a time when every major financial institution—with the possible exception of JPMC—urgently needed more capital? In November 2009, Bernanke advised the Financial Crisis Inquiry Commission that *all* of the thirteen largest U.S. financial institutions *except one* (presumably JPMC) would have failed without federal assistance during the post-Lehman panic. Geithner told the FCIC a month later that "none of [the biggest banks] would have survived a situation in which we had let that fire try to burn itself out."[138] Fed and Treasury officials said they offered generous terms to persuade the strongest megabanks to accept TARP capital so that their weaker peers would not be stigmatized when they received capital infusions.[139] That rationale is not entirely convincing, given the fragile condition of most megabanks and the frozen market conditions they faced in October 2008. A more plausible explanation is that the Fed and Treasury did not want to impose stringent terms that would have further weakened troubled financial giants.

———

TARP capital infusions and FDIC debt guarantees did not solve the severe problems afflicting many large U.S. banks. By November 21, Citigroup was on the brink of failure, only six weeks after receiving its first $25 billion bailout. To prevent Citigroup's collapse, Treasury bought $20 billion of additional TARP preferred stock from Citigroup on November 23, 2008. The Fed, FDIC, and Treasury also issued a joint guarantee to protect Citigroup against catastrophic losses on a $306 billion pool of troubled assets. As originally proposed, the guaranteed asset pool would have included $85 billion of second-lien mortgages, $74 billion of subprime and Alt-A mortgages, $12 billion of CDOs, $9 billion of SIV assets, $9.5 billion of auction-rate securities, and $16 billion of leveraged loans. The composition of the proposed asset pool showed that Citigroup was still exposed to massive losses from its reckless lending and high-risk securitizations, even though Citigroup had previously reported $70 billion of losses and write-downs from troubled assets.[140]

Citigroup's second bailout also proved to be insufficient, as the bank continued to suffer staggering losses. In February 2009, Treasury converted $25 billion of its preferred stock into 33.6% of Citigroup's common stock, and other Citigroup shareholders converted $33 billion of their preferred stock into common stock on the same terms. Treasury's third bailout significantly increased Citigroup's tangible common equity and helped to stabilize the bank.[141]

Notwithstanding its first $25 billion bailout, BofA also needed additional federal assistance to cope with crippling losses from its acquisitions of Countrywide and

Merrill Lynch. In January 2009, the Fed, FDIC, and Treasury gave BofA a second bailout similar to Citigroup's. Treasury bought $20 billion of additional TARP preferred stock from BofA, and the three agencies provided a joint guarantee to protect BofA from catastrophic losses on a $118 billion pool of troubled assets.[142]

The repeated bailouts of Citigroup and BofA undermined public confidence in the banking system. Investors, business owners, and consumers also lost faith in the general economy as the U.S. fell into a deep recession after Lehman failed. GDP dropped by 3% during the last quarter of 2008 and the first quarter of 2009. More than 6 million Americans lost their jobs during the last four months of 2008 and the first half of 2009. American household wealth fell by 16% in 2008, due to steep drops in home values and stock prices. Household consumption declined by 4.6% during the second half of 2008 and the first half of 2009.[143]

In late 2008, New York Fed staff members estimated that U.S. banks could suffer $840 billion of additional losses in a "stress scenario" and $1.25 trillion of additional losses in an "extreme stress scenario." They also projected that the fifteen largest U.S. banks could face a capital shortfall of more than $500 billion in an "extreme stress" situation. After President Obama appointed Geithner as Treasury Secretary in January 2009, Geithner decided that federal regulators should perform a public "stress test" of the largest banks, and the federal government should pledge to provide any capital those banks needed. In Geithner's view, the Obama administration "needed to make a more credible commitment that we would allow no more messy failures of systemic [financial] firms, and no more haircuts of senior bondholders—in other words, no more Lehmans or WaMus."[144]

On February 10, 2009, Geithner and senior federal bank regulators announced a stress test for the nineteen largest U.S. banks, each with more than $100 billion of assets. Geithner explained that the stress test would include "a new program of capital support for those institutions which need it."[145] On February 23, Geithner and his colleagues issued another joint statement, which repeated that the federal government would provide any needed capital that the nineteen banks could not raise on their own. That joint statement declared:

> The U.S. government stands firmly behind the banking system during this period of financial strain . . . [and] will ensure that banks have the capital and liquidity they need to provide the credit necessary to restore economic growth. Moreover, we reiterate our determination to preserve the viability of systemically important financial institutions so that they are able to meet their commitments.[146]

The regulators' joint statements made clear to investors and the general public that the nineteen largest U.S. banks were TBTF, at least for the duration of the financial crisis.[147] The federal government's TBTF guarantee "alleviated many of the widespread concerns about what the government might do with the banks." The TBTF guarantee encouraged investors to buy stock in the nineteen largest banks with the assurance that "there would not be a catastrophic failure at any other major institution."[148] Geithner's colleague Lee Sachs called the government's pledge of capital support "the Geithner Put." The Geithner Put effectively placed a floor under the stock prices of the nineteen largest banks as of February 2009.[149]

The federal regulators' stress test concluded that ten of the nineteen banks needed a total of $75 billion of additional capital. Nine banks (including Citigroup) succeeded in raising their prescribed amounts of new capital. However, FDIC chairman Sheila Bair questioned why Citigroup was only required to raise $5.5 billion of new capital after receiving three bailouts. GMAC (the financing unit of General Motors) could not satisfy its specified capital requirement. Treasury filled that gap by increasing its investment in GMAC to more than $16 billion.[150]

The 2009 stress test confirmed the U.S. government's policy of providing extraordinary support to large financial institutions during financial disruptions. Treasury provided $220 billion of TARP capital to the nineteen largest banks and $70 billion of capital to AIG. The nineteen largest banks issued $235 billion of FDIC-guaranteed debt. In addition, GE Capital (a systemically important nonbank financial company) issued $70 billion of FDIC-guaranteed debt after Paulson persuaded the FDIC to include GE Capital in its debt guarantee program. The liquidity support provided by the Fed under its emergency lending programs—including TAF, TSLF, and PDCF—reached a single-day peak of $1.2 trillion on December 5, 2008. The Fed provided most of those loans to the largest U.S. and European banks, and it did so at below-market interest rates. The total outstanding amount of emergency loans, capital infusions, guarantees, and other U.S. government assistance to financial institutions peaked at almost $7 trillion in early 2009.[151]

Residential mortgages, asset-backed securities, and private-label RMBS represented almost a third of the collateral that large financial institutions posted with the Fed under TAF, TSLF, and PDCF. Thus, the Fed allowed large banks and securities firms to obtain hundreds of billions of dollars of cash or Treasury securities by posting collateral consisting of high-risk, illiquid mortgages and structured finance securities. The Fed effectively acted as dealer (market maker) of last resort for those risky and illiquid assets. During the period following Bear Stearns' rescue—and especially after Lehman's failure—repo lenders and other private-sector creditors imposed large haircuts before accepting such assets as collateral, if they accepted them at all.[152]

Combining all of the separate loan transactions in the Fed's emergency lending programs produces a cumulative total of $19.5 trillion of liquidity support for financial institutions between 2007 and 2010. The Fed provided more than 80% of that cumulative total—$16.4 trillion—to AIG and thirteen other financial giants that were members of the Big Seventeen group of financial conglomerates.[153] The Big Seventeen and AIG were unquestionably the epicenter of the financial crisis, as they suffered $900 billion of the $1.5 trillion of total worldwide losses that banks, securities firms, and insurers reported between June 2007 and March 2010.[154]

In contrast to the federal government's massive support for troubled financial giants, federal agencies gave very limited help to smaller and midsized banks. Treasury provided only $45 billion of capital assistance to banks with assets under

$100 billion. Those banks issued only $11 billion of FDIC-guaranteed debt and received relatively small amounts of emergency loans from the Fed. Federal regulators allowed only two financial institutions larger than $100 billion (Lehman and WaMu) to fail without protecting all of their creditors. Meanwhile, more than 450 smaller banks failed and were placed in FDIC receiverships between 2008 and 2012. Federal regulators did not issue "prompt corrective action" orders against any of the nineteen largest banks for insufficient capital, even though several megabanks (including Citigroup and BofA) should have received such orders. Yet federal agencies issued more than 1,400 enforcement orders for inadequate capital against smaller banks.[155]

Thus, federal officials "ruled out forbearance" for "smaller, less complex institutions" and followed a deliberate policy of letting them fail when they became troubled.[156] The federal government's no-forbearance rule for smaller banks was completely at odds with its no-failure policy for large financial institutions. The stark disparity in the federal government's treatment of small and large banks cemented the TBTF policy as the cardinal rule of U.S. banking regulation in the minds of depositors, investors, and bank executives.

———

The Bush and Obama administrations were no more generous to struggling homeowners than they were to small and midsized banks. The TARP legislation authorized spending to prevent or mitigate home foreclosures, but Treasury Secretary Paulson did not use any TARP funds for that purpose. The Obama administration said it would use $50 billion of TARP funds to help homeowners avoid foreclosures, but by September 2016 it had spent only $32 billion on foreclosure mitigation programs.[157]

The Obama administration's primary program for reducing foreclosures, the Home Affordable Mortgage Program (HAMP), modified 1.6 million mortgages before it expired at the end of 2016. However, HAMP did not meaningfully reduce the principal amounts of modified mortgages for the great majority of participants. For most participants, HAMP left their principal balances unchanged while reducing their scheduled payments for five years (either by cutting their interest rates or by extending the maturity dates of their mortgages). In addition, more than two-thirds of homeowners who applied for HAMP modifications were rejected by their mortgage servicers. A third of homeowners who did receive HAMP modifications later re-defaulted, often because their modifications left them "underwater," with principal balances that significantly exceeded the market values of their homes.[158]

A 2018 Fed staff study determined that (1) less than 5% of a large sample of mortgages that were modified between 2008 and 2010 received substantial principal reductions, and (2) less than 15% of sampled mortgages that were modified in 2011 received substantial principal reductions.[159] The same study (as well as other studies) concluded that mortgage modifications were much more likely to be successful in avoiding re-defaults if they included significant principal reductions.[160]

Due to the lack of meaningful and widespread principal relief for underwater homeowners, about 12 million households lost their homes to foreclosures, short sales, and other distressed transactions between 2007 and 2016. That avalanche of foreclosures and distressed sales contributed to a $5.5 trillion drop in housing prices between 2006 and 2012. The resulting loss of household wealth depressed consumption, increased unemployment, and delayed economic recovery.[161] Sheila Bair, Alan Blinder, Atif Mian, and Amir Sufi strongly criticized the Bush and Obama administrations for not doing more to prevent foreclosures.[162]

The Bush and Obama administrations did not establish programs giving substantial principal relief to vulnerable homeowners because they knew that such an approach would impose large losses on major banks. The four largest banks—JPMC, BofA, Citigroup, and Wells Fargo—held $475 billion of second-lien home loans on their books at the end of 2008. Many of those second-lien loans were piggyback loans, which the banks extended to borrowers who took out nonprime first-lien mortgages. The banks securitized the first-lien nonprime mortgages, retained the second-lien loans, and acted as servicers for both sets of loans. Big banks strongly opposed principal reductions on first-lien mortgages because those reductions would have forced the banks to write off the accompanying second-lien loans. Paulson, Geithner, and other senior officials in the Bush and Obama administrations rejected proposals for principal reductions because they did not want to inflict additional losses on troubled megabanks. They feared that TARP would not provide enough funds to cover those losses.[163]

Federal regulators did not require big banks to start writing down their second-lien loans until 2012, even for loans secured by homes whose market values were substantially lower than the outstanding principal balances on their first mortgages. In March 2014, BofA, JPMC, and Wells Fargo still held $250 billion of second-lien loans on their books. Thus, federal officials provided extraordinary forbearance for megabanks and did everything necessary to ensure their survival. Geithner's top policy goal was to prevent the failures of any more systemically important financial institutions— "no more Lehmans or WaMus." The interests of other groups—including smaller banks and struggling underwater homeowners—were given a much lower priority.[164]

———

The first stress test in early 2009 stabilized the U.S. banking system, but did it not end the Great Recession. In February 2009, Congress passed an $800 billion fiscal stimulus bill to revive the U.S. economy.[165] The Fed adopted unconventional monetary policies to provide further help to the struggling economy. In December 2008, the FOMC adopted a zero-interest-rate policy (ZIRP) by reducing the Fed's target for short-term rates effectively to zero. The Fed also implemented three rounds of quantitative easing (QE) to push down interest rates on longer-term debt, including home mortgages. Under QE1, which lasted from November 2008 to March 2010, the Fed purchased $300 billion of longer-term Treasury securities as well as $1.45 trillion of agency RMBS and other debt obligations issued by Fannie Mae and Freddie Mac. Under QE2, the Fed bought $600 billion of longer-term Treasury securities in late 2010 and 2011. Under QE3, the Fed purchased over $1.6 trillion of additional agency RMBS and Treasury securities between October 2012 and September 2014. The three QE programs expanded the Fed's balance sheet from $900 billion in September 2008 to $4.5 trillion in October 2015.[166]

The Fed's ZIRP and QE policies supported economic recovery after the Great Recession, especially in the housing and financial markets. ZIRP and QE were successful in pushing down short-term and longer-term interest rates. They reduced financial stress by cutting the cost of short-term and longer-term debts for borrowers who could refinance their debts. ZIRP and QE were particularly helpful to troubled megabanks. Big banks relied for much of their funding on short-term wholesale (money market) liabilities, and they also held large portfolios of nonprime mortgages and mortgage-related securities. By cutting short-term interest rates, ZIRP reduced wholesale funding costs for megabanks. By reducing long-term rates, QE boosted the market values of nonprime assets held by megabanks. In addition, big banks that were primary dealers earned substantial commissions by arranging QE sales of Treasury bonds to the Fed.[167]

In contrast, ZIRP and QE were not helpful to savers and pension funds, as they significantly reduced yields on bank deposits and highly rated government and corporate bonds. By reducing yields on safer debt instruments, ZIRP and QE encouraged retail and institutional investors to "reach for yield" by investing in riskier assets, including equity stocks, residential and commercial real estate, leveraged corporate loans, and junk bonds. The resulting surge by investors into riskier investments generated significant gains in stock market prices and real estate values. As shown in Figure 9.1 in Chapter 9, home values rose significantly after 2012 for Americans who still owned homes. However, gains from higher-yielding investments accrued mainly to the richest households, thereby aggravating wealth disparities that had been widening since the early 1980s.[168]

Median U.S. household wealth fell by almost half between 2007 and 2010, reflecting the steep losses in housing values, incomes, and investments caused by the Great Recession. In 2016, median household wealth still remained a third below its 2007 level, despite ZIRP and QE. In contrast, the share of total household wealth held by the richest 1% of households rose from 34.6% to 39.6% between 2007 and 2016, while the share of total household wealth held by the most affluent 10% of households climbed from 71.5% to 77.4%.[169] Thus, ZIRP and QE produced an economic recovery in which most of the gains accrued to the wealthiest households.

In May 2019, Fed governor Lael Brainard provided data that confirmed and updated those trends. As shown in Figure 11.1, household wealth levels for families with the top 10% and top 30% of incomes were substantially higher in 2018 than they were in 2007. In contrast, household wealth levels were marginally lower for families with incomes in the 40–70% range and significantly lower for families with the lowest 40% of incomes, compared with 2007.[170]

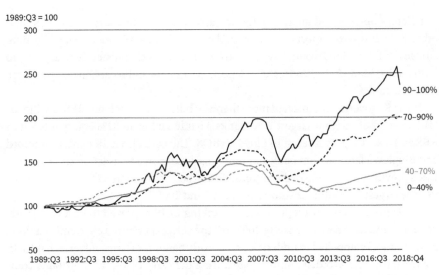

1989:Q3 = 100

Figure 11.1 Changes in U.S. Household Wealth by Income Percentiles, 1989–2018

Note: Wealth values are reported in 2018 dollars using personal consumption expenditures prices and indexed to 1989: Q3.

Source: Brainard (2019a: figure 1); data from Federal Reserve Board, Distributional Financial Accounts; Bureau of Economic Analysis

In sum, ZIRP and QE supported economic recovery after the Great Recession, and those policies definitely helped troubled megabanks to recover from their massive losses.[171] However, ZIRP and QE had highly skewed effects on the distribution of gains in investments and household wealth. Those asymmetric outcomes provoked vigorous debates about the longer-term benefits of ZIRP and QE. In addition, some experts warned that the Fed and other central banks were risking their legitimacy and political independence by adopting policies that moved beyond the established boundaries of monetary policy (the traditional purview of central banks) into areas affecting fiscal policy and credit allocation (the traditional responsibilities of politically accountable leaders, legislatures, and agencies).[172]

—————

The U.K. and other European nations followed the U.S. example by vigorously implementing the G7's pledge to support systemically important financial institutions. On September 29, 2008, Ireland guaranteed all deposits and other liabilities of its six largest banks. However, Irish banks proved to be "too big to save," as their total assets were equal to seven times Ireland's GDP. In November 2010, Ireland was obliged to accept a massive bailout package from the EU, ECB, and International Monetary Fund to finance its bank rescue program.[173]

Ireland's open-ended guarantee for its banks put great pressure on the U.K. and other EU nations to protect depositors in their own banks. Without such protection, citizens of EU nations would have had strong incentives to transfer their deposits to Irish banks. Many EU nations issued deposit guarantees and recapitalized their large troubled banks.[174]

The U.K. government injected more than $80 billion of capital into RBS and Lloyds HBOS—two of the four largest U.K. banks—while taking an 82% equity interest in RBS and a 43% equity interest in Lloyds HBOS. The U.K. also nationalized Bradford and Bingley, a large savings bank and mortgage lender, in a transaction similar to the U.K.'s previous rescue of Northern Rock. Thus, the U.K. was forced to bail out four of its nine largest depository institutions in 2007 and 2008.[175]

The U.K.'s decision to adopt universal banking in 1986 proved to be a very costly error. During the financial crisis of 2007–09, the U.K. experienced a systemic banking crisis and was compelled to undertake very costly bailouts of large universal banks. In contrast, the U.K. avoided a similar fate during the early 1930s, when Britain's commercial banks were separated from London's securities markets and did not fail.[176]

Switzerland recapitalized UBS and provided emergency loans to both UBS and Credit Suisse. France provided capital infusions and liquidity assistance to its six largest banks, including BNP Paribas and Société Générale. Germany bailed out Commerzbank and rescued several large regional banks, including BayernLB, HSH Nordbank, IKB, SachsenLB, WestLB, and Hypo Real Estate. The Netherlands bailed out ING. Belgium, France, and the Netherlands jointly rescued two large universal banks, Dexia and Fortis. Both banks were eventually separated into national units and restructured by their respective home countries.[177] Thus, troubled universal banks were at the center of the financial crisis in Europe in 2008 and 2009, as they had been during the early 1930s.[178]

The EU authorized almost €5 trillion of state aid for banks in the form of capital infusions, asset purchases, and financial guarantees. EU governments spent about €2 trillion to support more than 110 banks between 2008 and 2015. The recipients of state aid included twelve of the twenty largest EU banks.[179] Large European banks also received massive amounts of liquidity assistance from the ECB and the Fed, both directly through the Fed's emergency lending programs and indirectly through the Fed's dollar swap lines with the ECB and other European central banks. The ECB provided over €700 trillion of long-term loans to banks on very generous terms in exchange for a wide range of collateral (including illiquid mortgage-related securities).[180]

Greece, Portugal, and Spain entered the same "doom loop" that ensnared Ireland after all three nations ran huge budget deficits and assumed heavy debt burdens to rescue their banks. Like Ireland, all three countries accepted large bailouts from the EU, ECB, and IMF.[181] Ireland, Spain, and Portugal exited their financial assistance programs between 2013 and 2017. Greece made a similar exit in August 2018, after receiving two additional bailouts. However, many observers expressed concerns about Greece's ability to sustain its massive sovereign debt burden over the long term.[182]

The Bank of England, Bank of Japan (BoJ), and ECB followed the Fed's example by instituting QE programs to boost their economies after conventional monetary policies failed to generate strong recoveries. The BoE and ECB purchased government debt and corporate bonds, and the BoJ bought government debt as well as publicly traded equity and real estate funds. The Fed, ECB, BoE, and BoJ increased the total size of their balance sheets from $4 trillion to $15 trillion between 2008 and 2018. By pushing down yields on government bonds, the ECB's QE program enabled weaker Eurozone countries to issue bonds with lower interest rates, thereby easing their debt service costs and budget pressures.[183] The ECB's QE program effectively made the ECB "the de facto lender of last resort to [Eurozone] governments."[184]

———

The financial crisis left deep and painful scars on the economies, societies, and government budgets of the U.S., U.K., and EU. Almost 9 million Americans lost their jobs, and the U.S. unemployment rate rose from 4.4% to 10% between 2007 and 2009. The U.S. recorded a net loss of more than 270,000 small businesses (employing fewer than a hundred workers) between March 2007 and March 2010. U.S. GDP fell by 4.3% during 2008 and 2009 and did not return to its 2007 level until 2011.[185]

The impact of the financial crisis was at least as severe—and more prolonged—in the U.K. and the Eurozone. The unemployment rate peaked at 8.3% in the U.K. in 2011 and reached 12.1% in the Eurozone in 2013.[186] U.K. GDP dropped by 6% during 2008–09 and did not return to its 2007 level until 2013. Eurozone GDP also fell by 6% during 2008–09 and did not regain its 2007 level until 2015.[187] Total annual investments in buildings, infrastructure, machinery, and equipment did not recover their 2007 levels until 2013 in the U.S. and 2018 in the EU (including the U.K.).[188] Similarly, the Eurozone's unemployment rate did not fall back to its 2008 level until a decade later.[189]

Government debt burdens rose sharply as the U.S., U.K., and Eurozone struggled to rescue their financial systems and mitigate the impact of high unemployment and widespread business failures. Between 2007 and 2017, the ratio of government debt to GDP increased from 63% to 103% in the U.S., 33% to 83% in the U.K., and 65% to 88% in the Eurozone.[190] Losses of potential economic output probably exceeded 70% of GDP in all three regions between 2007 and 2017. The U.S. lost more than $10 trillion of potential output during that decade.[191] The Eurozone's loss of potential output was especially severe between 2011 and 2017, due to the sovereign debt crisis that the Eurozone struggled to contain during those years.[192]

Statistics for unemployment, budget deficits, and lost output cannot convey the enormous human costs of the financial crisis in terms of careers destroyed, homes and businesses lost, educational opportunities forgone, families disrupted, and physical and mental health shattered. The devastating economic and social consequences of the Great Recession created volatile political conditions on both sides of the Atlantic. The financial crisis destroyed the credibility of politicians, regulators, and bank executives who had eagerly touted the benefits of deregulated financial markets and light-touch regulation during the 2000s.

Insurgent political candidates used populist, anti-establishment appeals to defeat or weaken political elites in many countries after 2009. The Tea Party and Occupy Wall Street movements were early examples of that trend in the U.S. Later examples included Britain's vote for Brexit in 2016, Bernie Sanders' insurgent campaign and Donald Trump's election in 2016, victories by populist candidates in Hungary, Poland, and Italy, and street protests by the *gilets jaunes* (yellow vests) in France in late 2018 and early 2019, which forced President Emmanuel Macron to make significant policy concessions.[193]

Public anger over bailouts of megabanks generated strong public support for financial reforms in the U.S., U.K., and Europe. As discussed in Chapter 12, post-crisis reforms attempted to improve regulatory controls over systemically important financial institutions and markets. However, those reforms failed to make any fundamental changes to the structure and business models of the universal banks and shadow banks that caused the crisis.

12

Unfinished Business

Post-Crisis Reforms Have Not Removed the Systemic
Dangers Posed by Universal Banks and Shadow Banks

In early 2009, the Obama administration agreed with other leaders of the Group of 20 nations on a reform agenda designed to prevent another global financial crisis. The G20—which includes nineteen major developed countries and the European Union—gave top priority to the following reforms: (1) establishing stronger capital and liquidity requirements for internationally active banks, especially global systemically important banks (G-SIBs), (2) developing new strategies for resolving failures of G-SIBs and nonbanks that are systemically important financial institutions (SIFIs), (3) improving regulation of over-the-counter derivatives, (4) reforming compensation policies to discourage excessive risk-taking by executives, traders, and other key employees of G-SIBs and nonbank SIFIs, and (5) strengthening controls over potential sources of systemic risk in the shadow banking system, including hedge funds, private equity funds, and nonbank lenders. The G20 established the Financial Stability Board (FSB) to implement its reform agenda, working in partnership with the Basel Committee on Banking Supervision and the International Monetary Fund.[1]

The Obama administration and the G20 did not recommend fundamental changes to universal banks. They also did not try to shrink the shadow banking system significantly. Governments on both sides of the Atlantic decided that universal banks and shadow banks should continue to exist but should operate under "strengthened regulation and supervision" based on "internationally agreed high standards."[2] Thus, the G20's reform agenda preserved the existing system of large, global financial institutions but tried to improve the regulatory tools for overseeing those institutions.[3]

The G20 pledged to maintain "an open world economy based on market principles" and to encourage "innovation in the marketplace."[4] The G20's affirmation of market-based principles in 2009 was consistent with the "Wall Street–Treasury Consensus" (also known as the "Washington Consensus") of the 1990s. During that period, Robert Rubin, Lawrence Summers, and Alan Greenspan championed economic policies that discouraged "overregulation" of financial markets and promoted "free capital flows" across international borders, including international loans by global banks.

During the 1990s, Rubin, Summers, and Greenspan encouraged the IMF to act as "international lender of last resort" for "crisis-afflicted countries." The U.S. actively supported the IMF's loan programs for distressed countries during the emerging market debt crises of the 1990s. IMF loans helped distressed countries to repay their foreign obligations, thereby reducing losses suffered by global banks. The IMF imposed strict austerity requirements (including smaller budget deficits and lower levels of foreign debt) on countries that accepted its loans. Rubin, Summers, and Greenspan invoked free-market principles to defend the IMF's austerity requirements. However, the IMF loans they advocated provided "de facto bailouts" to global banks, thereby weakening market discipline over those institutions.[5]

The G20's reform agenda followed the Washington Consensus and the IMF loan programs of the 1990s by insisting that failures of G-SIBs and nonbank SIFIs must be avoided at all costs. In April 2009, the G20 pledged to "restore domestic lending and international capital flows" by taking "all necessary actions to ... ensure the soundness of systemically important institutions."[6] The G20 viewed the survival of megabanks and large nonbank financial institutions (shadow banks) as a prerequisite for restoring domestic and international prosperity. The G20 never considered the possibility of breaking up the interlocking system of universal banks and shadow banks that financed the toxic credit bubble of the 2000s. The carefully limited scope of the G20's reform agenda revealed that the pre-crisis status quo had powerful defenders and remarkable staying power, despite the massive costs that universal banks and shadow banks inflicted on governments and ordinary citizens during the financial crisis of 2007–09.

In June 2009, the U.S. Treasury Department issued the Obama administration's blueprint for financial reform. Treasury Secretary Timothy Geithner and National Economic Director Lawrence Summers took the lead in crafting Treasury's plan, which incorporated the G20's agenda and provided a template for the Dodd-Frank Wall Street Reform and Consumer Protection Act of 2010 (Dodd-Frank).[7] Neither Treasury's plan nor Dodd-Frank attempted to make any fundamental changes in the size or structure of the largest banks and nonbank financial companies. Geithner insisted that the only way to restore public confidence in the U.S. financial system was to ensure the survival of all major financial institutions, while improving their resilience and strengthening their oversight.[8]

The congressional leaders who drafted Dodd-Frank—Senator Christopher Dodd and Congressman Barney Frank—agreed with the Obama administration that "it would be enough to put the financial sector under stricter rules, without trying to undo the two decades of growth and concentration that had transformed American finance." Moreover, the stark realities of the "political money game"—in which the financial industry made huge contributions to friendly politicians and employed armies of lobbyists (including many former members of Congress)—meant that very few legislators were willing to challenge the status quo produced by the repeal of Glass-Steagall in 1999.[9]

Title I of Dodd-Frank established the Financial Stability Oversight Council (FSOC) as an umbrella super-agency to identify and control systemic financial risks.[10] Title I authorizes FSOC to designate large, complex nonbank financial companies as nonbank SIFIs. It enables the Fed to impose stricter regulations on large banks and nonbank SIFIs, including stress tests and stronger capital and liquidity rules. Title I also requires large banks and nonbank SIFIs to submit plans ("living wills") to the Fed and FDIC for their "orderly resolution in the event of material financial distress or failure."[11]

Title II of Dodd-Frank created the Orderly Liquidation Authority (OLA) to handle failures of large bank holding companies and nonbank financial companies. The Treasury Secretary, with the Fed's and FDIC's concurrence and after consulting with the President, may establish an OLA receivership for a troubled financial company if the Secretary determines that (1) "no viable private sector alternative is available to prevent" the company's failure, (2) the company's resolution under other insolvency regimes (such as the federal Bankruptcy Code) would have "serious adverse effects on financial stability," and (3) appointing the FDIC as receiver for the company would "avoid or mitigate such adverse effects."[12]

Title VII of Dodd-Frank prescribes standards for greater transparency in the pricing and trading of derivatives, and it also mandates stronger regulation of derivatives dealers and large end-users. Under Title VII, trading in "standardized" (non-customized) derivatives must occur on a designated contract market (DCM)—such as a swap exchange or a swap execution facility—and those trades must be settled through a clearinghouse. Title VII mandates capital requirements, margin rules, and stress tests for DCMs and clearinghouses. Title VII directs the Commodity Futures Trading Commission and the Securities and Exchange Commission to prescribe margin rules and other prudential standards for cleared derivatives as well as customized derivatives that are traded in over-the-counter (OTC) transactions with dealers. All derivatives trades (whether cleared or conducted through OTC transactions) must be reported to swap data repositories.[13]

Section 956(b) of Dodd-Frank requires federal regulators to issue rules prohibiting compensation policies that encourage excessive risk-taking by executive officers, directors, and other key insiders of banks, securities broker-dealers, and other financial institutions.[14] Title IV of Dodd-Frank requires advisers for hedge funds and private equity funds to register with the SEC and provide information to the SEC. Title IV does not give the SEC direct regulatory authority over the activities of hedge funds and private equity funds, even though those funds are leading participants in the shadow banking system.[15]

Title X of Dodd-Frank established the Consumer Financial Protection Bureau (CFPB), despite the vehement opposition of megabanks and Wall Street. Killing the CFPB was the top priority for big financial institutions and their Republican allies. However, the CFPB's supporters prevailed, due to Elizabeth Warren's persuasive advocacy and strong support from President Obama, Senator Dodd, and Representative Frank. Title X provides the CFPB with broad rulemaking, examination, and enforcement powers to protect consumers of financial services. The CFPB's supporters persuaded Congress that the new agency would be more effective in protecting consumers than the federal banking agencies had been during the toxic credit boom of the 2000s.[16]

The financial industry and its Republican allies could not defeat Dodd-Frank. However, the financial industry did block or weaken—often with the Obama administration's help—several provisions that would have imposed stronger restrictions on the size and activities of financial giants. For example, Senators Sherrod Brown (D-OH) and Ted Kaufman (D-DE) co-sponsored an amendment to impose maximum size limits on financial institutions. The Brown-Kaufman amendment would have forced the six largest U.S. banks—JPMorgan Chase (JPMC), Bank of America (BofA), Citigroup, Wells Fargo, Goldman Sachs, and Morgan Stanley—to reduce their size substantially.[17]

Treasury Secretary Geithner urged Senator Kaufman to withdraw the proposed amendment. Geithner promised that federal regulators would force big banks to hold more capital. Kaufman replied, "What happens when we get a president who says, 'no regulation'?" Geithner confidently predicted, "It'll be hard for them to reverse the rules we put in place." After extensive lobbying by Treasury officials together with megabanks and their political allies, the Senate rejected the Brown-Kaufman amendment by a vote of 61–33.[18]

Former Fed Chairman Paul Volcker proposed that banks should be barred from holding ownership interests in hedge funds and private equity funds, and from engaging in "proprietary trading" in securities, commodities, or derivatives. Volcker wanted to stop banks from using FDIC-insured deposits and Fed discount window loans to fund their speculative investments and trades in financial instruments. He argued that proprietary investing and trading by banks represented an unfair and dangerous exploitation of their federal safety net subsidies.[19]

In January 2010, President Obama endorsed the "Volcker Rule" to rally public support for Dodd-Frank.[20] The big-bank lobby vigorously attacked the Volcker Rule, and the Treasury Department provided only tepid support. The House-Senate conference committee on the Dodd-Frank Act substantially weakened the Volcker Rule. As enacted, the Volcker Rule allows banks to buy and sell financial instruments for the purpose of underwriting, "market making," and "risk-mitigating hedging." As discussed later, those three exempted activities are very difficult to distinguish in practice from prohibited proprietary trading. In addition, the Volcker Rule allows banks to invest up to 3% of their equity capital in minority interests in hedge funds and private equity funds.[21]

Senator Blanche Lincoln (D-AR) sponsored a "swaps push-out rule" to force banking organizations to transfer all of their derivatives to nonbank affiliates. Lincoln argued that the federal safety net should be protected from the risks of derivatives, and she repeated Volcker's argument that banks should not be allowed to use FDIC-insured deposits and Fed discount window loans to finance speculative capital markets activities. The Senate adopted the Lincoln Amendment despite intense opposition from the big-bank lobby and the Obama administration. However, the House-Senate conference committee greatly reduced the scope of the amendment. As enacted, the provision applied only to equity derivatives, commodity derivatives, and uncleared credit default swaps, and even those types of derivatives were exempted if they were used for "risk-mitigating hedging." Consequently, the Lincoln Amendment, as enacted, applied to less than 10% of derivatives held by banks.[22]

FDIC Chairman Sheila Bair proposed that megabanks and nonbank SIFIs should pay risk-based assessments to pre-fund the Orderly Liquidation Fund (OLF). The OLF provides a backup source of funding for resolving failing financial giants that are placed in OLA receiverships. The House bill included Bair's proposal and would have required megabanks, nonbank SIFIs, and large hedge funds to pay $150 billion of assessments over several years to pre-fund the OLF.[23]

Big banks and their Republican allies attacked the pre-funded OLF as a "bailout fund," and Geithner and Summers joined in those attacks. As Bair pointed out, the "bailout fund" epithet was truly an "Orwellian" claim. Pre-funding the OLF would have forced megabanks, nonbank SIFIs, and large hedge funds to help cover the future costs of resolving troubled financial giants, instead of imposing those costs on taxpayers. Bair's proposal also would have allowed the FDIC to discourage excessive risk-taking by imposing risk-adjusted OLF premiums on large financial firms. Megabanks and the Obama administration successfully blocked Bair's proposal, and the OLF currently has a zero balance. As a result, future resolutions of financial behemoths will depend on loans from the Treasury Department, as explained later.[24]

———

To implement the G20's mandate for stronger capital and liquidity requirements, the Basel Committee on Bank Supervision adopted the Basel III international capital accord. Basel III established new risk-weighted and leverage capital requirements for G-SIBs and other internationally active banks. To meet Basel III's risk-weighted standards, a bank must hold common equity Tier 1 capital equal to 4.5% of its risk-weighted assets (RWAs) plus a capital conservation buffer equal to 2.5% of its RWAs.[25]

Basel III imposes a capital surcharge on megabanks that have been designated as G-SIBs by the FSB. The FSB published a list of thirty G-SIBs in November 2019 that included eight U.S. banks, three U.K. banks, and ten Eurozone banks.[26] The Basel III capital surcharge requires G-SIBs to hold additional common equity Tier 1 capital ranging from 1% to 2.5% of their RWAs, based on the FSB's evaluation of each G-SIB's systemic significance. In November 2019, the FSB determined that only one bank (JPMC) needed to satisfy a 2.5% capital surcharge, while the other twenty-nine G-SIBs are required to meet smaller surcharges ranging from 1% to 2%.[27]

Basel III also includes a new leverage capital standard. The leverage standard requires each internationally active bank to hold total Tier 1 capital (including common equity Tier 1 capital, qualifying preferred stock, and "additional Tier 1 capital") equal to 3% of its total (unweighted) assets. Beginning in 2022, each G-SIB must maintain an additional leverage buffer equal to its 3% base rate multiplied by one-half of its G-SIB capital surcharge rate. For example, JPMC will be required to hold total Tier 1 leverage capital of 4.25% in 2022 (consisting of its 3% base rate plus a leverage buffer equal to one-half of its 2.5% G-SIB surcharge rate). In addition, U.S. G-SIBs must satisfy a higher leverage requirement. In 2014, federal bank regulators established a leverage capital standard of 5%—the highest leverage standard among major developed nations—for U.S. G-SIBs.[28]

Basel III allows national authorities to impose a discretionary countercyclical capital buffer during economic expansions, and to reduce or eliminate that buffer during recessions. The countercyclical buffer is designed to force banks to build up larger capital cushions during favorable economic conditions as extra protection against failure during crises. France and the U.K. were the only large developed countries that required their banks to maintain countercyclical buffers in 2019.[29]

In sum, Basel III requires the largest global banks (G-SIBs) to hold common equity Tier 1 capital equal to about 10% of their RWAs and to maintain total Tier 1 capital between 4% and 5% of their unweighted total assets. Basel III is substantially stronger than Basel II, but many analysts view Basel III's capital standards as far too low to prevent another financial crisis.[30] Two Fed staff economists determined that Basel III's capital surcharges for G-SIBs should be at least three times higher "to ensure the survival of G-SIBs through serious crises without extraordinary public assistance."[31] The Federal Reserve Bank of Minneapolis and numerous academic experts contend that G-SIBs should be required to hold Tier 1 equity capital of more than 20% on a risk-weighted basis and at least 15% on a leverage basis. Anat Admati and Martin Hellwig maintain that leverage capital requirements for G-SIBs should be even higher, in the range of 25–30%.[32]

Basel III (like its predecessors) allows banks to apply a risk-weighted capital requirement of zero to their holdings of sovereign debt issued by their home countries. Basel III therefore allows banks to purchase large amounts of their home country's sovereign debt without increasing their risk-weighted capital. That approach is frequently encouraged by their home country regulators, who face intense political pressures to help their governments finance big budget deficits.

Large holdings of sovereign debt by banks frequently create a "doom loop" between the banks and their home countries. That doom loop arises for two reasons. First, a heavily indebted country has strong incentives to rescue its banks to avoid any liquidation of their bond portfolios, as such a liquidation would cause market values for the country's outstanding bonds to fall sharply. Second, rescues of banks by a heavily indebted country are likely to trigger a sovereign debt crisis if the country issues large quantities of new bonds to pay for bailouts (as Ireland did) or loses access to international bond markets (as Greece did). In December 2017, the Basel Committee released a discussion paper requesting comments on possible approaches for assigning higher risk weights to bank holdings of home country sovereign debt. However, the Basel Committee did not adopt any of the suggested approaches. Consequently, Basel III does not prevent the continued existence of doom loops between undercapitalized banks and their heavily indebted home countries.[33]

Financial giants have repeatedly arbitraged risk-weighted capital requirements by using their internal risk models to reduce their RWAs (thereby reducing the denominator of their risk-weighted capital requirements). More than twenty megabanks and large securities firms failed or received bailouts on both sides of the Atlantic after they reported risk-weighted capital ratios that exceeded Basel II's standards. A 2017 study determined that megabanks were especially likely to manipulate their risk models and understate the risks of their trading portfolios when they had "lower equity capital, as well as during periods of high systemic stress." Basel III limits, but does not eliminate, the ability of megabanks to arbitrage their RWAs by using internal risk models.[34] As Patrick Jenkins explained, "Many banks have responded to the higher post-crisis regulatory capital demands by engaging in 'capital optimisation' programmes—a euphemism for tweaking [internal] models so that loans look less risky and thus attract as little capital as possible."[35]

Megabanks can manipulate their leverage capital requirements by investing in riskier assets, shifting assets to off-balance-sheet conduits, and postponing recognition of losses on assets. Several large international banks either failed or received bailouts during the financial crisis after reporting leverage ratios above 7%.[36] However, leverage capital requirements have generally been more effective than risk-weighted capital standards in restraining risk-taking by megabanks, as leverage requirements cannot be arbitraged by internal risk models.[37]

The greater binding effect of leverage capital requirements is indicated by the fact that, since the financial crisis, megabanks have increased their risk-weighted capital ratios to a much greater degree than their leverage capital ratios. According to the IMF, G-SIBs increased their average ratio of Tier 1 equity to RWAs by more than 5% between 2010 and 2017, while their average ratio of Tier 1 equity to total assets rose by only 1% during the same period. Similarly, the ratio of common equity to total assets for G-SIBs was only about 1% higher in 2017 than it was in 2003.[38]

In June 2017, the average reported Basel III leverage capital ratio was 6.95% for U.S. G-SIBs and 4.78% for G-SIBs headquartered in the U.K. and other EU nations.[39] Those ratios were far below the 15% level recommended by the Minneapolis Fed and many experts, and also below the 7–8% level at which several large international banks failed during the crisis.[40]

———

Unfortunately, the mid-2017 capital ratios for G-SIBs marked the high-water mark for post-crisis efforts to force U.S. and European megabanks to increase their capital. The Fed applied relatively tough annual stress tests from 2009 to 2016, during President Obama's tenure. Those tests compelled U.S. G-SIBs to retain most of their earnings to build sufficient capital levels to satisfy the Fed's scenarios for heightened financial and economic stress.

The lineup of senior federal banking regulators changed rapidly after President Trump took office in January 2017. Trump appointed Jerome Powell as the Fed's Chairman, Randal Quarles as the Fed's Vice Chairman for Supervision, and Richard Clarida as the Fed's other Vice Chairman. Trump also appointed Joseph Otting as

Comptroller of the Currency and Jelena McWilliams as the FDIC's Chairman. Those Trump-appointed regulators allowed megabanks to stop raising their capital levels.

In 2017 and 2018, Trump-appointed members of the Fed relaxed the stress tests and permitted big banks to distribute 100% or more of their earnings to shareholders. As a result, the risk-weighted and leverage capital ratios for U.S. G-SIBs and other large U.S. banks remained stagnant or declined slightly after 2017. A similar pattern emerged in Europe, as the risk-weighted and leverage capital ratios for large European banks showed very little growth after 2017.[41]

In November 2018, Fed vice chairman Quarles proposed that the Fed should provide "additional transparency" to big banks by disclosing more information in advance about the Fed's annual stress tests, including the Fed's "stress test scenarios" and "models." A prominent bank analyst stated that Quarles' proposal—which the Fed adopted in March 2019—would "permit mega banks to boost distribution levels while reducing the risk of an unexpected" failure in their stress tests.[42]

In defending his "transparency" plan, Quarles stated that U.S. megabanks were "healthy and profitable." Accordingly, he believed that big banks could "appropriately and safely tend to distribute much or all of [their] income in any given year." Quarles' speech clearly signaled his view that capital levels for U.S. G-SIBs did not need to rise any further.[43] In contrast, former Fed Governor Daniel Tarullo (appointed by President Obama) criticized the Fed's decision to provide more advance disclosures about its stress test scenarios and models. He warned that such disclosures would help megabanks to "reverse-engineer the models" and thereby weaken the stress tests' effectiveness.[44]

In February 2019, Fed chairman Jerome Powell told the House Financial Services Committee that "the overall level of capital, particularly at the largest firms, is about right."[45] Following the completion of its 2019 stress test, the Fed permitted the eighteen largest U.S. banks to distribute more than 100% of their expected earnings to shareholders through dividends and stock buybacks.[46] Thus, the Fed has allowed megabanks to stop increasing their capital levels and pay out 100% or more of their earnings since President Trump took office.[47] That pattern unfortunately resembles the behavior of the heedless grasshopper rather than the diligent ants in Aesop's fable.[48]

In March 2019, Powell, Quarles, and Clarida rejected proposals by Fed Governor Lael Brainard (appointed by President Obama) and five regional Federal Reserve Bank Presidents to establish a countercyclical capital buffer. The proposed buffer would have required large U.S. banks to follow the example of Aesop's ants and increase their risk-weighted capital ratios while economic conditions remained favorable. The banking industry strongly opposed any countercyclical buffer, and the three Trump-appointed Fed members agreed it was unnecessary.[49] Senator Sherrod Brown criticized the Fed for failing to implement a countercyclical buffer "to strengthen the resiliency of our financial system" against the risk of a future economic downturn.[50]

Basel III implemented the G20's mandate for stronger liquidity requirements by establishing two new liquidity standards. The liquidity coverage ratio (LCR) requires banks to hold enough high-quality liquid assets—assets that can quickly be converted into cash—to meet their projected liquidity needs for a thirty-day period under stressed financial conditions. The net stable funding ratio (NSFR) requires banks to maintain enough medium- and long-term sources of funding—including equity capital and long-term debt—to meet their estimated liquidity needs for one year.[51]

Average LCR and NSFR ratios for large U.S. and European banks rose substantially between 2012 and 2017. However, both ratios stopped rising in 2017 for large U.S. banks and declined slightly or remained stagnant in 2018 and 2019. Similarly, LCR and NSFR ratios for large European banks showed very little growth after 2017. Only about half of the twenty-four nations that are members of the Financial Stability Board have fully implemented Basel III's NSFR standards, and the U.S. is one of the laggards in that regard.[52]

In October 2019, the three Trump-appointed members of the Fed approved new regulations that significantly reduced LCR requirements for large U.S. banks other than G-SIBs. The new rules eliminated LCR requirements for banks with assets between $100 billion and $250 billion, and they cut LCR requirements by 15% for banks with assets between $250 billion and $700 billion. As a practical matter, the new rules have reduced mandatory liquidity levels by about $200 billion for large U.S. banks other than G-SIBs. Fed Governor Lael Brainard opposed the new rules because they "weaken core safeguards against the vulnerabilities that caused so much damage in the [financial] crisis."[53]

In sum, the post-crisis trend of requiring megabanks to increase their capital and liquidity effectively ended on both sides of the Atlantic in 2017. Given the lack of regulatory will to enforce higher capital and liquidity standards, Basel III will not be strong enough to prevent future financial crises. As shown above, Basel III's capital standards are much too low in light of our experience with large U.S., U.K., and EU financial institutions that failed during the financial crisis. In addition, large financial institutions have repeatedly arbitraged and evaded capital requirements since the 1980s, and regulators have often failed to enforce those requirements in a timely and effective manner.[54]

The erosion of regulatory will to impose stronger capital and liquidity standards under Basel III matches the predictions of John Coffee's "regulatory sine curve" theory as well as Erik Gerding's "regulatory instability" hypothesis. As Coffee and Gerding have shown, policymakers and regulators are likely to roll back post-crisis reforms as the adverse impacts of a financial crisis recede from the public's consciousness, and as the financial industry's lobbying efforts become more intense and effective.[55]

In October 2018, the IMF cautioned that "reform fatigue and rollback pressures [are] already visible" as "memories of the global financial crisis fade."[56] At the annual meeting of the Institute of International Finance in October 2019, Germany's top bank regulator warned that policymakers were being "pushed into a new cycle of downward regulation," which was "planting the seeds for the next financial crisis." At the same meeting, senior global bank executives called for regulatory "balance" that would give them more "capacity to run their businesses." Citigroup chairman (and former Comptroller of the Currency) John Dugan stated, "You can go too far (with regulation), the returns can become quite diminished."[57]

The following section highlights several areas in which U.S. policymakers and the financial industry have already eliminated or undermined key reforms mandated by the Dodd-Frank Act since its enactment in 2010.

Ending designations of nonbank SIFIs: In 2013, the Financial Stability Oversight Council designated three large nonbanks—AIG, GE Capital, and Prudential Insurance—as systemically important nonbank financial institutions (nonbank SIFIs). As a result of FSOC's designations, all three companies became subject to enhanced regulation by the Fed (including capital and liquidity requirements and resolution planning) under Title I of Dodd-Frank. In 2016, FSOC agreed to remove GE Capital's designation after GE Capital divested several business lines and reduced its size by more than half to diminish its systemic importance.

In 2014, FSOC designated MetLife as a fourth nonbank SIFI. MetLife sued FSOC to overturn that designation, and a federal district court upheld MetLife's challenge in 2016. In 2017—after President Trump appointed Steven Mnuchin as Treasury Secretary and FSOC chair—FSOC withdrew its appeal of the district court's decision and allowed that decision to become final. Under Mnuchin's leadership, FSOC also rescinded the designations of AIG and Prudential. Consequently, not a single nonbank SIFI remained subject to Fed supervision at the end of 2018.[58]

In March 2019, FSOC issued proposed guidance to govern future designations of nonbank SIFIs. Under the proposed guidance, FSOC would designate a nonbank SIFI only after completing a rigorous cost-benefit analysis, and only after determining that it would not be possible to control identified systemic risks by regulating activities instead of individual companies. The proposed guidance strongly indicates that FSOC does not intend to make any future designations of nonbank SIFIs. Such an outcome would ignore (1) the enormous threats that large securities firms and AIG posed to the global financial system during the financial crisis of 2007–09, and (2) the continuing systemic risks created by large nonbank financial institutions, including leading insurance companies and major private equity firms.[59]

Repealing the Lincoln Amendment and weakening derivatives regulation: In December 2014, the big-bank lobby won a major victory when Congress repealed almost all of the Lincoln Amendment. Megabanks and their Republican allies attached the repeal provision to a year-end appropriations bill. The Obama administration accepted that provision, due in part to the administration's long opposition to the Lincoln Amendment. The repeal provision gutted the amendment by reducing its coverage to less than 0.2% of all derivatives held by major banks. The repeal of the Lincoln Amendment permits large financial holding companies to conduct virtually all of their derivatives activities within their subsidiary banks, which enjoy the largest federal safety net subsidies and the lowest cost of funding within their respective holding company structures.[60]

The big-bank lobby scored another triumph—and significantly weakened Dodd-Frank's derivatives reforms—by convincing the CFTC to include a large loophole in a 2013 derivatives rule. Under that loophole, derivatives held by foreign subsidiaries of U.S. banks are not subject to regulation by the CFTC as long as the derivatives are not expressly guaranteed by the parent U.S. banks. The largest U.S. banks have exploited the loophole by transferring large volumes of their derivatives contracts to foreign subsidiaries while removing explicit guarantees from those contracts. However, parent U.S. banks remain exposed to significant legal and reputational risks because many customers expect that parent banks will stand behind their foreign subsidiaries' contracts. A recent study found that U.S. megabanks have engaged in "regulatory arbitrage" by shifting larger shares of their derivatives contracts to foreign subsidiaries located in jurisdictions with weaker oversight regimes for derivatives.[61]

In October 2019, Trump-appointed bank regulators proposed a new rule that would repeal a key Dodd-Frank reform and generate a significantly higher risk of losses for large banks engaged in derivatives activities. The proposed rule would rescind a regulation adopted in 2015 that requires nonbank affiliates to post collateral (margin) when they enter into derivatives contracts with affiliated banks. Removing that collateral requirement would allow nonbank affiliates to avoid posting about $40 billion of collateral for their derivatives contracts with affiliated banks. The elimination of that collateral requirement would expose big banks—as well as the FDIC and taxpayers—to substantial losses if nonbank affiliates default on their derivatives. Thus, like the repeal of the Lincoln Amendment, the proposal to rescind the affiliate margin requirement would save large financial holding companies tens of billions of dollars while imposing significantly higher risks on the FDIC and taxpayers.[62]

Weakening systemic risk protections: The financial industry achieved another significant legislative victory when Congress passed a "regulatory relief" bill in May 2018. The 2018 law effectively removes large banks with assets between $50 billion and $250 billion from the Fed's enhanced regulatory powers under Title I of Dodd-Frank. The new law also authorizes the Fed to "tailor"—properly translated as "weaken"—Title I's requirements for even bigger banks. The Trump-appointed members of the Fed relied on their new "tailoring" authority when they reduced liquidity requirements by 15% for banks with assets between $250 and $700 billion.[63] The 2018 "regulatory relief" law and the Fed's reduction of liquidity requirements ignored the fact that several deeply troubled U.S. financial institutions with assets between $100 billion and $700 billion—Bear Stearns, Countrywide, GE Capital, GMAC, Lehman Brothers, National City Bank, and Washington Mutual—posed major systemic threats to U.S. financial markets during the financial crisis.[64]

Undermining the Volcker Rule: The big-bank lobby has conducted a determined campaign to undermine the Volcker Rule since it was enacted as Section 619 of the Dodd-Frank Act in 2010. Aggressive lobbying by megabanks delayed the adoption of implementing regulations until December 2013. Those regulations were highly complex, due in part to demands by the big-bank lobby for dozens of safe harbors defining the activities permitted for banks under the Volcker Rule's exemptions for underwriting, market-making, and risk-mitigating hedging. Those exempted activities are notoriously difficult to distinguish in practice from the Volcker Rule's prohibition on proprietary trading.[65]

In June 2017, Treasury Secretary Mnuchin issued a report that criticized the Volcker Rule for being "unnecessarily burdensome," and he called for changes to "simplify" the rule. In May 2018, Trump-appointed federal regulators proposed new regulations to reduce the Volcker Rule's "compliance burdens."[66] As adopted in October 2019, the new regulations significantly weaken the Volcker Rule in several ways. First, the new regulations removed a previous rebuttable presumption, which treated matching buy-and-sale trades by a bank for its own account as forbidden proprietary trading if those trades occurred within a period of sixty days. Second, the new regulations add a new rebuttable presumption, which treats matching buy-and-sale trades occurring more than sixty days apart as *not* constituting proprietary trading.

Third, the new regulations substantially reduce the coverage of the Volcker Rule by eliminating its application to all bank assets valued on a mark-to-market basis that are not held in the bank's trading account. That change removes about one-quarter of mark-to-market assets held by banking organizations from the Volcker Rule's coverage. Fourth, the new regulations eliminate previous quantitative tests for applying the underwriting, market-making, and hedging exemptions. Instead, the new regulations establish much more lenient qualitative standards for applying those exemptions and allow banks to satisfy those standards based on their internal policies and procedures.

Two Obama appointees—FDIC Director and former Chairman Martin J. Gruenberg and Fed Governor Lael Brainard—opposed the new regulations and warned that they would seriously undermine the Volcker Rule's effectiveness. A Moody's analyst concluded that the new regulations would provide "an opportunity for some banks to take more risk, creating a credit negative for the industry."[67]

Hamstringing the CFPB: The CFPB has been the target of repeated attacks by the financial industry and the Trump administration since it was created by the Dodd-Frank Act. In 2017, the Republican-controlled Congress overturned a CFPB regulation that barred mandatory arbitration clauses in consumer financial contracts. The House of Representatives also passed bills to repeal the CFPB's examination authority, reduce its rulemaking and enforcement powers, eliminate its guaranteed funding from the Fed, give Congress full control over its budget, and allow the President to remove its Director without cause. The Senate failed to act on those proposals, and the Democratic Party captured control of the House in the 2018 midterm elections. It is therefore unlikely that Congress will pass similar legislation in 2020.[68]

Thus, the CFPB's opponents achieved only limited success in Congress. President Trump produced more dramatic results by installing former Congressman John "Mick" Mulvaney (R-SC) as the CFPB's Acting Director in 2017. Mulvaney—who was already serving as Director of the Office of Management and Budget (OMB)—received large campaign contributions from payday lenders during his tenure as a congressman. He described the CFPB as a "sad, sick joke," and he delayed the implementation of three major rules approved by his Obama-appointed predecessor, Richard Cordray. One of those rules would have mandated significant new consumer protections for payday loans. Mulvaney also drastically reduced the CFPB's examination and enforcement activities.[69]

In December 2018, the Senate confirmed Kathleen Kraninger as the CFPB's new Director. Kraninger served as Mulvaney's deputy at OMB, and she had no prior experience dealing with bank regulatory or consumer protection issues. In February 2019, Kraninger suspended the implementation of Cordray's payday lending rule, and she also proposed amendments that would remove several of its most important protections.[70] Kraninger also followed Mulvaney's lead by greatly decreasing the volume of the CFPB's enforcement actions, compared with the agency's previous enforcement record under Cordray.[71]

President Trump promised to "[do] a big number on Dodd-Frank" shortly after he became president.[72] The Trump administration has not succeeded with most of its efforts to repeal core provisions of the Dodd-Frank Act, and the Democratic Party's control of the House of Representatives will probably block further repeal efforts through the end of 2020. However, as has already been shown, Congress and Trump-appointed regulators have eliminated or undermined several of Dodd-Frank's key mandates. Most of Dodd-Frank's provisions rely on implementation by financial regulators, and those provisions can therefore be eroded further by new rules issued by Trump-appointed regulators.[73]

In addition, the Obama administration did not complete several very important regulations mandated by Dodd-Frank, including (1) a rule requiring the Fed to apply "early remediation" measures (prompt corrective action) against large bank holding companies and nonbank SIFIs that are undercapitalized or have other serious problems, and (2) a regulation prohibiting compensation policies that encourage excessive risk-taking by bank executives and other key insiders.[74] The unfinished implementation of Dodd-Frank and the continuing erosion of its mandates make clear that Dodd-Frank does *not* provide an adequate response to the dangers posed by universal banks and shadow banks.

The U.S., U.K., and EU have emphasized the importance of preventing future publicly financed bailouts of systemically important financial institutions (SIFIs), thereby ending their "too big to fail" (TBTF) status.[75] To achieve that goal, the U.S., U.K., and EU have established new regimes for resolving troubled SIFIs. The new resolution regimes are ostensibly designed to operate without using public funding. As described earlier, the U.S. established the Orderly Liquidation Authority under Title II of Dodd-Frank. In 2014, the EU promulgated the Bank Recovery and Resolution Directive (BRRD). The BRRD created the Single Resolution Mechanism (SRM) for large Eurozone banks, administered by a Single Resolution Board (SRB). The EU also authorized the European Central Bank to supervise large Eurozone banks. The

U.K. enacted bank resolution legislation in 2009 and subsequently amended that legislation to bring it into conformity with the BRRD.[76]

The new resolution regimes in the U.S., U.K., and EU attempt to solve two major problems that are very likely to arise in resolving the failure of a SIFI with international subsidiaries. First, the resolution should provide adequate funding to support the continued operations of the principal subsidiaries of the failed SIFI. Second, the resolution should enable the home country supervisor of the SIFI's parent holding company to manage the SIFI's failure without requiring the cooperation of host country supervisors of the SIFI's foreign subsidiaries. The Financial Stability Board and financial regulators in the U.S. and U.K. jointly developed a "single point of entry" (SPOE) resolution strategy to address both challenges. That strategy relies on funding provided by "total loss-absorbing capacity" (TLAC) in the form of equity and long-term debt securities issued by each SIFI's top-tier holding company.

Under the SPOE approach, the resolution authority will restructure only the top-tier holding company of a failed SIFI and will keep its principal subsidiaries in operation. The holding company's TLAC equity securities will be written off, and its TLAC debt securities will be converted into equity to recapitalize the SIFI's subsidiaries. The resolution authority will then transfer the subsidiaries from the original parent holding company to a new "bridge financial company" (BFC). Following that transfer, the resolution authority will either sell the BFC and its subsidiaries to another large financial institution or launch the BFC and its subsidiaries as a new financial holding company.

Thus, under the SPOE-TLAC strategy, a failed SIFI's principal subsidiaries (including banks and securities broker-dealers) will be kept in operation, and their creditors will not suffer any losses. Regulators hope that short-term creditors of those subsidiaries (including uninsured depositors, repo lenders, commercial paper holders, and derivatives counterparties) will not engage in panicked runs because they will receive full protection. The home country supervisor of the SIFI's parent holding company will maintain sole control over its resolution because the holding company will be the only entity placed in receivership. In theory, the home country supervisor will be able to complete the resolution without needing any approvals from regulators or courts in other countries where the SIFI's subsidiaries conduct business.[77]

Despite the claimed advantages of the SPOE-TLAC strategy, it is not likely to work during a systemic financial crisis. Regulators have made a very serious mistake by allowing SIFIs to rely on long-term debt securities, instead of equity stock, as their primary form of TLAC funding. Under the Fed's current TLAC rules, U.S. G-SIBs are permitted to operate with a Tier 1 leverage equity ratio of only 5%. They can satisfy the rest of their TLAC leverage requirement by issuing long-term debt securities. Other developed nations allow their G-SIBs to rely even more heavily on long-term debt.[78]

Due to regulators' very heavy reliance on TLAC debt, the SPOE-TLAC strategy depends on the ability of regulators to recapitalize a failed SIFI's important subsidiaries by "bailing in" the parent holding company's TLAC debt, either through write-offs or through conversions into equity. For example, the EU's BRRD mandates that bail-in debtholders must incur large losses (equal to at least 8% of the bank's risk-weighted assets) when a large Eurozone bank is rescued. However, past financial crises have demonstrated that equity capital is a far more resilient and effective resource for absorbing losses from bank failures, compared with hybrid or convertible instruments like bail-in debt.[79]

SPOE-TLAC's reliance on "bail-in" TLAC debt is likely to be a fatal flaw. Regulators do not want SIFIs to sell their TLAC debt to other SIFIs. Cross-holdings of TLAC debt among SIFIs would create a dangerous web of interdependence and contagion, as the collapse of one SIFI could cause serious losses for other SIFIs that own its TLAC debt. In 2016, the Basel Committee called upon its member nations to adopt strong capital penalties to discourage banks from holding TLAC debt issued by other banks.[80] Paul Tucker, a former Deputy Governor of the Bank of England and one of SPOE's leading architects, warned global financial regulators in 2018 that they should also impose strict limits on investments in TLAC debt by nonbank SIFIs, such as large insurance companies and leading money market mutual funds.[81]

Hedge funds are another group of potential buyers for TLAC debt securities. However, many hedge funds rely on large global banks for credit under "prime brokerage" relationships. Imposing "bail in" losses on TLAC debt held by hedge funds could trigger loan defaults by those funds, thereby inflicting serious losses on big banks. Regulators are therefore likely to discourage megabanks from selling large amounts of their TLAC debt to hedge funds.[82]

To avoid the foregoing problems, regulators have encouraged megabanks to sell most of their TLAC debt securities to mutual funds and pension funds.[83] As a practical matter, sales of TLAC debt to mutual funds and pension funds shift the future costs of rescuing megabanks from taxpayers to individual savers and pensioners. Regulators evidently view savers and pensioners as politically expedient target groups for bearing losses from megabank failures. That view seems to be based on the assumption that savers and pensioners will not have enough political clout to stop regulators from bailing in TLAC debt when megabanks fail.

If that is in fact the assumption behind the SPOE-TLAC strategy, it is severely mistaken. As described earlier, the SPOE-TLAC strategy will keep all important subsidiaries of failing financial giants in operation during SPOE resolutions, thereby providing full protection to the subsidiaries' short-term creditors. Those short-term creditors will include Wall Street investors like uninsured institutional depositors, repo lenders, institutional holders of commercial paper, and derivatives counterparties. Protecting Wall Street investors while inflicting losses from megabank failures on ordinary investors whose mutual funds and pension funds hold TLAC debt will be highly controversial as a political matter. I agree with Avinash Persaud that "pushing pensioners [and savers] under the bus" to save short-term Wall Street creditors will be no more palatable than forcing taxpayers to finance bailouts of megabanks.[84]

Thus, regulators will almost certainly face vehement political opposition if they try to impose large losses on mutual funds and pension funds that hold TLAC debt issued by failed SIFIs. Recent events have shown that imposing losses on retail bondholders in failed banks is just as "politically explosive" as forcing taxpayers to cover the cost of bailouts.[85] In addition, inflicting losses on bondholders is very likely to trigger panicked fire sales among holders of bail-in debt securities issued by other large banks that are viewed as troubled institutions. The market for European bail-in bonds was severely shaken by a cascade of selling in 2016, caused by investor concerns about the safety of bail-in bonds issued by Deutsche Bank and other weak European banks.[86]

In December 2015, Italy's government provoked a political firestorm by inflicting losses on individual holders of bail-in bonds issued by four failed Italian banks. Similarly, institutional bondholders filed lawsuits after (1) Portugal imposed losses on bail-in bonds issued by a large failed bank (Novo Banco) in 2016, and (2) the EU's Single Resolution Board (SRB) imposed losses on bail-in bonds as part of its emergency sale of Banco Popular to Santander in 2017. As a result of the intense controversies surrounding those transactions, the SRB has not forced bail-in bondholders to absorb losses since the Banco Popular sale.[87]

In mid-2017, Italy recapitalized Monte dei Paschi di Siena and provided financial support for Banca Intesa Sanpaolo's acquisitions of two troubled banks. The EU permitted Italian regulators to complete those rescues without inflicting losses on bondholders of the restructured banks. In 2019, the EU allowed Italian authorities to prop up Banca Carige and German officials to rescue Nord LB without imposing losses on bondholders of either bank. All of the foregoing rescues skirted the BRRD's bail-in mandate and severely undermined its credibility.[88] In December 2019, the *Financial Times* charged European authorities with "behaving like addicts unable to kick their habit" because they were "returning to their harmful practice of making taxpayers pay for bankers' and investors' poor lending choices."[89]

The EU's recent de facto waivers of the BRRD's bail-in mandate demonstrate that public officials will find it extremely difficult to inflict large losses on retail owners of TLAC debt. As a result, taxpayers remain on the hook for financing future rescues of failed financial giants. The continued exposure of taxpayers also arises from the fact that the SPOE-TLAC strategy depends crucially on the availability of public funding to cover the liquidity needs of operating subsidiaries of failing SIFIs until the resolution has been completed.

Converting the bail-in TLAC debt of a SIFI's holding company into equity stock would reduce the extent of its insolvency, but only from an accounting standpoint. Such conversions would not provide any new liquid funds to the SIFI's distressed operating subsidiaries. A failing SIFI would almost certainly lack enough liquidity reserves to support its subsidiaries because the SIFI would have to be insolvent (or nearly so) to justify an OLA receivership or a comparable resolution under U.K. or EU law.

In addition, a failing SIFI (or its successor BFC) would be very unlikely to attract significant new equity or debt funding from private investors or lenders, particularly during a financial crisis. Accordingly, the resolution authority would have to draw on public funding from the central bank or another government agency to furnish the liquidity needed by the SIFI's subsidiaries. For example, the FDIC and the Fed provided large amounts of funding to support the operations of Continental Illinois after they bailed out the troubled megabank in 1984.[90]

The Orderly Liquidation Fund, which is administered by the Treasury Department, provides the primary backup source of funding for an OLA receivership in the U.S. As previously discussed, the big-bank lobby, its Republican allies, and the Obama administration defeated efforts to require large financial institutions to pay risk-based premiums to pre-fund the OLF. Consequently, the OLF has a zero balance, and the FDIC will be forced to rely on Treasury-approved OLF loans whenever the assets of a failed SIFI do not cover its resolution costs.[91]

The FDIC is required to impose special assessments on large financial companies to repay Treasury's OLF loans over a five-year period. However, the FDIC (with the Treasury Secretary's approval) can postpone such assessments and extend OLF loans *indefinitely* if such postponements are necessary "to avoid a serious adverse effect on the [U.S.] financial system." During a financial crisis—when many large financial institutions are likely to face serious problems—the FDIC and Treasury would have very strong incentives to postpone assessments and extend the repayment period for OLF loans far beyond their presumptive five-year term. Under those circumstances, OLF loans would become long-term, Treasury-financed (and taxpayer-backed) bridge loans. Those long-term loans would protect short-term Wall Street creditors of failed SIFIs from suffering any losses, as explained previously. Critics would justifiably view such long-term loans as publicly financed bailouts.[92]

It is also highly doubtful whether the SPOE approach can successfully resolve failures of global SIFIs with extensive cross-border operations. During a future systemic crisis, at least some host country regulators would probably decide to "ring-fence" the assets of local subsidiaries of a failed SIFI to preserve those assets for claims asserted by their local consumers and businesses. Host country regulators repeatedly ring-fenced local assets of failing multinational SIFIs during 2008 and 2009. The threat of ring-fencing would make it very difficult for a SIFI's home country supervisor to complete an SPOE resolution without at least the tacit cooperation of host country regulators of the SIFI's significant foreign subsidiaries.[93]

In October 2018, the IMF acknowledged that "cross-border resolution remains an important gap ... there is a need for greater coordination and planning in how cross-border resolution for G-SIBs would be conducted."[94] A month earlier, the Group of 30—a body composed of former central bankers, former senior regulators, and top bank executives—reported that "there is a significant weakness in the collective ability [of home and host country regulators] to manage the cross-border failure of a large multinational institution (let alone several large multinational institutions)."[95]

SPOE-TLAC is a highly theoretical strategy that has never been tested during a major financial crisis. It might possibly succeed in resolving the failure of a single SIFI during relatively benign economic conditions. However, megabanks typically do not become financially distressed for idiosyncratic reasons. Most megabanks follow similar business strategies and have highly correlated risk exposures in the capital markets. As a result, financial giants are likely to suffer simultaneous and highly contagious losses during a systemic crisis, as was true during the banking crises of 1982–91 and 2007–09. When one megabank reaches the brink of insolvency during a crisis, several others will almost certainly be close behind. SPOE-TLAC is very unlikely to work under those circumstances.[96]

For all of the foregoing reasons, Stephen Lubben and I have argued that SPOE-TLAC does not provide a feasible approach for avoiding publicly funded bailouts of megabanks.[97] Pledges of "no more bailouts" by government officials are simply not credible after the events of 2007–09. Policymakers and regulators in the U.S., U.K., and EU authorized massive bailouts and protected all creditors of troubled SIFIs after they witnessed the devastating creditor runs triggered by the failures of Lehman Brothers and Washington Mutual. Based on his experiences as Assistant Treasury Secretary during the financial crisis, Neel Kashkari concluded that it is not realistic to expect "in the middle of economic distress . . . that the government will start imposing losses on debt holders [of megabanks], potentially increasing fear and panic among investors."[98]

Many analysts agree with Kashkari that bailouts of large, troubled financial institutions are inevitable during systemic crises.[99] Some experts maintain that the only practical way to avoid bailouts is to make sure that systemic crises never occur. Accordingly, they argue that governments and central banks must be prepared to provide a comprehensive backstop for the entire financial system—an approach that goes far beyond the traditional role of central banks as lenders of last resort for the banking industry. Their recommendations focus on vulnerabilities in the shadow banking system, where nonbank financial firms rely on repos, commercial paper, and other uninsured short-term liabilities to finance longer-term loans. As shown during the financial crisis of 2007–09, holders of uninsured short-term liabilities in the shadow banking system are very likely to engage in contagious, destabilizing runs whenever they perceive the threat of a serious crisis.[100]

Perry Mehrling contends that the Fed should act as "dealer of last resort" during a potential crisis by purchasing or guaranteeing financial assets that are used as collateral in shadow banking transactions. Eric Posner maintains that Congress should give the Fed even broader crisis-fighting powers, including the authority to provide unsecured loans to nonbank firms and to exercise regulatory control over nonbank firms that borrow from the Fed. Kathryn Judge recommends that Congress should authorize the Treasury to act as "guarantor of last resort" during threatened crises by issuing guarantees for designated classes of financial instruments (including uninsured short-term liabilities of shadow banks). Jeffrey Manns proposes that Congress should create a Federal Government Investment Corporation, which would act as "investor of last resort" by purchasing equity interests in troubled SIFIs during serious financial disruptions.[101]

The principal architects of the response to the last crisis—Ben Bernanke, Tim Geithner, and Hank Paulson—emphatically agree that federal agencies should have open-ended authority to prevent financial disruptions from becoming systemic crises. They have criticized the Dodd-Frank Act for cutting back on authorities that the Fed, FDIC, and Treasury used to prop up the entire financial system (including shadow banking markets) during the 2007–09 crisis.[102] Dodd-Frank amended Section 13(3) of the Federal Reserve Act to prevent the Fed from providing emergency loans in the future to individual nonbank firms like AIG. Under Section 13(3) as amended by Dodd-Frank, the Fed may provide such loans only to solvent firms and only through programs with "broad-based eligibility." Dodd-Frank also prohibits Treasury from using the Exchange Stabilization Fund to back future guarantee programs for money market mutual funds. In addition, Dodd-Frank bars the FDIC from establishing future debt guarantee programs for banks, bank holding companies, or their nonbank affiliates unless the FDIC first obtains approval from both the Treasury Secretary and Congress.[103]

Bernanke, Geithner, and Paulson contend that Congress should restore all of the authorities curtailed by Dodd-Frank so that "financial firefighters have the emergency powers they need to prevent the next fire from becoming a conflagration." They believe that the Fed, FDIC, and Treasury must be able to provide comprehensive guarantees for "uninsured, short-term funding" in shadow banking markets, as they did during the last crisis.[104] Geithner goes even further, stating that federal agencies must have authority not only "to guarantee liabilities at the core of the financial system" but also "to recapitalize that system if necessary."[105]

Thus, the leaders of the response to the last financial crisis and other experts agree that post-crisis reforms have *not* removed the need for publicly financed rescues of universal banks and shadow banks when the next systemic crisis occurs. Their proposals for unlimited government backstops confirm that we have *not* changed the fundamental financial conditions that caused the last crisis. Universal banks continue to benefit from open-ended TBTF subsidies. Shadow banks continue to maintain close connections with universal banks while relying on volatile, short-term, wholesale funding sources that pose serious threats to financial stability. Financial executives and investors expect that governments and central banks will intervene to support the entire financial system whenever the threat of a serious disruption appears.

During his testimony before a parliamentary subcommittee in 2014, HSBC chairman Douglas Flint described—with remarkable candor—precisely what the preservation of the status quo means for universal banks and society. Flint acknowledged that universal banks received an "implicit subsidy" during the financial crisis. He explained that governments provided that subsidy "because investment banking operations were alongside society's deposits, [and] there was an implicit underwriting of all the debt within the operation because one would not risk the systemic panic that would happen if people thought their deposits were at risk."

Flint also confirmed that post-crisis reforms have not changed the fundamental nature of the pre-crisis financial system. He asserted that "society" must continue to pay for the costs of resolving failed universal banks, and he noted that bail-in debt provides a method for "distributing the burden of failure" from taxpayers to pensioners and ordinary savers. As Flint bluntly pointed out, "Whether you take it out of society's future income through taxation or whether you take it out through their pensions or savings, *society is bearing the cost.*"[106]

Flint's testimony in 2014 provided a highly revealing glimpse into the mindset of financial leaders on Wall Street and in the City of London. Flint never mentioned the possibility that executives and other key insiders of failed megabanks might incur personal liability for authorizing or implementing high-risk strategies that result in the failure of their institutions. On the contrary, he and other top executives on Wall Street and in the City of London believed—both before *and* after the financial crisis—that megabanks and their insiders should keep their profits and bonuses from high-risk activities while "society"—including taxpayers, pensioners, and ordinary savers—should bear any losses. As indicated by Flint's statements, leaders of megabanks continue to assume that "privatizing the gains and socializing the losses" will remain a central (if unacknowledged) feature of financial regulatory policy. Their assumption is understandable, given the enormous bailouts that universal banks and shadow banks received during the last financial crisis and the widely shared view among policymakers and experts that similar measures must be taken in response to future crises.[107]

Studies have documented the massive TBTF subsidies that U.S., U.K., and European universal banks received during and after the crisis of 2007–09. The magnitude of those subsidies has decreased somewhat over the past several years, due to improving economic conditions and stronger post-crisis regulations. However, under the current regulatory framework, TBTF subsidies will undoubtedly expand again during the next crisis, when governments step in to provide "catastrophe insurance" that protects megabanks and large shadow banks from the risk of failure.[108] As shown by Flint's testimony and the views of many experts, expectations of future public bailouts for universal banks and large shadow banks remain firmly entrenched, and "society" remains on the hook for covering the costs of those bailouts.

———

In addition to bailing out megabanks during the financial crisis, governments allowed some megabanks to become significantly larger by acquiring troubled peers. In 2008 and 2009, the U.S. government provided extensive financial support that enabled (1) BofA to absorb Countrywide and Merrill Lynch, (2) JPMC to acquire Bear Stearns and Washington Mutual, and (3) Wells Fargo to acquire Wachovia. As a result of those transactions, BofA, JPMC and Wells Fargo expanded their combined share of U.S. deposits from 20% to 32% between 2007 and 2017. The same three banks and Citigroup increased their combined share of U.S. banking industry assets from 32%

to 44% between 2005 and 2018.[109] Similarly, the U.K. government supported Lloyds TSB's takeover of HBOS and also approved Santander's acquisitions of Alliance and Leicester.[110]

Government support helped JPMC, BofA, Citigroup, Goldman Sachs, and Morgan Stanley to achieve unquestioned dominance over the world's capital markets. Those five megabanks have been the five leading global investment banks since 2015, and they captured a third of all global investment banking revenues in 2017 and 2018. They have established a clear superiority in the world's capital markets over their U.K. and European competitors.[111] In addition, Wells Fargo significantly expanded its investment banking operations after acquiring Wachovia in 2008, and it is now a top-tier global universal bank.[112]

U.K. and European universal banks have produced disappointing results since 2010, due in large part to the EU's sovereign debt crises and weak recoveries in their domestic economies. Even so, seven big U.K. and European banks—Barclays, BNP Paribas, Credit Suisse, Deutsche Bank, HSBC, Société Générale, and UBS—continue to play significant roles in the world's capital markets. Those seven banks consistently ranked among the top dozen global investment banks between 2009 and 2018, despite losing ground to their U.S. competitors.[113]

Thus, the Big Seventeen group of financial conglomerates, which dominated the world's financial markets in 2007, has become a slightly smaller but equally dominant group of thirteen global universal banks. Bear Stearns, Lehman Brothers, and Merrill Lynch disappeared in 2008, and their investment banking operations were absorbed by larger universal banks (JPMC, Barclays, and BofA) with government help. RBS divested more than 60% of its assets and gave up its global investment banking ambitions at the insistence of its majority owner, the U.K. government. The remaining Big Thirteen universal banks—six from the U.S. and seven from the U.K. and Europe—remain the leaders in global capital markets activities.[114]

JPMC, BofA, Citigroup, and Goldman Sachs are the four largest global dealers in derivatives, followed by the rest of the Big Thirteen. The Big Thirteen are highly influential members of the three main clearinghouses for derivatives—LCH SwapClear, ICE Clear Credit, and ICE Clear Europe. LCH SwapClear controls over 95% of the worldwide market for centrally cleared interest-rate derivatives, while the two ICE clearinghouses jointly control over 95% of the global market for centrally cleared credit default swaps. In 2019, about four-fifths of interest-rate derivatives and half of credit derivatives were cleared in global markets.[115]

Representatives of the Big Thirteen control the membership rules and dominate the risk committees of the three principal derivatives clearinghouses. The biggest derivatives dealers have allegedly abused their controlling influence by (1) preventing smaller derivatives dealers from becoming members of the top clearinghouses and (2) blocking the growth of alternative trading venues.[116] In 2016, eleven members of the Big Thirteen and RBS paid $1.9 billion to settle claims of antitrust violations for "suppress[ing] price transparency and competition in the trading market for CDS," and for obstructing the creation of competing CDS trading facilities.[117]

The Big Thirteen also dominate the International Swaps and Derivatives Association, the trade association and standard-setting body for the derivatives industry. ISDA appoints representatives of the biggest dealers to serve as members of "determinations committees," which adjudicate CDS-related disputes. Those disputes include disagreements over the occurrence of designated "credit events" that require payouts by protection sellers to protection buyers under CDS.[118] Critics allege that ISDA's determinations committees have frequently issued decisions that are biased in favor of the trading positions of the largest banks.[119]

Thus, post-crisis reforms have not reduced the dominance of the largest universal banks as dealers in derivatives markets. The leading global derivatives dealers have extensive connections with the most important clearinghouses as members, custodians, brokers, and providers of credit, investment, and settlement services. A recent study showed that (1) five big U.S. banks held more than half of all customer funds connected to centrally cleared derivatives in U.S. markets, and (2) ten big banks—six from the U.S. and four from the U.K. and Europe—held more than three-quarters of those customer funds. Similarly, twenty large global banks maintained more than three-quarters of the total financial reserves for the world's three hundred top clearing facilities. Consequently, the failure of a top derivatives dealer could potentially threaten the solvency of major clearinghouses, thereby creating the potential for a systemic crisis in derivatives markets.[120]

Title VIII of Dodd-Frank empowers the Fed to regulate and provide emergency loans to systemically important clearing facilities. However, Dodd-Frank does not give the Fed (or any other agency) explicit authority to recapitalize and resolve a failed clearinghouse. Most other developed nations have similarly failed to establish explicit resolution regimes for large clearing facilities. In the absence of a viable resolution process, governments would probably be forced to arrange ad hoc bailouts of large troubled clearinghouses to prevent serious financial market disruptions.[121]

———

As shown by their central roles in derivatives markets, universal banks create extensive and complex networks with shadow banks through their capital markets activities. Universal banks work "in concert" with nonbank financial firms in the shadow banking system, and the two sectors are "strongly interrelated."[122]

Universal banks obtain a significant portion of their funding from the shadow banking system. In 2018, large U.S. and foreign banks sold more than $600 billion of commercial paper to wholesale investors, and their broker-dealer subsidiaries received over $2 trillion of additional funding from securities repurchase agreements (repos) and other securities lending arrangements. Money market mutual funds buy much of the commercial paper issued by the largest banks, and those funds also provide repo loans to the broker-dealer subsidiaries of the same banks.[123]

Megabanks are closely connected to shadow banks through a wide range of transactions. The largest banks act as prime brokers for hedge funds and provide credit, trading, and clearing services to those funds.[124] Big banks also make loans to many other shadow banks. Cross-border loans from large banks to shadow banks have risen at an annual rate of 7% since 2014 and totaled $7 trillion in mid-2019.[125]

Megabanks work in partnership with private equity firms to finance highly leveraged corporate buyouts and reorganizations by arranging syndicated leveraged loans and by underwriting high-yield, below-investment-grade (junk) bonds. Megabanks sell leveraged loans to institutional investors, including sponsors of collateralized loan obligations. CLOs securitize leveraged loans for sale to other investors. Private equity firms have established their own broker-dealer subsidiaries, and they finance highly leveraged corporate transactions alongside banks—and increasingly in competition with banks. In 2017, banks held $103 trillion of credit assets (loans and debt securities) on a worldwide basis. Insurance companies held $17 trillion of global credit assets, while other financial institutions (including private equity firms and hedge funds) held $41 trillion of global credit assets.[126]

Abundant credit provided by universal banks and shadow banks has encouraged explosive growth in private sector debts on a national (U.S.) and global basis since 2000. Public sector debts have also increased rapidly, especially after 2007 as governments spent huge sums to mitigate the social and economic impacts of the financial crisis. By 2019, business firms, households, and sovereigns confronted record-high debt burdens in the U.S. and in many other countries. [127]

Total debts owed by U.S. nonfinancial businesses climbed to an all-time high of $16.1 trillion in 2019. At least a third of those debts consisted of higher-risk obligations, including junk bonds, leveraged loans, and corporate bonds with the lowest investment-grade rating (BBB).[128] Similarly, U.S. household debts reached a record level of $14.1 trillion in 2019, due to significant growth in home mortgages, auto loans, credit card loans, and student loans.[129] Total U.S. private sector debts (including the obligations of nonprofits and financial firms) rose to $48.9 trillion in 2019, up from $22.5 trillion in 2000 and $41.6 trillion in 2007. Total U.S. public sector debts (federal, state, and local) equaled $26.3 trillion in 2019, a steep rise from $6.9 trillion in 2000 and $12.1 trillion in 2007.[130]

Global debt levels have followed the same trajectory of relentless growth. Worldwide private sector and public sector debts rose from $84 trillion in 2000 to $167 trillion in 2007 and $253 trillion in 2019. As reflected in Figure 12.1, the ratio of worldwide debts to global GDP increased from 225% in 2000 to 275% in 2007 and reached an all-time record of 322% in 2019.[131] Worldwide government debts in 2019 reached their highest level as a percentage of global GDP since World War II, "raising profound questions about the sustainability of the global debt pile."[132]

Central banks have supported the rapid expansion of global debts since 2008 by purchasing massive volumes of government bonds, mortgage-backed securities, and other private sector financial instruments under quantitative easing (QE) policies. The total balance sheets of central banks in the U.S., U.K., EU, and Japan grew from $4 trillion to $15 trillion between 2008 and 2018. The collective expansion of their balance sheets absorbed more than 10% of the total increase in global debts during

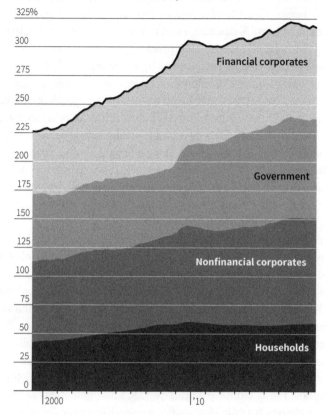

Global debt as a share of GDP, by sector

Figure 12.1 Increases in the Ratio of Global Debt to Global GDP, by Sector, 2000–2017
Source: Wall Street Journal (2019)

the same period. The balance sheets of the Fed and the Bank of England each grew from 6% to 25% of national GDP between 2006 and 2014. The balance sheet of the European Central Bank reached 34% of Eurozone GDP at the end of 2016, while the Bank of Japan's balance sheet equaled 88% of national GDP.[133]

As explained in Chapter 11, central banks adopted QE policies to push down long-term interest rates, thereby reducing debt service costs for heavily indebted households, business firms, and governments, while also supporting housing markets, stabilizing financial markets, and encouraging economic growth. By 2017, central banks around the world held on their balance sheets $30 trillion of financial assets (representing 8% of global financial assets), compared with $150 trillion of worldwide financial assets held by banks and an equivalent amount held by insurance companies and other nonbank financial institutions.[134]

Beginning in 2017, central banks tried to change their general policy approach from quantitative easing to quantitative tightening (QT). The Fed led that policy shift by raising its short-term interest rate target seven times in 2017 and 2018, and by shrinking its balance sheet from $4.5 trillion to less than $4 trillion during that period. The BoE raised its short-term interest rate target in August 2018. The ECB stopped buying Eurozone government bonds in December 2018.[135]

The coordinated moves by central banks toward a QT policy provoked widespread alarm in global financial markets. Many investors feared that central banks would stop supporting financial markets with fresh infusions of liquidity. Investors worried about the sustainability of economic growth and asset price levels without continued support from central banks. During the fourth quarter of 2018, rising pessimism among investors produced a sharp sell-off of risky assets in global markets and a strong move toward "safer" assets (such as U.S. Treasury bonds). The magnitude of that sell-off demonstrated that investor sentiment in the world's financial markets was highly dependent on investor confidence that central banks would continue to provide liquidity to those markets.[136]

The market turbulence in late 2018 jolted the Fed and other central banks. In January 2019, the Fed made "one of its sharpest U-turns in recent memory."[137] The Federal Open Market Committee announced that it would be "patient" before making any further increases in short-term interest rates. The FOMC also said that it would "stop reducing the Federal Reserve's asset holdings" and would be willing to expand the Fed's balance sheet "if future economic conditions warrant a more accommodative monetary policy."[138]

The FOMC strengthened its policy U-turn at its subsequent meetings in 2019. In March, the FOMC confirmed that it did not expect to raise short-term interest rates during the rest of the year. The FOMC then made a series of three interest rate cuts (each in the amount of 0.25%) in July, September, and October.[139]

In October, the Fed announced that it would again expand its balance sheet by purchasing short-term Treasury bills to increase bank reserves and improve liquidity in financial markets. The Fed's announcement followed a sudden and unexpected liquidity squeeze in the repo market in late September. The Fed injected almost $500 billion of fresh liquidity into financial markets between September and December 2019 by providing repo loans and purchasing short-term Treasury bills.[140]

Other central banks joined the Fed in easing their monetary policies. In March 2019, the ECB made its own U-turn by stating that it would not increase interest rates during the rest of the year and would maintain the existing size of its balance sheet. The ECB also announced a new program offering long-term loans to banks on favorable terms, thereby allowing banks (especially Italian and Spanish banks) to refinance their existing long-term loans from the ECB.[141] In September the ECB cut its short-term interest rate target to a record low of −0.5%. The ECB also restored its QE program and promised to purchase €20 billion of Eurozone bonds each month for the indefinite future.[142]

The dramatic U-turns by the Fed and other central banks in 2019 demonstrated their willingness "to extend a decade-long stance of easy money" in order to prevent "market turmoil [from] infecting the broader economy."[143] Those policy reversals "gave traders and investors everything they could have hoped for."[144] Global financial markets staged a strong rally in 2019 in response to the renewed support provided by central banks.[145]

The Powell Fed's U-turn in 2019 resembled (1) the Bernanke Fed's decision to maintain its QE3 program in 2013, after a "taper tantrum" broke out in emerging markets following rumors that the Fed might terminate that program, and (2) the Yellen Fed's postponement of further interest rate hikes after a similar market disruption occurred in 2016.[146] The Powell Fed's U-turn in 2019 represents the most recent example of the "Fed put"—namely, the Fed's willingness to ease monetary policy to calm distressed financial markets. The Powell Fed's actions in 2019 followed a pattern established by the Greenspan Fed's interventions in response to serious market disruptions in 1987, 1998, and the early 2000s, and by the Bernanke Fed's extraordinary measures to stabilize markets during the financial crisis and its aftermath.[147]

As Mohamed El-Erian pointed out, "The Powell-led Fed has now learned what its two predecessors did: that a highly levered economy means that, when push comes to shove, markets end up leading central banks rather than the other way around." Thus, central banks were "forced to abandon hopes of normalizing monetary policies" in 2019, and they resumed "unconventional monetary policies in a world awash in debt." El-Erian described the collective U-turn by central banks in 2019 as "the most accommodative global central bank policy stance since the global financial crisis."[148]

The coordinated easing of monetary policy by central banks in 2019 confirms that policymakers have *not* resolved the systemic problems in financial markets that led to the financial crisis of 2007–09. The same interlocking system of universal banks and shadow banks remains in place, and that system continues to inflate a global debt bubble comparable to the one that burst in 2007. As shown previously, universal banks and shadow banks are financing record volumes of private and public debt that pose grave threats to the stability of households, businesses, and governments. Market participants continue to believe—with considerable justification—that governments and central banks will intervene to support financial markets whenever they encounter serious problems.[149]

Central banks have severely distorted market signals by stabilizing financial markets whenever there are threats of significant disruptions. As one hedge fund manager observed, "capitalism is fast disappearing" as central banks keep interest rates artificially low and undermine the effectiveness of market discipline. Another hedge fund manager commented, "Modern financial systems have grown dependent on huge central bank balance sheets."[150] A Bloomberg analyst said that "the Fed has put a ceiling on bond yields and a floor under the S&P 500." William White, a leading international economist, warned that "markets were unable to allocate resources properly, due to the actions of central banks."[151]

As explained in Chapter 11, central banks pushed interest rates to record lows after 2008 to boost the values of mortgage-related assets held by banks, stabilize housing markets, and reduce debt service burdens for heavily indebted governments, businesses, and households. In spite of those benefits, the prolonged maintenance of ultra-low interest rates over the past decade has produced very disturbing side effects. Ultra-low interest rates reduce the profits earned by safer, lower-yielding loans and investments. Ultra-low rates therefore push investors and creditors (including banks) to pursue riskier, higher-yielding assets, thereby boosting the market values of those assets. The resulting "search for yield" has caused speculative loans, securities, and commercial real estate investments to reach dangerous levels in recent years.

In addition, ultra-low rates aggravate social inequality by widening the gap between the larger returns received by wealthy investors on riskier, higher-yielding assets and the very low returns received by risk-averse retail investors on deposits and government bonds. Investment gains for wealthy families have risen at a much faster rate than the savings and wages of middle-class families. Thus, ultra-low rates have widened the disparities in household income and wealth that existed before the financial crisis.[152]

Mike Mayo has argued that the Fed's post-crisis monetary policies produced a large "wealth transfer from prudent savers to the borrowers and risk takers." He calculated that American savers have lost $500 billion to $600 billion since 2008, due to abnormally low yields on their bank accounts and money market mutual funds.[153] The highly skewed wealth and income effects of unconventional central bank policies have provoked extensive debates about the wisdom and legitimacy of those policies.[154] Some commentators contend that ultra-low interest rates also undermine economic growth and create "secular stagnation" by enabling inefficient "zombie firms" to roll over their debts and remain in operation, thereby crowding out entry by more productive and profitable firms.[155]

———

In sum, post-crisis regulatory and monetary policies have produced a fragile and volatile global financial system, which depends on continuous infusions of central bank liquidity to support universal banks, large shadow banks, and the capital markets. Post-crisis policies have created what I call a "global doom loop," in which governments, central banks, universal banks, shadow banks, and capital markets are locked together in a dangerous web of mutual dependence. Governments and central banks must prevent disorderly failures of universal banks and large shadow banks to preserve the stability of capital markets. Governments and central banks must also prevent serious disruptions in capital markets to ensure the survival of systemically important financial institutions. Central banks must maintain unconventional monetary policies to keep interest rates low, boost asset prices, and support the continued growth of sovereign and private sector debts. Universal banks and shadow banks are more than happy to finance the continued expansion of those debts. William White has warned that "central-bank meddling" will be "a permanent fixture of 21st century financial markets" until a severe "growth shock" occurs.[156]

The perverse dynamics of the global doom loop were vividly illustrated in September 2019, when the Fed dramatically intervened in the U.S. repo market. The repo market experienced a sudden shortage of funding on September 17, and interest rates for overnight repo loans spiked. The primary reasons for that funding shortage were (1) increased demands by hedge funds for repo loans to finance highly leveraged arbitrage trades, and (2) refusals by the four largest U.S. banks—the dominant repo lenders—to satisfy those demands. The Fed intervened to stabilize the repo market by pouring almost $500 billion of additional liquidity into the financial markets (through repo loans and purchases of short-term Treasury bills) between September and December 2019.[157]

Thus, a collective breakdown in repo funding between megabanks and shadow banks forced the Fed to rescue the repo market and intensify its easing of monetary policy. Zoltan Pozsar described the Fed's intervention as a "repo bazooka."[158] Frances Coppola warned that "the repo market is becoming the principal market through which monetary policy is transmitted. But it is poorly understood and extremely concentrated. *Do we really want the transmission of monetary policy to depend entirely upon four large banks?*"[159]

The Fed's dramatic intervention in the repo market confirmed once again that universal banks are *not* superior risk-bearers, despite their claims to the contrary. The largest U.S. universal banks were unwilling to satisfy the repo market's liquidity needs in September 2019, even though a crisis did not exist in the financial markets. They refused to act and forced the Fed to step in.

The Fed's rescue of the repo market revealed that its monetary policy measures are inextricably tied to—and effectively held hostage by—universal banks, large shadow banks, and wholesale funding markets. As Gennadiy Goldberg pointed out in December 2019, "The Fed will not want to exit repo operations until they are absolutely certain the market can stand on its own two feet."[160] In January 2020, former New York Fed President Bill Dudley called on the Fed to establish a "standing repo facility," which would "address the potential problem of the Fed providing liquidity to primary dealers but primary dealers *not* lending the funds to other market participants that might need short-term repo financing."[161] Dudley's proposal, which other former Fed officials supported,[162] would permit big universal banks to shirk their roles as liquidity providers while committing the Fed to step in as the liquidity provider of last resort for all market participants.

As has been shown, the global doom loop connecting governments, central banks, universal banks, shadow banks, and the capital markets has supported a steady rise in global debt levels. A study by Oscar Jordà, Moritz Schularick, Alan Taylor, and Felix Ward concluded that the continuous growth in worldwide debts over the past three decades has intensified the "global risk appetite" of investors, boosted asset prices, and produced a "synchronization" of boom-bust cycles across global financial markets. Their study found that bank loans, housing prices, and equity prices have displayed significantly stronger "comovements" (correlations) across national borders since the early 1990s, as central banks, global megabanks, and shadow banks financed massive increases in private and public debts. The relentless growth of private and public debts has produced much higher ratios of credit to GDP on both national and global levels. Those elevated debt-to-credit ratios are leading risk indicators for future financial crises.[163]

Claudio Borio, Mathias Drehmann, and Dora Xia performed a similar study of the "global financial cycle." Their study showed that lenient monetary and regulatory regimes encouraged the expansion of credit, which in turn boosted asset values and produced more collateral to support more credit growth. The resulting credit cycle has generated a series of credit booms, financial crises, and severe recessions across the globe since 1980. In addition, the amplitude (volatility) of the global financial cycle has become much larger as central banks adopted low interest rate policies and developed and emerging countries implemented financial liberalization programs.[164]

The foregoing studies indicate that the global doom loop linking governments, central banks, universal banks, shadow banks, and capital markets is likely to trigger a future financial crisis that will be even more devastating than the last one. As shown by recent events, global financial markets rely heavily on "the promise of more QE"— an unhealthy addiction that makes markets "more fragile than we think."[165] At the same time, governments and central banks have exhausted much of their fiscal and monetary resources in dealing with the last financial crisis. Massive sovereign debt burdens, bloated central bank balance sheets, and ultra-low interest rates indicate that governments and central banks have only limited room to fight the next crisis.[166]

Bank of England Governor Mark Carney recently warned that "there's much less ammunition for all the major central banks than they previously had," and "it's not clear that monetary policy would have sufficient space" to deal with a future systemic crisis. Similarly, Ben Bernanke, Tim Geithner, and Hank Paulson cautioned that the U.S. government's "ability to respond to a collapse in economic demand with monetary and fiscal stimulus" has been "significantly depleted."[167] Thus, it is conceivable that governments and central banks might fail in their efforts to contain the next systemic crisis. Such a failure could potentially unleash a second Great Depression.

––––––

Large universal banks are unquestionably TBTF, due to their central roles in the global doom loop. They are also too big, too complex, and too opaque to be managed or regulated effectively. Global megabanks have sprawling and complex structures, with hundreds or thousands of subsidiaries operating in dozens of countries along with a multitude of off-balance-sheet entities. The risks of global megabanks are extremely difficult to evaluate, compared with large nonfinancial firms, because megabanks hold securities, derivatives, and other financial instruments whose values fluctuate rapidly based on sudden changes in market conditions.[168] Moreover, the largest global megabanks have not reduced their size, complexity, or opacity to any meaningful extent since the crisis of 2007–09.[169]

The continuing scandals and operational failures at global megabanks since the early 2000s demonstrate that their enormous risks cannot be controlled by either their managers or regulators. Eleven of the Big Seventeen financial conglomerates of the early 2000s were involved in the scandals surrounding Enron, WorldCom, biased research analysts, and corrupt practices in initial public offerings.[170] All of today's Big Thirteen universal banks have paid significant civil and/or criminal penalties and settlements during the past decade for a wide array of misconduct, including securities fraud, mortgage fraud, foreclosure abuses, other frauds and abuses related to consumer financial services, collusion in rigging benchmarks for interest rates and foreign exchange rates, facilitating tax evasion by clients, money laundering, and violations of international sanctions against terrorist states and organizations. Since 2008, large global banks have paid over $370 billion in penalties and settlements for such violations. All of the Big Thirteen universal banks and RBS appeared on a 2017 list of the twenty most heavily penalized global financial institutions.[171]

As John Griffin pointed out, "A careful examination of the empirical academic evidence indicates that conflicts of interest, misreporting, and fraud were central features of the securitization chain leading up to the financial crisis." Luigi Zingales similarly concluded that fraud has become a common occurrence within large financial institutions. As he explained, "Not only is the pervasiveness of fraud remarkable—from Libor fixing to exchange rate manipulation, there is hardly any activity untouched by fraud—but also the nonchalance of the people committing it." In 2018, New York Fed President William Dudley said that he was "struck by the fact that manipulation of the foreign exchange market occurred even after the LIBOR [collusion] scandal was well known."[172]

Megabanks that were once viewed as successful institutions have become embroiled in multiple scandals. JPMC paid almost $44 billion of fines and settlements between 2008 and 2018, and it suffered over $6 billion of losses from its "London Whale" derivatives trading debacle in 2012. JPMC was also criticized in 2019 for multiple conflicts of interest that severely compromised its ability to act objectively in managing the aborted initial public offering for WeWork. Wells Fargo paid over $17 billion of fines and settlements between 2008 and 2019, including large penalties for cross-selling abuses (such as the creation of 3.5 million fake accounts without customer consent) and exploitative practices in auto and mortgage lending.[173]

Australian banks were praised for their strong performance during the financial crisis.[174] However, a commission appointed by the Australian government reported in 2019 that the four largest Australian universal banks exhibited systematic "greed and dishonesty" as they charged "excessive commissions," imposed "charges for services never provided, even levied on the dead," and engaged in "rampant mis-selling" of unsuitable financial products. The commission determined that the "roots of the financial scandals" at the big Australian universal banks arose out of toxic cultures that encouraged executives and employees "to chase profits above all." Elizabeth Sheedy (an Australian scholar) stated that Australian banks "exploited their customers on an industrial scale, which helped them to generate super profits."[175]

The pervasiveness of fraud and other serious misconduct at global universal banks indicates that their cultures encourage (or at least tolerate) repeated violations of law and abuses of customers. A 2018 study by John Griffin, Samuel Kruger, and

Gonzalo Maturana found that the largest U.S. banks did not impose significant disciplinary sanctions on senior bankers who approved fraudulent offerings of residential mortgage-backed securities, even when those bankers were personally named in lawsuits filed by federal agencies against the banks. In addition, BofA, Citigroup, and JPMC were "particularly aggressive" in recruiting mortgage bankers from *other* large banks after those banks engaged in fraudulent RMBS offerings. The authors concluded that "these employment outcomes send a message ... that there is little, if any, price to pay for participating in fraudulent and abusive practices" at major banks. That message "reinforces cultural norms that allow and may even encourage employees to ignore warning signs of fraud and abuse."[176]

A 2015 survey of financial professionals working on Wall Street and in the City of London determined that (1) more than a third of high-income respondents (those with annual compensation of $500,000 or more) "witnessed or have first hand knowledge of wrongdoing in the workplace," (2) almost two-fifths of high-income respondents "disagree that the financial services industry puts the best interests of clients first," (3) nearly a third of all respondents believe that "compensation structures/ bonus plans at their company ... could incentivize employees to compromise ethical standards or violate the law," (4) nearly a fifth of all respondents "find it likely that their employer would retaliate if they were to report wrongdoing in the workplace," (5) almost half of high-income respondents "think law enforcement and regulatory authorities in their country are ineffective in detecting, investigating, and prosecuting securities violations," and (6) a third of all respondents "do not believe the financial services industry has changed for the better since the financial crisis."[177] Andrew Ross Sorkin commented that the survey "paints a troubling picture ... Rather than indicating that Wall Street has cleaned itself up, it suggests that ... the mind-boggling settlement numbers, as well as [Dodd-Frank's] stringent new rules, appear to have had little deterrent effect."[178]

Another revealing study reviewed surveys that measured the levels of "trust" expressed by various U.S. groups in the honesty of people and the effectiveness of public institutions between 1978 and 2016. The study found that trust levels declined to a much greater degree among financial industry workers during that period, compared with workers in other industries and the U.S. population as a whole. The decline in trust among financial industry workers was "particularly strong in the investment sector and among professionals with higher seniority, i.e., those who set the tone." The study concluded that the "unparalleled" drop in trust among financial industry workers was a matter of great concern, given the rising number of "financial scandals" and the "conflicts of interest, ... high complexity and informational asymmetry" generated by large financial institutions.[179]

In 2012, Greg Smith publicly resigned from his senior position at Goldman Sachs after criticizing the firm's "toxic and destructive" culture. As he explained:

I attend derivatives sales meetings where not one single minute is spent asking questions about how we can help clients. It's purely about how we can make the most possible money off of them.

It makes me ill how callously people talk about ripping their clients off. Over the past 12 months I have seen five different managing directors refer to their own clients as "muppets."[180]

In 2018, a Group of 30 study stated, "Skeptics wonder whether true change is possible in an industry that maintains large potential upsides to pushing the boundaries and [they] point to the example of Wall Street in 2017 recording its highest bonuses since 2006." New York Fed President William Dudley stated that post-crisis scandals "were particularly disturbing in terms of their scale and flagrancy ... These episodes underscore the tremendous power that incentives have to influence and distort behavior." Similarly, William Coen, Secretary General of the Basel Committee, observed, "The global financial crisis raised fundamental questions about ethics, incentives, and moral behaviour.... 10 years after the crisis, we continue to see episodes of bank practices that breach any basic ethical and moral principles."[181]

Despite strong evidence that universal bank cultures have *not* changed since the financial crisis, Trump-appointed bank regulators have relaxed their oversight while giving a "low priority" to efforts to improve "bank culture." Federal agencies have never issued final rules to prohibit compensation arrangements that encourage excessive risk-taking, despite the explicit mandate for such rules in Section 956(b) of Dodd-Frank.[182] In 2019, the Fed announced that its stress test reports would no longer include public disclosures of the Fed's "objections" to capital distributions by the largest U.S. banks based on "qualitative" failures in risk management or operational controls. The Fed said it would address such "qualitative" shortcomings on a confidential basis during private supervisory reviews with bank executives. Evidently the Fed's current leadership believes that megabanks should receive greater "transparency" from the Fed during stress tests but investors and citizens do *not* deserve similar treatment. A senior Fitch Ratings official commented that the Fed's "relaxed" approach for dealing with "qualitative" problems showed that "the regulatory environment is easing, which is a negative for bank creditors."[183]

The Fed reported in 2018 and 2019 that more than 40% of large bank holding companies (those with over $100 billion of assets) have received *unsatisfactory* supervisory ratings since 2009. Those unsatisfactory ratings reflect "weaknesses in one or more areas such as compliance, internal controls, model risk management, operational risk management, and/or data and information technology." The eight biggest U.S. banks and the largest foreign banks with U.S. operations have produced the highest number of unresolved supervisory findings for weaknesses in management controls and compliance.[184]

Despite the magnitude of those shortcomings, the Fed has never exercised its statutory authority to force large banks with unsatisfactory management ratings to divest subsidiaries or activities. The Fed's light-touch responses to legal violations and risk management failures at megabanks are part of a long-standing pattern of failures by federal regulators to supervise big banks effectively.[185] As Edward Kane has pointed out, federal regulators have treated megabanks as not just TBTF but also "too big to discipline adequately."[186]

––––––

Government officials have compounded the pernicious effects of their lax supervision of megabanks by failing to hold senior executives personally accountable for serious misconduct and failures in risk management at those institutions. Until 2019, authorities in developed countries did not pursue criminal charges against top executives of *any* of the Big Seventeen financial conglomerates or their Big Thirteen successors. Prior to 2019, officials brought only two criminal cases against even midlevel executives of those companies: (1) an unsuccessful case against two Bear Stearns officers who managed the two hedge funds that collapsed in July 2007 after investing in subprime mortgage-related securities and (2) a successful case against Kareem Serageldin of Credit Suisse, who "inflat[ed] the value of mortgage bonds in his trading portfolio ... in hopes of receiving a bigger bonus."[187]

In January 2019, four former senior executives of Barclays—including former CEO John Varley—went on trial in London for criminal fraud. U.K. prosecutors charged the four defendants with making more than £320 million of secret corrupt payments to Qatar's sovereign wealth fund and Qatari officials, in exchange for Qatar's agreement to buy £4 billion of Barclays stock in 2008. The four defendants allegedly approved the corrupt payments—and hid them from U.K. regulators and Barclays' shareholders—to secure Qatar's equity investment and thereby avoid a U.K. government bailout of Barclays. The defendants reportedly feared that a government bailout would threaten their jobs as well as their large compensation packages. The Barclays case represented "the first jury trial in the world" in which the CEO of a global megabank faced criminal charges for "actions taken during the 2008 crisis."[188]

In June 2019, a U.K. appellate court affirmed the trial court's dismissal of charges against former CEO Varley for lack of evidence. The appellate court also ordered a new trial for the other three former senior executives. The second trial resulted in a jury verdict acquitting all three defendants in February 2020. The defendants successfully argued that Barclays' directors and legal counsel had reviewed and approved their actions. As a result of their acquittals, "no British bankers will face prison for their actions during the 2008 financial crisis."[189]

A more successful departure from the pattern of non-prosecution of senior executives of global megabanks occurred in Italy. In November 2019, an Italian court convicted three bankers from Deutsche Bank—including Michele Faissola, the former head of Deutsche's asset management and commodities units—and two bankers from Nomura for crimes related to the collapse of Monte dei Paschi di Siena (MPS). The Italian court found that the defendants conspired with MPS's managers to create manipulative derivatives transactions that concealed the magnitude of MPS's losses between 2008 and 2012.[190]

The near-absence of prosecutions against top executives of global universal banks stands in sharp contrast with many successful criminal prosecutions against senior executives of smaller financial firms, lower-level employees of global banks, and other finance professionals for misconduct related to the crisis. Authorities in Iceland and Ireland convicted thirty-two senior bankers after the banking systems of both countries collapsed.[191] U.S. prosecutors convicted the former president and three other senior executives of Wilmington Trust (an $11 billion bank) for lending violations and securities fraud.[192] Former chairman Lee Farkas of the Taylor, Bean & Whitaker mortgage firm received a thirty-year jail sentence for defrauding Colonial Bank, a $25 billion bank that failed in 2009. Federal prosecutors convicted more than three hundred loan officers, real estate developers, mortgage brokers, and real estate brokers for mortgage fraud.[193] U.S. and U.K. prosecutors convicted several low-level and midlevel traders from global banks for colluding to rig benchmarks for interest rates and currency exchange rates and for manipulating prices in commodity markets.[194]

In light of those successful prosecutions, it is difficult to understand why the U.S. Justice Department did not pursue even one criminal prosecution against a top executive of the Big Seventeen financial conglomerates and AIG. As Judge Jed Rakoff pointed out, federal officials did not dispute "the widespread conclusion that fraud at every level permeated the bubble in mortgage-backed securities," in which all eighteen financial giants were implicated. Indeed, the Justice Department sued most of those companies for securities fraud related to their sales of nonprime RMBS and recovered over $100 billion in fines and settlements from them.[195]

The glaring disparity in treatment between senior executives of financial giants and less prominent defendants involved in the financial crisis is part of a broader trend. The Justice Department has brought very few cases against senior executives of Fortune 500 companies since the early 2000s.[196] Possible reasons for that trend include the following:

1. After the Justice Department brought successful prosecutions against senior officers of Enron, WorldCom, Adelphia, and Tyco during the early 2000s, corporate trade groups and the white-collar defense bar lobbied and litigated to obtain changes in law that made it significantly harder to prosecute top executives of big corporations.

2. The Justice Department's resources for investigating and trying complex corporate criminal cases did not keep pace with the rapid growth of white-collar defense practices at premier law firms over the past two decades. Anti-terrorist efforts occupied a much larger share of the Justice Department's attention and personnel after September 11, 2001. Federal prosecutors investigating corporate crimes found it increasingly difficult to match the firepower deployed by white-collar defense firms (which recruited many former senior prosecutors to join their teams).

3. The Justice Department's leaders became more risk-averse after the early 2000s and were reluctant to pursue trials against large corporations or senior executives without a high probability of success. The Justice Department increasingly used deferred prosecution agreements and plea agreements to resolve criminal charges against corporate defendants. Those agreements allowed corporate defendants to hire law firms and consultants to conduct internal investigations and institute compliance programs. Most internal investigations and compliance programs did not identify any wrongdoing by top executives.[197]

Judge Rakoff criticized the Justice Department for using deferred prosecution agreements as its primary tool for addressing misconduct at big banks. Before he became a federal judge, Rakoff represented many "high-level executives" during his career as a white-collar criminal defense lawyer. He observed that "the only thing [his clients] feared was the prospect of spending a day in jail ... whereas being fined, they couldn't care less." In Rakoff's view, "the future deterrent value of successfully prosecuting individuals far outweighs the prophylactic benefits of imposing internal compliance measures that are often little more than window-dressing."[198]

In a September 2014 speech, Attorney General Eric Holder provided a very disturbing rationale for the lack of criminal prosecutions of top financial executives. Holder said that it often was "not possible to establish knowledge of a particular scheme on the part of a high-ranking executive [in a large financial institution] who is far removed from a firm's day-to-day operations." According to Holder, "At some institutions that engaged in inappropriate conduct before, and may yet again, the buck still stops nowhere.... Responsibility remains so diffuse, and top executives so insulated, that any misconduct" could not be attributed to "the willful actions of any single individual."[199] Similarly, Bank of England Governor Mark Carney acknowledged in January 2019 that the threat of jail time for top executives of big banks was "a total bluff," even if a few bankers might be prosecuted "on the margin."[200]

EricHolder's statement that "the buck still stops nowhere" at large financial conglomerates provides the clinching argument for breaking them up. If top executives of universal banks cannot be held personally accountable for pervasive misconduct at their institutions, the only rational conclusion is that universal banks are too big to manage and regulate effectively and must be broken up.[201]

Federal agencies failed to pursue criminal charges or to impose severe civil money penalties against top-level executives of large financial institutions even when there *was* strong evidence of intentional misconduct. For example, Angelo Mozilo, Countrywide's CEO, described first-lien and second-lien subprime mortgages as "toxic" and "poison" in email messages that he sent to his top subordinates. Mozilo also warned his subordinates that Countrywide was "flying blind on how [option ARM] loans will perform in a stressed environment." The SEC filed civil securities fraud charges against Mozilo and two of his senior colleagues for "falsely assuring investors that Countrywide was primarily a prime quality mortgage lender" even though they "actually knew, and acknowledged internally, that Countrywide was writing increasingly risky loans and that defaults and delinquencies would rise as a result." The SEC also charged Mozilo with insider trading. The SEC alleged that he exercised stock options and sold the underlying stock for $140 million of gains during 2006 and 2007, "while he was aware of material, non-public information concerning Countrywide's increasing credit risk and the expected poor performance of Countrywide-originated loans."[202]

Thus, the SEC charged Mozilo and two senior colleagues with willful and knowing violations of federal securities laws. Yet the SEC did not take them to trial. Instead, the SEC entered into a settlement that required Mozilo personally to pay a $22.5 million civil penalty but allowed him to keep $500 million of compensation and profits from stock sales that he received between 2000 and 2008. Mozilo did not admit or deny the SEC's charges, although he did agree to be barred from serving again as an officer or director of a publicly traded company. The settlement provided comparable treatment for Mozilo's two subordinates. The relative leniency of the SEC's settlement with Countrywide's top executives is difficult to reconcile with the seriousness of their alleged violations as well as with the culpable knowledge they displayed in their email messages.[203] It also remains a mystery why the Justice Department decided not to pursue either criminal or civil fraud charges against Mozilo.[204]

The federal government's failure to impose meaningful personal sanctions on senior executives of megabanks for shocking misconduct at their institutions before and after the financial crisis should convince us that universal banks are too dangerous to exist.[205] Unless we break up those banks, we will not stop the infernal cycle of excessive risk-taking, relentless debt growth, boom-and-bust economic cycles, financial crises, massive bailouts, and near-blanket immunity for top executives. As shown in the Conclusion, a new Glass-Steagall Act provides the most feasible and effective way to remove the dangers posed by universal banks.

Conclusion

The Case for a New Glass-Steagall Act

National City Bank and its successor, Citigroup, were the prototypes for first- and second-generation American universal banks during the 1920s and the late 1990s. It is therefore significant that the founders of both universal banks eventually renounced their creations and called for a structural separation between the banking system and the capital markets. The experiences of the 1930s and the 2000s convinced them—and should also persuade us—that universal banks create intolerable risks and impose unacceptable costs on society. We must therefore restore the Glass-Steagall Act, which served our country so well after the Great Depression and World War II.

Citigroup was created by a merger between Citicorp and Travelers in 1998. As described in Chapter 8, that merger put great pressure on Congress to repeal the Glass-Steagall Act in 1999. Ten years later, John Reed (Citicorp's CEO) apologized for his role in creating Citigroup, and he argued that Congress made a serious error when it repealed Glass-Steagall. In a subsequent interview, Reed described the pernicious effects of the "clashing cultures" between Citigroup's investment bankers and commercial bankers. The investment bankers' high-risk trading culture was "infectious," and it quickly became the "dominant" ethos within Citigroup. The trading culture undermined Citigroup's internal risk management because the bank's risk officers were not willing to challenge capital markets deals that produced large bonuses for senior executives and investment bankers. In addition, the wide scope and enormous complexity of Citigroup's operations made it impossible to manage the bank effectively.[1]

At first, Sandy Weill (Travelers' CEO) defended his dual roles as Citigroup's co-founder and as leader of the financial industry's campaign to repeal Glass-Steagall. However, Weill changed his mind by 2012. During a televised interview on CNBC, he called on Congress to "split up investment banking from banking, have banks be deposit takers, have banks make commercial loans and real estate loans, have banks do something that's not going to risk the taxpayer dollars, that's not too big to fail." Weill recommended that universal banks should be "broken up so that the taxpayer will never be at risk, the depositors won't be at risk, the leverage of the banks will be something reasonable." He argued that securities firms should be separated from banks so that securities firms could "make some mistakes" without causing systemic crises.[2]

During the 1920s, Charles Mitchell built National City Bank into a vast "financial department store," which became the model for first-generation American universal banks. Mitchell strongly opposed the Glass-Steagall Act before he was forced to resign as National City's chairman in March 1933. However, he later decided that Glass-Steagall performed an important public service. In testimony before the Federal Monopoly Committee in December 1939, Mitchell described Glass-Steagall as a "great 'step' of progress" because it separated securities firms from commercial banks and thereby ensured the independence of the capital markets. Mitchell told the committee, "I am convinced today that if we had gone along with the development of the securities affiliates [of commercial banks] it would have resulted in monopoly."[3]

Reed, Weill, and Mitchell identified five important reasons for restoring Glass-Steagall's regime of structural separation between the banking system and the capital markets. First, a new Glass-Steagall Act would end the culture clash between investment bankers and commercial bankers within universal banks. Second, it would remove the conflicts of interest that make it impossible for universal banks to act as prudent, objective lenders or as impartial investment advisers. Third, it would reduce systemic risks and improve the stability and resilience of our financial system by creating strong structural buffers between the banking system and other financial sectors. Fourth, it would create a more competitive financial system by ending the control exercised by universal banks over capital markets and by encouraging the formation of new independent securities firms. Fifth, it would prevent large financial conglomerates from exercising an unhealthy dominance over our economy and our political and regulatory systems.

———

Former Fed Chairman Paul Volcker agreed with John Reed that universal banks generate dangerous culture clashes and destructive conflicts of interest. Volcker shared Reed's view that the cultural "cleavage" between investment banking and commercial banking undermines risk management in universal banks and creates "too many conflicts of interest." Volcker concluded that universal banks would never be able to fulfill a "fiduciary responsibility" to their clients because of their divided loyalties and manifold conflicts of interests.[4]

Conflicts of interest are deeply embedded in universal banks, as shown by their successful campaign in recent years to stop federal agencies from establishing a fiduciary duty standard for securities broker-dealers. The proposed fiduciary duty standard would have required securities broker-dealers to act with undivided loyalty when they provided investment recommendations to customers. Universal banks and their allies lobbied and litigated to prevent the Labor Department from establishing a fiduciary duty standard for firms offering investment advice to holders of retirement accounts. Their lobbying campaign also convinced the Securities and Exchange Commission to reject a fiduciary duty standard for all investment recommendations provided by broker-dealers and investment advisers.[5]

The SEC instead adopted a weak and poorly defined "best interest" standard, which allows securities broker-dealers to recommend investments in which they or their affiliates have significant financial interests. In a dissenting statement, Commissioner Robert Jackson criticized the SEC for issuing a standard that "failed to force Wall

Street to put investors first" and "exposes millions of Americans to the costs of con-
flicted advice."[6] As shown by their victorious campaign against the fiduciary duty
standard, universal banks will go to great lengths to defend their business model,
which is deeply compromised by pervasive conflicts of interest.

Conflicts of interest at universal banks produced disastrous sales of speculative
stocks and risky domestic and foreign bonds during the 1920s, as well as calamitous
sales of toxic securities related to nonprime mortgages during the 2000s. During both
periods, universal banks abandoned prudent lending standards and packaged enormous volumes of high-risk loans into purportedly safe securities. Universal banks
conducted high-pressure marketing campaigns, corrupted private sector gatekeepers
(including credit ratings agencies during the 2000s), and made fraudulent representations to sell those securities. Universal banks also undermined their own financial
soundness by making risky loans to support their securities affiliates and hazardous
investments in securities that their affiliates could not sell.[7]

A new Glass-Steagall Act would remove those conflicts of interest by separating
banks and their affiliates from securities firms and the capital markets generally. To
accomplish that separation, Congress should prohibit banks and their affiliates from
underwriting (distributing), dealing (trading), and making markets in securities, except for authorized "bank-eligible" securities such as federal, state, and local government bonds.[8]

A new Glass-Steagall Act should prohibit banks from making private placements
(sales to institutional and other qualified investors) as well as public offerings of securities, except for bank-eligible securities. Private placements create many of the
same conflicts of interest as public offerings, including the "salesman's stake" of a universal bank in marketing and supporting the financial investments that it originates.
Moreover, the disclosure standards for private placements are substantially weaker
than the disclosure requirements governing public offerings. Universal banks sold
most of the toxic CDOs created during the subprime lending boom through private
placements under the SEC's Rule 144A. Those CDOs inflicted devastating losses on
poorly informed institutional investors.[9]

A new Glass-Steagall Act should allow banks and their affiliates to syndicate loans
and to sell loans and loan participations to qualified institutional investors, such as
banks, insurance companies, securities broker-dealers, and asset managers. To encourage sound lending, Congress should require banks to retain at least 5–10% of
the credit risk for each loan they syndicate or sell. Risk retention ("skin in the game")
requirements would discourage banks from originating unsound loans for syndication or sale.[10]

Strong regulation of syndicated lending by banks is essential. Large banks arranged risky syndicated loans for domestic and foreign borrowers during the 1970s
and 1980s, and high default rates on those loans inflicted severe losses on banks.[11]
Regulators must ensure that the up-front fees generated by syndicated loans do not
tempt banks to originate and sell loans with excessive risks. Regulatory oversight
must include vigorous enforcement of both risk retention requirements and prudential safety-and-soundness standards.

While banks should be allowed to syndicate and sell loans, a new Glass-Steagall Act should prohibit banks and their affiliates from converting loans into asset-backed securities (ABS). As shown by the experiences of the 1920s and 2000s, the securitization process is riddled with conflicts of interest. It creates perverse incentives for banks to originate unsound, high-risk loans, package them into ABS, and then use deceptive marketing and fraudulent representations to sell those ABS to investors. A new Glass-Steagall Act should therefore bar banks and their affiliates from underwriting and selling ABS. It should also impose stronger risk retention requirements on securities broker-dealers and other nonbank financial institutions when they underwrite and sell ABS to investors.[12]

A new Glass-Steagall Act would promote higher-quality ABS by (1) imposing risk retention requirements on banks that sell loans to securities broker-dealers for securitization and (2) encouraging broker-dealers to enforce the loan covenants provided by those banks. Securities firms would be independent actors under a new Glass-Steagall Act because they would no longer be affiliated with banks.[13] Securities firms would also face liability risks if they sell unsound ABS to investors. Accordingly, securities firms would have strong incentives to enforce the loan covenants provided by banks. In combination, risk retention requirements and stronger incentives for enforcement of bank loan covenants should help to deter banks from originating and selling unsound or fraudulent loans.

In addition to prohibiting banks from underwriting and trading in securities, Congress should not allow banks and their affiliates to underwrite insurance products. Congress should reinstate the prohibition on insurance underwriting that previously applied to banks and their affiliates under the Bank Holding Company Act of 1956, as amended in 1970 and 1982. Prior to 1999, the BHC Act prevented banks and their affiliates from acting as principals (rather than agents) in providing insurance products, except for bona fide credit insurance sold to borrowers.[14]

Congress should allow banks and their affiliates to earn agency-based fees (1) by providing investment advice and securities brokerage services and (2) by acting as agents in selling insurance products. Brokerage and advisory services and other agency activities do not create the dangerous conflicts of interest and financial risks that are currently generated when universal banks underwrite (create) the financial products they sell. However, brokerage, advisory, and other agency activities must be strictly regulated to ensure that banks do not assume any legal duties or liabilities as principals in connection with those activities.[15]

Congress should also allow nonbank subsidiaries of bank holding companies to engage in activities that are "closely related to banking" under Section 4(c)(8) of the BHC Act. Congress could provide additional flexibility by allowing the Fed to approve new "closely related" activities that are reasonably related to traditional banking operations, such as deposit-taking, lending, payment and settlement services, and trust (wealth management) services. However, the Fed must not allow any "closely related" activities that would be equivalent—either legally or functionally—to the securities and insurance activities that a new Glass-Steagall Act would prohibit.[16]

To ensure the effectiveness of a new Glass-Steagall Act, Congress should forbid banks and their affiliates from creating derivatives that function as "synthetic" substitutes for securities or insurance products. To achieve that goal, Congress should prohibit banks and their affiliates from entering into derivatives—as either dealers or end-users—unless those derivatives qualify for hedge accounting treatment under standards issued by the Financial Accounting Standards Board. To satisfy hedge accounting standards, derivatives held by a bank or its affiliate must provide bona fide hedges against specifically identified risk exposures arising out of the bank's or affiliate's authorized assets, liabilities, and activities. Banks and their affiliates should not be allowed to enter into derivatives for vaguely defined purposes like "portfolio hedging" or "macro hedging." The broad parameters of those poorly defined concepts could potentially allow banks to evade the structural boundaries established by a new Glass-Steagall Act.[17]

———

In addition to ending culture clashes and removing dangerous conflicts of interest, a new Glass-Steagall Act would significantly reduce systemic risk and improve financial stability. The strong structural buffers established by the Glass-Steagall and BHC Acts prevented disruptions occurring in one financial sector from spilling over into other sectors and causing systemic crises after World War II. Those buffers also enabled financial institutions from one sector to help other sectors that experienced serious financial distress. For example, the Fed mobilized large banks (and supported them with discount window loans) to stabilize the commercial paper market following Penn Central's default in 1970, to help securities firms after the 1987 stock market crash, and to assist securities firms and nonfinancial companies after Russia's debt default in 1998. During all three episodes, the banking system provided much-needed support for other sectors because large banks were not exposed to crippling losses from capital markets activities. Conversely, securities firms provided an alternative source of credit to business firms in the early 1990s, when large banks were weakened by severe lending losses.[18]

In 1999, Congress repealed Glass-Steagall and destroyed the structural buffers that prevented contagious spillovers of financial risks and losses. The banking, securities, and insurance sectors became closely intertwined through the formation of giant financial conglomerates, and the risks created by those conglomerates spread across the entire span of the financial system. The financial crisis of 2007–09 was centered around the failures or threatened failures of giant financial conglomerates in *all three sectors*, including Citigroup, Bank of America, Wachovia, RBS, Lloyds-HBOS, ING, UBS, Commerzbank, Dexia, Fortis, the Big Five securities firms, and AIG.[19]

Restoring the precautionary buffers of the Glass-Steagall Act and the pre-1999 BHC Act would substantially reduce the threat of contagion from one financial sector into other sectors. Each sector could again serve as a potential source of financial support for distressed firms in other sectors. Federal regulators would be less likely to bail out troubled securities firms or insurance companies, as failures of nonbank financial firms would have a lower probability of disrupting the banking sector or destabilizing the entire financial system. Risk separation would be particularly effective if a new Glass-Steagall Act compels a substantial shrinkage of the shadow banking system, as will be described in the next section of this chapter. Thus, a new Glass-Steagall Act would establish a "precautionary principle" of great importance by strengthening the stability and resilience of the financial system and reducing the risks of a system-wide financial crisis.[20]

A new Glass-Steagall Act would also reduce systemic risks in the banking system by requiring banks to divest their capital markets operations. Studies have shown that universal banks created excessive risks and undermined financial stability during the boom-and-bust cycles that led to the Great Depression and the Great Recession. Large banks that engaged heavily in capital markets activities (including securitization, trading, and other investment banking services) during the 2000s experienced higher volatility in their earnings as well as greater risks of failure.[21] During the Great Recession, large diversified banks from countries with universal banking regimes performed much worse than traditional banks from countries that imposed limits on the ability of banks to engage in capital markets activities.[22] Similarly, universal banks in the U.S. and Europe performed much worse during the Great Depression, compared with specialized U.K. and Canadian commercial banks that were structurally separated from the capital markets.[23]

Large U.S. and foreign banks that focused on capital market activities during the 2000s generated higher levels of systemic risk and posed greater threats to financial and economic stability.[24] More than twenty large financial conglomerates in the U.S., U.K., and EU assumed enormous risks in their capital markets units during the 2000s, which led to huge losses and costly bailouts of those institutions during the Great Recession.[25] Restoring Glass-Steagall would reverse those dangerous trends in the U.S. and potentially in other countries that follow our lead by separating their banks from the capital markets.

A new Glass-Steagall Act would stop banks from using capital markets affiliates to exploit safety net subsidies, including deposit insurance, access to Fed discount window loans and payment system guarantees, and implicit TBTF guarantees. The current regulatory regime allows universal banks to use their significant cost-of-funding advantage from accepting deposits—the cheapest source of funding available in the private sector—to finance speculative investments and trading in the capital markets. JPMC, BofA, and Citigroup paid average interest rates of less than 0.2% on their savings deposits and money market accounts between 2013 and 2017. Ultra-low deposit rates give big universal banks a decisive cost-of-funding advantage over nonbank competitors in the capital markets.[26]

Universal banks have magnified their cost-of-funding advantages by persuading Congress to repeal the Lincoln Amendment in 2014 and by convincing regulators to weaken the Volcker Rule in 2019. The repeal of the Lincoln Amendment allows universal banks to conduct virtually all of their derivatives activities inside their subsidiary banks. JPMC's "London Whale" fiasco occurred in its largest subsidiary bank, which used "excess deposits" to finance disastrous trading in high-risk synthetic derivatives. By watering down the Volcker Rule, regulators have allowed universal banks to expand their opportunities to use deposits to finance their capital markets activities.[27]

A new Glass-Steagall Act would represent a major step toward stopping the transfer of safety net subsidies outside the banking system. It would significantly increase market discipline in the capital markets. Investors and creditors would have stronger incentives to monitor nonbank financial firms that engage in capital markets activities because those firms would not be affiliated with banks and regulators would be less likely to bail them out during a crisis. In addition, regulators could more effectively supervise banks, securities firms, and insurance companies because those institutions would be smaller and less complex.[28]

To address potential systemic risks among nonbanks, Congress should clarify and strengthen the authority of the Financial Stability Oversight Council to designate nonbank financial firms as systemically important financial institutions. Congress should clarify that FSOC has a duty—not merely a discretionary option—to designate nonbank firms as SIFIs if they pose significant risks to financial stability. Congress should also strengthen the Fed's authority to apply enhanced prudential regulation and oversight to designated nonbank SIFIs under Title I of Dodd-Frank.[29]

———

A new Glass-Steagall Act will not be successful unless it prevents nonbanks from continuing to fund their activities by issuing short-term financial claims that function as deposit substitutes. Section 21 of the Glass-Steagall Act of 1933 prohibits nonbanks from accepting "deposits," and it imposes criminal penalties for violating that prohibition. However, Section 21 does not define the term "deposits" with sufficient clarity. Beginning in the 1970s, federal regulators allowed nonbanks to offer short-term financial instruments that serve as substitutes for deposits, including money market mutual funds (MMMFs), commercial paper, and securities repurchase agreements (repos).[30]

Securities broker-dealers and other nonbank financial firms have used short-term deposit substitutes since the 1970s to finance longer-term consumer and commercial loans. Deposit substitutes grew at exponential rates after 1975 and allowed nonbanks to offer liquidity and lending services that were functionally equivalent to the deposits and loans provided by chartered banks. Assets held by MMMFs mushroomed from $3 billion in 1977 to $3.8 trillion in 2007. The commercial paper market swelled from $50 billion in 1975 to $2 trillion in 2007. The volume of repos issued by large securities firms expanded from $110 billion in 1981 to $3.5 trillion in 2007.[31]

Policymakers encouraged the growth of deposit substitutes (shadow deposits) by giving them preferential treatment. The Fed intervened to stabilize the commercial paper market in 1970 and the repo market in 1982. Congress created a bankruptcy safe harbor for repos in 1984 and expanded it in 2005. Shadow deposits made the capital markets more fragile by creating the potential for contagious runs by creditors who held short-term deposit substitutes issued by securities firms and other nonbank financial firms (shadow banks). During the financial crisis of 2007–09, the federal government provided trillions of dollars of emergency loans and guarantees to protect shadow deposits and shadow banks.[32]

Congress should amend Section 21 by defining "deposits" to include all short-term financial instruments that are payable in practice at par (100% of the amount invested) either on demand or within ninety days of issuance. Accounting principles treat debt instruments with maturities of less than three months as "cash equivalents."[33] My proposed definition of "deposits" would prohibit nonbanks from issuing short-term financial instruments that function as cash equivalents and deposit substitutes. My proposed definition would include MMMFs with a fixed net asset value (NAV) of $1 per share. MMMFs with fixed NAVs are deposit substitutes because they redeem their shares in practice at par on demand. Commercial paper and repos with terms of less than ninety-one days would also be treated as "deposits" under my proposed definition. Only chartered banks would be allowed to issue such short-term financial instruments because those instruments constitute "money claims," have very significant effects on financial stability and monetary policy, and are therefore matters of compelling public interest.[34]

Requiring all deposit substitutes to be issued by chartered banks would dramatically shrink the shadow banking system by forcing short-term financial claims to move from nonbanks to the regulated banking system. Nonbanks would be required to finance their operations by issuing either equity securities or debt obligations that have maturities longer than ninety days, or by obtaining loans from banks. Nonbanks would be subject to stronger market discipline and would have to pay higher interest rates on their longer-term obligations, because a new Glass-Steagall Act would substantially reduce the likelihood of government bailouts for nonbanks and holders of their securities.

The potential impact of defining "deposits" to include all short-term financial claims is illustrated by the response of institutional investors to a rule adopted by the SEC in 2014. Under that rule, MMMFs whose shares are held by institutional investors must redeem their shares based on a floating (market-value) NAV if those funds invest in either "prime" (nongovernment) securities or tax-exempt municipal bonds. The 2014 rule effectively removed deposit-like treatment from prime and tax-exempt MMMFs held by institutional investors. In contrast, the 2014 rule allows all MMMFs held by retail investors and government MMMFs (which invest in federal government securities) held by institutional investors to continue providing deposit-like treatment by redeeming their shares based on a fixed NAV of $1 per share.

When the 2014 rule took effect in 2016, institutional investors quickly withdrew over $1 trillion from prime and tax-exempt MMMFs and transferred those funds to either government MMMFs or bank deposit accounts. Meanwhile, there was no significant change in the amount of MMMFs held by retail investors because those funds continued to offer a fixed NAV of $1 per share.[35]

The dramatic response of institutional investors to the SEC's 2014 rule strongly indicates that MMMFs would probably disappear—and their funds would be transferred to bank deposit accounts—if *all* MMMFs were barred from offering deposit-like treatment (payment at par on demand, based on fixed NAVs). Similarly, the ability of nonbanks to fund their operations from commercial paper or repos would be significantly reduced if they were prohibited from issuing such instruments with maturities shorter than ninety-one days.

Preventing nonbanks from issuing deposit substitutes would greatly improve the ability of federal regulators to monitor the volume and potential risks of short-term claims in the financial system. Regulators could readily determine the volume of short-term claims through their supervision of banks that issue those claims. In contrast, regulators cannot adequately monitor and regulate the risks of short-term financial claims in shadow banking markets under present rules. In 2018, the Treasury Department's Office of Financial Research acknowledged that regulators could only roughly estimate the size of the market for uncleared bilateral repos, even though that market includes trillions of dollars of short-term obligations.[36]

Runs by holders of short-term financial claims have been a leading and recurrent cause of systemic financial crises.[37] My proposed definition of "deposits" under Section 21 would greatly improve the ability of regulators to prevent such runs. All short-term financial claims would be brought out of the shadows and into chartered banks, which are subject to periodic reporting requirements as well as supervision and examination by bank regulators. For example, regulators could (1) require banks to maintain stronger liquidity reserves for short-term claims, (2) specify the types of collateral that banks may pledge when they borrow funds under short-term repos, and (3) impose limits on the ability of repo lenders to rehypothecate (repledge) the collateral pledged by banks.

Moving all short-term financial claims inside banks would also enhance the Fed's ability to conduct monetary policy by adjusting bank reserve requirements in response to changing financial and economic conditions. For example, the Fed could impose higher reserve requirements on banks to prevent dangerous liquidity mismatches between their long-term assets and short-term liabilities. The Fed could establish higher reserve requirements without being concerned that short-term financial claims would migrate to nonbanks outside the banking system.[38] Studies have shown that the growth of shadow banks in the U.S. and Canada has undermined the effectiveness of monetary policy in both countries by allowing investors to transfer their funds from chartered banks to shadow banks whenever the Fed or the Bank of Canada attempts to tighten monetary policy.[39] Accordingly, prohibiting nonbanks from issuing short-term financial claims would substantially improve the effectiveness of the Fed's monetary policy actions.

Moving all short-term financial claims inside banks would also expand the FDIC's resources for dealing with banking crises. Banks pay deposit insurance assessments to the FDIC based on their total liabilities multiplied by their risk-adjusted premium rate.[40] In contrast, MMMFs have never paid government insurance premiums except for a minimal 0.3% guarantee fee for a relatively brief period after MMMFs were bailed out in 2008.[41] Under my proposed amendment to Section 21, the volume of short-term liabilities held by banks would increase by trillions of dollars (as funds move from MMMFs and broker-dealers to banks), and banks would pay correspondingly higher deposit insurance assessments. Higher assessments would increase the size of the deposit insurance fund, thereby providing the FDIC with additional resources for dealing with future bank failures.

———

A new Glass-Steagall Act would also promote greater competition in both the commercial banking sector and the capital markets. Universal banks would be required to divest their capital markets activities, thereby significantly reducing their size and complexity. Big banks would probably face additional pressures to shrink because their TBTF cost-of-funding advantages would likely diminish after they spin off their capital markets operations. Capital markets operations account for a much larger share of the assets of the biggest money center banks, compared with midsized regional banks. A new Glass-Steagall Act should therefore lead to a more competitive banking industry with smaller size disparities between money center banks and regional banks.[42]

Goldman Sachs and Morgan Stanley would probably decide to spin off their deposit banking operations and return to their former status as nonbank securities firms. Neither firm maintains a large network of deposit-taking branches, and deposits represent a relatively small percentage of their total liabilities. Both firms would therefore be likely to keep their large capital markets and wealth management operations and divest their much smaller banking functions. New securities firms would probably be organized from the capital markets operations spun off by JPMC, BofA, Citigroup, and Wells Fargo.[43] The result should be greater competition among a larger number of securities broker-dealers, including the broker-dealer subsidiaries of private equity firms.

A new Glass-Steagall Act should also expand the availability of bank credit to small and medium-sized businesses. Those businesses cannot obtain financing from public offerings of securities and depend on banks as their primary external sources of credit. After divesting their capital markets activities, large banks would have stronger incentives to increase their lending to bank-dependent business firms. In addition, the prohibition on the issuance of deposit substitutes by nonbanks would cause households, businesses, and institutional investors to shift trillions of dollars of short-term funds to banks of all sizes. Increased deposit funding for banks would enable them to make more loans to bank-dependent businesses.[44]

Policymakers should make special efforts to encourage growth within the community bank sector. Community banks (typically with assets under $10 billion) are the primary and preferred source of credit for small businesses, and they are much more reliable lenders to small firms through the business cycle. The four biggest U.S. banks slashed their small business lending by more than half between 2006 and 2014, while other large U.S. banks with over $50 billion of assets reduced their small business lending by more than a third. In contrast, banks smaller than $50 billion decreased their small business lending by only 12%, and community banks with assets under $10 billion increased their share of the small business lending market between 2006 and 2014.[45] Community banks continued to expand the amount of their small business lending more rapidly than the rest of the banking industry between 2014 and 2018.[46]

The very severe cutbacks in small business lending by big banks during the financial crisis inflicted worse than average job losses and higher failure rates on small businesses and discouraged the formation of new businesses. The steep reductions in small business lending by big banks contributed to above-average unemployment rates and below-average wage growth in counties where big banks held larger market shares.[47] Community banks could not fill the lending gap created by big banks because federal agencies provided very little help to smaller banks during the financial crisis. In contrast to the massive bailouts given to megabanks, federal officials "ruled out forbearance" for community banks and stood by while more than 450 smaller banks failed between 2008 and 2012.[48]

Federal regulators also created very high entry barriers that discouraged the formation of new community banks after the financial crisis. Fewer than twenty new banks opened for business between 2010 and 2018, in sharp contrast to the formation of over two thousand new banks between 1993 and 2008. Federal agencies required newly chartered banks to satisfy extremely high capital requirements, thereby making it almost impossible to establish new banks in smaller cities or rural areas.[49]

Failures of hundreds of community banks during the financial crisis and the very high regulatory barriers to new entry after the crisis accelerated a longer-term trend of shrinkage in the community bank sector. The number of community banks with assets under $10 billion fell by more than half—from more than 14,000 to fewer than 6,000—between 1984 and 2015. Community banks' share of total banking industry assets declined from 38% to 14% during that period, while the share of industry assets held by the four largest U.S. banks skyrocketed from 6% to 44%. Federal agencies encouraged both trends by (1) adopting very lenient antitrust review standards that permitted a rapid consolidation of the banking industry through mergers and acquisitions and (2) rescuing TBTF megabanks while doing little to help community banks during the banking crises of 1982–91 and 2007–09.[50]

The disappearance of community banks removed a crucial source of credit for new firms and contributed to an alarming drop in business startups. The annual formation rate for new U.S. business firms fell from 100,000 during the early 2000s to less than 25,000 in 2012 and 2013. That sharp decline in business start-ups should be a matter of great public concern because small businesses create a majority of new jobs and employ almost half of the private sector workforce.[51]

Many small firms have turned to online ("fintech") nonbank lenders for credit in recent years, due to the lack of adequate bank credit. However, fintech lenders charge much higher interest rates and insist on more onerous repayment terms. It is also doubtful whether fintech lenders will be able to maintain their small business lending during financial disruptions, given the heavy reliance of fintech lenders on volatile funding from the capital markets. Small businesses strongly prefer community banks—compared with larger banks and fintech lenders—because (1) community banks follow a long-term, customized, relationship-based approach instead of a short-term, transactional, "cookie-cutter" model and (2) community banks are much more reliable lenders through downturns in the business cycle.[52]

The declining market share of community banks and the increasing dominance of megabanks have also contributed to a growing inequality in economic outcomes between the largest metropolitan areas and smaller cities, towns, and rural areas. Since the financial crisis, the biggest U.S. banks have focused on serving the most affluent urban areas, and they have closed thousands of branches in smaller cities, towns, and rural counties. Branch closings by large banks have left many communities without any banking presence, a situation that often amounts to a "death sentence for a small town." Community banks are currently the only banks or the primary banks in about 40% of U.S. counties. Community banks are also the most important supporters of civic groups and charitable organizations in many smaller cities and towns.[53]

A new Glass-Steagall Act would be likely to encourage substantial inflows of deposits and capital into community banks as universal banks break up and nonbanks are barred from issuing short-term financial claims. Policymakers should promote additional growth in the community bank sector by reducing regulatory barriers to the formation of new banks. A stronger community banking sector would provide much-needed credit to existing small businesses, would help to finance new business start-ups, and would give vital support to smaller cities, towns, and rural areas, thereby improving economic and social welfare.[54]

A recent European study documented the highly positive impact of smaller banks on the economic performance of local regions in Austria, France, Germany, Italy, and Spain. The study found that regions in which smaller banks had a more substantial presence benefited from higher levels of household income and household wealth as well as lower unemployment rates. In contrast, regions dominated by larger banks suffered from lower levels of household income and household wealth as well as higher unemployment rates. The crucial difference was the willingness of smaller banks to invest a significantly higher percentage of their assets in making loans to borrowers in the regions they served. Increased lending by smaller banks made them much more effective as catalysts for economic growth within their local regions. The study concluded that further "consolidation of the European banking system is counterproductive" because "[a] diverse local banking structure improves regional supply of financial intermediation and could be the basis for more relationship lending."[55]

Federal bank regulators and the Justice Department should take further steps to promote a more decentralized, diverse, and competitive U.S. banking industry by applying much stricter scrutiny to bank mergers and acquisitions. Bank regulators and the Justice Department have encouraged bank consolidation over the past three decades by adopting very lax antitrust review standards. However, the anticipated benefits of a highly concentrated banking system have not been realized.[56]

Big banks have repeatedly failed to provide adequate and reliable credit to bank-dependent firms and smaller communities. Large banks have pursued aggressive expansion strategies to become megabanks so they can exploit TBTF subsidies and dominate local and regional geographic markets as well as specialized product markets. Megabanks have charged substantially higher fees for their services to consumers and small businesses compared with community banks.[57] The biggest banks have produced the highest levels of systemic risk in the U.S. and around the world since 2000, and many of them required costly bailouts during the financial crisis.[58] Accordingly, regulators should deny bank mergers and acquisitions that threaten to intensify TBTF problems, undermine financial stability, or weaken competition in geographic or product markets.[59]

———

A new Glass-Steagall Act would produce additional public benefits by reducing the excessive and dangerous influence that universal banks and their allies exercise over our political and regulatory systems. The financial (finance, insurance, and real estate) sector spent $14 billion on lobbying and political campaign contributions between 1998 and 2018. Those expenditures surpassed—by a very substantial margin—comparable spending on political influence by any other industry sector.[60]

Universal banks have magnified their influence by employing former members of Congress and former senior agency officials.[61] About 30% of the lawmakers and 40% of the senior legislative staff members who played the most important roles in drafting the Dodd-Frank Act subsequently left Congress to work for Wall Street institutions or firms that provide professional services to Wall Street. Many senior executive branch officials and regulators have taken the same path.

For example, former House Financial Services Committee Chairman Jeb Hensarling (R-TX) joined UBS as a vice chairman, following the route previously taken by his mentor, former Senate Banking Committee Chairman Phil Gramm (R-TX). Former White House Chief of Staff William Daley joined Wells Fargo as vice chairman of public affairs. Former Comptroller of the Currency John Dugan became chairman of the board of Citigroup. Former Treasury Secretaries Timothy Geithner and Jacob Lew became top executives in private equity firms. Former Fed Chairman Ben Bernanke became a senior advisor to Pimco and the Citadel hedge fund. Former Senate Banking Committee Chairman Christopher Dodd, former Attorney General Eric Holder, and former SEC Chairman Mary Jo White joined prominent law firms that represent many of the largest financial institutions.[62]

Passage of the Gramm-Leach-Bliley Act (GLBA) in 1999 greatly increased the financial industry's political clout, as it enabled large banks, securities firms, and insurance companies to combine forces by establishing financial holding companies. GLBA ended the internecine political warfare among the banking, securities, and insurance sectors, which blocked many deregulatory bills from advancing in Congress during the 1980s and the early and mid-1990s. Since 1999, the financial industry has shown a high degree of solidarity in advancing its political agenda, and the biggest universal banks have been the leaders in shaping that agenda.[63] In 2009 and 2010, the financial sector employed over 1,400 former federal officials as lobbyists, including 73 former members of Congress and two former Comptrollers of the Currency. During the same period, the six largest universal banks directly employed over 240 lobbyists who were former members of Congress, congressional staffers, or senior agency officials.[64]

Megabanks and the financial sector as a whole have received lucrative returns from their political investments. Large banks achieved an unbroken series of legislative victories between 1999 and 2007, including passage of GLBA, the Commodity Futures Modernization Act of 2000, and bankruptcy "reform" legislation in 2005. The financial industry also defeated several bills that would have imposed tighter restrictions on nonprime mortgage lending. The financial industry could not prevent Dodd-Frank's passage in 2010, but it defeated, watered down, or undermined the implementation of key provisions that threatened the interests of universal banks.[65]

Megabanks secured additional, individualized benefits from their lobbying efforts. Large banks that spent more on lobbying (including employing well-connected former government officials) were *more* likely to receive bailouts and *less* likely to be targeted with tough enforcement actions during the financial crisis and its aftermath. The favorable treatment they received was *not* due to either better business judgment or improved financial performance. In fact, large banks that spent more on lobbying also pursued riskier business strategies (including higher-risk mortgage lending), suffered larger losses during the financial crisis, and performed worse after the crisis, compared with banks that did relatively little lobbying.[66]

Efforts to restrain the political power of universal banks by imposing additional restrictions on lobbying, political contributions, or the employment of former government officials are not likely to be effective. Lobbying, political fundraising, and the "revolving door" between Washington and Wall Street are deeply entrenched features of our political landscape. Those trends have steadily grown in magnitude during the past half century, under both Democratic and Republican administrations.[67] The six largest U.S. universal banks enjoy a decisive advantage in political and economic influence over their domestic competitors. The same six banks and seven of their European peers dominate global financial markets as well as leading international financial trade associations.[68]

A new Glass-Steagall Act would offer a much more direct and promising approach for reducing the political influence of megabanks. Breaking up the financial industry into three distinct sectors would be likely to rekindle the heated political rivalries that existed among banks, securities firms, and insurance companies until the late 1990s. Each sector would have strong incentives to police the boundaries established by a new Glass-Steagall Act and to oppose regulatory or legislative efforts that could undermine those boundaries. Each sector would serve as a strong counterweight against the political and regulatory influence of the others.[69]

A new Glass-Steagall Act would incorporate the wisdom of James Madison and Louis Brandeis by dividing the political, economic, and financial power of large universal banks. Madison explained in Federalist No. 51 that the federal government should be divided into three separate branches to enable those branches to serve as "the means of keeping each other in their proper places."[70] In the early 1900s, Louis Brandeis argued that the "Money Trust" on Wall Street should be broken up by separating banks from the securities markets. Brandeis maintained that Wall Street's "financial oligarchy" threatened the political liberty of ordinary citizens as well as the social and economic welfare of local communities and small and medium-sized businesses. The Glass-Steagall Act of 1933 followed Brandeis' advice and "curb[ed] private financial power by fragmenting that power." Louis Brandeis and Carter Glass were both devoted followers of Woodrow Wilson, and there was a "striking similarity in [their] backgrounds and views."[71]

To defend the integrity of its structural barriers, a new Glass-Steagall Act should expressly authorize firms from each financial sector to file lawsuits challenging regulatory actions that threaten to weaken those barriers. Securities firms and insurance companies successfully filed lawsuits to defend the original Glass-Steagall Act until the Supreme Court issued its *Chevron* decision in 1984. As explained in Chapter 7, *Chevron* enabled bank regulators to undermine Glass-Steagall by claiming judicial deference for very questionable "interpretations" of purportedly "ambiguous" terms in the statute. Accordingly, a new Glass-Steagall Act should declare that future regulatory interpretations of the statute will *not* qualify for *Chevron* deference and will instead be subject to independent de novo review by the courts.[72]

––––––

Opponents of a new Glass-Steagall Act have raised three major objections. First, they argue that breaking up universal banks would destroy beneficial economies of scale and scope.[73] Analysts have long debated whether large, diversified banks produce beneficial economies of scale and scope, and a consensus has not been reached on that question.[74] However, there is compelling evidence that big universal banks do *not* generate positive synergies *through the business cycle*, especially if one excludes their cost-of-funding advantages from TBTF subsidies. Richard Davies and Belinda Tracey could not identify any favorable economies of scale at large international banks (with more than $50 billion of assets) between 2001 and 2010 after they controlled for the effects of TBTF cost-of-funding advantages.[75] Several studies determined that large U.S. banks with greater geographic and activity diversification had higher levels of earnings volatility and insolvency risk and lower market valuations even before the financial crisis began.[76] Other studies found that large U.S. and international banks with a heavy focus on capital markets activities had elevated levels of systemic risk and were more likely to fail or need bailouts out during the financial crisis.[77]

Many universal banks failed the acid test of the financial crisis of 2007–09, just as they failed the challenges of the Great Depression.[78] More than twenty large universal banks either collapsed or were bailed out in the U.S., U.K., and Europe during the financial crisis.[79] The four largest U.S. universal banks and the five largest U.S. securities firms—which were de facto universal banks, with a heavy reliance on short-term shadow deposits—either failed or received extensive government assistance. It is very doubtful whether any of those nine institutions (with the possible exception of JPMC) would have survived without government help.[80]

Only three of the top eleven global universal banks produced positive average annual returns for their shareholders between 2007 and 2016. A fourth bank broke even, and the other seven produced negative returns.[81] That dismal record reflected the very large losses that big universal banks suffered during the financial crisis as well as the additional losses and penalties they incurred after the crisis for misconduct and other operational failures

Widespread violations of law and other operational failures have tarnished the reputations and financial results of leading global universal banks since 2000. The twenty-six biggest U.S. banks reported more than $270 billion of losses from operational failures between 2002 and 2016, primarily due to sales of defective products and violations of other duties to clients. The six biggest U.S. universal banks paid $180 billion of misconduct penalties and settlements between 1998 and 2018, while major U.S. and foreign banks paid $370 billion of misconduct penalties and settlements between 2009 and 2018.[82]

Investors have discounted the values of large universal banks, given their disastrous performance during the financial crisis and their continuing operational failures over the past decade. In December 2018, only two U.S. universal banks—JPMC and Wells Fargo—had market values higher than their book values. The market values of BofA and Morgan Stanley were about equal to their book values, while Goldman Sachs, Citigroup, and sixteen European universal banks had market values that were lower—in many cases much lower—than their book values.[83] The very disappointing record of most universal banks in the U.S. and Europe since 2000 shows that universal banking is a boom-and-bust business model that does *not* produce positive synergies on any consistent, long-term basis.

———

The second argument made by opponents of a new Glass-Steagall Act is that a breakup of universal banks would undermine the ability of U.S. financial institutions to compete with foreign universal banks from Europe and Japan.[84] That argument rests on two deeply flawed premises: (1) the U.S. must allow foreign nations with the *weakest* standards of financial regulation to dictate the level of constraints on our financial institutions until *all* major countries agree on a common set of binding reforms, and

(2) in the meantime, the U.S. must tolerate universal banks despite the grave threats they pose to financial stability and the severe problems caused by their conflicts of interest, incentives for excessive risk-taking, and TBTF subsidies. Both premises are unacceptable and must be rejected.[85]

As shown previously, a new Glass-Steagall Act would improve financial stability, increase the transparency of financial institutions and markets, and enhance market discipline for banks and nonbank financial firms. Accordingly, a larger share of global investment capital should flow into the U.S. banking system and U.S. financial markets after the new statute is enacted. That likely shift of global investment capital into the U.S. financial system would place great pressure on foreign countries to abandon universal banking and adopt similar prudential safeguards for their own banks and securities markets. In any event, we must not allow the stability of our financial system, the health of our economy, and the welfare of our citizens and nonfinancial businesses to be held hostage to the decisions of other countries.

The claim that a new Glass-Steagall Act would place U.S. banks and securities firms at a competitive disadvantage is also contradicted by historical evidence. Large U.S. banks and securities firms were the most innovative and competitive financial institutions in global financial markets from the 1970s until the repeal of Glass-Steagall in 1999. The decentralized U.S. financial system produced more competitive, innovative, and dynamic financial institutions on both sides of Glass-Steagall's structural boundaries. In contrast, Europe's securities markets were completely dominated by large universal banks, and Europe's financial institutions and securities markets were therefore far less innovative and much less competitive.[86]

During the 1980s and 1990s, large U.S. banks and securities firms earned higher profits and maintained better efficiency ratios than European universal banks. An important reason for the superior international performance of large U.S. financial institutions was that they faced more vigorous competition at home. Accordingly, they had strong incentives to improve the quality of their products and services as well as the efficiency of their operations. When European banks tried to catch up with their U.S. rivals in the 1990s and early 2000s, they did so by acquiring American financial firms and by hiring American bankers. Credit Suisse bought First Boston and Donaldson, Lufkin & Jenrette, while Deutsche Bank purchased Bankers Trust and UBS acquired Paine Webber. Thus, leading European universal banks recognized that they could not compete with U.S. banks and securities firms without acquiring American expertise.[87]

European universal banks have also performed much worse since the financial crisis, compared with their U.S. rivals. Since 2010, the five American universal banks with the largest securities operations—JPMC, BofA, Citigroup, Goldman Sachs, and Morgan Stanley—have established a clear lead in global capital markets over their European competitors. Many European universal banks have reduced the size and scope of their investment banking operations after producing very disappointing results. According to Philipp Hildebrand, former head of the Swiss central bank, the "migration [of European universal banks] into US-style investment banking for the most part has turned out to be a very bad adventure."[88] Deutsche Bank announced in 2019 that it would divest its global equity trading operations and substantially reduce other investment banking activities, due to several years of poor results.[89] Nomura, the leading Japanese (and Asian) universal bank, experienced similar problems and also retreated from its previous ambition to compete with Wall Street banks on a global scale.[90]

It is very unlikely that the long record of superior performance of large U.S. financial institutions would change if those institutions were required to return to specialized business models resembling their operations from the 1970s through the mid-1990s. Past experience strongly indicates that specialized U.S. banks and securities firms would be more dynamic, innovative, and successful than European and Japanese universal banks. A renewal of the historic rivalry between large U.S. banks and securities firms in their home market would give them powerful incentives to provide superior services to both domestic and foreign customers.

———

Third, opponents of Glass-Steagall Act contend that only big universal banks can satisfy the financial needs of multinational corporations.[91] That claim is also contradicted by historical experience. From World War II through the 1990s, large U.S. and foreign corporations successfully obtained funding from U.S. banks through syndicated loans and from U.S. securities firms through syndicated offerings of equity and debt securities. Syndicated loans enable multiple banks to work together in providing large lines of credit and term loans to major corporations. Similarly, syndicated offerings of securities allow multiple securities firms to cooperate in selling large offerings of corporate equity and debt securities.[92]

The global syndicated lending market serves a wide range of business firms, including large multinational corporations. It is a growing market with almost $5 trillion of outstanding syndicated loans.[93] The syndicated lending market would be likely to expand—not shrink—if large U.S. banks were required to focus on syndicated lending as their primary method for providing financing to large corporations.

U.S. multinational corporations obtained most of their financing from U.S. banks and securities firms during the 1980s and 1990s. They did not rely substantially on European or Japanese universal banks during that period. As discussed earlier, a new Glass-Steagall Act would restore the decentralized system of banks and securities firms that performed very successfully during the 1980s and 1990s in financing business firms of all sizes, including the largest.[94]

Former Treasury Secretary and Citigroup chairman Robert Rubin vigorously defended the need for TBTF megabanks in an interview with David Rothkopf in 2012. Rothkopf asked Rubin whether "the biggest and most influential financial organizations ought to be broken up" to solve the TBTF "problem." Rubin replied: "No . . . don't you see? Too big to fail isn't a problem with the system. It *is* the system. . . . The bigger multinationals get, the bigger financial institutions will have to get."[95] Rubin's defense of universal banks mirrored the claim by HSBC chairman Douglas Flint in 2014 that universal banks were an essential part of modern finance. As previously discussed, Flint also argued that the "burden of failure" of universal banks "rests with society."[96] Thus, according to Rubin and Flint, TBTF subsidies and bailouts are the price society must pay to preserve the touted—but illusory—benefits of universal banks.

It is hardly surprising that top executives of universal banks are anxious to preserve those institutions. Rubin received $126 million of compensation from Citigroup between 1999 and 2009, despite Citigroup's near-collapse and its receipt of three government bailouts.[97] The CEOs of the five biggest U.S. universal banks (JPMC, BofA, Citigroup, Wells Fargo, and Goldman Sachs) received $900 million of compensation between 2008 and 2018, and their top subordinates received over $2.5 billion.[98] Large European universal banks have also provided very generous compensation to their senior executives over the past decade, particularly in view of the lackluster performance of those banks.[99]

Most universal banks display a stunning gap between the extraordinary levels of compensation paid to their executives and the subpar investment returns received by their long-term shareholders. That gap between executive pay and universal bank performance reflects a general failure by regulators and shareholders to restrain self-aggrandizement by insiders of those financial giants.[100] Deutsche Bank provides an extreme example of that trend. Deutsche Bank paid €71 billion of bonuses to its executives and key employees between 1995 and 2016, while producing total shareholder returns of only €17 billion during the same period. After reviewing those figures, a Deutsche investment banker asked, "Would the bank have been better off without hiring any of us?"[101]

———

We must adopt a new Glass-Steagall Act because the Dodd-Frank Act has failed to remove the enormous dangers posed by universal banks and shadow banks. As described in Chapter 12, the Obama administration and leading congressional sponsors of Dodd-Frank made conscious decisions *not* to break up universal banks or shadow banks. Instead, they tried to make universal banks and shadow banks safer by improving regulatory controls over those institutions.

From the outset, Dodd-Frank's success depended on the highly discretionary implementation of hundreds of complex and technical reforms by regulators who were subject to constant lobbying from universal banks and other Wall Street interests. Several of Dodd-Frank's key reforms have never been implemented, and a number of other mandates have been repealed or undermined by Congress and regulators (especially those appointed by President Trump). Consequently, Dodd-Frank has not solved the TBTF problem, and it has not significantly reduced the systemic dangers posed by universal banks and large shadow banks.[102] As Simon Johnson and James Kwak warned in 2010, "Solutions [like Dodd-Frank] that depend on smarter, better regulatory supervision and corrective action ignore the political constraints on regulation and the political power of the large banks," as well as the omnipresent threat of "regulatory capture."[103]

Unless we institute a new Glass-Steagall Act, our banking system and capital markets will continue to be dominated by giant universal banks and large shadow banks (including private equity firms and hedge funds), with their manifold conflicts of interest, excessive risk-taking, TBTF subsidies, and systemic dangers.[104] Universal banks and shadow banks will keep generating record levels of household, corporate, and sovereign debts, which could set the stage for the next financial crisis. Despite repeated calls for restraint by regulators, universal banks and shadow banks continue to churn out massive volumes of financing for risky transactions, including leveraged corporate loans and junk bonds as well as securitizations of speculative commercial real estate loans, nonprime auto loans, student loans, and credit card debts.[105]

The risky private sector debts produced by universal banks and shadow banks are part of an expanding global debt pile, which also includes unprecedented levels of sovereign debts during peacetime. Universal banks hold significant risk exposures to many of those debts.[106] Heavy sovereign debt burdens and huge budget deficits accumulated during the last financial crisis have left most developed nations with very limited room for fiscal stimulus. When the next crisis occurs, it is doubtful whether many developed countries will be able to issue large volumes of new government bonds without risking the outbreak of new sovereign debt crises.[107]

During the past decade, the U.S., U.K., EU, and Japan have relied heavily on their central banks to maintain financial stability and support economic growth by adopting unconventional monetary policies. However, those four central banks exhausted much of their unconventional policy arsenal by 2019. After completing huge quantitative easing programs, their balance sheets held over $15 trillion of assets, in 2018, compared with only $4 trillion in 2008. Many analysts therefore questioned whether central banks could undertake large new QE programs in response to a future crisis without straining their credibility and risking the soundness of the currencies they oversee.[108]

The interest rate tools of the four major central banks were similarly depleted by 2019. At the beginning of that year, baseline interest rates were 2.25–2.5% in the U.S., 0.75% in the U.K., and below zero in the EU and Japan. As discussed in Chapter 12, the Fed and other central banks conducted a coordinated easing of monetary policy after widespread turmoil occurred in global capital markets during the fourth quarter of 2018. The Fed reduced its target for short-term interest rates three times between July and October 2019, resulting in a baseline rate of only 1.50–1.75%. The ECB cut its baseline rate to an all-time low of –0.5% in September. Thus, the four leading central banks have very limited room to cut interest rates in response to future financial disruptions, in contrast to the rate reductions of 4–5% they implemented during the crisis of 2007–09.[109]

In October 2019, former IMF Chief Economist Olivier Blanchard warned, "Monetary policy is almost out of ammunition, but if central banks say this too explicitly, the markets may freak out."[110] Two months later, Bank of England Governor

Mark Carney acknowledged that "it's not clear that monetary policy would have sufficient space" to deal with a severe economic downturn.[111]

Thus, governments and central banks exhausted the greater part of their crisis-fighting ammunition when they rescued universal banks, large shadow banks, and their economies from the last financial crisis. Yet the three principal leaders of the response to the last crisis—Ben Bernanke, Tim Geithner, and Hank Paulson—and other experts maintain that governments and central banks must be prepared to use equally aggressive or even more dramatic measures to stop future financial disruptions from becoming systemic crises. Their proposals would effectively turn governments and central banks into guarantors of last resort for universal banks, shadow banks, and financial markets in general.[112] The Fed's intervention to stabilize the repo market in September 2019 suggests that the Fed is already prepared to act in accordance with those proposals.[113]

Investors and creditors expect that governments and central banks will provide comprehensive backstops for universal banks, shadow banks, and financial markets to prevent financial disturbances from becoming systemic crises. However, it is far from clear whether governments and central banks will be able to fulfill such expectations during a future systemic crisis. Investors and creditors would almost certainly panic if governments and central banks failed to preserve financial stability during a future crisis. The magnitude of such a panic would probably surpass the worldwide flight to safety that followed Lehman's unexpected collapse.

In sum, our existing financial system—with its "global doom loop" linking TBTF universal banks and run-prone shadow banks to heavily indebted governments and overcommitted central banks—poses an unacceptable risk of causing a global financial panic that could trigger a second Great Depression.[114] We must adopt a completely different approach to have any realistic hope of preventing such a catastrophe.

A new Glass-Steagall Act would provide the most direct and workable strategy for breaking the global doom loop and ending the infernal cycle of global debt expansion. A new Glass-Steagall Act would break up universal banks and shadow banks, thereby fostering more prudent and competitive banks and securities firms, more resilient and stable financial markets, and a more diverse and productive economy. It would stop banks from exploiting safety net subsidies to finance speculative capital markets activities. It would create strong structural buffers that would reduce the risks of contagion across financial sectors. It would stop securities firms and other nonbanks from continuing to offer run-prone shadow deposits, and it would force nonbanks to finance their operations with more stable, longer-term sources of funding. It would promote more effective regulatory and market discipline by reducing the size, scope, and complexity of large financial institutions. It would permit the Fed to fulfill its traditional role as lender of last resort for the banking system without being required to provide open-ended guarantees for the entire financial system.[115]

A new Glass-Steagall Act should be combined with a strengthened Dodd-Frank regime for regulating and resolving SIFIs. A strengthened Dodd-Frank regime should include clearly defined mandates for designating nonbank SIFIs in a timely manner, and it should give the Fed enhanced regulatory authority over nonbank SIFIs and large bank holding companies. Stronger capital and liquidity requirements should be central components of the Fed's enhanced powers for regulating large financial institutions. A more effective and credible Orderly Liquidation Authority should be established to resolve failures of large bank holding companies and nonbank SIFIs. Large financial companies should be required to pay risk-based premiums to prefund the Orderly Liquidation Fund, so that future resolutions of failed SIFIs are paid for by large financial firms instead of relying on long-term loans from the Treasury Department and taxpayers.[116]

The foregoing reforms would restore our banking system and our financial markets to their proper roles as servants—not masters—of businesses and consumers. Those reforms would establish improved supervision and stronger market discipline for all types of financial service providers. They would stop Wall Street megabanks and large shadow banks from continuing to exercise a dangerous and unwarranted influence over our political and regulatory systems. They would end the system of crony capitalism that severely distorts our financial markets and undermines market discipline with blanket guarantees and other TBTF subsidies for universal banks and shadow banks. They would return our financial markets to their rightful status as true markets.

Our choice is clear—we must break up universal banks and shadow banks or they will continue to dictate our government's policies and control the future direction of our economy and society. In 1914, Louis Brandeis warned the American people, "We must break the Money Trust or the Money Trust will break us."[117] Congress acted on his advice in 1933 by enacting the Glass-Steagall Act. Brandeis' warning is just as timely today as it was in 1914 and 1933.

Notes

Acknowledgments and Note on Statistics

1. FRED-CPI (2019).
2. FRED-Debt (2019); Historical Statistics (1975: 989) (Series X, 393–409) (providing the figure for total U.S. private and public debts in 1930).

Introduction

1. Santayana (1980 [1905], chapter XII).
2. Blinder (2013); Eichengreen (2015); FCIC (2011); Wigmore (1985).
3. Unless otherwise indicated, the terms "banks" and "banking organizations" refer to both banks and bank holding companies (companies that control banks). See Wilmarth (2002: 220–23).
4. A bank "underwrites" securities when it purchases securities from one or more issuers and promises to sell those securities to investors. A bank "trades" (or "deals") in securities when it purchases and sells securities for its own account. Carnell, Macey, & Miller (2017: 152–66, 314–20, 676–77, 691–93).
5. See Chapter 5, which discusses additional reasons for the greater resilience of the British and Canadian banking systems during the 1930s, including Britain's and Canada's departure from the international gold exchange standard in 1931 and the presence of effective lenders of last resort for banks in Britain and Canada.
6. See Eichengreen (2015: 66–67); Johnson & Kwak (2010: 34–37); Wilmarth (2017: 452–55, 502).
7. See Pozsar et al. (2010); Ricks (2016: 2–8, 93–101, 230–43).
8. See Chapter 11. For analysis of the potential risk that unconventional monetary policies could undermine the independence and legitimacy of central banks, see Tucker (2018a: 4–9, 391–545).
9. The G20 includes the U.S., the EU, the U.K., and seventeen other leading countries. Bernanke (2015: 181, 349–50).
10. Ricks (2019).
11. IMF-GFS (2018: 74); Noonan (2019) (quoting Felix Hufeld).
12. Wilmarth (2009, 2014, 2017); see also Chapters 2–4, 9–11, and the Conclusion.
13. Jordà, Schularick, & Taylor (2013, 2016a); Verner (2019); Wilmarth (2009, 2014, 2017).
14. Aikman et al. (2018: 2, 40–41 [charts 1 & 2]); see also Chapters 9–12. For another comparison of the U.S. economy's performance and the federal government's fiscal policies during the Great Depression and Great Recession, see Fishback (2016: 5–10, 61–63, 78–79 [figures 1 & 2]).
15. Baron, Verner, & Xiong (2019: table 5C and online appendix, part VI.B); Middleton (2010: 417, 419 [figures 1–3]) (showing the very significant difference in GDP performance between Britain and the U.S. during the Great Depression); ibid., at 419, 421, 437

(stating that there was "no banking crisis" and "no burst asset-price bubble" in Britain during the Depression, in contrast to the U.S.); see also Chapters 5–6.

16. Fraser (2014: 11, 170–71, 425); see also Chapters 8–11.

17. See Chapters 7 and 9–12, as well as Wilmarth (2009, 2014, 2017).

18. Eichengreen (2015: 69–77); Wilmarth (2009: 972–97, 1002–43); see also Chapters 2–4 and 9–11.

19. Haldane & Alessandri (2009); Haldane, Brennan, & Madouros (2010); Johnson & Kwak (2010); Wilmarth (2009, 2017); see also Chapters 1–6 and 10–12.

20. Philippon & Reshef (2012: 1552–58, 1578 [figure VIIIC], 1580–93, 1605); see also Chapters 1–3 and 7–11 (describing the federal government's deregulatory policies during the 1920s, 1990s, and 2000s).

21. Philippon & Reshef (2012: 1552, 1578 [figure VIIIC], 1586–90).

22. Ibid., 1553, 1562–65, 1590–93, 1605–06. A recent study by Thomas Piketty, Emmanuel Saez, and Gabriel Zucman complements the findings of Philippon and Reshef. Piketty, Saez, and Zucman determined that pretax national income shares for the top 1% and top 10% of U.S. adults peaked during the late 1920s and again during the mid-2000s. Piketty, Saez, and Zucman concluded that "widespread deregulation (particularly in the financial sector)" was a significant factor that helped to explain the remarkable rise in income levels for the top 1% and 10% of U.S. adults. Piketty, Saez, & Zucman (2018: 586–89, 604–05).

23. Hacker & Pierson (2010: 66–71); Wilmarth (2011a: 970–71).

24. Hacker & Pierson (2010: 66–71, 196–98, 224–30, 247–50); Johnson & Kwak (2010: 82–152); Mukunda (2014); Wilmarth (2009; 2011a: 970–79; 2013: 1328–45, 1359–64; 2017); see also Chapters 8–11.

25. Allen (1935: 222–24); Chernow (1990: 225–26, 254–55); see also Chapters 1–4.

26. See Chapters 1–4 and 9–12.

27. See Chapters 9–11 (describing a "big seventeen" group of financial conglomerates during the 2000s, which included JPMorgan Chase [JPMC], Bank of America [BofA], Citigroup, Wachovia, Bear Stearns, Goldman Sachs, Lehman Brothers, Merrill Lynch, Morgan Stanley, Barclays, BNP Paribas, Credit Suisse, Deutsche Bank, HSBC, Royal Bank of Scotland [RBS], Société Générale, and UBS); see also Chapter 12 (describing the successor "big thirteen" group that has dominated global financial markets since 2010, and explaining that the smaller group resulted from the acquisitions of Bear Stearns by JPMC, of Merrill Lynch by BofA, and of Wachovia by Wells Fargo, as well as Lehman's failure and RBS's large divestitures of assets from its global banking and capital markets units).

28. See Chapter 12 and the Conclusion, as well as Johnson & Kwak (2010).

29. IMF-GFS (2019: chapter 1); see also Chapter 12 (explaining that global private and public debts increased from $167 trillion to $253 trillion between 2007 and 2019); Stubbington (2019) (stating that global sovereign debts surpassed 70% of global GDP in 2019, their highest level since 1945).

30. See Gelpern (2009: 1064–67) (distinguishing between extraordinary "crisis containment" measures and ordinary "regulation" and "prevention" actions that promote "normal market functioning").

31. See Bernanke (2015: 538–67) (quote at 561); see also Chapter 12.

32. See Chapter 12.

33. Arnold, Stubbington, & Fletcher (2019); El-Erian (2019a, 2019b, 2019c) (quotes); Mackenzie (2019b); Rennison & Greeley (2019); Smith & Rennison (2019); Wigglesworth (2019); see also Chapter 12.

34. El-Erian (2019c).

35. Bernanke served as Fed Chairman from 2006 to 2014. Geithner served as President of the Federal Reserve Bank of New York from 2003 to 2009, and as Treasury Secretary from 2009 to 2013. Paulson served as Treasury Secretary from 2006 to 2009.

36. Bernanke, Geithner, & Paulson (2018; 2019: 111–12, 120–22, 127–28). See Bair (2019), Ricks (2019), Chapter 12, and the Conclusion for critical responses to the arguments of Bernanke, Geithner, and Paulson and other experts who share their views.

37. Ardagna (2019); Briançon (2019); Curran & Miller (2019); Summers & Stanbury (2019); see also the Conclusion.

38. Crawford (2017: 1–2); Finkle (2018b); Warren (2017) (announcing introduction of proposed legislation by Senators Warren, John McCain [R-AZ], Maria Cantwell [D-WA], and Angus King [I-ME]).

Chapter 1

1. Symons (1983: 688–705). Banks "discounted" negotiable instruments—obligations to pay money that could be transferred to other parties—by purchasing those instruments for less than their face amounts, or by making loans based on the security of those instruments for less than their face value. The amount of each "discount" below face value reflected the purchasing or lending bank's fee as well as the perceived riskiness of the party or parties who were obligated to pay the instrument. Conti-Brown (2016: 210–13); Eichengreen (1992: 42–43, 279–80).

2. After the charter of the Second Bank of the United States expired in 1836, state governments chartered and regulated all commercial banks until the Civil War. The National Bank Act of 1864 established a new system of federally chartered, privately owned national banks. The state banking system survived, and a "dual banking system" emerged, composed of both national and state banks. White (1983). Many state-chartered banks collapsed during a series of financial panics that occurred between 1837 and 1841. Some large state banks failed after suffering catastrophic losses from investments in public works projects, commercial enterprises, state bond underwritings, and cotton trading operations. In response to those failures, many states passed laws that prohibited state banks from underwriting or investing in corporate stocks, bonds, and commodities. Similarly, the National Bank Act of 1864 did not authorize national banks to engage in those activities. Consequently, private investment banks (described in note 4 below) controlled the securities underwriting and trading business after 1840. Carosso (1970: 2–3, 10–27, 43–51); Morrison & Wilhelm (2007: 145–54, 162–80); Peach (1941: 38–39, 43–51); Redlich (1968: 337–73); Symons (1983: 688–708); Wilmarth (2007: 1555–58).

3. In an "underwriting," one or more investment banks purchased securities from a government or corporate issuer and agreed to sell those securities to institutional or retail investors. The underwriting agreement required the issuer to pay fees to the bank underwriters for their services, including the risks they assumed in distributing the issuer's securities. In contrast, trading or "dealing" occurred when an investment bank bought and sold

securities for its own account for the purpose of making a profit. Carosso (1970: 13–28, 51–67); Morrison & Wilhelm (2007: 134–37, 162–74).

4. Carosso (1970: 29–67); Cleveland & Huertas (1985: 32–42); Redlich (1968: 381–92); Morrison & Wilhelm (2007: 121–23, 162–85). Most private investment banks were organized as partnerships. They did not have bank charters and were not subject to any oversight by federal or state agencies until the first state "blue sky" (anti-fraud) laws were enacted after 1910. Private investment banks accepted deposits from their business clients but not from the general public. In contrast, commercial banks were chartered as banking corporations under the National Bank Act or state banking laws, were supervised by federal or state regulators, and accepted deposits from the general public as well as their business clients. Carosso (1970: 85–98, 156–64); Chernow (1990: 256, 303–06); Cleveland & Huertas (1985: 32–42, 55–59, 83–88); Morrison & Wilhelm (2007: 162–70, 184–85, 201–02); U.S. Senate (1934: 221–26).

5. Allen (1935: 175–76); Carosso (1970: 23, 47–50, 73–74); Chernow (1990: 90–91); Cleveland & Huertas (1985: 32–42, 56–58, 356n17); Morrison & Wilhelm (2007: 169–70, 184–85); Redlich (1968: 380, 390–91).

6. Carosso (1970: 100, 107–08, 140–41); Chernow (1990: 151–54); Cleveland & Huertas (1985: 32–42, 56); Morrison & Wilhelm (2007: 184–85); Redlich (1968: 381, 391–92).

7. Peach (1941: 38–39, 43–45, 50); Redlich (1968: 389).

8. Carosso (1970: 97); Redlich (1968: 392–93). The relevant court decisions are discussed in Peach (1941: 45–48, 50–51) and Symons (1983: 703–08).

9. White (1983: 23–25, 38–42, 47).

10. Carosso (1970: 97–98); Peach (1941: 14–15, 21, 53–55, 59–66, 107); Redlich (1968: 393). When the First National Bank of New York organized its nonbank securities affiliate in 1908, president George Baker told the bank's shareholders that the affiliate would allow the bank to engage in "certain lines of profitable business which, though often transacted by bankers, are not expressly included within the corporate powers of national banks. Among these are the acquiring and holding of real estate, securities, stocks and other property." Peach (1941: 61–62) (quoting Baker's letter to the bank's shareholders in Feb. 1908). Similarly, when National City Bank established its nonbank securities affiliate in 1911, president Frank Vanderlip informed shareholders that the affiliate would be able to "make investments and transact other business, which though often very profitable, may not be within the express corporate powers of a National Bank." Cleveland & Huertas (1985: 63) (quoting Vanderlip's letter to shareholders dated June 28, 1911).

11. State-chartered trust companies expanded rapidly between 1890 and 1907, due to their more lenient oversight and their broader powers to provide fiduciary services, make real estate loans, and engage in securities activities. Neal (1971: 37–45); Moen & Tallman (1992: 612–16); Tallman & Moen (1990: 11–12); White (1983: 38–42). However, the growth of trust companies declined after fifteen trust companies failed during the Panic of 1907. Bruner & Carr (2007: 67–113, 122–25); Moen & Tallman (1992: 616–28); Tallman & Moen (1990: 7–8, 10–12); Wicker (2000: 85–113). Those failures caused many states to strengthen their oversight of trust companies. White (1983: 40–42, 81–82).

12. Peach (1941: 53–57, 60–61).

13. Between 1923 and 1933, the Securities Dealers of North America listed only eighteen national banks that operated securities affiliates organized as state-chartered banks or trust companies. Peach (1941: 56, 82–83).

14. Peach (1941: 61–64, 81–83).
15. Carosso (1970: 97–98, 272–75); Peach (1941: 61–70, 100–04).
16. Perino (2010: 203–06).
17. U.S. Senate (1933a: 2030, 2040, 2042) (reprinting Lehmann's opinion dated Nov. 6, 1911). For discussions of Wickersham's and Lehmann's opposition to NCC, see Carosso (1970: 98); Peach (1941: 151–53); Perino (2010: 203–06).
18. U.S. Senate (1933a: 2034–41) (reprinting Lehmann's 1911 opinion, including his discussion of *Concord National Bank v. Hawkins*, 174 U.S. 364 [1899], and the control that National City Bank's management exercised over NCC).
19. Cleveland & Huertas (1985: 64–66); Perino (2010: 204); see also White (1983: 14–15, 156–60) (explaining that the National Bank Act prohibited national banks from opening branch offices prior to the McFadden Act of 1927).
20. U.S. Senate (1933a: 2042) (reprinting Lehmann's 1911 opinion).
21. See Chapters 5 and 6. During the U.S. Senate's investigation of securities affiliates of commercial banks in 1933, Senator Peter Norbeck (R-SD) referred to Lehmann as "a prophet." U.S. Senate (1933a: 2044).
22. Perino (2010: 205–06); Cleveland & Huertas (1985: 62–63, 66); see also Carosso (1970: 98); Peach (1941: 144).
23. Carosso (1970: 274); Cleveland & Huertas (1985: 66–67, 84–85); Freeman & McKinley (2018: 126–27); Peach (1941: 147–48).
24. Allen (1935: 174–88); Carosso (1970: 136–53); Cleveland & Huertas (1985: 68–69, 359–60n53); Fink (2019: 28–29); Perino (2010: 205–06); U.S. House of Representatives (1913).
25. Carosso (1970: 107–08, 140–41) (quoting U.S. House of Representatives [1913: 56, 90]); see also U.S. House of Representatives (1913: 91–106, 130–35). During the Pujo Committee's hearings, George Baker, president of the First National Bank, acknowledged that he could not recall any securities underwriting of more than $10 million during the previous decade that occurred without the participation of at least one of the six leading institutions. Carosso (1970: 144–45); see U.S. House of Representatives (1913: 160).
26. Carosso (1970: 153); Fink (2019: 29) (quoting U.S. House of Representatives [1913: 133]). For analysis of the evidence produced by the Pujo Committee, see Allen (1935: 177–88); Carosso (1970: 140–53); Chernow (1990: 149–56); Cleveland & Huertas (1985: 67–68, 360n54).
27. Carosso (1970: 174–76, 180) (explaining that *Other People's Money* grew out of a series of articles that Louis Brandeis published in *Harper's Weekly*); see also Chernow (1990: 178–80); Rosen (2016: 67–77).
28. Brandeis (1933 [1914]: 18–19).
29. Ibid., 19–24.
30. Ibid., 3–5; see also ibid., 6–35, 137–41 (describing the dangers created by "our financial oligarchy").
31. Ibid., 26–28.
32. Carosso (1970: 153–54, 176–77); Cleveland & Huertas (1985: 74); Fink (2019: 29); Peach (1941: 101–04, 148); U.S. House of Representatives (1913: 151–53, 155–56, 164, 169–70). The Pujo Committee's recommendations helped to persuade Congress to adopt Section 8 of the Clayton Antitrust Act of 1914, which prohibited the sharing of common directors between large banks and large trust companies, or between banks and trust companies of any size located in the same local community. Carosso (1970: 176–77).

33. Carosso (1970: 174–76, 180); see also Chernow (1990: 378–79); Pecora (1939: 39, 75–76) (discussing the relevance of *Other People's Money* to the Senate investigation of Wall Street that Ferdinand Pecora led in 1933).

34. Brandeis (1933 [1914]: xxxvi–xxxvii) (editor's foreword by Norman Hapgood).

35. Carosso (1970: 211–16); Cleveland & Huertas (1985: 86–87).

36. Cleveland & Huertas (1985: 55, 86–88) (quoting letter from Vanderlip to Stillman); see also Peach (1941: 19, 87–88).

37. Peach (1941: 87–88) (quoting NCC's advertisement in the *Commercial and Financial Chronicle*, Oct. 14, 1916, p. 17).

38. Allen (1935: 310–12); Barton (1923); Cleveland & Huertas (1985: 87) (quoting Vanderlip's memoir); Perino (2010: 75–76) (quoting Mitchell); Puckette (1927).

39. Carosso (1970: 224–26); Chernow (1990: 201–03); Peach (1941: 31–33); Sutch (2015: 15–16, 25); see also Friedman & Schwartz (1963: 199, 216n29) (stating that the U.S. Treasury provided $9.5 billion of loans to the Allies between 1917 and 1920).

40. Carosso (1970: 224); Mitchell (2007: 251–54); Sutch (2015: 16–21).

41. Carosso (1970: 225); Ott (2008: 622); Sutch (2015: 13–15).

42. Carosso (1970: 226) (quoting Benjamin Ginzburg, "Wall Street Under the New Deal," 245 *North American Review* 70 [Spring 1938]).

43. Carosso (1970: 238–39) (quoting Edwin F. Gray, "The Great Depression," 10 *Foreign Affairs* 533–34 [July 1932]).

44. Carosso (1970: 225–27); Meltzer (2003: 85–87); Peach (1941: 31–33).

45. Carosso (1970: 227); Peach (1941: 32–33); see also Cleveland & Huertas (1985: 384n4) ("What the [National] City Company learned from the Liberty bond campaign was the technique of mass marketing"); Mitchell (2007: 255) ("The Liberty loan drives provided a graduate education for bankers and securities salesmen").

46. Carosso (1970: 228) (quoting Charles E. Mitchell, "Sound Inflation," 20 *Magazine of Wall Street* 295 [June 9, 1917]).

47. Cleveland & Huertas (1985: 136) (quoting Mitchell's lecture to National City's Banking III class for trainees on Mar. 18, 1919).

48. Carosso (1970: 224–27, 230–33) (noting that the CIC rejected more than $900 million of proposed new issues of corporate securities).

49. Ibid., 216–17 (showing that corporate loans by U.S. banks grew from $15.5 billion in 1914 to $20.9 billion in 1917); Cleveland & Huertas (1985: 76).

50. Cleveland & Huertas (1985: 104–05, 371n58); Friedman & Schwartz (1963: 222–24); Meltzer (2003: 86–103).

51. Cleveland & Huertas (1985: 104–05); Friedman & Schwartz (1963: 231–41, 287); Grant (2014); Meltzer (2003: 90–129).

52. Cleveland & Huertas (1985: 81, 99–103, 369n39); Freeman & McKinley (2018: 98–102); Winkler (1933: 39–41).

53. Cleveland & Huertas (1985: 79, 103–06); Hubbard (1995: 181–85); Perino (2010: 78–79).

54. Cleveland & Huertas (1985: 104–06) (noting that the market price for Cuban sugar fell from 22 cents per pound in 1920 to 3.75 cents per pound in 1921); Hubbard (1995: 185); Perino (2010: 79); U.S. Senate (1933a: 1792–93) (testimony of Charles E. Mitchell)).

55. Cleveland & Huertas (1985: 105–08) (quote); Chernow (1990: 237); Freeman & McKinley (2018: 104–08); Hubbard (1995: 185). As a result of National City's domestic and international problems, its annual net profits fell from $12.3 million to $900,000 between

1920 and 1922, its total assets declined from \$1.03 billion to \$850 million, and its capital accounts dropped from \$116 million to \$90 million. Cleveland & Huertas (1985: 321 [appendix B]).

56. Cleveland & Huertas (1985: 107–12); Perino (2010: 79); Puckette (1927).
57. Cleveland & Huertas (1985: 108–10); Freeman & McKinley (2018: 110–14); Hubbard (1995: 185); Perino (2010: 80, 159–60); U.S. Senate (1933a: 1789–95, 1798–99, 1835–36) (testimony of Charles E. Mitchell).
58. Allen (1935: 310–13); Wilson (1936: 57–58).
59. Cleveland & Huertas (1985: 112) (quoting Mitchell's speech).
60. Ibid., 113–14, 135, 156–58; New York Herald Tribune (1921b); Peach (1941: 13, 71–72, 87–95, 111–12); see also Chapter 2.
61. Grant (2014: 85–86); Kane (1922: chapter XVI); New York Times (1914c). From 1913 to 1935, the Secretary of the Treasury and the Comptroller of the Currency served as ex officio members of the Federal Reserve Board. In 1935, Congress amended the Federal Reserve Act to remove both officials from the reconstituted Board of Governors of the Federal Reserve System. Conti-Brown (2016: 21–31); Meltzer (2003: 4, 73–74, 484–85).
62. Grant (2014: 85–86); Kane (1922: chapter XVI); New York Times (1900).
63. Grant (2014: 85–87); Maccaro (2003); New York Times (1908a, 1908b, 1912); Slipek (2005).
64. New York Times (1914d).
65. Ibid. In 1916, Williams similarly warned a convention of Tennessee bankers that the growing concentration of wealth in an "ostentatious leisure class" was "the greatest danger threatening the nation." He urged bankers to expand economic opportunities throughout the nation by providing credit to small businessmen and farmers "so that no worthy man may be hopeless." New York Times (1916).
66. Comptroller of the Currency (1914: 93–94, 94n1); see also Grant (2014: 87) (stating that National City "had inserted a mole into the Department of the Treasury").
67. Comptroller of the Currency (1914: 93–95); Grant (2014: 87–88); Kane (1922: chapters XV and XVI); New York Times (1914a, 1914b, 1914c).
68. Comptroller of the Currency (1914: 93–94).
69. Kane (1922: chapter XVI).
70. Ibid.
71. Ibid.; New York Times (1915, 1920).
72. Kane (1922: chapter XVI); New York Times (1919b).
73. The original Federal Reserve Act of 1913 established the Federal Reserve Board and a decentralized system of twelve regional Federal Reserve Banks. The original statute gave the title of Governor to the head of the Federal Reserve Board and also to the head of each regional Bank. In 1935, Congress amended the Federal Reserve Act and reorganized the Federal Reserve System. The 1935 amendments gave the title of Chairman to the head of the reconstituted Board of Governors of the Federal Reserve System, while the head of each regional Bank was given the title of President. The Federal Reserve Bank of New York (New York Fed) continued to be the most important regional Bank, due to its location near Wall Street and its responsibility for conducting open market operations to implement the Fed's monetary policies. Conti-Brown (2016: 21–31); Meltzer (2003: 68–82, 474–86); White (1983: 96–99, 165–67).

74. Grant (2014: 92–108, 119–27); Meltzer (2003: 93–117, 127–29); New York Times (1921e). William P. G. Harding. an Alabama banker, was appointed as a member of the Federal Reserve Board by President Wilson in 1914 and became Governor of the Board in 1916. He was not related to Warren G. Harding, who succeeded Wilson as president in Mar. 1921. Grant (2014: 36, 92–94); Meltzer (2003: 74n18).

75. Grant (2014: 125–27); New York Times (1921c).

76. Grant (2014: 136–37, 142–44, 179–82, 190–91); Meltzer (2003: 112–31); New York Times (1921d, 1921e, 1921f).

77. Kane (1922: chapter XVI); White (1983: 130–34); White (2009: 41–42). Under the Federal Reserve Act (12 U.S.C. §§ 222, 321), all national banks were required to join the Federal Reserve System as member banks, while state banks could choose either to become member banks or to remain nonmember banks.

78. White (1983: 130–37, 165–67, 132 [table 3.1]) (showing that the number of state member banks increased from 53 in June 1917 to 1,648 in June 1922); White (2009: 41–42); New York Times (1921a). During the final two years of Williams' tenure as Comptroller of the Currency, Representative McFadden and others introduced bills in the House and the Senate to abolish the Office of the Comptroller of the Currency and transfer its bank supervisory responsibilities to the Fed. The proposed bills, which many bankers supported, represented attempts "to abolish John Skelton Williams." Efforts to pass those bills were abandoned after Williams stepped down as Comptroller in Mar. 1921. Kane (1922: chapter XIV); New York Times (1919a).

79. White (1983: 136–40) (reporting that national banks and state member banks held 70.3% of U.S. bank deposits in 1920 and 73.1% of U.S. bank deposits in 1929, with the remainder held by state nonmember banks).

80. U.S. Senate (1931: 301) (testimony of Charles E. Mitchell, chairman of National City and NCC); see also Freeman & McKinley (2018: 146–47); Peach (1941: 151n28).

81. Freeman & McKinley (2018: 100–06); Grant (2014: 87–91); see also Cleveland & Huertas (1985: 105–07, 321 [appendix A]) (showing that National City had $116 million of capital at the end of 1920).

82. Grant (2014: 109–10).

83. Ibid., 108–10 (discussing Williams' letter to Harding on Dec. 27, 1920); New York Times (1921f). In addition to making $144 million of loans to National City, the New York Fed provided more than $120 million of credit to Guaranty Trust. Grant (2014: 115–16). "Call money" loans were short-term loans to securities brokers, secured by pledges of securities or other collateral. Meltzer (2003: 70–71); see also Chapters 2 and 4.

84. Glass did not originally favor a presidentially appointed Federal Reserve Board, but he was persuaded by President Wilson and Louis Brandeis to include such a Board in his House bill, which ultimately was enacted as the Federal Reserve Act of 1913. Conti-Brown (2016: 17–22, 30–31); Fink (2019: 30–56, 170 [quote]); Meltzer (2003: 4, 73–74).

85. Conti-Brown (2016: 210–15); Fink (2019: 64–72); Meltzer (2003: 66–72, 92–103); White (1983: 115–25).

86. Fink (2019: 85–117); Perkins (1971: 494–95, 517–18, 524–25); Willis & Chapman (1934: 49–102); see also Chapter 6.

87. Comptroller of the Currency (1920: 57).

88. Ibid., 55–56.

89. Ibid., 56–57.

90. Grant (2014: 113–16).
91. Ibid., 115–17, 176–78; see also Chernow (1990: 237, 292).
92. New York Herald Tribune (1921a); New York Times (1921b).
93. The most controversial item inserted by Williams into the enlarged call report form required national banks to disclose the total amount of salaries paid to their executive officers. Many national banks refused to comply with that item, and Crissinger promptly rescinded it. Kane (1922: chapter XVI); New York Times (1921b).
94. Comptroller of the Currency (1922: 4); Kane (1922: chapter XVII).
95. First National Bank in St. Louis v. Missouri, 263 U.S. 640 (1924).
96. Henry Dawes was a Chicago businessman and the younger brother of Charles Dawes, a prominent Chicago banker who served as Comptroller of the Currency from 1898 to 1901 under President William McKinley. Henry Dawes resigned as Comptroller in Dec. 1924, after Charles was elected Vice President as Calvin Coolidge's running mate. See "Charles G. Dawes," available at http://www.occ.treas.gov/about/what-we-do/history/150th-comptroller-charles-dawes.html; "Henry M. Dawes," available at http://www.federalreservehistory.org/People/DetailView/250
97. McIntosh was appointed as Comptroller of the Currency by President Coolidge in Dec. 1924 and served until Nov. 1928. See "Joseph W. McIntosh," available at http://www.federalreservehistory.org/People/DetailView/251.
98. Allen (1935: 222–24) (during the Harding and Coolidge administrations, "business—and especially financial business—was king.... The 'hands off business' sentiment had a very real effect upon the relation between government and private enterprise"); Chernow (1990: 225–26, 254–55) ("During the Republican-dominated 1920s, bankers probably attained their peak of influence in American history").
99. Galbraith (1972: 31); Stabler (1927).
100. Comptroller of the Currency (1924: 2–12) (report submitted by Dawes).
101. Ibid.; Comptroller of the Currency (1927: 1–12) (report submitted by McIntosh); Peach (1941: 39–42, 150).
102. Cleveland & Huertas (1985: 384n12); Comptroller of the Currency (1924: 2–3, 12); Comptroller of the Currency (1927: 1–2, 11–12); Peach (1941: 39–42, 82–84, 148–51); Perino (2010: 207); Perkins (1971: 493–96, 494n27).
103. White (1983: 42–44).
104. Peach (1941: 39–42, 56–57, 150); Perkins (1971: 493–96); Willis & Chapman (1933: 48, 536–37).
105. For Erik Gerding's application of his "regulatory instability hypothesis" to events during the 1920s, see Gerding (2014: 8–15, 84–91, 104, 108).

Chapter 2

1. Allen (1935: 222–23, 232–39).
2. Ibid., 361–62, 390; Carosso (1970: 240–41); Chandler (1970: 15–16); Cleveland & Huertas (1985: 113–14); Friedman & Schwartz (1963: 240–42, 287–89): Kennedy (1973: 9); Galbraith (1972: 6–19); Shiller (2015: 130–34).
3. Chancellor (1999: 192–94); see also Eichengreen (2015: 3, 21) ("Creation of the Federal Reserve System in 1913 encouraged the belief that the business cycle instability that had traditionally plagued the country had been tamed"); White (2009: 3, 14–15) (the

Fed's success in "reducing the volatility of the financial markets" between 1914 and 1929 created widespread confidence in the Fed's ability to "prevent a financial crisis"). See Chapter 3 for discussion of the Fed's easy-money policies in 1924 and 1927.

4. Carosso (1970: 253–65, 271–80, 299); Chernow (1990: 225, 237, 302–10). See Chapter 4 for analysis of the sales of foreign bonds made by U.S. commercial and investment banks.

5. Allen (1935: 232); see also Perino (2010: 81) ("With the booming stock market, [Charles] Mitchell and other Wall Street leaders were celebrities, and the press chronicled their business pronouncements and their social lives with equal ardor").

6. Willis & Chapman (1934: 188–90, 199–200, 536–37, 586–89); Peach (1941: 38–42, 53–57, 148–51).

7. White (1983: 163–65).

8. Willis & Chapman (1934: 589–91) (noting that real estate loans held by national banks grew from less than $300 million to more than $1.4 billion between 1921 and 1929); see also Goldsmith (1933: 72–77, 293 [table 6]) (showing that real estate loans made by "All Incorporated Banks" rose from $5.5 billion in 1921 to $11.3 billion in 1929).

9. Calder (1999: 17–22, 211–37); Chandler (1970: 15–17); Eichengreen & Mitchener (2003: 23, 36–42); Gordon (1951: 176–79, 188–91, 196–97); Olney (1999: 320–23); Persons (1930: 108–15). The total value of consumer durable goods produced each year rose from $4.1 billion in 1919 to $6.3 billion in 1929. During the same period, the number of motor vehicles sold each year increased from 1.9 million to 5.3 million. Historical Statistics (1975: 700 [Series P 318–374], 716 [Series Q 148–162]).

10. Carosso (1970: 273); Cleveland & Huertas (1985: 128, 140–41); Goldsmith (1933: 55, 60–61, 64–66, 293 [table 6]); Peach (1941: 22–27); Willis & Chapman (1934: 611–15).

11. Peach (1941: 22–31, 82–84).

12. Goldsmith (1933: 86–89, 293 [table 6]); see also Cleveland & Huertas (1985: 130–32); Willis & Chapman (1934: 557–58, 615–28).

13. Wilmarth (2004a: 88–89).

14. Peach (1941: 108–10); see also Goldsmith (1933: 131–37).

15. Carosso (1970: 279).

16. Ibid., 278–29; Cleveland & Huertas (1985: 139–46, 153–58); Goldsmith (1933: 133–39); Peach (1941: 28–31, 72–81, 85–104, 111–12).

17. Peach (1941: 37, 142).

18. Mitchener & Richardson (2016: 4–6); Richardson (2007b: 644–45, 649–51); White (1983: 149–51).

19. Supporters of the Federal Reserve Act of 1913 believed that it would stop the "pyramiding of reserves" in New York and Chicago, which had occurred under the National Bank Act of 1864. During House debates on the Federal Reserve Act, Representative Carter Glass, Chairman of the House Banking and Currency Committee, denounced the pyramiding of reserves that allowed money center banks to act as "the legal custodians of all the reserve funds of the country [which] they put into the maelstrom of Wall Street stock operations." Glass predicted that the Federal Reserve Act would "break down the artificial connection between the banking business of this country and the stock speculative operations at the money centers." Smith & Rixley (1939: 453–54) (reprinting Glass's floor speech in the House of Representatives on Sept. 10, 1913). Contrary to those hopes, 90% of state banks chose not to become members of the Federal Reserve System. State nonmember banks could satisfy their reserve requirements under state law by maintaining deposits

with reserve city banks and money center banks. National banks and state member banks maintained their required reserves with regional Federal Reserve Banks. However, most of those banks also deposited surplus funds (excess reserves) in reserve city banks and money center banks. Unlike the Federal Reserve Banks, which did not pay interest on excess reserves, money center banks and reserve city banks paid interest to attract deposits from smaller banks. Smaller banks also maintained deposits with reserve city banks and money center banks as a condition of receiving correspondent banking services from those larger banks. As a result of the strong incentives for maintaining interbank deposits, the "pyramid of interbank balances remained in place on the eve of the Great Depression." Mitchener & Richardson (2016: 4–6); see also White (1983: 65–72, 149–51).

20. Carosso (1970: 369–70); Cleveland & Huertas (1985: 127–28, 380n45); Peach (1941: 13, 28–31, 76–77, 96, 111–12).

21. Carosso (1970: 85, 267); Goldsmith (1933: 26–27).

22. James (1938: 963–64).

23. Historical Statistics (1975: 1006 [Series X 510–515]) (showing that corporations issued $33 billion of debt securities and $21 billion of stocks between 1919 and 1930); see also Carosso (1970: 240–44, 243 [exhibit 7], 255, 271–79) (describing how aggressive competition between commercial and investment banks encouraged new securities issues during the 1920s).

24. Historical Statistics (1975: 1006 [Series X 516]); Peach (1941: 36–37).

25. Mintz (1951: 8–9, 9 [table 1]).

26. U.S. Senate (1931: 540) (testimony of Allan M. Pope, executive vice president of the First National Old Colony Corp.). The First National Old Colony Corporation was a securities affiliate of the First National Bank of Boston, which acquired the Old Colony Trust Company and its securities affiliate in 1930. Peach (1941: 78, 98).

27. 75 *Congressional Record* 9904–05 (1932) (remarks of Sen. Walcott); see also Cleveland & Huertas (1985: 141) (stating that "wholesale" investment banks such as J. P. Morgan and Kuhn, Loeb "had no retail distribution of their own, while National City had the country's best").

28. 75 *Congressional Record* 9888 (1932) (remarks of Sen. Glass).

29. In 1929, National City Bank had $1.65 billion of deposits and $240 million of capital, while its securities affiliate, National City Company, had $130 million of capital. Cleveland & Huertas (1985: 134 [table 7.8], 153 [table 8.6]). In 1930, following its merger with Equitable Trust, Chase National Bank had more than $2 billion of deposits and almost $300 million of capital, while its securities affiliate, Chase Securities Corporation, had $110 million of capital. In 1928, the Continental Illinois Bank and Trust Company of Chicago, which operated the third-largest securities affiliate, had more than $900 million of deposits and $150 million of capital, while its securities affiliate, the Continental Illinois Company, had $60 million of capital in 1930. Goldsmith (1933: 135–36); New York Times (1928); Peach (1941: 97–98); Pecora (1939: 132). J. P. Morgan & Co., the largest and most important private investment bank, had $490 million of deposits and $120 million of capital in 1929. In contrast, Kuhn, Loeb & Co., the second-most-important private investment bank, had only $90 million of deposits and $25 million of capital in 1929. Carosso (1970: 255–57).

30. Carosso (1970: 255–65, 271–79, 339); Chernow (1990: 225, 237, 303–04); Cleveland & Huertas (1985: 139–47, 152–58); Geisst (2012: 153, 159–62, 170–72); Peach (1941: 13–14, 74–75, 85–112, 139–42).

31. Carosso (1970: 283–95, 325, 344–46); Chernow (1990: 308); Goldsmith (1933: 142–46); U.S. Senate (1934: 333–62); see Chapter 4 for additional discussion of the growth and collapse of investment trusts.

32. Carosso (1970: 255, 254, 271); see also Chernow (1990: 225, 237) (stating that the "big New York City bankers scrambled for the new business" in foreign bond issues during the 1920s, with the result that "too many bankers … chased too few good deals, and credit standards eroded accordingly").

33. Cleveland & Huertas (1985: 87–88, 113–14, 156–58).

34. New York Herald Tribune (1921b).

35. Cleveland & Huertas (1985: 113–58); New York Herald Tribune (1921b).

36. Cleveland & Huertas (1985: 114–27).

37. Ibid., 113–30, 153–56, 376n40, 380n45; see also ibid., 134 (table 7.8) (showing that National City Bank's deposits increased from $650 million to $1.65 billion between 1921 and 1929, while its loans rose from $530 million to $1.24 billion and its assets grew from $820 million to $2.21 billion); Klein (2001: 58, 112); Peach (1941: 90–92).

38. Cleveland & Huertas (1985: 130–32, 131 [table 7.7]) (showing that the bank's call loans for its own account and the account of others rose from $140 million in June 1923 to $620 million in Oct. 1929).

39. U.S. Senate (1933a: 1879) (testimony of Gordon S. Rentschler, president of National City Bank).

40. Cleveland & Huertas (1985: 171).

41. Ibid., 156–57.

42. U.S. Senate (1933a: 1995, 1939) (colloquies between Ferdinand Pecora and Mitchell and Baker).

43. Pecora (1939: 82).

44. Cleveland & Huertas (1985: 110–11); Pecora (1939: 114–17); Perino (2010: 142–44, 146–48): U.S. Senate (1934: 205–07).

45. Freeman & McKinley (2018: 117–20, 163); see Chapter 6 for discussion of the Senate's investigation of National City.

46. Pecora (1939: 114, 117–18); see also Perino (2010: 142–44).

47. U.S. Senate (1933a: 1769–72).

48. Ibid., 1769–72.

49. Peach (1941: 19–20, 87–95); see also Cleveland & Huertas (1985: 135–53).

50. Cleveland & Huertas (1985: 152–53); Klein (2001: 54–58); Peach (1941: 89–95); U.S. Senate (1933a: 1863–65) (testimony of Charles Mitchell).

51. Barton (1923: 16, 132–33).

52. Allen (1935: 311–12).

53. U.S. Senate (1933a: 1772, 1887–88, 1926–27) (testimony of Charles Mitchell and Hugh Baker).

54. Cleveland & Huertas (1985: 137–46, 140 [table 8.1]) (showing that NCC was a lead or participating underwriter for $10.73 billion of the $50.27 billion of bonds issued in the U.S. between 1921 and 1929); New York Times (1927) (reporting on NCC's decision in early 1927 to begin selling common stock to investors).

55. Carosso (1970: 339, 344–45) (providing information for J. P. Morgan and Dillon, Read); U.S. Senate (1933b: 2281–82) (testimony of Chase National Bank chairman Albert

Wiggin, stating that Chase's securities affiliate sold $6.16 billion of securities between 1917 and 1933, with most sales occurring between 1927 and 1930).

56. Pecora (1939: 82–83).
57. Wilson (1936: 56, 57–58).
58. New York Herald Tribune (1927).
59. Cleveland & Huertas (1985: 127–31, 135–43, 156–58).
60. Ibid., 139, 385n14 (quoting Mitchell's lecture to National City Bank and NCC trainees, Mar. 18, 1919).
61. Ibid., 137.
62. Ibid., 138 (figure 8.1) (reproducing NCC advertisement entitled "I shouldn't decide it alone").
63. Perino (2010) (photo section following page 182, reproducing NCC advertisement entitled "Empire Builders—in your safe deposit box").
64. Ibid., 236 (quoting NCC advertisement).
65. Pecora (1939: 88–92); Perino (2010: 198–203); U.S. Senate (1933a: 2015–20) (testimony of NCC president Hugh Baker); U.S. Senate (1934: 167–68).
66. Perino (2010: 202, 199) (quoting Julian Sherrod, *Scapegoats* [New York: Brewer, Warren, & Putnam, 1931], 22–23, 39, 16).
67. Perino (2010: 202–03) (quoting Mitchell's telegram); Seligman (2003: 24–25) (same); see also Wilson (1936: 56) (stating that NCC's salesmen were "always afraid of being fired if they failed to sell more and more bonds," because Mitchell had told them, "You cannot stand still in this business—you fellows are not *Self Starters'*—till they would resort to faking orders merely to inflate their figures and invest their own salaries in these securities about whose value they knew as little as the people they were selling them to").
68. Cleveland & Huertas (1985: 108–10); Peach (1941: 131–33); Pecora (1939: 121–23); Perino (2010: 159–64); U.S. Senate (1933a: 1788–99, 1835) (testimony of Charles Mitchell); see also New York Times (1932) (reporting that NCC wrote down its capital from $55 million to $11 million as of Dec. 31, 1931, due in large part to NCC's decision to reduce the reported value of its investment in General Sugar from $25 million to $1). As described in Chapter 1, National City's shareholders held joint stock certificates representing ownership of both National City Bank and NCC. Accordingly, National City's shareholders suffered when either company incurred losses.
69. Perino (2010: 160–64); Pecora (1939: 121–23); U.S. Senate (1933a: 1796–97, 1833–34).
70. Perino (2010: 161).
71. Pecora (1939: 110–12); Perino (2010: 181–83); Seligman (2003: 47); U.S. Senate (1933a: 1919–24, 1970) (testimony of NCC president Hugh Baker); see also Geisst (2012: 159–60) (describing the curb exchange, which was organized by brokers to compete with the NYSE and later became the American Stock Exchange). NYSE rules during the 1920s prohibited corporations from becoming members of the NYSE, and corporations therefore could not trade in NYSE-listed stocks except through brokers who were members of the NYSE. Sissoko (2017: 60–61). By virtue of its status as a corporation, NCC could not trade directly in the stock of National City Bank as long as that stock was listed on the NYSE.
72. Pecora (1939: 110–12); Peach (1941: 92–94); Perino (2010: 179–84); U.S. Senate (1933a: 1879–84, 1890–92, 1919, 1938–40, 1971–80, 1983–85, 1989–97) (testimony of Gordon Rentschler, Hugh Baker, and Charles Mitchell).

73. U.S. Senate (1933a: 1938–40, 2006–09, 2019–21) (testimony of Hugh Baker). In Feb. 1929, NCC sent out a "flash" to its sales agents, which encouraged them to sell National City stock, promised to pay them the "usual" commission, and stressed the importance of recruiting new shareholders to provide "a substantial number of new business prospects for all of us." Ibid., 2013–14 (reprinting "Flash No. 3765," dated Feb. 1, 1929, from Hugh Baker); see also Perino (2010: 179) (explaining that NCC "intensely marketed [National City] stock to the public, not only to raise the price of the stock, but because broad stock ownership benefited the bank. Stockholders became just another group to whom the bank could cross-sell its other financial products").

74. U.S. Senate (1933a: 1921–23) (testimony of Hugh Baker); Wigmore (1985: 49 [table 1.14], 50, 468, 469 [table 14.6]).

75. Perino (2010: 135, 322n9) (quoting letter from Helen Kirst to Sen. Peter Norbeck).

76. Pecora (1939: 128–29); Perino (2010: 168–71); New York Herald Tribune (1929e). National City Bank established its stock purchase plan for ordinary employees at a time when both NCC and Charles Mitchell held large blocks of National City's stock following the collapse of a planned merger with the Corn Exchange Bank. National City's leadership evidently hoped that selling a large block of stock to ordinary employees would help to shield NCC and Mitchell from further trading losses. However, National City's stock price continued to fall, and the employee stock purchase plan inflicted large losses on participating employees. Perino (2010: 169–71).

77. Pecora (1939: 127–28); Perino (2010: 166–68); U.S. Senate (1933a: 1868–72, 1875) (testimony of Gordon Rentschler).

78. Pecora (1939: 128–30); Perino (2010: 168–69, 187, 325 (note 16) (quoting *New York Inquiry*, Mar. 5, 1933); U.S. Senate (1933a: 1872–75) (testimony of Gordon Rentschler). The *New York Herald Tribune* stated that the public was "shocked by the obvious injustice of making large loans to officers of the institution with which to carry stock and then writing off such loans, while lesser employees were compelled to continue installment payments on the bank's shares." ("Restoring Confidence" [editorial], *New York Herald Tribune*, Feb. 28, 1933, 14). Another newspaper stated that "the clerks of the bank, who had been urged, and in some cases really driven, to purchasing the bank stock ... lest they lose the favor of their superior officers, were given ... no aid whatsoever by the bank in carrying the shares they bought.... No loans to help them carry on!" (Perino 2010: 187, 325n16) (quoting 135 *Nation* 245, 248 [Mar. 8, 1933]).

79. Pecora (1939: 132–33).

80. Klein (2001: 59–60); Pecora (1939: 131–33). Wiggin finished high school but did not attend college. He began his career as a clerk in a Boston bank, served as a bank examiner for three years, and worked as a vice president in a Boston bank and a New York bank before joining Chase in 1904. New York Times (1926, 1951).

81. Klein (2001: 59–60); Pecora (1939: 132–36); Wigmore (1985: 50); U.S. Senate (1933b: 2410) (testimony of Albert Wiggin).

82. Carosso (1970: 346); Peach (1941: 63–68, 95–98).

83. New York Times (1926).

84. Cleveland & Huertas (1985: 157, 164–65); Goldsmith (1933: 161–62, 307 [table 23]); Klein (2001: 59–60); Peach (1941: 17n4, 95n58).

85. Peach (1941: 63–64, 67–68, 95–97); Pecora (1939: 137–40); U.S. Senate (1933b: 2281–82) (testimony of Albert Wiggin).

86. U.S. Senate (1933b: 2371–79) (testimony of Albert Wiggin).

87. Pecora (1939: 131–32, 149–51); Wigmore (1985: 49 [table 1.14], 50, 468, 469 [table 14.6]); U.S. Senate (1933b: 2837–39) (testimony of Albert Wiggin and Henry Hargreaves); U.S. Senate (1934: 174–81).

88. Wigmore (1985: 50).

89. U.S. Senate (1933b: 2921–25) (testimony of Albert Wiggin); U.S. Senate (1934: 182).

90. Pecora (1939: 92–93); U.S. Senate (1933a: 1843–55) (testimony of Charles Mitchell); U.S. Senate (1934: 166–67).

91. Pecora (1939: 92–95); U.S. Senate (1933a: 1843–55, 1862–66) (testimony of Charles Mitchell); see also U.S. Senate (1934: 107–09, 166–68) (describing NCC's purchases and sales of the stock of United Aircraft [Boeing] and Anaconda, and noting that "other common and preferred stock was sold by [NCC] throughout the country by means of this extensive selling organization").

92. Pecora (1939: 168–76); U.S. Senate (1933b: 3340–41) (colloquy between Sen. Duncan Fletcher and Elisha Walker); U.S. Senate (1934: 64–66).

93. Pecora (1939: 183–85); U.S. Senate (1933b: 2858–59) (providing a list of CSC's trading syndicates). Jiang, Mahoney, & Mei (2005) provide a more benign assessment of stock trading pools during the 1920s. Based on a data set consisting of pools for stocks traded on the NYSE in 1928 and 1929, they conclude that "while the pattern of stock price and trading volume could be consistent with market manipulation, there is no evidence that the stock pools' trades drove prices to artificially high levels. Therefore, we conclude that public investors were not harmed by pool operations." Ibid., 150. However, their data set did not include the trading pools for the stocks of National City, Chase, Anaconda, and Sinclair because those stocks were not traded on the NYSE. In addition, their data set did not include any of the other trading syndicates organized by CSC. Compare ibid., 153, 154–56 (table 1) with U.S. Senate (1933b: 2858–59).

94. Goldsmith (1933: 132–36, 147–78); Peach (1941: 19–20, 63–64, 87–99, 104).

95. James (1938: 947–52).

96. Allen (1935: 321–24); Goldsmith (1933: 130–37, 195–200); Hector (1988: 24–54); James (1938: 961–63); Peach (1941: 54–60, 65–66, 98–104).

97. Willis & Chapman (1934: 381–90); see also Goldsmith (1933: 147–83, 201–05, 305 [table 19]) (showing that bank holding companies and banks with branches collectively controlled $30 billion of assets at the end of 1929, compared with $28.4 billion of assets that were held by unit [non-branching] banks).

98. Goldsmith (1933: 133–36, 152–56); Peach (1941: 100–05).

99. Eichengreen (2015: 124–29); Goldsmith (1933: 225–26); Hamilton (1985: 583–84, 591–96, 599, 607); McFerrin (1969); Wicker (1996: 22, 32–36).

100. Goetzmann & Newman (2010: 3–9); Goldsmith (1933: 75–76); Graham & Dodd (1940: 138–44, 742–44nn19–21); Persons (1930: 98–101); Postel-Vinay (2016: 482–83); Snowden (2010: 59–60); White (2009: 29–32); Wiggers & Ashcraft (2012: 2–7).

101. Goetzmann & Newman (2010: 6–7, 12, 15, 18–19, 23 [figure 7]) (showing that the repayment rate for real estate bonds declined from 80% for bonds issued in 1920 to 60% for bonds issued in 1924 and 40% for bonds issued in 1927 and 1928); Graham & Dodd (1940: 138–41, 742–43n19); White (2009: 31–32); Wiggers & Ashcraft (2012: 7–9, 12–13, 17–18).

102. Wigmore (1985: 228–29, 430–31, 436–38); see also Rodkey (1935–36: 101–08, 134–38) (reporting that three-quarters of real estate bonds backed by Michigan properties defaulted by the end of 1932, and real estate bonds accounted for more than 40% of the investment securities held by 168 Michigan state-chartered banks that failed between Jan. 1930 and Feb. 1933).

103. U.S. Senate (1933b: 4050–52, 4058–64 [testimony of Leslie Snow], 4072–78 [reprinting prospectuses]).

104. Ibid., 4057–64, 4084–85, 4100–04 (testimony of Leslie Snow and George Ramsey).

105. Goldsmith (1933: 72–76, 296 [table 10]); Persons (1930: 96–98, 101–04); Historical Statistics (1975: 989 (Series X 393–409); White (2009: 25–29, 36–39). The total amount of farm mortgages remained essentially unchanged (at approximately $10 billion) during the 1920s, due in large part to the severe problems that plagued the farm economy throughout the decade. In 1930, commercial banks held about $1 billion of farm mortgages and $5 billion of urban nonfarm mortgages. Goldsmith (1933: 72–76, 296 [table 10]); Historical Statistics (1975: 989 [Series X 393–409]).

106. About a third of all farm and nonfarm mortgages were held by individuals in 1930, either as independent investors or as investors in real estate bonds or mortgage guarantee certificates. White (2009: 25).

107. More than $1 billion of mortgage guarantee participation certificates were issued by mortgage guarantee companies. Those companies originated commercial or residential mortgages, placed the mortgages in trusts, and sold participation certificates to investors with a guarantee of payment. Most mortgage guarantee companies failed during the 1930s and defaulted on their certificates. Goetzmann & Newman (2010: 5, 8–9); Snowden (2010: 58–59, 62–63); White (2009: 30–32).

108. Goetzmann & Newman (2010: 1–5, 16–19); White (2009: 2–3, 29–33, 50).

109. Brocker & Hanes (2013: 2–5, 12–13); Eichengreen & Mitchener (2003: 21–25, 33–35); Field (1992: 786–87, 795); Goetzmann & Newman (2010: 2–9); Goldsmith (1933: 77–79, 296 [table 10]); Gordon (1951: 201, 202 [table 13], 203–07); Nicholas & Scherbina (2013: 278–81, 296–300); Persons (1930: 125–27); White (2009: 3–14); Historical Statistics (1975: 618 [Series N 1–29], 640 [Series N 156–69]). For vivid descriptions of the spectacular housing boom in Florida, which peaked in 1925 and collapsed in 1927, see Allen (1931: chapter XI); Eichengreen (2015: 26–35) (noting that "this frenzied activity would not have been possible, of course, without the banks"; ibid., 28).

110. Goetzmann & Newman (2010: 3–4).

111. Chernow (1990: 302).

112. Allen (1931: chapter XI, § 4).

113. James (1938: 942–43, 964–66).

114. Postel-Vinay (2016: 482–83).

115. Goldsmith (1933: 296 [table 10]); Goetzmann & Newman (2010: 24 [table 1]); Postel-Vinay (2016: 483 [figure 1]).

116. Eichengreen & Mitchener (2003: 21–25, 33–35) (describing how the "credit boom" for real estate "fueled an orgy of construction that left the landscape littered with vacant apartment buildings, and with subdivisions that ... remained undeveloped for years"); Field (1992: 785–89, 792–95, 799–801) (explaining that "an enormous boom in real capital formation accompanied the speculative activity" in housing markets and produced "uncontrolled" development and overbuilding); Nicholas & Scherbina (2013: 281,

303) (stating that "speculation in real estate securities" helped to produce a "pre-crash construction boom" and an "oversupply of available housing" in New York City).

117. James (1938: 992).

118. Allen (1931: chapter XI, §4).

119. U.S. Senate (1933c: 7).

120. Brocker & Hanes (2013: 3–5, 31–33) (determining that a housing "bubble" was created by "excess investment" during the 1920s, because "cities which had experienced the biggest house construction booms in the mid-1920s, and the highest increases in house values and homeownership rates across the 1920s, [also] saw the greatest declines in house values and homeownership rates after 1930"); Goetzmann & Newman (2010: 18–19) (concluding that the market for real estate bonds "buckled under the top-heavy burden of greater demand for financial assets than for their underlying real properties ... Optimism in financial markets has the power to raise steel, but it does not make a building pay"); see also authorities cited in note 116.

121. Brocker & Hanes (2013: 2, 20 [figure 1]) (explaining that the increase in the ratio of non-farm mortgage debt to household income during the 1920s indicated "homebuyers' willingness to buy into the rising price environment" for homes).

122. Postel-Vinay (2017: 559–61, 570–72, 579–82); Snowden (2010: 51–52); White (2009: 26–27).

123. Olney (1999: 321 [table I]).

124. Beim (2009).

125. Fasianos, Guevara, & Pierros (2016: 21 [figure 7]); Historical Statistics (1975: 224 [Series F 1–5]) (showing that U.S. GNP was $84.0 billion in 1919 and $103.1 billion in 1929); Historical Statistics (1975: 989 [Series X 393–409]) (showing that between 1919 and 1929, total private sector debt grew from $97.2 billion to $161.8 billion).

126. Meltzer (2003: 14, 259); Historical Statistics (1975: 989 [Series X 393–409]) (showing that federal government debt declined from $25.6 billion to $16.5 billion between 1919 and 1929).

127. Historical Statistics (1975: 989 [Series X 393–409] (showing that state and local debt increased from $5.5 billion in 1919 to $13.6 billion in 1929).

128. Calomiris (1993: 76).

129. Peach (1941: 13–15, 18–23, 36–37, 82–84) (describing the growing role of commercial banks and their affiliates in underwriting and distributing the huge volume of debt securities that were issued by U.S. corporations and state and local governments during the 1920s).

130. Eichengreen & Mitchener (2003); see also Eichengreen (2015: 3) (describing how "the explosive growth of credit fuel[ed] property and asset-market booms" during the 1920s); Persons (1930: 94) (concluding that the "depression was due essentially to the great wave of credit expansion" during the 1920s); Postel-Vinay (2019) (providing additional evidence that the credit surge of the 1920s was a "credit boom gone wrong").

Chapter 3

1. Carosso (1970: 245–51, 261–63); Chernow (1990: 225–29, 236–38); Cleveland & Huertas (1985: 146–47, 387n24); Costigliola (1976: 477–79, 485–89, 494–95); Eichengreen

(2015: 52–57); Mintz (1951: 8–9); Rothbard (1975: 127–31); Stallings (1987: 67–68, 254–58); Wigmore (1985: 198–202, 417).

2. Accominotti & Eichengreen (2016: 475–76); Carosso (1970: 245–48); Mintz (1951: 8–13).
3. Chernow (1990: 236); New York Herald Tribune (1924).
4. Chernow (1990: 236–38).
5. Ahamed (2009: 90–91, 100); Costigliola (1976: 477–79); Crafts & Fearon (2010: 288–89).
6. Ahamed (2009: 11–13, 19–20); Eichengreen (1992: 29–32, 42–54).
7. Ahamed (2009: 90–91, 155–64); Bordo, Edelstein, & Rockoff (2003: 288–98); Eichengreen & Temin (2010: 371–74); Meltzer (2003: 5, 10–11, 49–51, 75–84).
8. Accominotti & Eichengreen (2016: 470–71); Ahamed (2009: 76, 83–84, 87, 90–91, 99–101, 130–32, 135–37, 157–61); Crafts & Fearon (2010: 288–90); see also Winkler (1933: 116–18, 125–26) (noting that the Allies spent almost $12 billion to acquire supplies from the U.S. during World War I). France owed $3 billion of war debts to Britain in addition to the $4 billion France owed to the U.S. Ahamed (2009: 130–31).
9. Ahamed (2009: 101–32, 135–44, 257); Chernow (1990: 227–28, 247–48, 251); Eichengreen (2015: 36–40); Eichengreen (1992: 127–42); Kindleberger (1986: 17–20, 25–27); Ritschl (2012: 7); Wolf (2010: 344–48). The Allies—especially Britain—might have been willing to reduce their demands for German reparations if the U.S. had forgiven a comparable portion of its loans to the Allies. However, President Woodrow Wilson firmly rejected any linkage between German reparations and Allied war debts. Ahamed (2009: 130–32); Harman (1931).
10. Ahamed (2009: 184–201); Chernow (1990: 247–49); Costigliola (1976: 480–85).
11. Ahamed (2009: 197–200); Chernow (1990: 243–44, 247–49); Costigliola (1976: 479, 483–86).
12. Ahamed (2009: 201–16); Chernow (1990: 249–53); Cleveland & Huertas (1985: 146–49, 388–89n32); Costigliola (1976: 485–94); Eichengreen (1992: 148–52, 223–24); Eichengreen (2015: 39–40, 52–54); Kindleberger (1986: 20–23).
13. Chernow (1990: 249–51); Cleveland & Huertas (1985: 148–49, 388–39n32); Eichengreen (2015: 53–54).
14. Costigliola (1976: 490–95); Eichengreen (1989: 115–16, 119–20).
15. Accominotti & Eichengreen (2016: 471–75); Ahamed (2009: 324–25); Cleveland & Huertas (1985: 149); Costigliola (1976: 485–89, 495–98); Wolf (2010: 346–47); Schuker (1988: 35–37).
16. Ahamed (2009: 283–84); Ritschl (2012: 8–9); Ritschl (1998: 53).
17. Ahamed (2009: 215–16, 325–26); Chernow (1990: 251–53, 310–11); Ritschl (2012: 6–11).
18. Ahamed (2009: 17–18, 155–64, 191–99, 209–16, 221, 227–28); Bordo, Edelstein, & Rockoff (2003: 288–301); Chernow (1990: 244–45, 274–75); Eichengreen (2015: 21–22, 36–46); Ritschl & Sarferaz (2014: 351–52).
19. Crafts & Fearon (2010: 289); Eichengreen (1992: 127–210); Kindleberger (1986: 27–39); Meltzer (2003: 165, 170); Wolf (2010: 346–49); see also authorities cited in note 18.
20. Ahamed (2009: 149–63, 168–69, 218–37); Chernow (1990: 244–46, 273–76); Eichengreen (2015: 21–24); Eichengreen (1992: 159–67, 190–92); Kindleberger (1986: 28–31); Wigmore (1985: 201–02).
21. Ahamed (2009: 92, 132–33, 219–28); Chernow (1990: 244–47, 273–76); Eichengreen (2015: 21–24); Meltzer (2003: 75, 110, 165, 170, 185).

22. Chernow (1990: 274–76); Eichengreen (2015: 21–24, 55); Friedman & Schwartz (1963: 287–88); Meltzer (2003: 125, 170–74, 202–04); Rothbard (1975: 132–34).

23. Eichengreen (1992: 187–203); Eichengreen & Flandreau (2009: 380–89) (explaining that the share of total reserves held by member countries in the form of foreign exchange increased from 28% in 1925 to 42% in 1928). Allan Meltzer provided the following summary description of the interwar gold exchange standard: "To conserve limited gold stocks (and earn interest on reserve balances), countries other than the United States, Britain, and later France held part or all of their reserves in dollar or pound securities, exchangeable for gold. These dollar or pound claims could be exchanged for gold reserves on demand as long as the United States and Britain maintained convertibility; hence the name gold exchange standard." Meltzer (2003: 171n47).

24. Eichengreen & Flandreau (2009: 392–403).

25. Eichengreen (1992: 203–23, 279–86, 293–98, 323–32); Eichengreen & Flandreau (2009: 382–86, 402–05).

26. Ahamed (2009: 287–89, 292–98); Eichengreen (1992: 210–13); Kindleberger (1986: 31–36, 49–50).

27. Ahamed (2009: 294–99); Eichengreen (1992: 212–13); James (1938: 972–76); Kindleberger (1986: 43, 49–53); Meltzer (2003: 174–79, 215–27). The regional Federal Reserve Banks in Chicago, Minneapolis, Philadelphia, and San Francisco vehemently opposed Strong's proposed discount rate cut, "insisting that such a move would only fuel stock market speculation." The Federal Reserve Board (by a 4–3 vote) imposed the rate reduction on Chicago after Chicago refused to implement it voluntarily. Ahamed (2009: 298–99); see also Meltzer (2003: 221–23).

28. Friedman & Schwartz (1963: 288n67): Meltzer (2003: 172–74).

29. See Chapter 2 for discussion of the U.S. credit boom during the 1920s.

30. Ahamed (2009: 274–78, 298–300); Eichengreen (2015: 21–25, 48); Kindleberger (1986: 53–54); Meltzer (2003: 226–27); Rothbard (1975: 142–43).

31. Eichengreen (2015: 25) (quoting Hoover's criticism of Strong); Jeansonne (2016: 179–81).

32. Ahamed (2009: 299) (quoting Hoover's memorandum); Kindleberger (1986: 53–54).

33. Chernow (1990: 313) (quoting letter from Leffingwell to Lamont dated Mar. 8, 1929).

34. Eichengreen (2015: 21); see also Ahamed (2009: 300) (concluding that the Fed's easing in 1927 was "the spark that lit the forest fire"); Jeansonne (2016: 179–81) (arguing that the Fed should have heeded Hoover's warnings about the risks created by the Fed's "easy money policies"); Rothbard (1975: 131–52, and "Introduction to the Second Edition") (contending, in line with Austrian business cycle theories, that the Federal Reserve's "easy money" policies in 1924 and 1927 promoted unsound "cheap credit," which in turn produced a "great inflationary boom" that "set the stage inevitably for the depression").

35. Costigliola (1976: 490, 495); Eichengreen (2015: 50, 55); Eichengreen (1989: 115–16, 120); Jeansonne (2016: 163–64); Mintz (1951: 8–9, 26–27). In 1927, a prominent American bond analyst described "the pronounced demand for and the ready absorption of large foreign [bond] issues, irrespective of quality." The analyst explained that American investors "crave for high rates of interest and unreasonable profits on the investment of their capital, and these cravings are, as is to be expected, being taken advantage of by dishonest contrivances of promoters." Winkler (1933: 85) (quoting Max Winkler's statements published in the *New York Tribune* on Mar. 17, 1927).

36. Bordo, Edelstein, & Rockoff (2003: 297–305, 313–14); Eichengreen (2015: 48–54); Eichengreen (1989: 117–20).

37. Costigliola (1976: 477–79, 494–95); Eichengreen (1989: 117–20); Stallings (1987: 67–68, 257–58, 261).

38. Kuczynski (1932: 26) (quoting Traylor's testimony during a Senate subcommittee hearing on Dec. 11, 1931); see also Cleveland & Huertas (1985: 387n24).

39. Carosso (1970: 248–49) (quoting Hoover); see also Jeansonne (2016: 163–64, 427n16) (citing Hoover's warnings in 1921 about the potential dangers of foreign bonds, including a "Hoover Memo to Harding Warning of Foreign Loans, Nov. 30, 1921"); Schuker (1988: 37–38).

40. Carosso (1970: 248–49); see also Costigliola (1976: 496); Cleveland & Huertas (1985: 147, 386–87n24); Stallings (1987: 74); Winkler (1933: 163–72) (quoting statement by Secretary of State Henry L. Stimson, dated Jan. 7, 1932, describing the State Department's informal review process for foreign bonds).

41. Cleveland & Huertas (1985: 147, 387–88n26); see also Chernow (1990: 225–28); Eichengreen (1989: 123–24).

42. Cleveland & Huertas (1985: 147, 386–87nn24, 26); see also Winkler (1933: 164–66) (quoting statement by Secretary of State Henry L. Stimson on Jan. 7, 1932, in which Stimson declared that the State Department "has never assumed responsibility for the wisdom or worth of the [foreign] loans of which it was informed. Its responses avoid all judgment of the matters of business risk involved, and in no way represent measurement of the merit of any foreign loan ... either for the bankers or investors").

43. Chernow (1990: 228–29) (quoting Thomas Lamont, a partner in J. P. Morgan & Co.); see also Cleveland & Huertas (1985: 388n26) (stating that the State Department's review process created a widespread public impression that each foreign bond "had the government's stamp of approval as an investment").

44. Chernow (1990: 228–29, 225); see also Rothbard (1975: 130) (the widespread belief that "every foreign loan had the Federal government's seal of approval and was therefore a good buy ... stimulated reckless foreign lending all the more").

45. Costigliola (1976: 496) (quoting a memorandum on "German Loans," dated Aug. 7, 1925, written by Arthur Young, the State Department's economic adviser, and summarizing a memorandum from Andrew Mellon, dated Nov. 3, 1925, and a letter from Herbert Hoover, dated Oct. 23, 1925); see also Schuker (1988: 37–38).

46. Kuczynski (1932: 14–17) (quoting from Gilbert's report of Dec. 10, 1927).

47. U.S. Treasury (1926: 4–5).

48. Eichengreen (1989: 125).

49. See Chapters 8–9 and 12.

50. Carosso (1970: 246–47); Costigliola (1976: 494–97); Eichengreen (2015: 52–57); Mintz (1951: 8–13, 26–28, 50–53); Schuker (1988: 35–38).

51. Winkler (1933: 86); see also Mintz (1951: 65). During Senate hearings on foreign bond sales in 1931–32, a U.S. government official described the "very keen competition" among American bankers that persuaded "a great many countries" to issue bonds during the 1920s. Mintz (1951: 65) (quoting testimony of James C. Corliss, a Latin American specialist at the U.S. Department of Commerce, printed in U.S. Senate [1931–32: 845–46]).

52. Carosso (1970: 257) (quoting Kahn).

53. Mintz (1951: 66) (quoting a 1927 speech by Lamont and a memorandum, dated Feb. 10, 1927, from Oliver C. Townsend, U.S. commercial attaché in Lima).

54. Winkler (1933: 86–87) (quoting Dr. Koepker-Aschoff, former Prussian minister of finance, and recounting the story of the bond issue by the small Bavarian town).

55. Carosso (1970: 248, 262) ("the expectation of large profits ... was the major inducement that attracted bankers to these [bond] issues").

56. Rippy (1950: 239–42); Seligman (2003: 10); Wigmore (1985: 198–204, 417).

57. Flandreau, Gaillard, & Panizza (2010: 44 [table A]).

58. Cleveland & Huertas (1985: 145–52); Horan (1931); New York Times (1931); see also Mintz (1951: 8–9) (showing that $12.1 billion of foreign bonds were issued in the U.S. between 1919 and 1930).

59. Horan (1931); New York Times (1931).

60. Flandreau, Gaillard, & Panizza (2010: 44 [table A]); Peach (1941: 87–97, 133–39); Rippy (1950: 239 [table 2]).

61. Mintz (1951: 84); see also ibid., 85 (stating that U.S. bankers "were assured of a market for any [foreign] loan they floated" during the second half of the 1920s); Carosso (1970: 245–54, 261–62, 299); Eichengreen (2015: 52–57).

62. Rippy (1950: 238); Carosso (1970: 254).

63. Mintz (1951: 33–34, 37–40, 43–45) (showing that 24% of all non-Canadian foreign bonds issued in the U.S. between 1920 and 1923 defaulted by the end of 1937, compared with 40% of such bonds issued between 1923 and 1927 and 68% of such bonds issued between 1927 and 1929).

64. Ibid., 51–58, 67–68.

65. Morrow (1927: 224–25); see also Carosso (1970: 224–28, 235–39, 249–51, 261–65); Cleveland & Huertas (1985: 135–39); Eichengreen (2015: 50, 55–57).

66. Carosso (1970: 251) (quoting "Is It Safe to Buy Foreign Securities?," 33 *Magazine of Wall Street* 1112–13 [Apr. 26, 1924]).

67. Eichengreen (1989: 122).

68. Morrow (1927: 220–24).

69. Mintz (1951: 80–81).

70. Cleveland & Huertas (1985: 127–31, 380n45) (stating that National City offered its correspondent banks "a complete investment service"); Goldsmith (1933: 22–25, 48–50, 105–07); Mintz (1951: 83–84); Peach (1941: 28–31, 75–77, 96); Wigmore (1985: 122–23, 123 [table 4.2], 293, 322–23) (showing that the average exposure of country banks to foreign bonds in 1930 was more than twice as high, as a percentage of their capital, as the exposure of large urban banks); 75 *Congressional Record* 9910 (1932) (remarks of Sen. Bulkley).

71. 75 *Congressional Record* 9883, 9887 (1932) (remarks of Sen. Glass).

72. U.S. Senate (1932: 434–35) (colloquy between Sen. Brookhart and Mr. Pole).

73. Sen. Glass endorsed Sen. Gore's position. U.S. Senate (1933b: 4028–29) (colloquy between Sens. Glass and Gore). Gore also claimed that bank examiners encouraged country banks to buy foreign bonds to increase their "secondary reserves" of liquidity. Ibid., 4029. Brookhart similarly contended that national bank examiners advised country banks to buy bonds instead of making loans to farmers. U.S. Senate (1932: 434).

74. Morrow (1927: 225–26).

75. Mintz (1951: 81) (quoting Mitchell's testimony as printed in U.S. Senate [1931–32: 325, 352]).

76. During the Senate hearings, Thomas Lamont of J. P. Morgan & Co. testified that "we never issue a bond unless we believe it to be good." Similarly, Otto Kahn of Kuhn, Loeb & Co. stated that "we always want to be sure that what we offer is intrinsically sound." Mintz (1951: 78) (quoting testimony by Lamont and Kahn as printed in U.S. Senate [1931–32]: 40, 49–50, 342).

77. Morrow (1927: 226, 232).

78. Cleveland & Huertas (1985: 136, 139) (quoting Mitchell's lecture to National City trainees on Mar. 18, 1919). See Chapter 2 for discussion of Mitchell's professed principles.

79. Carosso (1970: 224–28, 235–55, 261–65, 273–79), Cleveland & Huertas (1985: 113–14, 135–58); Costigliola (1976: 494–95); Peach (1941: 28–37, 71–77, 87–112).

80. Carosso (1970: 317–18, 330–31, 334–35); Kuczynski (1932: 63–65); Peach (1941: 112–16, 133–42); Winkler (1933: 51–112). Foreign bonds were not the only securities that underwriters sold to American investors based on inadequate and misleading prospectuses. Brent Horton reviewed prospectuses for twenty-five public offerings of stock by domestic U.S. corporations between 1910 and 1929, including seventeen offerings completed during the 1920s. Horton concluded that "there was a widespread failure [in those prospectuses] to provide financial statements, information about capital structure and voting rights, information about compensation of executives and underwriters, and information about risk factors." The underwriters for the public offerings studied by Horton included several leading commercial banks and trust companies. Horton (2017: 745–46, 800–03 [appendix A]).

81. Eichengreen (1989: 151n19) (quoting Lothrop Stoddard, *Europe and Our Money* [New York: Macmillan, 1932], 106).

82. Flandreau, Gaillard, & Panizza (2010; 12, 15, 44 [table A]) (showing that National City and Chase served as lead underwriters for forty-five issues of foreign government bonds sold in New York during the 1920s, and twenty-seven of those bond issues defaulted during the 1930s); see also Ang & Richardson (1994: 359–63, 364 [table 3]) (showing that National City and Chase were lead underwriters for fifty-six issues of foreign and domestic bonds between 1926 and 1930 for which the ultimate "fate" is "known," and twenty-nine of those bond issues defaulted during the 1930s). As discussed in the text accompanying note 132, more than half of all foreign bonds sold in the U.S. were in default by 1938.

83. Ang & Richardson (1994: 364 [table 3], 365); Flandreau, Gaillard, & Panniza (2010: 15–16, 44 [table A]); Puri (1994: 400–01, 404–09, 409 [table 4]).

84. Stallings (1987: 259–61); U.S. Senate (1934: 126–31).

85. U.S. Senate (1933a: 2053) (quoting letter dated Dec. 9, 1921, from C. W. Calvin to J. T. Cosby).

86. Ibid., 2058 (quoting memorandum dated July 12, 1923, from C. M. Bishop to A. W. Dunham).

87. Ibid., 2060–61 (quoting memorandum dated Dec. 16, 1925, from "E.A.K.").

88. Ibid., 2065–66 (quoting an undated handwritten memorandum prepared by Victor Schoepperle).

89. Ibid., 2070–71 (quoting letter dated July 27, 1927, from J. H. Durrell to Charles E. Mitchell). Durrell was "a vice president and overseas manager of the National City Bank." U.S. Senate (1934: 128–29).

90. U.S. Senate (1934: 130) (quoting report dated Mar. 4, 1928, from Frederick R. Kent).

91. U.S. Senate (1933a: 2113–14) (quoting letter dated Oct. 8, 1928, from H. E. Henneman to J. H. Durrell).

92. U.S. Senate (1931–32: 1599–600) (quoting Dennis' testimony).

93. Perino (2010: 234–37); U.S. Senate (1934: 126, 128, 129, 131).

94. U.S. Senate (1933a: 2132–33) (testimony of Ronald M. Byrnes).

95. Ibid., 2155 (quoting letter dated June 12, 1927, from George F. Train to Ronald M. Byrnes).

96. Ibid., 2152 (quoting letter dated Apr. 27, 1928, from Train to M. E. Squires).

97. Ibid., 2156–57 (testimony of George F. Train, quoting letter dated Sept. 14, 1927, from D. C. Baldwin to Train).

98. Ibid., 2157 (testimony of Train).

99. Ibid., 2135–36 (testimony of Ronald M. Byrnes); ibid., 2160–63 (testimony of George F. Train); see also Perino (2010: 247–53) (describing Pecora's investigation of the Minas Gerais bond offerings).

100. U.S. Senate (1933a: 2133) (quoting offering prospectus dated Sept. 16, 1929).

101. Ibid., 2135, 2137 (testimony of Byrnes); see also Perino (2010: 248–49 (explaining that National City "dictated the content of a Minas Gerais law in order to ensure the legality of paying itself back with the proceeds of bonds National City was offering to American investors").

102. U.S. Senate (1933a: 2166) (quoting letter dated July 12, 1929, from D. C. Baldwin to M. E. Squires).

103. Ibid., 2132–33 (testimony of Byrnes), 2112–13 (copy of National City Company's "Flash 5033," dated Sept. 27, 1929).

104. U.S. Senate (1934: 131, 133).

105. U.S. Senate (1933a: 2298–99, 2310–11) (testimony of Ronald M. Byrnes).

106. Ibid., 2317–19 (testimony of Ronald M. Byrnes).

107. Ibid., 2320–21 (quoting report from Sterling Bunnell).

108. Ibid., 2319–23 (testimony of Ronald M. Byrnes, acknowledging that National City underwrote the $30 billion bond offering for AIGC about two months before its offering of LNC bonds).

109. Ibid., 2112–13 (reprinting National City's "Flash" to its sales offices dated Sept. 27, 1929); ibid., 2309–17 (testimony of Ronald M. Byrnes); U.S. Senate (1934: 99–100).

110. U.S. Senate (1934: 134).

111. Ibid., 135. The Chase group sold $20 million of bonds ("serial certificates") to investors in two equal installments in Oct. 1928 and Jan. 1929.

112. Ibid., 138; U.S. Senate (1933b: 2711–12, 2714–16) (testimony of Shepard Morgan); ibid., 2747–48 (testimony of A. M. Williams).

113. Peach (1941: 136–37).

114. Pecora (1939: 164–65); U.S. Senate (1933b: 2630–48) (testimony of Adam K. Geiger); U.S. Senate (1934: 215).

115. U.S. Senate (1933b: 2630–31) (quoting letter dated Feb. 23, 1931, from Adam K. Geiger to Joseph Rovensky); Pecora (1939: 165–66) (same).

116. See U.S. Senate 1933b: 2812–13 (reprinting prospectus for the $40 million of bonds offered to the public in Feb. 1930).

117. U.S. Senate (1934: 135); U.S. Senate (1933b: 2666–67, 2684–87) (testimony of Shepard Morgan).

118. U.S. Senate (1934: 135–38). The designated revenues included gasoline taxes and sales of automobile license plates, which Cuba's public works program was expected to stimulate by building a central highway across Cuba. U.S. Senate (1933b: 2548–49) (testimony of Shepard Morgan).

119. U.S. Senate (1934: 140); U.S. Senate (1933b: 2716–17) (testimony of Shepard Morgan).

120. U.S. Senate (1934: 138, 141–42); U.S. Senate (1933b: 2748–55) (testimony of Shepard Morgan and A. M. Williams, with additional statements by Sen. Adams, Sen. Couzens, and Mr. Pecora).

121. U.S. Senate (1933b: 2762–63, 2772–73, 2798) (testimony of Shepard Morgan, stating that Chase's underwriting group provided short-term loans and purchased $867,000 of bonds to enable Cuba to pay off the 1928 bonds between 1931 and 1933); U.S. Senate (1934: 142); see also Mintz (1951: 29–30) (referring to Cuba's default on its "external obligations" in 1933).

122. U.S. Senate (1934: 145–50) (noting that National City participated in the underwriting syndicate organized by Kuhn, Loeb & Co. for the fourth issue of Chilean bonds in 1928).

123. Pecora (1939: 88–89).

124. Ibid., 135. See Chapter 6 for discussion of the Senate committee's investigation of abusive securities practices by commercial and investment banks.

125. Kuczynski (1932: 37–38) (quoting Lisman's testimony as printed in U.S. Senate [1931–32: 1775]).

126. Mintz (1951: 83) (quoting Breck's testimony as printed in U.S. Senate [1931–32: 1321]).

127. Stallings (1987: 74).

128. Cleveland & Huertas (1985: 174) (quoting Mitchell's testimony before the Senate Committee on Manufactures in Dec. 1931).

129. Ibid., 175 (same).

130. As discussed in Chapter 2, Mitchell presented the same justification for National City's conduct in 1933, when he was asked why National City had sold hundreds of thousands of shares of Anaconda stock to the public in 1929. According to Mitchell, "*It became our duty*, or so we conceived it, *so long as our customers viewed that stock as an investment stock*, to buy in the market and to sell additional shares to them. Which we did." U.S. Senate (1933a: 774, 1866) (emphasis added).

131. Seligman (2003: 10); Stallings (1987: 77, 78 [table 1]).

132. Eichengreen (1989: 137); Mintz (1951: 29–43).

133. Carosso (1970: 261–65, 330–31, 348, 353); Chernow (1990: 304, 355–56); Geisst (2012: 161–63, 207–11); Seligman (2003: 10, 26–28); Wigmore (1985: 291–93, 304–05, 417–20, 524–25).

134. Accominotti & Eichengreen (2016: 473–80); Eichengreen (1992: 224–27); Kindleberger (1986: 39–41); Stallings (1987: 63–75).

135. Ahamed (2009: 324–25); Eichengreen (1992: 226); Meltzer (2003: 228–30); Mintz (1951: 24–27); Kindleberger (1986: 54–55, 59–63); Rothbard (1975: 122, 144–45).

136. Ahamed (2009: 215–16, 283–86, 324–31); Eichengreen (1992: 223–27, 241–45); Ritschl (2012: 8–11).

137. Ahamed (2009: 328–37, 369–70, 395–99); Chernow (1990: 310–12); Costigliola (1976: 498–99); Eichengreen (1992: 245); Kindleberger (1986: 65–68); Partnoy (2009: 135–36, 151).

138. Ahamed (2009: 336, 401); Eichengreen (1992: 245, 263); Kindleberger (1986: 67–68); Ritschl (2012: 11–13).

139. Accominotti & Eichengreen (2016: 475–80); Ahamed (2009: 401); Ritschl (2012: 11–13); Ritschl (1998: 52–54, 64–65); Schuker (1988: 50–52). Ivar Kreuger (the "Match King") and a syndicate of U.S. commercial and investment banks provided $15 million of the Young Plan loan and agreed to make $125 million of additional loans to Germany in exchange for Kreuger's receipt of a long-term monopoly on the sale of German matches. Partnoy (2009: 135–57); Straumann, Kugler, & Weber (2017: 236).

140. Chernow (1990: 312); Kuczynski (1932: 65–66); Wigmore (1985: 203–04).

141. Kuczynski (1932: 67–77); see also Wigmore (1985: 204).

142. Eichengreen (1989: 135, 152n40) (quoting National City Company's circular dated June 14, 1930). See also Kuczynski (1932: 65) (stating that the Young Plan offering began on June 12, 1930).

143. Accominotti & Eichengreen (2016: 476); Wigmore (1985: 204–06, 304).

144. Chernow (1990: 394–99); Mintz (1951: 29–31, 37–40); Wigmore (1985: 291–93, 414–16); Winkler (1933: 93–112, 182–264); see also U.S. Senate (1934: 98) (stating that the market price of Young Plan bonds dropped from $90 to $35 by Apr. 1932). After Hitler seized power, Germany selectively defaulted in 1934 on its long-term debts, including Dawes Plan and Young Plan bonds that were held by American investors. Chernow (1990: 392–98); Mintz (1951: 29–30, 41–42); Schuker (1988: 64–81).

Chapter 4

1. Carosso (1970: 244 [exhibit 8]); "Dow Jones History … 1920–1929" (May 15, 2008), available at https://leduc998.wordpress.com/2008/05/15/dow-jones-history1920-1929.

2. Ahamed (2009: 292–99, 308); Allen (1931: chapter XII, §1); Eichengreen (2015: 21–26, 46–51); Kindleberger (1986: 43, 49–54); Meltzer (2003: 125, 170–79, 202–04, 215–27); Rothbard (1975: 131–45). See Chapter 3 for discussion of the Fed's decisions to adopt easy-money policies in 1924 and 1927.

3. New York Times (1927).

4. New York Herald Tribune (1927) (quoting Mitchell).

5. Allen (1935: 314–15, 336–43); Carosso (1970: 243–45, 249–51, 253–54).

6. Ahamed (2009: 306–11, 341–43); Allen (1931: chapter XII); DeLong & Shleifer (1991); Eichengreen (2015: 34–35, 58–59, 105–06); Galbraith (1972: 6–29); Rappaport & White (1993); White (1990); "Dow Jones History … 1920–1929" (May 15, 2008) (cited in note 1).

7. Ahamed (2009: 308–09); Galbraith (1972: 16–19); White (1990: 72–73); Wigmore (1985: 3–5).

8. Carosso (1970: 244 [exhibit 8]).

9. Wigmore (1985: 26). As discussed in Chapter 2, National City Bank and Chase National Bank moved their common stocks from the NYSE to the curb exchange in Jan. 1928.

10. Galbraith (1972: 25–26); Geisst (2012: 173–77); Rappoport & White (1993: 553–54); Willis & Chapman (1934: 623–26); U.S. Senate (1934: 9–16).

11. Wigmore (1985: 26, 648 [table A.22]).

12. Eichengreen (2015: 61–62); Rappoport & White (1993: 555, 555–56n20); White (1990: 75); Willis & Chapman (1934: 627–28); U.S. Senate (1934: 14–16).

13. Eichengreen (2015: 61–62).

14. Allen (1931: chapter XII, §2); Allen (1935: 350–58); Eichengreen (2015: 34–35); Galbraith (1972: 16–19, 84–85); Wigmore (1985: 27–31); U.S. Senate (1934: 30–41, 63–68).

15. U.S. Senate (1934: 17–18, 63–68, 166–68, 192–93). See Chapter 2 for discussions of National City's and Chase's participation in trading pools.

16. Ibid., 168–82. See Chapter 2 for descriptions of National City's and Chase's trading programs for their own stocks.

17. Wigmore (1985: xiv, 3, 49 [table 1.14], 50).

18. Allen (1935: 341–43); Carosso (1970: 281–99); DeLong & Shleifer (1991); Galbraith (1972: 51–70); Wigmore (1985: 40–46, 154–58, 193, 248–51, 348–51); U.S. Senate (1934: 333–62).

19. New York Herald Tribune (1928) (quoting Mitchell and summarizing his remarks).

20. Ibid. (paraphrasing resolutions adopted at the 1928 ABA convention).

21. New York Times (1929a) (quoting Mitchell's "year-end statement" to National City's shareholders).

22. Ahamed (2009: 299); Allen (1935: 360); Chernow (1990: 314); Galbraith (1972: 20–21). Hoover had privately warned Coolidge since 1925 about the dangers of stock market speculation fueled by easy credit, but Coolidge dismissed Hoover's concerns. Kindleberger (1986: 96); see also Jeansonne (2016: 179–81).

23. Ahamed (2009: 314); Galbraith (1972: 31).

24. Eichengreen (2015: 61); Meltzer (2003: 228–35, 249).

25. Friedman & Schwartz (1963: 193n, 266–69, 271 [chart 22]); Meltzer (2003: 75–76, 149–50, 232–36, 249). Under the Fed's "real bills" doctrine during the 1920s, the Fed preferred to provide credit to member banks by discounting bills of acceptances and bills of exchange, as those instruments were viewed as the products of "legitimate" commercial transactions. The Fed was less eager to provide credit by lending against government securities, because of concerns that such credit would be used to finance "speculation" in the securities markets. Ibid.

26. Eichengreen (2015: 61); Friedman & Schwartz (1963: 254–66); Meltzer (2003: 235–41, 249–52, 262–65); Wigmore (1985: 3–5, 91–92, 648 [table A.22]).

27. Friedman & Schwartz (1963: 254–66); Meltzer (2003: 235–41, 249–52, 262–65).

28. Ahamed (2009: 320–24); Eichengreen (2015: 61–62); Wigmore (1985: 92–95); Willis & Chapman (1934: 627–28).

29. Eichengreen (2015: 61–62, 171–78, 185–91).

30. Ahamed (2009: 323); Galbraith (1972: 40–42); see also Bell (1929a) (reporting that market participants feared that "the Federal Reserve Board was going to pursue relentlessly … its policy, clearly enunciated last February 6, of diverting to business a large portion of funds that were finding their way into the stock market").

31. Galbraith (1972: 42).

32. Bell (1929a).

33. Galbraith (1972: 42).

34. Bell (1929a, 1929b).

35. Galbraith (1972: 42); see also Bell (1929a) (reporting that after Mitchell's announcement on Mar. 26, the stock market's "rally continued without interruption for the rest of the day").

36. Cleveland & Huertas (1985: 132).

37. Bell (1929a).

38. Galbraith (1972: 43) (quoting Mitchell's message).
39. Bell (1929b).
40. Cleveland & Huertas (1985: 132, 383n57); Friedman & Schwartz (1963: 260). Under the Federal Reserve Act, each member bank must purchase stock in its regional Federal Reserve Bank. Each regional Bank has a board consisting of nine directors. The member banks of that region elect three Class A and three Class B directors, and the Federal Reserve Board appoints three Class C directors. Class A directors are required to be officers of member banks, while Class B and Class C directors may not serve as officers, directors, or employees of banks, and Class C directors may not own any bank stocks. Conti-Brown (2016: 104–06); Wilmarth (2012a: 941–46).
41. New York Herald Tribune (1929a) (quoting the public statement issued by Glass on Mar. 28, 1929).
42. Albert Wiggin, Chase's chairman, was elected to succeed Mitchell, and his term as a Class A director began in Jan. 1932. New York Herald Tribune (1931).
43. Conti-Brown (2016: 23–32); Friedman & Schwartz (1963: 260–66, 362–419, 445–49); Meltzer (2003: 235–66, 408–13, 470–86). Allan Meltzer attributed somewhat less significance to the intra-Fed policy disputes of the late 1920s and early 1930s, compared with Milton Friedman and Anna Schwartz. Meltzer concluded that the New York Fed and the Federal Reserve Board disagreed primarily over implementing procedures rather than the substantive goals of monetary policy. Meltzer (2003: 272–81, 288–89, 408–13).
44. Galbraith (1972: 37–47). For analysis of the Fed's indecisive monetary policies during 1929, see Friedman & Schwartz (1963: 260–66); Meltzer (2003: 241–43); Wigmore (1985: 95).
45. Allen (1931: chapter XII, §4).
46. Galbraith (1972: 47) ("Free at last from all threat of government reaction or retribution, the market sailed off into the wild blue yonder"); ibid., 71 (stating that the *New York Times* industrial index rose from 339 to 449 during June, July, and Aug. 1929). The Dow Jones Industrial Index rose by about 20% during the summer of 1929. Wigmore (1985: 4).
47. Allen (1931: chapter XII, §5).
48. Ahamed (2009: 312); Galbraith (1972: 74–77).
49. Galbraith (1972: 75, 57) (quoting Bruce Barton's interview of Baruch in *The American Magazine* and summarizing Raskob's article).
50. Ibid., 75 (noting that Lawrence's statements from his book were subsequently published in the *New York Times*).
51. Allen (1931: chapter XII, §5) (quoting from Dice's book); Galbraith (1972: 19) (same).
52. Ahamed (2009: 348–49); Eichengreen (2015: 105–06); Galbraith (1972: 88–90); Wigmore (1985: 5).
53. Ahamed (2009: 349–50); see also Galbraith (1972: 89–91) ("Wall Street ... promptly and soundly denounced [Babson]. *Barron's* ... said he should not be taken seriously by anyone acquainted with the 'notorious inaccuracy' of his past statements").
54. Ahamed (2009: 275–79, 299–300, 314, 354) (quoting Lamont's memorandum of Oct. 19 to Hoover); Chernow (1990: 314–15) (same); Galbraith (1972: 46); see also Jeansonne (2016: 179–81) (describing Hoover's great concerns since the mid-1920s about the speculative boom on Wall Street).
55. Ahamed (2009: 351–54); Galbraith (1972: 97–102); Wigmore (1985: 4–5).
56. Carosso (1970: 300, 269–70) (summarizing and quoting views expressed during the IBA's 1929 annual convention); see also ibid., 165–92, 265–70 (describing the formation and

activities of the IBA). The principal organizer and first president of the IBA in 1912 was George Caldwell, a vice president of Chicago's Continental and Commercial Trust & Savings Bank (later Continental Illinois). Ibid., 165–71.

57. Galbraith (1972: 99) (quoting Mitchell).

58. New York Herald Tribune (1929c); New York Times (1929b).

59. Galbraith (1972: 75, 99) (quoting Fisher).

60. Ahamed (2009: 353) (quoting Fisher); Eichengreen (2015: 106) (same); Galbraith (1972: 75, 102) (same). The quotations of Fisher's remarks on Oct. 15 and 21 differ slightly among the three works.

61. Ahamed (2009: 354); Galbraith (1972: 102–04).

62. Allen (1931: chapter XIII, §3); Galbraith (1972: 103); Wigmore (1985: 5).

63. Wigmore (1985: 6).

64. Allen (1931: chapter XIII, §3); Galbraith (1972: 104).

65. During the Panic of 1907, J. P. Morgan, Sr. convinced leading New York banks to con- tribute to a joint rescue program, which prevented the failures of several key New York trust companies. That rescue program helped to prevent the Panic of 1907 from becoming a full-fledged depression, although a severe recession did occur. Bruner & Carr (2007: 83– 147); Chernow (1990: 121–29).

66. Ahamed (2009: 355); Allen (1931: chapter XII, §3); Chernow (1990: 316); Galbraith (1972: 106–07).

67. Allen (1931: chapter XIII, §3); see also Galbraith (1972: 107–09).

68. Wigmore (1985: 7, 10, 12 [table 1.2]); see also Chernow (1990: 317) (quoting an article in the *Wall Street Journal* on Oct. 25, with the headline "Bankers Halt Stock Debacle: 2-Hour Selling Deluge Stopped After Conference at Morgan's Office"); New York Herald Tribune (1929d) (quoting article on Oct. 26, with the headline "Bankers Insure Market Against Another Rout").

69. Galbraith (1972: 109–10) (quoting the *New York Times* and the statements made by Mitchell and representatives of thirty-five brokerage firms).

70. Allen (1931: chapter XIII, §4) (quoting Hoover); Carosso (1970: 303–04) (same); Galbraith (1972: 111–12) (quoting Hoover and the Wall Street advertisement); Wigmore (1985: 11).

71. Ahamed (2009: 356–57); Galbraith (1972: 114–15); Wigmore (1985: 13).

72. Carosso (1970: 304).

73. Galbraith (1972: 115–16); see also Carosso (1970: 304–05) ("Lamont's statement that the [banking] pool's only purpose was to maintain orderly markets was quite different from what the press had led the public to believe was its function").

74. Galbraith (1972: 116–17); Carosso (1970: 305) (quoting description of Tragic Tuesday in the *New York Times*).

75. Carosso (1970: 305); Galbraith (1972: 118–19).

76. Galbraith (1972: 119).

77. Carosso (1970: 305–06).

78. Cleveland & Huertas (1985: 163, 393nn9, 10); Friedman & Schwartz (335–39, 363–64); Meltzer (2003: 283–86); Wigmore (1985: 89–90).

79. Wigmore (1985: 3–5, 24); see also Ahamed (2009: 308, 360).

80. Wigmore (1985: 648–49, 650) (table A.22 and note c).

81. Friedman & Schwartz (1963: 363–67); Meltzer (2003: 284–91); Wigmore (1985: 95–97). The New York Fed also reduced its discount rate for bankers' acceptances in three steps to 4%. Wigmore (1985: 97).

82. Wigmore (1985: 95–97, 625, 627 (table A.17) (showing that interest rates for commercial paper, acceptances, and renewals of call loans were 5%, 4%, and 5.5% on Dec. 28, 1929, compared with 4%, 3.25%, and 5.38% on Dec. 31, 1927; 4.88%, 4.13%, and 7% on June 30, 1928; and 6.13%, 5.13%, and 9% on Sept. 7, 1929).

83. Allen (1935: 398–99); Chernow (1990: 321); Fishback (2010: 401); Jeansonne (2016: 220–23, 233–34); Wigmore (1985: 90–91, 113–15).

84. Wigmore (1985: 116–18).

85. Ibid., 128–29.

86. Ahamed (2009: 370–71); Eichengreen (1985: 114–15, 118–19). Kindleberger (1986: 106–07); Wigmore (1985: 116–18).

87. Kindleberger (1986: 117–22); Wigmore (1985: 203–04). See Chapter 3 for discussion of the Young Plan.

88. Allen (1931: chapter XIV, §1); Galbraith (1972: 147–48); Wigmore (1985: 102, 113–15).

89. Lyon (1930).

90. New York Herald Tribune (1930).

91. Wigmore (1985: 3, 128–32, 138–43, 637 [table A.19]).

92. Ibid., 195–96, 203–04, 206–07.

93. Allen (1935: 278); Cudahy & Henderson (2005: 51–56, 62–63); Pecora (1939: 226–27); Platt (1991: 271–72); Taylor (1962: 188–89).

94. Allen (1935: 271–73, 285); Cudahy & Henderson (2005: 51–56); McDonald (1962: 182, 203–05). See Chapters 1 and 2 for descriptions of the Liberty Bond drives during World War I.

95. Carosso (1970: 328–29); Cudahy & Henderson (2005: 51–53); Pecora (1939: 232–33); Perino (2010: 123–24).

96. Cudahy & Henderson (2005: 51–53, 73); Perino (2010: 123–24); Taylor (1962: 195); see also Chapters 5 and 6 for further discussion of the collapse of Insull's utility empire in 1932.

97. Carosso (1970: 306); Cudahy & Henderson (2005: 58–59, 62–64, 94–97); McDonald (1962: 237, 278–86); Pecora (1939: 228–32); Wigmore (1985: 196); U.S. Senate (1933a: 1693–97).

98. McDonald (1962: 286).

99. Cudahy & Henderson (2005: 51–56, 63–65, 91–95) (contending that Insull's utility empire resembled Enron because their "operations and capital structures were staggeringly complex, yet the iconic stature of both of these companies … made it unnecessary for either Insull or Enron to simplify their disclosures in order to raise capital on favorable terms" [ibid., 93] and that as a result of that complexity, "no human being could have possibly assessed the financial risk that lurked within the Insull empire" [ibid., 94]); see also Allen (1935: 281) (noting "the bewilderment of any man who had tried to discover what Insull was really doing in his endlessly complex financial pyramid-building," yet the public still regarded Insull as "a miracle-worker" in 1929); Carosso (1970: 306, 328) ("Insull's credit still was so good that nearly every one of [the 1930 bond] issues was oversubscribed").

100. Cudahy & Henderson (2005: 64–65, 73–75); McDonald (1962: 287–90); Wigmore (1985: 152, 154, 247, 344–48); see also Taylor (1962: 193–95, 202–03 [appendix])

(showing that public investors lost more than $380 million of their total investments of $400 million in CSC, IUI, and Middle West).

101. Wigmore (1985: 203); U.S. Senate (1934: 138–43); see Chapter 3 for a more detailed discussion of Chase's 1930 offering of Cuban bonds.

102. Wigmore (1985: 174).

103. Ibid., 63, 171–75, 238, 357); see also Pecora (1939: 65–69); see Chapter 6 for discussion of the large losses that Chase suffered from its involvement with GTE.

104. Wigmore (1985: 133, 203, 291–92, 414–15); Winkler (1933: 58–60, 103–07, 189 [table], 248–49).

105. Wigmore (1985: 291–93); Winkler (1933: 203 [table]).

106. Wigmore (1985: 203–04).

107. Carosso (1970: 307); Wigmore (1985: 196–208).

108. The Dow Jones Industrial Index steadily declined during the second half of 1930 and closed at 164 at the end of 1930, well below its post-crash low of 198 in Nov. 1929. Allen (1931: chapter XIV); Romer (1990: 617); Wigmore (1985: 3–5, 128–32, 137–45, 207–08, 637 [table A.19]).

109. Chandler (1970: 19–21); Kindleberger (1986: 74–93, 103–04); Meltzer (2003: 282–83, 290, 297–303); Romer (1993: 21–22, 26–29); Wigmore (1985: 101–02, 130–35).

110. Romer (1993: 29–30).

111. Galbraith (1972: 180–83); Mishkin (1978: 931); Romer (1993: 30–31); Romer (1990: 606–11); Historical Statistics (1975: 699–700) (Series P 318–74).

112. Wigmore (1985: 130–31, 175–77, 182).

113. Ibid., 131; see also Chandler (1970: 20–21); Historical Statistics (1975: 618) (Series N 1–29) (showing that the total value of private construction declined from $8.3 billion to $5.9 billion between 1929 and 1930, while the total value of newly constructed housing units dropped from $3.2 billion to $1.7 billion).

114. Ahamed (2009: 362); Romer (1993: 29–31).

115. Chandler (1970: 27–28); Wigmore (1985: 132).

116. Chandler (1970: 5 [table 1-2]) (showing that the number of unemployed workers rose from 1.55 billion in 1929 to 4.34 billion in 1930, representing 8.7% of the total labor force of 49.8 million); Wigmore (1985: 130–32); Historical Statistics (1975: 241) (Series F 262–86) (showing that total personal income fell from $85.9 billion in 1929 to $77.0 billion in 1930).

117. Mishkin (1978: 921–23, 929–34); Olney (1999).

118. Ahamed (2009: 361–62); Galbraith (1972: 182–83); Mishkin (1978: 929–36).

119. Ahamed (2009: 362) (quoting Hirst's book, *Wall Street and Lombard Street* [New York: M acmillan, 1931], 59).

120. Romer (1990: 598–603, 616–17) (quoting *The Magazine of Wall Street*, Nov. 16, 1929, 94, and June 14, 1930, 254, and *Moody's Investors Service*, Dec. 16, 1929, I-257); Romer (1993: 29–31).

121. Allen (1931: chapters XIV, §1, XIII, §4, appendix).

122. Chandler (1970: 19–21); Olney (1999: 319–20, 324–25, 328–33); Romer (1993: 29–31); Romer (1990: 600–03).

123. Wigmore (1985: 122–23, 228–29); see also Chapters 5 and 6 for discussion of the losses that banks suffered during the 1930s from their risky exposures to real estate and securities.

124. See Chapter 2; see also Wigmore (1985: 115–23, 144–45, 160–61, 228–29).

125. Ahamed (2009: 365–66); Eichengreen (2015: 119–20); Friedman & Schwartz (1963: 367–75); Kindleberger (1986: 128–29); Meltzer (2003: 306–15).

126. Meltzer (2003: 312) (quoting Harrison's letter of July 17, 1930, to other Fed Governors).

127. Ibid., 315–22 (quoting Miller's and Harrison's comments during the meeting of the Fed's Open Market Policy Conference on Sept. 25, 1930); see also Friedman & Schwartz (1963: 374–75).

128. Friedman & Schwartz (1963: 371–74); Hetzel (2008: 17, 20–22); Meltzer (2003: 298, 309, 311–23).

129. Meltzer (2003: 322–23) (quoting Hamlin's speech); see also Bordo & Wheelock (2010: 22–23); Eichengreen (2015: 120).

130. Ahamed (2009: 366); see also Calomiris & Wilson (2004: 422, 425–26, 433–38, 452) (explaining that large New York City banks "scrambled to shed asset risk" and "reduce default risk" during the early 1930s by reducing their loans and increasing their cash reserves and holdings of Treasury bonds); Cleveland & Huertas (1985: 321 [appendix B]) (showing that National City Bank's loans declined from $1.25 billion to $1.15 billion between 1929 and 1930, while its holdings of cash increased from $366 million to $453 million).

131. Meltzer (2003: 321–22); see also Eichengreen (2015: 119–20); Fishback (2010: 390, 393–94); Friedman & Schwartz (1963: 371–75).

132. Eichengreen (2015: 123–24); Fishback (2010: 401–03; 2016: 6–7, 11, 20); Jeansonne (2016: 228–44); Wigmore (1985: 115–16, 145, 208, 308–13).

Chapter 5

1. Adalet (2009a: 4–5, 8–15); Battilossi (2009: 101–02, 119–28); Bernanke & James (1991: 51–56); Eichengreen (1992: 264–76, 359–60); James (1991: 7–11); Jonker & van Zanden (1995: 78, 81–91); Vanthemsche (1991: 105–07, 110–12, 117–18); Weber (1995: 339–54); Weber (1991: 20–24).

2. Forsyth (1991: 181–82).

3. McFerrin (1969: 3–36, 48–80); see also Eichengreen (2015: 124–25); Hamilton (1985: 591–93). For a listing of bonds sold by Caldwell and Company to the public, see McFerrin (1969: 252–55).

4. McFerrin (1969: 37–47, 81–98); see Chapters 2 and 4 for further discussion of investment trusts.

5. Ibid., 116–19; Richardson & Troost (2009: 1041).

6. McFerrin (1969: 62–63, 79–80, 116–19) (showing that Caldwell and Company controlled insurance companies with $232 million of assets, the largest chain of banks in the South with $213 million of assets, and industrial and commercial enterprises with $48 million of assets); see also Eichengreen (2015: 125); Hamilton (1985: 591–92).

7. McFerrin (1969: 99–115).

8. Ibid., 120–25, 140–42; Hamilton (1985: 592–93).

9. McFerrin (1969: 254 [appendix C]) (showing that Caldwell and Company had assets of $38 million and capital of $1.8 million at the end of 1929).

10. Ibid., 122–24, 235–36.

11. Ibid., 126–37; Hamilton (1985: 593); U.S. Senate (1931: 631–34) (Comptroller of the Currency's report on the failure of the National Bank of Kentucky in Nov. 1930).

12. Hamilton (1985: 593–608); McFerrin (1969: 176–88, 231–40); Richardson (2007: 644, 658–62); Wicker (1996: 28–36); U.S. Senate (1931: 634–35) (report on the failure of National Bank of Kentucky).

13. McFerrin (1969: 240–45).

14. Eichengreen (2015: 129–30); Trescott (1992: 384); Werner (1933: 2–9, 62–63).

15. Trescott (1992: 388–91); Werner (1933: 13–31, 117–23). The BUS-Bankus stock units were documented by stock certificates that showed the bank's shares on one side and the affiliate's shares on the other. Werner (1933: 24–27). See Chapter 2 for discussion of the trading operations conducted by National City and Chase in their own shares.

16. Trescott (1992: 389–90); Werner (1933: 33–61).

17. Trescott (1992: 391, 394); Werner (1933: 124–30).

18. Werner (1933: 97–123, 148–49).

19. Ibid., 154–55.

20. Ibid., 181–88.

21. Ibid., 196–211; Eichengreen (2015: 130–31); Wigmore (1985: 124–25). Scholars have debated whether the refusal by New York's banking leaders to rescue BUS was due in part to anti-Semitism, as suggested by Friedman & Schwartz (1986: 201–02, 201–02n2). That suggestion is supported by the fact that J. P. Morgan & Co. and several other large New York and Boston banks decided to rescue Kidder, Peabody & Co. during the same month (Dec. 1930). Kidder, Peabody was a large, troubled investment bank with predominantly WASP partners and strong business ties to the House of Morgan. Ahamed (2009: 386–89); Carosso (1970: 309–17); Chernow (1990: 325–27). For other views on that issue, see Eichengreen (2015: 130–31); Trescott (1992: 395–96); Werner (1933: 211–13); Wicker (1996: 55–56); Wigmore (1985: 124–25).

22. Ahamed (2009: 387, 391); Cleveland & Huertas (1985: 397n34); Eichengreen (2015: 131); Trescott (1992: 387).

23. Eichengreen (2015: 124–31); Trescott (1992: 392–95); Werner (1933: 181–88, 209, 214); compare McFerrin (1969: 246–51) (summarizing the reasons for Caldwell and Company's collapse).

24. Goldsmith (1933: 226–27); Wicker (1996: 29 [table 2.2]); Wigmore (1985: 125, 128, 250).

25. Chernow (1990: 326–27); Cleveland & Huertas (1985: 166–67, 395–97nn28–34); Friedman & Schwartz (1963: 308–11, 357) (quoting Owen Young). In contrast, Wicker (1996: 36–38) concluded that BUS's failure did not have important systemic effects.

26. Wicker (1996: 26 [table 2.1], 27, 32–38) (explaining that 806 banks, with $628 million of deposits, failed during the first banking crisis between Nov. 1930 and Jan. 1931).

27. Eichengreen (2015: 127–29, 132); Richardson & Troost (2009: 1033–34, 1038–45, 1064–71); Wicker (1996: 42–45, 53–55). The Atlanta Fed had previously acted as lender of last resort for threatened Fed member banks in central Florida during a short-lived local banking crisis in the summer of 1929. Carlson, Mitchener, & Richardson (2011).

28. Ahamed (2009: 391); Friedman & Schwartz (1963: 269–70, 358–59).

29. Alston, Grove, & Wheelock (1994: 410–15); Eichengreen (1992: 88–92); Friedman & Schwartz (1963: 196, 269–70, 358–59); Hamilton (1985: 585–89); White (1983: 123–24, 140–43, 149); Wicker (1996: 5–7).

30. Friedman & Schwartz (1963: 270); see also Fishback (2010: 394).

31. According to Meltzer (2003: 325, 325–26n54), the New York Fed purchased $200 million of government securities and discounted $160 million of acceptances during Dec. 1930.

32. Friedman & Schwartz (1963: 357–58, 376–77); Meltzer (2003: 325–29); Wigmore (1985: 125–26); Wicker (1996: 56–58).

33. Friedman & Schwartz (1963: 273 [chart 23], 302 [chart 27], 304 [chart 29], 308–13).

34. Ahamed (2009: 389–90); Bernanke (1983: 257, 260 [table 1], 264–66); Calomiris (1993: 68–75); Calomiris & Wilson (2004: 425 [table 1], 435–38, 452); Meltzer (2003: 325–26); Richardson (2007: 590, 597–99, 606); Wicker (1996: 40, 48–52, 58–59).

35. Eichengreen (1992: 260, 271–73); Friedman & Schwartz (1963: 313); Meltzer (2003: 329–34); Wigmore (1985: 228, 235–36).

36. Eichengreen (1992: 245–46, 260–63, 271–73); Kindleberger (1986: 130–34); Ritschl (1996, 2012: 11–13); Schnabel (2004: 842–46); Schuker (1988: 50–53).

37. Gissler (2015) (describing how Germany's central bank triggered the crash by attempting to deflate a suspected bubble in stock prices); Voth (2003) (same).

38. Ahamed (2009: 3–4, 374); Feinstein, Temin, & Toniolo (1995: 34–35); Hetzel (2002: 16–20); Kindleberger (1986: 103–04, 131–32); Romer (1993: 20–24); Schnabel (2004: 842–43); see also Adalet (2009b: 2, 24 [figure 1]) (explaining that the Great Depression was far more severe in Germany than it was in Britain, France, or Sweden).

39. Ahamed (2009: 3–4, 393–402); Eichengreen (2015; 137–40); Galofré-Vilà et al. (2017); Kindleberger (1986: 130–34); Schuker (1988: 53–54).

40. Aguado (2001: 207–08); Bernanke & James (1991: 55–56); Eichengreen (2015: 140–47); Eichengreen (1992: 264–73); Feinstein & Watson (1995: 98–103, 107–17); Gissler (2015: 5–12); Kindleberger (1986: 134–36, 144–53); Jonker & van Zanden (1995: 81–85, 90–91); Schnabel (2004: 830–43); Weber (1995: 340–53). In 1931, Austria had almost $900 million of foreign debts, and Germany had $4.2 billion of foreign debts, according to Feinstein & Watson (1995: 116 [table 3.4]).

41. Aguado (2001: 207–11); Ahamed (2009: 404–06); Kindleberger (1986: 145–46).

42. Aguado (2001: 201–07); Ahamed (2009: 405); Eichengreen (2015: 140); Kindleberger (1986: 145); Weber (1995: 351–52).

43. Ahamed (2009: 404–05); Eichengreen (2015: 140); Kindleberger (1986: 145); Weber (1995: 344–52). For a detailed analysis of Creditanstalt's equity investments and loans to Austrian companies, see Mosser & Teichova (1991: 138–52).

44. For analysis of the Creditanstalt crisis and Austria's departure from the gold standard, see Accominotti (2012: 5–6); Aguado (2001: 210–18); Eichengreen (2015: 141–42); Eichengreen (1992: 265–70); Kindleberger (1986: 145–47); Weber (1995: 337–39, 353–56).

45. According to Feinstein & Watson (1995: 100–02, 115–17), Germany had $4.2 billion of foreign debts in 1931. In contrast, Ahamed (2009: 402, 415) and Callender (1931) stated that Germany had $6 billion of foreign debts in 1931, including short-term debts of $3.0 to $3.5 billion. Eichengreen (1992: 244–46) and Schuker (1988: 72) agreed that more than half of Germany's foreign debts were short-term obligations, and Schuker determined that Germany had $5.7 billion of foreign debts in July 1931.

46. Schnabel (2004: 828–34).

47. Ibid., 835–42, 859–61 (quote at 842); Schnabel (2009: 13–17); see also Adalet (2009b: 7–9, 12–15, 18); Gissler (2015: 6–12).

48. Schnabel (2004: 848–51); see also Kindleberger (1986: 133–34).

49. Eichengreen (2015: 143–44); Galofré-Vilà et al. (2017); Kindleberger (1986: 148–49); Schnabel (2004: 852, 857–60).

50. Ahamed (2009: 407–14); Eichengreen (2015: 144–45); Eichengreen (1992: 275–78); Kindleberger (1986: 150–51).

51. Ahamed (2009: 414–20); Eichengreen (1992: 275–76); Hetzel (2002: 29–32); Kindleberger (1986: 142, 149–52).

52. Accominotti (2012: 2, 5–6); Ahamed (2009: 415–19); Cleveland & Huertas (1985: 168, 398n402); Eichengreen (2015: 146–47); Eichengreen (1992: 275–78); Forbes (1987: 574–77); Kindleberger (1986: 151–53).

53. Schnabel (2004: 852–67) (explaining that the German crisis of 1931 was a "twin crisis" in which the run on German banks became "intertwined" with a run on Germany's currency, and both runs forced Germany to abandon the gold exchange standard); Schnabel (2009: 3–7, 11–17, 19 [table A1]) (showing that Germany followed a too-big-to-fail policy by ensuring the survival of its ten largest universal banks through liquidity assistance, capital infusions, and assisted mergers).

54. For discussion of Italian universal banks and Italy's banking crisis of the 1930s, see Amidei & Giordano (2014); Battilossi (2009: 101–02, 108–28, 131–32 [appendix A]); Bernanke & James (1991: 51); Forsyth (1991: 179–82, 192–200); Jonker & van Zanden (1995: 78, 82); Toniolo (1995: 300–10); Toniolo & White (2016: 460–61). Italy created a state-owned holding company to acquire the banks' ownership stakes in industrial firms. That state-owned company issued long-term bonds (guaranteed by the Italian government) to finance those stock acquisitions and to provide additional support to the industrial firms. Amidei & Giordano (2014: 73).

55. Vanthemsche (1991: 104–07, 110–13, 117–18).

56. Amidei & Giordano (2014: 76–83) (discussing Italy's 1936 Banking Act); Forsyth (1991: 180, 200) (same); Vanthemsche (1991: 110–13) (describing Belgium's banking "reform" laws of 1934 and 1935).

57. Ahamed (2009: 210–12, 236–39, 292–99, 423–24); Eichengreen (1992: 210–17, 256–57, 279–83); Feinstein, Temin, & Toniolo (1995: 25–26); Kindleberger (1986: 42).

58. Ahamed (2009: 422–24); Eichengreen (1992: 256–57, 280–83); Feinstein, Temin, & Toniolo (1995: 40–42); Kindleberger (1986: 154–55).

59. Ahamed (2009: 423–24); Allen & Moessner (2012: 137 and note 24); Eichengreen (1992: 264, 280–81); Kunz (1991: 39).

60. Billings & Capie (2011: 196–97); Capie (1995a: 46–59); Capie (1995b: 395–99); Perkins (1971: 485); Scott & Newton (2007: 887–900).

61. Accominotti (2012: 6–11, 25–27); Billings & Capie (2011: 196–99); Capie (1995b: 395, 399–403).

62. Accominotti (2012: 10–20, 25–28); Accominotti (2016: 7–22) (stating that British banks held $316 million of short-term loans to German borrowers in 1931); Eichengreen (2015: 149–50); Grossman (1994: 673).

63. Accominotti (2012: 20–36); Accominotti (2016: 15–17, 21–22, 33–35); Billings & Capie (2011: 197–202, 211); Grossman (1994: 673).

64. Ahamed (2009: 424–26); Kindleberger (1986: 154–55); Kunz (1991: 41–42); Wigmore (1985: 298–99).

65. Ahamed (2009: 426–33); Chernow (1990: 329–36); Eichengreen (2015: 149–52); Kindleberger (1986: 155–59); Kunz (1991: 43–44); Wigmore (1985: 299–302).

66. Baron, Verner, & Xiong (2019: table 5C and online appendix, part VI.B) (confirming the absence of a systemic banking crisis in the U.K. during the 1930s); see also Middleton (2010: 418, 421, 437) (stating that there was "no banking crisis" and "no burst asset-price bubble" in Britain during the 1930s, unlike the U.S. experience).

67. Billings & Capie (2011: 199–202, 211); Forbes (1987: 577–85); Turner (2014: 159–63). Germany ultimately paid off its standstill obligations between 1953 and 1961, in accordance with the London Debt Agreement of 1953. Accominotti (2016: 8–9).

68. Romer (1993: 21 [figure 1], 22 [table 1]) (showing that industrial production declined during the Depression at a much lower rate in Britain than it did in the U.S. and Germany); see also Figure 0.1 in the Introduction (showing that GDP declined much less and recovered more quickly in Britain during the Depression, compared with the U.S.); Middleton (2010: 417, 419 [figures 1–3]) (showing the same very significant difference in GDP performance between Britain and the U.S. during the Depression).

69. Adalet (2009a: 4–5, 11–15); Adalet (2009b: 7–9, 12–15, 18); Battilossi (2009: 101–02, 119–28); Bernanke & James (1991: 51–56); Capie (1995b: 395–96, 405–06, 411); Eichengreen (1992: 264–76, 359–60); Feinstein, Temin, & Toniolo (1995: 20–23, 35, 38–39, 45); James (1991: 7–11); Jonker & van Zanden (1995: 81–91); Weber (1995: 339–54).

70. 76 Congressional Record 9911 (1932) (remarks of Sen. Bulkley).

71. Brean, Kryzanowski, & Roberts (2011: 255–56); Drummond (1991: 232–37, 245); Greer (1933: 722–26, 728–29); Haubrich (1990: 225–26); Kryzanowski & Roberts (1993: 364, 368nn11, 12); Thomas & Walter (1991: 110–13); Wagster (2012: 90–91). Canadian banks could invest in bonds and stocks issued by domestic and foreign nonbanking companies. However, investments by Canadian banks in corporate securities accounted for less than 2% of their total assets in 1929. Drummond (1991: 234 [table 13.1], 245); Greer (1933: 724).

72. Bordo, Redish, & Rockoff (2015: 219, 227–29); Grossman (1994: 658–64); Saunders & Wilson (1999: 538–50).

73. Ian Drummond concluded that nationwide branching in Canada was of secondary importance during the Depression because "risk spreading" produced by branching would have insulated banks against "localized" shocks but would not have been effective when "the whole economy is depressed." Drummond (1991: 233); see also Greer (1933: 722–26, 728–31) (contending that close cooperation between Canadian banks and the Canadian government, as well as the "sound banking principles" followed by Canadian banks, were more important than branching in ensuring their survival).

74. Capie (1995b: 395–403, 411); Brean, Kryzanowski, & Roberts (2011: 255–56); Drummond (1991: 237–38, 243–44); Eichengreen (1992: 284–85, 293–300, 328–29); Greer (1933: 722–26, 728–29); Haubrich (1990: 225–28).

75. Billings & Capie (2011: 196–202); Turner (2014: 161–62).

76. Bordo & Redish (1987: 407–08); Drummond (1991: 232–34, 241–45, 249); Haubrich (1990: 227); Wagster (2012: 92–93); see also the discussions in this chapter and Chapter 6 of the very limited support provided by the Fed and the RFC to U.S. banks.

77. Billings & Capie (2011: 196–202); Brean, Kryzanowski, & Roberts (2011: 252–54); Kryzanowski & Roberts (1993); Toniolo & White (2016: 453, 464–65); Turner (2014: 159–63). In 1928 and 1929, the Bank of England helped to rescue a failing regional clearing bank (William Deacon's) and a troubled British-owned Italian bank (Banca Italo-Britannica). Turner (2014: 160–61).

78. Drummond (1991: 246–49); Toniolo & White (2016: 464).

79. Drummond (1991: 237–42, 246–49; Kryzanowski & Roberts (1993: 364–66); see also Greer (1933: 730–31); Baron, Verner, & Xiong (2019: 23, panel 5C and online appendix, part VI.B) (concluding that a systemic banking crisis did not occur in Canada during the 1930s).

80. Haubrich (1990: 224, 229 [figure 4]); Wagster (2012: 93, 94 [table 1], 95 [table 2]).

81. Friedman & Schwartz (1963: 352–53); see also Drummond (1991: 234 [table 13.1], 235) (providing data for Canadian bank deposits).

82. Wicker (1996: 2 [table 1.1]) (showing that more than 9,000 of the 24,000 U.S. commercial banks in existence at the end of 1929 failed by the end of 1933); Historical Statistics (1975: 1019 (Series X 580–87) (showing that total assets of U.S. banks fell from $72.3 billion in 1929 to $51.4 billion in 1933).

83. Friedman & Schwartz (1963: 352–53); Historical Statistics (1975: 1019) (Series X 580–87) (showing that U.S. bank deposits fell from $58.3 billion in 1929 to $41.7 billion in 1933).

84. Historical Statistics (1975: 1019) (Series X 580–87) (showing that U.S. bank loans plummeted from $41.9 billion to $22.3 billion between 1929 and 1933, while bank holdings of securities and cash declined only slightly, from $26.5 billion to $25.9 billion).

85. Calomiris & Wilson (2004); Friedman & Schwartz (1963: 355–59, 457–58); Mitchener & Richardson (2013); see also Cleveland & Huertas (1985: 159, 171) (showing that National City Bank cut its loans by 50% and greatly increased its liquidity reserves between 1929 and 1932).

86. Friedman & Schwartz (1963: 352) (stating that that U.S. national output fell by 53% between 1929 and 1933, while Canadian national output dropped by 49%); Eichengreen (1992: 299–300, 300 [figure 10.3]) (showing similar declines in U.S. and Canadian industrial production between 1931 and 1933); Kindleberger (1986: 279 [figure 13]) (showing similar declines in industrial production for the U.S. and Canada between 1929 and 1930).

87. Drummond (1991: 232); Haubrich (1990: 225, 241–50); Kindleberger (1986: 74–80, 84–87, 122–23, 137–41, 188–90, 189 [table 18]) (showing that Canada's exports fell by 65–70% between 1928–29 and 1932–33); Wigmore (1985: 391) (stating that "new issues of foreign bonds ceased in 1932, even for Canadian issuers").

88. Calomiris (1993: 76); see also Chapter 2 for discussion of the U.S. credit boom of the 1920s.

89. Capie (1995b: 411) (concluding that the specialized commercial banking systems of Britain and Canada were much more resilient than universal banking systems during the Depression); James (1991: 7) (noting that "there was no universal banking tradition [in Canada during the 1920s], so one potential source of trouble [during the 1930s] was removed"); Jonker & van Zanden (1995: 82–86, 90–91) (describing the superior performance of specialized British clearing banks compared with European universal banks).

90. For analysis of the very poor performance of European universal banks during the early 1930s, see notes 42–56 and accompanying text.

91. Allen (1935: 412–13); James (1938: 1006–22); Kennedy (1973: 26–30); Wicker (1996: 72–73, 77–78, 96–99, 103); Wigmore (1985: 209–10, 235–37, 285–87, 304–05).

92. Wigmore (1985: 305); see also Richardson (2007a: 590) ("Following Britain's departure from the gold standard, the depression deepened").

93. Wigmore (1985: 236–37, 637–38 [table A.19]) (showing that the index peaked at 381 in Sept. 1929 and recorded its high point for 1931 at 194 in Feb.).

94. Ibid., 286–305 (quote at 286).

95. Ibid., 218–21, 286–305; see also Friedman & Schwartz (1963: 304 [chart 29] [showing changes in yield spreads during 1931], 312, 315, 355–56 [discussing efforts by weak banks to increase their liquidity by selling low-grade bonds]); Kennedy (1973: 20, 30) (same); Mintz (1951: 29–30) (describing defaults by foreign issuers on their bonds).

96. Ahamed (2009: 433–35); Eichengreen (2015: 152–53); Friedman & Schwartz (1963: 315–16); Kindleberger (1986: 157–58, 164–65); Wicker (1996: 86–88).

97. Friedman & Schwartz (1963: 317–18); Meltzer (2003: 344–45, 347–48); Richardson (2007a: 600); Wicker (1996: 86–94). Due to large-scale withdrawals by depositors, the amount of currency in circulation rose from $4.16 billion in Oct. 1930 to $5.13 billion in Oct. 1931. Wicker (1996: 26 [table 2.1], 67 [table 3.2], 86–87).

98. Fishback (2010: 390–92); Friedman & Schwartz (1963: 317–19, 378–83); Meltzer (2003: 335–45, 347–51); Wicker (1996: 82, 85–95); Wigmore (1985: 218–26).

99. Wicker (1996: 67 [table 3.2]).

100. Kennedy (1973: 26–30); Olson (1988: 9).

101. Ritschl & Sarferaz (2014: 352, 356–62, 366–68).

102. Richardson (2007a: 600, 606); see also Ahamed (2009: 434–35) (stating that Britain's decision to abandon the gold standard and the resulting outflow of gold from the U.S. "came at a particularly crucial juncture for the U.S. banking system, then reeling under the wave of failures" that began in Chicago in June).

103. Esbitt (1986); James (1938: 953–68, 992–93); Postel-Vinay (2016: 480–89).

104. James (1938: 945–66); Thomas (1933: 4–10).

105. Eichengreen (2015: 153–54); James (1938: 996–1006); Goldsmith (1933: 174–76, 229–30); Mather (1931); Wicker (1996: 66–72).

106. Goldsmith (1933: 230); Wicker (1996: 69).

107. Eichengreen (2015: 155); Friedman & Schwartz (1963: 358–59); Goldsmith (1933: 230–33); Wicker (1996: 72–93); Wigmore (1985: 127–28, 218–24).

108. Richardson (2007a: 600); see also Goldsmith (1933: 79–84, 103–07); Kennedy (1973: 20, 30, 80); Calomiris & Mason (2003b: 1630–32) (explaining that Fed member banks with higher levels of troubled loans, foreclosed real estate, and risky bonds were more likely to fail during the early 1930s); Calomiris & Mason (1997: 880) (stating that "bond depreciation" was a significant factor in the failures of three small Chicago national banks in June 1932); Postel-Vinay (2017: 488–501) (finding that Chicago banks with larger holdings of real estate mortgages experienced significantly higher failure rates between 1931 and 1933).

109. Wigmore (1985: 122–23, 123 [table 4.2], 287–88, 291–305, 322–23, 394–95, 409–19); see also Goldsmith (1933: 105–06); Willis & Chapman (1934: 537–40) (concluding that depreciated bond values contributed significantly to the failures of nineteen New York banks between 1930 and 1932).

110. See Chapters 1–3 for discussion of correspondent relationships between large money center banks and smaller banks.

111. See Chapters 2, 3, and 6.

112. Goldsmith (1933: 163–64, 232); Wicker (1996: 85–86); Wigmore (1985: 218); New York Times (1931a).

113. Kemmerer (1977: 139–51, 159–64); see also Cleveland & Huertas (1985: 169, 399–400n46); Hector (1988: 42–44, 47–50, 54).

114. Eichengreen (2015: 155–56); Kennedy (1973: 32–35); Wicker (1996: 95).

115. Ahamed (2009: 436–37); Cleveland & Huertas (1985: 169–70); Eichengreen (2015: 156–57); James (1938: 1025–26); Jeansonne (2016: 253); Kennedy (1973: 34–36); Olson (1977: 25–27); Wicker (1996: 95–96). The NCC ultimately approved $155 million of loans to banks before the Reconstruction Finance Corporation replaced the NCC in Jan. 1932 and took over the NCC's portfolio of outstanding loans. However, the NCC approved most of those loans after it was harshly criticized for its very conservative lending policies, and after the NCC knew that the RFC would assume responsibility for the NCC's loans. Meltzer (2003: 373–74); Olson (1977: 29–30); Upham and Lamke (1934: 6–8).

116. Eichengreen (2015: 157–58); Friedman & Schwartz (1963: 320–21); Kennedy (1973: 36–38); Olson (1988: 10–16).

117. Eichengreen (2015: 158–59); Kennedy (1973: 46–47); Meltzer (2003: 357–58). Under the Federal Reserve Act, as amended by the Glass-Steagall Act of 1932, each Federal Reserve Bank was required to maintain gold reserves equal to at least 40% of that bank's outstanding Federal Reserve notes (currency), plus additional reserves, including commercial bills of exchange and government securities, in amounts up to 60% of that bank's outstanding notes. Friedman & Schwartz (1963: 194); Kennedy (1973: 47).

118. Eichengreen (2015: 157–59); Fishback (2010: 391–94); Friedman & Schwartz (1963: 322–24, 384–89); Meltzer (2003: 359–77, 370 [table 5.23]).

119. The RFC extended $1.1 billion of loans to more than 6,500 banks between Feb. 1932 and Mar. 1933. Mason (2001a: 177 [table 8.1]).

120. Goldsmith (1933: 208, 233); Olson (1988: 18) (noting that the RFC provided $330 million of loans to twenty-six large banks in 1932); see also Calomiris & Mason (2013: 540–43 (finding that Michigan banks were more likely to receive RFC assistance if they were "important within the national network of banking"); Mason (2001b: 85–86) (finding that bank size had "a significant positive effect on whether [Illinois] banks receive[d] loans" from the RFC).

121. Allen (1935: 319–25); Cleveland & Huertas (1985: 169, 399–400nn43, 46); Goldsmith (1933: 195–99); Hector (1988: 24–50); James & James (1954: 268–311).

122. Cleveland & Huertas (1985: 169, 399–400nn43, 46); Goldsmith (1933: 197–99); Hector (1988: 47–50, 54–56); James & James (1954: 311–20, 325–31, 338); Kemmerer (1977: 160–64); Wigmore (1985: 253–54); see also Accominotti (2016: 56 [table 3]) (showing that Bank of America held more than $13 million of frozen loans to Germany, Austria, and Hungary in 1931, and lost 25% of its deposits during that year).

123. Goldsmith (1933: 199–200); Hector (1988: 42–45, 49–56); James & James (1954: 331–58); Jones (1951: 19–20, 37–38); Kennedy (1973: 39, 186–87); Wigmore (1985: 253–54) (stating that Bank of America "nearly collapsed" during the proxy fight between Giannini and Walker and "became the first bank to borrow from the [RFC] in 1932"). The RFC's loans allowed Bank of America to repay the loans it had previously received from the NCC and New York banks. Transamerica paid off the RFC's loans in 1934. James & James (1954: 351–58, 374).

124. Calomiris & Mason (1997: 866–68); Eichengreen (2015: 160–61); James (1938: 1028–31); Peach (1941: 54, 59–60n87, 98); Wigmore (1985: 344–48, 360–61); Wilmarth (2005: 597). See Chapter 4 for discussion of the Insull utility empire and its aggressive marketing of securities to retail investors.

125. U.S. Senate (1933a: 1529–33, 1555–57, 1564, 1684–87, 1693–99, 1741–42) (showing that Continental Illinois held $60 million of Insull-related loans, while First Chicago and

Central Republic held $20 million and $12 million, respectively, of such loans); see also Wilmarth (2005: 597).

126. Calomiris & Mason (1997: 865–68); James (1938: 1028–34); Wicker (1996: 111–14). After a ten-week trial, Bain and three of his family members were found guilty of conspiracy to defraud creditors of Bain's group of twelve banks. Chicago Daily Tribune (1932b).

127. James (1938: 1033–36); Jones (1951: 72–74).

128. James (1938: 1034–38); Jones (1951: 72–75); Kennedy (1973: 40–41); Upham & Lamke (1934: 158–59); Wicker (1996: 113–14); see also Reconstruction Finance Corp. v. Central Republic Trust Co., 17 F. Supp. 263, 267 (N.D. Ill. 1936) (hereinafter RFC v. Central Republic) (reporting that Central Republic's deposits fell from $240 million in July 1931 to less than $130 million on June 25, 1932).

129. Eichengreen (2015: 161–62); James (1938: 1038–40); Jones (1951: 75–79); Kennedy (1973: 41–42); Wicker (1996: 114); Wilmarth (2005: 598–99); see also RFC v. Central Republic at 270, note 2 (quoting the minutes of the meeting of RFC's board of directors on June 27, 1932, which described Central Republic's potential failure as a "grave emergency" and stated that "the closing of a bank as large as the Central Republic Bank and Trust Company would greatly aggravate the tense situation in Chicago and ... would cause repercussions that would be far reaching and would further impair public confidence throughout the country. In these circumstances, it was the view of the members of the [RFC] Board that the bank should be saved from closing and enabled to continue in business").

130. Bordo & Wheelock (2010: 20–33); Calomiris & Mason (1997: 868–69n4); James (1938: 1038–41); Jones (1951: 74–79); Wigmore (1985: 323); Wilmarth (2005: 596–99).

131. Mason (2001a: 173–74); see also James (1938: 1044); Olson (1988: 67–68); Olson (1977: 47–48, 55, 97); Wigmore (1985: 324). The RFC typically accepted collateral equal to only 80% of the market value of a bank's high-grade bonds and 50% of the market value of other assets. Olson (1977: 47–48).

132. Eichengreen (2015: 157–58); James (1938: 1040); Olson (1977: 47–48, 55, 97); Mason (2001a: 173–76); RFC v. Central Republic at 273–85; see also Calomiris et al. (2013: 527, 539–40, 546) (finding that RFC loans did not reduce the risk of failure among Michigan banks that received such loans during 1932 and early 1933); Mason (2001b: 79–80, 87–90) (finding that forty-four of the seventy-nine Illinois banks that received RFC loans during 1932 and early 1933 subsequently failed, and RFC loans significantly increased the probability of bank failure). The RFC ultimately received full repayment of its loan to Central Republic after liquidating the bank's assets and collecting shareholder assessments from Charles Dawes and about four thousand of the bank's other stockholders. Kennedy (1973: 42n68).

133. Wicker (1996: 110, 2 [table 1.1] [reporting that, between 1931 and 1932, the number of failed banks declined from 2,293 to 1,453, and deposits in failed banks dropped from $1.69 billion to $706 million], 117 [table 4.1] [showing that the amount of currency held by the public varied between $4.8 billion and $4.9 billion for most of 1932 and was $4.83 billion at the end of the year]); see also Friedman & Schwartz (1963: 302 [chart 27]) (showing trends in the nation's money stock and the amount of currency held by the public during 1932).

134. Olson (1988: 23–26).

135. Bank deposits fell from $60.3 billion in 1930 to $57.2 billion in 1931 and $45.6 billion in 1932, while bank loans plummeted from $41.0 billion in 1930 to $35.4 billion in 1931 and $28.0 billion in 1932. Historical Statistics (1975: 1019) (Series X 580–87).

136. Benmelech, Frydman, & Papanikolaou (2017); Bernanke (1983); Calomiris (1993: 68–79); Calomiris & Mason (2003a); Carlson & Rose (2015); Olson (1977: 56–57, 92–95); Wicker (1996: 2 [table 1.1]).

137. Historical Statistics (1975: 224) (Series F 6–9) (showing that GNP fell by 29.2% between 1929 and 1932 based on constant 1958 prices).

138. Wigmore (1985: 327–28).

139. Chandler (1970: 5 [table 1-2]) (reporting that the number of unemployed U.S. workers rose from 1.55 million in 1929 to 12.1 million in 1932, while the nation's unemployment rate increased from 3.2% to 23.6%).

140. Wigmore (1985: 307–08, 315–16) (stating that industrial output declined by 46% between 1929 and 1932, while auto production fell from 4.8 million cars to 1.2 million cars, and building contracts declined from $6.6 billion to $1.4 billion).

141. U.S. Senate (1934: 7) (stating that the total value of NYSE-listed stocks declined from $89.7 billion to $15.6 billion between Sept. 1929 and July 1932, while the total value of NYSE-listed bonds fell from $49.3 billion to $30.6 billion between Sept. 1930 and Apr. 1933).

142. Accominotti (2016: 11, 20, 56 [table 3]); Cleveland & Huertas (1985: 168, 399n43); Wigmore (1985: 172–75, 355 [table 11.6], 357–58).

143. Wigmore (1985: 172–75, 355 [table 11.6], 357–58). See Chapter 4 for discussion of Chase's involvement in GTE's hostile takeover of Fox. Chase reduced its capital by $106 million between 1929 and 1932 to create reserves for losses, while its securities affiliate (Chase Securities Corp.) reduced its capital by $73 million to create such reserves. U.S. Senate (1933b: 2317–19, 2355 (committee exhibit 6), 2383–87, 2388 (committee exhibit 8), 2390–98).

144. Cleveland & Huertas (1985: 159–60, 168–69, 171, 391–92n4, 399n43).

145. Wigmore (1985: 321, 354, 355 [table 11.6], 360).

146. Kindleberger (1986: 184–87); Wigmore (1985: 319–23); see also Calin (1942) (showing that loans by Chicago banks fell from $2.2 billion in Oct. 1929 to $1.1 billion at the end of 1931 and $700 million at the end of 1932); Cleveland & Huertas (1985: 171, 371 [appendix B]) (showing that National City Bank's loans declined from $1.25 billion at the end of 1929 to $1.0 billion at year-end 1931 and $700 million at year-end 1932, while its total investments and holdings of cash rose from $610 million in 1929 to $700 million in 1932).

147. Bordo & Wheelock (2010: 24–25); Kennedy (1973: 47–48); Meltzer (2003: 369).

148. Eichengreen (1992: 319–20); Kindleberger (1986: 175–76); Wigmore (1985: 410).

149. Eichengreen (1992: 319–20); Kindleberger (1986: 193–95); Meltzer (2003: 382); Schuker (1988: 63–70); Wigmore (1985: 410, 520–21). Britain did not make any further payments on its war debts after a "token" payment in June 1933. Wigmore (1985: 521).

150. The July 1932 statute required the RFC to provide monthly reports of loans that the RFC made to banks between July 21 and Dec. 31, 1932. Anbil & Vossmeyer (2017: 8–9); Butkiewicz (1995: 200–01); Kennedy (1973: 42–43).

151. Olson (1977: 53) (quoting Roosevelt's speech on Apr. 8, 1932).

152. Butkiewicz (1995: 200–01); Jones (1951: 74–79, 121–23); Kennedy (1973: 39–43); Olson (1977: 51–54, 58–60).

153. Anbil & Vossmeyer (2017); Ballantine (1948: 134); Butkiewicz (1995: 207–09, 214); Cleveland & Huertas (1985: 171–72, 402n61); James (1938: 1045–46).

154. Anbil & Vossmeyer (2017); Ballantine (1948: 134); Butkiewicz (1995: 207–09, 214); Eichengreen (2015: 163); Friedman & Schwartz (1963: 325); Olson (1977: 99–100).

155. Anbil (2017).

156. Olson (1977: 94–95); Wicker (1996: 111 [table 4.1], 115–16).

157. Kennedy (1973: 81–87); Olson (1977: 94–95); Wicker (1996: 115–16).

158. Wicker (1996: 115).

159. Olson (1977: 94–95, 100–01); see also Kennedy (1973: 74–76).

160. Kennedy (1973: 77–78); Historical Statistics (1975: 716) (Series Q 148–62).

161. Goldsmith (1933: 168–69); Kennedy (1973: 77–80); Pecora (1939: 234–41); Wigmore (1985: 51, 120–21, 434–37, 441–43); U.S. Senate (1934: 236, 241); see also Olson (1988: 28) (stating that Guardian and DBC "heavily invested in the securities markets and sustained major losses after 1929").

162. Jones (1951: 54–58); Wigmore (1985: 374, 407, 437–38, 514); Historical Statistics (1975: 716) (Series Q 148–62).

163. Kennedy (1973: 80–81); Pecora (1939: 241–48); Wigmore (1985: 435–36); U.S. Senate (1934: 247–55, 261–68, 270–77, 284–86).

164. Pecora (1939: 248–51); U.S. Senate (1934: 255–61, 268–70, 277–84); U.S. Senate (1933b: 5165–99, 5575–78).

165. Wigmore (1985: 437–38); see also Pecora (1939: 251–52).

166. Awalt (1969: 350–52); Ballantine (1948: 135–36); Eichengreen (2015: 164–65); Pecora (1939: 251–56); Wicker (1996: 118–19).

167. Awalt (1969: 350–54); Ballantine (1948: 135–36); Jones (1951: 56–63) (quoting Couzens and Ford); Kennedy (1973: 82–89); Pecora (1939: 251–56). Couzens was one of Henry Ford's original business partners. They dissolved their partnership in 1915, and Ford purchased Couzens' investments in Ford Motor Company for $29 million in 1919. Couzens and Ford became bitter rivals in both business and politics after their partnership ended. Jones (1951: 55–56); Kennedy (1973: 86).

168. Ballantine (1948: 136) (summarizing the conversation among himself, Chapin, and Ford); see also Awalt (1969: 350–54) (providing a more extensive summary of that conversation).

169. Awalt (1969: 353–54); Ballantine (1948: 136); Jones (1951: 61–64) (quoting Couzens and Ford); Kennedy (1973: 86–92).

170. Awalt (1969: 354–57); Ballantine (1948: 136); Jones (1951: 63–65); Kennedy (1973: 90–96).

171. Eichengreen (2015: 5–6, 162–66, 194–202); see also Olson (1977: 59) (stating that the RFC's loan to Central Republic "postponed the national banking disaster" until 1933). See Chapter 11 for discussions of the rescue of Bear Stearns and the failure of Lehman Brothers.

172. See Jones (1951: 56, 59–60) (discussing attacks by Coughlin and Couzens); Kennedy (1973: 82, 85) (describing attacks by Coughlin and Flynn); Olson (1977: 103) ("The [RFC's] Board of Directors realized immediately that a large loan to Guardian ... would raise the liberal ire and bring on another major controversy resembling the Dawes crisis

of June 1932"); Pecora (1939: 253) (quoting testimony in 1933 by the OCC's national bank examiner, Alfred Leyburn, who stated that RFC directors repeatedly asked, "What will Mr. Ford do?" and that they were deeply troubled by the question "Why should we bail out Mr. Ford?").

Chapter 6

1. Jones (1951: 54); see also Allen (1935: 423–24) (explaining that the "final abrupt collapse" of the nation's banking system "began in Detroit," where the failures of the two largest banks and Michigan's bank holiday "immediately set in motion the forces of panic elsewhere"); Awalt (1969: 349) (agreeing that Michigan's banking crisis "proved to be the straw that broke the camel's back"); Moley (1939: 138) (recalling that Michigan's bank holiday "jolted the nation into panic").
2. Kennedy (1973: 129–51).
3. Ballantine (1948: 136–37); Moley (1939: 139–42); Wigmore (1985: 422–23, 445–47). Before Hoover sent his letter of Feb. 18, 1933, he and Roosevelt had previously failed to reach agreement on several issues, including the handling of Allied war debts, the best way to respond to farmers' distress, and the desirability of imposing new excise taxes to reduce the federal budget deficit. Eichengreen (1992: 319–22); Moley (1939: 68–79, 84–105); Wigmore (1985: 314–15, 422–23).
4. Ahamed (2009: 442–44); Eichengreen (1992: 326–29); Kennedy (1973: 135–41); Meltzer (2003: 380–81); Moley (1939: 118–22, 139–43); Wigmore (1987: 742–44). Senator Carter Glass, who strongly supported the gold standard, drafted the plank of the Democratic Party platform that pledged to preserve "a sound currency . . . at all hazards." During the 1932 election campaign, Roosevelt publicly endorsed that plank and promised to follow a "sound money" policy if he were elected. Smith & Beasley (1939: 308, 314, 321–23).
5. Ballantine (1948: 137) (quoting Roosevelt's reply); Kennedy (1973: 141–42) (same). Roosevelt plainly recognized the severity of the banking panic. His letter to Hoover stated that "on present values, very few financial institutions anywhere in the country are actually able to pay off their deposits in full, and the knowledge of this fact is widely held." Kennedy (1973: 142) (quoting Roosevelt's letter).
6. Moley (1939: 141–43).
7. Awalt (1969: 364–66); Olson (1977: 107–08, 111–14); Seligman (2003: 7) (quote); Smith & Beasley (1939: 327–29, 339–40).
8. Kennedy (1973: 101–03); Wicker (1996: 123–24).
9. Wigmore (1985: 443–44) (quoting minutes of the RFC board's meeting on Feb. 23, 1933) (emphasis added). Roosevelt selected Woodin as Treasury Secretary-designate after Carter Glass refused Roosevelt's repeated offers of the position. Glass declined to serve as Treasury Secretary, ostensibly due to health concerns, but the real reason was that Roosevelt would not give Glass any assurances about maintaining the gold standard. Smith & Beasley (1939: 329–38).
10. Meltzer (2003: 383–84); see also Friedman & Schwartz (1963: 326–27, 389–91).
11. Kennedy (1973: 145–46); Meltzer (2003: 384). Shortly after midnight on Mar. 3, the Federal Reserve Board issued a formal recommendation for a national bank holiday. The board's recommendation did not reach the White House until 2 a.m. on Mar. 4, by which time Hoover was already asleep. Later that morning, Hoover sent an "angry" response to

the Board, stating that he was "at a loss to understand why such a communication should have been sent to me in the last few hours of this administration." Ahamed (2009: 446–47); Meltzer (2003: 385, 388).

12. Eichengreen (2015: 225); James (1938: 1053–60, 1072 [table XXX]); Kennedy (1973: 133–35, 144–47); Perino (2010: 117–18, 241–42, 257–60, 275–77); Silber (2009: 27); Wicker (1996: 116–17); Wigmore (1985: 672).

13. Eichengreen (2015: 163–66); Kennedy (1973: 147–49); Wicker (1996: 126–31); Wigmore (1987: 741–49); Wigmore (1985: 446–49).

14. Eichengreen (1992: 324–26); James (1938: 1059–64); Wicker (1996: 130–31); Wigmore (1987: 745–48).

15. Awalt (1969: 359); Kennedy (1973: 144–48); Meltzer (2003: 385–86n133); Moley (1939: 144–47); Olson (1988: 33–34). Carter Glass advised Hoover and Roosevelt that the Trading with the Enemy Act did not provide an adequate basis for declaring a national bank holiday. Smith & Beasley (1939: 340–42). According to Moley, Roosevelt told Hoover that "the risk of subsequent congressional disavowal would be no jot or tittle smaller whether he, Roosevelt, invoked the emergency powers or Hoover invoked them." (Moley 1939: 146). Moley acknowledged, however, that it was reasonable for Hoover to be concerned that "if his invocation of the Trading with the Enemy Act proved disastrous [the incoming] Congress would jump at the chance to blame him for invoking it and refuse to validate his action." Ibid., 145–46n11.

16. Awalt (1969: 359–60); Cleveland & Huertas (1985: 189–90); James (1938: 1064–66); Kennedy (1973: 149–51); Meltzer (2003: 384–88); Wigmore (1987: 747–49).

17. New York Times (1934b) (reporting that National City Bank held $1.26 billion of deposits in Feb. 1933); Cleveland & Huertas (1985: 160 [table 9.1], 172, 189) (stating that National City's deposits fell to a low point of $810 million on Mar. 3, 1933).

18. Ahamed (2009: 446) ("Roosevelt's strategy was to withhold his cooperation in the hope that conditions would deteriorate so badly before he took office that he would get the credit for any subsequent rebound."); Kennedy (1973: 141–43) (reporting that Roosevelt said to one of his advisers, "Let them bust; then we'll get things on a sound basis."); Olson (1988: 34–35) (concluding that Roosevelt wanted to "avoid being tainted by Hoover's 'kiss of death' reputation, and even exploit the seriousness of the situation. Things could not get any worse, only better, and he would reap credit for the inevitable improvement."); Wigmore (1985: 422–23, 443–47) (criticizing Roosevelt and contending that Roosevelt could have avoided a national bank holiday by cooperating with Hoover). In Barry Eichengreen's view, Roosevelt's behavior could be viewed as "Machiavellian" because "the worse the situation was on March 4, the more problems could be blamed on Hoover, and the more positive would be the reception of [Roosevelt's] initiatives." However, Eichengreen concluded that Roosevelt "was wise to refuse to cooperate with Hoover" because any "plan advanced by a discredited president" could have diminished the political capital that Roosevelt needed to resolve the banking emergency after Mar. 4. Eichengreen (2015: 226, 230).

19. In Mar. 1932, with Hoover's support, the Senate authorized an investigation of short-selling, bear raids, stock trading pools, and other manipulative practices on Wall Street. The Senate Banking and Currency Committee appointed a special subcommittee to conduct the investigation, and the subcommittee's inquiry ultimately expanded to cover a broad range of abusive practices on Wall Street. The subcommittee made very limited

progress until it hired Pecora as its new chief counsel in Jan. 1933. Carosso (1970: 322–38); Perino (2010: 11–23, 45–64); Seligman (2003: 11–21).

20. Carosso (1970: 325–29); Kennedy (1973: 107–08); Perino (2010: 112–25); see Chapters 4 and 5 for discussion of the marketing of Insull securities by Halsey, Stuart and its syndicate partners, including large Chicago banks.

21. Perino (2010: 88, 133–34, 221–26).

22. Ibid., 63–64, 88–94, 102–04, 137–38. After Pecora completed his inquest of National City, a group of National City's employees sent an anonymous letter to President Roosevelt, urging Roosevelt to investigate additional abuses by National City that Pecora did not uncover. Roosevelt's secretaries forwarded the letter to Senator Carter Glass, who was leading the Senate Banking Committee's work on the proposed Glass-Steagall Act. Kennedy (1973: 108–09, 126–27).

23. For descriptions of those securities transactions, see Chapters 2 and 3 as well as Perino (2010: 159–66, 179–86, 198–203, 231–41, 247–53, 273); and Wilmarth (2016: 1303–12, 1317–20, 1324–25). By the early 1930s, most states had enacted "blue sky laws," which prohibited fraudulent sales of securities. However, most "blue sky laws" were full of loopholes and poorly enforced, and they did not stop abusive and deceptive practices by National City and other universal banks and investment banks during the 1920s and early 1930s. Seligman (2003: 41–46).

24. See Chapter 2 for discussions of Pecora's investigation of National City's bonus plan, stock purchase plan, and "morale" loans for senior executives, as well as the bank's onerous treatment of ordinary employees who agreed to buy National City stock under installment contracts. See also Pecora (1939: 113–23, 127–29); Perino (2010: 142–49, 166–69); Wilmarth (2016: 1318–19, 1322–23); and U.S. Senate (1934: 172, 206–08). In Dec. 1932, National City's board of directors wrote off and forgave the $1.9 million of "advances" made to Mitchell and other senior executives during the first half of 1929. New York Herald Tribune (1933c).

25. Perino (2010: 147–49, 155–57, 186–89); Seligman (2003: 25–26); Wells (2010: 706–07, 713–15).

26. Pecora (1939: 123–26); Perino (2010: 274–75); U.S. Senate (1933a: 2327–42); U.S. Senate (1934: 106–07).

27. Perino (2010: 152–55); see also U.S. Senate (1934: 322–23); Washington Post (1933) (stating that "Mitchell's tax return for 1929 showed a purported net loss of $48,000 and that accordingly he had paid no tax"); *Helvering v. Mitchell*, 303 U.S. 391, 395 (1938).

28. Perino (2010: 224–26); see also Cleveland & Huertas (1985: 186–87). Hugh Baker similarly resigned as president of National City's securities affiliate. New York Herald Tribune (1933a).

29. Cleveland & Huertas (1985: 186) (quoting editorial published in the *New York Times* on Feb. 28, 1933).

30. Perino (2010: 189–91, 297–98); New York Herald Tribune (1933c); Washington Post (1933); *Mitchell v. Helvering*, 303 U.S. 391 (1938). Mitchell's counsel at his criminal trial was Max Steuer, "the greatest trial lawyer of his day." Steuer argued that Mitchell had engaged in legitimate "tax avoidance" based on the advice of his lawyers. Perino (2010: 297–98). Justice Louis Brandeis wrote the Supreme Court's opinion that upheld the validity of the Commissioner's civil assessment against Mitchell. *Mitchell v. Helvering*, at 395. In 1914, Brandeis identified National City as a key member of Wall Street's "financial

oligarchy" in his famous book, *Other People's Money*. Brandeis (1933 [1914]: 1–35, 137–41), discussed in Chapter 1.

31. Perino (2010: 2–6, 187–88, 225–26, 243–47, 281–83, 287–89, 292); Seligman (2003: 29–30).

32. Franklin D. Roosevelt, "Inaugural Address" (Mar. 4, 1933), available at Gerhard Peters & John Woolley, *The American Presidency Project*, https://www.presidency.ucsb.edu/documents/inaugural-address-8.

33. Awalt (1969: 360–66); Ballantine (1948: 138–39); Friedman & Schwartz (1963: 421–22); Kennedy (1973: 156–81); Meltzer (2003: 388–89, 421–25); see also Moley (1939: 151) (describing the "loyal support and superlative technical advice" that Roosevelt's financial team received from Ogden Mills [Hoover's former Treasury Secretary], Arthur Ballantine [Hoover's former Treasury Undersecretary], and Francis Awalt [acting Comptroller of the Currency under both Hoover and Roosevelt]); Olson (1977: 107, 113) ("It is important to remember that the Emergency Banking Act, while the first major proposal of the New Deal, was also the last major proposal of the Hoover administration," because key provisions of that Act were "formulated during the final weeks of the Hoover administration").

34. Federal Reserve Banks issued more than $200 million of short-term notes to reopened banks. Friedman & Schwartz (1963: 421–22). The Fed did not have to issue the full amount authorized by the Emergency Banking Act because the public quickly deposited $1.2 billion of hoarded currency in reopened banks. Silber (2009: 25–28); see also Eichengreen (2015: 231) (explaining that the liquidity support provided by Federal Reserve Banks provided an "implicit guarantee" to the reopened banks).

35. Kennedy (1973: 177–201, Olson (1988: 63–71).

36. Friedman & Schwartz (1963: 423–27); Kennedy (1973: 177–90); Olson (1988: 65–73); see also Historical Statistics (1975: 1019) (Series X 580–87) (stating that 15,918 banks were in operation at the end of 1934). Only 93 banks failed during 1934 and 1935. Kennedy (1973: 201–02); Olson (1988: 66, 81–82).

37. Hector (1988: 59–60); James & James (1954: 367–74); Kennedy (1973: 186–87); Moley (1939: 153–54).

38. Moley (1939: 154).

39. Eichengreen (1992: 329–47); Friedman & Schwartz (1963: 462–71); Meltzer (2003: 425–29, 442–58). In Jan. 1934, Congress passed legislation that authorized Roosevelt to establish the official price of gold. The legislation also created a $2 billion Exchange Stabilization Fund, which enabled the Treasury Department to buy gold at the new official price of $35 per ounce without any additional congressional appropriations. Meltzer (2003, 457–58).

40. Friedman & Schwartz (1963: 497–509); Mitchener & Mason (2010: 513–14); Romer (1992: 758–59, 772–83); see also Wigmore (1985: 682–83 [table A.35]) (showing that the U.S. government's holdings of gold increased from $4.04 billion at the end of 1933 to $10.12 billion at the end of 1935); Historical Statistics (1975: 1019) (Series X 580–87) (showing that U.S. bank deposits rose from $41.68 billion in 1933 to $51.27 billion in 1935).

41. Friedman & Schwartz (1963: 427–28, 434–42); Silber (2009); Wigmore (1985: 540).

42. Calomiris et al. (2013: 527, 539–47); Jones (1951: 25–40, 45–49); Mason (2001a: 87–91); Mason (2001b: 174–78, 185–91); Mitchener & Mason (2010: 518–22); see also Upham & Lamke (1934: 202–07) (explaining that large numbers of banks incurred severe losses during the early 1930s and faced serious threats to their survival in mid-1934).

43. See Chapter 11 for discussion of the federal government's rescue of the banking system during 2008–09.

44. Jones (1951: 25–28, 33–34); Mitchener & Mason (2010: 521–22); Olson (1988: 73, 77–79); see also Ballantine (1948: 134, 148–49).

45. Jones (1951: 35–36, 47–49); Olson (1988: 80–81); Upham & Lamke (1934: 237–38); New York Herald Tribune (1933g). By 1935, the RFC owned more than a third of the U.S. banking system's total capital. Olson (1988: 80–82).

46. Jones (1951: 34); see also Friedman & Schwartz (1963: 421) (stating that the RFC provided capital to 6,139 banks, including nearly half of all Fed member banks).

47. James (1938: 947–52); Peach (1941: 19–20, 59–68, 87–104); Wigmore (1985: 49–50, 171–75, 319–23, 354–61, 468–70); see Chapter 2 for descriptions of the rapid growth of all three banks during the 1920s).

48. After taking $167 million of charge-offs, National City Bank still held over $50 million of nonperforming assets at the end of 1934. Cleveland & Huertas (1985: 159–60, 191, 206, 210, 211 [table 10.5]); New York Times (1934b). The common equity capital of National City Bank dropped from $240 million in 1929 to $112 million in Jan. 1934, following the bank's sale of preferred stock to the RFC. Cleveland & Huertas (1985: 134 [table 7.8]); New York Herald Tribune (1933f).

49. Cleveland & Huertas (1985: 160, 161 [table 9.2]) (showing that the equity capital of National City Company dropped from $130 million in 1929 to $21 million in 1932); New York Times (1934b) (reporting that NCC further reduced its capital to $15 million in 1933). James Perkins, National City's chairman, stated that the RFC's purchase of preferred stock enabled the bank to establish necessary loss reserves without selling additional common stock. New York Times (1934b).

50. Jones (1951: 35–36).

51. U.S. Senate (1933b: 2317–19, 2355 [committee exhibit 6] [showing $212 million of losses for Chase National Bank between 1929 and 1933], 2383–87, 2388–89 [committee exhibit 8] [showing $120 million of losses for Chase Securities Corp. during the same period], 2390–99, 2829–30); New York Herald Tribune (1933d). The common equity capital of Chase National Bank fell from $368 million in May 1930 to $159 million in Jan. 1934, following the bank's sale of preferred stock to the RFC. U.S. Senate (1933b: 2355 [committee exhibit 6]); New York Herald Tribune (1933h). According to Chase chairman Winthrop Aldrich, the RFC's investment permitted Chase to reduce its capital without "jeopardizing the common stock dividends." New York Times (1934a).

52. Jones (1951: 47–49); Kennedy (1973: 191); Chicago Daily Tribune (1932a); Chicago Daily Tribune (1933); Chicago Daily Tribune (1935); FDIC (1984: 45–46, 139).

53. Olson (1988: 66–73, 77 [note 35], 80–82) (stating that the RFC provided $665 million of loans to all banks during 1933 and 1934).

54. See Wigmore (1985: 49–50, 171–75, 319–23, 354–61, 468–70) (stating that the National City, Chase, and Continental Illinois "had been the most aggressive banks" during the boom of the 1920s and "led the industry down in dividend cuts, write-offs, and stock price declines" during the Depression).

55. Chernow (1990: 353–54); Perino (2010: 149); Perkins (1971: 518–19); Seligman (2003: 39–42).

56. Fink (2019: 96) (quoting Glass' platform plank and Roosevelt's speech).

57. Chernow (1990: 359–60); Moley (1939: 176–78); Perino (2010: 286–88); Seligman (2003: 29–30, 50–54).

58. Chernow (1990: 360–61); Seligman (2003: 30–31).

59. Chernow (1990: 356–57, 360–77); Perino (2010: 283–90); Seligman (2003: 31–38).

60. Chernow (1990: 363–64) (quoting Mr. Morgan's testimony); Pecora (1939: 5–6) (same).

61. Pecora (1939: 5–6).

62. Chernow (1990: 366); see also Perino (2010: 284); Seligman (2003: 33–34).

63. Chernow (1990: 370–72); Pecora (1939: 27–31); Seligman (2003: 34–35); U.S. Senate (1934: 101–05).

64. Pecora (1939: 29–30) (quoting letter from William Ewing to William Woodin).

65. Ibid., 32 (quoting Wiggin's testimony).

66. Ibid., 32–33 (quoting letter from Raskob to George Whitney).

67. Ibid., 32, 40 (quoting Wiggin's testimony).

68. Ibid., 12–15, 35–37, 40 (quote); see also Carosso (1970: 340); Chernow (1990: 364–65); Seligman (2003: 31–32), as well as Chapter 1 for discussion of the Pujo hearings.

69. Carosso (1970: 297–98, 340–41); Chernow (1990: 308–10, 369–72); Pecora (1939: 20–34, 222–24); Seligman (2003: 35–37).

70. Wigmore (1985: 348–53, 465–68); see also Lorey (1933) (reporting that the stock price of Alleghany Corporation dropped from a high of $56.50 in 1929 to $2.50 by May 1933).

71. Chernow (1990: 373); see also Lorey (1933) (reporting that disclosure of the House of Morgan's preferred lists "caused quite a commotion").

72. Seligman (2003: 37) (quoting *New York Times*, May 27, 1933, and *New York World-Telegram*, May 26, 1933).

73. Carosso (1970: 348–53, 368–72); Chernow (1990: 355–75); Perino (2010: 4–7, 208–11, 221–26, 280–90); Perkins (1971: 522–23); Seligman (2003: 1–2, 22–38, 72). President Roosevelt signed the Securities Act into law on May 27, 1933, while Pecora's subcommittee was conducting its hearings on J. P. Morgan & Co. Perino (2010: 289). Roosevelt signed the Glass-Steagall Act on June 16, 1933, after the Morgan hearings ended. Chernow (1990: 362–76); Seligman (2003: 31–38).

74. Pecora (1939: 4).

75. Seligman (2003: 66).

76. Carosso (1970: 352–57); Seligman (2003: 38–42, 50–72).

77. Perino (2010: 287–89).

78. New York Times (1933f) (quoting the FTC). As explained in Chapter 2, a total of $81 billion of domestic and foreign corporate and government securities were issued in the U.S. between 1919 and 1930. In 1934, Congress created the Securities and Exchange Commission to administer the Securities Act of 1933 as well as the Securities Exchange Act of 1934. Carosso (1970: 356); Seligman (2003: 99).

79. Kennedy (1973: 203–05, 212–13); see also Fink (2019: 76–99); Perkins (1971: 510–15); Smith & Beasley (1939: 304–06); Willis & Chapman (1934: 84–95).

80. U.S. Senate (1931: 191 [Wiggin], 298–99 [Mitchell], 404 [Traylor], 540 [Pope]).

81. U.S. Senate (1932a: 16–17 [testimony by Pope], 56–59 [testimony by Haas], 485–89 [letter from Scott]). For descriptions of the IBA's membership and activities between 1912 and 1934, see Carosso (1970: 165–73, 183–92, 255–71, 300–01, 319–20, 357–61, 368–75).

82. U.S. Senate (1932a: 422–24 (testimony of Comptroller J. W. Pole), 501–02 (letter from Governor Harrison); see also Fink (2019: 83–85) (discussing the Hoover administration's

lack of support for the Glass bill); Perkins (1971: 510–11) (discussing Pole's and Harrison's strong opposition to the Glass bill).

83. U.S. Senate (1932a: 358, 387–94) (testimony of Governor Eugene Meyer); Fink (2019: 89) (quoting Hamlin's letter to Glass dated Sept. 29, 1932).

84. Chapman & Willis (1934: 84–96); Fink (2019: 79–80, 83–98); Kennedy (1973: 203–04, 211–12); Smith & Beasley (1939: 306). For a summary of the original Glass bill, see U.S. Senate (1932b).

85. 77 *Congressional Record* 3725–26, 4179–80 (1933) (remarks of Sen. Glass and Sen. Bulkley), 3835, 3907, 4027 (1933) (remarks of Rep. Steagall, Rep. Kopplemann, and Rep. Fish); U.S. Senate (1933c: 3–10); see also Symons (1983) (describing traditional banking activities); Wilmarth (2002: 225–30, 254–57) (same).

86. 77 *Congressional Record* 3725, 3726 (1933) (remarks of Sen. Glass); see also Chapters 2–5 for discussions of the underwriting and sale of speculative bonds and stocks by securities affiliates of commercial banks.

87. 77 *Congressional Record* 3835 (1933) (remarks of Rep. Steagall).

88. 75 *Congressional Record* 9904–06 (1932) (remarks of Sen. Walcott).

89. 77 *Congressional Record* 3907 (1933) (remarks of Rep. Kopplemann).

90. 77 *Congressional Record* 4028 (1933) (remarks of Rep. Fish).

91. Chernow (1990: 375); see Chapters 3 and 5 for discussion of conflicts of interest revealed by the foreign bond offerings conducted by National City and Chase.

92. 75 *Congressional Record* 9910–12 (remarks of Sen. Bulkley); 77 *Congressional Record* 4028 (remarks of Rep. Fish); U.S. Senate (1931: 1063–66 [appendix VII]) (staff report prepared by a Senate subcommittee chaired by Sen. Glass). For descriptions of conflicts of interest and other abusive practices that occurred at universal banks with securities affiliates during the 1920s, see Chapters 2–5, and see also Wilmarth (2016: 1306–22).

93. 75 *Congressional Record* 9911 (1932) (remarks of Sen. Bulkley).

94. 75 *Congressional Record* 9911–12 (1932).

95. 77 *Congressional Record* 3907 (1933) (remarks of Rep. Kopplemann, followed by applause).

96. See Chapter 1 for discussion of the McFadden Act.

97. U.S. Senate (1932b: 11, 16 [majority views], Part II [minority views]); see also Wilmarth (1992: 973–75).

98. Kennedy (1973: 207–09); Westerfield (1933: 742–44); Wilmarth (1992: 973–75).

99. Kennedy (1973: 214–17).

100. Ibid., 215–18; Westerfield (1933: 745–46); U.S. House of Representatives (1933: 5–7); U.S. Senate (1932b: 12, 14); 77 *Congressional Record* 3839–40 (1933) (remarks of Rep. Steagall).

101. U.S. Senate (1933c: 12, 14); see also FDIC (1984: 40–44). The provisions of the Glass-Steagall Act that established the deposit insurance program appear in 48 *Statutes at Large* 168–80 (1933).

102. Fink (2019: 105–08, 115–17); Kennedy (1973: 204–09, 214–23); Preston (1933: 597–603); Westerfield (1933: 742–49); Wilmarth (1992: 973–75); New York Times (1933g); see also 77 *Congressional Record* 3727–28 (1933) (remarks of Sen. Glass, explaining why he and President Roosevelt accepted partial deposit insurance with federal oversight); 77 *Congressional Record* 3836–38, 4033, 5894–98 (1933) (remarks of Rep. Steagall and other House members, explaining why they accepted partial deposit insurance and limited statewide branching).

103. New York Times (1933a) (quoting Perkins); see also Cleveland & Huertas (1985: 186–90, 197, 407n3).

104. New York Times (1933b) (quoting Aldrich). Aldrich was a lawyer who served as chairman of the Equitable Trust Company—a bank controlled by the Rockefeller family—before Equitable merged with Chase National Bank in June 1930. Aldrich quickly became an influential director of Chase, and Chase's board of directors elected Aldrich as chairman in Jan. 1933, after Albert Wiggin retired.

105. Ibid. (quoting Aldrich). The *New York Times* viewed Aldrich's proposals as an effort "to reduce the present overlords of the New York money market," including J. P. Morgan & Co. and Kuhn, Loeb & Co., to a position of "relative impotence."

106. Ibid. (quoting Wiggin); see also Peach (1941: 157–58) (explaining that Aldrich's views represented a "complete reversal of policies" that Chase followed under Wiggin's leadership). In Apr. and May 1933, Chase's board of directors and shareholders approved Chase's plan to divest its securities affiliate. New York Times (1933d); New York Herald Tribune (1933b).

107. Chernow (1990: 355–56, 362–75); Kennedy (1973: 212–13); Peach (1941: 157–59); Perino (2010: 287–90); Perkins (1971: 522–24); see also 76 *Congressional Record* 9910 (1932) (remarks of Sen. Bulkley, stating that Bank of Manhattan, Bankers Trust, Chatham Phenix Bank, and Chemical Bank either closed or sold their securities affiliates during 1931 and 1932).

108. New York Times (1933c) (quoting Potter). Guaranty Trust was the third-largest bank in New York City and the U.S. in the early 1930s. Goldsmith (1933: 161–62).

109. Chernow (1990: 354–55, 357) (quoting correspondence between Leffingwell and Roosevelt in 1932, and describing Lamont's telephone call to Roosevelt in early 1933). J. P. Morgan & Co. "campaigned to slip Leffingwell into a Treasury post" after Roosevelt won the 1932 election. However, Roosevelt rejected that proposal and stated his administration would not "tie up" with any partner from the House of Morgan. Ibid., 355.

110. 77 *Congressional Record* 4178–79 (1933) (remarks of Sen. Tydings). Thomas Lamont and Russell Leffingwell of J. P. Morgan & Co. publicly supported Tydings's proposal for an exemption shielding private investment banks from the application of the Glass-Steagall Act. Chernow (1990: 376).

111. 77 *Congressional Record* 4179–80 (1933) (remarks of Sen. Bulkley and Sen. Glass). Glass had previously informed the Senate that Section 21 encountered "bitter hostility" from "the large private banks, whose chief business is an investment business." Glass contended that it was essential to separate such institutions from "the deposit banking business" (quote at ibid., 3730).

112. 77 *Congressional Record* 4179–80 (1933) (remarks of Sen. Glass). In 1934, officers from Chase's securities affiliate joined with officers from the First National Bank of Boston's securities affiliate to create a new securities firm, called The First Boston Corporation. Chernow (1990: 375); Peach (1941: 165–66).

113. Kennedy (1973: 221–22); see also New York Times (1933g).

114. 48 *Statutes at Large* 165, 184. Sections 5(c) and 16 are codified at 12 U.S.C. §§335 & 24 (Seventh). For a description of "bank-eligible" securities that banks may underwrite and trade under Sections 5(c) and 16, see Wilmarth (2002: 225–26n30). Glass-Steagall's restrictions originally applied only to national banks and state member banks. Since

1992, those restrictions have also applied to state nonmember banks under the Federal Deposit Insurance Act. See 12 U.S.C. §1831a.

115. 48 *Statutes at Large* 165, 184, 188, 194. Sections 20 and 32 were repealed by the Gramm-Leach-Bliley Act of 1999, discussed in Chapter 8.

116. 48 *Statutes at Large* 189 (emphasis added), codified at 12 U.S.C. §378(a)(2).

117. Chernow (1990: 374–75); see also 77 *Congressional Record* 3835 (1933) (remarks of Rep. Steagall, explaining that the Glass-Steagall Act would "confine banks of deposit to legitimate functions and … separate them from affiliates of other organizations which have brought discredit and loss of public confidence"); 75 *Congressional Record* 9914 (1932) (remarks of Rep. Bulkley, stating that "by removing the bankers from the temptation of using credit in such a way to make a … foundation for the flotation of more security issues we are protecting the depositors").

118. 77 *Congressional Record* 3729, 4165–66 (1933) (remarks of Sen. Glass); 75 *Congressional Record* 9882–83 (1932) (remarks of Sen. Glass); see 48 *Statutes at Large* 181–82 (1933) (text of Section 11(b)). In 1980 and 1982, Congress repealed the Fed's authority to set maximum interest rates for time deposits under Regulation Q. FCIC (2011: 29). In 2010, Congress repealed the provision barring banks from paying interest on demand deposits. See 124 *Statutes at Large* 1640 (2010).

119. 77 *Congressional Record* 3729 (1933) (remarks of Rep. Glass); Madrick (2011: 13); see also Friedman & Schwartz (1963: 443–44).

120. U.S. Senate (1933c: 9, 15); 48 *Statutes at Large* 181, codified at 12 U.S.C. §374a (text of Section 11(a)); see also Chapter 4 for discussion of the significant role played by nonbanks and wealthy individuals in funding broker call loans during the stock market bubble of the late 1920s.

121. Friedman & Schwartz (1963: 444–45).

122. Beasley & Smith (1939: 304–05) (stating that the Glass bill imposed "severe restrictions" to "curb the use of Federal Reserve funds for speculative purposes"); Meltzer (2003: 248, 418, 431, 434 (explaining that Glass and other members of Congress believed that the Fed "permitted securities speculation" during the 1920s, which led to "financial collapse" during the Great Depression); 75 *Congressional Record* 9882–85 (1932) (remarks of Sen. Glass); U.S. Senate (1933c: 3–9, 13–14); see also 48 *Statutes at Large* 163, 180, codified at 12 U.S.C. §§301, 347 (text of Sections 3(a) and 9).

123. Meltzer (2003: 434); see also Beasley & Smith (1939: 304–05).

124. As amended in 2002, Section 201.3(c)(3) of the Fed's regulations provided that each Federal Reserve Bank should "keep itself informed of … the loans and investments" held by banks, and should "consider such information in determining whether to extend credit" to banks. However, Section 201.3(c)(3) did *not* say that the Fed should refrain from extending credit that would encourage speculative financing by banks. See 67 *Federal Register* 67786 (Nov. 7, 2002) (adopting 12 C.F.R. 201.3(c)(3)). See Chapter 11 for discussion of the Fed's huge emergency lending programs that supported the securities portfolios of large universal banks and securities firms during the financial crisis.

125. Carosso (1970: 344–45); Pecora (1939: 206–07); see also Flandreau, Gaillard, & Panizza (2010: 12–14, 44 [table A]) (showing that thirteen [81%] of the sixteen foreign government bond issues underwritten during the 1920s by Dillon, Read defaulted by 1940); U.S. Senate (1934: 145–48) (reporting that Dillon, Read sold $186 million of Brazilian government bonds to American investors during the 1920s; the prospectuses for those

bonds contained false and misleading statements, and $144 million of those bonds defaulted by October 1933).

126. U.S. Senate (1934: 334–50) (quote at 344); see also Carosso (1970: 345–46); Pecora (1939: 206–14); Seligman (2003: 224–25).

127. Pecora (1939: 134–35) (also stating that Chase, "behind its imposing façade of unassailable might and rectitude, was not a whit better than the National City Bank itself"); see also Carosso (1970: 346–47).

128. Pecora (1939: 162–68); U.S. Senate (1934: 133–43); Wilmarth (2016: 1312–16); see Chapters 2–5 for discussions of Chase's underwriting of high-risk securities.

129. Pecora (1939: 149–51, 168–87) (quote at 184–85); U.S. Senate (1934: 173–83, 187–95); Wilmarth (2016: 1319–21); see also Chapter 2 for descriptions of Chase's stock trading pools.

130. U.S. Senate (1934: 201–02, 208–10); Wilmarth (2016: 1324–25).

131. Pecora (1939: 146–52, 157–60); U.S. Senate (1934: 187–89, 325–28); Wilmarth (2016: 1325); New York Times (1933h).

132. Pecora (1939: 153–61) (quote at 161); see also U.S. Senate (1934: 188–92); Wilmarth (2016: 1325–26); New York Herald Tribune (1933e).

133. Carosso (1970: 328–79); Chernow (1990: 355–79); Perino (2010: 280–94); Seligman (2003: 20–38, 69–100).

134. Chernow (1990: 206, 355, 374); Fink (2019: 147–51); Perino (2010: 219, 285–86); Smith & Beasley (1939: 156–57, 160–62, 197–98, 231).

135. Seligman (2003: 78–83, 111–14).

136. Glass' proposed amendment would have limited the amount of any single bond issue to 10% of the bank underwriter's capital and the amount of all such issues to 200% of the bank's capital. 79 *Congressional Record* 11827 (1935); U.S. Senate (1935: 16); Fink (2019: 167–68).

137. Chernow (1990: 384–86); Seligman (2003: 114).

138. Fink (2019: 168) (quoting letters sent by Roosevelt to Glass in July and Aug. 1935).

139. 79 *Congressional Record* 11932–33 (1935) (remarks of Sen. La Follette).

140. 79 *Congressional Record* 11932–33 (1935) (remarks of Sen. La Follette).

141. Ibid. (remarks of Sen. La Follette and Sen. Vandenberg); see also 79 *Congressional Record* 11935 (1935) (showing that Senator Duncan Fletcher, who chaired the Pecora subcommittee's hearings after Mar. 1933, joined La Follette and Vandenberg in voting to strike Glass' amendment).

142. 79 *Congressional Record* 11934–35 (1935) (reporting the Senate's decision to reject La Follette's motion by a vote of 22–39); ibid. 13706 (remarks of Rep. Steagall, followed by applause); see also Chernow (1990: 384–87); U.S. House of Representatives (1935: 53). Glass had advised the Senate that he would sacrifice his amendment if that step was necessary to achieve passage of the Banking Act of 1935. 79 *Congressional Record* 11827 (1935) (remarks of Sen. Glass).

143. Chernow (1990: 386–89); see also Morrison & Wilhelm (2007: 209–10).

144. Carosso (1970: 373–74); Morrison & Wilhelm (2007: 209–10); Peach (1941: 165–68).

145. Carosso (1970: 243 [exhibit 7], 393–95); Seligman (2003: 114–17, 161); Historical Statistics (1975: 1005 [Series X: 499–509], 1006 [Series X 510–515]).

146. Historical Statistics (1975: 1019) (Series X 580–87).

147. Calomiris & Wilson (2004); Cleveland & Huertas (1985: 199–201) (quoting Perkins' letter to shareholders of Dec. 5, 1933).

148. Fishback (2010: 395); see also Mitchener & Mason (2010: 526, 530–31, 536).

149. Mitchener & Mason (2010: 524, 529–31); Olson (1988: 82, 132–38, 153–54) (quoting Jones' speech to the New York Bankers' Association on Feb. 5, 1934).

150. Cleveland & Huertas (1985: 201–04 [quoting Perkins's message to John Neylan], 415n49); Friedman & Schwartz (1963: 449–62); Jones (1951: 51–52, 183–84); Olson (1988: 132–38, 153–54).

151. Mitchener & Mason (2010: 524–25); Olson (1988: 156–78); Sablik (2013: 2–3).

152. Sastry (2018: 19–28).

153. Cleveland & Huertas (1985: 201, 204–05, 417n54); Mitchener & Mason (2010: 524–26, 528–31).

154. Cleveland & Huertas (1985: 417n54) (quoting Perkins' statements in National City Bank's *Economic Letter* of May 1938); see also Mitchener & Mason (2010: 525) (stating that "total bank lending remained below its 1921 levels until the 1940s," when "wartime production resuscitated economic activity").

155. Gordon & Krenn (2010); Meltzer (2003: 416, 560, 570–72); Vernon (1994); see also Romer (1992: 761 [figure 2]).

156. Mitchener & Mason (2010: 524–36) (describing the negative economic effects of risk aversion by banks and business firms during the Great Depression, and noting evidence of similar behavior during the global financial crisis of 2007–09). For discussions of the adverse economic impact of risk aversion during the 2007–09 crisis, see Benhima & Massenot (2013: 68–73, 89–97); DeDad (2017); Guiso, Sapienza, & Zingales (2017).

157. Benston (1990) (quotes at 41, 107).

158. White (1986: 40) (acknowledging that "the effects of bank size cannot be analyzed," due to data limitations in his study); see also Kroszner & Rajan (1994: 811n3) (stating that White's "evidence must be interpreted cautiously" because his study did not determine the effect of size on bank survival); Wilmarth (2005: 591–604) (providing several reasons to question whether banks with securities affiliates were safer than those that did not engage in securities activities). See Chapter 5 and this chapter for discussions of the systemic impacts of the failures of Caldwell and Company, Bank of United States, and the two largest Michigan banks. As also discussed in Chapter 5 and this chapter, several leading universal banks—including Bank of America, Central Republic, National City, Chase, and Continental Illinois—received extensive financial support from the RFC, the Fed, and/or other large banks.

159. Ang & Richardson (1994); Kroszner & Rajan (1994); Puri (1994, 1996); see also Wilmarth (2005: 605–06) (discussing the results of those studies).

160. See the discussion of Glass-Steagall's purposes in this chapter; see also Wilmarth (2005: 606–07).

Chapter 7

1. See Chapter 6, as well as Wilmarth (2017: 449–52) (summarizing Glass-Steagall's main provisions); Krishnamurthy (2018: 825, 841–43) (same).

2. As originally enacted in 1956, the BHC Act applied only to holding companies that controlled two or more banks. In 1970, Congress expanded the BHC Act's scope to include

one-bank holding companies, after it became clear that large banks were organizing one-bank holding companies to engage in nonbanking activities that were off-limits for multi-bank holding companies. The 1970 amendments also prevented insurance, commercial, or industrial firms from affiliating with banks through a one-bank holding company structure. Wilmarth (2007: 1567–68).

3. Public Law No. 84–511, 70 *Statutes at Large* 133 (1956). Prior to the BHC Act's passage, the Glass-Steagall Act required bank holding companies to register with the Fed and obtain the Fed's permission before they could vote the stock of national banks or state member banks. Most holding companies avoided those requirements by refraining from voting the stock of their subsidiary banks. The BHC Act replaced Glass-Steagall's ineffective holding company provisions. Wilmarth (2007: 1566); Wilmarth (1990: 1154, 1160–61).

4. Wilmarth (2007: 1566).

5. Herman (1959: 535–37).

6. Wilmarth (1992: 975–77).

7. Wilmarth (2007: 1566–69).

8. Hector (1988: 66–67); Herman (1959: 521, 537–38).

9. U.S. Treasury (1991: XVIII-9).

10. Ibid., XVIII-6 through XVIII-9; see also Krishnamurthy (2018: 825).

11. See Wilmarth (1990: 1157–58) (discussing (i) *Investment Co. Institute v. Camp*, 401 U.S. 617 [1971], which struck down an OCC regulation authorizing national banks to offer collective investment funds that resembled mutual funds; (ii) *Saxon v. Georgia Association of Independent Insurance Agents*, 399 F.2d 1010 [5th Cir. 1968], which invalidated an OCC rule allowing national banks to operate insurance agencies across the nation; and (iii) *Port of New York Authority v. Baker, Watts & Co.*, 392 F.2d 497 [D.C. Cir. 1968], which overruled an OCC regulation permitting national banks to underwrite municipal revenue bonds).

12. See Wilmarth (2002: 226–27) (discussing (i) *Alabama Association of Insurance Agents v. Board of Governors of the Federal Reserve System*, 533 F.2d 224, 241–42 [5th Cir. 1976], *modified on rehearing*, 558 F.2d 729 [5th Cir. 1977], *cert. denied*, 435 U.S. 904 [1978], which struck down a Fed rule allowing bank holding companies to sell various types of insurance as a "convenience" to their customers; and (ii) a 1982 federal statute that imposed strict limits on the permissible insurance activities of bank holding companies).

13. Eichengreen (2015: 66–67).

14. Barth, Brumbaugh, & Litan (1992: 59–61); Garten (1989: 513–21).

15. Carnell, Macey, & Miller (2017: 21); see also Garten (1989: 517–19).

16. Wilmarth (2002: 219–20, 224–27, 451, 475–76).

17. Ibid., 235–37, 375–77, 451; see also Brimmer (1989: 5–7, 11–15); Chernow (1990: 700–01); Davis (1992: 161–63, 250–51); Mishkin (1991: 98–104). Commercial paper is a short-term debt security that is issued by a business or financial firm and typically has a maturity of less than 90 days. Hahn (1993: 46–48).

18. Zingales (2012). In a Mar. 2010 interview, former Citigroup co-chairman John Reed stated that "the compartmentalization that was created by Glass-Steagall" was a "positive factor" because it reduced the risks of "a catastrophic failure" affecting the entire financial system. FCIC (2011: 55, 474n18) (quoting Reed).

19. Litan (1987: 34–45); Wilmarth (1990: 1141–44, 1157–58).

20. Hetzel (2008: 67–93); Meltzer (2005: 158–72); Weise (2012).

21. Under the Bretton Woods agreement, the U.S. promised to convert dollars into gold at a fixed price of $35 per ounce, and many other nations agreed to peg their currencies to the dollar. The Bretton Woods agreement permitted member nations to adjust their pegged exchange rates under the oversight of the International Monetary Fund. President Nixon's decision in Aug. 1971 to suspend convertibility of dollars into gold led to the complete breakdown of Bretton Woods in early 1973, when many developed countries adopted floating exchange rates. Bayoumi (2017: 161–64); Bordo (2017: 3–4, 21–26); Hetzel (2008: 100–07); Silber (2012: 86–92, 113–21).

22. Bernstein (1996: 246, 251, 320–22); Hetzel (2008: 150–54).

23. Hetzel (2008: 94–95, 150–65); Madrick (2011: 66, 104, 164–70); Silber (2012; 165–215, 222–24).

24. Cleveland & Huertas (1985: 253–57, 266–68, 432n35); Madrick (2011: 16–19); Morris & Walter (1993). Wriston's bank is referred to as "Citibank" in this chapter. However, the bank operated under the name "First National City Bank of New York" from 1962 to 1976, when it changed its name to "Citibank." Cleveland & Huertas (1985: iv).

25. Wilmarth (1990: 1143–44).

26. Taub (2014: 70–72, 125–31, 154–55, 224–28).

27. Black (2005: 29–38); Day (2019: chapters 12, 13); Taub (2014: 4–5, 50–72); Wilmarth (2007: 1573–75); FDIC (1997: 167–86).

28. Black (2005: 17–41, 243–67); Day (2019: chapter 14); Taub (2014: 76–107); Wilmarth (2007: 1575–79); FDIC (1997: 180–88).

29. FCIC (2011: 35–36); see also FDIC (1997: 167–88, 279–418).

30. Taub (2014: 5, 69–73, 87–89, 223–33); see also Chapters 9–11.

31. Cook & Duffield (1993: 156–59, 164–67); Eichengreen (2015: 67–68); Litan (1987: 34–35); Madrick (2011: 97–98); FCIC (2011: 29–30, 33).

32. Cook & Duffield (1993: 157); FCIC (2011: 30, 33).

33. Ricks (2016: 233); see also Eichengreen (2015: 69–70).

34. Cook & Duffield (1993: 164).

35. Ibid.

36. As explained in Chapters 5 and 6, Section 21 prohibits any person other than a chartered depository institution from engaging "in the business of accepting deposits subject to check or to repayment upon presentation of a pass book, certificate of deposit, or other evidence of debt, or upon request of the depositor." Violators of Section 21 are subject to criminal penalties, including fines and imprisonment. 12 U.S.C. § 378(a)(2), (b).

37. Undated letter (apparently written in Dec. 1979) from Philip E. Heymann, Assistant Attorney General for the DOJ's Criminal Division, and Lawrence Lippe, Chief of the Criminal Division's General Litigation and Legal Advice Section, to Martin Lybecker, Associate Director of the SEC's Division of Investment Management (rejecting allegations of violations of Section 21 of the Glass-Steagall Act made in letters sent to the SEC and the Attorney General in Oct. 1979 by Morris D. Crawford, Jr., chairman of the board of the Bowery Savings Bank of New York). I am indebted to Morgan Ricks for providing a photocopy of the Heymann-Lippe letter to me.

38. FCIC (2011: 30, 33).

39. Eichengreen (2015: 67–68); Taub (2014: 51–61); Wilmarth (2002: 239–40); FCIC (2011: 30–34); FDIC (1997: 91–94).

40. Cook & Duffield (1993: 157); FCIC (2011: 30); Peek & Rosengren (2015: 20 [figure 7]).

41. Pozsar et al. (2010: 11–20).
42. Hahn (1993: 46–48); Kacperczyk & Schnabl (2010: 30–32); FCIC (2011: 30–31).
43. Lumpkin (1993: 59–63); McLean & Nocera (2010: 241–42); Paulson (2010: 97–98, 227–28); FCIC (2011: 31). The repo market consists of two major segments: bilateral repos (two-party transactions between securities firms and cash lenders) and triparty repos (three-party transactions, in which a clearing bank acts as an intermediary in the transaction and serves as the agent for both the lender and the borrower). Baklanova, Copeland, & McCaughlin (2015: 7–20).
44. MMMFs owned about one-third of all outstanding commercial paper in both 1992 and 2007. Hahn (1993: 50–51); Kacperczyk & Schnabl (2010: 35). MMMFs were also among the most significant cash lenders for repos. Pozsar et al. (2010: 50–52).
45. Hahn (1993: 50–52, 52 [table 2]); Kacperczyk & Schnabl (2010: 32, 38 [figure 1]).
46. Lumpkin (1993: 73–74 [tables 1 and 2]); Fleming & Garbade (2003: 1); Logan, Nelson, & Parkinson (2018: 4 [figure 1]); Peek & Rosengren (2015: 19 [figure 6]).
47. Pozsar et al. (2010: 22–37).
48. Hockett & Omarova (2017: 1188–93) (quote at 1192).
49. Ricks (2016: 5–6, 226, 230–37, 301n7) (citing Section 21 of the Glass-Steagall Act, codified at 12 U.S.C. §378).
50. The check-writing privileges offered by MMMFs depended on the willingness of banks to clear their checks through the banking industry's check-clearing system, which the Fed regulated. The Fed could have instructed banks not to clear checks written on MMMF accounts. In a 1981 interview, Martin Mayer, a leading financial journalist, asked Fed chairman Paul Volcker why the Fed allowed banks to clear checks for MMMFs. According to Mayer, Volcker replied, "It was one of those things where you look and think, 'That's interesting, I wonder where it will go,' and the next time you look at it it's so big you don't dare to do anything about it." Mayer (2009: 10) (quoting Volcker).
51. Brimmer (1989: 5–7); Mishkin (1991: 98–101); Stojanovich & Vaughan (1998: 8–9); Wilmarth (2002: 235–36, 470–71); FCIC (2011: 30–31).
52. Lumpkin (1993: 63–65); Sissoko (2009: 5–7); FCIC (2011: 31–32).
53. Pozsar et al. (2010: 22–36, 46–53).
54. FCIC (2011: 32); see also Ricks (2016: 32–36, 34 [figure 1.2]). Ricks included uninsured bank deposits and Eurodollar deposits in his classification of "private-money claims," while the FCIC did not include those deposits in its calculation of sources of shadow bank funding.
55. FCIC (2011: 32); Pozsar et al. (2010: 50–52). At the end of 2007, FDIC-insured depository institutions held about $8.4 trillion of deposits, including $4.3 trillion of FDIC-insured deposits and $4.1 trillion of uninsured domestic and foreign deposits. FDIC (2008: 5 [table II-A], 15). Assets held by shadow banks in 2007 also exceeded assets held by traditional banks. Adrian & Shin (2009: 1 [figure 1]) (showing that lenders funded by the securities markets held $16.6 trillion of assets in mid-2007, compared with $12.8 trillion held by regulated depository institutions).
56. Ricks (2016: 36).
57. Gorton & Metrick (2012: 423–36, 443–48); Kacperczyk & Schnabl (2010: 36–48); Pozsar et al. (2010: 2–7, 58–66); see also Chapters 10 and 11.
58. Pozsar et al. (2010: 61, 64); see also Ricks (2016: 96–101), and Chapters 10 and 11.
59. Ricks (2016: 96–122, 184–99, 230–37); see also Chapter 11.

60. See Fein (2011: chapter 13); Schwarcz, Markell, & Broome (2004); *Federal Housing Finance Agency v. Nomura Holding America, Inc.*, 873 F.2d 85, 100–06 (2d Cir. 2017), *cert. denied*, 126 S. Ct. 2679 (2018) (hereinafter *FHFA v. Nomura*).

61. Engel & McCoy (2011: 43–51); Schwarcz, Markell, & Broome (2004: 6–16) (noting that a securitization may involve the creation of more than one SPE); *FHFA v. Nomura*, 873 F.2d at 100–06.

62. McConnell & Buser (2011: 176).

63. Ibid., 176–78.

64. Ibid., 178; Madrick (2011: 356–61); McLean & Nocera (2010: 4–13); Taub (2014: 42–45, 73–74).

65. Madrick (2011: 360–61); McLean & Nocera (2010: 14–16); Taub (2014: 74–75, 228–31).

66. Boemio & Edwards (1989: 659–60).

67. Cleveland & Huertas (1985: 294); see also Madrick (2011: 20) (describing Citibank's "plans to sell mutual funds").

68. *Investment Co. Institute v. Camp* (hereinafter *ICI v. Camp*), 401 U.S. 617, 622–23 (1971).

69. Ibid., at 634–36, 639; see also Cleveland & Huertas (1985: 294–95).

70. *ICI v. Camp*, 401 U.S. at 629–34, 636–38. For a detailed review of Glass-Steagall's legislative history, see Chapter 6.

71. *Securities Industry Association v. Board of Governors of the Federal Reserve System* (hereinafter *Bankers Trust I*), 468 U.S.137, 139–41 (1984).

72. Ibid., at 139–41, 149–57.

73. Ibid., at 155 (quoting *ICI v. Camp*, 401 U.S. at 634); see also ibid., at 154 (explaining that Congress's "concern about commercial-bank underwriting activities derived from the perception that the role of a bank as a promoter of securities was fundamentally incompatible with its role as a disinterested lender and adviser").

74. *Securities Industry Association v. Board of Governors of the Federal Reserve System* (hereinafter *Bankers Trust II*), 807 F.2d 1052 (D.C. Cir. 1986), *cert. denied*, 483 U.S. 1005 (1987).

75. Ibid., at 1056 (citing *Chevron U.S.A., Inc. v. NRDC*, 467 U.S. 837 (1984) [hereinafter *Chevron*]). The Supreme Court decided *Chevron* shortly before it issued its decision in *Bankers Trust I*. The Court gave "little deference" to the Fed's original order in *Bankers Trust I* because that order did not include any analysis of whether the Fed's position was consistent with the Glass-Steagall Act's purposes. *Bankers Trust I*, 468 U.S. at 143–44.

76. *Chevron*, 467 U.S. at 842–43 (under the first step of *Chevron*, the court asks "whether Congress has directly spoken to the precise question at issue. If the intent of Congress is clear, that is the end of the matter; for the court, as well as the agency, must give effect to the unambiguously expressed intent of Congress.").

77. Ibid., at 843, 844 (under the second step of *Chevron*, "if the statute is silent or ambiguous with respect to the specific issue, the question for the court is whether the agency's answer is based on a permissible construction of the statute." In that case, the court should defer to any "reasonable interpretation" made by the agency, even if the court would have reached a different result.).

78. See Wilmarth (2010: 37, 48).

79. *Bankers Trust II*, 807 F.2d at 1056, 1059.

80. Ibid., at 1056–66.

81. Ibid., at 1062–70.

82. Ibid., at 1069.

83. Ibid.

84. Engel & McCoy (2007: 2066–73); Muolo & Padilla (2008: 219–21); Wilmarth (2013: 1344–45, 1382); Wilmarth (2015a: 280–81 (note 104), 337); FCIC (2011: 170, 187, 224–26); see also the discussions of CDOs in this chapter and Chapters 9–11. In fairness to the D.C. Circuit, the SEC issued Rule 144A in 1990, four years after the D.C. Circuit issued its decision in *Bankers Trust II*. Rule 144A substantially relaxed the rules governing sales of securities in private placements to institutional and other qualified investors. Prior to 1990, private placements were required to comply with the more restrictive provisions of the SEC's Rule 144. Engel & McCoy (2007: 2071–72).

85. Carnell, Macey, & Miller (2017: 153) (stating that the undermining of "Glass-Steagall restrictions on banks' securities activities ... is a tale of legal ingenuity, and agency persistence, and the power of *Chevron* deference"); Fein (2011: §§1.05, 4.05[A]) (explaining that federal courts "played a major role in dismantling the Glass-Steagall Act" by issuing more than a dozen decisions that affirmed rulings by federal agencies, frequently "based on the *Chevron* rule of agency deference").

86. Wilmarth (2002: 318); Federal Reserve Board (1997: 45296).

87. *Citicorp, J. P. Morgan & Co, and Bankers Trust N.Y. Corp.* (hereinafter *Citicorp*), 73 *Federal Reserve Bulletin* 487 (1987).

88. Section 20 of Glass-Steagall prohibited banks from affiliating with companies that were "engaged principally" in "underwriting ... stocks, bonds, debentures, notes, or other [bank-ineligible] securities." *Citicorp*, at 474n6.

89. Ibid., at 475–77, 485–86.

90. Ibid., at 505. H. Robert Heller, Manuel Johnson, and Martha Seger voted in favor of the *Citicorp* order. All three of those Governors were appointed by President Reagan. Volcker was appointed by President Carter in 1979 and reappointed by President Reagan in 1983, while Angell was appointed by Reagan in 1986. See federalreservehistory.org/people.

91. *Citicorp*, 73 *Federal Reserve Bulletin* at 505.

92. Silber (2012: 259–62); see also Uchitelle (2010) (reporting that Volcker's "reluctance to deregulate contributed in part to his departure" from the Fed).

93. Bennett (1984) (quoting in part Volcker's testimony before a congressional committee); Uchitelle (2010).

94. Nash (1987).

95. *Securities Industry Association v. Board of Governors of the Federal Reserve System*, 839 F.2d 47 (2d Cir.), *cert. denied*, 486 U.S. 1059 (1988).

96. Ibid., at 49.

97. Ibid., at 52.

98. Ibid., at 49 (see also the quotation from Santayana on the first page of the Introduction of this book).

99. Ibid., at 52–54.

100. Ibid., at 60, 63, 67.

101. *Securities Industry Association v. Board of Governors of the Federal Reserve System*, 900 F.2d 360, 365 (D.C. Cir. 1990).

102. Wilmarth (2002: 318–19).

103. Ibid., at 319; Federal Reserve Board (1997) (approving removal of Section 20 "firewalls").

104. Wilmarth (2002: 319).

105. Fein (2011: §1.06[E] (stating that the Fed relaxed its Section 20 rules in 1996 and 1997 in an "attempt to regain favor as a friendly regulator and to outdo the OCC," which had been in "the vanguard" of deregulatory efforts during the 1980s and 1990s); Wilmarth (2012: 933) (stating that the Fed and the OCC "each sought to attract the patronage of major banks by approving new activities and reducing regulatory requirements" during the 1990s).

106. *Securities Industry Association v. Clarke* (hereinafter *Security Pacific*), 703 F. Supp. 256 (S.D.N.Y. 1988), *vacated and remanded*, 885 F.2d 1034 (2d Cir. 1989), *cert. denied*, 493 U.S. 1070 (1990).

107. *Security Pacific,* 703 F. Supp. at 259–60.

108. Ibid., at 259, 261.

109. Ibid., at 260–61.

110. Ibid.

111. *Security Pacific*, 885 F.2d at 1042, 1044–49.

112. Ibid., at 1051.

113. *Security Pacific*, 885 F.2d at 1046 (quoting the OCC's opinion).

114. Engel & McCoy (2011: 25–41); McLean & Nocera (2010: 126–28, 134–37, 216–29); Taub (2014: 228–33); Wilmarth (2009: 1015–24); FCIC (2011: xxii, 42–45, 104–18, 165–70, 187, 224–26). See Chapters 9–12 for discussion of the nonprime mortgage lending and securitization boom as well as the pervasive fraud that took place during the boom.

115. Fein (2011: §§13.02[A], 7.02[G] and [H], 9.04[D]).

116. FCIC (2011: 43–45, 45 [figure 3.1]); Wilmarth (2002: 388–90, 403–05).

117. Duca (2016: 515–16); Hockett & Omarova (2017: 1176–77); Wilmarth (2009: 984–85).

118. See Chapter 8 for discussion of GLBA.

119. Hockett & Omarova (2017: 1193–201); Wilmarth (2009: 1017–19, 1027–30).

120. Claessens et al. (2012: 8, 9 [figure 2]); Griffin, Lowery, & Saretto (2014: 2885–92). See Chapter 10 for discussion of the growth of markets for structured-finance securities during the 2000s.

121. Filler & Markham (2014: 1–9, 24–27); Stout (2011: 7–10); Tett (2009: 12).

122. Tett (2009: 24–25); Wilmarth (2002: 333n486).

123. Filler & Markham (2014: 1–9); Wilmarth (2002: 333n485); PWGFM (1999b: 4–5).

124. Bernstein (1996: 246, 251, 304–05, 320–22); Filler & Markham (2014: 40–41); Madrick (2011: 96–97); Tett (2009: 10–11).

125. Stout (1999: 722–24).

126. PWGFM (1999b: 7–8, 24–26) (discussing the 1974 "Treasury Amendment"). In 1981, Salomon Brothers pioneered the first OTC currency swap, a $210 million contract between IBM and the World Bank. Funk & Hirschman (2014: 3, 22–23); Tett (2009: 11–12). In 1997, the Supreme Court held that the Treasury Amendment barred the CFTC from regulating OTC options to buy or sell foreign currencies. *Dunn v. CFTC*, 519 U.S. 465 (1997).

127. Funk & Hirschman (2014: 22–26) (explaining that "the swaps market in the 1980s–1990s [was] dominated by a small number of increasingly large commercial banks in competition with a small number of prominent investment banks").

128. CFTC (1998: 26116–17).

129. Funk & Hirschman (2014: 28–29); Greenspan (1997a); ISDA (1999): Stout (2011: 19–20); PWGFM (1999b: 8–12).

130. Omarova (2009).

131. Ibid., 1058–59; OCC (2000: 6n17).

132. Omarova (2009: 1060–61).

133. Ibid., 1060–63, 1065.

134. Ibid., 1077.

135. Ibid., 1063–64.

136. Ibid., 1063–65; *Investment Company Institute v. Ludwig* (hereinafter *ICI v. Ludwig*), 884 F. Supp. 4 (D.D.C. 1995).

137. *ICI v. Ludwig*, 884 F. Supp. at 5.

138. Ibid. (rejecting the mutual fund trade association's "attempts to equate ownership of stock index futures to stock speculation through its analysis of the comparative risks of each investment").

139. Wilmarth (2017: 483–84).

140. Ibid., 484, 484n304).

141. Tett (2009: 17–18).

142. OCC (2000: 6–7); Omarova (2009: 1069–72).

143. OCC (2000: 9–10). Before 2000, a national bank typically hedged its exposure under a "long" or "short" equity swap by entering into an offsetting "mirror transaction" with an affiliated securities broker-dealer. The broker-dealer affiliate then hedged its exposure to the bank by purchasing or shorting the relevant equity stock. The OCC's ruling allowed national banks to avoid the transaction costs created by those "mirror image" hedges. Ibid., 2–3.

144. Ibid., 3.

145. Wilmarth (2011a: 1044–45); Wilmarth (2017: 486 and note 326); see also Carpenter & Murphy (2010: 3) (describing the federal safety net for banks). The significant cost-of-funding advantage enjoyed by major banks, compared with their nonbank holding company affiliates, was vividly illustrated in 2011. The Fed allowed Bank of America to transfer a large portfolio of derivatives contracts from its Merrill Lynch broker-dealer subsidiary to its subsidiary national bank. That transfer of derivatives allowed BofA to avoid posting $3.3 billion of additional collateral with its derivatives counterparties. The reduced collateral requirements for BofA's subsidiary bank were based on the fact that the bank was explicitly protected by the federal safety net and received a significantly higher credit rating than Merrill. Wilmarth (2015a: 349).

146. Wilmarth (2011a: 1045).

147. Omarova (2009: 1097–106).

148. Funk & Hirschman (2014: 28–31); Wilmarth (2002: 337–38); see also *Caiola v. Citibank, N.A.*, 295 F.3d 312, 315–18 (2d Cir. 2002) (explaining that Citibank's sale of OTC equity swaps and cash-settled stock options to plaintiff Caiola created a "synthetic portfolio" of "synthetic positions,... the values of which are pegged to the market prices of the related physical shares or options").

149. Funk & Hirschman (2014: 30).

150. Ibid., 31, 34.

151. Carnell, Macey, & Miller (2017: 175, 179, 857); Wilmarth (1990: 1166–68).

152. Tett (2009: 44–49); see also McLean & Nocera (2010: 60–62).

153. Carnell, Macey, & Miller (2017: 857, 878–79); see also Taub (2014: 192–93).

154. Blinder (2013: 66); see also McLean & Nocera (2010: 60) ("A credit default swap is essentially an insurance policy against the possibility of default.").

155. FCIC (2011: 50, 352); Skeel (1999: 441, 441n30). As amended in 1992, the Commodity Exchange Act preempted the application of state laws to OTC derivatives that were covered by the CFTC's 1993 exemption. As discussed in Chapter 8, Congress significantly expanded the preemption of state laws when it passed the Commodity Futures Modernization Act in 2000. Stout (2011: 19–22); FCIC (2011: 46–50).

156. FCIC (2011: 50–51); Taub (2014: 235–37); see also Chapter 10.

157. Tett (2009: 51–56, 60–64); see also McLean & Nocera (2010: 78–81).

158. Tett (2009: 54–55, 62–64).

159. Ibid., 64.

160. McLean & Nocera (2010: 80–81, 120–24, 263–68); Tett (2009: 66–69, 94–103, 132–39); Wilmarth (2011a: 964–67); FCIC (2011: xxiv–xxv, 142–46, 190–95).

161. Roe (2011: 541–49); Sissoko (2009: 7–9); see also the discussion earlier in this chapter of the bankruptcy safe harbor for certain types of repos that Congress created in 1984.

162. Wilmarth (2009: 991–92, 993).

163. Wilmarth (2002: 336–37).

164. The combined notional values of OTC derivatives contracts held by major U.S. banks rose from $5 trillion in 1990 to $38 trillion in 2000 and $159 trillion in 2007 (including $14 trillion of credit derivatives). Wilmarth (2002: 334) (providing figures for the top seven U.S. bank dealers in OTC derivatives in 1990 and 2000); OCC (2007: graph 4) (providing figures for the top five U.S. bank dealers in 2007).

165. Wilmarth (2002: 337).

166. Wilmarth (2017: 491–92, 541–43).

Chapter 8

1. Wilmarth (2017: 445–49, 491–92, 542–43).

2. Wilmarth (1990: 1154–55n87) (explaining that, in 1989, Congress authorized interstate acquisitions of failed banks with assets of $500 million or more, as President Carter proposed in 1980); FDIC (1997: 129–30) (describing unsuccessful efforts to pass broader interstate banking legislation during the 1980s).

3. Gerth (1981).

4. American Banker (1981); Douglas (2019: 322).

5. Bennett (1984); see also Douglas (2019: 316–22).

6. Madrick (2011: 10–11, 14, 19, 23) (quoting Albert Wojinlower).

7. Bennett (1984, 1985).

8. Cleveland & Huertas (1985: 277–79, 308–09).

9. Ibid., 156–58, 258–60, 276–79, 302–04, 308–09); Madrick (2011: 12–14, 20); see Chapters 1–4 and 6 for discussions of Charles Mitchell's leadership of National City Bank.

10. See Chapter 7 for discussion of negotiable CDs, Eurodollar deposits, and Regulation Q.

11. Cleveland & Huertas (1985: 267–68); see also Madrick (2011: 101–03).

12. Cleveland & Huertas (1985: 268–71, 438nn31, 32); Wilmarth (2002: 378–81).

13. FDIC (1997: 194 [figure 5.3], 196 [table 5.1b], 199); Madrick (2011: 101–06). Between 1973 and 1980, oil-exporting countries deposited much of their aggregate current account surplus of $366 billion into large U.S., U.K., and European banks. Those banks

loaned a large portion of the deposited funds to LDCs, which needed to finance an aggregate current account deficit of $267 billion. Schuker (1988: 133).

14. For discussions of the recycling of oil payments into syndicated LDC loans, see Bayoumi (2017: 164–66); FDIC (1997: 192–204); Madrick (2011: 101–06). For comparisons between the LDC debt cycle and the European reparations cycle, see Chernow (1990: 207–08, 225–29, 237, 247–53, 637–48); Schuker (1988: 1–2, 14–46, 131–47).

15. Schuker (1988: 134); see also Madrick (2011: 104) ("Throughout the late 1970s, Wriston insisted that sovereign nations did not go broke and [nations] fully understood they had to pay back their debt in order to retain access to international financing.").

16. FDIC (1997: 204) (quoting a 1987 book by Philip A. Wellons); see also Bayoumi (2017: 165).

17. Guill (2016: 25, 25n22).

18. For discussions of the LDC debt crisis, see Bayoumi (2017: 166–67); FDIC (1997: 191–210); Guill (2016: 25); Madrick (2011: 101–09, 172–73); Silber (2012: 218–27, 242–47); Wilmarth (2002: 312–16, 378–81).

19. For comparisons of the LDC debt crisis to the foreign lending spree of the 1920s and the sovereign debt defaults of the 1930s, see Chernow (1990: 225–29, 237, 304, 637–48); Schuker (1988: 1–2, 131–47).

20. Schuker (1988: 133) (explaining that during the 1970s, bankers had perverse incentives to arrange high-risk LDC loans because they could "earn lucrative up-front management fees by serving as intermediaries in the recycling of oil revenues" from oil-producing nations to LDCs); see Chapter 3 for discussion of the similar fee-based incentives for underwriters of foreign bonds during the 1920s.

21. FDIC (1997: 208–09).

22. Schuker (1988: 138–39).

23. Wilmarth (2002: 313); see also U.S. Treasury (1991: XVIII-11 and figures 2, 3); FDIC (1997: 199–206, 291–378).

24. Feldstein (2013: 112–15) (quoting Volcker).

25. Bennett (1984); Madrick (2011: 99–101, 106–09, 311–15); Stevenson (1998); Wilmarth (2014: 72–77). See Chapter 7 for a discussion of *ICI v. Camp*.

26. Chernow (1990: 538–41, 593, 653–56, 704–05); see also Tett (2009: 16) (JPMC "built up a good capital markets business" in its London branch, where "Glass-Steagall didn't apply"). For analysis of the authority of U.S. banks to engage in securities activities through foreign offices prior to the repeal of Glass-Steagall, see Fein (2011: §16.01).

27. Chernow (1990: 654–56, 716) (quoting comment by an unnamed "insider" about JPMC's preparation of *Rethinking Glass-Steagall*).

28. Funk & Hirschman (2014: 18–19). See Chapter 7 for discussion of the Fed's *Citicorp* order approving Section 20 subsidiaries.

29. Chernow (1990: 716–17); McLean & Nocera (2010: 53–54); Tett (2009: 73, 76).

30. Engel & McCoy (2011: 189–92); Madrick (2011: 14, 228); McLean & Nocera (2010: 85).

31. Madrick (2011: 228).

32. Engel & McCoy (2011: 190).

33. Greenspan (1997b).

34. Nash (1987) (describing views of Greenspan and Gould).

35. Bennett (1984) (quoting Volcker's congressional testimony).

36. Greenspan (1987: 91–92, 96–97).

37. Ibid., 92, 95–98.

38. Ibid., 97–98.

39. Wilmarth (2017: 498–99).

40. Fein (2011: §1.04[B]); Rehm (1990).

41. Greenspan (1990); see also Wilmarth (2007: 1607) ("When Drexel Burnham declared bankruptcy in February 1990, following the collapse of the junk bond market, its problems quickly spread" to its broker-dealer subsidiaries, which the SEC was "obliged to liquidate ... after they could not obtain even short-term credit from counterparties or banks").

42. Greenspan (1990).

43. Corman (1990) (quoting Richard Whiting, general counsel of the Association of Bank Holding Companies, and Robert Dugger, chief economist of the ABA).

44. Fein (2011: § 1.06[A]); Suarez & Kolodny (2010: part II); Nash (1988); Wayne (1991); see 77 *Congressional Record* 3906–07 (1933) (remarks of Rep. John Dingell, Sr., in support of the Glass-Steagall Act).

45. Trigaux (1987b) (reporting that " 'Glass-Steagall Saved U.S. Again' is emblazoned on large round buttons appearing in Washington now"); see Chapter 7 for discussion of Glass-Steagall's beneficial effects during the Oct. 1987 stock market crash, when Glass-Steagall shielded commercial banks from the losses suffered by securities firms.

46. Atlas (1988); Dale (1992: 53–54); Trigaux (1987a, 1987b).

47. U.S. Treasury (1991: 49–61); Nash (1987) (describing Gould's proposals).

48. Congress has not yet adopted Treasury's third recommendation to remove the BHC Act's restrictions on combinations between banks and commercial or industrial firms. However, GLBA permits financial holding companies to make "merchant banking" investments in nonfinancial firms, subject to specified limits. "Merchant banking" investments are private-equity-style transactions that could potentially undermine the separation of banking and commerce. Wilmarth (2007: 1579–84, 1587); see also Omarova (2013).

49. U.S. Treasury (1991: 51, XVII-8).

50. Ibid., 51–52; Wilmarth (1992: 963, 978–79).

51. U.S. Treasury (1991: XVII-8 through XVII-13).

52. Wilmarth (1992: 980–82).

53. Ibid., 983–94; Wilmarth (1995: 41–46); Wilmarth (2002: 313–16); FCIC (2010: 6–9). For additional analysis of the severe problems faced by large U.S. banks during the 1980s and 1990s, see Barth, Brumbaugh, & Litan (1992); Freeman & McKinley (2018: 211–26, 236–50).

54. Barth, Brumbaugh, & Litan (1992: 25–56, 115).

55. Wagner (2010); see also Kroszner & Strahan (2014: 527) (noting that "a larger and more developed financial sector could improve risk sharing and diversification and thereby reduce [economic] volatility," but it also could "allow greater concentrations of risk and generate interconnections, thereby potentially making the entire system more fragile and vulnerable to shocks").

56. Goetz, Laeven, & Levine (2013).

57. Demsetz & Strahan (1997); Dick (2006).

58. Calomiris & Mason (2003b: 1630–32); Carlson (2004).

59. Mian, Sufi, & Verner (2017).

60. Chen, Hanson, & Stein (2017): table 1, panel A (showing that small business lending by the four biggest U.S. banks plunged by 59% between 2006 and 2010, compared to an average decline of 34% at other banks).

61. Wilmarth (1992: 994–1004): see also FCIC (2010: 6–10); FDIC (1997: 243–52, 373–78); Freeman & McKinley (2018: 221–26).

62. Barth, Brumbaugh, & Litan (1992: 115, 32, 41–44, 54–56).

63. Wilmarth (1995: 44–45, 44–45n210); see also Barth, Brumbaugh, & Litan (1992: 32, 41, 54–56); Freeman & McKinley (2018: 217–20, 235–51).

64. Barth, Brumbaugh, & Litan (1992: 28–56, 89–90, 94); Phillips (1992); Wilmarth (1995: 44–46); Wilmarth (2002: 315–16, 470–73).

65. U.S. Treasury (1991: 26–28) ("The government must *always* maintain the flexibility to protect the banking system and the economy in circumstances of genuine systemic risk" [emphasis added]).

66. Pub. L. No. 102-242, 105 *Statutes at Large* 2236 (1991); see Wilmarth (1992: 979) (discussing FDICIA).

67. Carnell (1993: 327–57); see also U.S. Treasury (1991: 37–41).

68. Carnell (1993: 363–64); Wilmarth (1992: 995–96); see also U.S. Treasury (1991: 26–27) (recommending that "the FDIC should be required to use the least expensive resolution method" for failed banks, which would probably "result in more losses for uninsured depositors").

69. Carnell (1993: 367–68); Wilmarth (1992: 996–97) (quoting 12 U.S.C. §1823(c)(4)(G)).

70. Wilmarth (1992: 997).

71. FCIC (2010: 19) (quoting 137 *Cong. Rec.* S18619 [daily ed., Nov. 27, 1991]) (remarks of Sen. Dodd); see also Ricks (2016: 197–99); FCIC (2010: 19); Johnson & Kwak (2010: 150–53); Wilmarth (2002: 304, 304n369).

72. Ricks (2016: 32–37, 198–99).

73. Wilmarth (1992: 979–80); Labaton (1991a, 1991b, 1991c).

74. Garsson (1992).

75. Wilmarth (1995: 3–4, 9–10); Garsson (1994); New Hampshire Union Leader (1994); Scism (1994).

76. Allentown Morning Call (1994).

77. Garsson (1994).

78. Wilmarth (1995: 13–14).

79. Kress (2019b: 19–27; Wilmarth (2009: 975–76, 1011–13; 2015: 256–57); see also FCIC (2011: 52–53) (reporting that the total assets of the five largest U.S. banking organizations [including Wells Fargo] increased from $2.2 trillion to $6.8 trillion between 1998 and 2007).

80. Johnson & Kwak (2010: 7–11, 78–82, 89–92, 121–26, 133–37); Malone (1996).

81. U.S. Treasury (1991: 54–56).

82. Ibid., XVIII-25, XVIII-26. See Saunders & Walter (1994: 120–24) (discussing the impact of the EU's Second Banking Directive).

83. U.S. Treasury (1991: XVIII-12 through XVIII-16, XVIII-19).

84. Ibid., XVIII-27, XVIII-32.

85. Ibid., XVIII-31, 58–60.

86. Benkelman (1991); Fein (2011: §1.06[C]); Labaton (1991a); Suarez & Kolodny (2010: part II ["The Bush Years"]); Wayne (1991).

87. Bradsher (1995); Fein (2011: §1.06[D]–[F]); Suarez & Kolodny (2010: part II ["The Clinton Years"]).

88. Wilmarth (2002: 220); Wilmarth (2014: 70).

89. Lipin & Frank (1998).

90. Kantrow & Moyer (1998) (quoting Weill); see also Siconolfi (1998) (reporting that Reed and Weill were "betting that the broad services of the huge new firm could weather any future market swoons").

91. Barth, Brumbaugh, & Wilcox (2000); Benston (1994); Santos (1998); Saunders & Walter (1994).

92. Wilmarth (2014: 73–74) (quoting Edward J. Kane, "Implications of Superhero Metaphors for the Issue of Banking Powers," 23 *Journal of Banking and Finance* 663, 666 [1999]).

93. Wilmarth (2014: 74); see also Wilmarth (2002: 221, 221n12) (discussing Section 4(a) (2) of the BHC Act, 12 U.S.C. § 1841(a)(2), which allows newly organized bank holding companies to retain nonconforming assets for a two-year period and to obtain three one-year extensions of that period from the Fed).

94. Rehm (1998) (quoting an unnamed "banking lawyer").

95. Wilmarth (2014: 74).

96. Madrick (2011: 311–13); Rehm (1998); Wilmarth (2014: 74). Weill had approached Greenspan in connection with Travelers' unsuccessful attempt to acquire JPMC in 1997. At that time, Greenspan advised Weill that the Fed would give Travelers the benefit of the BHC Act's temporary exemption. Madrick (2011: 309).

97. Rehm (1998). A federal appeals court upheld the Fed's approval of the merger. *Independent Community Bankers of America v. Board of Governors*, 195 F.3d 28, 31–32 (D.C. Cir. 1999) (upholding the Fed's order approving the Citigroup merger because the order was in "literal compliance with §4(a)(2)" of the BHC Act, and dismissing as irrelevant the claim that the merger "put pressure on Congress to amend" the BHC Act).

98. Wilmarth (2002: 221, 306); Wilmarth (2014: 74).

99. Madrick (2011: 313).

100. Ibid., 314–15; Scheer (1999); Wilmarth (2014: 74–75, 74–75n43); Wilmarth (2002: 306–07).

101. Greenspan (1997c, 1999a).

102. Rubin (1995). Rubin and Greenspan disagreed on the question of which agency should exercise primary supervisory authority over universal banks. Rubin argued that national banks should be allowed to conduct expanded powers through directly owned financial subsidiaries, which would be regulated by the OCC (a bureau within the Treasury Department). Greenspan maintained that broader powers should be granted only to nonbank subsidiaries of financial holding companies, which the Fed would regulate. Greenspan largely prevailed. GLBA granted much broader powers to nonbank subsidiaries of financial holding companies, compared with financial subsidiaries of banks. GLBA also gave the Fed the leading role in determining the scope of those new powers. Suarez & Kolodny (2010: part II ["The Clinton Years"; "The End of an Era"]); Wilmarth (2004b: 277n203).

103. Hacker & Pierson (2010: 247–50); Hirsh (2013); Johnson & Kwak (2010: 93–104, 185–87); Madrick (2011: 313–15); Malone (1996); Scism (1994).

104. Labaton (1997).

105. Parks (1999a, 1999b); Suarez & Kolodny (2010: part II ["The End of an Era"]).

106. 145 *Congressional Record* S13783 (daily ed., Nov. 3, 1999) (remarks of Sen. Gramm); ibid., S13888 (daily ed., Nov. 4, 1999) (remarks of Sen. Reed, stating that GLBA would provide an "important ratification" of prior developments, and would "allow our financial institutions to be more efficient and more effective"); ibid., S13907 (daily ed., Nov. 4, 1999) (remarks of Sen. Lieberman, stating that GLBA would establish a "rational financial structure" to replace "regulatory loopholes").

107. Clinton (1999).

108. Ibid. (quoting remarks of Summers).

109. Ibid. (quoting remarks of Sen. Gramm); see also Lipton & Labaton (2008) (describing Gramm, a former economics professor at Texas A&M, as a "fierce opponent of government intervention in the marketplace").

110. Lipton & Labaton (2008) (quoting Gramm's remarks at a Senate hearing in Apr. 2000).

111. Wilmarth (2009: 974) (summarizing arguments made by GLBA's opponents); see 145 *Congressional Record* S13871–74 (daily ed., Nov. 4, 1999) (remarks of Sen. Wellstone); ibid., S13896–97 (remarks of Sen. Dorgan); ibid., H11530, H11542 (daily ed., Nov. 4, 1999) (remarks of Rep. Dingell).

112. 145 *Congressional Record* S13872 (daily ed., Nov. 4, 1999) (remarks of Sen. Wellstone).

113. U.S. Senate (1999: 7–8) (citing the "safeguards" provided by "the holding company structure"); ibid., 66 ("Additional Views" of nine Democratic Senators, expressing confidence in the "strict limits" provided by Sections 23A and 23B). In 2002, I questioned "whether regulators and lobbyists for the financial services industry actually believed in the virtues of corporate separation during the 1990s, or whether they simply viewed the 'firewall' argument as a convenient tool to help persuade Congress that [GLBA] would not create undue risks." Wilmarth (2002: 454–57).

114. Stiglitz (2003: 159–61).

115. 145 *Congressional Record* S13872 (daily ed., Nov. 4, 1999) (remarks of Sen. Wellstone).

116. Silber (2012: 275, 419n5) (quoting Volcker's testimony before the House Committee on Banking and Financial Services in Apr. 1995).

117. Omarova (2011: 1692–94, 1701–08). Section 23B requires affiliate transactions to be conducted on arm's-length, market-based terms. However, Section 23B does not impose additional quantitative limits on affiliate transactions. Ibid., 1693–94; Carpenter & Murphy (2010: 23–25). The Dodd-Frank Act limited, but did not abolish, the Fed's authority to grant exemptions and waivers from Section 23A's requirements. Omarova (2011: 1766–68).

118. Wilmarth (2002: 456–57, 472); see also New York Fed (2001: 3, 7–9) ("Report of the President: Responding to September 11 and Future Prospects for the New York Regional Economy").

119. Wilmarth (2002: 472).

120. Omarova (2011: 1729–61); Wilmarth (2008: 8–9, 11). In addition, the Fed granted waivers of Section 23A in 2006 that allowed Citigroup to transfer more than $17 billion of subprime mortgages from its nonbank mortgage lending subsidiaries to Citibank, its flagship bank. Those transfers significantly increased Citibank's losses from subprime mortgage defaults after the financial crisis broke out in mid-2007. Omarova (2011: 1712–17).

121. Omarova (2011: 1762–63).

122. Wilmarth (2014: 70–72, 132–37).

123. 145 *Congressional Record* H11542 (daily ed., Nov. 4, 1999) (remarks of Rep. Dingell); see also ibid., S13896–97 (daily ed., Nov. 4, 1999) (remarks of Sen. Dorgan, expressing a similar warning).

124. Wilmarth (2002: 446–47, 476).

125. PWGFM (1999b: 4) (reporting that total notional values of OTC derivatives reached $80 trillion in 1998, compared with total notional values of $13.5 trillion for exchange-traded futures and options); see also Wilmarth (2002: 334n489) (stating that total notional values of OTC derivatives grew from $7 trillion in 1989 to $88 trillion in 1999).

126. Greenspan (1999b).

127. See Chapter 7 for discussion of the CFTC's 1993 exemption for OTC derivatives.

128. Bookstaber (2007: 9–11).

129. Ibid., 14–31.

130. Wilmarth (2002: 341).

131. Ibid., 362–65. For a detailed account of the scandals, lawsuits, and enforcement actions involving Bankers Trust and Merrill Lynch, see Partnoy (2003: 49–61, 112–22, 162–71).

132. Partnoy (2003: 228–29, 240–44); Wilmarth (2002: 351–52, 370).

133. McLean & Nocera (2010: 66–68); Partnoy (2003: 141–55); Tett (2009: 36–37).

134. Tett (2009: 28–29, 31–32, 36–39); see also ISDA (1999) (describing ISDA as "an international organization whose membership includes more than 400 of the world's largest commercial, merchant and investment banks and other corporations and institutions that conduct significant activities in swaps and other privately negotiated derivatives transactions").

135. McLean & Nocera (2010: 64, 66–68); see also Partnoy (2003: 141–55).

136. Tett (2009: 38–40) (quoting Greenspan's testimony in 1994).

137. Partnoy (2003: 228–29, 235–61); Wilmarth (2002: 311, 346. 365).

138. CFTC (1998); Faiola, Nakashima, & Drew (2008); Goodman (2008); McLean & Nocera (2010: 103–05).

139. CFTC (1998: 26115–19).

140. Rubin, Greenspan, & Levitt (1998).

141. Faiola, Nakashima, & Drew (2008); McLean & Nocera (2010: 106).

142. Summers (1998).

143. Greenspan (1998). SEC Chairman Arthur Levitt also testified at the July 1998 hearing. He praised OTC derivatives as reflections of "the unique strength and innovation of American capital markets," and he called on Congress to block any attempt by the CFTC to regulate OTC derivatives because "imposition of new regulatory costs also may stifle innovation and push transactions offshore." Levitt (1998).

144. Wilmarth (2002: 346); see also Partnoy (2003: 86, 110–11) (describing LTCM's formation).

145. Roukema (1999).

146. Wilmarth (2002: 346–47, 360); see also PWGFM (1999a: 11–12, 14–16, 30–31) (describing LTCM's financial position in 1998).

147. Wilmarth (2002: 312n391, 347); see also PWGFM (1999a: 12–13, 16) (describing LTCM's trading strategy in 1998).

148. Wilmarth (2002: 236–37, 312, 347–48); see also Fahlenbach, Prilmeier, & Stulz (2011: 7–8) (describing the global financial crisis that followed Russia's devaluation and default).

149. Wilmarth (2002: 370–72).

150. Ibid., 348–49, 370–71. For additional analysis of the LTCM crisis, see FCIC (2011: 56–57); McLean & Nocera (2010: 96, 106–07); Partnoy (2003: 251–64).

151. Wilmarth (2002: 236–37, 368–72; see also Stout (2011: 3–4n10) (citing warnings issued by corporate law professor Lynn Stout and others during the 1990s about the hazards of OTC derivatives); PWGFM (1999a: 12–14, 17–18, 19–20) (describing the circumstances that led federal officials to organize a rescue of LTCM).

152. Wilmarth (1995: 51–55).

153. Wilmarth (2002: 347–50, 358, 370–72, 375–77) (describing large losses suffered by Citigroup, BofA, Bankers Trust, Credit Suisse, UBS, Merrill Lynch, Goldman Sachs, and Barclays during the 1998 crisis); see also Guill (2016: 28–29) (discussing Bankers Trust's predicament in 1998–99).

154. McLean & Nocera (2010: 107); Partnoy (2003: 2–4, 228–29); Wilmarth (2002: 348–49, 358–61.

155. Wilmarth (2017: 533).

156. Fahlenbach, Prilmeier, & Stulz (2011: 1–5, 25–26). The worst performers during both periods were institutions that grew faster, operated with higher leverage, and relied more heavily on short-term funding sources. Ibid., 5, 18–22. Remarkably, financial institutions with the same CEOs in 1998 and 2006 performed no better than institutions that changed their CEOs after 1998. Ibid., 15–16. CEOs who experienced the 1998 crisis apparently did not take meaningful steps to reduce the risks of their institutions prior to 2007. The correlation between bad performance in 1998 and poor performance in 2007–08 was strongest among large financial institutions, thereby indicating that big institutions assumed they were TBTF and "felt less compelled to change their business model after the 1998 crisis, because they were reasonably certain to receive federal assistance during the next crisis." Ibid., 15.

157. FCIC (2011: 47–48, 56–59, 74–75).

158. Wilmarth (2017: 533–34); see also FCIC (2011): 57–58 (quoting leading bankruptcy attorney Harvey Miller, who stated that market participants "expected the Fed to save Lehman [in 2008], based on the Fed's involvement in LTCM's rescue").

159. Born (1999); FCIC (2011: 47–48); see also Faiola, Nakashima, & Drew (2008); McLean & Nocera (2010: 107–08); Stout (2011: 20–21); Wilmarth (2017: 534). For examples of arguments opposing any new rules for OTC derivatives, see Coalition of OTC Derivatives Dealers (1999); Lugar (1998).

160. PWGFM (1999b: cover letter and 1).

161. Greenspan (1999b).

162. Ibid.

163. Ibid. The VAR risk models used by LTCM and most major financial institutions during the 1990s and 2000s were based on the standard Black-Scholes assumptions of highly liquid markets, constant volatility, and a "normal" (symmetric) distribution of prices. All three of those assumptions are very likely to fail during financial panics, when markets are characterized by illiquidity, high volatility, risk aversion, and extremely negative outcomes (fat tails). In addition, most VAR models of the 1990s and 2000s used historical data samples from recent, benign economic periods, which did not provide reliable predictions about the potential range and volatility of asset returns during financial crises. VAR models also encouraged managers to concentrate on predicting the *probability of loss* with "confidence levels" ranging from 95% to 99%, while ignoring the *potential*

magnitude of loss that could occur during extreme "tail events." Wilmarth (2002: 342–50); see also Partnoy (2003: 243, 257, 263–64, 325).

164. Greenspan (1999b). See Greenspan (1996) for similar arguments.
165. PWGFM (1999a: viii–ix, 11–12, 14, 17–18, 29–32).
166. Ibid., 14–16.
167. Ibid., 16, 31.
168. Ibid., 25, 26.
169. Wilmarth (2017: 536–37).
170. PWGFM (1999a: 24, 29, 31–40); see also McLean & Nocera (2010: 107–08); Wilmarth (2017: 537, 537n733).
171. PWGFM (1999b) (cover letters to Speaker of the House J. Dennis Hastert and President of the Senate Al Gore).
172. Ibid., 1–13.
173. Ibid., 15–16.
174. Wilmarth (2017: 536–39).
175. PWGFM (1999b: 34).
176. Ibid., 16n40, 34–35 (referring briefly to the working group's first report on LTCM).
177. Wilmarth (2017: 539).
178. Faiola, Nakashima, & Drew (2008); ISDA (2000); Lipton & Labaton (2008).
179. Faiola, Nakashima, & Drew (2008); FCIC (2011: 48); Lipton & Labaton (2008); Stout (2011: 21–22); Wilmarth (2017: 539–40).
180. 146 *Cong. Rec.* S11897 (daily ed., Dec. 15, 2000) (remarks of Sen. Harkin, reprinting letter dated Dec. 15, 2000, from Treasury Secretary Summers, SEC Chairman Levitt, Fed Chairman Greenspan, and CFTC Chairman William Rainer).
181. 146 *Cong. Rec.* S11866 (daily ed., Dec. 15, 2000) (remarks of Sen. Gramm).
182. Wilmarth (2017: 541).
183. Ibid.
184. Ibid., 541–42; Johnson & Kwak (2010: 88–121, 133–37).
185. Mahoney (2018: 237–40, 253–77); Markham (2010: 1082, 1118–28, 1134); Wallison (2009: 5–14); White (2010: 940–46). Alan Blinder reached a split decision on this question, as he concluded that GLBA did not play an important role in triggering the financial crisis but CFMA did. Blinder (2013: 64–64, 132, 266–67, 274).
186. Wilmarth (2017: 542).
187. Ibid., 542–43; see also Johnson & Kwak (2010: 133–37).
188. Kingson (2000); Prial (2000); Rehm (2000); Wilmarth (2002: 252, 319–20, 323, 376–77).
189. Wilmarth (2017: 543); Rehm (2000) (quoting an unnamed "federal regulator").
190. Kroszner & Strahan (2014: 499–500).
191. FCIC (2011:30); Peek & Rosengren (2015: 20 [figure 7]); Kacperczyk & Schnabl (2010: 32. 38 [figure 1]).
192. Fleming & Garbade (2003: 1); Logan, Nelson, & Parkinson (2018: 4 [figure 1]); Peek & Rosengren (2015: 19 [figure 6]); Bhidé (2017: 107–08 [tables 1, 2]); Claessens et al. (2012: 8, 9 [figure 2]).
193. FCIC (2011; 48–51); Greenspan (1999b); Wilmarth (2009: 991–94).
194. Eichengreen (2015: 70–76); Stout (2011: 22–29); Wilmarth (2017: 544–46).
195. FCIC (2011: 55, 65–66, 150–51); Wilmarth (2009: 977).

196. Wilmarth (2009: 977–84; 2017: 543–44); see also Pozsar et al. (2010: 1–6, 11–20, 34–36, 58–66).
197. Bayoumi (2017: 18–22, 27–41); Eichengreen (2015: 70–73); Dale (1992: 106–16, 156–72); Llewellyn (1996: 161–68, 177–86); Saunders & Walter (1994: 116–24); Wilmarth (2009: 976–77).
198. Wilmarth (2009: 976–77); see also Barth, Caprio, & Levine (2012: 65); Bayoumi (2017: 33–41, 86–90, 95–97); Cordell (2016); Kay (2015: 24–27, 31–33, 126–29, 248–50); Robertson (2016); Tooze (2018: 80–84).
199. Wilmarth (2009: 975–94); Wilmarth (2011a: 966, 966n45). For AIG's importance in the credit default swap market, see FCIC (2011: 139–42, 200–02, 265–70); McLean & Nocera (2010: 188–91); Tett (2009: 62–63).
200. Bayoumi (2017: 18–22, 27–41, 86–90, 95–97); Wilmarth (2017: 544–45).
201. Eichengreen (2015: 73).

Chapter 9

1. Beim (2009); Mian & Sufi (2014: 4–7); Wilmarth (2011a: 957–82); see also Bhidé (2017: 96, 107–08 [tables 1, 2]) (showing that the outstanding volume of private-label securitizations of home mortgages and other consumer credit in the U.S. grew from less than $500 billion to $4.5 trillion between 1999 and 2007, and the outstanding volume of similar securitizations in Europe increased from $100 billion to $1.7 trillion during the same period).
2. Federal Reserve Board (2020:7 [table D.3]); FRED-GDP (2020). The credit boom of the 2000s continued a longer-term trend of rapid growth in private sector debts. Total U.S. private sector debts increased from $10.4 trillion to $20.4 trillion between 1991 and 1999, and the ratio of private sector debts to GDP rose from 169% to 212% during that period. Ibid.; see also Wilmarth (2011a: 963–71); Wilmarth (2009: 1000–20).
3. Aikman, Haldane, & Nelson (2015); Barth, Caprio, & Levine (2012: 121–40); Blinder (2013: 168–71, 410–12); Eichengreen (2015: 354–63); Jordà, Schularick, & Taylor (2014: 5–14); Sayek & Taskin (2014: 460–70); Tooze (2018: 102–09); Turner (2014: 93–101).
4. For the U.K., see FSA (2009: 18 [top panel of exhibit 1.10]), reproduced in Figure 0.3 (top panel) in the Introduction; see also Turner (2014: 93, 94 [table 4.6]). For Ireland, Portugal, and Spain, see Sayek & Taskin (2014: 462–64, 465 [figure 2], 466–70).
5. As described in Chapter 8, the Big Seventeen included the four largest U.S. banks (Bank of America, Citigroup, JPMorgan Chase, and Wachovia), the five largest U.S. securities firms (Bear Stearns, Goldman Sachs, Lehman Brothers, Merrill Lynch, and Morgan Stanley), and eight large European universal banks (Barclays, BNP Paribas, Credit Suisse, Deutsche Bank, HSBC, RBS, Société Générale, and UBS).
6. Wilmarth (2011a: 963–71); Wilmarth (2009: 980–94).
7. Griffin, Lowery, & Saretto (2014) compiled a comprehensive data set of $10.2 trillion of structured finance securities that were issued between 2000 and 2010 and recorded in Bloomberg's data system. About $9.1 trillion of those securities were issued between 2000 and 2007. Ibid., 2885–86, 2887 [table 1], 2891–92, Internet Appendix [table A.1]). Cordell, Huang, & Williams (2012: 4–6) compiled a separate data set of structured finance securities that were issued between 1998 and 2007 and recorded on Intex. Their data set included $3.3 trillion of RMBS, $2.5 trillion of securitized home equity loans, and $640 billion of CDOs, but it did not include CMBS or CLOs.

8. Griffin, Lowery, & Saretto (2014: 2921 [table 9]); Internet Appendix [table A.2]). Société Générale was the seventeenth-ranked underwriter of structured finance securities during the 2000s, just behind Santander Bank. RBS was also a significant underwriter, but it was not included in the study conducted by Griffin, Lowery, & Saretto (2014: 2885–86, 2891–92, Internet Appendix [table A.2]). See DOJ-RBS (2018: 1) (stating that RBS was the third-largest global underwriter of private-label RMBS by dollar volume). For additional discussions of the dominance of the Big Seventeen in securitization markets during the 2000s, see Dunbar & Donald (2009); Wilmarth (2009: 994–95, 1011–20).

9. FCIC (2011: 139–42); McLean & Nocera (2010: 188–91).

10. Bakk-Simon et al. (2012: 11–15, 19–23, 27–28); Turner (2014: 93–101).

11. Field (2011: 231–76); Sornette & Cauwels (2014: 106–22); see also Perez (2009) (analyzing the "double bubble" that occurred during the late 1990s and 2000s); Chapters 2 and 4 (discussing the real estate boom and stock market bubble of the 1920s).

12. Lowenstein (2004: 101–26, 147–55); Partnoy (2003: 267–94); Perez (2009: 784–90); Shiller (2015: 1–9, 39–43, 123–26, 136–38).

13. Lowenstein (2004: 101–26, 147–55, 219); Partnoy (2003: 267–94); Shiller (2015: 1–9, 39–43, 123–26, 129–32, 136–38); Wilmarth (2009: 997–98).

14. Gasparino (2005); Lowenstein (2004); Partnoy (2003); Sullivan (2006); Wilmarth (2009: 997–1002); Wilmarth (2006).

15. Lowenstein (2004: 127–204); Partnoy (2003: 295–373); Wilmarth (2006: 6–8).

16. Wilmarth (2006: 8–10); see generally Bratton (2002).

17. McLean & Elkind (2003: 162, 164).

18. Ibid., 165; see also Wilmarth (2006: 11).

19. Wilmarth (2009: 999); Wilmarth (2006: 10–16).

20. Wilmarth (2006: 17–20) (quoting bankers' statements); see also Wilmarth (2014: 78–80).

21. Lowenstein (2004: 150–55, 164–66); Wilmarth (2009: 998–99); Wilmarth (2006: 25–29).

22. Wilmarth (2006: 30–36); *In re WorldCom, Inc. Securities Litigation*, 346 F. Supp. 2d 628, 650–55 (S.D.N.Y. 2004) (quoting the underwriters' "road show" script).

23. Wilmarth (2009: 999–1000); Wilmarth (2006: 30–39).

24. Wilmarth (2006: 37–39, 54n137) (quoting Grubman's interview published in *Business Week* on May 15, 2000).

25. Wilmarth (2006: 38, 55n139 [quoting Grubman]); see also Gasparino (2005: 144–48); Lowenstein (2004: 152–55).

26. Wilmarth (2006: 39–41); see also Gasparino (2005: 161–64, 169–85).

27. Wilmarth (2006: 39); see also Gasparino (2005: 177–85); Stiglitz (2003: 91–101, 164–67).

28. Wilmarth (2014: 78–83); Wilmarth (2009: 1000).

29. Wilmarth (2014: 81–82, 82n101) (quoting Citigroup's head of global equity research); Wilmarth (2009: 1000); see also Gasparino (2005).

30. Smith (2009: 103–09, 206–11) (quoting Credit Suisse analyst Erach Desai on page 209).

31. Gasparino (2005: 219, 232–33); Wilmarth (2006: 22).

32. Gasparino (2005: 40–41, 125–26, 210–11, 219, 223–24, 235–36, 239) (noting that Blodget worked at Merrill Lynch from Feb. 1999 to Dec. 2001).

33. Wilmarth (2006: 22–24); see also Lowenstein (2004: 84–85, 212–13, 218–19).

34. Gasparino (2005: 151–61, 167–69, 288–97); Wilmarth (2014: 82).

35. Lowenstein (2004: 111–12, 125–26); Partnoy (2003: 267–85) (quoting Credit Suisse banker's statement on page 281); Smith (2009: 89–95, 110–34); Wilmarth (2014: 80–83).

36. Lowenstein (2004: 4, 208). See Chapters 2–6 for analysis of conflicts of interest and abusive practices at universal banks during the 1920s.

37. Stiglitz (2003: 158–61).

38. Wilmarth (2014: 79–83); Wilmarth (2009: 1000–02) (stating that enforcement orders were issued against BofA, Citigroup, Credit Suisse, Deutsche Bank, JPMC, Bear Stearns, Goldman Sachs, Lehman Brothers, Merrill Lynch, Morgan Stanley, and UBS for their involvement in scandals related to Enron, biased research, and/or IPO spinning); see also Fein (2011: ¶3.05[G][21]–[23], [25], and [27]) (providing descriptions of many of those enforcement orders); Securities and Exchange Commission, "Spotlight on the Global Research Analyst Settlement" (same), available at https://www.sec.gov/spotlight/global-settlement.htm.

39. Gasparino (2005: 225–30, 235–38, 246–50, 276–78, 293–97, 304–09); Wilmarth (2014: 82–83).

40. Gasparino (2005: 282–83, 299–307); Johnson & Kwak (2010: 148–49); Lowenstein (2004: 201–13, 223–25); Partnoy (2003: 393–95, 405–06); Smith (2009: 237–315); Wilmarth (2009: 1001–02); see also "Spotlight on the Global Research Analyst Settlement," cited in note 38.

41. FCIC (2011: 204–05); Wilmarth (2013: 1342–44) (quoting Interagency Statement, "Sound Practices Concerning Elevated Risk Complex Structured Finance Activities," 72 *Federal Register* 1372, 1374–77 [Jan. 11, 2007]).

42. Wilmarth (2006: 44); see also Wilmarth (2009: 997–1002).

43. Wilmarth (2009: 996–97) (summarizing the results of several studies by U.S. and European economists published between 2001 and 2006). A 2012 New York Fed staff study confirmed that the ten largest U.S. bank holding companies significantly increased their reliance on "nontraditional" sources of income (securitization, investment banking, trading, and other capital markets activities) between 2001 and 2006. Copeland (2012). See Chapter 8 for discussion of the failures by federal policymakers to adopt strong regulatory measures after the 1998 LTCM crisis.

44. Bernanke (2002b); Ferguson (2002, 2003); Greenspan (2002a, 2002c, 2004a); see also Bernanke (2015: 70–81, 90–91); FCIC (2011: 84–85); Fleckenstein & Sheehan (2008: 108–48); Tett (2009: 85–86). See Chapter 8 for a description of the Fed's response to the terrorist attacks on Sept. 11.

45. Bair (2010) (section entitled "Low Interest Rates Stimulate the Demand for Mortgage Debt and Housing"); FCIC (2011: 60, 103); Wilmarth (2009: 1005).

46. Taylor (2009: 1–13) (quote at 4) (presenting a critique of the Fed's monetary policy during the 2000s); see also ibid., 3 (figure 1) (showing the gap between the Fed's targets for short-term interest rates and the rates implied by the Taylor rule). In his 2015 memoir, Ben Bernanke defended the Fed's ultra-low interest rate policy during the early 2000s. Bernanke argued that it was "highly implausible" that the Fed's monetary policy during that period could have been "easy enough to achieve our employment and inflation goals while simultaneously tight enough to significantly moderate the housing boom." Bernanke (2015: 90–92).

47. Catte et al. (2010: 6–7, 11–16, 19–29); see also Bair (2010); Eichengreen (2015: 83–85); Maddaloni & Peydró (2010: 9–10, 14–15, 24–26); Rajan (2010: 105–12); Wessel (2009: 56–59); Wilmarth (2009: 1005–06).

48. Fleckenstein & Sheehan (2008: 129–76, 181 [quote]). Similarly, Carlota Perez concluded that the dotcom–telecom bust did not cause a major economic recession because the Fed created an "easy liquidity bubble," which stimulated the subprime lending boom. Perez (2009: 780, 784–803).

49. U.S. Census Bureau, "New Privately Owned Housing Units Completed," available at https://www.census.gov/construction/nrc/pdf/compann.pdf (accessed July 31, 2018) (showing that the number of completed new homes rose from 1.41 million in 1996 to 1.57 million in 2001 and 1.98 million in 2006).

50. Greenspan (2002b) (quote); Greenspan (2003); see also FCIC (2011: 85–88).

51. Wilmarth (2002: 236–37, 314–15, 347–48, 370–72, 470–72); see also Greenspan (2004a); Kohn (2004); and Chapters 7 and 8 for analysis of the Fed's interventions to stabilize financial markets after serious disruptions.

52. Wilmarth (2002: 471) (quoting "First the Put, Then the Cut?," *Economist* [Dec. 16, 2000: 81]); see also Authers (2018); FCIC (2011: 60–61); Fleckenstein & Sheehan (2008: 110–14).

53. Greenspan (2002b, 2002d, 2004a); see also Bernanke (2002a); Ferguson (2003); Kohn (2004). New York Fed President (and later Treasury Secretary) Tim Geithner concurred with the "conventional wisdom in central banks" that "it would be irresponsible and ineffective to try to use monetary policy to pop bubbles." Geithner also agreed that the Fed and other federal agencies should use "overwhelming force" to "arrest a financial panic" in order to prevent "an economic disaster." Geithner (2014: 110–11, 518–19).

54. Blinder & Reis (2005: 67–68, 81) (emphasis in original).

55. Rajan (2010: 110–16, 149–51); Wilmarth (2002: 470–76); see also FCIC (2011: 60–61); Johnson & Kwak (2010: 101–02); Morris (2008: 62–65); Wessel (2009: 60–61). A recent study determined that the "Greenspan put" provided significant benefits to equity market investors between 1996 and 2008. The study found that put options on the S&P 500 index rose significantly in value during periods when the Fed followed a "Greenspan put" monetary policy and established short-term rates that fell below levels implied by the Taylor rule. Dahiya et al. (2017).

56. Bayoumi (2017: 134, 140–46); Eichengreen (2015: 3, 21, 84–86, 168–69); Johnson & Kwak (2010: 39–40, 54–56, 118–19); Kay (2015: 38–39, 54–56, 63–64, 99–100); see also IMF (2011: 7 [¶12]) (describing the "complacency" created by the widely shared view that "serious recessions could be avoided, and that the global economy had entered a period of 'Great Moderation'"); McLean & Nocera (2010: 96–97, and the seventh page of photos after page 236) (summarizing the Feb. 1999 article in *Time*, and showing the magazine's cover, which identified Greenspan, Rubin, and Summers as "The Committee to Save the World"); Bernanke (2015: 92) (stating that the Fed's "generally successful monetary policies" and "the remarkable economic stability … [during] 'the Great Moderation' … likely bred complacency"); Geithner (2014: 389) (concluding that "the optimism of the Great Moderation [and] the delusion of indefinite stability" encouraged a "mania of overconfidence [that] fueled an explosion of credit in the economy and leverage in the financial system").

57. FCIC (2011: 61) (quoting interview with Lindsey on Sept. 20, 2010).

58. Barwell & Burrows (2011: 17).

59. Turner (2014: 93–95).

60. Maddaloni & Pedró (2010: 14–15, 31 [figure 1]); Taylor (2009: 1–3, 8–10).

61. Maddloni & Peydró (2010: 18–28).

62. Taylor (2009: 7–10); see also Barth, Caprio, & Levine (2012: 123–28, 137–38); Bayoumi (2017: 97–101); Jordà, Schularick, & Taylor (2014: 11–14).

63. For analysis of the economic impact of large inflows of funds from Asian and oil-producing countries into Western nations during the 2000s, see Barwell & Burrows (2011: 4, 18, 32–33); Catte et al. (2010: 6–16, 27–29); Eichengreen (2015: 50–58, 86–88, 427n31); FCIC (2011: 9, 38–39, 103–04); Kay (2015: 140–45, 247–54); Mian & Sufi (2014: 93–95); Morris (2008: 65–71, 88–104); Rajan (2010: 6–13, 80–82, 109, 118); see also Edwards (2005) (including the responses to Edwards' paper at pages 269–99). See Chapter 10 for discussion of investments by European banks in private-label RMBS and other U.S. structured finance securities. See Chapter 3 for analysis of the role played by foreign bonds in supporting investment and consumption in Central Europe and South America during the 1920s.

64. Levitin & Wachter (2012: 1187–95). "Subprime" mortgages were loans made to borrowers whose credit histories were tarnished by bankruptcy, foreclosure, or other serious defaults. "Alt-A" mortgages were loans made to borrowers who had less serious credit problems but were not willing or able to provide full documentation of their assets and income. GAO (2010: 5); Sengupta (2010: 55–56); Scott (2010: 22–23); Wilmarth (2009: 1015–16).

65. Bernanke (2015: 122–28); Levitin & Wachter (2012: 1192–95).

66. Bair (2010: section entitled "Low Interest Rates Stimulate the Demand for Mortgage Debt and Housing"); Engel & McCoy (2011: 19–21, 28–33); FCIC (2011: 103–05); Levitin & Wachter (2012: 1192–202); Taub (2014: 140–46); Wilmarth (2009: 1016–17).

67. Fannie Mae and Freddie Mac could not purchase nonprime mortgages because those loans did not satisfy Fannie's and Freddie's underwriting standards for "conforming" mortgages. In addition, nonprime mortgages could not be securitized to create "agency" RMBS that were issued and guaranteed by Fannie and Freddie. Securities firms and banks therefore created "private-label" (also called "nonagency") RMBS to securitize nonprime mortgages. FCIC (2011: 68–72); Levitin & Wachter (2012: 1182–83, 1189–95); Robertson (2011: 6–14); Wilmarth (2014: 83–84, 90–91); Wilmarth (2013: 1331–32); Wilmarth (2009: 988–90, 1015–17). See Chapter 7 for a description of the securitization process.

68. FCIC (2011: 74–75); McLean & Nocera (2010: 82–88, 125–28); Wilmarth (2013: 1332–33); Wilmarth (2009: 1017–18); Wilmarth (2004b: 312–14); Wilmarth (2002: 396–401).

69. FCIC (2011: 75, 88); Taub (2014: 146–50); Wilmarth (2009: 1017–18).

70. Wilmarth (2014: 84); Wilmarth (2009: 1017–18); Wilmarth (2004b: 314–15).

71. FCIC (2011: 78) (summarizing findings of the HUD-Treasury joint study): Wilmarth (2004b: 308–09) (same).

72. FCIC (2011: 79); Lipton & Labaton (2008); McLean & Nocera (2010: 88). Representative John LaFalce (D-NY) introduced another anti-predatory-lending bill in early 2000, and Senator Sarbanes introduced his second anti-predatory-lending bill in 2002. Both of those bills were blocked by Republicans and never received a committee vote. Aaron (2009).

73. FCIC (2011: 9–11, 16–17, 22, 93–95); see also Andrews (2008); Bair (2012: 48); Engel & McCoy (2011: 194–96); Wilmarth (2011b: 898–900).

74. Wilmarth (2013: 1330–32); Wilmarth (2004b: 309–10).

75. Wilmarth (2011b: 906, 906n93) (quoting "Bank Activities and Operations: Real Estate Lending and Appraisals," 69 Federal Register 1904, 1913n55, 1916–17 [Jan. 13, 2004]).

76. Engel & McCoy (2011: 168).

77. FCIC (2011: 20–22, 172). In 1982, as described in Chapter 7, Congress authorized banks and nonbank lenders to offer alternative mortgages with nontraditional terms, including adjustable interest rates, interest-only payments, and balloon payments. That 1982 statute preempted state laws prohibiting such mortgages. FCIC (2011: 34–35); McLean & Nocera (2010: 29); Taub (2014: 62–63, 69–71, 125, 224–25).

78. Bair (2012: 44–45) (stating that in 2006 and early 2007, hybrid subprime ARMs had a "typical starter rate [of] 7% to 9%, with an interest rate jump of 4 to 6 percentage points after two to three years").

79. For descriptions of hybrid ARMs and option ARMs, see Engel & McCoy (2011: 34–39); FCIC (2011: 6–7, 11, 20–22, 172); McLean & Nocera (2010: 135–36); Taub (2014: 124–30).

80. FCIC (2011: 20–22, 172–73); Engel & McCoy (2011: 165–68, 176); McLean & Nocera (2010: 214–16); see also Bair (2012: 43–45) (describing the FDIC's unsuccessful efforts to broaden the scope and strengthen the terms of the 2006 guidance).

81. Wilmarth (2011b: 901–02); see also Bair (2012: 45–47) (describing the OCC's and Fed's refusal to issue stronger guidance for hybrid subprime ARMs); Bernanke (2015: 97–98) ("Most of the guidance and rules [issued by federal banking agencies] weren't tough enough or timely enough").

82. Engel & McCoy (2011: 165–66) (quoting speech by Dugan to the American Bankers Association on Oct. 17, 2006 [emphasis in original]); see also Bernanke (2015: 103) ("To preserve the ability of bankers to make character loans, ... the Fed did not ban low-documentation loans").

83. Bair (2012: 45–46); FCIC (2011: 21–22, 173); Wilmarth (2013: 1340–41). For example, the American Bankers Association claimed that the 2006 guidance "overstates the risks of [nontraditional] mortgage products" because those mortgages "simply present different types of risks that may be well-managed by prudent lenders." McLean & Nocera (2010: 214) (quoting the ABA). Similarly, the Financial Services Roundtable—a trade association representing the largest banks—declared it was "not aware of any empirical evidence that supports the need for further consumer protection standards." Wilmarth (2013: 1341) (quoting the Roundtable's letter dated Mar. 29, 2006).

84. U.S. Senate (2010: 13) (quoting answer by Countrywide's general counsel to a question from Senator Christopher Dodd [D-CT] during a Senate committee hearing on Mar. 22, 2008).

85. Associated Press (2007); Engel & McCoy (2011: 33–35, 228–29); Levitin & Wachter (2012: 1201–02); McLean & Nocera (2010: 135–36, 253–57); Tett (2009: 123–24); see also Bernanke (2015: 93–94) (stating that the Fed was "aware" of the risks of nontraditional mortgages with introductory "teaser" rates, "but, in retrospect, we responded too slowly and cautiously").

86. Buzenberg (2009); Dunbar & Donald (2009); Engel & McCoy (2011: 198–203); FCIC (2011: 77, 94–95); Wilmarth (2011b: 900–01).

87. FCIC (2011: 77, 94–95) (quoting from interviews with Greenspan and Braunstein); see also Bernanke (2015: 104–06) ("While not foreseeing all that would occur, Ned [Gramlich] unquestionably did see more, and do more, than the rest of us" on the Fed's Board of Governors); Engel & McCoy (2011: 198–99); Wilmarth (2011b: 900–01).

88. FCIC (2011: 96) (quoting interview with Alvarez); Wilmarth (2014: 125–27) (same); see also Greenspan (2005b) (praising "self-correction" by "forces of the marketplace," and arguing that government regulations "have often have come too late or have been

misguided"); Bernanke (2015: 94) (acknowledging that during the 2000s, the Fed was "open to arguments that regulatory burden should not be excessive and that competitive market forces would to some extent deter poor lending practices.... [T]he Fed and other regulators probably tipped too far in the direction of credit availability").

89. Andrews (2008) (quoting Greenspan's testimony on Oct. 23, 2008); Clark & Treanor (2008) (same).

90. Greenspan (2002a).

91. FCIC (2011: 9–11, 15–16, 95) (quoting Margot Saunders of the National Consumer Law Center); see also Engel & McCoy (2011: 61–62); Wessel (2009: 62–63). Fed officials also dismissed repeated warnings from Professor Patricia McCoy about the dangers posed by subprime mortgages and subprime RMBS during her service on the Fed's Consumer Advisory Council between 2002 and 2004. Engel & McCoy (2011: 7); FCIC (2011: 95).

92. FCIC (2011: 93–94) (quoting Greenspan); Bernanke (2015: 102–03).

93. Blinder (2013: 59); Engel & McCoy (2011: 20–21); FCIC (2011: 41–42, 72–74); McLean & Nocera (2010: 32–37, 48–51, 168).

94. Bair (2012: 44–46).

95. Barth, Caprio, & Levine (2012: 6, 89–91); Engel & McCoy (2011: 189–96); FCIC (2011: 94–94); McLean & Nocera (2010: 84–91); Wessel (2009: 64–65); Wilmarth (2011b: 903–04).

96. Engel & McCoy (2011: 196–204); FCIC (2011: 93–94); Wilmarth (2014: 84–85); see also Bernanke (2015: 103–05) (acknowledging that the Fed's order against Citigroup was an "exception," and the Fed "failed to stop some questionable practices").

97. (FCIC 2011: 171–72) (quoting interview with Ludwig on Sept. 2, 2010); Greenspan (1997c) (advising Congress that the Fed had adopted "a more risk-focused/less transaction-testing approach" in examining large bank holding companies in order to avoid "unduly intrusive" supervision); see also Menand (2018: 1566–67) ("Ludwig pulled back on-site, hands-on bank examinations from large firms and 'directed a concerted effort to streamline' supervision and 'lower its cost'") (quoting Ludwig's testimony before a congressional committee in 1995).

98. FCIC (2011: 171–72, 307) (quoting the OCC's *Large Bank Supervision Handbook*); Menand (2018: 1531–32, 1562–74); Wilmarth (2014: 122–32). According to the Financial Crisis Inquiry Commission, examiners became "something like consultants" under the Fed's and OCC's policy of "risk-focused supervision." FCIC (2011: 307).

99. Menand (2018: 1571) (quoting 2000 GAO report); Wilmarth (2014: 99–101, 114–32); see note 129 and accompanying text for a description of the off-balance-sheet vehicles established by Citigroup and other megabanks, and see Chapter 10 for discussion of the Fed's and OCC's failures to recognize the on-balance-sheet and off-balance-sheet risks of those banks until the fall of 2007.

100. Wilmarth (2011b: 905) (quoting speech by Williams in May 2005 and congressional testimony by Dugan in Sept. 2007); see also Engel & McCoy (2011: 167–74) analyzing the OCC's record of lax regulation).

101. Turner (2014: 199).

102. Engel & McCoy (2011: 176) (quoting two speeches by Reich in 2006); Wilmarth (2011b: 905) (quoting Gilleran's statement in 2004); Taub (2014: 220) (describing the photo with Gilleran and Reich); see also Engel & McCoy (2011: 174–84) (reviewing the OTS's record of extremely lax regulation).

103. Engel & McCoy (2011: 167–84); Mencimer (2007); Nalder (2008); Wilmarth (2011b: 905–06, 906n98) ("During 2004, ten large [national] banks accounted for four-fifths of all complaints" filed by consumers with the OCC); compare Wilmarth (2009: 975–76) (stating that the ten largest U.S. banks controlled 55% of the industry's assets in 2005).

104. For analysis of state APL laws, see Ding et al. (2012: 369–73); Li & Ernst (2006: 6–7, 22 [appendix I]); White et al. (2011: 248, 251–53, 257, 262–64, 268).

105. Li & Ernst (2006: 8, 12, 18); White et al. (2011: 249, 262–70). Similarly, Griffin & Maturana (2016a: 1687–89) found that state APL laws decreased the number of non-prime loans made by the worst mortgage lenders (i.e., the lenders most likely to falsify loan documents), and reduced the ability of those lenders to distort home prices in local markets.

106. FCIC (2011: 11–13, 96); Madigan (2010: 4–9); Nalder (2008); Wilmarth (2011b: 910); Wilmarth (2004b: 315–16).

107. Madigan (2010: 9–10); Nalder (2008); Wilmarth (2011b: 910–12). The OCC vigorously supported national banks when they filed lawsuits to stop state enforcement actions. In early 2007, national banks and the OCC won a major victory when the Supreme Court upheld the validity of the OCC's rules that preempted most state consumer protection laws from applying to national banks and their subsidiaries. *Watters v. Wachovia Bank, N.A.*, 550 U.S. 1 (2007). More than two years later, the Supreme Court reversed course and upheld the authority of state attorneys general to file lawsuits to enforce valid state laws against national banks. *Cuomo v. Clearing House Association, L.L.C.*, 557 U.S. 519 (2009). However, the financial crisis of 2007–09 had already occurred by that time. See Wilmarth (2010).

108. Engel & McCoy (2011: 162); Madigan (2010: 11); Wilmarth (2011b: 913–14).

109. Madigan (2010: 9–10); FCIC (2011: 13, 96–97, 111–13, 126); U.S. Senate (2010: 16–17). See also Berner & Grow (2008: 38) (concluding that the OCC contributed to the financial crisis of 2007–09 by "stifling … prescient state enforcers and legislators").

110. Ding et al. (2012: 368, 379, 382–85); Di Maggio, Kermani, & Korgaonkar (2016: 3–7, 21, 33); Di Maggio & Kermani (2017: 3711, 3713–15, 3734–45).

111. Bravin & Beckett (2002) (quoting Hawke); see also U.S. Senate (2010: 16) ("At a hearing on the OCC's preemption rule, Comptroller Hawke acknowledged, in response to a question from Senator Sarbanes, that one reason Hawke issued the preemption rule was to attract additional charters, which helps to bolster the budget of the OCC."); Bar-Gill & Warren (2008: 91–95) (stating that the OCC has "a direct financial stake in keeping its bank clients happy"); Bernanke (2015: 95–96) (agreeing that competition for bank charters among regulators "created an incentive for regulators to be less strict so as not to lose their regulatory 'clients'—and the exam fees they paid").

112. Wilmarth (2011b: 915–16) (discussing the conversions of JPMC and the U.S. bank subsidiaries of HSBC and Bank of Montreal from state banks into national banks).

113. Appelbaum & Nakashima (2008); McLean & Nocera (2010: 215); Taub (2014: 215–18); see also Wilmarth (2013: 1390–92) (describing the OTS's efforts to persuade Countrywide and other institutions to convert to federal thrift charters); Wilmarth (2011b: 915–16) (same).

114. Bair (2012: 30–36); Barr, Jackson, & Tahyar (2018: 278–84, 291–311); Engel & McCoy (2011: 211–13); FCIC (2011: 49, 171); Schooner & Taylor (2010: chapters 10–12); Tarullo (2008: 55–65, 122–30).

115. Engel & McCoy (2011: 211–12); FCIC (2011: 139–42, 200–02, 266–73, 276–78, 300–01); Herring (2018: 187–89); Kling (2009: 23–25); McLean & Nocera (2010: 81, 240); Tarullo (2008: 80–83, 88, 158–59); Tett (2009: 51–56, 62–65, 97–98); Tooze (2018: 85–87).

116. Bair (2012: 30–33); Bayoumi (2017: 78–86, 250–51); Engel & McCoy (2011: 212–13); Herring (2018: 188–91); Tarullo (2008: 117–21, 160–72); Schooner & Taylor (2010: chapters 11–12); Turner (2014: 197–99); Wilmarth (2002: 458–65).

117. FCIC (2011: 171) (quoting memorandum from Spillenkothen dated May 31, 2010).

118. Hoenig (2016); see also Herring (2018: 192 and figure 1) (showing the decline in the ratio of risk-weighted assets to total assets at a group of large global banks that included ABN Amro, BofA, Banco Santander, Barclays, BNP Paribas, Citigroup, Credit Agricole, Credit Suisse, Deutsche Bank, HSBC, ING Bank, RBS, Société Générale, UBS, and Unicredit).

119. Turner (2014: 197–201); see also Haldane, Brennan, & Madouros (2010: 99–100, 115–17 [charts 24–25, table 4]) (describing the rise in leverage at major UK and European banks between 1997 and 2008).

120. FCIC (2011: 150–54); Johnson & Kwak (2010: 140–41); Stowell (2010: 186, 187 [exhibit 10.2], 408, 410 [exhibit 3]); Taub (2014: 240–42).

121. Admati & Hellwig (2013: 176–78, 184–85); Bayoumi (2017: 37–41, 88–90); Haldane, Brennan, & Madouros (2010: 99–100, 115–17 [charts 24–25, table 4]) (documenting leverage ratios for large U.K. and European banks); Stowell (2010: 187 [exhibit 10.2]) (showing leverage ratios for Barclays, Deutsche Bank, and UBS from 2006 to 2009); Tooze (2018: 87–88); see also Noeth & Sengupta (2012: 464–66) (explaining that large European banks—including Barclays, BNP Paribas, Deutsche Bank, and Société Générale—greatly expanded their balance sheets and increased their leverage ratios by acquiring assets with relatively low risk weights).

122. Haldane, Brennan, & Madouros (2010: 117 [table 4]) (showing leverage ratios of 20.6:1 for BofA and 24.5:1 for Citigroup in 2007, compared with a leverage ratio of 17.6:1 for JPMC).

123. The 2001 joint rule's higher capital requirements for equity tranches responded to the failures of Superior Bank and several other FDIC-insured banks between 1997 and 2002. Those banks failed after suffering large losses on their holdings of equity (first loss) tranches from securitizations of subprime mortgages and other subprime consumer loans. Engel & McCoy (2011: 155); Wilmarth (2013: 1332–33). See Chapters 7 and 10 for descriptions of the tranched structures of RMBS and CDOs.

124. Engel & McCoy (2007: 2065–68); Wilmarth (2013: 1333). Large banks frequently provided loans to hedge funds to finance those funds' purchases of equity tranches of RMBS and CDOs underwritten by the lending banks. In many cases, the lending banks later suffered significant losses when the hedge funds defaulted on their loans during the financial crisis. Morris (2008: 113–23); Wilmarth (2009: 1026).

125. Bair (2010) (section titled "Failure of Regulation"); FCIC (2011: 99–100); Kling (2009: 25–26); Taub (2014: 232–33); Wilmarth (2013: 1333–34).

126. Bolton, Freixas, & Shapiro (2012: 86–87, 107–09); Kling (2009: 25–26); McLean & Nocera (2010: 110–24); Taub (2014: 232–33); Wilmarth (2013: 1334). See Chapter 10 for further analysis of conflicts of interest at credit ratings agencies.

127. Kling (2009: 26); McLean & Nocera (2010: 188–91, 200–03); Tett (2009: 62–63, 126–27); Wilmarth (2013: 1334); Wilmarth (2009: 1031). See Chapter 7 for discussion of CDS, and Chapters 10–11 for descriptions of the failures of monoline insurers and AIG during the financial crisis, and the contagious impact of those failures.

128. For analysis of the 2004 joint capital rule and similar capital rules in Europe, see Acharya, Schnabl, & Suarez (2013: 522–25); FCIC (2011: 114); Wilmarth (2013: 1334–36). For a detailed comparison of Enron's SPE abuses to the use of SPEs by large banks to minimize their capital requirements for securitizations of nonprime mortgages, see Bratton & Levitin (2013: 785–94, 821–47). Federal regulators also permitted U.S. banks to avoid leverage capital requirements for their exposures to off-balance-sheet SPEs if the banks shared the risks of those exposures by selling "expected loss notes" to investors. However, those notes typically provided the banks with only 0.1% of protection against potential defaults by SPEs, and they therefore proved to be woefully inadequate during the financial crisis. Acharya, Schnabl, & Suarez (2013: 524).

129. Acharya, Schnabl, & Suarez (2013: 521–22, table 1) (describing sponsored ABCP conduits); Gorton (2009: 29–30) (describing SIVs); Wilmarth (2014: 100) (same).

130. For analysis of BAPCA's impact, see Campbell (2005: 697, 701–09); FCIC (2011: 114–15); Lubben (2010): 320–26); Roe (2011: 546–49); Wilmarth (2013: 1360–61.

131. Campbell (2005: 712); Lubben (2010: 320–22, 328–35); Peek & Rosengren (2015: 8–9, 19 [figure 6]); Roe (2011: 544–45, 549–64); Taub (2014: 243–45); Wilmarth (2013: 1362).

132. Robertson (2011: 15–16).

133. Ashcraft & Schuermann (2008: 2 [table 1]); FCIC (2011: 104–11); GAO (2009: 11–13, 24–26 [tables 2, 5]); Levitin & Wachter (2012: 1196–201); Mayer, Pence, & Sherlund (2009: 32 [table 2, panel C]).

134. Bernanke (2015: 84–98); FCIC (2011: 13–17, 20–22, 171–73, 214–15); Wilmarth (2013: 1328–45).

135. Wilmarth (2013: 1406–07); see also Haldane, Brennan, & Madouros (2010: 89–90, 97–102, 119 [chart 35]); Johnson & Kwak (2010: 58–60, 80–87, 201–02) (showing that the six largest U.S. banks held assets equal to 60% of U.S. GDP in 2008, compared with only 18% of GDP in 1995).

136. Haldane, Brennan, & Madouros (2010: 89–90, 98, 102, 109 [charts 2, 3], 114 [chart 19]).

137. Alex Glorioso, "Finance/Insurance/Real Estate: Background" (Center for Public Integrity, Mar. 2016), available at https://www.opensecrets.org/industries/background.php?cycle=2016&ind=F (visited on June 30, 2018); Center for Public Integrity, "Lobbying: Ranked Sectors," available at https://www.opensecrets.org/lobby/top.php?indexType=c&showYear=2018; see also Wilmarth (2013: 1363).

138. Center for Public Integrity, "Finance, Insurance, and Real Estate: Long-Term Contribution Trends," available at http://www.opensecrets.org/industries/totals.php?cycle=2018&ind=F; and "Annual Lobbying," available at http://www.opensecrets.org/lobby/indus.php?id=F&year=2018 (visited on June 30, 2018).

139. Wilmarth (2013: 1363–64); see also Johnson & Kwak (2010: 88–100, 118–19).

140. FCIC (2011: 307) (quoting interview with Cole).

141. Bair (2010) (section titled "Failure of Regulation").

142. Bernanke (2015: 97–98).

143. Wilmarth (2013: 1394) (quoting statements by Brown in Apr. 2010 and by Davies in Nov. 2010).

144. Johnson & Kwak (2010: 58–62, 92–100, 113–19); Philippon & Reshef (2012: 1557–58, 1572–93, 1605–06); Wilmarth (2013: 1406–12). In 1980, average compensation in the financial industry was about the same as average wages in the rest of the U.S. economy. By 2006, average compensation in the financial industry was more than 70% higher than average U.S. wages. Philippon & Reshef (2012: 1552–58, 1578 [figure VIII.C], reproduced as Figure 0.4 in the Introduction).

145. Wilmarth (2013: 1407–11; 2014: 74–75); see also Barth, Caprio, & Levine (2012: 6–7, 89, 105, 209–10); Hirsh (2013); Johnson & Kwak (2010: 92–110, 114–19). Dugan subsequently became chairman of Citigroup in 2018. Armstrong (2018).

146. Johnson & Kwak (2010: 97); see also Wilmarth (2013: 1417–23).

147. Kwak (2014: 83–91); see also Barth, Caprio, & Levine (2012: 6–9, 15, 38–40, 89–91, 209–12).

148. Geithner (2014: 85); Braithwaite (2013).

149. Johnson & Kwak (2010: 92–94, 97–100); Wilmarth (2013: 1420–24).

150. Geithner (2014: 89); see also Wilmarth (2012a: 943–47) (citing "conflicts of interest that have resulted from close linkages between the Fed and top financial executives," including the fact that "the New York Fed provided emergency assistance to a major bank and three large financial firms [in 2008] while executives of all four organizations served as directors of the New York Fed").

151. Fraser (2014: 181–82) (quoting Gordon Brown's Mansion House speech in June 2007); Wilmarth (2013: 1394–95) (quoting a press release from the U.K. Treasury on May 24, 2005, containing Brown's remarks [italics in original], and also quoting the speech delivered by Cole on Oct. 17, 2006); see also Kay (2015: 234) ("From 1998 to 2012, Britain's Financial Services Authority was under political pressure to capture business for London from New York by imposing 'lighter-touch' regulation"); Tooze (2018: 80–84) (describing the intense competition for "financial hegemony" between New York and London).

152. Wilmarth (2013: 1395, 1395n536) (quoting (i) the op-ed "To Save New York, Learn from London," published by Bloomberg and Schumer in the *Wall Street Journal*, Nov. 1, 2006, A18, and (ii) Paulson's speech, "On the Competitiveness of the U.S. Capital Markets," delivered on Nov. 20, 2006). See also Lipton & Hernandez (2008) (reporting that Schumer received more than $6.1 million of contributions from securities and investment firms between 1989 and 2006, and stating that he "embraced the [securities] industry's free-market, deregulatory agenda more than almost any other Democrat in Congress").

153. Wilmarth (2013: 1395–96) (quoting and summarizing the McKinsey report published in Jan. 2007). As a result of strong advocacy by FDIC Chairman Sheila Bair and support from Senators Christopher Dodd (D-CT) and Richard Shelby (R-AL), federal regulators maintained the leverage capital requirement for U.S. banks. See Bair (2012: 16–17, 22–24, 27, 30–39) (describing her refusal, as FDIC Chairman, to apply "lighter touch regulation" and her successful efforts to preserve the leverage capital requirement for U.S. banks in 2006 and 2007, despite intense lobbying from the banking industry and pressure from Senator Schumer and other U.S. bank regulators).

154. Kwak (2014: 74–75); Wilmarth (2013: 1423–24); see also Bair (2012: 16–17, 27) (describing the "deregulatory dogma" and "groupthink" that prevailed among most U.S. and European financial regulators before the financial crisis). In May 2010, Richard Spillenkothen, the Fed's Director of Bank Supervision from 1991 to 2006, explained that

federal regulators had "a high degree of faith that financial markets were largely effi- cient and self-correcting and, therefore, that counterparty and market discipline were generally more effective 'regulators' of risk-taking and improper practices than gov- ernment rules and supervisors." Wilmarth (2013: 1424) (quoting memorandum from Spillenkothen dated May 31, 2010).

155. Greenspan (2005b, 2004b).

156. Geithner said that he saw "little prospect that supervision will have the capacity to iden- tify and address potential concentrations in exposure to individual risk factors, whether through changes to capital charges or other means." Geithner also said that federal reg- ulators "do not have the capacity to eliminate the risk of excess leverage or asset price misalignments, nor do we have the ability to act preemptively to diffuse them." Geithner (2007).

157. Ibid.; see also Wilmarth (2014: 124–27) (comparing the two speeches by Greenspan and Geithner). Geithner later said that he "greatly admired [Robert] Rubin, [Lawrence] Summers, and Greenspan, and I shared their general approval of markets and finan- cial innovation." In contrast, Geithner did not agree with Paul Volcker's position as a "thundering critic of modern Wall Street," and Geithner did not have "the strength of [Volcker's] convictions" regarding "the conflicts of interest, the mind-boggling compen- sation, [and] the elevation of risky trading of newfangled products over careful and con- servative banking." Geithner (2014: 85–86, 89–90).

158. Geithner (2007) (warning of the potential dangers of complacency after "a sustained pe- riod of relative stability and low credit losses"); Greenspan (2005b) (stating that "success at stabilization carries its own risks" because "it is difficult to suppress growing market exuberance").

159. Geithner (2007); see also Greenspan (2005b) (contending that "the flexibility of our market-driven economy" has made the economy "more resilient to shocks and more stable overall during the past couple of decades").

160. FSA (2009: §1.4, at 39).

161. Parker (2016) (quoting an interview with Macpherson); Giles (2012) (quoting a speech by King).

162. IMF (2011: 17 [¶¶ 40, 42]); see also ibid., 34 (annex 7) ("The Fund's *general mindset that markets know best* and financial innovation reduces risk would have made it difficult for the staff to see the build-up of systemic risks") (emphasis in original).

163. Cooper (2015) (identifying six economists who issued warnings about a potential housing crash and economic recession prior to 2007, including Dean Baker and Nouriel Roubini, and noting that Roubini was "often derided as Dr. Doom"); Rajan (2010: 1) (listing Kenneth Rogoff, Robert Shiller, and William White as economists who "repeat- edly sounded warnings about the levels of U.S. housing prices and household indebt- edness," and noting that "critics were often written off as Cassandras or 'permabears' "). For examples of legal academics who issued warnings prior to 2006 about the dangers of nonprime lending and the risks of a systemic financial crisis, see Engel & McCoy (2002); Peterson (2005, 3–4n4) (listing articles by legal academics warning about the hazards of predatory nonprime lending); Wilmarth (2002: 392–407, 444–76); Wilmarth (2004b: 308–16, 348–56, 363–64).

164. Suskind (2011: 56–57) (quoting an interview with Shiller, and noting that Shiller served on the New York Fed's Economic Advisory Panel for fourteen years). Shiller presented

similar evidence of a housing "bubble" in the 2005 edition of his book *Irrational Exuberance*. The "Advisory Groups" section of the New York Fed's Annual Reports list Shiller as a member of the Economic Advisory Panel at the end of 2003, but not at the end of 2004. See https://www.newyorkfed.org/medialibrary/media/aboutthefed/annual/annual03/advisory.pdf, and https://www.newyorkfed.org/medialibrary/media/about-thefed/annual/annual04/advisory.pdf.

165. Borio & White (2003: 140–44, 149–58).

166. Ibid., 167–77.

167. See "Commentary" by Mark Gertler and "General Discussion" following Borio & White (2003), at pages 213–40; see also Tett (2009: 153–54) (describing the hostile response to Borio's and White's paper at the 2003 Jackson Hole conference).

168. Rajan (2005: 343–53).

169. Rajan (2010: 2–3); see also Bernanke (2015: 81) ("The Kansas City Fed's annual Jackson Hole symposium in August 2005 ... hailed [Greenspan] as the greatest central banker in history").

170. Kohn (2005: 371–72).

171. Rajan (2010: 3); see also "General Discussion" following Kohn (2005), at pages 387–97 (quoting Summers at 387, 389). FDIC Chairman Sheila Bair was similarly called a "Luddite" for her opposition to Basel II's heavy reliance on internal risk models developed by major banks. Bair (2012: 36).

172. Geithner (2005, 2007); Greenspan (2004b, 2005b); Kohn (2005: 371–75); see also IMF (2011: 9–10 [¶ 21]) (noting that Rajan's warnings "did not influence" the International Monetary Fund, even though he was then serving as the IMF's economic counselor); Menand (2018: 1531–32, 1555–58) (discussing Greenspan's strong commitment to universal banking, which was shared by Robert Rubin and other key U.S. regulators and policymakers). See Chapter 8 for discussion of the enactment of GLBA and CFMA.

173. FCIC (2011: 13–17, 20–22, 93–96, 170–73); Johnson & Kwak (2010: 100–09, 118–19, 140–44, 147–50).

174. Federal Reserve Board (2020: 7 [table D.3]) (showing that U.S. residential mortgage debt rose from $2.7 trillion in 1991 to $10.6 trillion in 2007, while consumer nonmortgage debt increased from $815 billion in 1991 to $2.6 trillion in 2007); see also Garriga, Noeth, & Schlagenhauf (2017: 184 [figure 1]) (showing the increase in the ratio of household debt to disposable income).

175. Hacker & Pierson (2010: 20–24) (showing that total after-tax incomes, including public and private benefits, grew by 256% for households with the top 1% of incomes between 1979 and 2006, while total after-tax incomes of households in the 80th to 99th percentiles rose by 55%; in contrast, total after-tax incomes grew by only 11% for households in the lowest income quintile, 18% for households in the second-lowest quintile, 21% for households in the third-lowest quintile, and 32% for households in the fourth-lowest quintile). See also Suskind (2011: 62) (stating that the wealthiest 1% of U.S. households received 23% of total national income in 2007, up from 9% in 1980).

176. Barba & Pivetti (2009; 113–18); Hacker & Pierson (2010: 31–33, 197–98); Rajan (2010: 8–9, 24–26, 38–40); Wilmarth (2009: 1009–11).

177. Greenspan (2002c, 2003); see also Wilmarth (2009: 997–98, 1002–06, 1009–11).

178. Greenspan & Kennedy (2007: 1–3, 9–11, 16–17 [table 2]).

179. Bernanke (2015: 86–87); see also Rajan (2010: 8–9, 24–26, 38–40); Wilmarth (2009: 1002–06, 1009–11).
180. A. Turner (2010: 16–18, 55, 60 [charts 7 and 12]) (showing that total lending by U.K. banks and building societies rose from 27% to 402% of U.K. GDP between 1964 and 2007); Jordà, Schularick, & Taylor (2016a: 115–20) (showing that real estate lending by banks and household mortgage debts rose significantly after 1970, and even more rapidly after 1990, especially in the U.S., U.K., Spain, the Netherlands, Denmark, Portugal, and Switzerland); Jordà, Schularick, & Taylor (2014: 11–14) (describing the housing booms and the rapid growth of mortgage debts in Spain and Ireland during the 2000s); Bayoumi (2017: 71–101) (describing how large European banks financed credit booms in several EU nations); McCauley (2018: 52–53) (same); Noeth & Sengupta (2012: 466–68) (same); Shin (2012: 187–90) (same); J. Turner (2014: 93, 94 [table 4.6]) (showing that the annual volume of new U.K. mortgages tripled between 2000 and 2007); see also OECD (2015: 21 ["In 2008, the OECD rang the alarm bells about the pervasive, decades-long increase in income inequality"], 21 [figure 1.2] [showing that disposable household income rose much more rapidly for the top 10% of households in seventeen OECD countries between 1985 and 2007, compared with households in lower income deciles]).

Chapter 10

1. Jordà, Schularick, & Taylor (2016a: 113–20, 127–30); Mian & Sufi (2018a: 7–15); Tooze (2018: 102–09); Turner (2014: 93–96). See Chapter 9 for a discussion of monetary and regulatory policies that encouraged the credit boom of the 2000s. See also Bhidé (2017: 108 [table 2]) (showing that the outstanding volume of mortgage-backed securities in Europe [including the U.K.] increased from $110 billion in 2000 to $2 trillion in 2008).
2. Ashcraft & Schuermann (2008: 2 [table 1]); Sengupta (2010: 57 [figure 1]).
3. Ashcraft & Schuermann (2008: 2 [table 1]); Gorton (2009: 15 [table 3], 17, 18 [table 4]).
4. Mian & Sufi (2018b). The two types of lenders that relied most heavily on funding from private-label RMBS were financial conglomerates (including Citigroup, JPMorgan Chase JPMC, and Countrywide) and specialized nonbank lenders (including Ameriquest and New Century). Financial conglomerates obtained most of their funding from deposits, sales of RMBS to investors, repos, and sales of short-term commercial paper. Ibid., 8–14.
5. See Chapter 9 for a discussion of the leading roles of the Big Seventeen financial conglomerates in underwriting nonprime RMBS and CDOs; see also Dunbar & Donald (2009); Wilmarth (2011a: 966, 966n45); Wilmarth (2009: 1019, 1019n280); Griffin & Maturana (2016: Internet Appendix 44 [table I.A.12]) (showing that fourteen of the Big Seventeen conglomerates—all *except* BNP Paribas, Société Générale, and Wachovia—ranked among the top eighteen underwriters of nonprime RMBS, along with Countrywide, WaMu, GMAC, and Nomura); Cordell, Feldberg, & Sass (2019: 17 [exhibit 10]) (showing that fifteen of the Big Seventeen conglomerates—all *except* BNP Paribas and HSBC—ranked among the eighteen top underwriters of CDOs, along with Credit Agricole, WestLB, and Dresdner Bank; and also noting that the top eighteen underwriters issued 89% of all CDOs).
6. Dunbar & Donald (2009); Engel & McCoy (2011: 44–45, 56–58); FCIC (2011: 113–15); McLean & Nocera (2010: 134–35); Wilmarth (2009: 1019–20).

7. Coval, Jurek, & Stafford (2009: 22); Engel & McCoy (2011: 27–47, 51); FCIC (2011: 88–91, 102–04, 113–18); McLean & Nocera (2010: 125–45); Taub (2014: 140–45, 155–59); Wilmarth (2009: 1025). See Chapters 7 and 9 for descriptions of the securitization process, hybrid subprime ARMs, and option ARMs.

8. Coval, Jurek, & Stafford (2009: 22); Engel & McCoy (2011: 56–58); FCIC (2011: 102–04, 113–18); McLean & Nocera (2010: 126–27, 134–35, 217–18); Wilmarth (2014: 90–95, 114–17).

9. FCIC (2011: 102–03) (quoting interview with Prince on Mar. 17, 2010).

10. Ibid., 165–68; Wilmarth (2014: 92).

11. FCIC (2011: 19, 168–69); Wilmarth (2014: 92–94).

12. FCIC (2011: 18–19) (discussing the harsh treatment received by Lehman Brothers' chief risk officer, Madelyn Antoncic, after she objected to Lehman's excessive risk-taking); Suskind (2011: 38–39) (describing Stan O'Neal's firing of Jeff Kronthal after Kronthal tried to reduce the risks Merrill Lynch was taking with nonprime mortgages and CDOs); Taub (2014: 144) (stating that WaMu forced Greg Saffer to leave his job after he refused to encourage customers to accept high-risk option ARMs); Taibbi (2014a) (reporting that JPMC dismissed Alayne Fleischmann, a due diligence review manager, after she warned her supervisors that JPMC was committing "massive criminal securities fraud" by securitizing materially defective mortgages to create nonprime RMBS); see also Cohan (2016a) (stating that "Wall Street whistle-blowers [were] shunned, ostracized, and ignored," and were "often fired from their jobs and blackballed from the industry"; and describing the punitive treatment received by Richard Bowen, Alayne Fleishmann, and Michael Winston, a former managing director at Countrywide who was "punished, isolated . . . and ultimately dismissed" after he tried to stop "wrongdoing").

13. FCIC (2011: 167) (table showing Clayton's rejection rates as well as the "waived in" rates for mortgages Clayton reviewed for Credit Suisse, Deutsche Bank, Goldman Sachs, JPMC, Lehman Brothers, Merrill Lynch, UBS, and WaMu).

14. *Federal Housing Finance Agency v. Nomura Holdings America, Inc.*, 104 F. Supp. 3d 441, 471–84, 559–61, 571–73 (S.D.N.Y. 2015), *affirmed*, 873 F.3d 85, 125–34 (2d Cir. 2017), *cert. denied*, 126 S. Ct. 2679 (2018) (hereinafter *FHFA v. Nomura*). In mid-2006, "Nomura told Clayton that it needed to relax its due diligence process" because Nomura wanted to "increase approval rate, . . . improve [mortgage] seller satisfaction with the due diligence process, and decrease efforts all around." *FHFA v. Nomura*, 104 F. Supp. 3d at 474; see also DOJ-RBS (2018: 7) ("One due diligence vendor . . . concluded that RBS waived [defective mortgages] 30% more frequently than the industry average").

15. *FHFA v. Nomura*, 104 F. Supp. 3d at 520–22, 531–33 (quotes at 533, 521), *affirmed*, 873 F.3d at 140–47; *see also* 104 F. Supp. 3d at 572 (describing Nomura's and RBS's "wholesale abandonment of underwriting guidelines").

16. DOJ-RBS (2018: 1, 5–6) (quoting RBS's chief U.S. credit officer and other RBS employees).

17. DOJ-UBS (2018: 2, 7, 57–59).

18. DOJ (2015: 12–13) (quoting internal emails from and to Mozilo dated Aug. 1 and Aug. 2, 2005); see Dunbar & Donald (2009) (stating that Countrywide originated the largest amount of subprime mortgages between 2005 and 2007 and underwrote the third-largest amount of subprime RMBS in 2005 and 2006).

19. *SEC v. Mozilo* (C.D. Cal. Sept. 16, 2010), available on Westlaw at 2010 WL 3656068 (quoting internal emails from Mozilo dated Mar. 27 and Sept. 26, 2006); DOJ (2015: 14) (quoting email dated Sept. 26, 2006); SEC (2009c) (quoting emails dated Apr. 13, 2006, and Sept. 26, 2006).

20. Demyanyk & Van Hemert (2011: 1852–53, 1864–66, 1875–76) (study using the LoanPerformance database, which included 85–90% of securitized subprime loans); Mayer, Pence, & Sherlund (2009: 40–44) (study using the same database); see also FCIC (2011: 104–11, 214–19).

21. Mayer, Pence, & Sherlund (2009: 31, 32 [table 2, panel C]) (showing that between 2003 and 2006, the portion of subprime mortgages with piggyback loans increased from 7% to 28% while the share of Alt-A mortgages with piggyback loans rose from 12% to 42%); see also Engel & McCoy (2011: 35–36); FCIC (2011: 109–10); LaCour-Little, Calhoun, & Yu (2011); GAO (2009: 8–9) (stating that the portion of subprime mortgages with combined loan-to-value ratios above 100% increased from 2.4% in 2000 to 29.3% in 2006, while the share of Alt-A mortgages with similarly high ratios grew from 8.6% in 2000 to 19.5% in 2006).

22. Demyanyk & Van Hemert (2011: 1854 [table 1], 1855); Mayer, Pence, & Sherlund (2009: 32 [table 2, panel C]); see also Engel & McCoy (2011: 36–37); FCIC (2011: 110–11); Jiang, Nelson, & Vytlacil (2014).

23. Mayer, Pence, & Sherlund (2009: 32 [table 2, panel C]); see also Engel & McCoy (2011: 34–35); FCIC (2011: 106–09); Taub (2014: 126–27); and Chapter 9 for discussion of the payment shock created by hybrid subprime ARMs and option ARMs with interest-only payments or negative amortization terms.

24. Mian & Sufi (2014: 75–85). Mian and Sufi also determined that housing prices in low-credit-score zip codes rose twice as fast as housing prices in high-credit-score zip codes between 2002 and 2006. The trend reversed in 2007, when housing prices in low-credit-score zip codes dropped at a much faster rate. Ibid., 80–81. In addition, households with the lowest quintile of net worth suffered the greatest relative loss of wealth between 2007 and 2010, while households in the middle quintile of the net worth spectrum experienced a significantly higher relative loss of wealth compared with the richest quintile of households. Ibid., 19–25.

25. Mian & Sufi (2015); Mian & Sufi (2014: 75–80, 97–105).

26. Bar-Gill (2009); Engel & McCoy (2011: 21–42); FCIC (2011: 105–09); McLean & Nocera (2010: 126–27); Mian & Sufi (2014: 86–88); Wilmarth (2009: 1021–24); see also GAO (2009: 24–25 [tables 3, 4]) (showing that (i) 59% of all nonprime mortgage loans between 2000 and 2007 were refinanced mortgages, and (ii) 86% of subprime refinanced mortgages and 67% of Alt-A refinanced mortgages were cash-out refinancings). For examples of repeated refinancings, see Mian & Sufi (2014: 86) (describing an elderly woman in Detroit who refinanced her mortgage five times between 2001 and 2007); Wilmarth (2009: 1023–24n305) (describing an elderly woman in Hackensack, New Jersey, who refinanced her mortgage thirteen times with no-doc loans between 1999 and 2007, increasing the principal amount of her mortgage from $142,000 to $544,000).

27. Coval, Jurek, & Stafford (2009: 19–20); Engel & McCoy (2011: 47–49, 58–59); FCIC (2011: 118–20).

28. Acharya & Schnabl (2010); Bayoumi (2017: 86–90); Bertaut et al. (2011: 5–18, figure 11); Errico et al. (2014: 12–20); Noeth & Sengupta (2012: 459–66); Shin (2012: 162–74); Tooze (2018: 73–79).

29. FCIC (2011: 118–20, 169–70) (quoting testimony by Jerome Fons before a congressional committee on Oct. 22, 2008); see also Coval, Jurek, & Stafford (2009: 19–20); Engel & McCoy (2011: 47, 58–61); McLean & Nocera (2010: 110–13); *FHFA v. Nomura*, 873 F.3d

at 104, 148–50 (stating that Nomura and RBS did not provide final prospectuses with general descriptions of the underlying mortgage pools until *after* investors purchased their nonprime RMBS). See Chapter 7 for further description of the securitization process.

30. FCIC (2011: 130); Taub (2014: 157); Wilmarth (2014: 96).

31. FCIC (2011: 127–30, 202–03) (quoting, on page 130, Credit Suisse banker Joe Donovan, who said "we created the investor" by inventing cash flow CDOs); see also Cordell, Feldberg, & Sass (2019: 12–14); Engel & McCoy (2011: 51–53); McLean & Nocera (2010: 120–23); Taub (2014: 157–58, 233–35); Wilmarth (2014: 96).

32. FCIC (2011: 130–33, 203 [quote]); see also Engel & McCoy (2011: 51–53); McLean & Nocera (2010: 122–23); Taub (2014: 157–58, 233–35).

33. Bernstein & Eisinger (2010); see also FCIC (2011: 202–04).

34. Chernenko (2017) (quotes at 1894).

35. FCIC (2011: 127–29, 148 [quoting Kyle Bass], 193 [quoting analyst James Grant's description of the "mysterious alchemical processes" by which "Wall Street transforms BBB-minus-rated mortgages into AAA-rated tranches of mortgage securities" through the production of CDOs]).

36. McLean & Nocera (2010: 122–23).

37. FCIC (2011: 48, 139–42, 200–02, 266–67) (quote at 140); McLean & Nocera (188–91, 200–03) (quote at 189). See Chapter 8 for discussion of CFMA's exemption of CDS and other OTC derivatives from virtually all types of federal and state regulation.

38. FCIC (2011: 204, 276–77) (quote); see also Engel & McCoy (2011: 48, 86); Gasparino (2009: 246, 347–50); Tett (2009: 126–27, 134–35, 138).

39. Bolton, Freixas, & Shapiro (2012: 85–89, 106–10); Engel & McCoy (2011: 47–51); FCIC (2011: 146–50, 206–11); McLean & Nocera (2010: 111–24, 297–98); Tett (2009: 100–01); Wilmarth (2011a: 967–68).

40. Coval, Jurek, & Stafford (2009: 21–22) (quoting emails sent by CRA analysts on Apr. 5, 2007, and Dec. 15, 2006); see also Engel & McCoy (2011: 47–51, 55–56); FCIC (2011: 146–50, 206–11); Levitin & Wachter (2012: 1235–37).

41. Griffin & Tang (2012).

42. FCIC (2011: 210, 207) (quoting interview with Jerome Fons on Apr. 22, 2010).

43. Geithner (2014: 134).

44. Lewis (2010: 54–55, 88–89 (quote), 154–58); FCIC (2011: 120–21); Wilmarth (2014: 101–04); see also McLean & Nocera (2010: 124) (quoting a former Moody's executive, who said, "It seems to me that we had blinders on and never questioned the information we were given.... Why didn't we envision that credit would tighten after being loose and housing prices would fall after rising? After all, most economic cycles are cyclical and bubbles inevitably burst").

45. FCIC (2011: 146–49, 193–95) (citing Grant's newsletter of Oct. 6, 2006); Wilmarth (2014: 103, 103n279); see also Gasparino (2009: 199–203) (discussing faulty assumptions made by CRAs).

46. Benmelech & Dlugosz (2009: 1–15, 21–25); Coval, Jurek, & Stafford (2009: 3–4, 8–21); Engel & McCoy (2011: 47–51); FCIC (2011: 118–22, 146–50, 193–94); Lewis (2010: 98–103, 154–60, 165–77, 205–17); McLean & Nocera (2010: 117–24).

47. FCIC (2011: 142–46, 190–95); see also Cordell, Feldberg, & Sass (2019: 13–16); Wilmarth (2011a: 965–66).

48. FCIC (2011: 142–46, 190–95); Eisinger & Bernstein (2010); McLean & Nocera (2010: 260–66).

49. SEC (2010a, 2010b); see also FCIC (2011: 190–95); McLean & Nocera (2010: 278–82); Bratton & Levitin (2013: 847–58) (providing a detailed analysis of the Abacus deal).

50. SEC (2011a) (consent order requiring JPMC to pay $154 million to settle charges that JPMC misled the long investors in a $1 billion synthetic CDO in early 2007; the SEC alleged that JPMC did not disclose that Magnetar Capital played a significant role in selecting $600 million of the referenced CDO securities, which Magnetar then shorted through CDS arranged by JPMC); SEC (2011c) (consent order requiring Citigroup to pay $285 million to settle charges that it misled the long investors in a $1 billion synthetic CDO in early 2007; the SEC alleged that Citigroup did not disclose that it took short positions against $500 million of the referenced subprime assets).

51. Griffin & Maturana (2016: 385–90, 413–16). See note 5 in this chapter for a description of the eighteen largest underwriters of RMBS included in their study.

52. Ibid., 387. Darcy Palmer, a former quality assurance and fraud analyst at Wells Fargo, told the Financial Crisis Inquiry Commission that Wells Fargo funded "at least half the loans she flagged for fraud … over her objections." FCIC (2011: 162); see also DOJ-RBS (2018: 13–14) (alleging that RBS knew that 33% of the nonprime mortgages underlying an offering of RMBS in Sept. 2007 had inflated appraisals).

53. Piskorski, Seru, & Witkin (2015: 2642–53, 2671–72).

54. Ibid., 2658–61, 2672 (emphasis in original).

55. Griffin, Lowery, & Saretto (2014: 2873–76, 2893–922).

56. Cordell, Huang, & Williams (2012: 18, 36 [table 14]) (showing that the worst losses were recorded by CDOs arranged by Morgan Stanley, Citigroup, Bear Stearns, UBS, Bank of America, and Goldman Sachs).

57. Griffin, Lowery, & Saretto (2014: 2873–76, 2915–22).

58. DOJ-RBS (2018: 9–20) (quotes at 10, 19–20).

59. DOJ (2016). The Justice Department's complaint alleged that (i) Barclays conducted sham due diligence on thousands of mortgages included in securitized pools backing the nonprime RMBS that Barclays underwrote between 2005 and 2007, (ii) Barclays "routinely ignored" evidence that high percentages of those mortgages did not conform to Barclays' representations in its offering documents, and (iii) Barclays "systematically and intentionally misrepresented key characteristics" of the underlying mortgages, including loan-to-value ratios, appraisals, and the borrowers' ability to repay. The complaint alleged that "more than half of the underlying residential mortgages defaulted, resulting in billions of dollars in losses to investors," including "investors in AAA-rated tranches of those securities." DOJ (2016); see also DOJ-RBS (2018: 1) (alleging that RBS "underwrote RMBS backed by home mortgages with a high risk of default, and then made false and misleading representations to sell those RMBS to investors," resulting in losses to investors of "over $49 billion, with more than $5.6 billion in losses still forecast to occur"); DOJ-UBS (2018: 2) (alleging that UBS knew that "large percentages" of the mortgages it securitized did not meet the loan originators' guidelines, did not comply with applicable laws, and were based on "inaccurate, inflated or fraudulent appraisals of the properties underlying the loans").

60. Griffin, Kruger, & Maturana (2018: 1, 1n1; Internet Appendix table I.A.1) (providing information about settlements completed between 2012 and 2017). In 2018, Barclays, Wells Fargo, RBS, and HSBC collectively paid $9.8 billion of civil penalties to resolve the Justice

Department's claims against them. DOJ (2018a) (Barclays settlement for $2 billion); DOJ (2018b) (Wells Fargo settlement for $2.1 billion); DOJ (2018c) (RBS settlement for $4.9 billion); DOJ-HSBC (2018) (HSBC's settlement for $765 million).

61. *FHFA v. Nomura*, 441 F. Supp. 3d at 453 (quote), 520 (quote), 532 (quote), 559–66.

62. *FHFA v. Nomura*, 873 F.3d at 96–97, 108–09, 143–48, 159. The district court also concluded that Nomura and RBS made material misstatements about the combined loan-to-value ratios of the underlying mortgages (which were significantly understated) and the credit ratings assigned to the RMBS (which were falsely represented as being based on accurate information about the underlying loan pools). The Second Circuit did not consider it necessary to review those findings in its decision. *FHFA v. Nomura*, 441 F. Supp. 3d at 533–36, 566–68, *affirmed*, 873 F.3d at 108–09; see also DOJ-RBS (2018) (containing the Justice Department's allegations of systematic fraud by RBS in underwriting and selling nonprime RMBS).

63. FCIC (2011: 15, 161–63) (quoting Swecker).

64. Ibid., 172 (quoting interview with Snow on Oct. 7, 2010). See Chapter 9 for a review of systematic failures by federal regulators to prevent unsound and predatory lending by federally regulated institutions.

65. Becker, Stolberg, & Labaton (2008) (quoting Lindsey). See Chapter 9 for discussion of the Fed's use of ultra-low interest rates to stimulate the housing market and support economic growth between 2001 and 2004.

66. Greenspan (2005a) (testimony before the House Committee on Financial Services on July 21, 2005).

67. Mian & Sufi (2014: 78) (quoting Bernanke's testimony before the Joint Economic Committee as Chairman of the Council of Economic Advisers on Oct. 20, 2005). Hank Paulson was concerned about the risk of a potential financial crisis when he became Treasury Secretary in July 2006. However, he did *not* expect that the housing market would be the cause of the crisis that began in Aug. 2007. Paulson (2010: 42–47, 61).

68. Eichengreen (2015: 169–70) (quoting Bernanke's interview on CNBC on July 1, 2005). Michael Burry, a hedge fund manager who began shorting the nonprime mortgage market in early 2005, viewed the collapse of housing prices during the 1930s as a key reference point for his analysis. Lewis (2010: 54–55).

69. See Geithner (2014: 110) ("A lot of internal Fed work and academic studies suggested that the run-up in home prices was justified by economic fundamentals, and that in any case sharp nationwide price drops had little historical precedent"). At a special meeting in June 2005, the Fed's staff gave reports to the Federal Open Market Committee about the potential risks and effects of a significant drop in housing prices. Bernanke did not attend that meeting, but he later said, "Today, the transcript of that meeting makes for painful reading.... Most [Fed] policymakers at the meeting, like most staff economists, downplayed the risks." Bernanke (2015: 88–89).

70. FCIC (2011: 188–91, 195–204, 214–15, 238); Gasparino (2009: 238–39, 246–50); McLean & Nocera (2010: 253–60); see also Griffin, Lowery, & Saretto (2014: Internet Appendix, table A.1) (showing that annual issuances of CLOs, MBS, ABS, and CDOs rose from $1.28 trillion in 2004 to $1.86 trillion in 2005 and $2.15 trillion in 2006, before declining slightly to $1.96 trillion in 2007).

71. For discussions of ABCP conduits and SIVs, see Acharya, Schnabel, & Suarez (2013: 514–22); FCIC (2011: 138–39, 252–53); Acharya & Schnabl (2009: 86–98); Gasparino (2009: 250, 307); Geithner (2014: 550n); Tooze (2018: 73–74); Wilmarth (2014: 99–101).

72. FCIC (2011: 195–99); Tett (2009: 136, 203–06); Wilmarth (2014: 98–100).

73. Clementi et al. (2009: 198–200); McLean & Nocera (2010: 163–67, 234–38, 303–11); Tett (2009: 134–39, 206–09); see also Griffin, Lowery, & Saretto (2014: Internet Appendix, table A.12, panel D) (showing that Merrill Lynch and Citigroup were the two top-ranked underwriters of CDOs during the 2000s, while Deutsche Bank and UBS were the two leading European bank underwriters of CDOs).

74. Acharya & Schnabl (2009: 83–86, 97–98, table 2.2); FCIC (2011: 202–04, 257–59); Gasparino (2009: 235–37, 259–61, 292–97).

75. Bair (2010: "Failure of Regulation" section); Bernanke (2015: 85–86, 96–97, 134–40).

76. Tett (2009: 151–53); see also Wessel (2009: 103).

77. Acharya & Schnabl (2009); Wilmarth (2011a: 975); Wilmarth (2009: 1034–35); see also Wessel (2009: 103–04) ("A more apt description might have been 'originate and hide' ").

78. Associated Press (2007); Engel & McCoy (2011: 69–71); FCIC (2011: 214–16, 233–34); Gasparino (2009: 246–48); Robertson (2011: 5–6); Wilmarth (2009: 1019–20).

79. Appelbaum & Cho (2009); Dunbar & Donald (2009); FCIC (2011: 206, 257–62, 281, 304–06); Gasparino (2009: 167–69, 235–36, 247–49); McLean & Nocera (2010: 238–39); Wilmarth (2009: 1018).

80. Wilmarth (2014: 91–92, 107–08) (quoting statement on Sept. 12, 2007, by Jeffrey Perlowitz, Citigroup's head of global securitized markets); see also Gasparino (2009: 167–69, 235–36, 247–49); Wilmarth (2009: 1017–18).

81. FCIC (2011: 175–76); Wilmarth (2009: 1037–39); see also Griffin, Lowery, & Saretto (2014: Internet Appendix, table A.1) (showing that underwriters issued almost $600 billion of CMBS between 2003 and 2007).

82. FCIC (2011: 174–75); Wilmarth (2014: 105–06); Wilmarth (2009: 1039–41) (explaining that (i) interest-only loans allowed the borrower to defer payments of principal, (ii) payment-in-kind loans permitted the borrower to defer the payment of interest by issuing new debt to cover accrued interest, and (iii) "covenant lite" loans did not contain standard covenants that limited the borrower's outstanding debt and required the borrower to maintain minimum levels of cash flow coverage and interest payment coverage).

83. Wilmarth (2014: 106–07) (quoting from notes of a meeting of federal regulators with Citigroup officials on Nov. 19, 2007).

84. Wilmarth (2014: 107) (quoting Kate Kelly et al., "Two Big Funds at Bear Stearns Face Shutdown," *Wall Street Journal*, June 20, 2007, A1; and Michael Hudson, "Is Corporate-Credit Party About Over?," *Wall Street Journal*, July 2, 2007, C5); see also FCIC (2011: 238–41) (describing the severe problems at two hedge funds owned by Bear Stearns in June and July 2007).

85. Nakamoto & Wighton (2007) (quoting interview with Prince). Prince defended his "still dancing" view by stating that the "depth of the pools of liquidity" in the capital markets "is so much larger than it used to be that a disruptive event now needs to be much more disruptive than it used to be." Prince said he did not believe markets were "at that point" where liquidity could disappear.

86. Ibid.; Wilmarth (2014: 107–08) (quoting Eric Dash, "Is the Dance Over? Citigroup Is Upbeat," *New York Times*, Aug. 3, 2007, C1).

87. Paulson (2010: 69).

88. Ibid., 69–70.

89. In a May 2007 speech, Bank of America CEO Kenneth Lewis described the "tremendous value" his bank created by "being able to provide a strong balance sheet to arrange large, complex financial transactions." Lewis boasted that BofA participated in seven of the fifteen largest leveraged buyout deals during 2006. However, Lewis admitted, "We are close to a time when we'll look back and say we did some stupid things.... We need a little more sanity in a period in which everyone feels invincible and thinks this is different." Ip (2007) (quoting Lewis).

90. Gasparino (2009: 189–92, 237–38); UNCTAD (2010: 63–66); Wilmarth (2014: 90–91, 98–105). According to Gillian Tett, JPMC's Jamie Dimon was the rare CEO who had "the supreme self-confidence" to reject demands by analysts and investors for more risk-taking to produce higher short-term revenues and profits. Dimon told Tett, "One of the problems of being a CEO is the constant pressure on you to grow, grow, and grow.... But if you are in the risk business, you can get into terrible trouble if you just keep growing." Tett (2009: 140–41).

91. FCIC (2011: xix [quote], 198–99, 279 [quote], 291, 343); see also Bebchuk & Spamann (2010: 262–66); Clementi et al. (2009: 198–206).

92. Bhattacharyya & Purnanandam (2011: 1–12, 17–19, 26–31).

93. Bhagat & Bolton (2013). Lucian Bebchuk, Alma Cohen, and Holger Spamann found that the five highest-paid executives at Bear Stearns and Lehman Brothers received large net gains from their incentive compensation plans between 2000 and 2008, even though both firms failed in 2008. The five top-earning executives at Bear Stearns received more than $1.4 billion in cash bonuses and cash proceeds from sales of equity awards between 2000 and 2008, while the five top-earning executives at Lehman Brothers received over $1 billion. After accounting for their investment losses in 2008, the five highest-paid managers of Bear Stearns still received net non-salary gains of $650 million, while the five top-earning managers of Lehman Brothers received net non-salary gains of $400 million. Bebchuk, Cohen, & Spamann (2010: 266–73).

94. DeYoung, Peng, & Yan (2013).

95. Wilmarth (2014: 116–17). See Chapters 2 and 6 for descriptions of the compensation received by Mitchell and Wiggin.

96. FCIC (2011: 63, 259); Ligi & Holland (2009).

97. Wilmarth (2013: 1382–87).

98. Clementi et al. (2009: 204) (describing increases in compensation for employees of investment banks and investment banking divisions of financial conglomerates between 2002 and 2007); Philippon & Reshef (2012: 1557–58, 1572–93, 1605) (analyzing the gap between employee compensation in the financial sector and other industries between 1909 and 2006).

99. FCIC (2011: 259); Gasparino (2009: 229, 235); Wilmarth (2014: 99, 117).

100. FCIC (2011: 274) (discussing the compensation paid by AIG to Cassano between 1987 and 2008); see also McLean & Nocera (2010: 329, 340) (stating that Cassano's lawyers subsequently claimed that $70 million of his compensation was deferred and not paid to Cassano after AIG failed).

101. Bank One's CEO, John McCoy, resigned under pressure in Dec. 1999, after his bank's earnings and stock price repeatedly disappointed investors and Wall Street analysts. Wahl

(1999). JPMC acquired Bank One in 2003. Tett (2009: 104–07). Morgan Stanley's CEO, Philip Purcell, stepped down under pressure in June 2005, due in part to widespread unhappiness about the firm's "lackluster earnings and weak stock price." Hamilton (2005).

102. Geithner (2014: 93).

103. FCIC (2011: 142–45); Gasparino (2009: 177–80, 187–92, 235–38); McLean & Nocera (2010: 153–67) (stating that Goldman's revenues rose from $16 billion in 2003 to almost $38 billion in 2006, and proprietary trading accounted for 75% of Goldman's profits); Tett (2009: 133–39).

104. Giannone (2007) (stating that Goldman earned record profits of $9.4 billion in 2006 and paid $54 million to CEO Blankfein, $54 million to former CEO Paulson, and $53 million to each of its two co-presidents, Gary Cohn and Jon Winkelreid); McLean & Nocera (2010: 157) (stating that Goldman paid $51.2 million to Paulson and $49.6 million to Blankfein in 2003 and 2004).

105. Gasparino (2009: 177–80, 187–92, 235–38); Lambe (2010); Tett (2009: 133–39); Wilmarth (2014: 98–106, 114–16).

106. FCIC (2011: 235) (quoting emails dated Dec. 14 and 15, 2006, from Kevin Gasvoda and David Viniar).

107. FCIC (2011: 236) (quoting emails dated Jan. 31 and Feb. 11, 2007, from Daniel Sparks and Lloyd Blankfein).

108. Ibid., 236–38.

109. Ibid., 191–95, 235–38; Lewis (2010); McLean & Nocera (2010: 260–66, 299); Tett (2009: 121–28, 138–51).

110. Zandi (2008: 44) (stating that $1.25 trillion of subprime mortgages, $1 trillion of Alt-A mortgages, and $500 billion of jumbo ARMs were outstanding in 2007); Gorton (2009: 14 [table 2]) (showing that $1.96 trillion of private-label RMBS backed by such mortgages were outstanding in 2007).

111. Altman & Karlin (2008: 6, 7 [figure 1]); Cordell, Huang, & Williams (2012: 4–6); Dugan (2008: 2); Griffin, Lowery, & Saretto (2014: Internet Appendix, table A.1); Wilmarth (2009: 1035–42); see also "Household Debt and Credit Report," available at https://ycharts.com/indicators/reports/household_debt_and_credit_report (accessed on July 31, 2018).

112. Claessens et al. (2012: 9 [figure 2]) (showing growth of the private-label securitization market during the 2000s); Wilmarth (2011: 966–67).

113. See Chapters 2, 3, and 5 for discussions of the underwriting and sale of risky corporate and foreign bonds by universal banks during the 1920s.

114. See notes 170–72 (stating that AIG provided $80 billion of CDS protection, while monoline insurers provided $780 billion of protection through CDS and other guarantees).

115. Morris (2008: 131–32) (citing estimate by Peter Bernstein). As described in Chapters 7 and 8, CDS were private contracts negotiated between dealers and end-users, and those contracts were not reported to or supervised by any regulator prior to the Dodd-Frank Act. A more precise estimate of the volume of CDS connected to securitized assets in 2007 is not available from public sources.

116. Wilmarth (2011a: 966–67); Wilmarth (2009: 1027–32).

117. See the discussion of the commercial paper and repo markets in Chapter 7, and the description of ABCP conduits and SIVs earlier in this chapter; see also Kacperczyk & Schnabl (2010: 34–37) (stating that European and U.S. financial institutions had issued

more than $530 billion of outstanding commercial paper in 2007, and money market mutual funds were the largest investors in that paper).

118. For a concise presentation of Minsky's concept of "Ponzi finance" and the role that Ponzi finance played in his financial instability hypothesis, see Minsky (1992). For discussions of the strong parallels between Minsky's financial instability hypothesis and the credit boom of the 2000s, see Aliber & Kindleberger (2015: 39–52, 315–22); Field (2011: 243–58); Gerding (2014: 44, 414–19, 439–54); Wilmarth (2009: 1021–35).

119. Mian & Sufi (2018b: 20–22, 42 [figure 6]).

120. FCIC (2011: 174–76, 213–16, 226–34, 246–54, 397–98); Wilmarth (2014: 99–101, 109–14); Wilmarth (2009: 1032–43).

121. Bernanke (2007a, 2007b). During a Senate committee hearing on July 18, Bernanke cited estimates that financial institutions would experience subprime-related losses in the range of $50 to $100 billion. Those estimates "understated the problem enormously." Wessel (2009: 93).

122. Reuters (2007) (quoting and summarizing Paulson's comments in mid-April to the Committee of 100, a New York business group); FCIC (2011: 246) (quoting Paulson's remarks as reported in a Bloomberg article on July 26, 2007).

123. Bernanke (2015: 134–36); Geithner (2014: 110–14). Geithner received a staff report in Mar. 2007 that stated: "Signs of strain in the subprime area have continued to increase, but appear to remain contained to this sector." Geithner (2014: 114); see also Eichengreen (2015: 168–71) (discussing the Fed's relatively benign view of the subprime mortgage market during the first half of 2007); Wessel (2009: 88–89) (stating that most members of the Federal Open Market Committee believed in Mar. 2007 that "the economy was likely to expand at a moderate pace" and that the troubled subprime mortgage market "wasn't big enough to overturn the entire U.S. economy").

124. Swagel (2009: 9–10); see also Paulson (2010: 65–70); Becker, Stolberg, & Labaton (2008).

125. Bernanke (2015: 82–90, 96–98, 134–42); Eichengreen (2015: 168–71); Gasparino (2009: 279–81); Geithner (2014: 109–15); Paulson (2010: 64–69); Swagel (2009: 6–10). IMF (2011: 7–13).

126. Bernanke (2015: 97); Wessel (2009: 129) (quoting interview with Bernanke).

127. Geithner (2014: 114).

128. IMF (2011: 7–13).

129. Bernanke (2018: 1–2, 5, 14–15); Kohn & Sack (2018: 4, 12–13) ("Models provided limited guidance because they had elementary financial sectors").

130. Bernanke (2013: 9–10, 10n9); see also FOMC (2008a: 114) (statement by Fed Governor Frederic Mishkin during the Federal Open Market Committee's meeting on Jan. 29, 2008, warning that the risk of an "adverse feedback loop"—a contagious spillover of problems from the credit markets into the general economy—was "just not built into the [Fed's macroeconomic] model").

131. Eichengreen (2015: 171).

132. Stiglitz (2018: 70, 79, 80, 81, 84, 85, 90 [quotes; emphasis in original]). Stiglitz also criticized the Fed's forecasting model for failing to consider real-world problems created by "imperfect and asymmetric information" and "differences in beliefs" across a wide range of economic actors, including consumers, investors, lenders, and business firms. Ibid., 74–77, 87–90. David Hendry and John Muellbauer pointed to similar shortcomings in

the forecasting model used by the Bank of England during the pre-crisis period. Hendry & Muellbauer (2018: 287–90, 295–305).

133. Benmelech & Dlugosz (2009: 10–12, 33–34 [tables 4, 5]); FCIC (2011: 242–43).

134. FCIC (2011: 246–48); see also Bernanke (2015: 140–41); Eichengreen (2015: 173–76); Tett (2009: 175–78).

135. FCIC (2011: 250–51) (quoting BNP announcement on Aug. 9, 2007); see also Bernanke (2015: 140–43); Paulson (2010: 61).

136. Blinder (2013: 90–91); Eichengreen (2015: 176–77); Judge (2016: 876–78, 877n137 (listing authorities who have identified July 9 as the starting date for the financial crisis); Shin (2009: 102); Tooze (2018: 144–45).

137. Geithner (2014: 117).

138. Ibid., 194–95, 551n (explaining that the TED spread is the difference between (1) interest rates for three-month loans between banks, as determined by the London Interbank Offered Rate (LIBOR), and (2) yields on three-month Treasury bills); see also Blinder (2013: 114).

139. Bernanke (2015: 142–45); Eichengreen (2015: 176–77); Wessel (2009: 100–03).

140. FCIC (2011: 248–49); Geithner (2014: 122–25, 549nn); Wessel (2009: 118). Countrywide acquired a bank and became a bank holding company in 2000. Its holding company was supervised by the Fed until Mar. 2007, when Countrywide converted to a thrift holding company supervised by the OTS. Bernanke (2015: 95–96); McLean & Nocera (2010: 140). In December 2007, Countrywide funded over two-thirds of its assets from non-deposit sources. Federal Reserve Board (2008: 2) (stating that Countrywide had $200 billion of assets and $62 billion of deposits). Countrywide became a "primary dealer" in Jan. 2004 and traded Treasury securities with the New York Fed until July 2008, when Bank of America acquired Countrywide's operations. Federal Reserve Bank of New York, "Primary Dealers List Archive," available at https://www.newyorkfed.org/markets/pridealers_listing.html.

141. Bernanke (2015: 152–53); FCIC (2011: 249–50); Geithner (2014: 125–28); Wessel (2009: 117–18). In 2007, triparty repos were a $2.7 trillion market. The clearing banks for that market—BNY Mellon and JPMC—acted as intermediaries between repo lenders and repo borrowers, and they also provided intraday credit to repo borrowers between the unwinding of expiring repo loans in the morning and the commencement of new repo loans in the afternoon. Geithner (2014: 549n); Krishnamurthy, Nagel, & Orlov (2014: 2387–88).

142. Geithner (2014: 127).

143. Ibid., 127.

144. Ibid., 127–28.

145. Ibid., 513 (acknowledging that he "could have tried to use the indirect channel of [Fed] supervision more aggressively to rein in other parts of the shadow banking system that were connected to traditional banks, like tri-party repo [and] asset-backed commercial paper"); Wessel (2009: 118) ("Countrywide was an early warning of the susceptibility of the tri-party repo market to sudden bouts of distrust among big players in financial markets, the same virulent distrust that would sink Bear Stearns seven months later"). See also Chapter 9 for discussion of Congress's expansion of the bankruptcy "safe harbor" for repos in 2005.

146. Wilmarth (2011a: 1004) (discussing the large advances that Federal Home Loan Banks provided to WaMu and Wachovia [which both failed], Countrywide and Merrill [which were both acquired by Bank of America in emergency transactions], and Citigroup and Bank of America [which both received "exceptional assistance" from the TARP program]); see also Bernanke (2015: 147–51); FCIC (2011: 274); Wessel (2009: 119–21).

147. Bernanke (2015: 168–69); Eichengreen (2015: 178–83); Shin (2009: 101–10); Tett (2009: 194–96); Tooze (2018: 145–46); Turner (2014: 96–99).

148. Benmelech & Dlugosz (2009: 10–15). By Jan. 2008, S&P had downgraded 3,400 tranches of nonprime RMBS and 1,400 tranches of CDOs. (FCIC: 264, 276).

149. Bernanke (2015: 159–70); FCIC (2011: 264); Judge (2016: 864–66); Kacperczyk & Schnabl (2010: 37–40).

150. Bernanke (2015: 159–65, 169–70); Eichengreen (2015: 185–91); Geithner (2014: 128–33, 140–42).

151. Paulson (2010: 78–79); Swagel (2009: 10–13).

152. Geithner (2014: 140); Paulson (2010: 79); Swagel (2009: 13).

153. FCIC (2011: 252–53); Geithner (2014: 136, 140); Tett (2009: 196–99, 208–09); Wilmarth (2014: 99–101); Wilmarth (2009: 1032–34).

154. See Chapter 5 for discussion of Hoover's NCC proposal.

155. Swagel (2015: 108, 109); see also Gasparino (2009: 314–15) (reporting that people who spoke with Treasury Secretary Paulson reported that "his mood toward the end of [2007] was still pretty upbeat, as if the worst of the crisis had passed").

156. Geithner (2014: 132–33).

157. Bernanke (2015: 168–69, 176–78); FCIC (2011: 256–74); Geithner (2014: 133–35); Wilmarth (2014: 99–104).

158. FCIC (2011: 260–65); Geithner (2014: 132, 135–37); Wilmarth (2014: 101–05, 117–24).

159. Geithner (2014: 135–38).

160. Ibid., 135.

161. FCIC (2011: 256).

162. FOMC (2008a: 8) (remarks of Dudley).

163. Ibid., 184–88 (presentations by Jon Greenlee, the Fed's Associate Director for the Division of Banking, and Art Angulo, the New York Fed's Senior Vice President for banking supervision).

164. Judge (2016: 884–85); see also FCIC (2011: 302–03) (stating that "much of the toughest language" from the senior supervisors' review "was reserved for Citigroup").

165. FOMC (2008a: 189–90) (remarks of Rosengren); see also Judge (2016: 886–87) (discussing Rosengren's recommendations).

166. FOMC (2008a: 192) (remarks of Hoenig).

167. See Chapter 11 for discussion of the Feb. 2009 stress test.

168. FOMC (2008a: 80–81) (remarks of Geithner).

169. Ibid., 86–88 (remarks of Warsh).

170. Ibid., 7–8, 18 (remarks of Dudley).

171. FOMC (2008a: 17–18) (comments by Geithner).

172. FCIC (2011: 268–72); McLean & Nocera (2010: 330–31, 336–38).

173. Judge (2016: 883–84).

174. FCIC (2011: 272–74, 345–36); Gasparino (2009: 346); Geithner (2014: 184); McLean & Nocera (2010: 339–41). The New York State Insurance Department "was largely

oblivious to the massive risk taking" at AIG, in part because CFMA's federal preemption meant that the Department had no authority to regulate CDS and other derivatives. The Department therefore lacked jurisdiction over AIG Financial Products (AIGFP), which issued the CDS protection for CDOs. Gasparino (2009: 351). The Office of Thrift Supervision supervised AIG and its subsidiaries (including AIGFP) because AIG owned a thrift institution, but the OTS's supervision was extremely lax and woefully inadequate. Engel & McCoy (2011: 221–23); FCIC (2011: 274, 350–51).

175. Jon Greenlee, the Fed's Associate Director for the Division of Banking, told the FOMC in Jan. 2008 that Bear Stearns and Morgan Stanley were *not* included in the senior supervisors' review of risk management practices at eleven major financial institutions. Greenlee did not give any reason for the exclusion of those two firms from the review. FOMC (2008a: 184) (remarks by Jon Greenlee).

176. FCIC (2011: 280–88); Gasparino (2009: 269–77, 286–88, 325–29); Geithner (2014: 147–48); Paulson (2010: 94); Swagel (2015: 110).

177. Gasparino (2009: 358–63); Geithner (2014: 147–48); Swagel (2015: 110).

178. Gasparino (2009: 363).

179. Judge (2016: 913–14); see also Sarin (2019: 13–33).

180. Bernanke (2015: 157, 162–63, 183–85); Eichengreen (2015: 186–87); Geithner (2014: 141); Tooze (2018: 210–15). By December 2008, the Fed was "lending $450 billion to banks through the [TAF] auctions versus $90 billion through the traditional discount window," and the outstanding amount of dollar swap lines with foreign central banks reached $580 billion. Wessel (2009: 137–39) (quote); Tooze (2018: 212).

181. FOMC (2008a: 21–33, 37–38 (Fed staff members' comments on consensus forecast). For expressions of concern about "downside risks," see ibid., 51–55 (remarks by San Francisco Fed President Janet Yellen), 65–67 (comments by Atlanta Fed President Dennis Lockhart), 69–70 (remarks by Chicago Fed President Gary Stern), 78–80 (comments by Boston Fed President Eric Rosengren), 86–89 (remarks by Fed Governor Kevin Warsh), 93–101 (comments by Fed Governor Frederic Mishkin and Chairman Bernanke).

182. Bernanke (2008a) (testimony on Feb. 14, 2008).

183. Bernanke (2015: 199–200).

184. Isidore (2008) (quoting comments by Paulson and Schumer and summarizing remarks by Bernanke).

185. Bernanke (2015: 182, 405–07); Blinder (2013: 11, 35–36); Eichengreen (2015: 187–91).

186. FCIC (2011: 277–78). The SEC issued consent orders requiring BofA, Citigroup, Deutsche Bank, Raymond James, Royal Bank of Canada, TD Ameritrade, UBS, and Wachovia to pay $67 billion to retail investors who suffered losses after the auction-rate securities market shut down. SEC (2011b). However, many investors failed to recover all or even part of their losses. Foley & Lardner (2010).

187. FCIC (2011: 248–55, 276–86); Gasparino (2009: 344–53, 357–64); Wessel (2009: 149–51).

188. McCulley (2010) (describing his warning about "shadow banking" risks at the Jackson Hole conference).

189. McCulley (2007).

190. McCulley (2008) (emphasis in original).

191. See Chapter 7 for discussion of the markets for commercial paper, money market mutual funds, and repos, as well as the support provided by Congress and federal regulators to those markets. See also Gelpern & Gerding (2016: 387–406) (explaining that "safe

assets"—including bank deposits and shadow bank substitutes—are "products of legal intervention to reduce risks, attract buyers with risk-free labels, and ratify assumptions about safety with guarantees") (quote at 405).

Chapter 11

1. Bernanke (2015: 203–06).
2. FOMC (2008b: 1–2) (remarks of Bernanke); see also Bernanke (2015: 207–08).
3. FOMC (2008b: 4–7) (remarks of Dudley).
4. During the Great Depression, the Fed made $1.5 million of loans to commercial firms under Section 13(3). Prior to 1991, Fed could not accept securities (except for government bonds) as collateral for loans under Section 13(3). As described in Chapter 8, Goldman Sachs organized a successful lobbying campaign that persuaded Congress to amend Section 13(3) in 1991. The 1991 amendment authorized the Fed to accept private-sector securities as collateral for loans under Section 13(3). The Fed did not exercise its expanded authority under Section 13(3) until Mar. 2008. See 12 U.S.C. §343; Sastry (2018: 19–29); Wessel (2009: 159–62).
5. Bernanke (2015: 208–09); Wessel (2009: 147–48, 152).
6. FOMC (2008b: 20, 9–10) (remarks of Hoenig). In his memoir, Bernanke stated, "I was mindful of the dangers of moral hazard—the risk that rescuing investors and financial institutions from the consequences of their bad decisions could encourage more bad decisions in the future." Bernanke (2015: 147) (explaining that "moral hazard" refers to "the tendency of people whose property is insured to make less effort to avoid loss or accident").
7. FOMC (2008b: 13–14) (remarks of Plosser).
8. Ibid., 20–22 (remarks of Lacker).
9. Ibid., 20, 22–24 (remarks of Hoenig and Kohn).
10. Ibid., 10–11, 16 (remarks of Fisher).
11. Ibid., 16–17 (remarks of Geithner).
12. FCIC (2011: 287–88); Geithner (2014: 146–48).
13. Bernanke (2015: 211–17); Wessel (2009: 157–59) (stating that the Fed's loan to JPMC was secured by $14 billion of assets pledged by Bear).
14. Bernanke (2015: 217–22); Eichengreen (2015: 191–96); FCIC (2011: 286–91); Geithner (2014: 147–58); Wessel (2009: 162–73). According to Bernanke, the Fed's judgment that its loan was adequately secured under Section 13(3) was "founded on our confidence that we would ultimately be able to stabilize the financial system. If we succeeded, then the value of the assets … should ultimately be sufficient to repay the Fed's loan with interest. If we did not succeed, the outcome was uncertain." Bernanke (2015: 220); see also Wessel (2009: 172–73) (stating that the assets sold by Bear Stearns to Maiden Lane lost over $4 billion of their market value between Mar. and Dec. 2008).
15. Labaton (2008a) (reporting that "regulators were unaware of Bear's precarious health" until shortly before Bear failed).
16. Geithner (2014: 147–49) (noting that SEC Chairman Cox told reporters on Mar. 12 that the SEC had "a good deal of comfort" with Bear's level of capital).
17. FCIC (2011: 290); see also Judge (2016: 889) (SEC Chairman Cox acknowledged that the SEC did not anticipate Bear's sudden collapse).
18. Swagel (2015: 110); Swagel (2009: 31–32).

19. Judge (2016: 889); see also Sarin (2019: 2–4, 13–33) (explaining that regulators "missed warning signs" and did not use their available authority to force large banks and securities firms to increase their capital between the outbreak of the financial crisis in Aug. 2007 and the collapse of Lehman Brothers in Sept. 2008).

20. Wessel (2009: 170–71).

21. Bernanke (2015: 220–21); FCIC (2011: 294–95); see also FOMC (2008c: 4) (comments of William Dudley). See Chapter 9 for discussion of the triparty repo market.

22. Bernanke (2015: 215–16 [quotes], 223–25); Bernanke (2008b) (testimony before the Senate Banking Committee on Apr. 2, 2008); see also Geithner (2014: 149–51); Paulson (2010: 98–103, 117–18); FCIC (2011: 290–91); Labaton (2008a).

23. Geithner (2014: 159); Wessel (2009: 148) (emphasis in original).

24. Bernanke (2015: 223–25); Blinder (2013: 109–11); Gasparino (2009: 384–86); Geithner (2014: 159–61); Wessel (2009: 173–75).

25. Bernanke (2015: 215); Paulson (2010: 102).

26. See Chapters 7 and 8 for analysis of the breakdown of Glass-Steagall's structural barriers during the 1990s.

27. Eichengreen (2015: 196); see also Swagel (2009: 32). See Chapter 5 for discussion of the RFC's rescue of Central Republic Bank in June 1932.

28. Bernanke (2015: 222–23, 226); Blinder (2013: 114–15); FCIC (2011: 292–93).

29. Engel & McCoy (2011: 91–94); FCIC (2011: 292–95, 301–06); Gasparino (2009: 385, 390–91); Geithner (2014: 162–63); Tett (2009: 225–30).

30. Bernanke (2015: 222–23).

31. FOMC (2008d).

32. Ibid., 4–5, 94 (remarks of Dudley and Bernanke); see also 139–40 (comments of Angulo), 253 (appendix) (indicating that each of the four investment banks had a leverage ratio of about 25:1).

33. Ibid., 140–44, 148, 248–49 (remarks of Angulo and appendix).

34. Ibid., 164, 166, 170–71 (remarks of Lacker and Hoenig).

35. Ibid., 175–76, 178 (comments of Stern and Plosser).

36. Ibid., 171–72 (remarks of Geithner), 182–83 (remarks of Kohn), 189–90 (comments of Mishkin), 162–63, 172, 196 (statements by Bernanke).

37. Ibid., 180, 181–82, 187 (comments by Lockhart, Kohn, and Kroszner).

38. Ibid., 168–70 (remarks of Rosengren); see also Engel & McCoy (2011: 92) (discussing UBS's problems); Lambe (2010) (same); McCauley (2018: 49 [table 4]) (showing that UBS held $68 billion of nonprime mortgage-backed securities on its balance sheet at the end of 2007).

39. FOMC (2008d: 176–77) (remarks of Yellen).

40. Bernanke (2015: 231); Paulson (2010: 138–39); Wessel (2009: 178–80).

41. Geithner (2014: 165–66); see also Bernanke (2015: 251–53); FCIC (2011: 296–98, 328); Judge (2016: 901).

42. Geithner (2014: 165–67); Paulson (2010: 136–38, 173).

43. Sarin (2019: 3, 18–27).

44. Bernanke (2015: 255) (summarizing Parkinson's statement).

45. Judge (2016: 900–03).

46. FCIC (2011: 328–29) (quoting and summarizing emails to and from Parkinson).

47. Judge (2016: 899–900); Valukas (2010: 5–10). Lehman did not disclose its use of Repo 105 transactions to government regulators before it failed. Valukas (2010: 5–8, 8n27, 17–21).

48. Judge (2016: 894–903, 913–16); see also Sarin (2019: 13–33).

49. Bair (2012: 80–84); Engel & McCoy (2011: 94); Geithner (2014: 168–69).

50. FCIC (2011: 310–11); Frame et al. (2015: 31–32). The third-largest source of mortgage funding after the private-label RMBS market collapsed was the Government National Mortgage Association (Ginnie Mae), a federal government agency that guaranteed mortgages issued by the Federal Housing Authority and the Veterans Administration. Engel & McCoy (2011: 136); FCIC (2011: 38–39).

51. FCIC (2011: 182–83, 310–12); Ferguson & Johnson (2009: 7, 12); Frame et al. (2015: 32); McLean & Nocera (2010: 342–43); Paulson (2010: 127–28).

52. Engel & McCoy (2011: 91–95); FCIC (2011: 180–87, 311–16); Frame et al. (2015: 32–33); Geithner (2015: 170).

53. Engel & McCoy (2011: 93–95) (quoting Paulson's testimony before the Senate Banking Committee on July 15, 2008); FCIC (2011: 316–17) (same); Paulson (2010: 142–56) (quotes on 153).

54. Bernanke (2015: 230–41, 244–45); Engel & McCoy (2011: 99–100); FCIC (2011: 317–19); Paulson (2010: 156–61).

55. Bernanke (2015: 245–47); FCIC (2011: 319–21); Frame et al. (2015: 38–39, 47); Paulson (2010: 167–70).

56. Bernanke (2015: 271, 371–72) (quote on 271); FCIC (2011: 321) (quoting interview with Paulson); Ferguson & Johnson (2009: 17–18); Frame et al. (2015: 42–44, 47); Paulson (2010: 159–70).

57. FCIC (2011: 321) (quoting interviews with former Treasury Assistant Secretary Neel Kashkari and Fed Governor Kevin Warsh); Paulson (2010: 173).

58. Morgenson & Rosner (2011); Wallison (2015).

59. FCIC (2011: 178–82); Frame et al. (2015: 28–31); Thomas (2009: 8–15).

60. FCIC (2011: 178–80); Levitin & Wachter (2012: 1189–94); McLean & Nocera (2010: 181–83); Thomas (2009: 18–19).

61. FCIC (2011: 68–72, 88–93, 104–18, 180–83); Levitin & Wachter (2012: 1189–210); McLean & Nocera (2010: 180–86, 211–30); Thomas (2009: 7–13, 18–19, 24–25). See Chapter 10 for discussion of the dominant roles that large banks and securities firms played in the non-prime mortgage market and the private-label RMBS market.

62. FCIC (2011: 217–19); Thomas (2009: 22–23).

63. FCIC (2011: 122–25); Frame et al. (2015: 30–31); Thomas (2009: 15–17). See FHFA (2017: 61, 61n36; 2018: 45) (describing FHFA's successful claims on behalf of Fannie and Freddie against eighteen leading underwriters of private-label RMBS for violations of federal and state securities laws).

64. Zandi & deRitis (2013: 5 [table 1]).

65. Engel & McCoy (2011); Levitin & Wachter (2012). In Oct. 2008, Alan Greenspan told the House Oversight Committee that Wall Street underwriters of private-label RMBS were primarily responsible for the subprime mortgage crisis because they "pressured lenders to lower their standards and produce more 'paper.'" Greenspan said that without the demand created by Wall Street underwriters, the volume of subprime mortgage originations "would have been far smaller and defaults accordingly far lower." Andrews (2008) (quoting and paraphrasing Greenspan's testimony on Oct. 23, 2008).

66. As shown in Chapter 10, note 5, thirteen of the Big Seventeen financial conglomerates—all *except* BNP Paribas, HSBC, Société Générale, and Wachovia—ranked among the top eighteen underwriters for *both* private-label RMBS *and* CDOs. The largest losses from CDOs were suffered by three CDO underwriters that retained significant exposures to super-senior tranches of CDOs (Citigroup, Merrill Lynch, and UBS) and two insurance companies that provided financial guarantees for CDO tranches (AIG and Ambac). Benmelech & Dlugosz (2009: 15–16, 38 [table 9]) (providing information on losses from CDO investments as of 2009); Cordell, Feldberg, & Sass (2019: 16–17) (providing information on losses from CDO investments as of 2018); Cordell, Huang, & Williams (2012: 6, 27 [table 1]) (providing information on outstanding CDOs in 2007).

67. Ball (2018: 32–37. 81–92); Bernanke (2015: 254–59); FCIC (2011: 330–35); Geithner (2014: 175–78); Paulson (2010: 173–88); Valukas (2010: 9–11).

68. Bernanke (2015: 262–63); FCIC (2011: 333–34); Geithner (2014: 175); Hilsenrath, Solomon, & Paletta (2008); Paulson (2010: 181–83); Wessel (2009: 14–15) (quoting Paulson).

69. Paulson (2010: 185–86); see also Andrews & Anderson (2008); Geithner (2014: 178–79).

70. Wessel (2009: 16) (quoting Paulson and Geithner).

71. FCIC (2011: 334–35); Geithner (2014: 180–82) Paulson (2010: 191–93); Wessel (2009: 16–17) (quoting Paulson and Geithner).

72. Paulson (2010: 197–206, 210, 219–20); see also FCIC (2011: 335); Geithner (2014: 182–85).

73. FCIC (2011: 335–37); Geithner (2014: 185–87) (quoting Paulson's paraphrase of Darling's comment); Paulson (2010: 207–10); see also Bernanke (2015: 265–67).

74. FCIC (2011: 336–37) (quoting email from Wilkinson to JPMC executive Jes Staley); see also Bernanke (2015: 266–68); Geithner (2014: 180–87); Paulson (2010: 197, 208–14); Wessel (2009: 20–21).

75. Bernanke (2015: 268–69); Geithner (2014: 187–88); Paulson (2010: 218).

76. Ball (2018: 145–64); FCIC (2011: 337); Sorkin (2009: 355).

77. Ball (2018: 145–51); Blinder (2013: 168); FCIC (2011: 330, 337–40); Fleming & Sarkar (2014: 175–79); Sorkin (2009: 355–59, 366–69).

78. Bernanke (2008c).

79. Paulson (2010: 187); Wessel (2009: 11).

80. Swagel (2015: 112).

81. Andrews & Anderson (2008).

82. Sorkin (2009: 373–74) (paraphrasing and quoting Paulson's comments to Bush).

83. Labaton (2008b).

84. Andrew & Anderson (2008) (quoting Hintz); Bernanke (2015: 265–66) (quoting Trichet).

85. Sorkin (2009: 356–59) (quoting Miller, Baxter, and Beller); see also FCIC (2011: 338) (quoting part of Miller's warning and paraphrasing Baxter's response to Miller).

86. Blinder (2013: 128); Wessel (2009: 23) (quoting Blinder).

87. Tett (2009: 239 (quoting Lagarde); Wessel (2009: 22) (same).

88. Eichengreen (2015: 196–97, 202). See Chapters 5 and 6 for discussion of Union Guardian's failure in Feb. 1933 and its role in precipitating a nationwide banking panic.

89. Bernanke (2015: 270–71); Eichengreen (2015: 201–02); FCIC (2011: 349); Geithner (2014: 190–91); Labaton (2008b).

90. Paulson (2010: 223–28) (describing telephone call from Ken Brody).

91. Labaton (2008b); Paulson (2010: 227–28) (quoting Paulson's statement to Immelt).

92. Engel & McCoy (2011: 73–74, 104); FCIC (2011: 265–74, 344–45); McDonald & Paulson (2015: 82–95). In its securities lending deals, AIG provided corporate bonds as collateral and invested the loan proceeds in riskier and more illiquid securities. About two-thirds of those securities were private-label RMBS, CDOs, and other mortgage-related securities. McDonald & Paulson (2015: 84–87).

93. FCIC (2011: 346–47) (quoting message from Kevin Coffey); Geithner (2014: 176).

94. FCIC (2011: 347–48) (quoting messages from Boesky and LaTorre); Geithner (2014: 181).

95. Bernanke (2015: 274–77); FCIC (2011: 348–49); Geithner (2014: 191–93); Sorkin (2009: 330, 364, 380–91).

96. Paulson (2010: 230–31); Swagel (2015: 113); see also Wessel (2009: 189) (stating that Lehman's bankruptcy was "messier than anyone had contemplated").

97. Paulson (2010: 233–34); Swagel (2015: 112–13); Swagel (2009: 40–41); Wessel (2009: 206–08); see also Geithner (2014: 195–96) (stating that "money market funds were widely viewed as virtually indistinguishable from bank deposits as similarly safe vehicles for storing cash with slightly better interest rates").

98. Paulson (2010: 233–35) (describing telephone call from Bill Osborn, chairman of Northern Trust Co.); Swagel (2015: 112–13); Swagel (2009: 40–41); Nocera & Andrews (2008) (quoting Rosner); Wessel (2009: 206–08).

99. Geithner (2014: 194–97) (quotes on 194, 197); Paulson (2010: 234–41) (quoting Bush at 235); see also Bernanke (2015: 279–85); Dash & Sorkin (2008); McDonald & Paulson (2015: 89) (stating that $13.3 billion of the Fed's $85 billion loan was used to recapitalize AIG's life insurance subsidiaries); Wessel (2009: 189–97).

100. Andrews, de la Merced, & Walsh (2008).

101. Ball (2018: 121–44); Bernanke (2015: 281–83, 287–91); Geithner (2014: 187, 192–93); Nocera & Andrews (2008) (quoting Paulson's claim that "we didn't have the powers" to save Lehman); Paulson (2010: 209).

102. FCIC (2011: 340–42); Nocera & Andrews (2008); Stewart & Eavis (2014).

103. Ball (2018: 121–41); FCIC (2011: 340–41); Stewart & Eavis (2014).

104. Ball (2018: 95–111); Stewart & Eavis (2014) (describing unpublished assessments of Lehman's assets and liabilities by two teams of New York Fed staff members).

105. Dash & Sorkin (2008).

106. Bernanke (2015: 364–68, 421–22); Geithner (2014: 227–28, 245–46, 315); Swagel (2009: 42).

107. Paulson (2010: 393–94) (quoting Bush and Jim Lambright).

108. Ball (2018: 177, 185–89); Stewart (2014) (quoting Geithner's testimony in a lawsuit filed by former AIG chairman Maurice "Hank" Greenberg, in which Greenberg claimed damages for the federal government's allegedly unlawful takeover of AIG).

109. McDonald & Paulson (2015: 103).

110. FCIC (2011: 347–48); McDonald & Paulson (2015: 85, 91).

111. FCIC (2011: 376–79); see also Bernanke (2015: 365–67) ("we were pilloried by Congress and the media for conducting 'backdoor bailouts'"); Geithner (2014: 246–48) ("our failure to impose haircuts on AIG's counterparties would become Exhibit A for the populist outrage and critique of our crisis response").

112. Paulson (2010: 131–32 [stating that in Apr. 2008, "the state of the markets was not yet so dire, nor was Congress anywhere near ready to consider granting us [the] powers" provided by the subsequent TARP legislation], 139–55 [describing Congress's reluctance

to grant additional powers during the summer of 2008]); Wessel (2009: 176–80, 205–06) ("Bernanke and Paulson agreed that there was no point offering Congress a plan so far-reaching unless the crisis was so severe that Congress would see no other option"); Swagel (2015: 111–12) (describing Treasury's belief that Congress would not grant TARP-like powers until "a broader market crisis . . . actually arose").

113. Geithner (2014: 192 [summarizing and quoting Rep. Frank's telephone call], 201 [explaining Geithner's views]).

114. Paulson (2010: 244–45); Sorkin (2009: 419–20).

115. Paulson (2010: 244–45 [quotes], 255–61, 265–68); Bernanke (2015: 291 [quote], 302–07, 312–13); see also Wessel (2009: 26, 279n) (quoting Bernanke's statement that "if Lehman hadn't failed, the public would not have seen the resulting damage and the story line would have been that [TARP] was unnecessary").

116. Nocera (2009).

117. Bernanke (2015: 332–35); Paulson (2010: 317–28).

118. Blinder (2013: 145–46); see also Paulson (2010: 252–53, 262–63); Swagel (2009: 43–44) (describing Treasury's reliance on the ESF as a "drastic" step).

119. Paulson (2010: 263).

120. Blinder (2013: 147–48) (describing the Fed's Asset-Backed Commercial Paper Money Market Mutual Fund Liquidity Facility); Logan, Nelson, & Parkinson (2018: 9–11) (same).

121. Blinder (2013: 148–49); Logan, Nelson, & Parkinson (2018: 12–14); Swagel (2015: 114) (quote).

122. Pozsar et al. (2010: 61–64); Ricks (2016: 96–101); see also Nersisyan (2015).

123. Logan, Nelson, & Parkinson (2018: 14–19) (discussing the Fed's Term Asset-Backed Securities Loan Facility).

124. FCIC (2011: 360–62); Geithner (2014: 203–04); Paulson (2010: 264, 269, 271) (quoting Blankfein); Sorkin (2009: 427–28, 442–48).

125. Better Markets (2018) (quoting email message from Silva to Christine Cummings).

126. FCIC (2011: 362–63) (quoting Mack); Wessel (2009: 217–18) (quote); see also Bernanke (2015: 310–11); Geithner (2014: 204–06).

127. Bair (2012: 84–94); FCIC (2011: 306–07, 365–66); Geithner (2014: 213–16); see also Blinder (2013: 155–57). See Chapter 8 for discussion of the "systemic risk exception" in the Federal Deposit Insurance Act.

128. FCIC (2011: 366–71) (describing IRS Notice 2008-83 [repealed by Congress in 2009], which "encourage[d] strong banks to acquire weak banks by removing limitations on the use of tax losses"); see also Bair (2012: 95–105); Bernanke (2015: 327–32); Blinder (2013: 157–61); Geithner (2014: 217–24).

129. Blinder (2013: 161).

130. Geithner (2014: 219).

131. Paulson (2010: 339, 343, 349–50); see also Bernanke (2015: 346–52); Wessel (2009: 231–36).

132. Bair (2012: 110–12); Bernanke (2015: 240–41); Blinder (2013: 161–62); Paulson (2010: 340–41).

133. Bair (2012: 112–14); Bernanke (2015: 241–43); Geithner (2015: 232–34).

134. Swagel (2009: 51–53); see also Paulson (2010: 170, 358–64).

135. Swagel (2009: 53–54); Paulson (2010: 363–67). When Kovacevich balked at accepting $25 billion of TARP capital, Geithner and Paulson warned him that Wells Fargo could later become undercapitalized, due to problems from its acquisition of Wachovia, and Wells would then find it very difficult to raise new capital. Paulson also told Kovacevich that any future capital investments from the government would carry much tougher terms. Kovacevich ultimately agreed to sell $25 billion of preferred stock to Treasury. Geithner (2014: 238–39); Paulson (2010: 364–65); Sorkin (2009: 525).

136. Sorkin (2009: 485–87); Paulson (2010: 284).

137. Wilmarth (2012b: 5, 20n40) (discussing four studies showing that the eight largest U.S. banks and their shareholders received more than $100 billion of gains from TARP capital infusions and FDIC debt guarantees); see also Wilmarth (2015a: 263n29) (describing additional studies confirming that the largest U.S. banks received substantial benefits from the federal government's financial rescue programs).

138. FCIC (2011: 353–54) (quoting interviews with Bernanke and Geithner). In Feb. 2009, Geithner and Lawrence Summers sent President Obama a memo stating that JPMC was the only top-four bank that was not "in distress," and there was a "significant chance" that the government would have to take control of Citigroup and BofA. Geithner (2014: 308–09).

139. Bernanke (2015: 352–54); Geithner (2014: 235–39); Paulson (2010: 362–67); Swagel (2009: 51–54).

140. Bair (2012: 121–26); FCIC (2011: 379–82); Paulson (2010: 402–14); Wilmarth (2014: 110–12) (explaining that Citigroup's guaranteed asset pool was subsequently modified by removing the CDO assets, reducing the amount of corporate loans, and increasing the amount of residential mortgages).

141. Bair (2012: 165–68); Wilmarth (2014: 110–13) (stating that Citigroup recorded $130 billion of losses and write-downs between June 2007 and Mar. 2010, including $25 billion of losses in Jan. 2009).

142. In May 2009, BofA decided not to activate its asset guarantee, and it paid $425 million to compensate the three federal agencies for the risks they assumed under the terms of the second bailout. Bair (2012: 126–28); Bernanke (2015: 373–76); FCIC (2011: 382–86); Paulson (2010: 425–32). BofA recorded $97 billion of losses and write-downs between June 2007 and Mar. 2010. Acharya, Kulkarni, & Richardson (2011: 147 [table 6.1]).

143. Bernanke (2015: 363, 404–07); Blinder (2013: 19–22); Geithner (2014: 276–77).

144. Geithner (2014: 286–92); see also Clark, Kabaker, & Sachs (2018: 5–6, 11–15).

145. Blinder (2013: 257–58) (quoting Geithner).

146. Federal Reserve Board (2009) (joint statement of the Fed, FDIC, OCC, OTS, and Treasury).

147. Wilmarth (2015a: 261); see also Geithner (2014: 309).

148. Clark, Kabaker, & Sachs (2018: 14–15).

149. Geithner (2014: 312–14).

150. Bair (2012: 159–61); Bernanke (2015: 395–97);

151. Geithner (2014: 369) (graph); Wilmarth (2015a: 261–63); Wilmarth (2013: 1345–46); see also Keoun & Kuntz (2011) (describing the Fed's emergency loan programs). A majority of the Fed's liquidity assistance under TAF was provided to European banks. Gorton, Laarits, & Metrick (2018: 4).

152. Carlson & Macchiavelli (2018); Gorton, Laarits, & Metrick (2018: 3–8, 14 [table 2]).

153. Wilmarth (2015a: 260–62); see also Felkerson (2011: 31–33) (showing that the top four-teen recipients of the Fed's emergency lending programs were Citigroup, Merrill Lynch, Morgan Stanley, AIG, Barclays, BofA, BNP Paribas, Goldman Sachs, Bear Stearns, Credit Suisse, Deutsche Bank, RBS, JPMC, and UBS); Keoun & Kuntz (2011).

154. Wilmarth (2011a: 977–78).

155. Wilmarth (2015a: 261–62, 269–76) (commenting that Citigroup and BofA received "confidential memoranda of understanding" instead of public enforcement orders); Wilmarth (2013: 1346–47, 1346n289) (citing congressional testimony by Marc Jarsulic, stating that the tangible common equity ratios for BofA and Citigroup at the end of 2008 were only 2.8% and 1.3%, which would have warranted public prompt corrective action orders).

156. Clark, Kabaker, & Sachs (2018: 6–8).

157. Geithner (2015: 300–03, 376–84); Liang, McConnell, & Swagel (2018: 15); Paulson (2010: 376–79, 396–99, 406, 419–20); SIGTARP (2016: 98–106).

158. For a highly critical evaluation of HAMP, see SIGTARP (2016: 98–132); see also Blinder (2013: 335–36); Mian & Sufi (2014: 133–42).

159. Calem et al. (2018: 8–13, 38 [table 1]).

160. Ibid., 2, 4–5, 24, 27, 29 (finding that modified mortgages had a significantly higher likeli-hood of avoiding redefaults if they included substantial principal reductions, and citing other studies reaching the same conclusion).

161. Mian & Sufi (2014: 19–71); Piskorski & Seru (2018); see also Gittelsohn (2015) (stating that four million short sales, deeds in lieu of foreclosure, and other distressed home sales occurred between 2007 and 2015); Vandevelde et al. (2018) (reporting that 7.8 million foreclosures were completed between 2007 and 2016).

162. Bair (2012: 67–71, 131–53); Blinder (2013: 320–42); Mian & Sufi (2014: 133–42, 146–48); see also Wilmarth (2013: 1351–59).

163. Bair (2012: 131–53); Blinder (2013: 322–23, 329–36); Engel & McCoy (2011: 133); FCIC (2011: 406); Geithner (2014: 300–03, 376–84); Wilmarth (2013: 1356–59).

164. Bair (2012: 242–56); Geithner (2014: 286–92, 300–03, 309–14, 376–84); Mian & Sufi (2014: 133–42); Schreiber (2011: 236–42); Tooze (2018: 281–82, 305–07); Wilmarth (2013: 1351–59); Wilmarth (2015: 272–73); see also Blinder (2013: 320–42) (criticizing the Obama administration's unwillingness to create a large-scale principal reduction program for "underwater" homeowners, and noting the effectiveness of the New Deal's Home Owners' Loan Corporation, which prevented foreclosures by refinancing over 1 million mortgages during the 1930s); Fishback (2016: 3–4, 46–47, 56–59) (describing the HOLC's strong record of preventing home foreclosures during the 1930s).

165. Bernanke (2015: 406 [figure 2]); Blinder (2013: 223–26, 232–34); Geithner (2014: 318, 336).

166. Bernanke (2015: 377–39, 420–21, 490–92, 531–33, 565–66); Blinder (2013: 207, 251–52, 368–72); Kuttner (2018: 121–25); Wilmarth (2015a: 265–66).

167. Eisinger (2011); Feldstein (2018: 416–17); Kuttner (2018: 127–40); Huszar (2013); Wilmarth (2015a: 266–67).

168. Authers & Fox (2018); Feldstein (2018: 417–19); Tooze (2018: 156–57, 451–63, 472–75); Webb (2018a, 2018b).

169. Kuhn, Schularick, & Steins (2018: 21–22, 29–30); Wolff (2017: 2, 7–14, 36–39).

170. Brainard (2019a: 2, figure 1).

171. Dell'Ariccia, Rabanal, & Sandri (2018); Huszar (2013); Kuttner (2018).

172. Authers & Fox (2018); Fletcher (2019a); Giles & Jones (2018); Taylor (2018); Tucker (2018a: 527–37); Webb (2018b).

173. Blinder (2013: 170, 411–12); Eichengreen (2015: 354–59); Geithner (2014: 227, 446–50); Millaruelo & Del-Rio (2017: 5 [table 1]); Tooze (2018: 185–86, 322–23, 359–66); Véron (2018: 4–9); Woll (2014: 143–47, 152–63).

174. Millaruelo & Del-Rio (2017: 3–4, 5 [table 1]); Tooze (2018: 185–95).

175. Blinder (2013: 170); Fraser (2014: 320–36, 349–52, 389–90); Tooze (2018: 189–91); Turner (2014: 48–49, 54–55, 93–100); Woll (2014: 86–88, 91–94, 102–10); see also McCauley (2018: 49) [table 4]) (showing that RBS held $84 billion of nonprime mortgage-backed securities on its balance sheet at the end of 2007).

176. In 1985, David Willetts, a policy adviser to Prime Minister Margaret Thatcher, warned that the "Big Bang" reforms—which allowed banks to acquire securities brokers and dealers in 1986—could lead to "fraud" and "unethical behavior" in Britain's financial markets. Pickard & Thompson (2014). See Chapter 5 for discussion of Britain's ability to avoid bailouts of its major commercial banks during the early 1930s as a result of the structural separation between those banks and London's securities markets. See Chapter 8 for discussion of Britain's "Big Bang" reforms in 1986.

177. Eichengreen (2015: 213–15); IMF (2014: 25–30, 36–37); Tooze (2018: 154–55, 167, 193–95, 215); Woll (2014: 113–16, 119–21, 127–36); see also Carbó-Valverde, Cuadros-Solas, & Rodriguez-Fernández (2019: 47 [appendix B, table B]) (listing capital infusions provided by European governments to thirty large European banks).

178. See Chapter 5 for discussion of the central roles played by large universal banks in the European banking crises of the early 1930s.

179. Adamczyk & Windisch (2015: 1); Millaruelo & Del-Rio (2017: 5 [table 1], 7–11); see also Laeven & Valencia (2018: 34–38 [table 2]).

180. Blinder (2013: 424–25); Geithner (2014: 235–36, 443, 477); Hale (2016a, 2018); Tooze (2018: 207–19, 285–86, 420–21).

181. Blinder (2013: 410–28); Brunnermeier & Reis (2019: 8–10, 13, 29–36); Eichengreen (2015: 341–76); Geithner (2014: 441–50, 472–77, 481–85); Tooze (2018: 322–45, 396–446).

182. Brunsden & Khan (2018); Frayer (2014); Hall & Hope (2020); Inman (2018). The four EU nations could not devalue their currencies to mitigate the impact of their banking and sovereign debt crises. Their membership in the Eurozone locked them into a single-currency, fixed-exchange-rate regime with deflationary effects similar to the interwar gold exchange standard. Eichengreen (2015: 11–13, 89–100, 337–87).

183. Authers & Fox (2018); Curran & Miller (2019); Darrah (2018); Dell'Ariccia, Rabanal, & Sandri (2018); Gros, Alcidi, & De Groen (2015); Haldane et al. (2016); Lewis & Dunkley (2018); Sternberg (2019); Webb (2018a).

184. Romei & Arnold (2019) (quoting Christian Odendahl).

185. Blinder (2013: 10–12, 354–55); Fox News (2012); Geithner (2014: 495); Liang, McConnell, & Swagel (2018: 3); Kuttner (2018: 138).

186. "United Kingdom Unemployment Rate, 1971–2019," available at https://tradingeconomics.com/united-kingdom/unemployment-rate; "Euro Area Unemployment Rate, 1995–2019," available at https://tradingeconomics.com/euro-area/unemployment-rate.

187. Dell'Arriccia, Rabanal, & Sandri (2018: 148 [figure 1, panel A]), 153–56, 160–61). In 2018, GDP for Italy and Greece remained below their pre-crisis levels. Wise (2018).

188. Romei (2019).

189. Romei & Arnold (2019).

190. "Federal Debt: Total Public Debt as Percent of Gross Domestic Product," available at https://fred.stlouisfed.org/series/GFDEGDQ188S; "United Kingdom Public Sector Debt to GDP, 1995–2019," available at https://tradingeconomics.com/united-kingdom/government-debt-to-gdp; "Euro Area Government Debt to GDP, 1995–2019," available at https://tradingeconomics.com/euro-area/government-debt-to-gdp.

191. Atkinson, Luttrell, & Rosenblum (2013: 3–9, 19); Barnichon, Matthes, & Ziegenbein (2018); Better Markets (2015: 1–2, 97–98).

192. IMF-WEO (2018: 82, figure 2.11).

193. Barber (2018); Hall (2018, 2019); Mallet (2019); Mallet & Agnew (2019); Stephens (2018); Tooze (2018: 304–07, 352–53, 394–95, 458–70, 491–92, 538–58, 564–80); Viscusi (2018).

Chapter 12

1. G20 (2009a, 2009b, 2009c); see also Armour et al. (2016: 619–23); FSB (2018: 6); IMF-GFS (2018: 59); Tooze (2018: 269–70, 296–301); Wolf (2014: 224–25).

2. G20 (2009a: 14); see Wolf (2014: 232–34) (explaining that "the thrust [of the post-crisis reform agenda] has been to preserve the system that existed prior to the crisis").

3. Geithner (2014: 339–45, 390–400, 409–10); Tooze (2018: 293–301).

4. G20 (2009a: 3, 14).

5. Bhagwati (1998); Johnson & Kwak (2010: 39–46, 51–52); Stiglitz (2003: 215–31); see also Ngo & Diego (2020) (concluding, based on a study of 269 IMF loans to 47 developing countries between 1983 and 2016, that the IMF's loans frequently provided "de facto bailouts" to big U.S. banks and their shareholders).

6. G20 (2009a: 2 [¶8]).

7. Act of July 21, 2010, Pub. L. No. 111–203, 124 *Statutes at Large* 1376.

8. Geithner (2014: 263–64, 291–92, 319–27, 390–411, 419–29); Heckinger & Steigerwald (2011); Kaiser (2013: 90–94, 129–30, 374–75); Schreiber (2011: 171–75, 228–30); Suskind (2011: 233–42, 280–82, 290–92, 303–05, 311–12, 428–33, 437–40).

9. Kaiser (2013: 90–91, 129–33); see also Suskind (2011: 233–42, 280–92, 311–12); Wilmarth (2013: 1359–69), and Chapters 8 and 9 for discussions of the enormous political influence wielded by the financial sector after the repeal of Glass-Steagall.

10. FSOC is chaired by the Treasury Secretary and includes nine other voting members: the Comptroller of the Currency; the Directors of the Consumer Financial Protection Bureau and the Federal Housing Finance Agency; the Chairmen of the Commodity Futures Trading Commission, FDIC, Fed, National Credit Union Administration, and Securities and Exchange Commission; and an independent member with insurance expertise. The FSOC also includes five nonvoting members: the Directors of the Federal Insurance Office and the Office of Financial Research as well as three state regulators of insurance, banking, and securities. Dodd-Frank §111 (codified at 12 U.S.C. §5321).

11. Dodd-Frank §§113, 120, 165 (codified at 12 U.S.C. §§5323, 5330, 5365). For discussions of Dodd-Frank's provisions governing large banks and nonbank SIFIs, see Metrick &

Rhee (2018: 156, 165–66); Wilmarth (2011a: 1006–09). Dodd-Frank originally provided that banks larger than $50 billion would be subject to enhanced supervision and regulation by the Fed. Congress raised that asset threshold to $250 billion in 2018. Richardson, Schoenholtz, & White (2018: 204–06); Sullivan & Cromwell (2018: 2–3). In Oct. 2019, the Fed eliminated resolution planning (living will) requirements for U.S. banks smaller than $250 billion and significantly relaxed those requirements for banks with assets between $250 billion and $700 billion. Brainard (2019c).

12. Dodd-Frank §203 (codified at 12 U.S.C. §5383). For discussions of OLA, see Metrick & Rhee (2018: 166–67); Wilmarth (2011a: 993–97).

13. Barr, Jackson, & Tahyar (2018: 1175–204). Under Title VII, the SEC regulates "security-based swaps" and the CFTC regulates other types of swaps (which represent about 90% of the total swaps market). Ibid., 1177–79; see also Baker (2016: 14–16).

14. Dodd-Frank §956(b). See Wilmarth (2015a: 363–68).

15. Barr, Jackson & Tahyar (2018: 1125–27, 1147–51); Vandevelde (2018); U.S. Senate (2010: 38–39).

16. Bar-Gill & Warren (2008); Geithner (2014: 403, 423, 427); Kaiser (2013: 112–15, 133–37, 222–25, 339, 343–44, 377–79); Suskind (2011: 4–6, 77–81, 343–45, 439–40); Wilmarth (2012a: 886–89, 926–40); U.S. Senate (2010: 9–23, 161–74). See Chapters 9 and 10 for discussion of regulatory failures by federal banking agencies during the 1990s and 2000s.

17. The Brown-Kaufman amendment would have imposed (i) a size cap on banks equal to 10% of nationwide deposits (about $750 billion), and (ii) a size limit on non-deposit liabilities equal to 2% of GDP for banks and 3% of GDP for nonbanks. Schreiber (2011: 225–28); Wilmarth (2011a: 1055, 1055n454).

18. Schreiber (2011: 225–28); Suskind (2011: 428–29).

19. Suskind (2011: 144–45, 287–90, 341–43, 349–50, 396–97); U.S. Senate (2010: 90–92).

20. Schreiber (2011: 212–15); Suskind (2011: 341–42, 349–50, 396–97); Wilmarth (2011a: 1025, 1025n317).

21. Bair (2012: 222, 227); Fletcher (2014: 860–62); Kaiser (2013: 310–13, 339–42); Schreiber (2011: 213–15, 223, 229, 244); Suskind (2011: 430–33, 438–39); Wilmarth (2011a: 1025–30). See notes 65–67 in this chapter and accompanying text for further discussion of the Volcker Rule's three major exceptions.

22. GAO (2017: 9–13, 19–22); Geithner (2014: 419–20, 423); Kaiser (2013: 292–97, 344–51); Schreiber (2011: 216–24); Suskind (2011: 398–400, 413, 430–32, 438–39); Wilmarth (2011a: 1030–34).

23. Bair (2012: 185, 196–99); Wilmarth (2011a: 1015–16).

24. Bair (2012: 214–19); see also Geithner (2014: 409, 422–23); Kaiser (2013: 206–08, 268–72); Wilmarth (2011a: 1015–22). See notes 91–92 and accompanying text later in this chapter for further discussion of the consequences of Congress' decision to allow the OLF to operate without any pre-funding, so that it will have a zero balance when a failed SIFI is placed in a future OLA receivership.

25. Armour et al. (2016: 299–307); Gerding (2016: 367–79); IMF-GFS (2018: 59–65); Sironi (2018: 10–15); see also Barr, Jackson, & Tahyar (2018: 321–25) (explaining that (i) common equity Tier 1 capital consists of common stock and retained earnings, and (ii) Basel III's capital conservation buffer limits the ability of banks to pay dividends or repurchase their stock).

26. FSB (2019b) (also listing four Chinese banks, three Japanese banks, and two Canadian banks as G-SIBs). The eight U.S. G-SIBs are BofA, Bank of New York Mellon, Citigroup, Goldman Sachs, JPMC, Morgan Stanley, State Street, and Wells Fargo.

27. Armour et al. (2016: 305–09); Barr, Jackson & Tahyar (2018: 324–27); FSB (2019a); Sironi (2018: 26–29).

28. Barr, Jackson, & Tahyar (2018: 326–27); BIS (2017: 140–42).

29. Armour et al. (2016: 304–09); Binham (2018); Keohane (2019); see also Hamilton (2018) (reporting that Norway and Sweden required countercyclical buffers); Sironi (2018: 16) (stating that the Czech Republic, Iceland, and Slovakia also imposed such buffers).

30. Acharya, Kulkarni, & Richardson (2011: 144–58); Admati & Hellwig (2013); Armour et al. (2016: 304–14); Haldane & Madouros (2012); Hoenig (2016); Vickers (2018: 2–4).

31. Passmore & von Hafften (2017).

32. Admati & Hellwig (2013: 176–91); Egan, Hortaçsu, & Matvos (2017: 203–06); FT letter from 20 scholars (2010); Jordà et al. (2017: 23–31); Minneapolis Fed (2017: 88–99).

33. Basel Committee (2017: 1, 18–22) (stating that "the Committee has not reached a consensus to make any changes to the treatment of sovereign exposures," and the committee therefore issued the discussion paper for comment but did not initiate a formal consultation). For discussions of the "doom loop" linking heavily indebted nations and their undercapitalized banks, see Brunnermeier & Reis (2019: 21–22, 29–36); Cooper & Nikolov (2018: 4–9, 29–31); Haldane & Allesandri (2009); Theodore & Fischer (2018); van Riet (2018: 3–5).

34. Armour et al. (2016: 300–05); Begley, Purnanandam, & Zheng (2017) (quote at 3410); Gerding (2016: 375–81); Haldane & Madouros (2012: 6–8, 10–12); Sironi (2018: 22–25, 31–33); Vickers (2018: 2–4); see Chapter 9 for a discussion of how big banks used internal risk models to reduce their RWAs under Basel II.

35. Jenkins (2019a).

36. Armour et al. (2016: 304); Haldane & Madouros (2012: 15–16, 29 [chart 5]); Richardson, Schoenholtz, & White (2018: 204–06).

37. Admati & Hellwig (2013: 176–91); Haldane & Madouros (2012: 10–12, 15–16); Hoenig (2016).

38. IMF-GFS (2018: 61, 68 [figure 2.2, panels 3 and 4, and figure 2.6, panel 1]); see also Quarles (2018a) (stating that the leverage capital requirement for U.S. G-SIBs was "the primary capital constraint for some of the largest firms").

39. Adrian, Kiff, & Shin (2017: 2); FDIC (2017a).

40. Haldane & Madouros (2012: 15–16, 29 [chart 5]); Rocha (2018); see also the authorities cited in notes 32 and 36 in this chapter.

41. Basel Committee (2020: 4, 6, 8 [graphs 1, 3 & 5], 115, 126 [tables C.3 & C.16]); Federal Reserve Board (2018c: 14 [figures 10 and 11]); Federal Reserve Board (2019a: 30); Federal Reserve Board (2019b: 5, figure 6); Federal Reserve Board (2019c: 13 [figure 10]); FSOC (2018: 57 [chart 4.11.2]); FSOC (2019: 67–68 & accompanying charts); Gray & Jopson (2017); Kane (2018: 23–26, 41 [figure 8]); Kansas City Fed (2019); Sironi (2018: 38–40 [figures 1–3]); Whitehouse (2017, 2018).

42. Quarles (2018b); Clozel (2018b) (quoting Jaret Seiberg); Heltman (2019d).

43. Quarles (2018b).

44. Heltman (2019d) (quoting Tarullo).

45. Heltman (2019a) (quoting Powell's testimony on Feb. 26, 2019).

46. FSOC (2019: 68, chart 4.11.4); Sweet (2019).

47. Federal Reserve Board (2019b: 5, figure 6); FSOC (2019: 68, chart 4.11.4); Kansas City Fed (2019).

48. See "Aesop's Fable of the Ants and the Grasshopper," available at http://read.gov/aesop/052.html.

49. See Fleming (2018); Hamilton (2018); Heltman (2018b); Lang (2019b).

50. Brown (2019).

51. Barr, Jackson, & Tahyar (2018: 327–29).

52. Basel Committee (2020: 14 [graph 11], 174 [table C.87]); Federal Reserve Board (2018c: 15 [figure 12]); Federal Reserve Board (2019b: 20 [figure 10]); Federal Reserve Board (2019c: 14 [figure 12]); FSB (2018: 3 [graph], 9–10); FSOC (2018: 61 [chart 4.11.13]); Sironi (2018: 42 [figure 6]).

53. Brainard (2019c); Heltman (2019e).

54. Admati (2014: 538–40, 544–57); Admati & Hellwig (2013: 169–207); Gerding (2016: 365–78); Haldane & Madouros (2012); Hoenig (2016); Kress (2019a: 210–11); Skeel (2011: 82–84); Wilmarth (2011a: 1009–15); see also notes 30–40 and accompanying text earlier in this chapter.

55. Coffee (2012: 1029–37); Gerding (2014: 137–79); see also Wolf (2019b) ("Over time, [financial] regulation degrades, as the forces against it strengthen and those in its favour corrode").

56. IMF-GFS (2018: 74).

57. Noonan (2019) (quoting BaFin president Felix Hufeld, and paraphrasing and quoting remarks by Dugan and top executives of Société Générale and Santander at the IIF annual meeting).

58. FSOC (2018: 104); Kelleher (2018: 6–9); Kress, McCoy, & Schwarcz (2019).

59. Kress, McCoy, & Schwarcz (2019); Schwarcz & Schwarcz (2014); Schwarcz & Zaring (2017); Tuch (2017: 362–73); see also Heltman (2019b) (describing FSOC's proposed new guidance for dealing with designations of nonbank SIFIs).

60. Blackwell (2014); GAO (2017: 9–27) (describing the 2014 provision that effectively repealed the Lincoln Amendment, 12 U.S.C. §8305); Wilmarth (2015a: 329–32, 350–52). See Chapter 8 for discussion of the lower costs of funding for banks (compared with their nonbank affiliates), due to the greater availability of federal safety net subsidies for banks in the form of FDIC insurance, Fed discount window loans, and Fed guarantees of payments made on Fedwire.

61. Gandré et al. (2019); Levinson (2015b).

62. FDIC Director and former Chairman Martin J. Gruenberg and Fed Governor Lael Brainard—both Obama appointees—voted against the proposed rule to repeal the affiliate margin requirement. Brainard (2019c); Gruenberg (2019b).

63. Federal Reserve Board (2018a: 3–12); Brainard (2019c); Sullivan & Cromwell (2018) (describing the Economic Growth, Regulatory Relief, and Consumer Protection Act, Public Law No. 115–174). See note 53 and accompanying text earlier in this chapter for discussion of the Fed's reduction of LCR requirements for large banks other than G-SIBs.

64. Wilmarth (2018); see also Chapters 10 and 11 for descriptions of the problems caused by the named institutions.

65. Cockburn (2018); Fletcher (2014: 861–62, 888–89); Wilmarth (2011a: 1025–30); Wilmarth (2015a: 323–29). See note 21 and accompanying text earlier in this chapter, discussing the Volcker Rule's exemptions for those three types of activities.

66. Bain & Hamilton (2018); Jopson & Wigglesworth (2018); Madison, Lewis, & Shirley (2018) (quoting the Treasury report).

67. Brainard (2019b) (concluding that the new regulations "substantially weaken the Volcker Rule" because they "materially reduce the scope of covered activity" and "excessively rely on firms' self-policing"); Gruenberg (2019a) (contending that the new regulations "no longer impose a meaningful constraint on speculative proprietary trading by banks and bank holding companies"); see also Fanger (2019) (quote from Moody's analyst); Rodriguez Valladares (2019d).

68. McCoy (2019: 2567–72); see also Wilmarth (2012a: 884–900) (describing previous attacks on the CFPB by the financial industry and its Republican supporters).

69. Brown (2018); Keefe (2018); McCoy (2019: 2574–2600); see also Peterson (2017) (describing the CFPB's vigorous enforcement record under Director Cordray).

70. Berry (2019a); Kelleher (2019); McCoy (2019: 2579); Weinberger (2018); Weinberger & Beyoud (2019).

71. Lazarus (2019); Berry (2019b); Willis (2019).

72. Bain & Hamilton (2017) (quoting Trump); Protess & Davis (2017) (same).

73. Hamilton (2019); Onaran (2018); Kelleher (2018: 5–6); Wooten (2019).

74. Anderson & Naylor (2018); Coffee (2012: 1067–72); Heltman (2018a, 2019c); Wilmarth (2015a: 323–40, 363–68); see Sections 166 and 956(b) of the Dodd-Frank Act, 124 *Statutes at Large* 1432, 1905.

75. FSB (2018: 6, 11–12); IMF-GFS (2018: 71–72). The declared purpose of the Dodd-Frank Act is "to end 'too big to fail' [and] to protect the American taxpayer by ending bailouts." 124 *Statutes at Large* 1376 (2010) (preamble).

76. Bank of England (2017); Barr, Jackson, & Tahyar (2018: 985–96); Gordon & Ringe (2015: 1305–10, 1341–48); Group of 30 (2018a: 9–11, 30–34); Metrick & Rhee (2018: 966–69); Véron (2018: 9–10); Wilmarth (2011a: 993–1000).

77. For discussions of the SPOE-TLAC strategy, see Armour et al. (2016: 363–65); Barr, Jackson, & Tahyar (2018: 999–1004); Gordon & Ringe (2015: 1310–30); Guynn (2014); Lubben & Wilmarth (2017: 1213–23); Tucker (2018b).

78. Armour et al. (2016: 361–65); Lubben & Wilmarth (2017: 1221–23, 1244–47). U.S. G-SIBs sold almost $700 billion of TLAC debt securities between 2015 and 2018. Boston (2019a).

79. Barr, Jackson, & Tahyar (2018: 1003) (quoting John Vickers and Thomas Hoenig); see also Admati & Hellwig (2013: 187–88, 316nn80–81); Hale (2016b); Hoenig (2016); Lubben & Wilmarth (2017: 1235–38, 1246–47); Minneapolis Fed (2017: 154–55) (quoting Neel Kashkari's op-ed dated Apr. 4, 2017).

80. Armour et al. (2016: 361); FSB (2018: 11); Lubben & Wilmarth (2017: 1231–32).

81. Tucker (2018b: 9–10); see also Group of 30 (2018a: 11–12).

82. Fortado & Noonan (2019); Lubben & Wilmarth (2017: 1232).

83. Hale (2019b); Tucker (2018b: 9–10, 13–14); Wilmarth (2015b: 63–64).

84. Wilmarth (2015b: 63–65 [quoting Persaud (2013)]); see also Hale (2019b) (questioning the assumption by regulators that bondholders will be "a less politically explosive cohort than taxpayers" if they are forced to bear large losses from bank failures); Minneapolis Fed (2017: 154–58) (quoting op-eds by Neel Kashkari dated Apr. 4 and July 9, 2017).

85. Hale (2019b); see also Hale (2016b); Weber & Chrysoloras (2019).

86. Goodhart & Avgouleas (2014: 30–32); Lubben & Wilmarth (2017: 1235–38); Tarullo (2019: 69).

87. Comfort & Glover (2018); Group of 30 (2018a: 12, 23); Hale (2016b); Lubben & Wilmarth (2017: 1235–38); Smith (2018); Tarullo (2019: 69); Weber (2017); Weber & Chrysoloras (2019).

88. Bowman (2017); Brunsden et al. (2017); Espinoza & Storbeck (2019); Weber & Chrysoloras (2019); see also Group of 30 (2018a: 12); Lubben & Wilmarth (2017: 1237–38); Minneapolis Fed (2017: 157–58) (reprinting op-ed by Neel Kashkari dated July 9, 2017).

89. Financial Times (2019b).

90. Lubben & Wilmarth (2017: 1226–29, 1233–35); see also Tucker (2018b: 5) (indicating that central banks should be prepared to "provid[e] liquidity assistance *post-resolution* to firms that have been restored to solvency and viability" through an SPOE transaction).

91. See notes 23–24 and accompanying text earlier in this chapter.

92. Bair (2012: 214–19, 226–28); Geithner (2014: 409, 422–23); Kaiser (2013: 277–83, 356–61); Labonte (2018: 28–29, 32); Wilmarth (2015a: 311–13, 358–63) (quoting 12 U.S.C. §5390(o)(1)(C).

93. Bolton & Oehmke (2018); Bright et al. (2016); Faia & Weder di Mauro (2015); Herring (2014); Wilmarth (2015b: 70–71); see also Tucker (2018b: 9) ("Where home and host authorities cannot agree on the terms of [an SPOE resolution], the [SIFI] would need to be broken up in some fashion or restructured into ring-fenced silos.").

94. IMF-GFS (2018: 72).

95. Group of 30 (2018a: 23).

96. Geithner (2017); Group of 30 (2018a: 22–23); Herring (2014: 879); Kashkari (2016); Tarullo (2019: 69–70); Wilmarth (2015a: 332–40); Wilmarth (2015b: 76–82).

97. Lubben & Wilmarth (2017); see also Minneapolis Fed (2017: 78–79) ("We believe this [SPOE-TLAC] proposal is fundamentally unsound and will not work in practice"). For more favorable assessments of SPOE-TLAC, see Guynn (2014) and Tucker (2018b).

98. Geithner (2014: 286–88, 291–92 [quote], 308–15, 338–39, 343); Minneapolis Fed (2017: 78–79) (quoting Neel Kashkari's speech on June 10, 2016); Kashkari (2016: 4–5); Wilmarth (2015a: 256–67, 319–23).

99. Casey & Posner (2015: 482–87, 522–23); Geithner (2014: 286–88, 291–92, 308–15, 338–39, 343); Labonte (2018: 9–11, 32–33); Levitin (2012: 437–43, 513–14); Mehrling (2012); Wilmarth (2015a: 319–23).

100. See Geithner (2017); Gorton (2018); Group of 30 (2018a: 24); Judge (2019); Mehrling (2012).

101. Judge (2019); Manns (2011); Mehrling (2012); Posner (2017). For critical responses to Professor Judge's proposal, see Cecchetti & Schoenholtz (2019); Ricks (2019); Steele (2019).

102. Bernanke, Geithner, & Paulson (2018): Bernanke, Geithner, & Paulson (2019: 111–12, 120–22, 127–28). See Chapter 11 for discussion of how U.S. agencies (under the leadership of Bernanke, Geithner, and Paulson) aggressively exercised their pre-Dodd-Frank authorities to rescue the entire financial system during 2008 and 2009.

103. Geithner (2014: 429–32, 515–16); Posner (2017: 1574); Wilmarth (2011a: 1001–03).

104. Bernanke, Geithner, & Paulson (2018) (quotes); Bernanke, Geithner, & Paulson (2019: 120–22, 127–28); Geithner (2017). For a critical response to their arguments, see Bair (2019). For discussion of the "360 [degree] backstop" that federal agencies provided for shadow banking liabilities during 2008–09, see Pozsar et al. (2010: 58–64) and Chapter 11.

105. Geithner (2017).

106. Wilmarth (2015b: 78, 64) (quoting Flint's testimony before a House of Lords subcommittee on Oct. 21, 2014) (emphasis added).

107. Haldane & Alessandri (2009); Johnson & Kwak (2010: 10–12, 133–34, 150–74, 178–82); Labonte (2018: 5, 33); Wilmarth (2015b: 64–65, 79–82); see also authorities cited in notes 98–105 in this chapter.

108. Acharya, Anginer, & Warburton (2011); Gandhi & Lustig (2015); GAO (2014: 40–54); Haldane (2010: 2–3, 16–17 [tables 2–4]); IMF-GFS (2014: chapter 3); Kelly, Lustig, & Van Nieuwerburgh (2016); Roe (2014: 1432–39, 1454–60); Santos (2014); see also Wilmarth (2015a: 256–67) (discussing additional studies and empirical data confirming the existence of TBTF subsidies for megabanks); Wilmarth (2011a: 980–86) (same).

109. Ensign (2018); Wilmarth (2015a: 258, 263); see also "Top Banks and Holding Companies" as of Dec. 31, 2018 (Federal Reserve Bank of Chicago), available at https://www.chicago-fed.org/banking/financial-institution-reports/top-banks-bhcs. Total assets held by the four largest U.S. megabanks—JPMC, BofA, Citigroup, and Wachovia in 2007, with Wells Fargo replacing Wachovia in 2008—increased from $6.2 trillion in 2007 to $8.7 trillion in 2017 and $8.8 trillion in 2018. Ibid; Kress (2019a: 185–87 & tables 3, 4). The reported total assets of the four biggest U.S. banks would be almost twice as large under international accounting standards. Those standards would require U.S. megabanks to include on their balance sheets many assets they sell to investors for securitization, and to report their derivatives exposures on a gross basis instead of netting exposures with counterparties. Onaran (2013); Wilmarth (2015a: 264); see also Levinson (2015a).

110. Turner (2014: 95–100, 167–70); Woll (2014: 105–08).

111. Arnold (2018); Goodhart & Schoenmaker (2016); McGeever (2017); Morris & Crow (2019); Morris & Noonan (2018); Robinson, Nguyen, & Onaran (2018); S&P Global (2018, 2019); Tuttle (2019).

112. Levitt (2018); Noonan (2018b); see also "League Tables," *Financial Times* (as of Sept. 25, 2019), available at https://markets.ft.com/data/league-tables/tables-and-trends (visited on Dec. 26, 2019) (showing that Wells Fargo ranked ninth among global banks for investment banking fees during the first nine months of 2019).

113. Arnold (2018); Crow (2019); Crow & Morris (2019); Morris & Crow (2019); Morris & Keohane (2019); Noonan (2018a); S&P Global (2018, 2019); Storbeck (2018); Weber (2019); see also "League Tables" cited in note 112 (showing that Barclays, Credit Suisse, Deutsche Bank, and HSBC were in the bottom half of the top ten global banks for investment banking fees during the first nine months of 2019).

114. Arnold (2018); Crow & Morris (2019); MacAskill & White (2017); Morris & Crow (2019); Noonan (2019); see Chapters 8–10 for discussions of the global dominance of the Big Seventeen financial conglomerates during the 2000s.

115. Awrey (2014: 202–04, 232–34); Baker (2016: 32–34); Chang (2016: 692–708); Dodds (2018); FSOC (2019: 61–62); Lubben (2016: 128, 141–42).

116. Chang (2016: 711–16); Story (2010); *In re Credit Default Swaps Antitrust Litigation*, 2014 WL 4379112 (S.D.N.Y. Sept. 4, 2014); *In re Interest Rate Swaps Antitrust Litigation*, 261 F. Supp. 3d. 430 (S.D.N.Y. 2017).

117. *In re Credit Default Swaps Antitrust Litigation*, 2016 WL 2731524, at *1–*2 (S.D.N.Y. Apr. 26, 2016).

118. Awrey (2014: 198–222, 232–43); G. Fletcher (2019: 116–28, 156–59).

119. Linsell (2018); R. Smith (2019a); see also Boston (2019b).

120. Alvarez & McPartland (2019: 11–19) (showing that Citigroup, JPMC, Morgan Stanley, Goldman Sachs, and BofA were the top five banks based on customer funds for centrally cleared derivatives in the U.S., while the next five banks were Société Générale, Credit Suisse, Barclays, Wells Fargo, and UBS); see also Baker (2016: 32–40); Basel Committees et al. (2018); Dodds (2018); Faruqui, Huang, & Takàts (2018); FSOC (2018: 53–56, 99, 107–08); IMF-GFS (2018: 74).

121. Baker (2016: 65–69); Dodds (2018); FSB (2018: 12); Duffie (2019: 96, 101–02); Lubben (2016: 145–56); Skeel (2017).

122. Culp (2013) (quotes at 63).

123. Ibid., 67–68; FSB (2019a: 24–34); FSOC (2018: 43–46, 72–74, 78–79); Pozsar et al. (2010: 47–52). See Chapters 7, 10, and 11 for discussions of the commercial paper and repo markets.

124. Fortado & Noonan (2019).

125. Hale (2019a) (citing "Statistical release: BIS international banking statistics at end-June 2019" [Oct. 24, 2019], available at https://www.bis.org/statistics/rppb1910.pdf).

126. Culp (2013); de Fontenay (2013: 155–57); FSB (2019a: 22–34, 73–78); FSOC (2019: 31–35); Gottfried (2019); Indap & Vandevelde (2018); Lee (2019); Tuch (2017: 340–50); Vandevelde (2018). In 2019, six leading U.S. private equity firms held over $500 billion of outstanding loans to businesses. Basak, Scigliuzzo, & Willmer (2019).

127. Chappatta (2018); Das (2018); FSB (2019a: 13–34); Henderson (2019); IMF-GFS (2019: chapter 1); Kuriloff (2019); R. Smith (2019b).

128. Armstrong & Wigglesworth (2019); FSOC (2019: 29–35, 121); Federal Reserve Board (2020: 7 [table D.3.]); IMF-GFS (2019: chapter 1); Rodriguez Valladares (2018, 2019c); Smith (2018).

129. New York Fed (2020) (reporting that U.S. household credit in Dec. 2019 was $14.1 trillion—$1.5 trillion higher than its peak level in 2008).

130. Federal Reserve Board (2020: 7 [table D.3]) (showing U.S. private sector debt levels); FRED-Government Debt (2019) (showing amounts of U.S. public sector obligations).

131. Chappatta (2018); Das (2018); IIF (2020); Kuriloff (2019); Wall Street Journal (2019); see also Wigglesworth (2019) (reporting that only eight of 37 nations managed to reduce their total debt-to-GDP ratios between 2007 and 2017).

132. Stubbington (2019); see also IIF (2020); IMF-GFS (2019: Chapter 1).

133. Chappatta (2018); Curran & Miller (2019); Das (2018); Haldane (2015: 11); Haldane & Allesandri (2009: 16 [chart 5]); Rennison (2018); Stacey (2019); Williamson (2017).

134. FSB (2019a: 13) (exhibit 2.1). See Chapter 11 for additional discussion of central bank QE policies.

135. Allen & Fray (2018); BIS (2019: 1–6); Darrah (2018); Debter (2017); El-Erian (2019a); Giles & Jones (2018); IMF-WEO (2018: 5–8); Wigglesworth (2019).

136. Authers (2018); Authers & Fox (2018); BIS (2019: 1–6); El-Erian (2018); Fleming & Giles (2018); L. Fletcher (2019a, 2019b); Mackenzie (2018); Rennison (2018); Wigglesworth, Samson & Hunter (2018).

137. Fleming (2019b); see also El-Erian (2019a).

138. FOMC (2019a: 17–20, 10–12); see also Authers (2019); Fleming & Smyth (2019).

139. El-Erian (2019b); Politi (2019); Greeley & Smith (2019b); Schneider & Saphir (2019)

140. El-Erian (2019c); FOMC (2019b); Greeley & Smith (2019a); Rennison & Greeley (2019); Smith & Rennison (2019); Wigglesworth (2019).

141. Allen (2019); Economist (2019); Financial Times (2019a); Fleming & Smyth (2019); Jones (2019); Jones & Hunter (2019).

142. Barber & Jones (2019).

143. Hunter & Dunkley (2019); Mackenzie (2019a, 2019b).

144. Hunter & Dunkley (2019).

145. BIS (2019: 6–11); El-Erian (2019c); Wigglesworth (2019).

146. Fleming (2019a, 2019b); Pesek (2019a, 2019b); Tooze (2018: 475–84, 601–08); see also Bernanke (2015: 547–57) (discussing the "taper tantrum" that occurred in financial markets in 2013).

147. Authers (2020); Fletcher (2019a); Mackenzie (2019a, 2019b); Pesek (2019b); see Chapters 7, 9, and 11 for additional discussions of "puts" by the Greenspan Fed and Bernanke Fed.

148. El-Erian (2019a, 2019c); see also Mackenzie (2019a, 2019b); Pesek (2019a, 2019b).

149. Das (2018); Fletcher (2019a, 2019b); Stubbington (2019); Tett (2018a, 2018b); White (2018a, 2018b); Wolf (2019a).

150. Fletcher (2019a) (quoting Crispin Odey); Howell (2019) (quote).

151. Chappatta (2019) (quoting Ye Xie); White (2018a).

152. Fletcher (2019a); Green (2018); McWilliams (2019); Summers & Stansbury (2019); Tett (2018a, 2018b); Webb (2019); Wolf (2018, 2019a); see also Faroohar (2019a, 2019b) ("since the beginning of 2010, real hourly wages in the US have grown by only 6 per cent, while real housing prices have grown by over 20 per cent and inflation-adjusted stock market valuations have doubled"). A study by Asgari (2019) found that £100 placed in a U.K. savings account in 2009 had an inflation-adjusted value of only £84 in 2019, while £100 invested in the FTSE 250 stock index in 2009 had an inflation-adjusted value (including reinvested dividends) of £314 in 2019. U.S. banks paid average annual interest rates of only 0.14% on their savings accounts between 2013 and 2017. In contrast, the S&P 500 stock index rose by 67% on an inflation-adjusted basis during that period. Broughton (2018); S&P 500 Index (2019). See Chapter 9 for discussion of the increase in wealth and income inequality after 1980, and Chapter 11 for further analysis of the adverse side effects of central bank QE policies.

153. Son (2019) (quoting Mayo, a leading financial analyst, and summarizing his research note).

154. Faroohar (2019a) ("The dysfunctional divide between incomes and asset prices is not just an American problem. It is observable in many international markets as well [and] may require a rethink of monetary policy"); L. Fletcher (2019a) (quoting Michael Hintze's view that "the roots of populism lie in part in QE, driving asset prices up"); McWilliams (2019) (arguing that QE policies "drove up asset prices and bailed out baby boomers at the profound political cost of pricing out millennials from that most divisive of asset

markets, property"); see also Tett (2018c) (describing Paul Volcker's critique of central bank QE policies); Tucker (2018a: 482–540) (discussing critiques of the legitimacy of central bank QE policies).

155. Banerjee & Hofmann (2018); Summers & Stansbury (2019).

156. Chappatta (2019); Das (2018); El-Erian (2019a, 2019b, 2019c); White (2018b); see also White (2018a) (warning that "ultra-easy" global monetary policy "is now caught in a debt trap of its own making").

157. Alloway, Boesler, & McCormick (2019); Authers (2020); Avalos, Ehlers, & Eren (2019); FSOC (2019: 54–56, 117); Harris (2019); Kaminska (2019); Rennison (2019); C. Smith (2019); Wigglesworth (2019).

158. Alloway, Boesler, & McCormick (2019) (quoting Pozsar, a financial analyst).

159. Kaminska (2019) (quoting Coppolla, a financial commentator) (emphasis in original).

160. Harris (2019) (quoting Goldberg, a financial analyst).

161. Dudley (2020) (emphasis added).

162. Harris & Boesler (2020).

163. Jordà et al. (2018); see also Aikman, Haldane & Nelson (2015); Allen (2019).

164. Borio, Drehmann, & Xia (2018).

165. L. Fletcher (2019b); see also authorities cited in notes 133–52 and 157–62 in this chapter.

166. Briançon (2019); Jones (2019); Summers & Stansbury (2019); Turner (2018); White (2018b); Wolf (2019a).

167. Barber & Giles (2020) (quoting Carney's remarks during an interview on Jan. 7, 2020); Bernanke, Geithner, & Paulson (2019: 111–12, 123–25); see also Rodriguez Valladares (2019a) (quoting Alessio De Longis' opinion that the ECB "has used up its monetary policy arsenal" and has "no more room to ease").

168. Avraham, Selvaggi, & Vickery (2012); Carmassi & Herring (2016); Jones, Lee, & Yeager (2012); Kress (2019a: 188–92); Morgan (2002); Partnoy & Eisinger (2013); Roca et al. (2017).

169. Bright et al. (2016); Collins (2014); Ford (2018); Haldane (2015); Kress (2019a: 185–87, 193–94); Lenzner (2015); Mui & Niepmann (2015); Partnoy & Eisinger (2013); see also Goldberg & Meehl (2019: 19) (stating that the largest U.S. banks "remain highly complex on organizational, business, and geographic dimensions").

170. See Chapter 9 for a discussion of those scandals.

171. Better Markets (2019); CCP Research (2017); Group of 30 (2018b: 1–7); Griffin (2019: 3, 12–15, 21–23, 27–31); Griffin, Kruger, & Maturana (2017) (Internet Appendix, table IA.1, and Internet Appendix C); Jenkins (2015); Van Hoof (2019); Wilmarth (2013: 1323–25, 1374–82); Zingales (2015: 1329–38, 1347–49); see also Chapters 10–11.

172. Dudley (2018); Griffin (2019: 36); Zingales (2015: 1348); see also Chapters 10–11.

173. Goldstein (2018); Kress (2019a: 197–200); McLannahan (2019); Roe (2014: 1424–28, 1459); Tayan (2019); Wack (2016a, 2016b); Wilmarth (2013: 1430–37); see also Good Jobs First–WF (2019). JPMC was one of the largest lenders to WeWork as JPMC competed with Goldman Sachs and other universal banks to become the lead underwriter for WeWork's ill-fated initial public offering (which was abandoned in Sept. 2019). A JPMC-managed fund made a large investment in WeWork, thereby supporting JPMC's declaration of a high market valuation for the company. JPMC also provided extensive personal loans to Adam Neumann, WeWork's CEO. JPMC's loans to Neumann were comparable in magnitude to the loans and other personal benefits provided by Citigroup to Bernie

Ebbers, WorldCom's CEO, as described in Chapter 9. A corporate governance expert criticized JPMC's web of relationships with WeWork and Neumann as "an all-time Gordian knot of conflicts of interest." Benoit, Farrell, & Brown (2019); Platt et al. (2019); Sorkin (2019) (quoting Neil Minow). JPMC's conflicts of interest seriously undermined its ability to act as an objective lender or as a faithful adviser to its investment clients regarding WeWork.

174. Reuters (2014). Australian banks avoided severe problems during the financial crisis for several reasons. They were not involved to any significant extent in originating or securitizing nonprime mortgage loans. In addition, they benefited from the following major advantages: (i) the Australian government provided blanket guarantees for deposits and wholesale liabilities of Australian banks in 2008, (ii) the Australian central bank aggressively cut interest rates to support Australia's economy in 2008 and 2009, and (iii) Australia's economy enjoyed a prolonged boom from 1992 to 2018 and did not fall into a recession during the financial crisis, due to massive purchases of Australian commodities by Chinese enterprises and large-scale purchases of Australian homes by Chinese investors. Bollen et al. (2015); Bruce-Lockhart (2019); Hill (2012); Hume (2012); Knox (2010).

175. Financial Times (2018) (summarizing and quoting the Australian commission's report); Smyth (2019a) (same); Smyth (2019b) (quoting Sheedy); see also Group of 30 (2018b: 7, 16) (discussing scandals and misconduct at Australian banks); Sy (2019) (criticizing "anti-competitive oligopoly pricing" practices at the four largest Australian banks, and charging that "Australian financial regulation has never been properly enforced") (quotes at 5).

176. Griffin, Kruger, & Maturana (2018: 1–5, 25–36) (quotes at 3, 35–36); see also Kyger & Kodjak (2014) (reporting that four senior mortgage executives who worked at Bear Stearns were subsequently employed by other big banks, including BofA and JPMC, even though they were personally named as defendants in a lawsuit that the Federal Housing Finance Agency filed against Bear Stearns for mortgage fraud).

177. Tenbrunsel & Thomas (2015: 3–8).

178. Sorkin (2015).

179. Limbach, Rau, & Schürmann (2020) (quotes at 1–4).

180. Smith (2012) (explaining why he resigned as executive director and head of Goldman's U.S. equity derivatives business in Europe, the Middle East, and Africa).

181. Group of 30 (2018b: 8); Dudley (2018); Coen (2018: 4)

182. Heltman (2018a, 2019c); Wilmarth (2015a: 367–68); see also Clozel (2018c) (reporting that FDIC Chairman Jelena McWilliams and Fed Vice Chairman Randal Quarles "spent several months touring the country, visiting bank examiners in regional cities, and asking them to adopt a less-aggressive tone when flagging risk practices").

183. Rodriguez Valladares (2019b) (quoting Christopher Wolfe, and also quoting Gregg Gelznis' comment that "transparency only cuts in one direction" for the Fed's leaders); see also Lang (2019a), and notes 42–44 and accompanying text earlier in this chapter (discussing the Fed's new policy of providing megabanks with greater "transparency" about the Fed's stress test models and scenarios).

184. Federal Reserve Board (2018c: 14–16); Federal Reserve Board (2019c: "Supervisory Developments," including figures 13, 14).

185. Kress (2019a: 219–27, 238–39) (discussing the Fed's failure to exercise its divestiture authority under 12 U.S.C. §1843(m) and other statutes); Menand (2018) (describing repeated failures by federal regulators to supervise megabanks effectively); see also Chapters 9–11 (discussing the federal agencies' extremely lax regulation during the 1990s and 2000s).

186. Kane (2018: 21–24).

187. Cohan (2016b) (quote); see also Eisinger (2017: 232–33, 289–93, 317–30); Noonan et al. (2018); Rakoff (2014).

188. Binham (2019a, 2019c); Binham & Croft (2019) (quotes).

189. Binham (2019b, 2019c); Croft (2019); Croft & Binham (2020) (quote).

190. Sanderson & Crow (2019).

191. Milne (2016); Noonan et al. (2019); Treanor (2015, 2016).

192. Chase (2018); Peterson et al. (2018).

193. Protess (2011); Stewart (2015); Scannell & Milne (2017).

194. Dolmetsch (2018); Giel & Mangan (2018); Mathis & Wild (2019); Treanor (2016).

195. Rakoff (2014); see Chapters 9–11 for descriptions of mortgage-related misconduct by the Big Seventeen and AIG and the lawsuits brought against most of those companies by the Justice Department.

196. Eisinger (2017: xvi–xxi, 315–30); Garrett (2015, 2019).

197. Eisinger (2017: xvi–xxi, 91–92, 99–110, 139–45, 180–201, 214–26, 230–43, 250–63, 280–93, 315–30); Cohan (2016b); FCIC (2011: 15, 161–64); Garrett (2015: 1790–95, 1801–37, 1849–53); Protess & Apuzzo (2015); Rakoff (2014); Stewart (2015); Taibbi (2014a: chapters 1, 4, 8, 9).

198. Scannell (2015) (quoting Judge Rakoff); Rakoff (2014); see also Eisinger (2017: 202–04, 214–27, 294–304) (describing Judge Rakoff's objections to the SEC's settlements with Bank of America and Citigroup).

199. Holder (2014).

200. O'Brien (2019) (quoting Carney). Carney argued that it would be more effective to discipline bankers by making sure that their "deferred compensation" is "clawed back" if they violate their legal duties. However, as discussed earlier, federal agencies have never adopted rules requiring financial institutions to establish compensation policies that discourage excessive risk-taking by bankers, despite the explicit mandate for such rules in Section 956(b) of the Dodd-Frank Act. See notes 14, 74, 183 and accompanying text earlier in this chapter.

201. Robert Jenkins, a former member of the Bank of England's Financial Policy Committee, stated: "If the banks are so large and complex that [senior executives] cannot be expected to know" about serious misconduct, "then they are a walking argument for breaking up the banks." Treanor (2015) (quoting Jenkins).

202. SEC (2009a, 2009b [quotes], 2009c [quoting email messages sent by Mozilo on Mar. 28, 2006, Apr. 13, 2006, and Sept. 26, 2006]). See also Chapter 10 and Wilmarth (2013: 1382–85) for additional analysis of Mozilo's and Countrywide's misconduct.

203. Chicago Tribune (2016); Dobuzinskis & Levine (2010); Wilmarth (2013: 1383–85). The SEC required Mozilo to disgorge $45 million of gains from his stock sales, but BofA and its liability insurers paid that amount on Mozilo's behalf. The SEC required Mozilo's subordinates, Richard Sambol and Eric Sieracki, to pay $650,000 in civil penalties. Sambol agreed to disgorge $5 million of gains from his stock sales, but BofA and its insurers

paid that sum on Sambol's behalf. Sambol and Sieracki did not admit or deny the SEC's charges, but they agreed to be temporarily banned from serving as officers or directors of publicly traded companies. SEC (2010c); Wilmarth (2013: 1383–85).

204. Chicago Tribune (2016); Eisinger (2017: 237–43, 269–80, 287–93); Raymond (2016); Wilmarth (2013: 1372–90).

205. In January 2020, the Office of the Comptroller of the Currency filed administrative enforcement actions seeking almost $60 million of civil penalties from eight former senior executives of Wells Fargo. The OCC's enforcement actions arose out of Wells Fargo's massive and wide-ranging customer abuses, including the opening of millions of unauthorized accounts. Former CEO John Stumpf agreed to pay $17.5 million of civil penalties and accepted a lifetime ban from the banking industry. It remains to be seen whether the OCC's Wells Fargo enforcement actions will mark the beginning of a new trend in which federal agencies are more willing to impose meaningful sanctions on senior executives of megabanks for serious wrongdoing at their institutions. Los Angeles Times (2020); Schroeder & Prentice (2020).

Conclusion

1. Authers (2013) (quoting Reed); Ivry (2009); see also Wilmarth (2014: 70–71, 102–05, 114–20, 134–35; 2017: 513–17, 546). See Chapter 8 for discussion of the role played by Citigroup's creation in repealing the Glass-Steagall Act.

2. Booker (2010); Wack (2012) (quoting Weill's statements on CNBC); see also Wilmarth (2014: 135–36; 2017: 546).

3. Wilmarth (2017: 546–47) (quoting Mitchell); see Chapters 1–6 for analysis of Mitchell's career at National City Bank between 1916 and 1933.

4. Feldstein (2013: 116) (quoting Volcker); Mayo (2019) (same). A recent study found evidence of significant and detrimental conflicts of interest in German universal banks with retail banking and proprietary trading operations. The study determined that German universal banks with proprietary trading units sold large amounts of underperforming stocks in their portfolios to retail customers between 2005 and 2009. The largest sales of underperforming stocks to retail customers occurred after Lehman Brothers collapsed in September 2008, when German universal banks were under severe stress. In addition, investment returns for retail customers of German universal banks with proprietary trading units were much worse than the returns received by retail customers of other large German banks that did not have trading units. Fecht, Hackethal, & Karabulut (2018).

5. Kelleher & Hall (2019); Leonhardt (2017); Michaels (2015); Welsch (2018).

6. Jackson (2019); see also Kelleher & Hall (2019).

7. See Chapters 2–5 and 9–10.

8. See Wilmarth (2017: 443–44n5) (describing "bank-eligible" securities that banks were allowed to invest in and underwrite under the original Glass-Steagall Act).

9. For discussions of private placements of CDOs that occurred under the SEC's Rule 144A during the 2000s and their catastrophic impact on institutional investors, see Chapters 7 and 9–11. As a result of vigorous lobbying by Wall Street, the SEC issued rules in 2014 that did not strengthen the weak and inadequate disclosure standards for private placements of asset-backed securities. Levinson (2015a).

10. Elisabeth de Fontenay has shown that leveraged syndicated loans are similar to high-yield (junk) bonds. However, syndicated loans are not treated as securities, in part because banks sell participation interests in syndicated loans only to banks and other institutional investors. In addition, lead banks typically retain a portion of the credit risk for the loans they syndicate, thereby certifying the creditworthiness of their loans. Risk retention creates positive incentives for banks to make sound loans. Those incentives may explain why syndicated leveraged loans generally experienced lower default rates and produced higher recovery rates for investors during and after the financial crisis, compared with high-yield bonds. See de Fontenay (2014: 728–39, 738–57, 760–62). A new Glass-Steagall Act should require banks to retain a significant portion of the credit risk from their syndicated loans and should not allow banks to sell loans or loan participations to persons other than qualified institutional investors. Strong risk retention requirements and investor restrictions would help to maintain the existing legal distinction between syndicated lending and securities underwriting.

11. See Chapter 7 for discussion of problems caused by risky domestic and foreign syndicated loans that banks arranged during the 1970s and 1980s.

12. Section 941(b) of the Dodd-Frank Act required federal regulators to issue rules that would require sponsors (underwriters) of ABS to retain at least 5% of the credit risk of the loans underlying those securities. Sweet & Hall (2017). However, federal agencies did not implement Section 941(b) in accordance with congressional intent. Regulators adopted weak rules that exempted many sponsors of securitizations from any type of meaningful risk retention, thereby weakening the sponsors' incentives to securitize only sound loans. Ahmed, Bakewell, & Marsh (2017); Norris (2014); Pozen (2018).

13. A new Glass-Steagall Act should prohibit joint control of banks and securities firms and should also prevent banks and securities firms from sharing directors or officers. See Chapter 6 (discussing Sections 20 and 32 of the original Glass-Steagall Act, which prohibited such links between banks and securities firms); Fink (2019: 114) (same).

14. See Chapter 7 for discussion of the BHC Act's prohibition on insurance underwriting by banks and their affiliates. That prohibition (like the ban on securities underwriting and trading) was repealed by the Gramm-Leach-Bliley Act in 1999, as described in Chapter 8.

15. See DeYoung & Torna (2013) (finding that insurance agency sales and securities brokerage activities improved the profitability and stability of bank holding companies by providing diversified sources of fee-based revenues without creating market risks or significant liability risks).

16. Wilmarth (2011a: 1035–37); Wilmarth (2015a: 344–45) (explaining that in 1999 Congress prohibited the Fed from approving any new "closely related" activities beyond those previously authorized under Section 4(c)(8) of the BHC Act, 12 U.S.C. §1843(c)(8)).

17. FASB's hedge accounting standards would allow a bank to enter into derivatives that establish bona fide hedges against the bank's specific exposures to risks from its traditional activities, such as potential changes in interest rates or currency exchange rates. Wilmarth (2015a: 344, 350–51); see also Fletcher (2014: 859). See Chapter 7 for discussion of how banks used derivatives to create "synthetic" securities and insurance products.

18. See Chapter 7 for discussion of the positive impact of the Glass-Steagall and BHC Acts after World War II.

19. Wilmarth (2011a: 957–60, 978–83; 2017: 453–55, 543–45); see also Duffie (2019) and Chapters 10 and 11.

20. Allen (2013).
21. Demirgüç-Kunt & Huizinga (2010); DeYoung & Rice (2004); DeYoung & Torna (2013); Stiroh (2006a, 2006b); Stiroh & Rumble (2006).
22. Beltratti & Stultz (2012).
23. See Chapters 5 and 6.
24. Brunnermeier, Dong, & Palia (2019); DeYoung & Torna (2013); Haldane (2010: 8, 11–13, 19); Moore & Zhou (2014).
25. Masciantonio & Tiseno (2013); Molyneux, Schaeck, & Zhou (2014); Wilmarth (2011a: 957–86); see also Chapters 9–12.
26. Broughton (2018); Ensign (2018); Ensign & Hoffman (2017); Wilmarth (2015a: 348, 357–58, 369).
27. See Chapter 12 for discussion of universal banks' successful efforts to repeal the Lincoln Amendment and undermine the Volcker Rule, as well as JPMC's London Whale debacle. See also Wilmarth (2013: 1430–37) (describing JPMC's use of "excess deposits" to finance its London Whale bets on synthetic derivatives).
28. Sitaraman (2018).
29. For discussions of the need to strengthen FSOC's authority to designate nonbank SIFIs and the Fed's powers to supervise those institutions, see Kress, McCoy, & Schwarcz (2018); Schwarcz & Zaring (2017).
30. Crawford (2017); Ricks (2016); see Chapters 7 and 8 for discussion of regulatory failures to enforce Section 21 of the Glass-Steagall Act (12 U.S.C. §378) after 1970.
31. Wilmarth (2017: 456–64); see also Chapters 7 and 11.
32. Duffie (2019: 88–93, 99–100); Gelpern & Gerding (2016: 387–88, 399–405); Gorton (2016, 2018); Pozsar et al. (2010: 2, 58–64, 70); Ricks (2016: 96–101); Wilmarth (2017: 463–64); OFR (2018: 31897–98); see also Chapters 7, 9, and 11.
33. Ricks (2016: 37–38); see also Crawford (2017: 7–8).
34. Ricks (2016: 5–6, 42–46, 225–26, 301n7); see also Ricks (2018: 763–67, 771–72, 809–16). Ricks' argument that short-term financial instruments should be treated as "money claims" finds substantial support in a study by Greenwood, Hanson, & Stein (2015). They determined that yields paid on short-term U.S. Treasury bills were much lower than yields paid on longer-term U.S. Treasury bonds. Short-term Treasury bills included a "money premium"—a large reduction in yield—because they offered immediate or near-term liquidity to investors. The money premium was greatest for Treasury bills with maturities of less than thirty days, but it remained significant for maturities up to ninety days. Greenwood, Hanson, & Stein (2015: 1683–94); see also Ricks (2016: 42–46).
35. Cecchetti & Schoenholtz (2018); FSOC (2017: 87–90).
36. OFR (2018: 31900). The OFR issued a rule in 2019, which mandates the collection of data for centrally cleared bilateral repos, but it does *not* require any similar collection of data for uncleared bilateral repos. Uncleared bilateral repos are securities repurchase agreements that are individually negotiated between two parties and are not cleared through any central counterparty. OFR (2018, 2019).
37. Crawford (2017: 5–8); Ricks (2016: 94–142); see also Gorton (2016, 2018).
38. See Ricks (2018: 772–801, 806–16).
39. Kronick & Wu (2019) (studying the impact of shadow deposits on Canadian monetary policy); Xiao (2018) (reviewing the effects of shadow deposits on U.S. monetary policy).

40. Barr, Jackson, & Tahyar (2018: 250–53) (explaining that the deposit insurance assessment base for each bank is equal to its "average total consolidated assets, minus average tangible equity, which essentially ties the assessment base to total liabilities").

41. See Chapter 11 (discussing the bailout of MMMFs in Oct. 2008).

42. Paul Kupiec estimated in 2017 that JPMC, BofA, and Citigroup would be required to divest 20–30% of their assets to comply with a new Glass-Steagall Act. In contrast, three large regional banks—Capital One, PNC, and U.S. Bancorp—would need to spin off less than 6% of their assets. However, Kupiec concluded that a new Glass-Steagall Act would not have a significant impact on the TBTF status of the largest U.S. banks. Kupiec (2017).

43. After the original Glass-Steagall Act was enacted in 1933, Morgan Stanley separated from J. P. Morgan & Co., and First Boston was created by officers of the former securities affiliates of First National Bank of Boston and Chase National Bank. See Chernow (1990: 384–91); Peach (1941: 164–66); and Chapter 6.

44. Wilmarth (2015a: 288–303); see also Mitchell (2015).

45. Bord, Ivashina, & Taliaferro (2017); Chen, Hanson, & Stein (2017) (including table 1); Wilmarth (2015a: 277–80, 291–98).

46. FDIC (2015: 16–17); FDIC (2016: 16–17); FDIC (2017b: 16–17); FDIC (2018: 17); Wilmarth (2015a: 293) (providing data for 2014); see also Wilmarth (1995: 34–41) (describing the inferior record of large U.S. banks in providing credit to small businesses during the regional banking crises of the 1980s and early 1990s).

47. Bord, Ivashina, & Taliaferro (2017); Chen, Hanson, & Stein (2017); McCarthy (2019); Simon (2015); Wilmarth (2015a: 292–97).

48. Clark, Kabaker, & Sachs (2018: 6–8, 12–14) (quote at 7); Wilmarth (2015a: 256–81); see also Chapter 11.

49. Lettieri (2016: 17); Mitchell (2015); Witkowski (2018); see also Burns (2019) (reporting that federal regulators required organizers to invest at least $20–$25 million of capital in a newly chartered bank after the financial crisis, compared with a required capital investment of less than $10 million before 2009).

50. Wilmarth (2002: 250–57, 300–08, 312–15; 2015a: 256–81) (including the trend data described in 2015a: 256); see also Kress (2019b: 3–6, 17–27, 39–40) (describing the very lax federal antitrust policies for bank mergers after the early 1980s).

51. Lettieri (2016); McCarthy (2019); Wilmarth (2015a: 256–57, 288–300).

52. Fed SBCS (2019: 17–21, 25); Shubber (2017); Simon (2015); U.S. Treasury (2016); Wilmarth (2015a: 288–303) (describing the strong preference among small businesses for community-based financial institutions as their primary source of credit in the U.S., Canada, and U.K.).

53. Ensign & Jones (2017); Hendrickson, Muro, & Galston (2018: 12–13, 22–23); Mitchell (2015); Simon & Jones (2017) (quoting Tommy Davis); Wilmarth (2015a: 288–300).

54. Lettieri (2016); McCarthy (2019); Mitchell (2015); Wilmarth (2015a: 298–303).

55. Burghof, Schmidt, & Gehrung (2019) (quote at 18).

56. See Chapter 8, note 79 and accompanying text (describing how very lenient federal antitrust review standards encouraged a massive consolidation of the U.S. banking industry after the early 1980s).

57. Baxter (2011: 794–801, 827–31); Brewer & Jagtiani (2013); Carow, Kane, & Narayanan (2006); Kane (2000); Kress (2019b: 27–29); Molyneux, Schaeck, & Zhou (2014); Wilmarth (2002: 250–57, 293–309; 2015a: 298–303).

58. Laeven, Ratnovski, & Tong (2016); Kress (2019b: 29–30); Lorenc & Zhang (2018); Masciantonio & Tiseno (2013); Moore & Zhou (2014); Wilmarth (2015a: 256–75).

59. Baxter (2011: 870–74); Kress (2019b). Federal statutes require regulators to deny bank mergers and acquisitions that have significant adverse effects on competition, and to determine whether those transactions would create "greater or more concentrated risks" to U.S. financial stability. 12 U.S.C. §§ 1828(c)(5), 1842(c)(1) and (7) (quote).

60. Center for Responsive Politics (2019); Igan & Lambert (2018: 4, 4n4); see Chapters 7–9 and 12 for discussion of the financial industry's immense political clout.

61. Johnson & Kwak (2010: 92–100, 185–88); Wilmarth (2013: 1406–17).

62. Armstrong (2018); da Costa (2015); Dayen (2017); Fang (2015); Haggerty (2019); Levitt (2019); Ramonas (2017); Stein (2018); see also Tadena (2012) (reporting that Gramm was a vice chairman of UBS from 2003 to 2012).

63. Clozel (2018a); Finkle (2018a); Johnson & Kwak (2010: 90–92, 97–100, 120–21, 133–37); Mukunda (2014); Wilmarth (2013: 1359–69); see also the discussions of how large financial conglomerates used their political and regulatory influence to advance their interests in Chapters 8, 9, and 12.

64. Wilmarth (2013: 1366) (noting that the lobbyists hired by the financial industry included former Speaker of the House Dennis Hastert [R-IL]; former Senate majority leaders Bob Dole [R-KS] and Trent Lott [R-MS], and former House majority leaders Dick Armey [R-TX] and Dick Gephardt [D-MO]).

65. Igan & Lambert (2018: 13–15); Wilmarth (2013: 1359–69); see also Chapters 8, 9, and 12.

66. Igan & Lambert (2018: 16–22) (reviewing studies); Wilmarth (2013: 1364–67, 1401–04) (same).

67. Hacker & Pierson (2010: 170–252, 273–77); Johnson & Kwak (2010: 89–113, 133–37, 185–92); Mukunda (2014); Stein (2018); Wilmarth (2013: 1359–69, 1406–17); see also Shive & Forster (2017: 1446–47) (showing that financial institutions significantly increased their hiring of former regulators between 2001 and 2015). The entire commercial banking industry employed fewer than 40 lobbyists in 1969. In contrast, the six largest banks employed more than 240 former government officials as lobbyists in 2009–10. Douglas (2019: 291–92); Wilmarth (2013: 1366).

68. See Chapter 12 for discussion of the dominant roles played in global financial markets by the Big Thirteen universal banks (JPMC, BofA, Citigroup, Wells Fargo, Goldman Sachs, Morgan Stanley, Barclays, BNP Paribas, Credit Suisse, Deutsche Bank, HSBC, Société Générale, and UBS) in global financial markets. In Apr. 2019, representatives of the Big Thirteen occupied more than a third of the board seats—including both chairs—at two leading international financial trade associations: the Institute of International Finance and the Global Financial Markets Association. See https://www.iif.com/About-Us/Our-Board and http://www.gfma.org/About/Board (both visited on Apr. 30, 2019). In addition, representatives of the Big Thirteen occupied a majority of the board seats—including a vice chair—at the Association for Financial Markets in Europe, a trade association representing "leading global and European banks and other significant capital market players" in Europe's wholesale financial markets. See https://www.afme.eu/en/about-us (visited on Apr. 30, 2019).

69. Sitaraman (2017: 288–89); Sitaraman (2018); see also Chapter 8.

70. Federalist No. 51 (James Madison).

71. Brandeis (1933 [1914]: 1–36, 91–152); Fink (2019: xiv, 28–31, 90–118, 169–74) (quotes at xiv, 173–74); Johnson & Kwak (2010: 22–37); Rosen (2016: 62–80).

72. For example, Congress included a provision denying *Chevron* deference in the Dodd-Frank Act. That provision stipulates that the Office of the Comptroller of the Currency will *not* receive *Chevron* deference when it issues regulations or orders that seek to pre-empt state consumer financial laws. See Wilmarth (2011b: 932–34) (discussing 12 U.S.C. §25b(b)(5)(A)).

73. Baxter (2011: 786n81) (quoting Jamie Dimon); Guynn (2014); Kress (2019a: 204–12); Newell (2017).

74. For discussions of the inconclusive results of studies of economies of scale and scope at banks, see Baxter (2011: 787–811); Chernobai, Ozdagli, & Wang (2016: 3–7); Davies & Tracey (2014: 220–21, 225–26); Haldane (2010: 11–12); Hughes & Mester (2018); Kress (2019a: 204–05, 207–09).

75. Davies & Tracey (2014).

76. DeYoung & Rice (2004); Goetz, Laeven, & Levine (2013); Laeven & Levine (2007); Minton, Stulz, & Taboada (2017); Stiroh (2006a, 2006b); Stiroh & Rumble (2006).

77. Brunnermeier, Dong, & Palia (2019); DeYoung & Torna (2013); Haldane (2010: 8, 11–13, 19); Masciantonio & Tiseno (2013); Moore & Zhou (2014).

78. See Chapters 5 and 6 for discussion of the very poor performance of universal banks in the U.S. and Europe during the Great Depression, and Chapters 10 and 11 for analysis of the woeful performance of universal banks on both sides of the Atlantic during 2007–09.

79. Haldane (2010: 8, 12–13); Masciantonio & Tiseno (2013); Molyneux, Schaeck, & Zhou (2014); Wilmarth (2011a: 957–60, 977–86).

80. See Chapter 11 for discussion of failures and bailouts of universal banks and large securities firms during the financial crisis.

81. Arnold (2017: "Total shareholder returns at top-tier banks" graph) (showing that JPMC produced an 8% average annual return for shareholders between 2007 and 2016, while HSBC and Goldman Sachs produced average annual returns of less than 5%, BNP Paribas broke even, and Morgan Stanley, BofA, Barclays, UBS, Deutsche Bank, Credit Suisse, and Citigroup recorded negative average annual returns).

82. Berger et al. (2018: 8–10, 35 [figure 2]); Better Markets (2019); Curti & Mihov (2018: 9–11); Van Hoof (2019); see also Chapter 12 for discussion of legal violations and other operational failures at universal banks.

83. Morris (2018); see also Baxter (2011: 796–98, 847–51, 876–77 [charts 2, 3]) (analyzing the very poor performance of large universal banks between 2007 and 2010). Book values reflect the historical costs of a bank's assets and liabilities on its balance sheet, rather than the current market values of those assets and liabilities.

84. Baxter (2011: 816–17) (quoting Jamie Dimon); Borak (2012) (quoting Tony Fratto and Mark Calabria).

85. Wilmarth (2011a: 1050–52).

86. Kutler (1998); Sesit (1996); Wilmarth (2002: 440–43).

87. Baxter (2011: 817, 817n191); Gapper (2019); Jenkins & Noonan (2017); Kutler (1998); Sesit (1996); Wilmarth (2002: 322–23, 440–43).

88. Arons (2019); Arnold (2018); Crow & Morris (2019); Gapper (2019); Morris (2018) (quoting Hillebrand); Morris & Crow (2019); see also Chapter 12 for discussion of the superiority of U.S. universal banks over their European rivals since 2010.

89. Morris & Storbeck (2019); Storbeck, Morris, & Noonan (2019).

90. Lewis (2019); Lewis, Morris, & Martin (2019).

91. Baxter (2011: 812–13) (quoting Jamie Dimon); Borak (2012) (quoting Fratto and Calabria); Wilmarth (2014: 136–37n521) (quoting Rob Nichols)).

92. de Fontenay (2014); Lipin (1995); Sesit (1996); Wilmarth (2002: 326–30, 378–88).

93. Cumming et al. (2019).

94. Sesit (1996); Wilmarth (1992: 1060–63; 2002: 440–43).

95. Rothkopf (2012: 266) (quoting Rubin).

96. Wilmarth (2015b: 64) (quoting Flint's testimony before a subcommittee of the House of Lords on Oct. 21, 2014); see Chapter 12 for discussion of Flint's testimony.

97. Wilmarth (2014: 116–17; 2015b: 81–82); see Chapters 10 and 11 for discussion of Citigroup's near failure and repeated bailouts during the financial crisis of 2007–09.

98. Peters (2019); Public Citizen (2018).

99. Jenkins (2019b); Noonan & Blood (2017).

100. Johnson & Kwak (2010); Roe (2014); Wilmarth (2013, 2014).

101. Jenkins & Noonan (2017) (quoting an unnamed "top investment banker" hired by Deutsche in the 1990s).

102. See Chapter 12 for analysis of serious shortcomings in Dodd-Frank's design and implementation.

103. Johnson & Kwak (2010: 205–08) (quote at 207); see also Wilmarth (2011a: 986–1034, 1052–56); Wilmarth (2017: 544–48).

104. See Chapter 12. In view of the ongoing and highly successful campaign by universal banks to undermine Dodd-Frank, I no longer advocate my previous proposals for more limited structural reforms. In earlier works, I proposed an "internal Glass-Steagall" approach, which I believed would be more politically feasible than an "external Glass-Steagall" regime like the original 1933 act. My internal Glass-Steagall approach would have allowed financial holding companies to remain in existence but would have required their subsidiary banks to operate as "narrow banks," with strong "firewalls" separating those banks from their nonbank affiliates. Under that approach, narrow banks could not have made any loans or other transfers of funds to their nonbank affiliates except for the payment of lawful dividends to their parent holding companies. I hoped that strong firewalls and tight restrictions on transfers of funds would prevent narrow banks from transferring their safety net subsidies to their holding company affiliates. However, after observing Dodd-Frank's shortcomings as well as the weak implementation of the U.K.'s ring-fencing regime for large U.K. banks, I no longer have confidence in the internal Glass-Steagall approach. U.K. authorities adopted lenient rules that allow ring-fenced banks to provide loans to their capital markets affiliates and to engage in other transactions with those affiliates, subject to restrictions similar to Sections 23A and 23B of the Federal Reserve Act for U.S. financial holding companies. As discussed in Chapters 8 and 11, Sections 23A and 23B create very porous firewalls. In addition, the Fed granted numerous waivers of Section 23A that allowed subsidiary banks of financial holding companies to make very large transfers of funds to their capital markets affiliates during the financial crisis. I have therefore concluded that only a strict external Glass-Steagall approach, comparable to the original 1933 act, will be successful in establishing a clear separation between the banking system and the capital markets. See Britton et al. (2016) (describing the implementation of the U.K.'s ring-fencing legislation for large

U.K. banks); see also Wilmarth (2011a: 1034–57; 2015a: 342–70; 2017: 443–49, 546–48) (describing my previous internal Glass-Steagall proposal and contrasting that proposal with a stronger external Glass-Steagall approach comparable to the original 1933 act).

105. Boston (2019c); Federal Reserve Board (2019: 17–28); Hamilton & Torres (2019); Rodriguez Valladares (2019a, 2019c); Rushe (2019); Torres & Lee (2019); see also Chapter 12 for discussion of the relentless growth in U.S. and global debt levels since 2000.

106. Allen (2019); Boston (2019c); Federal Reserve Board (2019a: 22–28); Rodriguez Valladares (2019a, 2019c); van Riet (2018); see also Chapter 12 for discussion of the rapid growth of sovereign debts since 2007.

107. Ardagna (2019); Briançon (2019); Curran & Miller (2019); Reinhart, Reinhart, & Rogoff (2015); van Riet (2018).

108. Arnold (2019); Curran & Miller (2019); Jones (2019); Rogoff (2017: 48–54); Summers & Stansbury (2019); see Chapters 11 and 12 for discussion of the QE policies adopted by the four leading central banks after the financial crisis.

109. Arnold (2019); Briançon (2019); Curran & Miller (2019); Greeley & Smith (2019b); Jones (2019); Rogoff (2017: 48–54); N. Smith (2019); see Chapter 12 for discussion of the policy U-turn that central banks made in 2019 after their attempts at quantitative tightening in 2018 triggered a sharp selloff in global financial markets.

110. Arnold (2019) (quoting Blanchard).

111. Barber & Giles (2020) (quoting Carney).

112. See Chapter 12 for discussion of "guarantor of last resort" proposals and their implications.

113. See Chapter 12 for discussion of the Fed's intervention in the repo market between Sept. and Dec. 2019.

114. See Chapter 12 for analysis of the "global doom loop" linking universal banks and shadow banks to heavily burdened sovereigns and overstretched central banks.

115. See Nersisyan (2015). A new Glass-Steagall Act and a restored BHC Act should also prohibit banks from engaging in commercial activities, and should prevent commercial and industrial firms from owning or controlling banks. Establishing a strict separation between banking and commerce is essential to (i) maintain the independence and objectivity of banks as lenders and investment advisers, (ii) prevent the spread of the deposit insurance subsidy and other federal safety net subsidies outside the banking system, and (iii) avoid the systemic risks and TBTF problems that would be created by combinations between banks and commercial or industrial firms. See Federal Reserve Board (2016: 28–35); Wilmarth (2007, 2008).

116. Wilmarth (2015a: 358–63); see Chapter 12 for discussion of the OLA and OLF and the shortcomings in the federal agencies' current strategies for resolving failures of SIFIs.

117. Brandeis (1933 [1914]: 137).

References

Aaron, Kat (2009). "Predatory Lending: A Decade of Warnings—Congress, Fed Fiddled as Subprime Crisis Spread" (Center for Public Integrity, May 6, 2009), available at https://www.publicintegrity.org/2009/05/06/5452/predatory-lending-decade-warnings.

Accominotti, Olivier (2016). "International Banking and Transmission of the 1931 Financial Crisis" (Working Paper, Nov. 2016), available at http://ssrn.com/abstract=2867133.

Accominotti, Olivier (2012). "London Merchant Banks, the Central European Panic, and the Sterling Crisis of 1931," 72(1) *Journal of Economic History* 1–43.

Accominotti, Olivier, and Barry Eichengreen (2016). "The Mother of All Sudden Stops: Capital Flows and Reversals in Europe, 1919–32," 69(2) *Economic History Review* 469–92.

Acharya, Viral V., Deniz Anginer, and A. Joseph Warburton (2011). "The End of Market Discipline? Investor Expectations of Implicit Government Guarantees" (May 2016), available at http://ssrn.com/abstract=1961656.

Acharya, Viral V., Nirupama Kulkarni, and Matthew Richardson (2011). "Capital, Contingent Capital, and Liquidity Requirements," in Viral V. Acharya et al., *Regulating Wall Street: The Dodd-Frank Act and the New Architecture of Global Finance* 143–80. New York: John Wiley & Sons, Inc.

Acharya, Viral V., and Philipp Schnabl (2010). "Do Global Banks Spread Global Imbalances? Asset-Backed Commercial Paper During the Financial Crisis of 2007–09," 58(1) *IMF Economic Review* 37–73.

Acharya, Viral V., and Philipp Schnabl (2009). "How Banks Played the Leverage Game," in Viral V. Acharya and Matthew Richardson, eds., *Restoring Financial Stability: How to Repair a Failed System* 83–100. New York: John Wiley & Sons.

Acharya, Viral V., Philipp Schnabl, and Gustavo Suarez (2013). "Securitization Without Risk Transfer," 107 *Journal of Financial Economics* 515–36.

Adalet, Müge (2009a). "The Effect of Financial Structure on Crises: Universal Banking in Interwar Europe" (ERF Working Paper 0910, Nov. 2009), available at https://eaf.ku.edu.tr/sites/eaf.ku.edu.tr/files/erf_wp_0910.pdf.

Adalet, Müge (2009b). "Were Universal Banks More Vulnerable to Banking Failures?" (ERF Working Paper 0911, Nov. 2009), available at https://eaf.ku.edu.tr/sites/eaf.ku.edu.tr/files/erf_wp_0911.pdf.

Adamczyk, Guillaume, and Bernhard Windisch (2015). "State Aid to European Banks: Returning to Viability," *Competition State Aid Brief* (European Commission) (Issue 2015-01, Feb. 2015), available at http://ec.europa.eu/competition/publications/csb/csb2015_001_en.pdf.

Admati, Anat (2014). "The Compelling Case for Stronger and More Effective Leverage Regulation in Banking," 43 *Journal of Legal Studies* 535–61.

Admati, Anat, and Martin Hellwig (2013). *The Bankers' New Clothes: What's Wrong with Banking and What to Do About It*. Princeton: Princeton University Press.

Adrian, Tobias, John Kiff, and Hyun Song Shin (2018). "Liquidity, Leverage, and Regulation 10 Years After the Global Financial Crisis," 10(1) *Annual Review of Financial Economics* 1–24.

Adrian, Tobias, and Hyun Song Shin (2009). "Money, Liquidity, and Monetary Policy" (Federal Reserve Bank of New York Staff Report No. 360, Jan. 2009), available at http://ssrn.com/abstract=1331004.

Aguado, Iago Gil (2001). "The Creditanstalt Crisis of 1931 and the Failure of the Austro-German Customs Union Project," 44(1) *Historical Journal* 199–221.

Ahamed, Liaquat (2009). *Lords of Finance: The Bankers Who Broke the World*. New York: Penguin Books.

Ahmed, Nabila, Sally Bakewell, and Alastair Marsh (2017). "Banks Told to Keep Skin in Game. They Securitized That Too," *Bloomberg* (June 19, 2017).

Aikman, David, Andrew G. Haldane, Marc Hinterschweiger, and Sujit Kapadia (2018). "Rethinking Financial Stability" (Bank of England Staff Working Paper No. 712, Feb. 2018), available at http://ssrn.com/abstract=3130053.

Aikman, David, Andrew G. Haldane, and Benjamin Nelson (2015). "Curbing the Credit Cycle," 125 *Economic Journal* 1072–109 (June).

Aliber, Robert Z., and Charles P. Kindleberger (2015). *Manias, Panics, and Crashes.* 7th Edition. New York: Palgrave Macmillan.

Allen, Frederick Lewis (1935). *The Lords of Creation.* New York: Harper.

Allen, Frederick Lewis (1931). *Only Yesterday: An Informal History of the 1920s.* New York: Harper & Row.

Allen, Hilary J. (2013). "A New Philosophy for Financial Stability Regulation," 45(1) *Loyola University Chicago Law Journal* 173–231.

Allen, Kate (2019). "Eurozone Banks Buy Sovereign Bonds, Reviving 'Doom Loop' Fear," *Financial Times* (Mar. 7, 2019), available at https://www.ft.com/content/c6a13390-40e9-11e9-9bee-efab61506f44.

Allen, Kate, and Keith Fray (2018). "The QE Retreat: Central Banks' Balance Sheets Start to Shrink," *Financial Times* (Aug. 27, 2018), available at https://www.ft.com/content/34bf4d1e-a787-11e8-926a-7342fe5e173f.

Allen, William A., and Richhild Moessner (2012). "The International Propagation of the Financial Crisis of 2008, and a Comparison with 1931," 19(2) *Financial History Review* 123–47.

Allentown Morning Call (1994). "Clinton Signs Interstate Banking Bill," *Allentown Morning Call* (Sept. 30, 1994), A10, available on Westlaw at 1994 WLNR 1953028.

Alloway, Tracy, Matthew Boesler, and Liz Capo McCormick (2019). "Repo Oracle Zoltan Pozsar Expects Even More Turmoil," *Bloomberg Law* (Dec. 20, 2019).

Alston, Lee J., Wayne A. Grove, and David C. Wheelock (1994). "Why Do Banks Fail? Evidence from the 1920s," 31 *Explorations in Economic History* 409–31.

Altman, Edward I., with Brenda J. Karlin (2008). "Defaults and Returns in the High-Yield Bond Market: The Year 2007 in Review and Outlook" (New York University Salomon Center, Leonard N. Stern School of Business, Feb. 7, 2008), available at https://www.iiiglobal.org/sites/default/files/27defaultsandreturns.pdf.

Alvarez, Nahiomy, and John McPartland (2019). "The Concentration of Cleared Derivatives: Can Access to Direct CCP Clearing for End-Users Address the Challenge?" (Federal Reserve Bank of Chicago Working Paper 2019-06, Aug. 20, 2019), available at https://www.chicagofed.org/publications/working-papers/2019/2019-06.

American Banker (1981). "'Marketplace' Era Is at Hand for Financial Institutions," *American Banker* (Dec. 16, 1981), 4 (reprinting speech by Treasury Secretary Donald T. Regan before the Securities Industry Ass'n), available on Westlaw at 1981 WLNR 76809.

Amidei, Federico B., and Claire Giordano (2014). "The Redesign of the Bank-Industry-Financial Market Ties in the US Glass-Steagall and 1936 Italian Banking Acts," in Pier Clement, Harold James, and Herman Van der Wee, eds., *Financial Innovation, Regulation and Crises in History* 65–83. London: Pickering & Chatto.

Anbil, Sriya (2017). "Managing Stigma During a Financial Crisis" (Federal Reserve Board, Finance and Discussion Series 2017-007, Dec. 2016), available at https://doi.org/10.17016/FEDS.2017.007.

Anbil, Sriya, and Angela Vossmeyer (2017). "Liquidity from Two Lending Facilities" (Working paper, Aug. 11, 2017), available at http://ssrn.com/abstract=3021272.

Anderson, Sarah, and Bart Naylor (2018). "CEO-Worker Pay Ratios in the Banking Industry" (Institute for Policy Studies and Public Citizen, Apr. 2018), available at https://ips-dc.org/wp-content/uploads/2018/04/Bank-Pay-Ratios.pdf.

Andrews, Edmund L. (2008). "Greenspan Concedes Flaws in Deregulatory Approach," *New York Times* (Oct. 24, 2008), B1.

Andrews, Edmund L., and Jenny Anderson (2008). "Tough Love for Lehman," *New York Times* (Sept. 13, 2008), A1.

Andrews, Edmund L., Michael J. de la Merced, and Mary Williams Walsh (2008). "Fed in an $85 Billion Rescue of an Insurer Near Failure," *New York Times* (Sept. 17, 2008), A1.

Ang, James S., and Terry Richardson (1994). "The Underwriting Experience of Commercial Bank Affiliates Prior to the Glass-Steagall Act: A Re-examination of Evidence for Passage of the Act," 18 *Journal of Banking and Finance* 351–95.

Appelbaum, Binyamin, and David Cho (2009). "Fed's Approach to Regulation Left Banks Exposed to crisis," *Washington Post* (Dec. 21, 2009), A01.

Appelbaum, Binyamin, and Ellen Nakashima (2008). "Banking Regulator Played Advocate over Enforcer: Agency Let Lenders Grow Out of Control, Then Fail," *Washington Post* (Nov. 23, 2008), A1.

Ardagna, Silvia (2019). "Eurozone Is Running Low on Ways to Boost Growth," *Financial Times* (May 6, 2019), available at https://www.ft.com/content/a641891e-6fd9-11e9-bf5c-6eeb837566c5?.

Armour, John, Dan Awrey, Paul Davies, Luca Enriques, Jeffrey N. Gordon, Colin Mayer, and Jennifer Payne (2016). *Principles of Financial Regulation*. Oxford: Oxford University Press.

Armstrong, Robert (2018). "Citigroup Appoints Washington Insider as Its Next Chairman," *Financial Times* (Nov. 5, 2018), available at https://www.ft.com/content/a3cc0338-e08e-11e8-a6e5-792428919cee.

Armstrong, Robert, and Robin Wigglesworth (2019). "Triple-B Movie: 'Big Short' Star Fears for Debt-Laden Companies," *Financial Times* (Jan. 7, 2019), available at https://www.ft.com/content/4cdf8792-056f-11e9-9d01-cd4d49afbbe3.

Arnold, Martin (2019). "What Will Christine Lagarde's ECB Look Like?," *Financial Times* (Oct. 27, 2019), available at https://www.ft.com/content/1683ea12-f4f7-11e9-a79c-bc9acae3b654.

Arnold, Martin (2018). "How US Banks Took Over the Financial World," *Financial Times* (Sept. 16, 2018), available at https://www.ft.com/content/6d9ba066-9eee-11e8-85da-eeb7a9ce36e4.

Arnold, Martin (2017). "Barclays Chief Shows Growing Confidence by Shaking Up Bonuses," *Financial Times* (Feb. 23, 2017), available at https://www.ft.com/content/4155c220-f9e5-11e6-9516-2d969e0d3b65.

Arnold, Martin, Tommy Stubbington, and Laurence Fletcher (2019). "How Mario Draghi Brought Determination to Calm Market Turmoil," *Financial Times* (Oct. 14, 2019), available at https://www.ft.com/content/b9d004a4-ec40-11e9-a240-3b065ef5fc55?segmentId=a7371401-027d-d8bf-8a7f-2a746e767d56.

Arons, Steven (2019). "Europe's Banks Say Goodbye to Trading Dreams as U.S. Pulls Away," *Bloomberg Law* (Feb. 14, 2019).

Asgari, Nikou (2019). "Cash Savings: A Decade of Value Erosion," *Financial Times* (Mar. 8, 2019), available at https://www.ft.com/content/5630edaa-3ea3-11e9-b896-fe36ec32aece.

Ashcraft, Adam B., and Til Schuermann (2008). "Understanding the Securitization of Subprime Mortgage Credit" (Federal Reserve Bank of New York Staff Report No. 318, Mar. 2008), available at http://www.newyorkfed.org/research/staff_reports/sr318.html.

Associated Press (2007). "Will Subprime Mess Ripple Through Economy?" (Mar. 13, 2007), available at http://www.nbcnews.com/id/17584725/ns/business-real_estate/t/will-subprime-mess-ripple-through-economy/#.W1uyAPZFyUk.

Atkinson, Tyler, David Luttrell, and Harvey Rosenblum (2013). "How Bad Was It? The Costs and Consequences of the 2007–09 Financial Crisis" (Federal Reserve Bank of Dallas Staff Paper No. 20, July 2013), available at https://www.dallasfed.org/~/media/Documents/research/staff/staff1301.ashx.

Atlas, Terry (1988). "Lawmakers Take Continental to Task," *Chicago Tribune* (Feb. 4, 1988), 1, available on Westlaw at 1988 WLNR 1724293.

Authers, John (2020). "Happy New Year for Markets in 2020? History Argues Against It," *Bloomberg* (Jan. 6, 2020), available at https://www.bloomberg.com/opinion/articles/2020-01-06/2020-u-s-stock-rally-will-be-hard-to-achieve-if-history-is-guide.

Authers, John (2019). "This Is What It Sounds Like When Fed Doves Cry," *Bloomberg* (Jan. 31, 2019), available at https://www.bloomberg.com/opinion/articles/2019-01-31/this-is-what-it-sounds-like-when-fed-doves-cry-jrk5jzig.

Authers, John (2018). "Markets Can No Longer Rely on the Fed 'Put,'" *Bloomberg* (Nov. 25, 2018), available at https://www.bloomberg.com/opinion/articles/2018-11-25/stocks-tumble-the-fed-won-t-bail-out-markets-this-time.

Authers, John (2013). "Culture Clash Means Banks Must Split, Says Former Citi Chief," *Financial Times* (Sept. 8, 2013), available at https://www.ft.com/content/2cfa6f18-1575-11e3-950a-00144feabdc0.

Authers, John, and Brooke Fox (2018). "Legacy of Lehman Brothers Is a Global Pensions Mess," *Financial Times* (Sept. 24, 2018), available at https://www.ft.com/content/aecfbd18-bc0f-11e8-94b2-17176fbf93f5.

Avalos, Fernando, Torsten Ehlers, and Egemen Eren (2019). "September Stress in Dollar Repo Markets: Passing or Structural?," *BIS Quarterly Review* (Dec. 2019), 12–14, available at https://www.bis.org/publ/qtrpdf/r_qt1912.pdf.

Avraham, Dafna, Patricia Selvaggi, and James Vickery (2012). "A Structural View of U.S. Bank Holding Companies," 18(2) *Economic Policy Review* 65–81 (Federal Reserve Bank of New York, July 2012), available at https://www.newyorkfed.org/medialibrary/media/research/epr/12v18n2/1207avra.pdf.

Awalt, Francis Gloyd (1969). "Recollection of the Banking Crisis of 1933," 43(3) *Business History Review* 347–71.

Awrey, Dan (2014). "The Limits of Private Ordering Within Modern Financial Markets," 34(1) *Review of Banking and Financial Law* 183–254.

Bain, Ben, and Jesse Hamilton (2018). "Banks to Get Another Volcker Rule Win as Hedging Demands Eased (1)," *Bloomberg Law Banking Daily* (May 22, 2018).

Bain, Ben, and Jesse Hamilton (2017). "Regulatory Reform: Trump Pledges 'Big Number' on Dodd-Frank in Anti-Rule Push," 108 *Bloomberg BNA's Banking Report* 202 (Feb. 6, 2017).

Bair, Sheila C. (2019). "Bailing Out Big Banks Again Would Be a Disaster," *Washington Post* (May 26, 2019), B01, available on Westlaw at 2019 WLNR 16156754.

Bair, Sheila C. (2012). *Bull by the Horns: Fighting to Save Main Street from Wall Street and Wall Street from Itself.* New York: Free Press.

Bair, Sheila C. (2010). "Statement of FDIC Chairman Sheila C. Bair on the Causes and Current State of the Financial Crisis Before the Financial Crisis Inquiry Commission" (Jan. 14, 2010), available at https://www.fdic.gov/news/news/speeches/archives/2010/spjan1410.html.

Baker, Colleen M. (2016). "Clearinghouses for Over-the-Counter Derivatives" (Volcker Alliance Working Paper, Nov. 2016), available at https://www.volckeralliance.org/sites/default/files/attachments/VolckerAlliance_ClearinghouseForOverTheCounterDerivatives.pdf.

Bakk-Simon, Klara, et al. (2012). "Shadow Banking in the Euro Area: An Overview" (European Central Bank Occasional Paper No. 133, Apr. 2012), available at http://ssrn.com/abstract=1932063.

Baklanova, Viktoria, Adam M. Copeland, and Rebecca McCaughlin (2015). "Reference Guide to U.S. Repo and Securities Lending Markets" (Office of Financial Research Working Paper No. 15-17, Sept. 9, 2015), available at http://ssrn.com/abstract=2664207.

Ball, Laurence M. (2018). *The Fed and Lehman Brothers: Setting the Record Straight on a Financial Disaster*. New York: Cambridge University Press.

Ballantine, Arthur A. (1948). "When All the Banks Closed," 26(2) *Harvard Business Review* 129–43.

Banerjee, Ryan, and Boris Hofmann (2018). "The Rise of Zombie Firms: Causes and Consequences," *BIS Quarterly Review* (Sept. 2018), 67–78.

Bank of England (2017). "The Bank of England's Approach to Resolution" (Oct. 2017), available at https://www.bankofengland.co.uk/-/media/boe/files/news/2017/october/the-bank-of-england-approach-to-resolution.pdf?la=en&hash=FC806900972DDE7246AD8CD1DF8B8C324BE7652F.

Barba, Aldo, and Massimo Pivetti (2009). "Rising Household Debt: Its Causes and Macroeconomic Implications—a Long-Period Analysis," 33(1) *Cambridge Journal of Economics* 113–37.

Barber, Lionel, and Chris Giles (2020). "Central Banks Running Low on Ways to Fight Recession, Warns Mark Carney," *Financial Times* (Jan. 7, 2020), available at https://www.ft.com/content/713a70b4-315d-11ea-a329-0bcf87a328f2.

Barber, Tony (2018). "Emmanuel Macron's European Ambitions Are Hobbled by Troubles at Home," *Financial Times* (Dec. 15, 2018), available at https://www.ft.com/content/ea998530-fe32-11e8-ac00-57a2a826423e.

Barber, Tony, and Claire Jones (2019). "Interview: Mario Draghi declares victory in battle over the euro," *Financial Times* (Sept. 30, 2019), available at https://www.ft.com/content/b59a4a04-9b26-11e9-9c06-a4640c9feebb.

Bar-Gill, Oren (2009). "The Law, Economics and Psychology of Subprime Mortgage Contracts," 94(5) *Cornell Law Review* 1073–151.

Bar-Gill, Oren, and Elizabeth Warren (2008). "Making Credit Safer," 157(1) *University of Pennsylvania Law Review* 1–101.

Barnichon, Regis, Christian Matthes, and Alexander Ziegenbein (2018). "Are the Effects of Financial Market Disruptions Big or Small?" (June 7, 2018), available at https://www.frbsf.org/economic-research/publications/economic-letter/2018/august/financial-crisis-at-10-years-will-we-ever-recover/ [see list of references].

Baron, Matthew, Emil Verner, and Wei Xiong (2019). "Salient Crises, Quiet Crises" (Apr. 2019), available at http://ssrn.com/abstract=3116148.

Barr, Michael S., Howell E. Jackson, and Margaret E. Tahyar (2018). *Financial Regulation: Law and Policy*. Second edition. St. Paul, MN: Foundation Press.

Barth, James R., R. Dan Brumbaugh, and Robert E. Litan (1992). *The Future of American Banking*. Armonk, NY: M. E. Sharpe, Inc.

Barth, James R., R. Dan Brumbaugh, and James A. Wilcox (2000). "Policy Watch: The Repeal of Glass-Steagall and the Advent of Broad Banking," 14(2) *Journal of Economic Perspectives* 191–204.

Barth, James R., Gerard Caprio Jr., and Ross Levine (2012). *Guardians of Finance: Making Regulators Work for Us*. Cambridge, MA: MIT Press.

Barton, Bruce (1923). "Is There Anything Here That Other Men Couldn't Do?," 95(2) *American Magazine* 16–17, 128–35 (Feb.).

Barwell, Richard, and Oliver Burrows (2011). "Growing Fragilities? Balance Sheets in the Great Moderation" (Bank of England Financial Stability Paper No. 10, Apr. 2011), available at https://www.bankofengland.co.uk/-/media/boe/files/financial-stability-paper/2011/growing-fragilities-balance-sheets-in-the-great-moderation.

Basak, Sonali, Davide Scigliuzzo, and Sabrina Willmer (2019). "Apollo Is Betting It Can Do GE Capital Better than GE Could (1)," *Bloomberg Law* (Mar. 7, 2019).

Basel Committee (2020). Basel Committee (2020). "Basel III Monitoring Report" (Basel Committee on Bank Supervision, April 2020), available at https://www.bis.org/bcbs/publ/d500.pdf.

Basel Committee (2017). "Discussion Paper: The Regulatory Treatment of Sovereign Exposures" (Basel Committee on Bank Supervision, Dec. 2017) (issued for comment by Mar. 9, 2018), available at https://www.bis.org/bcbs/publ/d425.pdf.

Basel Committees et al. (2018). "Analysis of Central Clearing Interdependencies" (Basel Committees on Banking Supervision and on Payments and Market Infrastructures, Financial Stability Board, and OICU-IOSCO, Aug. 9, 2018), available at https://www.bis.org/cpmi/publ/d181.pdf.

Batillossi, Stefano (2009). "Did governance fail universal banks? Moral hazard, risk taking and banking crises in interwar Italy," 62 (S1) *Economic History Review* 101–34.

Baxter, Lawrence (2011). "Betting Big: Value, Caution, and Accountability in an Era of Large Banks and Complex Finance," 31(1) *Review of Banking and Financial Law* 765–879.

Bayoumi, Tamim (2017). *Unfinished Business: The Unexplored Causes of the Financial Crisis and the Lessons Yet to Be Learned*. New Haven: Yale University Press.

Bebchuk, Lucian A., Alma Cohen, and Holger Spamann (2010). "The Wages of Failure: Executive Compensation at Bear Stearns and Lehman, 2000–2008," 27(2) *Yale Journal on Regulation* 257–82.

Bebchuk, Lucian A., and Holger Spamann (2010). "Regulating Bankers' Pay," 98(2) *Georgetown Law Journal* 247–87.

Becker, Jo, Sheryl Gay Stolberg, and Stephen Labaton (2008). "White House Philosophy Stoked Mortgage Bonfire," *New York Times* (Dec. 21, 2008), §1, 1.

Begley, Taylor A., Amiyatosh Purnanandam, and Kuncheng Zheng (2017). "The Strategic Underreporting of Bank Risk," 30(10) *Review of Financial Studies* 3376–415.

Beim, David O. (2009). "It's All About Debt," *Forbes* (Mar. 13, 2009), available at http://www.forbes.com/2009/03/19/household-debt-gdp-markets-beim.html.

Bell, Elliott V. (1929a). "National City Throws in Funds to Avert Money Crisis," *New York Herald Tribune* (Mar. 27, 1929), 1.

Bell, Elliott V. (1929b). "Mitchell Stand Brings Relief to Wall Street," *New York Herald Tribune* (Mar. 28, 1929), 33.

Beltratti, Andrea, and René M. Stulz (2012). "The Credit Crisis Around the Globe: Why Did Some Banks Perform Better?," 105 *Journal of Financial Economics* 1–17.

Benhima, Kenza, and Baptiste Massenot (2013). "Safety Traps," 5(4) *American Economic Journal: Macroeconomics* 68–106.

Benkelman, Susan (1991). "Compromised to Death Bank Reform Plan Ended Up Pleasing Next to No One," *Newsday* (Nov. 6, 1991), 43, available on Westlaw at 1991 WLNR 339349.

Benmelech, Efraim, and Jennifer Dlugosz (2009). "The Credit Rating Crisis" (National Bureau of Economic Research Working Paper No. 15045, June 2009), available at http://www.nber.org/papers/w15045.

Benmelech, Efraim, Carola Frydman, and Dimitris Papanikolaou (2017). "Financial Frictions and Employment During the Great Depression" (National Bureau of Economic Research Working Paper No. w23216, Mar. 2017), available at http://www.nber.org/papers/w23216.

Bennett, Robert A. (1985). "Sanford's New Banking Vision," *New York Times* (Mar. 17, 1985), F1.

Bennett, Robert A. (1984). "A Banking Puzzle: Mixing Freedom and Protection," *New York Times* (Feb. 19, 1984), F1.

Benoit, David, Maureen Farrell, and Eliot Brown (2019). "Startup's Troubles Entangle JPMorgan," *Wall Street Journal* (Sept. 25, 2019), A14.

Benston, George J. (1994). "Universal Banking," 8(3) *Journal of Economic Perspectives* 121–43 (1994).

Benston, George J. (1990). *The Separation of Commercial and Investment Banking: The Glass-Steagall Act Revisited and Reconsidered*. New York: Oxford University Press.

Berger, Allen N., Filippo Curti, Atanas Mihov, and John Sedunov (2018). "Operational Risk Is More Systemic than You Think: Evidence from U.S. Bank Holding Companies" (Sept. 15, 2018), available at http://ssrn.com/abstract=3210808.

Bernanke, Ben S. (2018). "The Real Effects of the Financial Crisis" (Working paper, Sept. 13, 2018), available at https://www.brookings.edu/wp-content/uploads/2018/09/BPEA_Fall2018_The-real-effects-of-the-financial-crisis.pdf.

Bernanke, Ben S. (2015). *The Courage to Act: A Memoir of a Crisis and Its Aftermath*. New York: W. W. Norton & Co.

Bernanke, Ben S. (2013). "A Century of US Central Banking: Goals, Frameworks, Accountability," 27(4) *Journal of Economic Perspectives* 3–16.

Bernanke, Ben S. (2010). "Swearing-In Ceremony Remarks" (Feb. 3, 2010), available at https://www.federalreserve.gov/newsevents/speech/bernanke20100203a.htm.

Bernanke, Ben S. (2008a). "The Economy and Financial Markets: Testimony of Chairman Ben S. Bernanke Before the Committee on Banking, Housing, and Urban Affairs, U.S. Senate" (Feb. 14, 2008), available at https://www.federalreserve.gov/newsevents/testimony/bernanke20080214a.htm.

Bernanke, Ben S. (2008b). "The Economic Outlook: Testimony of Chairman Ben S. Bernanke Before the Joint Economic Committee, U.S. Congress" (Apr. 2, 2008), available at https://www.federalreserve.gov/newsevents/testimony/bernanke20080402a.htm.

Bernanke, Ben S. (2008c). "U.S. Financial Markets: Testimony of Chairman Ben S. Bernanke Before the Committee on Banking, Housing, and Urban Affairs, U.S. Senate" (Sept. 23, 2008), available at https://www.federalreserve.gov/newsevents/testimony/bernanke20080923a1.htm.

Bernanke, Ben S. (2007a). "The Economic Outlook: Testimony of Chairman Ben S. BERNANKE before the Joint Economic Committee, U.S. Congress" (Mar. 28, 2007), available at https://www.federalreserve.gov/newsevents/testimony/bernanke20070328a.htm.

Bernanke, Ben S. (2007b). "The Housing Market and Subprime Lending: Speech by Chairman Ben S. Bernanke to the 2007 International Monetary Conference" (June 5, 2007), available at https://www.federalreserve.gov/newsevents/speech/bernanke20070605a.htm.

Bernanke, Ben S. (2002a). "Asset-Price 'Bubbles' and Monetary Policy: Remarks by Governor Ben S. Bernanke Before the New York Chapter of the National Association of Business Economics" (Oct. 15, 2002), available at https://www.federalreserve.gov/boarddocs/speeches/2002/20021015/default.htm.

Bernanke, Ben S. (2002b). "Deflation: Making Sure 'It' Doesn't Happen Here: Remarks by Governor Ben S. Bernanke Before the National Economists Club" (Nov. 21, 2002), available at https://www.federalreserve.gov/boarddocs/speeches/2002/20021121/default.htm.

Bernanke, Ben S. (1983). "Nonmonetary Effects of the Financial Crisis in the Propagation of the Great Depression," 73(3) *American Economic Review* 257–76.

Bernanke, Ben S., Timothy F. Geithner, and Henry M. Paulson, Jr. (2019). *Firefighting: The Financial Crisis and Its Lessons*. New York: Penguin Books.

Bernanke, Ben S., Timothy F. Geithner, and Henry M. Paulson, Jr. (2018). "Prepping for the Next Crisis," *New York Times* (Sept. 9, 2018), SR2.

Bernanke, Ben S., and Harold James. "The Gold Standard, Deflation, and Financial Crisis in the Great Depression: An International Comparison," in R. G. Hubbard, ed., *Financial Markets and Financial Crises* 33–68. Chicago: University of Chicago Press, 1991.

Berner, Robert, and Brian Grow (2008). "They Warned Us: The Watchdogs Who Saw the Subprime Disaster Coming—and How They Were Thwarted by the Banks and Washington," *Business Week* (Oct. 20, 2008), 36.

Bernstein, Jake, and Jesse Eisinger (2010). "The Wall Street Money Machine: Banks' Self-Dealing Super-Charged Financial Crisis," *ProPublica* (Aug. 26, 2010), available at https://www.propublica.org/article/banks-self-dealing-super-charged-financial-crisis.

Bernstein, Peter L. (1996). *Against the Gods: The Remarkable Story of Risk*. New York: John Wiley & Sons.

Berry, Kate (2019a). "CFPB Takes Big Step Toward Unwinding Payday Lending Rule," *Credit Union Journal* (Feb. 6, 2019), available on Westlaw at 2019 WLNR 3897486.

Berry, Kate (2019b). "Where Have All the CFPB Fair-Lending Cases Gone?," *Credit Union Journal* (Dec. 17, 2019), available on Westlaw at 2019 WLNR 37740486.

Bertaut, Carol, Laurie Pounder DeMarco, Steven B. Kamin, and Ralph Tryon (2011). "ABS Inflows to the United States and the Global Financial Crisis" (Board of Governors of the Federal Reserve System International Finance Discussion Paper No. 2011-1028, Aug. 2011), available at https://www.federalreserve.gov/pubs/ifdp/2011/1028/default.htm.

Better Markets (2019). "Wall Street's Biggest Bailed-Out Banks: Their Rap Sheets and Their Ongoing Crime Spree" (Apr. 9, 2019), available at https://bettermarkets.com/sites/default/files/Better%20Markets%20-%20Wall%20Street%27s%20Six%20Biggest%20Bailed-Out%20Banks%20FINAL.pdf.

Better Markets (2018). "Goldman Sachs Failed 10 Years Ago Today" (Sept. 20, 2018), available at https://bettermarkets.com/newsroom/goldman-sachs-failed-10-years-ago-today.

Better Markets (2015). "The Cost of the Crisis: $20 Trillion and Counting" (July 2015), available at https://bettermarkets.com/sites/default/files/Better%20Markets%20-%20Cost%20of%20the%20Crisis.pdf.

Bhagat, Sanjai, and Brian J. Bolton (2013). "Misaligned Bank Executive Incentive Compensation" (June 2013), available at http://ssrn.com/abstract=2277917.

Bhagwati, Jagdish N. (1998). "The Capital Myth: The Difference Between Trade in Widgets and Dollars," *Foreign Affairs* 7–12 (May/June 1998), available at https://www.foreignaffairs.com/articles/asia/1998-05-01/capital-myth-difference-between-trade-widgets-and-dollars.

Bhattacharyya, Sugato, and Amiyatosh K. Purnanandam (2011). "Risk-Taking by Banks: What Did We Know and When Did We Know It?" (Nov. 28, 2011), available at http://ssrn.com/abstract-1619472.

Bhidé, Amar (2017). "Formulaic Transparency: The Hidden Enabler of Exceptional U.S. Securitization," 29(4) *Journal of Applied Corporate Finance* 96–111.

Billings, Mark, and Forrest Capie (2011). "Financial Crisis, Contagion, and the British Banking System Between the World Wars," 53(2) *Business History* 193–215.

Binham, Caroline (2019a). "Barclays Executive Said Bank 'Dead' Without Qatari Funds, Court Told," *Financial Times* (Jan. 24, 2019), available at https://www.ft.com/content/31286928-1fd8-11e9-b2f7-97e4dbd3580d.

Binham, Caroline (2019b). "Barclays Executives Accused of Lying to Avoid 2008 Crisis Bail-out," *Financial Times* (Oct. 8, 2019), available at https://www.ft.com/content/6d75166c-e9ca-11e9-85f4-d00e5018f061.

Binham, Caroline (2019c). "Former Barclays Chiefs 'Scared to Death' of Bailout Prospect," *Financial Times* (Oct. 15, 2019), available at https://www.ft.com/content/41ad2ec2-ef5e-11e9-ad1e-4367d8281195.

Binham, Caroline (2018). "BofE Ready to Loosen Bank 'Rainy-Day' Buffers on Brexit Upheaval," *Financial Times* (Dec. 5, 2018), available at https://www.ft.com/content/c2c2f7c0-f870-11e8-af46-2022a0b02a6c.

Binham, Caroline, and Jane Croft (2019). "Jury to hear groundbreaking charges against top UK Bankers," *Financial Times* (Jan. 22, 2019), available at https://www.ft.com/content/e92e99fe-1b1c-11e9-9e64-d150b3105d21.

BIS (2019). "Markets Retreat and Rebound," *BIS Quarterly Review* (Mar. 2019), 1–14, available at http://ssrn.com/abstract=3348182.

BIS (2017). "Basel III: Finalising Post-Crisis Reforms" (Dec. 2017), available at https://www.bis.org/bcbs/publ/d424.pdf,

Black, William K. (2005). *The Best Way to Rob a Bank Is to Own One: How Corporate Executives and Politicians Looted the S&L Industry.* Austin: University of Texas Press.

Blackwell, Rob (2014). "Why Citi May Soon Regret Its Big Victory on Capitol Hill," *American Banker* (Dec. 15, 2014).

Blinder, Alan S. (2013). *After the Music Stopped: The Financial Crisis, the Response, and the Work Ahead.* New York: Penguin Group (USA), LLC.

Blinder, Alan S., and Ricardo Reis (2005). "Understanding the Greenspan Standard," in *The Greenspan Era: Lessons for the Future* 11–96 (Proceedings of an Economic Policy Symposium, Federal Reserve Bank of Kansas City, Aug. 2005), available at https://www.kansascityfed.org/publicat/sympos/2005/pdf/Blinder-Reis2005.pdf.

Boemio, Thomas R., and Gerald A. Edwards, Jr. (1989). "Asset Securitization: A Supervisory Perspective," 75 *Federal Reserve Bulletin* 659–69 (Oct.).

Bollen, Bernard, et al. (2015). "The Global Financial Crisis and Its Impact on Australian Bank Risk," 15(1) *International Review of Finance* 89–111.

Bolton, Patrick, Xavier Freixas, and Joel Shapiro (2012). "The Credit Ratings Game," 67(1) *Journal of Finance* 85–111.

Bolton, Patrick, and Martin Oehmke (2018). "Bank Resolution and the Structure of Global Banks" (Columbia Business School Working Paper No. 18-39, Aug. 17, 2018), available at http://ssrn.com/abstract=3169138.

Booker, Katrina (2010). "Citi's Creator, Alone with His Regrets," *New York Times* (Jan. 3, 2010), §BU, 1.

Bookstaber, Richard (2007). *A Demon of Our Own Design: Markets, Hedge Funds, and the Perils of Financial Innovation.* Hoboken, NJ: John Wiley & Sons, Inc.

Borak, Donna (2012). "The Case Against Restoring Glass-Steagall," *American Banker* (Aug. 8, 2012), available on Westlaw at 2012 WLNR 16728061.

Bord, Vitaly, Victoria Ivashina, and Ryan Taliaferro (2017). "Large Banks and the Transmission of Financial Shocks" (Jan. 18, 2017), available at http://ssrn.com/abstract=2688738.

Bordo, Michael D. (2017). "The Operation and Demise of the Bretton Woods System, 1958 to 1971" (National Bureau of Economic Research Working Paper 23189, Feb. 2017), available at http://www.nber.org/papers/w23189.

Bordo, Michael, Michael Edelstein, and Hugh Rockoff (2003). "Was Adherence to the Gold Standard a 'Good Housekeeping Seal of Approval' During the Interwar Period?," in Stanley L. Engerman et al., eds., *Finance, Intermediaries, and Economic Development* 288–318. Cambridge: Cambridge University Press.

Bordo, Michael D., and Angela Redish (1987). "Why Did the Bank of Canada Emerge in 1935?," 47(2) *Journal of Economic History* 405–17.

Bordo, Michael D., Angela Redish, and Hugh Rockoff (2015). "Why Didn't Canada Have a Banking Crisis in 2008 (or in 1930, or 1907, or …)?," 68(1) *Economic History Review* 218–43.

Bordo, Michael D., and David C. Wheelock (2010). "The Promise and Performance of the Federal Reserve as Lender of Last Resort, 1914–1933" (Federal Reserve Bank of St. Louis Working Paper No. 2010-036A, Oct. 2010), available at http://ssrn.com/abstract=1693898.

Borio, Claudio, Mathias Drehmann, and Dora Xia (2018). "The Financial Cycle and Recession Risk," *BIS Quarterly Review* (Dec. 2018), 59–71.

Borio, Claudio, and William R. White (2003). "Whither Monetary and Financial Stability? The Implications of Evolving Policy Regimes," in *Monetary Policy and Uncertainty: Adapting to a Changing Economy* 131–211 (Proceedings of an Economic Policy Symposium, Federal Reserve Bank of Kansas City, Aug. 2003), available at https://www.kansascityfed.org/publications/research/escp/symposiums/escp-2003.

Born, Brooksley (1999). "Testimony of Brooksley Born, Chairperson, Commodity Futures Trading Commission, Before the Subcommittee on Capital Markets, Securities, and Government Sponsored Enterprises of the Committee on Banking and Financial Services, U.S. House of Representatives" (Mar. 25, 1999), available on Westlaw at 1999 WL 191046.

Boston, Claire (2019a). "Banks Presence Shrinks in the U.S. Company Bond Market," *Bloomberg Law* (Jan. 25, 2019).

Boston, Claire (2019b). "Wall Street Wants to Reform CDS. Here's Why That'll Be Tough (1)," *Bloomberg Law* (Mar. 7, 2019).

Boston, Claire (2019c). "Banks Keeping Riskier Credit Card Loans with Losses Creeping Higher," *Bloomberg* (May 6, 2019).

Bowman, Louise (2017). "Banking: Throwing the Bail-in Out with the Bath Water," *Euromoney* (Sept. 18, 2017), available at https://www.euromoney.com/article/b14q7hcxq7pm49/banking-throwing-the-bail-in-out-with-the-bath-water.

Bradsher, Keith (1995). "No New Deal for Banking: Efforts to Drop Depression-Era Barriers Stall, Again," *New York Times* (Nov. 2, 1995), D1.

Brainard, Lael (2019a). "Is the Middle Class Within Reach for Middle-Income Families" (May 10, 2019), available at https://www.federalreserve.gov/newsevents/speech/brainard20190510a.htm.

Brainard, Lael (2019b). "Statement on Final Rule to Modify the Volcker Rule by Governor Lael Brainard" (Oct. 8, 2019), available at https://www.federalreserve.gov/newsevents/pressreleases/brainard-statement-20191008.htm.

Brainard, Lael (2019c). "Statement by Governor Lael Brainard" (Oct. 10, 2019), available at https://www.federalreserve.gov/newsevents/pressreleases/brainard-statement-20191010.htm.

Brainard, Lael (2019d). "Statement by Governor Lael Brainard" (Oct. 28, 2019), available at https://www.federalreserve.gov/newsevents/pressreleases/brainard-statement-20191028.htm.

Braithwaite, Tom (2013). "Geithner to Take Strategy Role at Warburg Pincus," *Financial Times* (Nov. 16, 2013), available at https://www.ft.com/content/da749cde-4eca-11e3-a6f4-00144feabdc0.

Brandeis, Louis (1933 [1914]). *Other People's Money: And How the Bankers Use It*. Washington, DC: National Home Library Foundation.

Bratton, William W. (2002). "Enron and the Dark Side of Shareholder Value," 76(5–6) *Tulane Law Review* 1275–361.

Bratton, William W., and Adam J. Levitin (2013). "A Transactional Genealogy of Scandal: From Michael Milken to Enron to Goldman Sachs," 86(4) *Southern California Law Review* 783–868.

Bravin, Jess, and Paul Beckett (2002). "Friendly Watchdog: Federal Regulator Often Helps Banks Fighting Consumers," *Wall Street Journal* (Jan. 28, 2002), A1.

Brean, Donald J.S., Lawrence Kryzanowski, and Gordon S. Roberts (2011). "Canada and the United States: Different roots, different routes to financial sector regulation," 53(1) *Business History* 249–69.

Brewer III, Elijah, and Julapa Jagtiani (2013). "How Much Did Banks Pay to Become Too-Big-To-Fail and to Become Systemically Important?," 43 *Journal of Financial Services Research* 1–35 (2013).

Briançon, Pierre (2019). "Is Europe Ready for the Next Crisis?," *Barron's* (Mar. 29, 2019), available at https://www.barrons.com/articles/is-europe-ready-for-the-next-economic-crisis-51553901914.

Bright, Steve, Paul Glasserman, Christopher Gregg, and Hashim Hamandi (2016). "What Can We Learn from Publicly Available Data in Banks' Living Wills?" (Office of Financial Research Brief 16-05, May 25, 2016), available at https://www.financialresearch.gov/briefs/2016/05/25/living-wills.

Brimmer, Andrew F. (1989). "Distinguished Lecture on Economics in Government: Central Banking and Systemic Risks in Capital Markets," 3(2) *Journal of Economic Perspectives* 3–18.

Britton, Katie, Lindsey Dawkes, Simon Debbage, and Talib Idris (2016). "Ring-Fencing: What It Is and How Will It Affect Banks and Their Customers?," 56(4) *Quarterly Bulletin* 164–72 (Bank of England, 4th Qtr. 2016).

Brocker, Michael, and Christopher Hanes (2013). "The 1920s Real Estate Boom and the Downturn of the Great Depression: Evidence from City Cross Sections" (National Bureau of Economic Research Working Paper 18852), available at www.nber.org/papers/w18852.

Broughton, Kristin (2018). "The Battle for Deposits Intensifies," *American Banker Magazine* (May 1, 2018), available on Westlaw at 2018 WLNR 13248381.

Brown, Sherrod (2019). "Brown Calls on Fed to Protect Taxpayers by Increasing Big Bank Capital" (Jan. 30, 2019), available at https://www.banking.senate.gov/newsroom/minority/brown-calls-on-fed-to-protect-taxpayers-by-increasing-big-bank-capital.

Brown, Sherrod (2018). "Pushing the Envelope: The Consumer Financial Protection Bureau Under the Trump Administration" (U.S. Senate Committee on Banking, Housing, and Urban Affairs, Minority Staff Report, Nov. 2018), available at https://www.banking.senate.gov/imo/media/doc/Pushing%20the%20Envelope%20-%20Mick%20Mulvaney%20at%20CFPB%20FINAL.pdf.

Bruce-Lockhart, Chelsea (2019). "Australia's Stuttering Economy Is Hot Election Topic," *Financial Times* (May 15, 2019), available at https://www.ft.com/content/25700d04-7620-11e9-bbad-7c18c0ea0201.

Bruner, Robert F., and Sean D. Carr (2007). *The Panic of 1907: Lessons Learned from the Market's Perfect Storm*. Hoboken, NJ: John Wiley & Sons, Inc.

Brunnermeier, Markus K., Gang Dong, and Darius Palia (2019). "Banks' Non-Interest Income and Systemic Risk" (Working Paper, Jan. 2019), available at https://scholar.princeton.edu/markus/publications/banks-non-interest-income-and-systemic-risk.

Brunnermeier, Markus K., and Ricardo Reis (2019). "A Crash Course on the Euro Crisis" (National Bureau of Economic Research Working Paper 26229, Sept. 2019), available at http://www.nber.org/papers/w26229.

Brunsden, Jim (2018). "Eurozone Economy: Draghi Confirms Plan to End QE Despite Weak Economic Data," *Financial Times* (Nov. 26, 2018), available at https://www.ft.com/content/1f4f31ec-f197-11e8-9623-d7f9881e729f?emailId=5bfc5eef210413000440ffa4&segmentId=60a126e8-df3c-b524-c979-f90bde8a67cd.

Brunsden, Jim, et al. (2017). "Italian Banks: Why Italy's €17bn Bank Rescue Deal Is Making Waves Across Europe," *Financial Times* (June 26, 2017), available at https://www.ft.com/content/03a1c7d0-5a61-11e7-b553-e2df1b0c3220.

Brunsden, Jim, and Mehreen Khan (2018). "Greece Debt Crisis: Eurozone Hails Greece's Exit from Bailout as End of crisis," *Financial Times* (Aug. 20, 2018), available at https://www.ft.com/content/aeb930e0-a475-11e8-926a-7342fe5e173f.

Burghof, Hans-Peter, Daniel Schmidt, and Marcel Gehrung (2019). "Banking Systems and Their Effects on Regional Inequality and Wealth" (Apr. 30, 2019), available at http://ssrn.com/abstract=3380669.

Burns, Hilary (2019). "Post-Crisis Organizers Find a Whole New De Novo Ballgame," *American Banker* (Apr. 1, 2019), available on Westlaw at 2019 WLNR 10106883.

Butkiewicz, James (1995). "The Impact of a Lender of Last Resort During the Great Depression: The Case of the Reconstruction Finance Corporation," 32(2) *Explorations in Economic History* 197–216.

Buzenberg, Bill (2009). "Commentary: The Mega-Banks Behind the Meltdown: How Wall Street's Greed Fueled the Subprime Disaster" (Center for Public Integrity, May 6, 2009), available at https://www.publicintegrity.org/2009/05/06/5455/commentary-mega-banks-behind-meltdown.

Calder, Lendol (1999). *Financing the American Dream: A Cultural History of Consumer Credit*. Princeton: Princeton University Press.

Calem, Paul, Julapa Jagtiani, Ramain Quinn Maingi, and David Abell (2018). "Redefault Risk in the Aftermath of the Mortgage Crisis: Why Did Modifications Improve More than Self-Cures?" (Federal Reserve Bank of Philadelphia Working Paper 18-26, Nov. 2018), available at http://ssrn.com/abstract=3289013.

Calin, R.D. (1942). "Chicago Bank Loans Since 1914," *Chicago Tribune* (Jan. 3, 1942), 21.

Callender, Harold (1931). "The German Crisis as Seen from Germany," *New York Times* (Nov. 29, 1931), XXI.

Calomiris, Charles W. (1993). "Financial Factors in the Great Depression," 7(2) *Journal of Economic Perspectives* 61–85.

Calomiris, Charles W., and Joseph R. Mason (2003a). "Consequences of Bank Distress During the Great Depression," 93(3) *American Economic Review* 937–47.

Calomiris, Charles W., and Joseph R. Mason (2003b). "Fundamentals, Panics, and Bank Distress During the Depression," 93(5) *American Economic Review* 1615–47.

Calomiris, Charles W., and Joseph R. Mason (1997). "Contagion and Bank Failures During the Great Depression: The June 1932 Chicago Banking Panic," 87(5) *American Economic Review* 863–83.

Calomiris, Charles W., Joseph R. Mason, Marc Weidenmier, and Katherine Bobroff (2013). "The Effects of Reconstruction Finance Corporation Assistance on Michigan's Banks' Survival in the 1930s," 50 *Explorations in Economic History* 526–47.

Calomiris, Charles W., and Berry Wilson (2004). "Bank Capital and Portfolio Management: The 1930s 'Capital Crunch' and the 'Scramble to Shed Risk,'" 77(3) *Journal of Business* 421–55.

Campbell, Rhett G. (2005). "Financial Market Contracts and BAPCPA," 79(3) *American Bankruptcy Law Journal* 697–712.

Capie, Forrest (1995a). "Prudent and Stable (but Inefficient?): Commercial Banks in Britain, 1890–1940," in Michael D. Bordo and Richard Sylla, eds., *Anglo-American Financial Systems: Institutions and Markets in the Twentieth Century* 41–64. New York: Irwin Professional Publishing.

Capie, Forrest (1995b). "Commercial Banking in Britain Between the Wars," in Charles H. Feinstein, ed., *Banking, Currency, and Finance in Europe Between the Wars* 395–413. Oxford: Clarendon Press.

Carbó-Valverde, Santiago, Pedro Cuadros-Solas, and Francisco Rodriguez-Fernández (2019). "Do Bank Bailouts Have an Impact on the Underwriting Business?" (Aug. 2019), available at http://ssrn.com/abstract=3252421.

Carlson, Mark (2004). "Are Branch Banks Better Survivors? Evidence from the Depression Era," 42(1) *Economic Inquiry* 111–26.

Carlson, Mark A., and Marco Macchiavelli (2018). "Emergency Collateral Upgrades" (Federal Reserve Board Finance and Economics Discussion Series Working Paper 2018-078, Nov. 14, 2018), available at http://ssrn.com/abstract=3286488.

Carlson, Mark A., Kris James Mitchener, and Gary Richardson, "Arresting Bank Panics: Federal Reserve Liquidity Provision and the Forgotten Panic of 1929," 119(5) *Journal of Political Economy* 889–924.

Carlson, Mark, and Jonathan D. Rose (2015). "Credit Availability and the Collapse of the Banking Sector in the 1930s," 47(7) *Journal of Money, Credit and Banking* 1239–71.

Carmassi, Jacopo, and Richard Herring (2016). "The Corporate Complexity of Global Systemically Important Banks," 49 *Journal of Financial Services Research* 175–201.

Carnell, Richard Scott (1993). "A Partial Antidote to Perverse Incentives: The FDIC Improvement Act of 1991," 12 *Annual Review of Banking Law* 317–71.

Carnell, Richard Scott, Jonathan R. Macey, and Geoffrey P. Miller (2017). *The Law of Financial Institutions*. Sixth edition. New York: Wolters Kluwer.

Carosso, Vincent P. (1970). *Investment Banking in America: A History*. Cambridge: Harvard University Press.

Carow, Kenneth A., Edward J. Kane, and Rajesh P. Narayanan (2006). "How Have Borrowers Fared in Banking Megamergers?," 38(3) *Journal of Money, Credit, and Banking* 821–36 (2006).

Carpenter, David H., and M. Maureen Murphy (2010). "Permissible Securities Activities of Commercial Banks Under the Glass-Steagall Act (GSA) and the Gramm-Leach-Bliley Act (GLBA)" (Congressional Research Service, Report No. 7-5700, Apr. 12, 2010), available at http://digital.library.unt.edu/ark:/67531/metadc503609/m1/1/high_res_d/R41181_2010Apr12.pdf.

Casey, Anthony J., and Eric A. Posner (2015). "A Framework for Bailout Regulation," 91(2) *Notre Dame Law Review* 479–536.

Catte, Pietro, Pietro Cova, Patrizio Pagano, and Ignazio Visco (2010). "The Role of Macroeconomic Policies in the Global Crisis" (Bank of Italy Occasional Paper No. 69, July 2010), available at http://ssrn.com/abstract=1721429.

CCP Research (2017). "Conduct Costs Results" (CCP Research Foundation, 2017), available at http://conductcosts.ccpresearchfoundation.com/conduct-costs-results.

Cecchetti, Stephen G., and Kermit L. Schoenholtz (2019). "Emergency Guarantee Authority: A FEMA for Finance," *CLS Blue Sky Blog* (May 15, 2019), available at http://clsbluesky.law.columbia.edu/2019/05/15/emergency-guarantee-authority-a-fema-for-finance.

Cecchetti, Stephen G., and Kermit L. Schoenholtz (2018). "Money Funds—The Empire Strikes Back?," *Money and Banking* (Jan. 15, 2018) (blog post), available at https://www.moneyandbanking.com/commentary/2018/1/12/money-funds-the-empire-strikes-back.

Center for Responsive Politics (2019). "Finance/Insurance/Real Estate: Background," available at https://www.opensecrets.org/industries/background.php?cycle=2018&ind=F; "Lobbying: Ranked Sectors, 1998–2018," available athttps://www.opensecrets.org/lobby/top.php?indexType=c&showYear=a; "Finance/Insurance/Real Estate: Long-Term Contribution Trends," available athttps://www.opensecrets.org/industries/totals.php?cycle=2018&ind=F (visited on Apr. 12, 2019).

CFTC (1998). Commodity Futures Trading Commission, "Over-the-Counter Derivatives: Concept Release" (May 12, 1998), 63 *Federal Register* 26114 (1998), available on Westlaw at 1998 WL 232368 (F.R.).

Chancellor, Edward (1999). *Devil Take the Hindmost: A History of Financial Speculation*. New York: Farrar, Straus & Giroux.

Chandler, Lester V. (1970). *America's Greatest Depression*. New York: Harper & Row.

Chang, Felix B. (2016). "Second-Generation Monopolization: Parallel Exclusion in Derivatives Markets," 2016(3) *Columbia Business Law Review* 657–739.

Chappatta, Brian (2019). "Can Stocks and Bonds Both Be Right? Actually, Yes," *Bloomberg* (Apr. 4, 2019), available at https://www.bloomberg.com/opinion/articles/2019-04-04/a-world-of-leverage-heats-up-stocks-and-bonds.

Chappatta, Brian (2018). "$250 Trillion in Debt: The World's Post-Lehman Legacy," *Bloomberg* (Sept. 13, 2018), available at https://www.bloomberg.com/graphics/2018-lehman-debt/.

Chase, Randall J. (2018). "Ex-Wilmington Trust Official Convicted of Fraud, Conspiracy," *AP Business News* (May 3, 2018), available on Westlaw.

Chen, Brian S., Samuel G. Hanson, and Jeremy C. Stein (2017). "The Decline of Big-Bank Lending to Small Business: Dynamic Impacts on Local Credit and Labor Markets" (National Bureau of Economic Research Working Paper 23843, Sept. 2017), available at http://www.nber.org/papers/w23843.

Chernenko, Sergey (2017). "The Front Men of Wall Street: The Role of CDO Collateral Managers in the CDO Boom and Bust," 72(5) *Journal of Finance* 1893–935.

Chernobai, Anna, Ali Ozdagli, and Jianlin Wang (2016). "Business Complexity and Risk Management: Evidence from Operational Risk Events in U.S. Bank Holding Companies" (Federal Reserve of Boston Working Paper No. 16-16, Oct. 2016), available at http://ssrn.com/abstract=2874730.

Chernow, Ron (1990). *The House of Morgan: An American Banking Dynasty and the Rise of Modern Finance*. New York: Simon & Schuster.

Chicago Daily Tribune (1935). "1935 Earnings of Continental Bank Show Gain," *Chicago Daily Tribune* (Dec. 24, 1935), 21.

Chicago Daily Tribune (1933). "Continental Bank Approves RFC Stock Sale," *Chicago Daily Tribune* (Dec. 21, 1933), 25.

Chicago Daily Tribune (1932a). "Chicago Banks Earn Smaller Profits in 1931," *Chicago Daily Tribune* (Jan. 2, 1932), 15.

Chicago Daily Tribune (1932b). "Bain to Prison; Sons Fined," *Chicago Daily Tribune* (Aug. 25, 1932), 1.

Chicago Tribune (2016). "Feds Won't File Fraud Suit Against Countrywide's Mozilo," *Chicago Tribune* (June 17, 2016), available at https://www.chicagotribune.com/business/ct-countrywide-angelo-mozilo-feds-20160617-story.html.

Claessens, Stijn, Zoltan Pozsar, Lev Ratnovski, and Manmohan Singh (2012). "Shadow Banking: Economics and Policy" (IMF Staff Discussion Note SDN/12/12, Dec. 4, 2012), available at http://ssrn.com/abstract=2187661.

Clark, Andrew, and Jill Treanor (2008). "Greenspan—I Was Wrong About the Economy. Sort of," *The Guardian* (Oct. 23, 2008), available at https://www.theguardian.com/business/2008/oct/24/economics-creditcrunch-federal-reserve-greenspan.

Clark, Tim, Matt Kabaker, and Lee Sachs (2018). "Bank Capital, Phase 2—The Banks: Reviving the System" (Working paper, Sept. 2018), available at https://www.brookings.edu/wp-content/uploads/2018/08/06-Banks-II-9_10-REV-Prelim-Disc-Draft-2018.09.11.pdf.

Clementi, Gian Luca, Thomas E. Cooley, Matthew Richardson, and Ingo Walter (2009). "Rethinking Compensation in Financial Firms," in Viral V. Acharya and Matthew Richardson, eds., *Restoring Financial Stability: How to Repair a Failed System* 197–214. New York: John Wiley & Sons.

Cleveland, Harold van B., and Thomas F. Huertas (1985). *Citibank, 1812–1970*. Cambridge: Harvard University Press.

Clinton, William J. (1999). "Statement by President Bill Clinton at the Signing of the Financial Modernization Bill" (Nov. 12, 1999), available at http://www.treas.gov/press-center/press-releases/Pages/ls241.aspx.

Clozel, Lalita (2018a). "Big Banks Revamp Lobbying for New Regulatory Climate," *Wall Street Journal* (July 17, 2018), A4.

Clozel, Lalita (2018b). "Banking and Finance News: Fed Pushes for Easier Bank Stress Tests," *Wall Street Journal* (Nov. 10, 2018), B10.

Clozel, Lalita (2018c). "Fed, FDIC Seek Reset With Banks," *Wall Street Journal* (Dec. 13, 2018), A2.

Coalition of OTC Derivatives Dealers (1999). "Testimony of a Coalition of Investment and Commercial Banks Regarding Commodity Exchange Act Reauthorization Before the

Subcommittee on Risk Management, Research and Specialty Crops, United States House of Representatives" (May 20, 1999), available on Westlaw at 1999 WL 321618.

Cockburn, Andrew (2018). "Swap Meet: Wall Street's War on the Volcker Rule," *Harper's Magazine* (Jan. 2018), available at https://harpers.org/archive/2018/01/swap-meet.

Coen, William (2018). "Looking Ahead by Looking Back" (Speech at the 20th International Conference of Banking Supervisors, Nov. 28, 2018), available at https://www.bis.org/speeches/sp181128.pdf.

Coffee, John C., Jr. (2012). "The Political Economy of Dodd-Frank: Why Financial Reform Tends to Be Frustrated and Systemic Risk Perpetuated," 97 *Cornell Law Review* 1019–82.

Cohan, William D. (2016a). "Wall St. Whistle-Blowers, Often Scorned, Get New Support," *New York Times (DealBook)* (Feb. 11, 2016), available at https://www.nytimes.com/2016/02/12/business/dealbook/wall-st-whistle-blowers-often-scorned-get-new-support.html.

Cohan, William D. (2016b). "A Clue to the Scarcity of Financial Crisis Prosecutions," *New York Times (DealBook)* (July 21, 2016), available at https://www.nytimes.com/2016/07/22/business/dealbook/a-clue-to-the-scarcity-of-financial-crisis-prosecutions.html.

Collins, Neil (2014). "Banks Have Become Too Complex to Grasp," *Financial Times* (Nov. 7, 2014), available at https://www.ft.com/content/f94edb04-65c8-11e4-aba7-00144feabdc0.

Comfort, Nicholas, and John Glover (2018). "Riskiest Bank Debt Could Spark Market Turmoil, Bundesbank Says," *Bloomberg* (Mar. 27, 2018).

Comptroller of the Currency (1927). *Annual Report of the Comptroller of the Currency* (Dec. 12, 1927), available at https://fraser.stlouisfed.org/docs/publications/comp/1920s/compcurr_1927.pdf.

Comptroller of the Currency (1924). *Annual Report of the Comptroller of the Currency* (Dec. 1, 1923), available at https://fraser.stlouisfed.org/docs/publications/comp/1920s/compcurr_1924.pdf.

Comptroller of the Currency (1922). *Annual Report of the Comptroller of the Currency* (Dec. 4, 1922), available at https://fraser.stlouisfed.org/docs/publications/comp/1920s/compcurr_1922.pdf.

Comptroller of the Currency (1920). *Annual Report of the Comptroller of the Currency* (Dec. 6, 1920), Volume I, available at https://fraser.stlouisfed.org/docs/publications/comp/1920s/compcurr_1920_Vol1.pdf.

Comptroller of the Currency (1914). *Annual Report of the Comptroller of the Currency* (Dec. 7, 1914), Volume I, available at https://fraser.stlouisfed.org/docs/publications/comp/1910s/1914/compcurr_1914_Vol1.pdf.

Conti-Brown, Peter (2016). *The Power and Independence of the Federal Reserve*. Princeton: Princeton University Press.

Cook, Timothy Q., and Jeremy G. Duffield (1993). "Money Market Mutual Funds and Other Short-Term Investment Pools," in Timothy Q. Cook and Robert K. LaRoche, eds., *Instruments of the Money Market* 156–72. Seventh edition. Richmond: Federal Reserve Bank of Richmond, available at https://www.richmondfed.org/~/media/richmondfedorg/publications/research/special_reports/instruments_of_the_money_market/pdf/full_publication.pdf.

Cooper, Cameron (2015). "6 Economists Who Predicted the Global Financial Crisis" (July 7, 2015), available at https://www.intheblack.com/articles/2015/07/07/6-economists-who-predicted-the-global-financial-crisis-and-why-we-should-listen-to-them-from-now-on.

Cooper, Russell, and Kalin Nikolov (2018). "Government Debt and Banking Fragility: The Spreading of Strategic Uncertainty" (European Central Bank Working Paper No. 2195, Nov. 2018), available at https://www.ecb.europa.eu/pub/pdf/scpwps/ecb.wp2195.en.pdf?89346e644b718bbd7b9399a24b080459.

Copeland, Adam (2012). "Evolution and Heterogeneity Among Larger Bank Holding Companies: 1994 to 2010," 18(2) *FRBNY Economic Policy Review* 83–93, available at https://www.newyorkfed.org/medialibrary/media/research/epr/12v18n2/1207cope.pdf.

Cordell, Jake (2016). "The Big Bang 30 Years On: How the City of London Has Changed Since 1986" (Oct. 26, 2016), available at http://www.cityam.com/252351/big-bang-30-can-1986-hold-key-seizing-citys-brexit.

Cordell, Larry, Greg Feldberg, and Danielle Sass (2019). "The Role of ABS CDOs in the Financial Crisis," 25(2) *Journal of Structured Finance* 10–27.

Cordell, Larry, Yilin Huang, and Meredith Williams (2012). "Collateral Damage: Sizing and Assessing the Subprime CDO Crisis" (Federal Reserve Bank of Philadelphia Working Paper No. 11-30/R, May 2012), available at https://philadelphiafed.org/-/media/research-and-data/publications/working-papers/2011/wp11-30R.pdf.

Corman, Linda (1990). "Firewalls May Have Outlived Their Usefulness," *American Banker* (July 26, 1990), 1, available on Westlaw at 1990 WLNR 1840266.

Costigliola, Frank (1976). "The United States and the Reconstruction of Germany in the 1920s," 50(4) *Business History Review* 487–502.

Coval, Joshua, Jakub Jurek, and Erik Stafford (2009). "The Economics of Structured Finance," 23(1) *Journal of Economic Perspectives* 3–25.

Crafts, Nicholas, and Peter Fearon (2010). "Lessons from the 1930s Great Depression," 26(3) *Oxford Review of Economic Policy* 285–317.

Crawford, John (2017). "A Better Way to Revive Glass-Steagall," 70 *Stanford Law Review Online* 1–8 (May 2017), available at http://ssrn.com/abstract=2972203.

Croft, Jane (2019). "Barclays Bosses Were 'Scared to Death' About Risk of State Bailout," *Financial Times* (Jan. 28, 2019), available at https://www.ft.com/content/3f913eae-2316-11e9-8ce6-5db4543da632.

Croft, Jane, and Caroline Binham (2020). "Barclays acquittals leave SFO facing the questions," *Financial Times* (Feb. 28, 2020), available at https://www.ft.com/content/6e434190-5a3b-11ea-abe5-8e03987b7b20.

Crow, David (2019). "Barclays Boosts Case for Investment Banking After Strong Results," *Financial Times* (Oct. 25, 2019), available at https://www.ft.com/content/e3761e8e-f6f3-11e9-a79c-bc9acae3b654.

Crow, David, and Stephen Morris (2019). "Investment Banking: The Battle for Barclays," *Financial Times* (Jan. 19, 2019), available at https://www.ft.com/content/035be220-199a-11e9-b93e-f4351a53f1c3.

Cudahy, Richard D., and William D. Henderson (2005). "From Insull to Enron: Corporate (Re) Regulation after the Rise and Fall of Two Energy Icons," 26(1) *Energy Law Journal* 35–110.

Culp, Christopher L. (2013). "Syndicated leveraged loans during and after the crisis and the role of the shadow banking system," 25(2) *Journal of Applied Corporate Finance* 63–85.

Cumming, Douglas, Florencio Lopez-de-Silanes, Joseph A. McCahery, and Armin Schweinbacher (2019). "Tranching in the Syndicated Loan Market Around the World" (May 26, 2019), available at http://ssrn.com/abstract=3395114.

Curran, Enda, and Rich Miller (2019). "Central Banks' Window to Restock Ammo Is Closing," *Bloomberg* (Jan. 20, 2019), available at https://www.bloomberg.com/news/articles/2019-01-20/central-banks-window-to-restock-ammo-is-closing-as-growth-slows.

Curti, Filippo, and Atanas Mihov (2018). "Diseconomies of Scale in Banking: Evidence from Operational Risk" (Apr. 15, 2018), available at http://ssrn.com/abstract=3210206.

da Costa, Pedro Nicolaci (2015). "How to Break the Wall Street to Washington Merry-Go-Round," *Foreign Policy* (Dec. 10, 2015), available at https://foreignpolicy.com/2015/12/10/wall-street-to-washington-and-back-again-bernanke-revolving-door-federal-reserve.

Dahiya, Sandeep, Bardia Kamrad, Valerio Potì, and Akhtar R. Siddique (2017). "The Greenspan Put" (June 27, 2017), available at http://ssrn.com/abstract=2993325.

Dale, Richard (1992). *International Banking Deregulation: The Great Banking Experiment*. Oxford: Blackwell Publishers.

Darrah, Kim (2018). "The QE Reversal," *World Finance* (Apr. 26, 2018), available at https://www.worldfinance.com/banking/the-qe-reversal.

Das, Satyajit (2018). "The World Will Pay for Not Dealing with Debt," *Bloomberg* (Dec. 22, 2018), available at https://www.bloomberg.com/opinion/articles/2018-12-23/world-will-pay-for-not-reining-in-debt-growth?utm_medium=email&utm_source=newsletter&utm_term=181228&utm_campaign=sharetheview.

Dash, Eric, and Andrew Ross Sorkin (2008). "Throwing a Lifeline to a Troubled Giant: Fed's Bailout of A.I.G. Came After Frantic Search for Rescuer," *New York Times* (Sept. 18, 2008), C1.

Davies, Richard, and Belinda Tracey (2014). "Too Big to Be Efficient? The Impact of Implicit Subsidies on Estimates of Scale Economies for Banks," 46(1) *Journal of Money, Credit and Banking* 219–53.

Davis, E. P. (1992). *Debt, Financial Fragility, and Systemic Risk*. Oxford: Clarendon Press.

Day, Kathleen (2019). *Broken Bargain: Bankers, Bailouts, and the Struggle to Tame Wall Street*. New Haven: Yale University Press.

Dayen, David (2017). "A Corporate Defender at Heart, Former SEC Chair Mary Jo White Returns to Her Happy Place," *The Intercept* (Feb. 17, 2017), available at https://theintercept.com/2017/02/17/a-corporate-defender-at-heart-former-sec-chair-mary-jo-white-returns-to-her-happy-place.

Debter, Lauren (2017). "Fed Raises Rates for Third Time in 2017 as U.S. Economy Chugs Along," *Forbes* (Dec. 13, 2017), available at https://www.forbes.com/sites/laurengensler/2017/12/13/federal-reserve-raises-interest-rates-for-third-time-in-2017/#50af9027a531.

DeDad, Michael (2017). "Risk Aversion in Lending Following the Financial Crisis" (Working Paper, Apr. 21, 2017), available at https://economics.indiana.edu/home/conferences/2017-jordan-river-economics-conference/files/2017-04-28-13.pdf.

de Fontenay, Elisabeth (2014). "Do the Securities Laws Matter? The Rise of the Leveraged Loan Market," 39(4) *Journal of Corporation Law* 725–68.

de Fontenay, Elisabeth (2013). "Private Equity Firms as Gatekeepers," 33(1) *Review of Banking and Financial Law* 115–89.

Dell'Ariccia, Giovanni, Pau Rabanal, and Damiano Sandri (2018). "Unconventional Monetary Policies in the Euro Area, Japan, and the United Kingdom," 32(4) *Journal of Economic Perspectives* 147–72.

DeLong, J. Bradford, and Andrei Shleifer (1991). "The Stock Market Bubble of 1929: Evidence from Closed-End Mutual Funds," 51(3) *Journal of Economic History* 675–700.

Demirgüç-Kunt, Asli, and Harry Huizinga (2010). "Bank Activity and Funding Strategies: The Impact of Risk and Returns," 98 *Journal of Financial Economics* 626–50.

Demsetz, Rebecca S., and Philip E. Strahan (1997). "Diversification, Size, and Risk at Bank Holding Companies," 29(3) *Journal of Money, Credit, and Banking* 300–13.

Demyanyk, Yuliya, and Otto Van Hemert (2011). "Understanding the Subprime Mortgage Crisis," 24(6) *Review of Financial Studies* 1848–80.

DeYoung, Robert, Emma Y. Peng, and Meng Yan (2013). "Executive Compensation and Business Policy Choices at U.S. Commercial Banks," 48(1) *Journal of Financial and Quantitative Analysis* 165–96.

DeYoung, Robert, and Tara Rice (2004). "Noninterest Income and Financial Performance at U.S. Commercial Banks," 39(1) *Financial Review* 101–27.

DeYoung, Robert, and Gökhan Torna (2013). "Nontraditional Banking Activities and Bank Failures During the Financial Crisis," 22 *Journal of Financial Intermediation* 397–421.

Dick, Astrid A. (2006). "Nationwide Branching and Its Impact on Market Structure, Quality, and Bank Performance," 79(2) *Journal of Business* 567–92.

Di Maggio, Marco, and Amir Kermani (2017). "Credit-Induced Boom and Bust," 30(11) *Review of Financial Studies* 3711–58.

Di Maggio, Marco, Amir Kermani, and Sanket Korgaonkar (2016). "Partial Deregulation and Competition: Effects on Risky Mortgage Origination" (Harvard Business School Finance Working Paper, Nov. 17, 2016), available at http://ssrn.com/abstract=2591434.

Ding, Lei, Roberto G. Quercia, Carolina K. Reid, and Alan M. White (2012). "The Impact of Federal Preemption of State Antipredatory Lending Laws on the Foreclosure Crisis," 31(2) *Journal of Policy Analysis and Management* 367–89.

Dobuzinskis, Alex, and Dan Levine (2010). "Mozilo Settles Countrywide Fraud Case at $67.5 Million," *Reuters* (Oct. 15, 2010), available at https://www.reuters.com/article/us-sec-mozilo-idUSTRE69E4KN20101015.

Dodds, Lynn Strongin (2018). "Ten Years On: Are Derivatives Markets Safer?" (Sept. 18, 2018), available at https://derivsource.com/2018/09/18/ten-years-on-are-derivatives-markets-safer.

DOJ (2018a). United States Department of Justice, Press Release: "Barclays Agrees to Pay $2 Billion in Civil Penalties to Resolve Claims for Fraud in the Sale of Residential Mortgage-Backed Securities" (Mar. 29, 2018), available at https://www.justice.gov/opa/pr/barclays-agrees-pay-2-billion-civil-penalties-resolve-claims-fraud-sale-residential-mortgage.

DOJ (2018b). United States Department of Justice, Press Release: "Wells Fargo Agrees to Pay $2.09 Billion Penalty for Allegedly Misrepresenting Quality of Loans Used in Residential Mortgage-Backed Securities" (Aug. 1, 2018), available at http://www.justice.gov/opa/pr/wells-fargo-agrees-pay-209-billion-penalty-allegedly-misrepresenting-quality-loans-used.

DOJ (2018c). United States Department of Justice, Press Release: "Royal Bank of Scotland Agrees to Pay $4.9 Billion for Financial Crisis-Era Misconduct" (Aug. 14, 2018), available at https://www.justice.gov/opa/pr/royal-bank-scotland-agrees-pay-49-billion-financial-crisis-era-misconduct.

DOJ (2016). United States Department of Justice, Press Release: "United States Sues Barclays Bank to Recover Civil Penalties for Fraud in the Sale of Residential Mortgage-Backed Securities" (Dec. 22, 2018), and "Complaint of the United States," available at https://www.justice.gov/opa/pr/united-states-sues-barclays-bank-recover-civil-penalties-fraud-sale-residential-mortgage.

DOJ (2015). United States Department of Justice, Settlement Agreement between Bank of America (including Countrywide and Merrill Lynch) and the United States, "Annex 1—Statement of Facts" (Aug. 19, 2015), available at https://www.justice.gov/opa/pr/bank-america-pay-1665-billion-historic-justice-department-settlement-financial-fraud-leading.

DOJ-HSBC (2018). United States Department of Justice, Press Release: "HSBC Agrees to Pay $765 Million in Connection with Its Sale of Residential Mortgage-Backed Securities" (Oct. 9, 2018), available at https://www.justice.gov/usao-co/pr/hsbc-agrees-pay-765-million-connection-its-sale-residential-mortgage-backed-securities.

DOJ-RBS (2018). United States Department of Justice, Settlement Agreement between Royal Bank of Scotland and the United States, "Annex 1—Statement of Facts" (Aug. 14, 2018), available at https://www.justice.gov/opa/press-release/file/1087151/download.

DOJ-UBS (2018). Complaint of the United States of America versus UBS Securities LLC et al. (Nov. 8, 2018), available at https://www.justice.gov/usao-edny/press-release/file/1109561/download.

Dolmetsch, Chris (2018). "Libor-Rigging Guilty Verdicts Bolster U.S. Bid to Punish Traders," *Bloomberg* (Oct. 17, 2018), available at https://www.bloomberg.com/news/articles/2018-10-17/ex-deutsche-bank-traders-convicted-in-libor-rigging-case.

Douglas, Justin (2019). "Translating the Blueprint for Financial Deregulation: The American Bank Lobby's Unyielding Quest for Legislative Profits, 1968–1982," 20(2) *Enterprise and Society* 281–327.

Drummond, Ian W. (1991). "Why Canadian Banks Did Not Collapse in the 1930s," in Harold James et al., eds., *The Role of Banks in the Interwar Economy*. New York: Cambridge University Press.

Duca, John V. (2016). "How Capital Regulation and Other Factors Drive the Role of Shadow Banking in Funding Short-Term Business Credit," 69 *Journal of Banking and Finance* S10–S24.

Dudley, Bill (2020). "The Fed Should Keep Looking Forward, Not Retreat to the Past," *Bloomberg* (Jan. 6, 2020), available at https://www.bloomberg.com/opinion/articles/2020-01-06/fed-should-keep-looking-forward-not-retreat-to-the-past?srnd=opinion.

Dudley, William C. (2018). "The Importance of Incentives in Ensuring a Resilient and Robust Financial System" (Remarks at the U.S. Chamber of Commerce, Mar. 26, 2018), available at https://www.newyorkfed.org/newsevents/speeches/2018/dud180326.

Duffie, Darrell (2019). "Prone to Fail: The Pre-Crisis Financial System," 33(1) *Journal of Economic Perspectives* 81–106.

Dugan, John C. (2008). "Remarks by Comptroller of the Currency John C. Dugan Before the Housing Policy Council of the Financial Services Roundtable" (May 22, 2008), available at https://www.occ.treas.gov/news-issuances/speeches/2008/pub-speech-2008-58.pdf.

Dunbar, John, and David Donald (2009). "The Roots of the Financial Crisis: Who Is to Blame?" (Center for Public Integrity, May 6, 2009), available at https://www.publicintegrity.org/2009/05/06/5449/roots-financial-crisis-who-blame.

Economist (2019). "Care Package: Spooked by Slowdown, the ECB Rolls Stimulus," *Economist* (Mar. 7, 2019).

Economist (2009). "Mortgage Losses: Move Over, Subprime," *Economist* (Feb. 5, 2009), available at https://www.economist.com/finance-and-economics/2009/02/05/move-over-subprime.

Edwards, Sebastian (2005). "The End of Large Current Account Deficits," in *The Greenspan Era: Lessons for the Future* 205–68 (Proceedings of an Economic Policy Symposium, Federal Reserve Bank of Kansas City, Aug. 2005), available at https://www.kansascityfed.org/publicat/sympos/2005/pdf/Edwards2005.pdf.

Egan, Mark, Ali Hortaçsu, and Gregor Matvos (2017). "Deposit Competition and Financial Fragility: Evidence from the US Banking Sector," 107(1) *American Economic Review* 169–216.

Eichengreen, Barry (2015). *Hall of Mirrors: The Great Depression, the Great Recession, and the Uses—and Misuses—of History*. New York: Oxford University Press.

Eichengreen, Barry (1992). *Golden Fetters: The Gold Standard and the Great Depression, 1919–1939*. New York: Oxford University Press.

Eichengreen, Barry (1989). "The U.S. Capital Market and Foreign Lending, 1920–1955," in Jeffrey D. Sachs, ed., *Developing Country Debt and Economic Performance, Volume 1: The International Financial System* 107–55. Chicago: University of Chicago Press.

Eichengreen, Barry, and Marc Flandreau (2009). "The rise and fall of the dollar (or when did the dollar replace sterling as the leading reserve currency?)," 13 *Review of Economic History* 377–411.

Eichengreen, Barry, and Kris Mitchener (2003). "The Great Depression as a Credit Boom Gone Wrong" (Bank for International Settlements, Working Paper No. 137, Sept. 2003), available at http://ssrn.com/abstract=959644.

Eichengreen, Barry, and Peter Temin (2010). "Fetters of Gold and Paper," 26(3) *Oxford Review of Economic Policy* 370–84.

Eisinger, Jesse (2017). *The Chickenshit Club: Why the Justice Department Fails to Prosecute Executives*. New York: Simon & Schuster.

Eisinger, Jesse (2011). "In U.S. Monetary Policy, a Boon to Banks," *ProPublica* (June 29, 2011), available at https://www.propublica.org/article/in-u.s.-monetary-policy-a-boon-to-banks.

Eisinger, Jesse, and Jake Bernstein (2010). "The Magnetar Trade: How One Hedge Fund Kept the Bubble Going," *ProPublica* (Apr. 9, 2010), available at https://www.propublica.org/article/all-the-magnetar-trade-how-one-hedge-fund-helped-keep-the-housing-bubble.

El-Erian, Mohamed A. (2019a). "Fed Gives Markets What They Want," *Bloomberg* (Jan. 30, 2019), available at https://www.bloomberg.com/opinion/articles/2019-01-30/fed-signals-patience-on-rates-flexibility-on-its-balance-sheet.

El-Erian, Mohamed A. (2019b). "Why the Fed Solidified Its Policy U-Turn," *Bloomberg* (Mar. 20, 2019), available at https://www.bloomberg.com/opinion/articles/2019-03-20/fed-signals-no-rate-hikes-in-2019-new-approach-to-balance-sheet.

El-Erian, Mohamed A. (2019c). "Investors Rely on Short-Term Supports at Their Peril," *Financial Times* (Dec. 17, 2019), available at https://www.ft.com/content/8e9782d6-20a6-11ea-92da-f0c92e957a96.

El-Erian, Mohamed A. (2018). "Three Key Takeaways from a Volatile Year for 2019," *Financial Times* (Dec. 27, 2018), available at https://www.ft.com/content/07517d74-09e9-11e9-9fe8-acdb36967cfc.

Engel, Kathleen C., and Patricia A. McCoy (2011). *The Subprime Virus: Reckless Credit, Regulatory Failure, and Next Steps.* New York: Oxford University Press.

Engel, Kathleen C., and Patricia A. McCoy (2007). "Turning a Blind Eye: Wall Street Finance of Predatory Lending," 75(4) *Fordham Law Review* 2039–103.

Engel, Kathleen C., and Patricia A. McCoy (2002). "A Tale of Three Markets: The Law and Economics of Predatory Lending," 80(6) *Texas Law Review* 1255–381.

Ensign, Rachel Louise (2018). "Largest U.S. Banks Extend Their Dominance in Deposits," *Wall Street Journal* (Mar. 23, 2018), A1.

Ensign, Rachel Louise, and Liz Hoffman (2017). "Stingy Banks Pull In Depositors," *Wall Street Journal* (May 9, 2017), B1.

Ensign, Rachel Louise, and Coulter Jones (2017). "BofA's Rural Branch Exodus—Bank Shut 1,600 Sites Since Financial Crisis," *Wall Street Journal* (Sept. 18, 2017), A1.

Errico, Luca, et al. (2014). "Mapping the Shadow Banking System Through a Global Flow of Funds Analysis" (International Monetary Fund Working Paper 14/10, Jan. 2014), available at http://www.imf.org/external/pubs/ft/wp/2014/wp1410.pdf.

Esbitt, Milton (1986). "Bank Portfolios and Bank Failures During the Great Depression: Chicago," 46(2) *Journal of Economic History* 455–62.

Espinoza, Javier, and Olaf Storbeck (2019). "EU's Green Light for NordLB Rescue Provokes Backlash," *Financial Times* (Dec. 8, 2019), available at https://www.ft.com/content/18bff16e-1990-11ea-97df-cc63de1d73f4.

Fahlenbach, Rüdiger, Robert Prilmeier, and René Stulz (2011). "This Time Is the Same: Using Bank Performance in 1998 to Explain Bank Performance During the Recent Financial Crisis" (Charles A. Dice Center Working Paper 2011-10, June 2011), available at http://ssrn.com/abstract=1779406.

Faia, Ester, and Beatrice Weder di Mauro (2015). "Cross-Border Resolution of Global Banks" (Federal Reserve Bank of Dallas Working Paper No. 236, May 2015), available at http://ssrn.com/abstract=2643962.

Faiola, Anthony, Ellen Nakashima, and Jill Drew (2008). "What Went Wrong," *Washington Post* (Oct. 15, 2008), available at http://www.washingtonpost.com/wp-dyn/content/article/2008/10/14/AR2008101403343.html.

Fang, Lee (2015). "Eric Holder Returns as Hero to Law Firm That Lobbies for Big Banks," *The Intercept* (July 6, 2015), available at https://theintercept.com/2015/07/06/eric-holder-returns-law-firm-lobbies-big-banks.

Fanger, David (2019). "Streamlined Volcker Rule could encourage some banks to take bigger risks," *American Banker* (Sept. 23, 2019, available on Westlaw at 2019 WLNR 28945646.

Faroohar, Rana (2019a). "The Fed Has Exacerbated America's New Housing Bubble," *Financial Times* (Mar. 17, 2019), available at https://www.ft.com/content/219aaa52-4675-11e9-b168-96a37d002cd3?segmentId=a7371401-027d-d8bf-8a7f-2a746e767d56.

Faroohar, Rana (2019b). "What Donald Trump Gets Right About the US Economy," *Financial Times* (Apr. 14, 2019), available at https://www.ft.com/content/842d36d8-5d0b-11e9-939a-341f5ada9d40.

Faruqui, Umar, Wenqian Huang, and Előd Takàts (2018). "Clearing Risks in OTC Derivatives Markets: The CCP-Bank Nexus," *BIS Quarterly Review* (Dec. 2018), 73–90.

Fasianos, Apostolos, Diego Guevara, and Christos Pierros (2016). "Have We Been Here Before? Phases of Financialization Within the 20th Century in the United States" (Levy Economics Institute Working Paper No. 869, June 2016), available at http://ssrn.com/abstract=2801088).

FCIC (2011). Financial Crisis Inquiry Commission, *The Financial Crisis Inquiry Report: Final Report of the National Commission on the Causes of the Financial and Economic Crisis in the United States* (Jan. 2011). New York: Public Affairs.

FCIC (2010). Financial Crisis Inquiry Commission, *Preliminary Staff Report: Governmental Rescues of "Too-Big-to-Fail" Financial Institutions* (Aug. 31, 2010), available at http://fcic-static.law.stanford.edu/cdn_media/fcic-reports/2010-0831-Governmental-Rescues.pdf.

FDIC (2018). 12 *FDIC Quarterly* No. 3 (2d Qtr. 2018), available at https://www.fdic.gov/bank/analytical/quarterly/2018-vol12-3/fdic-v12n3-2q2018.pdf.

FDIC (2017a). Federal Deposit Insurance Corporation, *Global Capital Index* (as of June 30, 2017), available at https://www.fdic.gov/about/learn/board/hoenig/capitalizationratio2q2017.pdf.

FDIC (2017b). 11 *FDIC Quarterly* No. 3 (2d Quarter 2017), available at https://www.fdic.gov/bank/analytical/quarterly/2017-vol11-3/fdic-v11n3-2q2017.pdf.

FDIC (2016). 10 *FDIC Quarterly* No. 3 (2d Qtr. 2016), available at https://www.fdic.gov/bank/analytical/quarterly/2016-vol10-3/fdic-v10n3-1q16-quarterly.pdf.

FDIC (2015). 9 *FDIC Quarterly* No. 3 (2d Qtr. 2015), available at https://www.fdic.gov/bank/analytical/quarterly/2015-vol9-3/fdic-2q2015-v9n3.pdf.

FDIC (2008). Federal Deposit Insurance Corp., *Quarterly Banking Profile, First Quarter 2008*, available at https://www5.fdic.gov/qbp/2008mar/qbp.pdf.

FDIC (1997). *History of the Eighties: Lessons for the Future: Volume I: An Examination of the Banking Crises of the 1980s and Early 1990s*. Washington, DC: Federal Deposit Insurance Corp.

FDIC (1984). *The First Fifty Years: A History of the FDIC, 1933-1983*. Washington, DC: Federal Deposit Insurance Corp.

Fecht, Falko, Andreas Hackethal, and Yigitcan Karabulut (2018). "Is Proprietary Trading Detrimental to Retail Investors?," 73(3) *Journal of Finance* 1323–61.

Federal Reserve Bank of St. Louis (2016). "Gross Domestic Product (Implicit Price Deflator)," FRED Economic Data (Index 2009=100, Not Seasonally Adjusted, Updated July 27, 2018), available at https://fred.stlouisfed.org/series/A191RD3A086NBEA.

Federal Reserve Board (2020). *Financial Accounts of the United States* (Z.1), Fourth Quarter 2019 (Mar. 12, 2020), available at https://www.federalreserve.gov/releases/z1/20200312/z1.pdf.

Federal Reserve Board (2019a). *Financial Stability Report* (May 2019), available at https://www.federalreserve.gov/publications/files/financial-stability-report-201905.pdf.

Federal Reserve Board (2019b). *Supervision and Regulation Report* (May 2019), available at https://www.federalreserve.gov/publications/files/201905-supervision-and-regulation-report.pdf.

Federal Reserve Board (2019c). *Supervision and Regulation Report* (Nov. 2019), available at https://www.federalreserve.gov/publications/files/201911-supervision-and-regulation-report.pdf.

Federal Reserve Board (2018a). "Joint Notice of Proposed Rulemaking to Modify the Enhanced Supplementary Leverage Ratio Standards Applicable to U.S. Global Systemically Important

Bank Holding Companies and Certain of Their Insured Depository Institution Subsidiaries" (Apr. 5, 2018), available at https://www.federalreserve.gov/newsevents/pressreleases/files/bcreg20180411a1.pdf.

Federal Reserve Board (2018b). "Notices of Proposed Rulemaking to Tailor Prudential Standards" (Memorandum from Vice Chairman for Supervision Quarles, Oct. 24, 2018), available at https://www.federalreserve.gov/aboutthefed/boardmeetings/files/board-memo-20181031.pdf.

Federal Reserve Board (2018c). *Supervision and Regulation Report* (Nov. 2018), available at https://www.federalreserve.gov/publications/files/201811-supervision-and-regulation-report.pdf.

Federal Reserve Board (2016). *Report to the Congress and the Financial Stability Board Pursuant to Section 620 of the Dodd-Frank Act, Section I* (Sept. 2016), 1–45, available at https://www.federalreserve.gov/newsevents/pressreleases/files/bcreg20160908a1.pdf.

Federal Reserve Board (2009). "Joint Press Release: Joint Statement by the Treasury, FDIC, OCC, OTS, and the Federal Reserve" (Feb. 23, 2009), available at https://www.federalreserve.gov/newsevents/pressreleases/bcreg20090223a.htm.

Federal Reserve Board (2008). "Bank of America Corporation: Order Approving the Acquisition of a Savings Association and Other Nonbanking Activities" (June 5, 2008), available at https://www.federalreserve.gov/newsevents/pressreleases/files/orders20080605a1.pdf.

Federal Reserve Board (1997). "Bank Holding Companies and Change in Bank Control (Regulation Y): Amendments to Restrictions in the Board's Section 20 Orders," 62 *Federal Register* 45295 (Aug. 27, 1997).

Fed SBCS (2019). "Small Business Credit Survey: 2019 Report on Employer Firms" (Federal Reserve Banks of Atlanta et al.), available at https://www.fedsmallbusiness.org/survey/2019/report-on-employer-firms.

Fein, Melanie (2011). *Securities Activities of Banks.* Third edition, 2002, with supplements through 2011. Boston: Wolters Kluwer Law & Business.

Feinstein, Charles H., Peter Temin, and Gianni Toniolo (1995). "International Economic Organization: Banking, Finance, and Trade in Europe between the Wars," in Charles H. Feinstein, ed., *Banking, Currency, and Finance in Europe Between the Wars* 9–76. Oxford: Clarendon Press.

Feinstein, Charles H., and Katherine Watson (1995). "Private International Capital Flows in Europe in the Inter-War Period," in Charles H. Feinstein, ed., *Banking, Currency, and Finance in Europe Between the Wars* 94–130. Oxford: Clarendon Press.

Feldstein, Martin (2018). "Normalizing Monetary Policy," 38(2) *Cato Journal* 415–28.

Feldstein, Martin (2013). "An Interview with Paul Volcker," 27(4) *Journal of Economic Perspectives* 105–20 (Fall).

Felkerson, James (2011). "$29,000,000,000,000: A Detailed Look at the Fed's Bailout by Funding Facility and Recipient" (Levy Economic Institute of Bard College, Working Paper No. 698, Dec. 2011), available at http://ssrn.com/abstract=1970414.

Ferguson, Roger W., Jr. (2003). "Rules and Flexibility in Monetary Policy: Remarks by Vice Chairman Roger W. Ferguson, Jr. at the University of Georgia" (Feb. 12, 2003), available at https://www.federalreserve.gov/boarddocs/speeches/2003/20030212/default.htm.

Ferguson, Roger W., Jr. (2002). "Recent Experience and Economic Outlook: Remarks by Vice Chairman Roger W. Ferguson, Jr. at the 2003 Global Economic and Investment Outlook Conference" (Nov. 12, 2002), available at https://www.federalreserve.gov/boarddocs/speeches/2002/200211122/default.htm.

Ferguson, Thomas, and Robert Johnson (2009). "Too Big to Bail: The 'Paulson Put,' Presidential Politics, and the Global Financial Meltdown; Part II: Fatal Reversal—Single Payer and Back," 38(2) *International Journal of Political Economy* 5–45.

FHFA (2018). Federal Housing Finance Agency, *2017 Report to Congress* (May 23, 2018), available at https://www.fhfa.gov/AboutUs/Reports/ReportDocuments/FHFA_2017_Report-to-Congress.pdf

FHFA (2017). Federal Housing Finance Agency, *2016 Report to Congress* (June 15, 2017), available at https://www.fhfa.gov/AboutUs/Reports/ReportDocuments/FHFA_2016_Report-to-Congress.pdf.

Field, Alexander J. (2011). *Great Leap Forward: 1930s Depression and U.S. Economic Growth.* New Haven: Yale University Press.

Field, Alexander J. (1992). "Uncontrolled Land Development and the Duration of the Depression in the United States," 52(4) *Journal of Economic History* 785–805.

Filler, Ronald H., and Jerry W. Markham (2014). *Regulation of Derivative Financial Instruments (Swaps, Options, and Futures): Cases and Materials.* St. Paul, MN: West Academic Press.

Financial Times (2019a). "The ECB Is Attempting to Get Ahead of Events," *Financial Times* (Mar. 8, 2019) (editorial), available at https://www.ft.com/content/b2225c56-419c-11e9-b896-fe36ec32aece.

Financial Times (2019b). "A German Bailout Tests EU Bank Rules to the Limit," *Financial Times* (Dec. 10, 2019) (editorial), available at https://www.ft.com/content/8024e7dc-1b62-11ea-97df-cc63de1d73f4.

Financial Times (2018). "Australia Must Begin to Rebuild Trust in Its Banks," *Financial Times*, Feb. 5, 2019 (editorial), available at https://www.ft.com/content/f37bce5c-288e-11e9-88a4-c32129756dd8.

Fink, Matthew P. (2019). *The Unlikely Reformer: Carter Glass and Financial Regulation.* Fairfax, VA: George Mason University Press.

Finkle, Victoria (2018a). "They're Baaack: Big Banks Are Flexing Their Lobbying Muscle," *American Banker* (Aug. 22, 2018), available on Westlaw at 2018 WLNR 25639120.

Finkle, Victoria (2018b). "Is Glass-Steagall Poised for a Political Comeback?," *American Banker* (Sept. 10, 2018), available on Westlaw at 2018 WLNR 27443751.

Fishback, Price V. (2016). "How Successful Was the New Deal? The Microeconomic Impact of New Deal Spending and Lending Policies in the 1930s" (National Bureau of Economic Research Working Paper 21925, Jan. 2016), available at http://www.nber.org/papers/w21925.

Fishback, Price (2010). "US Monetary and Fiscal Policy in the 1930s," 26(3) *Oxford Review of Economic Policy* 385–413.

Flandreau, Marc, Norbert Gaillard, and Ugo Panizza (2010). "Conflicts of Interest, Reputation, and the Interwar Debt Crisis: Banksters or Bad Luck?" (HEID Working Paper No. 02/2010, Feb. 2010), available at http://ssrn.com/abstract=1558402.

Fleckenstein, William A., with Frederick Sheehan (2008). *Greenspan's Bubbles: The Age of Ignorance at the Federal Reserve.* New York: McGraw-Hill.

Fleming, Michael J., and Kenneth D. Garbade (2003). "The Repurchase Agreement Refined: GCF Repo," 9(6) *Current Issues in Economics and Finance* 1–7. Federal Reserve Bank of New York (June).

Fleming, Michael J., and Asani Sarkar (2014). "The Failure Resolution of Lehman Brothers," *Economic Policy Review* 175–206. Federal Reserve Bank of New York (Dec.).

Fleming, Sam (2019a). "Powell Backed Slowdown in Fed Bond Buying in 2013," *Financial Times* (Jan. 11, 2019), available at https://www.ft.com/content/462bc8a2-15be-11e9-a581-4ff78404524e.

Fleming, Sam (2019b). "Federal Reserve's 'Momentous' U-Turn Prompts Puzzlement," *Financial Times* (Jan. 31, 2019), available at https://www.ft.com/content/36cb58ba-24ef-11e9-8ce6-5db4543da632.

Fleming, Sam (2018). "Federal Reserve Debated Banks' Capital Buffers as Markets Surge," *Financial Times* (Aug. 29, 2018), available at https://www.ft.com/content/ec8e07ee-ab08-11e8-94bd-cba20d67390c.

Fleming, Sam, and Chris Giles (2018). "The Federal Reserve versus the markets: who has it wrong?" *Financial Times* (Dec. 30, 2018), available at https://www.ft.com/content/3401af9e-09ec-11e9-9fe8-acdb36967cfc.

Fleming, Sam, and Jamie Smyth (2019). "Global Economy: Why Central Bankers Blinked," *Financial Times* (Feb. 8, 2019), available at https://www.ft.com/content/24508f0e-2b91-11e9-88a4-c32129756dd8.

Fletcher, Gina-Gail S. (2019). "Engineered Credit Default Swaps: Innovative or Manipulative?" *New York University Law Review* (forthcoming) (Draft of Sept. 23, 2019), available at http://ssrn.com/abstract=3155504.

Fletcher, Gina-Gail S. (2014). "Hazardous Hedging: The (Unacknowledged) Risks of Hedging with Credit Derivatives," 33(2) *Review of Banking and Financial Law* 813–98.

Fletcher, Laurence (2019a). "Markets Should Be Careful What They Wish For," *Financial Times* (Feb. 12, 2019), available at https://www.ft.com/content/163a3784-2edf-11e9-8744-e7016697f225.

Fletcher, Laurence (2019b). "Investors' Herd Behaviour Makes Markets More Fragile," *Financial Times* (Feb. 25, 2019), available at https://www.ft.com/content/2fb89b16-38f2-11e9-b72b-2c7f526ca5d0.

Foley & Lardner (2010). Barry J. Mandel, Jonathan H. Friedmann, and Alicia L. Pitts, "Auction Rate Securities Litigation: From Multi-Billion Dollar Regulatory Settlements to Dismissals of Private Actions," available at https://www.foley.com/files/Publication/eea56262-e7b4-49f3-9a0e-be63e587ae64/Presentation/PublicationAttachment/5800b1a5-5953-40f2-8393-c0ced4f4f9a3/foley_lardner_mandel_friedman_pitts_article.pdf.

FOMC (2019a). "Minutes of the Federal Open Market Committee, January 29–30, 2019," available at https://www.federalreserve.gov/monetarypolicy/files/fomcminutes20190130.pdf.

FOMC (2019b). "Statement Regarding Monetary Policy Implementation" (Federal Open Market Committee, Oct. 11, 2019), available at https://www.federalreserve.gov/newsevents/pressreleases/monetary20191011a.htm.

FOMC (2008a). Transcript of the Meeting of the Federal Open Market Committee on Jan/ 29–30, 2008, available at https://www.federalreserve.gov/monetarypolicy/files/FOMC20080130meeting.pdf.

FOMC (2008b). Transcript of the Federal Open Market Committee Conference Call on Mar. 10, 2008, available at https://www.federalreserve.gov/monetarypolicy/files/FOMC20080310confcall.pdf.

FOMC (2008c). Transcript of the Meeting of the Federal Open Market Committee on Mar. 18, 2008, available at https://www.federalreserve.gov/monetarypolicy/files/FOMC20080318meeting.pdf.

FOMC (2008d). Transcript of the Meeting of the Federal Open Market Committee on Apr. 24–25, 2008, available at https://www.federalreserve.gov/monetarypolicy/files/FOMC20080625meeting.pdf.

Forbes, Neil (1987). "London Banks, the German Standstill Agreements, and 'Economic Appeasement' in the 1930s," 40(4) *Economic History Review* 371–87.

Ford, Jonathan (2018). "Financial Sector Remains an Impenetrable Black Box," *Financial Times* (Sept. 16, 2018), available at https://www.ft.com/content/234c6290-b99a-11e8-94b2-17176fbf93f5.

Forsyth, Douglas J. (1991). "The Rise and Fall of German-Inspired Mixed Banking in Italy, 1894–1936," in Harold James et al., eds., *The Role of Banks in the Interwar Economy*. New York: Cambridge University Press.

Fortado, Lindsay, and Laura Noonan (2019). "Banks Raise Bets on Prime Broking for Struggling Hedge Funds," *Financial Times* (Jan. 9, 2019), available at https://www.ft.com/content/7b8ea2cc-078f-11e9-9fe8-acdb36967cfc.

Fox News (2012). "Economy lost more than 200,000 small businesses in recession, Census shows," *Fox News* (July 26, 2012), available at https://www.foxnews.com/politics/economy-lost-more-than-200000-small-businesses-in-recession-census-shows.

Frame, W. Scott, Andreas Fuster, Joseph Tracy, and James Vickery (2015). "The Rescue of Fannie Mae and Freddie Mac," 29(2) *Journal of Financial Perspectives* 25–52.

Fraser, Ian (2014). *Shredded: Inside RBS, the Bank That Broke Britain.* Edinburgh: Birlinn.

Frayer, Lauren (2014). "Spain Exits Bailout Program; Second Eurozone Country to Do So," *Los Angeles Times* (Jan. 23, 2014), available at http://www.latimes.com/world/worldnow/la-fg-wn-spain-exits-international-bailout-20140123-story.html.

FRED-CPI (2019). FRED Economic Data, Federal Reserve Bank of St. Louis, chart entitled "Consumer Price Index for All Urban Consumers" (updated Mar. 2020), available at https://fred.stlouisfed.org/series/CPIAUCNS.

FRED-Debt (2019). FRED Economic Data, Federal Reserve Bank of St. Louis, chart entitled "All Sectors: Debt Securities and Loans" (updated Mar. 2020), available at https://fred.stlouisfed.org/series/TCMDO.

FRED-GDP (2020). FRED Economic Data, Federal Reserve Bank of St. Louis, chart entitled "Gross Domestic Product," covering the years 1929–2019 (updated Mar. 2020), available at https://fred.stlouisfed.org/series/GDPA.

FRED-Government Debt (2019). FRED Economic Data, Federal Reserve Bank of St. Louis, chart entitled "Federal Debt: Total Public Debt" (updated Mar. 2020), available at https://fred.stlouisfed.org/series/GFDEBTN, and chart entitled "State and Local Governments: Debt Securities and Loans" (updated Mar. 2020), available at https://fred.stlouisfed.org/series/SLGSDODNS.

Freeman, James, and Vern McKinley (2018). *Borrowed Time: Two Centuries of Booms, Busts, and Bailouts at Citi.* New York: HarperCollins.

Friedman, Milton, and Anna J. Schwartz (1986). "The Failure of the Bank of United States: A Reappraisal—A Reply," 23 *Explorations in Economic History* 199–204.

Friedman, Milton, and Anna J. Schwartz (1963). *A Monetary History of the United States, 1867–1960.* Princeton: Princeton University Press.

FSA (2009). U.K. Financial Services Authority, *The Turner Review: A Regulatory Response to the Global Banking Crisis* (Mar. 2009), available at https://webarchive.nationalarchives.gov.uk/20090320232953/http://www.fsa.gov.uk/pubs/other/turner_review.pdf.

FSB (2019a). Financial Stability Board, *Global Monitoring Report on Non-Bank Financial Intermediation 2018* (Feb. 4, 2019), available at http://www.fsb.org/wp-content/uploads/P040219.pdf.

FSB (2019b). Financial Stability Board, "2019 List of Global Systemically Important Banks (G-SIBs)" (Nov. 22, 2019), available at https://www.fsb.org/wp-content/uploads/P221119-1.pdf.

FSB (2018). Financial Stability Board, *Implementation and Effects of the G20 Financial Regulatory Reforms: 28 November 2018 4th Annual Report*, available at http://www.fsb.org/wp-content/uploads/P281118-1.pdf.

FSOC (2019). Financial Stability Oversight Council, *2019 Annual Report*, available at https://home.treasury.gov/system/files/261/FSOC2019AnnualReport.pdf.

FSOC (2018). Financial Stability Oversight Council, *2018 Annual Report*, available at https://home.treasury.gov/system/files/261/FSOC2018AnnualReport.pdf.

FSOC (2017). Financial Stability Oversight Council, *2017 Annual Report*, available at https://www.treasury.gov/initiatives/fsoc/studies-reports/Documents/FSOC_2017_Annual_Report.pdf.

FT League Tables (2018). "League Tables: Year to Date 2018," *Financial Times*, available at https://markets.ft.com/data/league-tables/tables-and-trends.

FT letter from 20 scholars (2010). "Healthy Banking System Is the Goal, Not Profitable Banks," *Financial Times* (Nov. 8, 2010) (letter from 20 prominent scholars in economics and finance), available at https://www.ft.com/content/63fa6b9e-eb8e-11df-bbb5-00144feab49a,

Funk, Russell J., and Daniel Hirschman (2014). "Derivatives and Deregulation: Financial Innovation and the Demise of Glass-Steagall" (Working paper, Jan. 4, 2014), available at https://osf.io/preprints/socarxiv/wpwe6.

G20 (2009a). Group of Twenty, "London Summit—Leaders' Statement" (Apr. 2, 2009), available at https://www.imf.org/external/np/sec/pr/2009/pdf/g20_040209.pdf.

G20 (2009b). Group of Twenty, "Declaration on Strengthening the Financial System—London Summit" (Apr. 2, 2009), available at http://www.fsb.org/wp-content/uploads/london_summit_declaration_on_str_financial_system.pdf.

G20 (2009c). Group of Twenty, "Leaders' Statement—The Pittsburgh Summit" (Sept. 24–25, 2009), available at https://www.treasury.gov/resource-center/international/g7-g20/Documents/pittsburgh_summit_leaders_statement_250909.pdf.

Galbraith, John Kenneth (1972). *The Great Crash; 1929*. Third edition. Boston: Houghton Mifflin.

Galofré-Vilà, Gregori, Christopher M. Meissner, Martin McKee, and David Stuckler (2017). "Austerity and the Rise of the Nazi Party," National Bureau of Economic Research Working Paper 24106 (Dec. 2017), available at http://www.nber.org/papers/w24106.

Gandhi, Priyank, and Hanno Lustig (2015). "Size Anomalies in U.S. Bank Stock Returns," 70(2) *Journal of Finance* 733–68.

Gandré, Pauline, Mike Mariathasan, Ouarda Merrouche, and Steven Ongena (2019). "Unintended Consequences of the Global Derivatives Market Reform" (Swiss Finance Institute Research Paper No. 20-02, Dec. 2019), available at http://ssrn.com/abstract=3518411.

GAO (2017). *Financial Regulation: Perspectives on the Swaps Push-Out Rule* (U.S. Government Accountability Office, Sept. 2017, GAO-17-607), available at https://www.gao.gov/assets/690/686903.pdf.

GAO (2014). *Large Bank Holding Companies: Expectations of Government Support* (U.S. Government Accountability Office, July 2014, GAO-14-621), available at https://www.gao.gov/assets/670/665162.pdf.

GAO (2010). *Nonprime Mortgages: Analysis of Loan Performance, Factors Associated with Defaults, and Data Sources* (U.S. Government Accountability Office, Aug. 2010, GAO-10-805), available at https://www.gao.gov/assets/310/308845.pdf.

GAO (2009). *Characteristics and Performance of Nonprime Mortgages* (U.S. Government Accountability Office, July 28, 2009, GAO-09-848R), available at https://www.gao.gov/products/GAO-09-848R.

Gapper, John (2019). "Why European Banks Repeatedly Fall Short on Wall Street," *Financial Times* (Feb. 15, 2019), available at https://www.ft.com/content/6edeaaa4-3048-11e9-ba00-0251022932c8.

Garrett, Brandon L. (2019). "Declining Corporate Prosecutions," *American Criminal Law Review* (forthcoming, draft of Mar. 26, 2019), available at http://ssrn.com/abstract=3360456.

Garrett, Brandon L. (2015). "The Corporate Criminal as Scapegoat," 101(7) *Virginia Law Review* 1789–853.

Garriga, Carlos, Bryan Noeth, and Don E. Schlagenhauf (2017). "Household Debt and the Great Recession," 99(2) *Review* 183–206 (Federal Reserve Bank of St. Louis, Second Quarter 2017).

Garrson, Robert M. (1994). "President Clinton Signs Interstate Bill into Law, Sayings It's a First Step," *American Banker* (Sept. 30, 1994), 2, available on Westlaw at 1994 WLNR 2195295.

Garrson, Robert M. (1992). "Banking Lobby Gearing Up for Clinton-Era Victories," *American Banker* (Dec. 24, 1992), 1, available on Westlaw at 1992 WLNR 2114795.

Garten, Helen (1989). "Regulatory Growing Pains: A Perspective on Bank Regulation in a Deregulatory Age," 57(4) *Fordham Law Review* 501–78.

Gasparino, Charles (2009). *The Sellout: How Three Decades of Wall Street Greed and Government Mismanagement Destroyed the Global Financial System*. New York: Harper Business.

Gasparino, Charles (2005). *Blood on the Street: The Inside Story of How Wall Street Analysts Duped a Generation of Investors*. New York: Free Press.

Geisst, Charles R. (2012). *Wall Street: A History*. Updated edition. New York: Oxford University Press.

Geithner, Timothy F. (2017). "Are We Safe Yet? How to Manage Financial Crises," *Foreign Affairs* (Jan./Feb. 2017), available at https://www.foreignaffairs.com/articles/united-states/2016-12-12/are-we-safe-yet.

Geithner, Timothy F. (2014). *Stress Test: Reflections on Financial Crises*. New York: Broadway Books.

Geithner, Timothy F. (2007). "Liquidity Risk and the Global Economy: Remarks at the Federal Reserve Bank of Atlanta's Financial Markets Conference" (May 15, 2007), available at https://www.newyorkfed.org/newsevents/speeches/2007/gei070515.

Geithner, Timothy F. (2005). "Remarks Before the Economic Club of Washington, DC" (Feb. 9, 2005), available at https://www.newyorkfed.org/newsevents/speeches/2005/gei050209.

Gelpern, Anna (2009). "Financial Crisis Containment," 41(4) *Connecticut Law Review* 1051–106.

Gelpern, Anna, and Erik F. Gerding (2016). "Inside Safe Assets," 33(2) *Yale Journal on Financial Regulation* 363–421.

Gerding, Erik F. (2016). "The Dialectics of Bank Capital: Regulation and Regulatory Capital Arbitrage," 55 *Washburn Law Review* 357–84.

Gerding, Erik F. (2014). *Law, Bubbles, and Financial Regulation*. London: Routledge.

Gerth, Jeff (1981). "Bank Target: Glass-Steagall Act," *New York Times* (Mar. 3, 1981), D1.

Giannone, Joseph A. (2009). "Goldman CEO Reaped Record $54.3 mln in Pay in 2006," *Reuters* (Feb. 21, 2007), available at https://www.reuters.com/article/us-goldmansachs-compensation/goldman-ceo-reaped-record-54-3-mln-in-pay-in-2006-idUSN2124847120070221.

Giel, Dawn, and Dan Mangan (2018). "How Ex–JP Morgan Silver Trader's Guilty Plea Could Boost Manipulation Claim Against Bank," CNBC (Nov. 13, 2018), available at https://www.cnbc.com/2018/11/12/ex-jp-morgan-silver-traders-guilty-plea-could-boost-manipulation-suit.html.

Giles, Chris (2012). "King Admits Failing to 'Shout' About Risk," *Financial Times* (May 3, 2012), available at https://www.ft.com/content/9cd39a3e-9480-11e1-8e90-00144feab49a.

Giles, Chris, and Claire Jones (2018). "The QE Retreat: Central Banks Assess Next Steps as ECB Joins Retreat from QE," *Financial Times* (Dec. 13, 2018), available at https://www.ft.com/content/eb6f41ca-fef5-11e8-ac00-57a2a826423e.

Gissler, Stefan (2015). "A Margin Call Gone Wrong: Stock Prices and Germany's Black Friday 1927" (FEDS Working Paper No. FEDGFE20150-54, Feb. 15, 2015), available at http://ssrn.com/abstract=2671000.

Gittelsohn, John (2015). "Real Estate: Few Who Lost Homes in U.S. Will Buy Again Soon amid Tight Credit," 104 *Bloomberg BNA's Banking Report* 825 (Apr. 28, 2015).

Goetz, Martin R., Luc Laeven and Ross Levine (2013). "Identifying the Valuation Effects and Agency Costs of Corporate Diversification: Evidence from the Geographic Diversification of U.S. Banks," 26(7) *Review of Financial Studies* 1787–1823.

Goetzmann, William N., and Frank Newman (2010). "Securitization in the 1920s" (National Bureau of Economic Research Working Paper 15650), available at www.nber.org/papers/w15650.

Goldberg, Linda, and April Meehl (2019). "Complexity in Large U.S. Banks" (Federal Reserve Bank of New York Staff Report No. 880, Feb. 2019), available at https://www.newyorkfed. org/research/staff_reports/sr880.

Goldsmith [né Goldschmidt], Raymond W. (1933). *The Changing Structure of American Banking.* London: George Routledge & Sons, Ltd.

Goldstein, Steve (2018). "Here's the Staggering Amount Banks Have Been Fined Since the Financial Crisis," *MarketWatch* (Feb. 24, 2018), available at https://www.marketwatch.com/story/ banks-have-been-fined-a-staggering-243-billion-since-the-financial-crisis-2018-02-20.

Goodhart, Charles, and Emilios Avgouleas (2014). "A Critical Evaluation of Bail-Ins as Bank Recapitalization Mechanisms" (Center for Economic Policy Research Discussion Paper 10065, July 2014), available at http://ssrn.com/abstract=2478647.

Goodhart, Charles, and Dirk Schoenmaker (2016). "The Global Investment Banks Are Now All Becoming American: Does That Matter for Europeans?," 2 *Journal of Financial Regulation* 163–81.

Good Jobs First–WF (2019). "Violation Tracker Parent Company Summary: Wells Fargo" (Good Jobs First, 2019), available at https://violationtracker.goodjobsfirst.org/parent/ wells-fargo.

Goodman, Peter S. (2008). "Taking Hard New Look at a Greenspan Legacy," *New York Times* (Oct. 9, 2008), A1.

Gordon, Jeffrey N., and Wolf-Georg Ringe (2015). "Bank Resolution in the European Banking Union: A Transatlantic Perspective on What It Would Take," 115(5) *Columbia Law Review* 1297–1369.

Gordon, Robert A. (1951). "Cyclical Experience in the Interwar Period: The Investment Boom of the Twenties," in *Conference on Business Cycles* 163. New York: National Bureau of Economic Research.

Gordon, Robert J., and Robert Krenn (2010). "The End of the Great Depression, 1939–41: Policy Contributions and Fiscal Multipliers" (National Bureau of Economic Research Working Paper 16380, Sept. 2010), available at http://www.nber.org/papers/w16380.

Gorton, Gary (2018). "Financial Crises," 10 *Annual Review of Financial Economics* 43–58.

Gorton, Gary (2016). "The History and Economics of Safe Assets" (Apr. 26, 2016), available at http://ssrn.com/abstract=22770569.

Gorton, Gary (2009). "The Subprime Panic," 15(1) *European Financial Management* 10–46.

Gorton, Gary B., Toomas Laarits, and Andrew Metrick (2018). "The Run on Repo and the Fed's Response" (July 18, 2018), available at http://ssrn.com/abstract=3216581.

Gorton, Gary, and Andrew Metrick (2012). "Securitized Banking and the Run on Repo," 104 *Journal of Financial Economics* 425–51.

Gottfried, Miriam (2019). "KKR Quietly Builds Wall Street Contender," *Wall Street Journal* (Sept. 26, 2019), B10.

Graham, Benjamin and David L. Dodd (1940). *Security Analysis: Principles and Technique.* Second edition. New York: McGraw-Hill.

Grant, James (2014). *The Forgotten Depression, 1921: The Crash That Cured Itself.* New York: Simon and Shuster.

Gray, Alistair, and Barney Jopson (2017). "Stress tests clear big US banks for $100bn payout" (June 28, 2017), available at https://www.ft.com/content/7c385452-5c41-11e7-b553-e2df1b0c3220.

Greeley, Brendan, and Colby Smith (2019a). "Fed to Resume Asset Purchases to Prevent a Cash Crunch," *Financial Times* (Oct. 8, 2019), available at https://www.ft.com/content/ f228f44c-e9f6-11e9-a240-3b065ef5fc55.

Greeley, Brendan, and Colby Smith (2019b). "Federal Reserve Delivers Third Rate Cut but Signals It Is Done for Now," *Financial Times* (Oct. 30, 2019), available at https://www.ft.com/ content/f80253b8-fb35-11e9-98fd-4d6c20050229.

Green, Joshua (2018). "The Biggest Legacy of the Financial Crisis Is the Trump Presidency," *Bloomberg Businessweek* (Aug. 30, 2018), available at https://www.bloomberg.com/news/articles/2018-08-30/the-biggest-legacy-of-the-financial-crisis-is-the-trump-presidency.

Greenspan, Alan (2005a). "Federal Reserve Board's Semiannual Monetary Policy Report to the Congress: Testimony of Chairman Alan Greenspan Before the Committee on Financial Services, U.S. House of Representatives" (July 20, 2005), available at https://www.federalreserve.gov/boarddocs/hh/2005/july/testimony.htm.

Greenspan, Alan (2005b). "Economic Flexibility: Remarks by Chairman Alan Greenspan to the National Association of Business Economics Annual Meeting" (Sept. 27, 2005), available at https://www.federalreserve.gov/boarddocs/speeches/2005/20050927/default.htm.

Greenspan, Alan (2004a). "Risk and Uncertainty in Monetary Policy: Remarks by Chairman Alan Greenspan at the Meetings of the American Economic Association" (Jan. 3, 2004), available at https://www.federalreserve.gov/boarddocs/speeches/2004/20040103/default.htm.

Greenspan, Alan (2004b). "Banking: Remarks by Chairman Alan Greenspan at the American Bankers Association Annual Convention" (Oct. 5, 2004), available at https://www.federalreserve.gov/boarddocs/speeches/2004/20041005/default.htm.

Greenspan, Alan (2003). "Federal Reserve Board's Semiannual Monetary Policy Report to the Congress: Testimony of Chairman Alan Greenspan Before the Committee on Financial Services, U.S. House of Representatives" (July 15, 2003), available at https://www.federalreserve.gov/boarddocs/hh/2003/july/testimony.htm.

Greenspan, Alan (2002a). "Federal Reserve Board's Semiannual Monetary Policy Report to the Congress: Testimony of Chairman Alan Greenspan Before the Committee on Banking, Housing, and Urban Affairs" (July 16, 2002), available at https://www.federalreserve.gov/boarddocs/hh/2002/july/testimony.htm.

Greenspan, Alan (2002b). "Economic Volatility: Remarks by Chairman Alan Greenspan at a Symposium Sponsored by the Federal Reserve Bank of Kansas City" (Aug. 30, 2002), available at https://www.federalreserve.gov/boarddocs/speeches/2002/20020830/default.htm.

Greenspan, Alan (2002c). "The Economic Outlook: Testimony of Chairman Alan Greenspan Before the Joint Economic Committee, U.S. Congress" (Nov. 13, 2002), available at https://www.federalreserve.gov/boarddocs/testimony/2002/20021113/default.htm.

Greenspan, Alan (2002d). "Issues for Monetary Policy: Remarks by Chairman Alan Greenspan Before the Economic Club of New York" (Dec. 19, 2002), available at https://www.federalreserve.gov/boarddocs/speeches/2002/20021219/default.htm.

Greenspan, Alan (1999a). "H.R. 10 and the Need for Financial Reform: Testimony of Chairman Alan Greenspan Before the Committee on Banking and Financial Services, U.S. House of Representatives" (Feb. 11, 1999), available at http://www.federalreserve.gov/boarddocs/testimony/1999/19990211.htm.

Greenspan, Alan (1999b). "Financial Derivatives: Remarks by Chairman Alan Greenspan Before the Futures Industry Association" (Mar. 19, 1999), available at http://www.federalreserve.gov/boarddocs/speeches/1999/19990319.htm.

Greenspan, Alan (1999c). "Remarks by Fed Chairman Alan Greenspan Before the World Bank Group and International Monetary Fund, Program of Seminars" (Sept. 27, 1999), available at https://www.federalreserve.gov/boarddocs/speeches/1999/199909272.htm.

Greenspan, Alan (1998). "Testimony by Alan Greenspan, Chairman, Board of Governors of the Federal Reserve System, Before the Committee on Agriculture, Nutrition, and Forestry, U.S. Senate" (July 30, 1998), available on Westlaw at 1998 WL 427687 (F.R.B.).

Greenspan, Alan (1997a). "Government Regulation and Derivatives Contracts: Remarks by Chairman Alan Greenspan at the Financial Markets Conference of the Federal Reserve Bank of Atlanta" (Feb. 21, 1997), available at http://www.federalreserve.gov/boarddocs/speeches/1997/19970221.htm.

Greenspan, Alan (1997b). "Remarks by Chairman Alan Greenspan at the Annual Conference of the Association of Private Enterprise Education" (Apr. 12, 1997), available at http://www.federalreserve.gov/boarddocs/speeches/1997/19970412.htm.

Greenspan, Alan (1997c). "Statement by Alan Greenspan, Chairman Board of Governors of the Federal Reserve System, Before the Committee on Banking and Financial Services, U.S. House of Representatives" (May 22, 1997), reprinted in 83 *Federal Reserve Bulletin* 578–83 (1997).

Greenspan, Alan (1996). "Bank Supervision in a World Economy: Remarks by Chairman Alan Greenspan at the International Conference of Banking Supervisors" (June 13, 1996), available at http://www.federalreserve/gov/boarddocs/speeches/1996/19960613.htm.

Greenspan, Alan (1990). "Statement by Alan Greenspan, Chairman, Board of Governors of the Federal Reserve System, Before the Committee on Banking, Housing, and Urban Affairs, U.S. Senate" (July 12, 1990), reprinted in 76 *Federal Reserve Bulletin* 731–38 (1990).

Greenspan, Alan (1987). "Statement by Alan Greenspan, Chairman, Board of Governors of the Federal Reserve System, Before the Committee on Banking, Housing, and Urban Affairs, U.S. Senate" (Dec. 1, 1987), reprinted in 74 *Federal Reserve Bulletin* 91–103 (1988).

Greenspan, Alan, and James Kennedy (2007). "Sources and Uses of Equity Extracted from Homes" (Fed. Res. Bd. Finance & Economics Discussion Series Working Paper 2007–20, Mar. 2007), available at https://www.federalreserve.gov/pubs/feds/2007/200720/200720pap.pdf.

Greenwood, Robin, Samuel G. Hanson, and Jeremy C. Stein (2015). "A Comparative-Advantage Approach to Government Debt Maturity," 70(4) *Journal of Finance* 1683–722.

Greer, Guy (1933). "Why Canadian Banks Don't Fail," 166 *Harper's Magazine* 722–34 (May 1933).

Griffin, John M. (2019). "Ten Years of Evidence: Was Fraud a Force in the Financial Crisis?" (Jan. 23, 2019), available at http://ssrn.com/abstract=3320979.

Griffin, John M., Samuel A. Kruger, and Gonzalo Maturana (2018). "Do Labor Markets Discipline? Evidence from RMBS Bankers" (Jan. 12, 2018), available at http://ssrn.com/abstract=2977741.

Griffin, John M., Richard Lowery, and Alessio Saretto (2014). "Complex Securities and Underwriter Reputation: Do Reputable Underwriters Produce Better Securities?," 27(10) *Review of Financial Studies* 2872–925.

Griffin, John M., and Gonzalo Maturana (2016a). "Did Dubious Mortgage Origination Practices Distort Housing Prices?" 29(7) *Review of Financial Studies* 1671–1708.

Griffin, John M., and Gonzalo Maturana (2016b). "Who Facilitated Misreporting in Securitized Loans?," 29(2) *Review of Financial Studies* 384–419.

Griffin, John M., and Dragon Y. Tang (2012). "Did Subjectivity Play a Role in CDO Credit Ratings?" 67(4) *Journal of Finance* 1293–1328.

Gros, Daniel, Cinzia Alcidi, and Willem Pieter De Groen (2015). "Lessons from Quantitative Easing: Much Ado About So Little?" (CEPS Policy Brief No. 330, Mar. 2015), available at https://www.ceps.eu/system/files/PB330_QuantitativeEasingwithbreaks_0.pdf.

Grossman, Richard S. (1994). "The Shoe That Didn't Drop: Explaining Banking Stability During the Great Depression," 54(2) *Journal of Economic History* 654–82.

Group of 30 (2018a). *Managing the Next Financial Crisis: An Assessment of Emergency Arrangements in the Major Economies* (Group of Thirty, Sept. 2018), available at http://group30.org/images/uploads/publications/G30_Managing_the_Next_Financial_Crisis.pdf.

Group of 30 (2018b). *Banking Conduct and Culture: A Permanent Mindset Change* (Group of Thirty, Nov. 2018), available at https://group30.org/images/uploads/publications/G30_Culture2018_FNL3lo-compressed.pdf.

Gruenberg, Martin J. (2019a). "Statement by Martin J. Gruenberg: The Volcker Rule" (Aug. 20, 2019), available at https://www.fdic.gov/news/news/speeches/spaug2019b.pdf.

Gruenberg, Martin J. (2019b). "Statement by Martin J. Gruenberg, Member, FDIC Board of Directors on the Notice of Proposed Rulemaking: Swap Margin Requirements" (Sept. 17, 2019), available at https://www.fdic.gov/news/news/speeches/spsep1719.html.

Guill, Gene D. (2016). "Bankers Trust and the Birth of Modern Risk Management," 28(1) *Journal of Applied Corporate Finance* 19–29.

Guiso, Luigi, Paola Sapienza, and Luigi Zingales (2017). "Time Varying Risk Aversion" (Working Paper, June 2017), available at http://faculty.chicagobooth.edu/luigi.zingales/papers/research/RiskAversion.pdf.

Guynn, Randall D. (2014). "Framing the TBTF Problem: The Path to a Solution," in Martin Neil Baily and John B. Taylor, eds., *Across the Great Divide: New Perspectives on the Financial Crisis* 281–301. Stanford, CA: Hoover Institution, available at http://ssrn.com/abstract=2535915.

Hacker, Jacob S., and Paul Pierson (2010). *Winner-Take-All Politics: How Washington Made the Rich Richer—And Turned Its Back on the Middle Class*. New York: Simon & Schuster.

Haggerty, Neil (2019). "Hensarling to Join UBS as Executive Vice Chairman," *American Banker* (Apr. 12, 2019), available on Westlaw at 2019 WLNR 11407592.

Hahn, Thomas K. (1993). "Commercial Paper," 79(2) *Economic Quarterly* 45–67. Federal Reserve Bank of Richmond, VA.

Haldane, Andrew G. (2015). "On Microscopes and Telescopes" (Mar. 27, 2015), available at https://www.bankofengland.co.uk/speech/2015/on-microscopes-and-telescopes.

Haldane, Andrew G. (2010). "The $100 Billion Question" (Mar. 30, 2010), *BIS Review* 40/2010, available at https://www.bis.org/review/r100406d.pdf.

Haldane, Andrew G., and Piergiorgio Alessandri (2009). "Banking on the State" (Sept. 25, 2009), *BIS Review* 139/2009, available at https://www.bis.org/review/r091111e.pdf.

Haldane, Andrew, Simon Brennan, and Vasileios Madouros (2010). "What Is the Contribution of the Financial Sector: Miracle or Mirage?," in *The Future of Finance: The LSE Report* 87–120. London: London School of Economics and Political Science.

Haldane, Andrew G., and Vasileios Madouros (2012). "The Dog and the Frisbee" (Aug. 31, 2012), available at https://www.bis.org/review/r120905a.pdf.

Haldane, Andrew G., Matt Roberts-Sklar, Tomasz Wieladek, and Chris Young (2016). "QE: The Story So Far" (Bank of England Staff Working Paper No. 624, Oct. 2016), available at https://www.bankofengland.co.uk/working-paper/2016/qe-the-story-so-far.

Hale, Thomas (2019a). "The Global Boom in Non-Bank Finance," *Financial Times* (Oct. 24, 2019), available at https://ftalphaville.ft.com/2019/10/24/1571906229000/The-global-boom-in--non-bank-finance.

Hale, Thomas (2019b). "Italian Bailouts: Follow the Retail Bonds," *Financial Times* (Dec. 16, 2019), available at https://ftalphaville.ft.com/2019/12/16/1576497767000/Italian-bailouts--follow-the-retail-bonds.

Hale, Thomas (2018). "Weaning European Banks off ECB support," *Financial Times* (Dec. 7, 2018), available at https://ftalphaville.ft.com/2018/12/07/1544194183000/Weaning-European-banks-off-ECB-support.

Hale, Thomas (2016a). "Draghi Offers Bank Sweetener to Encourage Lending," *Financial Times* (Mar. 10, 2016), available at https://www.ft.com/content/063886f6-e6e4-11e5-bc31-138df2ae9ee6.

Hale, Thomas (2016b). "The Role of Retail Investors in Italian Banking Woes: A Q&A," *Financial Times* (July 14, 2016), available at https://www.ft.com/content/5aabd08c-4916-11e6-8d68-72e9211e86ab.

Hall, Ben (2019). "Europe Shaken as Political Systems Splinter," *Financial Times* (Jan. 8, 2019), available at https://www.ft.com/content/9cbb5e0e-0555-11e9-9d01-cd4d49afbbe3.

Hall, Ben (2018). "Macron v. Salvini: The Battle over Europe's Political Future," *Financial Times* (Dec. 27, 2018), available at https://www.ft.com/content/79d1d422-f3e4-11e8-9623-d7f9881e729f.

Hall, Ben, and Kerin Hope (2020). "Greek Economy: Will Reality Collide with Fresh Optimism in Athens?," *Financial Times* (Jan. 7, 2020), available at https://www.ft.com/content/3ec23fe6-30b2-11ea-9703-eea0cae3f0de.

Hamilton, David E. (1985). "The Causes of the Banking Panic of 1930: Another View," 51(4) *Journal of Southern History* 581–608.

Hamilton, Jesse (2019). "Trump's Push to Ease Wall Street Rules Hindered by Missteps (1)," *Bloomberg Law* (Mar. 11, 2019).

Hamilton, Jesse (2018). "Fed Said to Resist Adding Capital Demand for Biggest Banks," 110 *Bloomberg BNA's Banking Report* 729 (May 21, 2018).

Hamilton, Jesse, and Craig Torres (2019). "Fed Issues More Warnings on Hazards of High-Risk Corporate Debt," *Bloomberg Law* (May 6, 2019).

Hamilton, Walter (2005). "CEO of Morgan Stanley to Retire," *Los Angeles Times* (June 14, 2005), available at http://articles.latimes.com/2005/jun/14/business/fi-morgan14.

Harman, S. Palmer (1931). "The World's War Debts: A Debate Reopened," *New York Times* (Feb. 15, 1931), 125.

Harris, Alexandra (2019). "Fed Wins Year-End Repo Battle, but War to Control Rates Drags On," *Bloomberg News* (Dec. 31, 2019).

Harris, Alexandra, and Matthew Boesler (2020). "Ex-New York Fed Boss Says It's Time to Overhaul Repo Toolkit (3)," *Bloomberg Law* (Jan. 6, 2020).

Haubrich, Joseph G. (1990). "Nonmonetary Effects of Financial Crises: Lessons from the Great Depression in Canada," 25(2) *Journal of Monetary Economics* 223–52.

Heckinger, Richard, and Robert S. Steigerwald (2011). "International Regulatory Cooperation After the Crisis," *Chicago Fed Letter* (No. 292, Nov. 2011), available at https://www.chicago-fed.org/publications/chicago-fed-letter/2011/november-292.

Hector, Gary (1988). *Breaking the Bank: The Decline of BankAmerica*. Boston: Little, Brown & Company.

Heltman, John (2019a). "Capital Levels Are Just Right, Powell Tells House Members," *American Banker* (Feb. 27, 2019), available on Westlaw at 2019 WLNR 6349707.

Heltman, John (2019b). "Dodd-Frank Oversight Council Wants to Make It Harder to Designate Nonbanks," *American Banker* (Mar. 6, 2019), available on Westlaw at 2019 WLNR 7189127.

Heltman, John (2019c). "Don't Hold Your Breath for an Executive Compensation Rule," *American Banker* (Mar. 14, 2019), available on Westlaw at 2019 WLNR 8024264.

Heltman, John (2019d). "Small Changes to Stress Testing Could Have Big Impact on Risk, Tarullo Says," *American Banker* (May 22, 2019), available at 2019 WLNR 15668567.

Heltman, John (2019e). "Fed Finishes Overhaul of post-Crisis Supervisory Regime," *American Banker* (Oct. 11, 2019), available on Westlaw at 2019 WLNR 30685275.

Heltman, John (2018a). "If Regulators Can't Fix Bank Culture, Who Can?," *American Banker*, Apr. 2, 2018, available on Westlaw at 2018 WLNR 9575645.

Heltman, John (2018b). "Would Raising Capital Requirements for a Rainy Day Hasten One?," *American Banker* (Dec. 14, 2018), available on Westlaw at 2018 WLNR 38667324.

Hendrickson, Clara, Mark Muro, and William A. Galston (2018). *Countering the Geography of Discontent: Strategies for Left-Behind Places*, Brookings (Nov. 2018), available at https://www.brookings.edu/wp-content/uploads/2018/11/2018.11_Report_Countering-geography-of-discontent_Hendrickson-Muro-Galston.pdf.

Hendry, David F., and John N. J. Muellbauer (2018). "The Future of Macroeconomics: Macro Theory and Models at the Bank of England," 34(1–2) *Oxford Review of Economic Policy* 285–328.

Herman, Edward S. (1959). "Board of Governors v. Transamerica: Victory out of Defeat," 4(4) *Antitrust Bulletin* 521–39.

Herring, Richard J. (2018). "The Evolving Complexity of Capital Regulation," 53 *Journal of Financial Services Research* 183–205.

Herring, Richard (2014). "The Challenge of Resolving Cross-Border Financial Institutions," 31 *Yale Journal of Regulation* 853–81.

Hetzel, Robert L. (2008). *The Monetary Policy of the Federal Reserve: A History.* New York: Cambridge University Press.

Hetzel, Robert L. (2002). "German Monetary History in the First Half of the Twentieth Century," 88(1) *Economic Quarterly* 1–35. Federal Reserve Bank of Richmond, VA (Winter).

Hill, Jennifer (2012). "Why Did Australia Fare So Well in the Global Financial Crisis?" (Sydney Law School Legal Studies Research Paper No. 12/35, May 2012), available at http://ssrn.com/abstract=2063267.

Hilsenrath, Jon, Deborah Solomon, and Damian Paletta (2008). "Crisis Mode: Paulson, Bernanke Strained for Consensus in Bailout," *Wall Street Journal* (Nov. 10, 2008), A1.

Hirsh, Michael (2013). "In Bob We Trust," *National Journal* (Jan. 19, 2013), 12.

Historical Statistics (1975). *Historical Statistics of the United States: Colonial Times to 1970.* U.S. Department of Commerce, Sept. 1975, available at https://fraser.stlouisfed.org/docs/publications/histstatus/hstat1970_cen_1975_v2.pdf.

Hockett, Robert C., and Saule T. Omarova (2017). "The Finance Franchise," 102(5) *Cornell Law Review* 1143–218.

Hoenig, Thomas M. (2016). "Strengthening Global Capital: An Opportunity Not to Be Lost," Remarks by FDIC Vice Chairman Thomas M. Hoenig at the 22nd Annual Risk USA Conference (Nov. 9, 2016), available at https://www.fdic.gov/news/news/speeches/spnov0916.html.

Holder, Eric H., Jr. (2014). "Remarks on Financial Fraud Prosecutions at NYU School of Law" (Sept. 17, 2014), available at https://www.justice.gov/opa/speech/attorney-general-holder-remarks-financial-fraud-prosecutions-nyu-school-law.

Horan, Harold J. T. (1931). "Mitchell Reveals $24,000,000 Profit," *Washington Post* (Dec. 20, 1931), M1.

Horton, Brent J. (2017). "In Defense of a Federally-Mandated Disclosure System: Observing Pre–Securities Act Prospectuses," 54(4) *American Business Law Journal* 743–806.

Howell, Michael (2019). "Why Markets Should Get Set for 'QE4,'" *Financial Times* (Feb. 18, 2019), available at https://www.ft.com/content/71801c80-3353-11e9-bb0c-42459962a812.

Hubbard, J.T.W. (1995). *For Each the Strength of All: A History of Banking in the State of New York.* New York: New York University Press.

Hughes, Joseph P., and Loretta J. Mester (2018). "The Performance of Financial Institutions: Modeling, Evidence, and Some Policy Implications" (June 25, 2018), available at http://ssrn.com/abstract=3247813.

Hume, Neil (2012). "Australia: Mine, All Mine," *Financial Times* (June 17, 2012), available at https://www.ft.com/content/f88223fe-b6d7-11e1-8c96-00144feabdc0.

Hunter, Michael, and Emma Dunkley (2019). "Fed Shift Helps Global Stocks Close In on Best Month Since 2016," *Financial Times* (Jan. 31, 2019), available at https://www.ft.com/content/0c81666a-2505-11e9-b329-c7e6ceb5ffdf.

Huszar, Andrew (2013). "Confessions of a Quantitative Easer," *Wall Street Journal* (Nov. 12, 2013), A17.

Igan, Deniz, and Thomas Lambert (2018). "Bank Lobbying: Regulatory Capture and Beyond" (Feb. 2018), available at http://ssrn.com/abstract=3128829.

IIF (2020). Institute of International Finance, *Global Debt Monitor: Sustainability Matters* (Jan. 13, 2020), available at https://www.iif.com/Portals/0/Files/content/Global%20Debt%20Monitor_January2020_vf.pdf.

IMF (2014). *Cross-Border Resolution: Recent Developments* (International Monetary Fund, June 2014), available at https://www.imf.org/external/np/pp/eng/2014/060214.pdf.

IMF (2011). International Monetary Fund, Independent Evaluation Office, *Evaluation Report, IMF Performance in the Run-Up to the Financial and Economic Crisis: IMF Surveillance in 2004–07* (2011), available at http://www.ieo-imf.org/ieo/files/completedevaluations/Crisis-%20Main%20Report%20(without%20Moises%20Signature).pdf.

IMF-GFS (2019). International Monetary Fund, *Global Financial Stability Report—Vulnerabilities in a Maturing Credit Cycle* (Apr. 2019), available at https://www.imf.org/en/Publications/GFSR/Issues/2019/03/27/Global-Financial-Stability-Report-April-2019.

IMF-GFS (2018). International Monetary Fund, *Global Financial Stability Report—A Decade after the Global Financial Crisis: Are We Safer?* (Oct. 2018), available at https://www.imf.org/en/Publications/GFSR/Issues/2018/09/25/Global-Financial-Stability-Report-October-2018.

IMF-GFS (2014). International Monetary Fund, *Global Financial Stability Report—Moving from Liquidity- to Growth-Driven Markets* (Apr. 2014), available at https://www.imf.org/en/Publications/GFSR/Issues/2016/12/31/Moving-from-Liquidity-to-Growth-Driven-Markets.

IMF-GFS (2008). International Monetary Fund, *Global Financial Stability Report—Containing Systemic Risks and Restoring Financial Soundness* (Apr. 2008), available at https://www.imf.org/en/Publications/GFSR/Issues/2016/12/31/Containing-Systemic-Risks-and-Restoring-Financial-Soundness.

IMF-WEO (2018). International Monetary Fund, *World Economic Outlook: Challenges to Steady Growth* (Oct. 2018), available at https://www.imf.org/en/Publications/WEO/Issues/2018/09/24/world-economic-outlook-october-2018.

Indap, Sujeet, and Mark Vandevelde (2018). "Private Equity: Apollo's Lucrative but Controversial Bet on Insurance," *Financial Times* (Oct. 31, 2018), available at https://www.ft.com/content/a7cb24ec-cae9-11e8-9fe5-24ad351828ab.

Inman, Phillip (2018). "Ten Years On, How Countries That Crashed Are Faring," *The Guardian* (June 16, 2018), available at https://www.theguardian.com/business/2018/jun/16/ireland-portugal-greece-spain-ten-years-after-crash-austerity.

Ip, Greg (2007). "Fed, Other Regulators Turn Attention to Risk in Banks' LBO Lending," *Wall Street Journal* (May 18, 2007), C1.

ISDA (2000). "Statement of the International Swaps and Derivatives Association, Inc. Before the Committee on Agriculture, Nutrition and Forestry, United States Senate" (Feb. 10, 2000) (submitted by Richard Grove), available on Westlaw at 2000 WL 156248.

ISDA (1999). "Statement Submitted on Behalf of The International Swaps and Derivatives Association, Inc. to the Subcommittee of Risk Management and Specialty Crops, Committee on Agriculture, United States House of Representatives" (May 20, 1999) (submitted by Joseph P. Bauman), available on Westlaw at 1999 WL 321621.

Isidore, Chris (2008). "Paulsen, Bernanke: Slow Growth Ahead," *CNNMoney* (Feb. 14, 2008), available at https://money.cnn.com/2008/02/14/news/economy/bernanke_paulson/index.htm.

Ivry, Bob (2009). "Reed Says 'I'm Sorry' for Role in Creating Citigroup (Update 1)," *Bloomberg* (Nov. 6, 2009), available at https://perma.cc/6WM6-PJYX.

Jackson, Robert (2019). "Statement of Commissioner Robert J. Jackson, Jr. on Final Rules Governing Investment Advice" (June 5, 2019), available at https://www.sec.gov/news/public-statement/statement-jackson-060519-iabd.

James, F. Cyril (1938). *The Growth of Chicago Banks*. New York: Harper & Brothers.

James, Harold (1991). "Introduction," in Harold James et al., eds., *The Role of Banks in the Interwar Economy* 1–12. New York: Cambridge University Press.

James, Marquis, and Bessie Rowland James (1954). *Biography of a Bank: The Story of Bank of America N.T. & S.A.* New York: Harper & Brothers.

Jeansonne, Glen (with David Luhrssen) (2016). *Herbert Hoover: A Life*. New York: New American Library.

Jenkins, Patrick (2019a). "Metro Gaffe Highlights Banks' Flimsy Risk Arithmetic," *Financial Times* (Mar. 4, 2019), available at https://www.ft.com/content/21605fe8-3c55-11e9-b856-5404d3811663.

Jenkins, Patrick (2019b). "Investors Must Keep Up Pressure on Runaway Banker Pay," *Financial Times* (Mar. 24, 2019), available at https://www.ft.com/content/6b207862-4cd0-11e9-bbc9-6917dce3dc62.

Jenkins, Patrick, and Laura Noonan (2017). "How Deutsche Bank's High-Stakes Gamble Went Wrong," *Financial Times* (Nov. 9, 2017), available at https://www.ft.com/content/60fa7da6-c414-11e7-a1d2-6786f39ef675.

Jenkins, Robert (2015). "Punish Errant Bankers—or We Are Doomed to Repeat the Past," *Independent* (Nov. 28, 2015), available at https://www.independent.co.uk/news/business/comment/punish-errant-bankers-or-we-are-doomed-to-repeat-the-past-a6752411.html.

Jiang, Guolin, Paul G. Mahoney, and Jianping Mei (2005). "Market Manipulation: A Comprehensive Study of Stock Pools," 77(1) *Journal of Financial Economics* 147–70.

Jiang, Wei, Ashlyn Aiko Nelson, and Edward Vytlacil (2014). "Liar's Loan? Effects of Origination Channel and Information Falsification on Mortgage Delinquency," 96(1) *Review of Economics and Statistics* 1–18.

Johnson, Simon, and James Kwak (2010). *13 Bankers: The Wall Street Takeover and the Next Meltdown*. New York: Pantheon Books.

Jones, Claire (2019). "The ECB After Draghi: 'You Need an Actor Who Can Act Fast,'" *Financial Times* (Mar. 13, 2019), available at https://www.ft.com/content/911665fe-41b8-11e9-9bee-efab61506f44.

Jones, Claire, and Michael Hunter (2019). "ECB Unveils Fresh Bank Stimulus amid Rising Eurozone Gloom," *Financial Times* (Mar. 7, 2019), available at https://www.ft.com/content/7ceb815e-40cd-11e9-b896-fe36ec32aece.

Jones, Jeffrey S., Wayne Y. Lee, and Timothy J. Yeager (2012). "Opaque Banks, Price Discovery, and Financial Instability," 21 *Journal of Financial Intermediation* 383–408.

Jones, Jesse H. (with Edward Angly) (1951). *Fifty Billion Dollars: My Thirteen Years with the RFC (1932–1945)*. New York: Macmillan Company.

Jonker, Joost, and Jan Luiten van Zanden (1995). "Method in the Madness? Banking Crises Between the Wars, an International Comparison," in Charles H. Feinstein, ed., *Banking, Currency, and Finance in Europe Between the Wars* 77–93. Oxford: Clarendon Press.

Jopson, Barney, and Robin Wigglesworth (2018). "US Regulators Begin to Ease Volcker Rule," *Financial Times* (May 30, 2018), available at https://www.ft.com/content/2536a362-6437-11e8-90c2-9563a0613e56.

Jordà, Òscar, Björn Richter, Moritz Schularick, and Alan M. Taylor (2017). "Bank Capital Redux: Solvency, Liquidity, and Crisis" (National Bureau of Economic Research Working Paper 23287, Mar. 2017), available at http://www.nber.org/papers/23287.

Jordà, Òscar, Moritz Schularick, and Alan M. Taylor (2016a). "The Great Mortgaging: Housing Finance, Crises and Business Cycles," 2016 *Economic Policy* 107–52.

Jordà, Òscar, Moritz Schularick, and Alan M. Taylor (2016b). "Sovereigns Versus Banks: Credit, Crises, and Consequences," 14(1) *Journal of the European Economic Association* 45–79.

Jordà, Òscar, Moritz Schularick, and Alan M. Taylor (2014). "Betting the House" (National Bureau of Economic Research Working Paper 20771, Dec. 2014), available at http://www.nber.org/papers/w20771.

Jordà, Òscar, Moritz Schularick, and Alan M. Taylor (2013). "When Credit Bites Back," 45(2) *Journal of Money, Credit and Banking* S2–S28.

Jordà, Òscar, Moritz Schularick, Alan M. Taylor, and Felix Ward (2018). "Global Financial Cycles and Risk Premiums" (National Bureau of Economic Research Working Paper 24677, June 2018), available at http://www.nber.org/papers/w24677.

Judge, Kathryn (2019). "Guarantor of Last Resort," 77(4) *Texas Law Review* 707–66.

Judge, Kathryn (2016). "The First Year: The Role of a Modern Lender of Last Resort," 116(3) *Columbia Law Review* 843–925.

Justiniano, Alejandro, Giorgio E. Primiceri, and Andrea Tambalotti (2017). "The Mortgage Rate Conundrum" (Federal Reserve Bank of New York Staff Report No. 829, Nov. 2017), available at https://papers.ssrn.com/sol3/papers.cfm?abstract_id=3072926.

Kacperczyk, Martin, and Philipp Schnabl (2010). "When Safe Proved Risky: Commercial Paper During the Financial Crisis of 2007-2009," 24(1) *Journal of Economic Perspectives* 29–50.

Kaiser, Robert G. (2013). *Act of Congress: How America's Essential Institution Works, and How It Doesn't*. New York: Alfred A. Knopf.

Kaminska, Izabella (2019). "A Summary of Recent Repo Chatter, Plus a Chart That Matters," *Financial Times* (Dec. 13, 2019), available at https://ftalphaville.ft.com/2019/12/12/1576161128000/A-summary-of-recent-repo-market-chatter--plus-a-chart-that-matters.

Kane, Edward J. (2018). "Double Whammy: Implicit Subsidies and the Great Financial Crisis" (Institute for New Economic Thinking Working Paper No. 81, Sept. 2018), available at https://www.ineteconomics.org/uploads/papers/WP_81-Kane-Double-Whammy.pdf.

Kane, Edward J. (2000). "Incentives for Banking Megamergers: What Motives Might Regulators Infer from Event-Study Evidence?," 32(3) *Journal of Money, Credit, and Banking* 671–701 (2000).

Kane, Thomas P. (1922). *The Romance and Tragedy of Banking: Problems and Incidents of Governmental Supervision of National Banks*. New York: The Bankers Publishing Co., available at http://chestofbooks.com/finance/banking/Romance-Tragedy/index.html.

Kansas City Fed (2019). "Bank Capital Analysis" as of June 30, 2019 [including "BCA news release (Nov. 5, 2019)," "BCA table" and "BCA trend chart"], available at https://www.kansascityfed.org/research/bankingandpayments/bca.

Kantrow, Yvette D., and Liz Moyer (1998). "Citi, Travelers: A Global Leader Takes Shape," *American Banker* (Apr. 7, 1998), A1, available on Westlaw at 1998 WLNR 2763775.

Kashkari, Neel (2016). "Lessons from the Crisis: Ending Too Big to Fail," Remarks by Neel Kashkari, President, Federal Reserve Bank of Minneapolis, at the Brookings Institution (Feb. 16, 2016), available at https://www.minneapolisfed.org/~/media/files/news_events/pres/kashkari-ending-tbtf-02-16-2016.pdf.

Kay, John (2015). *Other People's Money: The Real Business of Finance*. New York: PublicAffairs.

Keefe, Josh (2018). "CFPB Drops Investigation into Payday Lender That Contributed to Mick Mulvaney's Campaigns," *International Business Times* (Jan. 23, 2018), available at https://www.ibtimes.com/political-capital/cfpb-drops-investigation-payday-lender-contributed-mick-mulvaneys-campaigns.

Kelleher, Dennis (2019). "CFPB Is Looking Out for Financial Predators Instead of Main Street," *The Hill* (Feb. 22, 2019), available at https://thehill.com/opinion/finance/429349-cfpb-looking-out-for-financial-predators-not-main-street-americans#bottom-story-socials.

Kelleher, Dennis (2018). "The State of Financial Reform: November 2018," available at https://bettermarkets.com/sites/default/files/State%20of%20Financial%20Reform.pdf.

Kelleher, Dennis, and Stephen Hall (2019). "New SEC Rule Aids and Abets Wall Street Predators," *The Hill* (June 6, 2019), available at https://thehill.com/opinion/finance/447282-new-sec-rule-aids-and-abets-wall-street-predators.

Kelly, Bryan, Hanno Lustig, and Stijn Van Nieuwerburgh (2016). "Too-Systemic-to-Fail: What Option Markets Imply About Sector-Wide Guarantees," 106(6) *American Economic Review* 1278–319.

Kemmerer, Donald L. (1977). *The Life of John E. Rovensky, Banker and Industrialist*. Champaign, IL: Stipes Publishing Co.

Kennedy, Susan Eastabrook (1973). *The Banking Crisis of 1933*. Lexington: University Press of Kentucky.

Keohane, David (2019). "France Tells Banks to Set Aside More Capital," *Financial Times* (Mar. 18, 2019), available at https://www.ft.com/content/5c575cfc-49a5-11e9-8b7f-d49067e0f50d?desktop=true&segmentId=d8d3e364-5197-20eb-17cf-2437841d178a.

Keoun, Bradley, and Philip Kuntz (2011). "Wall Street Aristocracy Got $1.2 Trillion in Secret Loans," *Bloomberg* (Aug. 21, 2011).

Kindleberger, Charles (1986). *The World in Depression, 1929–1939*. Revised and enlarged edition. Berkeley: University of California Press.

Kingson, Jennifer A. (2000). "A New Law, New Bankers, a Few Notable Deals Highlight Pivotal Year," *American Banker* (Dec. 28, 2000), 1, available on Westlaw at 2000 WLNR 2821473.

Klein, Maury (2001). *Rainbow's End: The Crash of 1929*. New York: Oxford University Press.

Kling, Arnold (2009). "Not What They Had in Mind: A History of Policies That Produced the Financial Crisis of 2008" (Sept. 15, 2009), available at http://ssrn.com/abstract=1474430.

Knox, Malcolm (2010). "The Deal Is Simple. Australia Gets Money, China Gets Australia," *Bloomberg Business Week* (Sept. 6–12, 2010), 44–49.

Kohn, Donald L. (2005). "Commentary: Has Financial Development Made the World Riskier?," in *The Greenspan Era: Lessons for the Future* 371–79 (Proceedings of an Economic Policy Symposium, Federal Reserve Bank of Kansas City, Aug. 2005), available at https://www.kansascityfed.org/publicat/sympos/2005/pdf/Kohn2005.pdf.

Kohn, Donald L. (2004). "How Should Policymakers Deal with Low-Probability, High-Impact Events? Remarks by Governor Donald L. Kohn at the European Central Bank Conference on Monetary Policy and Imperfect Knowledge" (Oct. 15, 2004), available at https://www.federalreserve.gov/boarddocs/speeches/2004/20041015/default.htm.

Kohn, Donald, and Brian Sack (2018). "Monetary Policy During the Financial Crisis" (Working paper, Sept. 2018), available at https://www.brookings.edu/wp-content/uploads/2018/08/13-Monetary-Policy-Prelim-Disc-Draft-2018.09.11.pdf.

Kress, Jeremy C. (2019a). "Solving Banking's 'Too Big to Manage' Problem," 104(1) *Minnesota Law Review* 171–241.

Kress, Jeremy C. (2019b). "Modernizing Bank Merger Review," *Yale Journal on Regulation* (2020) (forthcoming) (draft of Sept. 1, 2019), available at http://ssrn.com/abstract=3440914.

Kress, Jeremy C., Patricia A. McCoy, and Daniel Schwarcz (2019). "Regulating Entities and Activities: Complementary Approaches to Nonbank Systemic Risk," 92(6) *Southern California Law Review* 1455–1527.

Krishnamurthy, Arvind, Stefan Nagel, and Dmitry Orlov (2014). "Sizing Up Repo," 69(6) *Journal of Finance* 2381–417.

Krishnamurthy, Prasad (2018). "George Stigler on His Head: The Consequences of Restrictions on Competition in (Bank) Regulation," 35 *Yale Journal on Regulation* 823–73.

Kronick, Jeremy, and Yan Wendy Wu (2019). "Shadow Banking and Canada's Monetary Policy" (Sept. 2019), available at http://ssrn.com/abstract=3451287.

Kroszner, Randall S., and Raghuram G. Rajan (1994). "Is the Glass-Steagall Act Justified? A Study of the U.S. Experience with Universal Banking Before 1933," 84(4) *American Economic Review* 810–32.

Kroszner, Randall S., and Philip E. Strahan (2014). "Regulation and Deregulation of the US Banking Industry: Causes, Consequences, and Implications for the Future," in Nancy L. Rose, ed., *Economic Regulation and Its Reform: What Have We Learned?* 485–543. Chicago: University of Chicago Press.

Kryzanowski, Lawrence, and Gordon S. Roberts (1993). "Canadian Banking Solvency, 1922–1940," 25(3) *Journal of Money, Credit, and Banking* 361–76.

Kuczynski, Robert R. (1932). *Bankers' Profits from German Loans*. Washington, DC: Brookings Institution.

Kuhn, Moritz, Moritz Schularick, and Ulrike I. Steins (2018). "Income and Wealth Inequality in America, 1949–2016" (Federal Reserve Bank of Minneapolis, Opportunity and Inclusive

Growth Institute Working Paper 9, June 2018), available at https://www.minneapolisfed.org/institute/working-papers-institute/iwp9.pdf.

Kunz, Diane B. (1991). "American Bankers and Britain's Fall from Gold," in Harold James et al., eds., *The Role of Banks in the Interwar Economy* 35–48. New York: Cambridge University Press.

Kupiec, Paul (2017). "Big Banks Will Always Be Too Big, Glass-Steagall or Not," *American Banker* (Apr. 24, 2017), available at https://www.americanbanker.com/opinion/big-banks-will-always-be-too-big-glass-steagall-or-not.

Kuriloff, Aaron (2019). "Taking Stock of the World's Growing Debt," *Wall Street Journal* (Jan. 2, 2019), R1.

Kutler, Jeffrey (1998). "U.S. Firms Seen Best-Placed on World Financial Speedway," *American Banker*, June 4, 1998, at 1, available on Westlaw at 1998 WLNR 2766748.

Kuttner, Kenneth N. (2018). "Outside the Box: Unconventional Monetary Policy in the Great Recession and Beyond," 32(4) *Journal of Economic Perspectives* 121–46.

Kwak, James (2014). "Cultural Capture and the Financial Crisis," in Daniel Carpenter and David A. Moss, eds., *Preventing Regulatory Capture: Special Interest Influence and How to Limit It* 71–98. New York: Cambridge University Press.

Kyger, Lauren, and Alison Fitzgerald Kodjak (2014). "Bear Stearns Mortgage Executives Have Plum Jobs on Wall Street" (Center for Public Integrity, Mar. 19, 2014), available at https://publicintegrity.org/business/bear-stearns-mortgage-executives-have-plum-jobs-on-wall-street.

Labaton, Stephen (2008a). "Bear Stearns in the Committee Room: Testimony About Chief's Misunderstanding and Treasury's Push for a Low Purchase Price," *New York Times* (Apr. 4, 2008), C1.

Labaton, Stephen (2008b). "Wall St. in Worst Loss Since '01 Despite Reassurances by Bush," *New York Times* (Sept. 16, 2008), A1.

Labaton, Stephen (1997). "A Clinton Social with Bankers Included a Leading Regulator," *New York Times* (Jan. 25, 1997), 1.

Labaton, Stephen (1991a). "House Turns Down Banking Overhaul by 324-to-89 Vote," *New York Times* (Nov. 5, 1991), A1.

Labaton, Stephen (1991b). "Lawmakers Still Split on Interstate Banking," *New York Times* (Nov. 25, 1991), D3.

Labaton, Stephen (1991c). "Congress Votes $100 Billion Bank and S.& L. Aid," *New York Times* (Nov 28, 1991).

Labonte, Marc (2018). "Systemically Important or 'Too Big to Fail' Financial Institutions" (Congressional Research Service Report 7-5700, R42150, Sept. 24, 2018), available at https://fas.org/sgp/crs/misc/R42150.pdf.

LaCour-Little, Michael, Charles A. Calhoun, and Wei Yu (2011). "What Role Did Piggyback Lending Play in the Housing Bubble and Mortgage Collapse?," 20(2) *Journal of Housing Economics* 81–100.

Laeven, Luc, and Ross Levine (2007). "Is there a diversification discount in financial conglomerates?" 85(2) *Journal of Financial Economics* 331–67.

Laeven, Luc, Lev Ratnovski, and Hui Tong (2016). "Bank Size, Capital, and Systemic Risk: Some International Evidence," 69 *Journal of Banking and Finance* S25–S34 (2016).

Laeven, Luc, and Fabian Valencia (2018). "Systemic Banking Crises Revisited" (IMF Working Paper No. 18-206, Sept. 2018), available at http://ssrn.com/abstract=3267233.

Lambe, Geraldine (2010). "Rebuilding UBS," *The Banker* (Mar. 1, 2010), available on Westlaw at 2010 WLNR 4332821.

Lang, Hannah (2019a). "Fed Curbs Stress Test Requirement for Most Big Banks," *American Banker* (Mar. 7, 2019), available on Westlaw at 2019 WLNR 7187170.

Lang, Hannah (2019b). "Fed Votes Against Deploying Big-Bank Capital Buffer," *American Banker* (Mar. 7, 2019), available on Westlaw at 2019 WLNR 7188115.

Lazarus, David (2019). "CFPB Celebrates Record of Consumer Protection—Except for the Whole Watchdog Thing," *Los Angeles Times* (June 14, 2019), available at https://www.latimes.com/business/lazarus/la-fi-lazarus-cfpb-kraninger-anniversary-20190614-story.html.

Lee, Lisa (2019). "Apollo and Blackstone Are Stealing Wall Street Loan Business (1)," *Bloomberg Law* (Dec. 18, 2019).

Lenzner, Robert (2015). "Hidden Dangers That Banking Regulators Fail to Chart," *Financial Times* (Apr. 20, 2015), available at https://www.ft.com/content/e09b49d6-e1fa-11e4-bb7f-00144feab7de.

Leonhardt, Megan (2017). "Inside Wall Street's Secret War on American Investors," *Money* (Jan. 24, 2017), available at http://money.com/money/4640730/wall-street-fights-fiduciary.

Lettieri, John W. (2016). "America Without Entrepreneurs: The Consequences of Dwindling Startup Activity," Testimony before the Committee on Small Business and Entrepreneurship, U.S. Senate (June 29, 2016), available at https://www.sbc.senate.gov/public/_cache/files/0/d/0d8d1a51-ee1d-4f83-b740-515e46e861dc/7F75741C1A2E6182E1A5D21B61D278F3.lettieri-testimony.pdf.

Levinson, Charles (2015a). "How Wall Street Captured Washington's Effort to Rein In Banks," *Reuters* (Apr. 9, 2015), available at https://www.reuters.com/investigates/special-report/usa-bankrules-weakening.

Levinson, Charles (2015b). "U.S. banks moved billions of dollars in trades beyond Washington's reach," *Reuters* (Aug. 21, 2015); available at https://www.reuters.com/investigates/special-report/usa-swaps/.

Levitin, Adam J. (2012). "In Defense of Bailouts," 99 *Georgetown Law Journal* 435–514.

Levitin, Adam J., and Susan M. Wachter (2012). "Explaining the Housing Bubble," 100(4) *Georgetown Law Journal* 1177–258.

Levitt, Arthur (1998). "Testimony of Chairman Arthur Levitt Before the Senate Committee on Agriculture, Nutrition, and Forestry, Concerning the Regulation of the Over-the-Counter Derivatives Market and Hybrid Instruments" (July 30, 1998), available on Westlaw at 1998 WL 468780 (S.E.C.).

Levitt, Hannah (2019). "Wells Fargo CEO Scharf Taps Daley to Help Fix Bank's Image (1)," *Bloomberg* (Nov. 7, 2019).

Levitt, Hannah (2018). "Wells Fargo CFO Sees Doubling Investment-Banking Fees in 5 Years," *Bloomberg* (Nov. 6, 2018), available at https://www.bloomberg.com/news/articles/2018-11-06/wells-fargo-cfo-sees-doubling-investment-banking-fees-in-5-years.

Lewis, Leo (2019). "Nomura Reports First Full-Year Loss in a Decade," *Financial Times* (Apr. 25, 2019), available at https://www.ft.com/content/24c9c99c-6736-11e9-9adc-98bf1d35a056.

Lewis, Leo, and Emma Dunkley (2018). "Bank of Japan Tweaks QE but Fails to Join Global Tightening Train," *Financial Times* (July 31, 2018), available at https://www.ft.com/content/b9a75a02-94b9-11e8-b67b-b8205561c3fe.

Lewis, Leo, Stephen Morris, and Katie Martin (2019). "Nomura Boss Says Bank Has 'No Choice' but to Change," *Financial Times* (Apr. 19, 2019), available at https://www.ft.com/content/5939e6f8-61dc-11e9-a27a-fdd51850994c.

Lewis, Michael (2010). *The Big Short: Inside the Doomsday Machine*. New York: W. W. Norton & Co.

Li, Wei, and Keith S. Ernst (2006). *The Best Value in the Subprime Market: State Predatory Lending Reforms* (Center for Responsible Lending, Feb. 23, 2006), available at https://www.responsiblelending.org/mortgage-lending/research-analysis/rr010-State_Effects-0206.pdf.

Liang, Nellie, Margaret M. McConnell, and Philip Swagel (2018). "Evidence on Outcomes" (Working paper, Nov. 2, 2018), available at https://www.brookings.edu/wp-content/uploads/2018/08/15-Outcomes-Prelim-Disc-Draft-2018.12.11.pdf.

Ligi, Antonio, and Ben Holland (2009). "Why Bernie Madoff Is No Marcel Ospel as Man Swiss Love to Hate," *Bloomberg* (Feb. 24, 2009).

Limbach, Peter, P. Raghavendra Rau, and Henrik Schürmann (2020). "The Death of Trust Across the Financial Industry" (Working paper, Mar. 2020), available at http://ssrn.com/abstract=3559047.

Linsell, Katie (2018). "Derivatives: ISDA Delays Transferring Oversight of Credit-Swap Payout Panels," 50 *Securities Regulation and Law Report (BNA)* 692 (May 7, 2018).

Lipin, Steven (1995). "For New Chase, Fresh Challenges—Chemical Merger Seen as Tactic to Compete with Financial Firms," *Wall Street Journal*, Aug. 29, 1995, A3.

Lipin, Steven, and Stephen E. Frank (1998). "The Big Umbrella: Travelers/Citicorp Merger—One-Stop Shopping Is the Reason for Deal," *Wall Street Journal* (Apr. 7, 1998), at C14.

Lipton, Eric, and Raymond Hernandez (2008). "A Champion of Wall Street Reaps the Benefits," *New York Times* (Dec. 14, 2008), 1.

Lipton, Eric, and Stephen Labaton (2008). "A Deregulator Looks Back, Unswayed," *New York Times* (Nov. 17, 2008), A1.

Litan, Robert E. (1987). *What Should Banks Do?* Washington, DC: Brookings Institution.

Llewellyn, David T. (1996). "Universal Banking and the Public Interest: A British Perspective," in Anthony Saunders and Ingo Walter, ed., *Universal Banking: Financial System Design Reconsidered* 161–204. Chicago: Irwin Professional Publishing.

Logan, Lorie, William Nelson, and Patrick Parkinson (2018). "Novel Lender of Last Resort Programs" (Sept. 2018), available at https://www.brookings.edu/wp-content/uploads/2018/08/02-Novel-LOLR-Prelim-Disc-Draft-2018.09.11.pdf.

Lorenc, Amy G., and Jeffery Y. Zhang (2018). "The Differential Impact of Bank Size on Systemic Risk" (Finance and Economics Discussion Series No. 2018-066, Federal Reserve Board, Aug. 21, 2018), available at https://www.federalreserve.gov/econres/feds/files/2018066pap.pdf.

Lorey, Eugene M. (1933). "Along the Highways of Finance," *New York Times* (May 28, 1933), N11.

Los Angeles Times (2020). "Hammer Falls in Wells Fargo Scandal," *Los Angeles Times* (Jan. 24, 2020), available on Westlaw at 2020 WLNR 2314668.

Lowenstein, Roger (2004). *Origins of the Crash: The Great Bubble and Its Undoing.* New York: Penguin Press.

Lubben, Stephen J. (2016). "Failure of the Clearinghouse: Dodd-Frank's Fatal Flaw?," 10(1) *Virginia Law and Business Review* 127–60.

Lubben, Stephen J. (2010). "Repeal the Safe Harbors," 18(1) *American Bankruptcy Institute Law Review* 319–35.

Lubben, Stephen J., and Arthur E. Wilmarth, Jr. (2017). "Too Big and Unable to Fail," 69(5) *Florida Law Review* 1205–49, available at http://ssrn.com/abstract=2839946.

Lugar, Richard (1998). "Opening Statement of Senator Dick Lugar, Senate Agriculture Committee CFTC Hearing" (Dec. 16, 1998), available on Westlaw at 1998 WL 876994.

Lumpkin, Stephen A. (1993). "Repurchase and Reverse Repurchase Agreements," in Timothy Q. Cook and Robert K. LaRoche, eds., *Instruments of the Money Market*, 59–74. Seventh edition. Richmond: Federal Reserve Bank of Richmond, available at https://www.richmond-fed.org/~/media/richmondfedorg/publications/research/special_reports/instruments_of_the_money_market/pdf/full_publication.pdf.

Lyon, W. A. (1930). "National City Is Now Biggest Bank in World," *New York Herald Tribune* (Jan. 15, 1930), 1.

MacAskill, Andrew, and Lawrence White (2017). "RBS Rising from Ruins as Shadow of Former Self," *Reuters* (Apr. 3, 2017), available at https://www.reuters.com/article/us-rbs-restructuring/rbs-rising-from-ruins-as-shadow-of-former-self-idUSKBN1750U6.

Maccaro, James (2003). "Thomas Fortune Ryan: The Great Opportunist," *Working Money* (Dec. 23, 2003), available at http://premium.working-money.com/wm/display.asp?art=440.

Mackenzie, Michael (2019a). "Federal Reserve at Early Stages of Pivot Towards Next Easing Cycle," *Financial Times* (Feb. 1, 2019), available at https://www.ft.com/content/fb3b78ec-2607-11e9-b329-c7e6ceb5ffdf.

Mackenzie, Michael (2019b). "Federal Reserve Shifts to Assessing the Situation," *Financial Times* (Oct. 30, 2019), available at https://www.ft.com/content/b28b18a2-fb48-11e9-a354-36acbbb0d9b6.

Mackenzie, Michael (2018). "December Drama Ends Bleak Year for Markets," *Financial Times* (Dec. 27, 2018), available at https://www.ft.com/content/80dea1b6-0120-11e9-9d01-cd4d49afbbe3.

Maddaloni, Angela, and José-Luis Peydró (2010). "Bank Risk-Taking, Securitization, Supervision and Low Interest Rates: Evidence from the Euro Area and the U.S. Lending Standards" (European Central Bank Working Paper No. 1248), available at http://ssrn.com/abstract=1679689.

Madigan, Lisa (2010). Testimony of Illinois Attorney General Lisa Madigan Before the Financial Crisis Inquiry Commission (Jan. 14, 2010), available at https://fraser.stlouisfed.org/files/docs/historical/fct/fcic/fcic_testimony_madigan_20100114.pdf.

Madison, George W., Michael D. Lewis, and William Shirley (2018). "Insight: Volcker Rule 2.0: A Significant but Unfinished Proposal," 110 *Bloomberg BNA's Banking Report* 1171 (Aug. 20, 2018).

Madrick, Jeff (2011). *The Age of Greed: The Triumph of Finance and the Decline of America, 1970 to the Present*. New York: Vintage Books.

Mahoney, Paul G. (2018). "Deregulation and the Subprime Crisis," 104(2) *Virginia Law Review* 235–300.

Mallet, Victor (2019). "France's gilets jaunes are marching to a different beat," *Financial Times* (Jan. 28, 2019), available at https://www.ft.com/content/6cac1ec8-22ed-11e9-b329-c7e6ceb5ffdf.

Mallet, Victor, and Harriet Agnew (2019). "Emanuel Macron promises tax cuts in new round of French reforms," *Financial Times* (Apr. 25, 2019), available at https://www.ft.com/content/2d5a32e4-6750-11e9-9adc-98bf1d35a056.

Malone, Julia (1996). "'The Buying of the President': Big Donors Wield Big Influence, Study Says," *Atlanta Journal and Constitution* (Jan. 12, 1996), A7, available on Westlaw at 1996 WLNR 2948804.

Manns, Jeffrey D. (2011). "Building Better Bailouts: The Case for a Long-Term Investment Approach," 63 *Florida Law Review* 1349–406.

Markham, Jerry W. (2010). "The Subprime Crisis—A Test Match for the Bankers: Glass-Steagall vs. Gramm-Leach-Bliley," 12(4) *University of Pennsylvania Journal of Business Law* 1081–134.

Masciantonio, Sergio, and Andrea Tiseno (2013). "The Rise and Fall of Universal Banking" (Bank of Italy Occasional Paper No. 164, June 2013), available at http://ssrn.com/abstract=2283099.

Mason, Joseph R. (2001a). "Reconstruction Finance Corporation Assistance to Financial Intermediaries and Commercial and Industrial Enterprises in the United States, 1932–37," in Stijn Claessens et al., eds., *Resolution of Financial Distress: An International Perspective on the Design of Bankruptcy Laws* 167–204. Washington, DC: World Bank.

Mason, Joseph R. (2001b). "Do Lender of Last Resort Policies Matter? The Effects of Reconstruction Finance Corporation Assistance to Banks During the Great Depression," 20(1) *Journal of Financial Services Research* 77–95.

Mather, O.A. (1931). "Big Loop Banks in 2 Mergers," *Chicago Daily Tribune* (June 8, 1931), 1.

Mathis, William, and Franz Wild (2019). "Second Ex-Barclays Trader Found Guilty of Rigging Euribor (3)," *Bloomberg Law* (Mar. 28, 2019).

Mayer, Christopher, Karen Pence, and Shane M. Sherlund (2009). "The Rise in Mortgage Defaults," 23(1) *Journal of Economic Perspectives* 27–50.

Mayer, Martin (2009). "Glass-Steagall in Our Future: How Straight, How Narrow" (Networks Financial Institution Public Policy Brief 2009-PB-07, Nov. 2009), available at http://ssrn.com/abstract=1505488.

Mayo, Mike (2019). "Paul Volcker on Conflicts, Ethics, and the US Banking Industry" (Feb. 25, 2019) (CFA Institute blog post), available at https://blogs.cfainstitute.org/investor/2019/02/25/paul-volcker-on-conflicts-ethics-and-the-us-banking-industry.

McCarthy, Brayden (2019). "Why Bank Lending to Small Businesses Isn't Recovering" (Feb. 6, 2019), available at https://www.fundera.com/blog/bank-lending-small-businesses-isnt-recovering.

McCauley, Robert (2018). "The 2008 Crisis: Transpacific or Transatlantic?," *BIS Quarterly Review* (Dec. 2018), 39–58.

McConnell, John J., and Stephen A. Buser (2011). "The Origins and Evolution of the Market for Mortgage-Backed Securities," 3 *Annual Review of Financial Economics* 173–92.

McCoy, Patricia A. (2019). "Inside Job: The Assault on the Structure of the Consumer Financial Protection Bureau," 103(6) *Minnesota Law Review* 2543–2615.

McCulley, Paul (2010). "After the Crisis: Planning a New Financial Structure" (May 25, 2010) (blog post), available at https://pro.creditwritedowns.com/2010/05/mcculley-after-the-crisis-planning-a-new-financial-structure.html.

McCulley, Paul (2008). "The Paradox of Deleveraging Will Be Broken" (Nov. 24, 2008) (blog post), available at http://www.mauldineconomics.com/outsidethebox/the-paradox-of-deleveraging-will-be-broken-2466.

McCulley, Paul (2007). "Teton Reflections" (Sept. 10, 2007) (blog post), available at http://www.mauldineconomics.com/outsidethebox/teton-reflections-342#.

McDonald, Forrest (1962). *Insull*. Chicago: University of Chicago Press.

McDonald, Robert, and Anna Paulson (2015). "AIG in Hindsight," 29(2) *Journal of Economic Perspectives* 81–106.

McFerrin, John B. (1969). *Caldwell and Company: A Southern Financial Empire*. Nashville: Vanderbilt University Press (reprint of original 1939 edition).

McGeever, Jamie (2017). "U.S. Investment Banks Strengthen Global Lead over Europe," *Reuters* (Mar. 21, 2017), available at https://www.reuters.com/article/us-global-banks-ranking-idUSKBN16T009.

McLannahan, Ben (2019). "Why Wells Fargo Is Struggling to Put Its Past Behind It," *Financial Times* (Mar. 20, 2019), available at https://www.ft.com/content/b20b0994-4a47-11e9-8b7f-d49067e0f50d.

McLean, Bethany, and Peter Elkind (2003). *The Smartest Guys in the Room: The Amazing Rise and Scandalous Fall of Enron*. New York: Portfolio.

McLean, Bethany, and Joe Nocera (2010). *All the Devils Are Here: The Hidden History of the Financial Crisis*. New York: Penguin Group (USA), Inc.

McWilliams, David (2019). "Quantitative Easing Was the Father of Millennial Socialism," *Financial Times* (Mar. 1, 2019), available at https://www.ft.com/content/cbed81fc-3b56-11e9-9988-28303f70fcff.

Mehrling, Perry (2012). "Three Principles for Market-Based Credit Regulation," 102(3) *American Economic Review: Papers and Proceedings* 107–12.

Meltzer, Allan H. (2005). "Origins of the Great Inflation," 87(2) *Review* (Federal Reserve Bank of St. Louis, Mar./Apr., Part 2) 145–75.

Meltzer, Allan H. (2003). *A History of the Federal Reserve: Volume I, 1913–1951*. Chicago: University of Chicago Press.

Menand, Lev (2018). "Too Big to Supervise: The Rise of Financial Conglomerates and the Decline of Discretionary Oversight in Banking," 103(6) *Cornell Law Review* 1527–88.

Mencimer, Stephanie (2007). "No Account: The Nefarious Bureaucrat Who's Helping Banks Rip You Off," *New Republic* (Aug. 27, 2007), 14, available at https://newrepublic.com/article/64918/no-account-0.

Metrick, Andrew, and June Rhee (2018). "Regulatory Reform," 10 *Annual Review of Financial Economics* 153–72.

Mian, Atif R., and Amir Sufi (2018a). "Finance and Business Cycles: The Credit-Driven Household Demand Channel" (National Bureau of Economic Research Working Paper 24322, Feb. 2018), available at http://www.nber.org/papers/w24322.

Mian, Atif R., and Amir Sufi (2018b). "Credit Supply and Housing Speculation" (National Bureau of Economic Research Working Paper 24823, July 2018), available at http://www.nber.org/papers/w24823.

Mian, Atif R., and Amir Sufi (2015). "Household Debt and Defaults from 2000 to 2010: Facts from Credit Bureau Data" (National Bureau of Economic Research Working Paper 21203, May 2015), available at http://www.nber.org/papers/w21203.

Mian, Atif R., and Amir Sufi (2014). *House of Debt: How They (and You) Caused the Great Recession, and How We Can Prevent It from Happening Again.* Chicago: University of Chicago Press.

Mian, Atif, Amir Sufi, and Emil Verner (2017). "How Do Credit Supply Shocks Affect the Real Economy? Evidence from the United States in the 1980s" (National Bureau of Economic Research Working Paper 23802, Oct. 2017), available at http://www.nber.org/papers/w23802.

Michaels, Dave (2015). "Securities: Perez Rallies Support for Broker Rules as Wall Street Pushes Back," 104 *Bloomberg BNA's Banking Report* 534 (Mar. 17, 2015).

Middleton, Roger (2010). "British monetary and fiscal policy during the 1930s," 26(3) *Oxford Review of Economic Policy* 414–41.

Millaruelo, Antonio, and Ana Del-Rio (2017). "The Cost of Interventions in the Financial Sector Since 2008 in the EU" (Banco de Espana Analytical Article, Apr. 6, 2017), available at http://ssrn.com/abstract=2948576.

Milne, Richard (2016). "Olafur Hauksson, the Man Who Jailed Iceland's Bankers," *Financial Times* (Dec. 9, 2016), available at https://www.ft.com/content/dcdb43d4-bd52-11e6-8b45-b8b81dd5d080.

Minneapolis Fed (2017). *The Minneapolis Plan to End Too Big to Fail* (Federal Reserve Bank of Minneapolis, Dec. 2017), available at https://www.minneapolisfed.org/~/media/files/publications/studies/endingtbtf/the-minneapolis-plan/the-minneapolis-plan-to-end-too-big-to-fail-final.pdf?la=en.

Minsky, Hyman P. (1992). "The Financial Instability Hypothesis" (Jerome Levy Economics Institute of Bard College Working Paper No. 74, May 1992), available at http://www.levyinstitute.org/pubs/wp74.pdf.

Minton, Bernadette A., René M. Stulz, and Alvaro G. Taboada (2017). "Are Larger Banks Valued More Highly?" (National Bureau of Economic Research Working Paper 23212, Mar. 2017), available at http://www.nber.org/papers/w23212.

Mintz, Ilse (1951). *Deterioration in the Quality of Foreign Bonds Issued in the United States, 1920–1930.* New York: National Bureau of Economic Research.

Mishkin, Frederic S. (1991). "Asymmetric Information and Financial Crises: A Historical Perspective," in R. Glenn Hubbard, ed., *Financial Markets and Financial Crises* 69–108. Chicago: University of Chicago Press.

Mishkin, Frederic S. (1978). "The Household Balance Sheet and the Great Depression," 38(4) *Journal of Economic History* 918–37.

Mitchell, Lawrence E. (2007). *The Speculation Economy: How Finance Triumphed over Industry.* San Francisco: Berrett-Koehler Publishers, Inc.

Mitchell, Stacy (2015). "One in Four Local Banks Has Vanished Since 2008. Here's What's Causing the Decline and Why We Should Treat It as a National Crisis" (Institute for Local Self-Reliance, May 5, 2015), available at https://ilsr.org/vanishing-community-banks-national-crisis.

Mitchener, Kris James, and Joseph Mason (2010). "'Blood and Treasure': Exiting from the Great Depression and Lessons for Today," 26(3) *Oxford Review of Economic Policy* 510–39.

Mitchener, Kris James, and Gary Richardson (2016). "Network Contagion and Interbank Amplification during the Great Depression" (National Bureau of Economic Research Working Paper 22074, Mar. 2016), available at www.nber.org/papers/w22074.

Mitchener, Kris James, and Gary Richardson (2013). "Shadowy Banks and Financial Contagion During the Great Depression: A Retrospective on Friedman and Schwartz," 103(3) *American Economic Review: Papers and Proceedings* 73–78 (May).

Moen, Jon, and Ellis W. Tallman (1992). "The Bank Panic of 1907: The Role of Trust Companies," 52(3) *Journal of Economic History* 611–30.

Moley, Raymond (1939). *After Seven Years*. New York: Harper & Brothers.

Molyneux, Philip, Klaus Schaeck, and Tim Mi Zhou (2014). "'Too Systemically Important to Fail' in Banking—Evidence from Bank Mergers and Acquisitions," 49 *Journal of International Money and Finance* 258–82.

Moore, Kyle, and Chen Zhou (2014). "The Determinants of Systemic Importance" (Systemic Risk Centre Discussion Paper No. 19, Aug. 2014), available at http://eprints.lse.ac.uk/59289/1/__lse.ac.uk_storage_LIBRARY_Secondary_libfile_shared_repository_Content_System%20Risk%20Center_Discussion%20Papers_dp-19_0.pdf.

Morgan, Donald P. (2002). "Rating Banks: Risk and Uncertainty in an Opaque Industry," 92(4) *American Economic Review* 874–88.

Morgenson, Gretchen, and Joshua Rosner (2011). *Reckless Endangerment: How Outsized Ambition, Greed, and Corruption Led to Economic Armageddon*. New York: Times Books.

Morris, Charles R. (2008). *The Two Trillion Dollar Meltdown: Easy Money, High Rollers, and the Great Credit Crash*. New York: PublicAffairs.

Morris, Marc D., and John R. Walter (1993). "Large Negotiable Certificates of Deposit," in Timothy Q. Cook and Robert K. LaRoche, eds., *Instruments of the Money Market* 34–47. Seventh edition. Richmond: Federal Reserve Bank of Richmond, available at https://www.richmondfed.org/~/media/richmondfedorg/publications/research/special_reports/instruments_of_the_money_market/pdf/full_publication.pdf.

Morris, Stephen (2018). "The Year When Hits Just Kept Coming for European Banks," *Financial Times* (Dec. 27, 2018), available at https://www.ft.com/content/15946d6e-0215-11e9-99df-6183d3002ee1.

Morris, Stephen, and David Crow (2019). "European Banks Wield Axe After Bleak Fourth Quarter," *Financial Times* (Feb. 21, 2019), available at https://www.ft.com/content/a24ba26c-35fb-11e9-bd3a-8b2a211d90d5.

Morris, Stephen, and David Keohane (2019). "Volatile Markets Cause Havoc at BNP Paribas Investment Bank," *Financial Times* (Feb. 6, 2019), available at https://www.ft.com/content/8c95b910-29dc-11e9-a5ab-ff8ef2b976c7.

Morris, Stephen, and Laura Noonan (2018). "Goldman Sachs Passes Citigroup in Investment Bank Ratings," *Financial Times* (Sept. 19, 2018), available at https://www.ft.com/content/4b8cced4-bc33-11e8-94b2-17176fbf93f5.

Morris, Stephen, and Olaf Storbeck (2019). "Deutsche Bank to Exit Equities Trading in Radical Overhaul," *Financial Times* (July 7, 2019), available at https://www.ft.com/content/94f979d8-a0a2-11e9-974c-ad1c6ab5efd1.

Morrison, Alan D., and William J. Wilhelm, Jr. (2007). *Investment Banking: Institutions, Politics, and Law*. New York: Oxford University Press.

Morrow, Dwight W. (1927). "Who Buys Foreign Bonds?" *Foreign Affairs* (Jan. 1927), available at https://www.foreignaffairs.com/articles/1927-01-01/who-buys-foreign-bonds.

Mosser, Alois, and Alice Teichova (1991). "Investment Behavior of Industrial Joint-Stock Companies and Industrial Shareholding by the Österreichische Credit-Anstalt: Inducement or Obstacle to Renewal and Change in Industry in Interwar Austria," in Harold James et al., eds., *The Role of Banks in the Interwar Economy* 122–57. New York: Cambridge University Press.

Mui, Preston, and Friederike Niepmann (2015). "Around the World in 8,379 Foreign Entities," *Liberty Street Economics* (Federal Reserve Bank of New York, Aug. 31, 2015), available at https://libertystreeteconomics.newyorkfed.org/2015/08/around-the-world-in-8379-foreign-entities.html.

Mukunda, Gautam (2014). "The Price of Wall Street's Power," *Harvard Business Review* (June 2014), available at https://hbr.org/2014/06/the-price-of-wall-streets-power.

Muolo, Paul, and Matthew Padilla (2008). *Chain of Blame: How Wall Street Caused the Mortgage and Credit Crisis.* Hoboken, NJ: John Wiley & Sons, Inc.

Nakamoto, Michiyo, and David Wighton (2007). "Citigroup Chief Stays Bullish on Buy-outs," *Financial Times* (July 9, 2007), available at https://www.ft.com/content/80e2987a-2e50-11dc-821c-0000779fd2ac.

Nalder, Eric (2008). "Mortgage System Crumbled While Regulators Jousted," *Seattle Post-Intelligencer* (Oct. 11, 2008), A1, available on Westlaw at 2008 WLNR 19502385.

Nash, Nathaniel C. (1988). "Greenspan Can Accept Bank Curb," *New York Times* (Sept. 15, 1988), D1.

Nash, Nathaniel C. (1987). "Treasury Now Favors Creation of Huge Banks," *New York Times* (June 7, 1987), A1.

Neal, Larry (1971). "Trust Companies and Financial Innovation, 1897–1914," 45(1) *Business History Review* 35–51.

Nersisyan, Yeva (2015). "The Repeal of the Glass-Steagall Act and the Federal Reserve's Extraordinary Intervention During the Global Financial Crisis" (Levy Economics Institute of Bard College Working Paper No. 829, Jan. 2015), available at http://ssrn.com/abstract=2554066.

Newell, Jeremy (2017). "Reinstating Glass-Steagall Is Unnecessary and Doesn't Make Sense" (Apr. 26, 2017) (The Clearing House Ass'n, LLC blog post), available at https://bpi.com/reinstating-glass-steagall-is-unnecessary-and-doesnt-make-sense.

New Hampshire Union Leader (1994). "Interstate Banking Bill Hits Clinton's Desk," *New Hampshire Union Leader* (Sept. 15, 1994), available on Westlaw at 1994 WLNR 5510909.

New York Fed (2020). Press Release: "Household Debt Tops $14 Trillion as Mortgage Originations Reach Highest Level Since 2005" (Feb. 11, 2020), available at https://www.newyorkfed.org/newsevents/news/research/2020/20200211.

New York Fed (2001). *2001 Annual Report* (Federal Reserve Bank of New York), available at http://www.newyorkfed.org/abouthtefed/annual/annual01/index.html.

New York Herald Tribune (1939). "Mitchell Terms Bank Act of '33 Progress Step," *New York Herald Tribune* (Dec. 15, 1939), 35.

New York Herald Tribune (1933a). "Perkins New Head of National City: Hugh Baker Quits," *New York Herald Tribune* (Feb. 28, 1933), 1.

New York Herald Tribune (1933b). "Chase Holders Give Aldrich's Plan Approval," *New York Herald Tribune* (May 17, 1933), 25.

New York Herald Tribune (1933c). "Bank Wrote Off Mitchell Debit, Trial Jury Told," *New York Herald Tribune* (June 2, 1933), 36.

New York Herald Tribune (1933d). "Chase Affiliate Stock Loss Put at 120 Millions," *New York Herald Tribune* (Oct. 19, 1933), 1.

New York Herald Tribune (1933e). "Wiggin Sold Chase Short Before Break," *New York Herald Tribune* (Nov. 1, 1933), 1.

New York Herald Tribune (1933f). "National City Cuts Capital Stock and Aids R.F.C. Plan," *New York Herald Tribune* (Dec. 6, 1933), 1.

New York Herald Tribune (1933g). "12 N.Y. Banks to Sell Capital Notes to R.F.C.," *New York Herald Tribune* (Dec. 6, 1933).

New York Herald Tribune (1933h). "Chase to Offer $50,000,000 of Senior Shares," *New York Herald Tribune* (Dec. 28, 1933), 1.

New York Herald Tribune (1931). "Albert H. Wiggin Nominated: Named to Succeed Mitchell on Reserve Board," *New York Herald Tribune* (Oct. 3, 1931), 23.

New York Herald Tribune (1930). "Morale of U.S. Business Good, Wiggin Finds," *New York Herald Tribune* (Jan. 13, 1930), 22.

New York Herald Tribune (1929a). "Glass Advises Mitchell Quit Reserve Post," *New York Herald Tribune* (Mar. 29, 1929), 1.

New York Herald Tribune (1929b). "Join Anaconda Board: Mitchell and Charles T. Fisher Are Elected Directors," *New York Herald Tribune* (May 24, 1929), 41.

New York Herald Tribune (1929c). "Stock Decline Went 'Too Far,' Mitchell Holds," *New York Herald Tribune* (Oct. 23, 1929), 37.

New York Herald Tribune (1929d). "Bankers Insure Market Against Another Rout," *New York Times* (Oct. 26, 1929), 23.

New York Herald Tribune (1929e). "National City Employees Get Stock Rights," *New York Herald Tribune* (Dec. 4, 1929), 37.

New York Herald Tribune (1928). "Credit Situation Not Alarming, Says Mitchell," *New York Herald Tribune* (Oct. 11, 1928), 33.

New York Herald Tribune (1927). "Mitchell Sees Common Stocks Gaining in Favor," *New York Herald Tribune* (Mar. 12, 1927), 19.

New York Herald Tribune (1924). "$150,000,000 Japanese Loan Out To-morrow," *New York Herald Tribune* (Feb. 24, 1924), 21.

New York Herald Tribune (1921a). "Williams Quits Currency Post; Scores McLean," *New York Herald Tribune* (Mar. 3, 1921), 18.

New York Herald Tribune (1921b). "In Wall Street: From Cradle to Grave," *New York Herald Tribune* (Dec. 24, 1921), 12.

New York Times (1951). "Albert H. Wiggin, Financier, 83, Dies," *New York Times* (May 22, 1951), 31.

New York Times (1934a). "Chase Bank Plans to Sue for Redress from Ex-Officials," *New York Times* (Jan. 10, 1934), 1.

New York Times (1934b). "City Bank Changes Voted by Holders," *New York Times* (Jan. 10, 1934), 31.

New York Times (1933a). "National City Bank to Drop Affiliate," *New York Times* (Mar. 8, 1933), 1.

New York Times (1933b). "Aldrich Hits at Private Bankers In Sweeping Plan for Reforms," *New York Times* (Mar. 9, 1933), 1.

New York Times (1933c). "Aldrich Proposals Stir Private Banks," *New York Times* (Mar. 10, 1933), 27.

New York Times (1933d). "Chase Bank Speeds End of Affiliates," *New York Times* (Apr. 6, 1933), 1.

New York Times (1933e). "Selling of Securities at Special Rates Is Covered in Bill Passed by Congress," *New York Times* (May 26, 1933), 8.

New York Times (1933f). "Roosevelt Signs the Securities Bill," *New York Times* (May 28, 1933), 2.

New York Times (1933g). "Bank Reform Bill Swiftly Approved," *New York Times* (June 14, 1933), 1.

New York Times (1933h). "Chase Stock Sold Short by Wiggin Before 1929 Crash," *New York Times* (Nov. 1, 1933), 1.

New York Times (1932). "Mitchell Warns Against Isolation," *New York Times* (Jan. 13, 1932), 39.

New York Times (1931a). "$550,000,000 Merger for Chatham Phenix and Manufacturers," *New York Times* (Dec. 4, 1931), 1.

New York Times (1931b). "Mitchell Forecasts Debts, Revision: Fears Reich, if Pressed Will Revolt," *New York Times* (Dec. 20, 1931), 1.

New York Times (1930). "Insull Bond Offer Is at Yield of 6.07%," *New York Times* (Jan. 3, 1930), 35.

New York Times (1929a). "C. E. Mitchell Sees Business as Sound: President of National City Bank Is Not Alarmed by High Level of Stocks," *New York Times* (Jan. 1, 1929), 37.

New York Times (1929b). "Mitchell Decries Decline in Stocks," *New York Times* (Oct. 23, 1929), 16.

New York Times (1928). "Billion-Dollar Bank Formed in Chicago," *New York Times* (Sept. 8, 1928), 27.

New York Times (1927). "National City Co. Widens Its Field," *New York Times* (Feb. 19, 1927), 21.

New York Times (1926). "A. H. Wiggin Becomes Head of Chase Bank," *New York Times* (Apr. 12, 1926), 36.

New York Times (1921a). "Order by Williams Raises Bank Storm," *New York Times* (Feb. 26, 1921), 3.

New York Times (1921b). "Williams Resigns; Assails McLean," *New York Times* (Mar. 3, 1921), 9.

New York Times (1921c). "Williams Renews Attacks on Bankers," *New York Times* (July 15, 1921), 3.

New York Times (1921d). "Williams Clashes with Ogden Mills," *New York Times* (Aug. 3, 1921), 23.

New York Times (1921e). "Stop Gov. Harding in Rush with Fist upon J. S. Williams," *New York Times* (Aug. 4, 1921), 1.

New York Times (1921f). "Williams Charges Bank 'Favoritism,'" *New York Times* (Sept. 21, 1921), 27.

New York Times (1920). "Williams Strikes at High Interest," *New York Timex* (Aug. 11, 1920), 24.

New York Times (1919a). "Move in Congress to Oust Williams," *New York Times* (Feb. 16, 1919), 1.

New York Times (1919b). "Williams Answers One of His Critics: Controller Assails Congressman McFadden's Methods as Banker," *New York Times* (Mar. 2, 1919), 14.

New York Times (1916). "Fears Control of Wealth," *New York Times* (May 20, 1916), 6.

New York Times (1915). "Williams Repeats His Usury Charges," *New York Times* (Nov. 27, 1915), 7.

New York Times (1914a). "National City Bank in Williams' Fight," *New York Times* (Jan. 16, 1914), 1.

New York Times (1914b). "Vindicate Williams in Confirming Him," *New York Times* (Jan. 20, 1914), 2.

New York Times (1914c). "New Controller of the Currency as a Storm Source," *New York Times* (Feb. 1, 1914), SM14.

New York Times (1914d). "Paints New York as Money Citadel," *New York Times* (May 14, 1914), 13.

New York Times (1912). "Southerners Buy Seaboard," *New York Times* (June 7, 1912), 14.

New York Times (1908a). "Pritchard Names Seaboard Receivers," *New York Times* (Jan. 3, 1908), 5.

New York Times (1908b). "Says a Williams Victory: Railroad Commissioner McLendon Says Ryan Mismanaged," *New York Times* (Jan. 3, 1908), 5.

New York Times (1900). "Seaboard in Control," *New York Times* (July 1, 1900), 11.

Ngo, Phong T. H., and Puente M. Diego (2020). "De Facto Bank Bailouts" (Working paper, Mar. 25, 2020), available at http://ssrn.com/abstract=3560858).

Nicholas, Tom, and Anna Scherbina (2013). "Real Estate Prices During the Roaring Twenties and the Great Depression," 41(2) *Real Estate Economics* 278–309.

Nocera, Joe (2009). "Lehman Had to Die, It Seems, So Global Finance Could Live," *New York Times* (Sept. 12, 2009), A1.

Nocera, Joe, and Edmund L. Andrews (2008). "Running a Step Behind as a Crisis Raged," *New York Times* (Oct. 23, 2008), A1.

Noeth, Bryan, and Rajdeep Sengupta (2012). "Global European Banks and the Financial Crisis," 94(6) *Review* 457–79 (Federal Reserve Bank of St. Louis, Nov./Dec. 2012).

Noonan, Laura (2019). "German Banks Supervisor Warns of New Cycle of Deregulation," *Financial Times* (Oct. 19, 2019), available at https://www.ft.com/content/0effd096-f293-11e9-b018-3ef8794b17c6.

Noonan, Laura (2018a). "Europe's Top 4 Investment Banks Hire Staff for Busier Times," *Financial Times* (Feb. 26, 2018), available at https://www.ft.com/content/6df8e92a-18ab-11e8-9376-4a6390addb44.

Noonan, Laura (2018b). "Wells Fargo Looking to Hire 20 Managing Directors," *Financial Times* (May 6, 2018), available at https://www.ft.com/content/f85e25be-4ff9-11e8-a7a9-37318e776bab.

Noonan, Laura, et al. (2018). "Who Went to Jail for Their Role in the Financial Crisis?," *Financial Times* (Sept. 20, 2018), available at https://ig.ft.com/jailed-bankers.

Noonan, Laura, and David Blood (2017). "Bank Chief Executives' Pay 2016," *Financial Times* (Aug. 20, 2017), available at https://ig.ft.com/bank-ceo-pay/2017.

Norris, Floyd (2014). "Banks Again Avoid Having Any Skin in the Game," *New York Times* (Oct. 24, 2014), B1.

O'Brien, Fergal (2019). "Carney Says Jail for Bankers a Bluff, Hitting Pay Is Best Weapon," *Bloomberg Law* (Jan. 24, 2019), available at https://www.americanbanker.com/articles/boes-carney-says-jail-for-bankers-a-bluff-hitting-pay-is-best-weapon.

OCC (2007). Office of the Comptroller of the Currency, "OCC's Quarterly Report on Bank Trading and Derivatives Activities, Fourth Quarter 2007," available at http://www.occ.treas.gov/topics/capital-markets/financial-markets/derivatives/dq407.pdf.

OCC (2000). Office of the Comptroller of the Currency, "Interpretive Letter No. 892" (Letter from Comptroller of the Currency John D. Hawke, Jr. to Rep. James A. Leach, Sept. 13, 2000), available at http://www.occ.gov/static/interpretations-and-precedents/sep00/int892.pdf.

OECD (2015). *In It Together: Why Less Inequality Benefits All* (Organization for Economic Co-operation and Development, 2015). Paris: OECD Publishing, available at https://read.oecd-ilibrary.org/employment/in-it-together-why-less-inequality-benefits-all_9789264235120-en#page3.

OFR (2019). Office of Financial Research (Treasury Dept.), "Ongoing Data Collection of Centrally Cleared Transactions in the U.S. Repurchase Agreement Market: Final rule," 84 *Federal Register* 4975–4987 (Feb. 20, 2019).

OFR (2018). Office of Financial Research (Treasury Dept.), "Ongoing Data Collection of Centrally Cleared Transactions in the U.S. Repurchase Agreement Market: Proposed rule," 83 *Federal Register* 31896–1911 (July 10, 2018).

Olney, Martha L. (1999). "Avoiding Default: The Role of Credit in the Consumption Collapse of 1930," 114(1) *Quarterly Journal of Economics* 319–35.

Olson, James S. (1988). *Saving Capitalism: The Reconstruction Finance Corporation and the New Deal, 1933–1940*. Princeton: Princeton University Press.

Olson, James S. (1977). *Herbert Hoover and the Reconstruction Finance Corporation, 1931–1933*. Ames: Iowa State University Press.

Omarova, Saule T. (2013). "The Merchants of Wall Street: Banking, Commerce, and Commodities," 98(1) *Minnesota Law Review* 265–355.

Omarova, Saule T. (2011). "From Gramm-Leach-Bliley to Dodd-Frank: The Unfulfilled Promise of Section 23A of the Federal Reserve Act," 89(5) *North Carolina Law Review* 1683–776.

Omarova, Saule T. (2009). "The Quiet Metamorphosis: How Derivatives Changed the 'Business of Banking,'" 63(4) *University of Miami Law Review* 1041–109.

Onaran, Yalman (2018). "Bank Rules Are Seen Easing Further Even if Democrats Seize House," *Bloomberg Banking Law News* (Nov. 1, 2018).

Onaran, Yalman (2013). "U.S. Banks Bigger than GDP as Accounting Rift Masks Risk," *Bloomberg* (Feb. 19, 2013), available at https://www.bloomberg.com/news/articles/2013-02-20/u-s-banks-bigger-than-gdp-as-accounting-rift-masks-risk.

Ott, Julia Cathleen (2008). "When Wall Street Met Main Street: The Quest for an Investors' Democracy and the Emergence of the Retail Investor in the United States, 1890–1930," 9(4) *Enterprise and Society* 619–30.

Parker, George (2016). "UK Treasury: Veteran of Treasury Battles Tots up a Decade's Wins and Losses," *Financial Times* (Apr. 14, 2016), available at https://www.ft.com/content/295dd92e-ff21-11e5-99cb-83242733f755.

Parks, Daniel J. (1999a). "United at Last, Financial Industry Pressures Hill to Clear Overhaul," 57 *CQ Weekly* 2373 (Oct. 9, 1999).

Parks, Daniel J. (1999b). "Financial Services Overhaul Bill Clears After Final Skirmishing over Community Reinvestment," 57 *CQ Weekly* 2654 (Nov. 6, 1999).

Partnoy, Frank (2009). *The Match King: Ivar Kreuger, The Financial Genius Behind a Century of Wall Street Scandals*. New York: PublicAffairs.

Partnoy, Frank (2003). *Infectious Greed: How Deceit and Risk Corrupted the Financial Markets*. New York: Henry Holt.

Partnoy, Frank, and Jesse Eisinger (2013). "What's Inside America's Banks?," *Atlantic* (Jan./Feb. 2013), available at http://www.theatlantic.com/magazine/archive/2013/01/whats-inside-americas-banks/309196.

Passmore, Wayne, and Alexander H. von Hafften (2017). "Are Basel's Capital Surcharges for Global Systemically Important Banks Too Small?" (FEDS Notes, Feb. 27, 2017), available at https://www.federalreserve.gov/econresdata/notes/feds-notes/2017/are-basels-capital-surcharges-for-global-systemically-important-banks-too-small-20170223.html#f4.

Paulson, Henry M., Jr. (2010). *On the Brink: Inside the Race to Stop the Collapse of the Global Financial System*. New York: Business Plus.

Peach, W. Nelson (1941). *The Security Affiliates of National Banks*. Baltimore: Johns Hopkins Press.

Pecora, Ferdinand (1939). *Wall Street Under Oath*. New York: Simon and Schuster.

Peek, Joe, and Eric Rosengren (2015). "Credit Supply Disruptions: From Credit Crunches to Financial Crisis" (Federal Reserve Bank of Boston Current Policy Perspectives Paper No. 15-5, Oct. 2015), available at http://ssrn.com/abstract=2687395.

Perez, Carlota (2009). "The Double Bubble at the Turn of the Century: Technological Roots and Structural Implications," 33(4) *Cambridge Journal of Economics* 779–805.

Perino, Michael (2010). *The Hellhound of Wall Street: How Ferdinand Pecora's Investigation of the Great Crash Forever Changed American Finance*. New York: Penguin Press.

Perkins, Edwin J. (1971). "The Divorce of Commercial and Investment Banking: A History," 86(6) *Banking Law Journal* 483–528.

Persaud, Avinash (2013). "Bail-ins Are No Better than Fool's Gold," *Financial Times* (Oct. 21, 2013), available at https://www.ft.com/content/686dfa94-27a7-11e3-8feb-00144feab7de.

Persons, Charles E. (1930). "Credit Expansion, 1920 to 1929, and Its Consequences," 45(1) *Quarterly Journal of Economics* 94–130.

Pesek, William (2019a). "How the Federal Reserve Turned Japanese," *Forbes* (Jan. 29, 2019), available at https://www.forbes.com/sites/williampesek/2019/01/29/how-the-federal-reserve-turned-japanese/#43db015778f8.

Pesek, William (2019b). "'Trumpified' Federal Reserve Reopens the Bar," *Forbes* (July 12, 2019), available at https://www.forbes.com/sites/williampesek/2019/07/12/trumpified-federal-reserve-reopens-the-bar/#2b6467ee62f5.

Peters, Andy (2019). "Which Bank CEOs Received the Biggest Raises in 2018?," *American Banker* (Mar. 17, 2019), available at https://www.americanbanker.com/list/which-bank-ceos-received-the-biggest-raises-in-2018.

Peterson, Christopher L. (2017). "Consumer Financial Protection Bureau Law Enforcement: An Empirical Review," 90(5) *Tulane Law Review* 1057–112.

Peterson, Christopher L. (2005). "Federalism and Predatory Lending: Unmasking the Deregulatory Agenda," 78(1) *Temple Law Review* 1–98.

Peterson, Josephine, et al. (2018). "Ex-Wilmington Trust Officials Are Guilty of 15 Counts of Fraud, Conspiracy," *News-Journal* (Wilmington, DE) (May 4, 2018), available on Westlaw at 2018 WLNR 13977048.

Philippon, Thomas, and Ariell Reshef (2012). "Wages and Human Capital in the U.S. Finance Industry," 127(4) *Quarterly Journal of Economics* 1551–609.

Phillips, Richard (1992). "How Greenspan Saved the Day," *American Banker* (Nov. 3, 1992), 4.

Pickard, Jim, and Barney Thompson (2014). "Archives 1985 and 1986: Thatcher Policy Fight over 'Big Bang' Laid Bare," *Financial Times* (Dec. 29, 2014), available at https://www.ft.com/content/f3c0d500-8537-11e4-bb63-00144feabdc0.

Piketty, Thomas, Emmanuel Saez, and Gabriel Zucman (2018). "Distributional "National Accounts: Methods and Estimates for the United States," 133(2) *Quarterly Journal of Economics* 553–609.

Piskorski, Tomasz, and Amit Seru (2018). "Debt Relief and Slow Recovery: A Decade After Lehman" (National Bureau of Economic Research Working Paper 25403, Dec. 2018), available at http://www.nber.org/papers/w25403.

Piskorski, Tomasz, Amit Seru, and James Witkin (2015). "Asset Quality Misrepresentation by Financial Intermediaries: Evidence from the RMBS Market," 70(6) *Journal of Finance* 2635–78.

Platt, Eric et al. (2019). "WeWork turmoil puts spotlight on JPMorgan Chase and Goldman Sachs," *Financial Times* (Sept. 24, 2019), available at https://www.ft.com/content/272d408e-de40-11e9-b112-9624ec9edc59.

Platt, Harold L. (1991). *The Electric City: Energy and the Growth of the Chicago Area, 1880–1930.* Chicago: University of Chicago Press.

Plender, John (2019). "ECB Critics Are Right to Worry About Ultra-Loose Monetary Policy," *Financial Times* (Oct. 15, 2019), available at https://www.ft.com/content/d8ab77a6-ef23-11e9-ad1e-4367d8281195?shareType=nongift.

Politi, James (2019). "Fed Sees No Further Rate Rises in 2019," *Financial Times* (Mar. 20, 2019), available at https://www.ft.com/content/92b45b78-4b36-11e9-8b7f-d49067e0f50d.

Posner, Eric A. (2017). "What Legal Authority Does the Fed Need During a Financial Crisis?," 101 *Minnesota Law Review* 1529–78.

Postel-Vinay, Natacha (2019). "Was the U.S. Great Depression a Credit Boom Gone Wrong?" (Working paper, July 2, 2019), available at http://ssrn.com/abstract=3413697.

Postel-Vinay, Natacha (2017). "Debt Dilution in 1920s America: Lighting the Fuse of a Mortgage Crisis," 70(2) *Economic History Review* 559–85.

Postel-Vinay, Natacha (2016). "What Caused Chicago Bank Failures in the Great Depression? A Look at the 1920s," 76(2) *Journal of Economic History* 478–519.

Pozen, Robert C. (2018). "Loan Originators No Longer Must Have 'Skin in the Game'" (Mar. 15, 2018), available at https://www.brookings.edu/blog/up-front/2018/03/15/loan-originators-no-longer-must-have-skin-in-the-game.

Pozsar, Zoltan, Tobias Adrian, Adam Ashcraft, and Hayley Boesky (2010). "Shadow Banking" (Federal Reserve Bank of New York Staff Report No. 458, July 2010), available at http://ssrn.com/abstract=1645337.

Preston, Howard H. (1933). "The Banking Act of 1933," 23(4) *American Economic Review* 585–607.

Prial, Dunstan (2000). "Merger Is Rich in Banking Heritage: Chase Manhattan, J. P. Morgan Tie Knot," *St. Louis Post-Dispatch* (Sept. 14, 2000), C1, available on Westlaw at 2000 WLNR 887697.

Protess, Ben (2011). "Mortgage Executive Receives 30-Year Sentence," *New York Times (DealBook)* (June 30, 2011), available at https://dealbook.nytimes.com/2011/06/30/mortgage-executive-receives-30-year-sentence.

Protess, Ben, and Matt Apuzzo (2015). "Justice Dept. Vow to Go After Bankers May Prove a Promise Hard to Keep," *New York Times* (Sept. 11, 2015), B1.

Protess, Ben, and Julie Hirschfeld Davis (2017). "Trump Vows Cuts in Wall St. Rules from Obama Era," *New York Times* (Feb. 4, 2017), A9.

Public Citizen (2018). "A Decade After Sinking the Economy, Five Biggest Banks' Executives Have Raked in $3.38B" (Public Citizen, Sept. 12, 2018), available at https://www.citizen.org/news/a-decade-after-sinking-the-economy-five-biggest-banks-executives-have-raked-in-3-38b.

Puckette, Charles McD. (1927). "Wall Street Harkens to C. E. Mitchell," *New York Times* (Feb. 13, 1927), SM12.

Puri, Manju (1996). "Commercial Banks in Investment Banking: Conflict of Interest or Certification Role?," 40 *Journal of Financial Economics* 373–401.

Puri, Manju (1994). "The Long-Term Default Performance of Bank Underwritten Security Issues," 18 *Journal of Banking and Finance* 397–418.

PWGFM (1999a). "Hedge Funds, Leverage, and the Lessons of Long-Term Capital Management: Report of The President's Working Group on Financial Markets" (Apr. 1999), available at http://www.treasury.gov/resource-center/fin-mkts/Documents/hedgfund.pdf.

PWGFM (1999b). "Over-the-Counter Derivatives Markets and the Commodity Exchange Act: Report of the President's Working Group on Financial Markets" (Nov. 1999), available at https://www.treasury.gov/resource-center/fin-mkts/Documents/otcact.pdf.

Quarles, Randal K. (2018a). "Semiannual Supervision and Regulation Testimony," Statement by Fed Vice Chairman for Supervision Randal K. Quarles before the Committee on Financial Services, U.S. House of Representatives (Apr. 17, 2018), available at https://www.federalreserve.gov/newsevents/testimony/quarles20180417a.htm.

Quarles, Randal K. (2018b). "A New Chapter in Stress Testing," Remarks by Fed Vice Chairman for Supervision Randal K. Quarles at the Brookings Institution (Nov. 9, 2018), available at https://www.federalreserve.gov/newsevents/speech/quarles20181109a.htm.

Rajan, Raghuram G. (2010). *Fault Lines: How Hidden Fractures Still Threaten the World Economy*. Princeton: Princeton University Press.

Rajan, Raghuram G. (2005). "Has Financial Development Made the World Riskier?," in *The Greenspan Era: Lessons for the Future* 313–69 (Proceedings of an Economic Policy Symposium, Federal Reserve Bank of Kansas City, Aug. 2005), available at https://www.kansascityfed.org/publicat/sympos/2005/pdf/Rajan2005.pdf.

Rakoff, Jed (2014). "The Financial Crisis: Why Have No High-Level Executives Been Prosecuted?," *New York Review of Books* (Jan. 9, 2014), available at http://www.nybooks.com/articles/archives/2014/jan09/financial-crisis-why-no-executive-prosecutions.

Ramonas, Andrew (2017). "New SEC Alums Swam 'Revolving Door' to Financial, Law Firms," 108 *Bloomberg BNA's Banking Report* 607 (Apr. 24, 2017).

Rappoport, Peter, and Eugene N. White (1993). "Was There a Bubble in the 1929 Stock Market?," 53(3) *Journal of Economic History* 549–574.

Raymond, Nate (2016). "Ex–Countrywide CEO Mozilo Will Not Face U.S. Fraud Case: Sources," *Reuters* (June 17, 2016), available at https://www.reuters.com/article/us-countrywide-lawsuit-mozilo-idUSKCN0Z326X.

Redlich, Fritz (1968). *The Molding of American Banking: Men and Ideas.* New York: Johnson Reprint Corp.

Rehm, Barbara (2000). "No Merger Wave, but Money Saved," *American Banker* (Nov. 7, 2000), 1, available on Westlaw at 2000 WLNR 2817824.

Rehm, Barbara (1998). "Megamerger Plan Hinges on Congress," *American Banker* (Apr. 7, 1998), 1, available on Westlaw at 1998 WLNR 2763791.

Rehm, Barbara (1990). "Coalition Presses Congress to Stop Building 'Firewalls,'" *American Banker* (May 10, 1990), 4, available on Westlaw at 1990 WLNR 1842348.

Reinhart, Carmen, Vincent Reinhart, and Kenneth Rogoff (2015). "Dealing with Debt" (Harvard Kennedy School Faculty Research Working Paper 15-009, Feb. 2015), available at http://ssrn.com/abstract=2577359.

Rennison, Joe (2019). "Repo Blame Game Moves Focus to Hedge Funds," *Financial Times* (Dec. 13, 2019), available at https://www.ft.com/content/6427f16a-1d05-11ea-97df-cc63de1d73f4.

Rennison, Joe (2018). "Investors Raise Alarm over Fed's Shrinking Balance Sheet," *Financial Times* (Dec. 20, 2018), available at https://www.ft.com/content/1459cdc4-040c-11e9-99df-6183d3002ee1.

Rennison, Joe, and Brendan Greeley (2019). "Federal Reserve to Buy $60 Billion of Treasury Bills per Month," *Financial Times* (Oct. 11, 2019), available at https://www.ft.com/content/baa7e796-ec38-11e9-85f4-d00e5018f061.

Reuters (2014). "Australian bank regulator happy to be seen as tougher than the rest," *Reuters* (Nov. 10, 2014), available at https://www.reuters.com/article/australia-banking-regulations/australian-bank-regulator-happy-to-be-seen-as-tougher-than-the-rest-idUSL3N0T113C20141111.

Reuters (2007). "Subprime Woes Likely Contained: Treasury's Paulson," *Reuters* (Apr. 20, 2007), available at https://www.reuters.com/article/us-usa-subprime-paulson-idUSWBT00686520070420.

Richardson, Gary (2007a). "Categories and Causes of Bank Distress During the Great Depression, 1929–1933: The Illiquidity Versus Insolvency Debate Revisited," 44 *Explorations in Economic History* 588–607.

Richardson, Gary (2007b). "The Check Is in the Mail: Correspondent Clearing and the Banking Panics of the Great Depression," 67(3) *Journal of Economic History* 643–71.

Richardson, Gary, and William Troost (2009). "Monetary Intervention Mitigated Banking Panics During the Great Depression: Quasi-Experimental Evidence from a Federal Reserve District Border," 117(6) *Journal of Political Economy* 1031–73.

Richardson, Matthew P., Kermit L. Schoenholtz, and Lawrence J. White (2018). "Deregulating Wall Street," 10 *Annual Review of Financial Economics* 199–217.

Ricks, Morgan (2019). "Guarantor of Last Resort: Is There a Better Alternative?," *CLS Blue Sky Blog* (May 15, 2019), available at http://clsbluesky.law.columbia.edu/2019/05/15/guarantor-of-last-resort-is-there-a-better-alternative.

Ricks, Morgan (2018). "Money as Infrastructure," 2018(3) *Columbia Business Law Review* 757–851.

Ricks, Morgan (2016). *The Money Problem: Rethinking Financial Regulation.* Chicago: University of Chicago Press.

Rippy, J. Fred (1950). "A Bond-Selling Extravaganza of the 1920's," 23(4) *Journal of Business* 238–47.

Ritschl, Albrecht (2012). "The German Transfer Problem, 1920–1933: A Sovereign Debt Perspective" (Centre for Economic Performance Discussion Paper No. 1155, July 2012), available at http://cep.lse.ac.uk/pubs/download/dp1155.pdf.

Ritschl, Albrecht (1998). "Reparations Transfers, the Borchardt Hypothesis, and the Great Depression in Germany, 1929–32," 2(1) *European Review of Economic History* 49–72.

Ritschl, Albrecht (1996). "Was Schacht Right? Reparations, the Young Plan, and the Great Depression in Germany" (Universitat Pompeu Fabra and CEPR Working Paper, Nov. 1996), available at http://personal.lse.ac.uk/ritschl/pdf_files/Schacht2.pdf.

Ritschl, Albrecht, and Samad Sarferaz (2014). "Currency Versus Banking in the Financial Crisis of 1931," 55(2) *International Economic Review* 349–73.

Robertson, Douglas (2011). "So That's Operational Risk" (Office of the Comptroller of the Currency Economic Working Paper 2011-1, Mar. 2011), available at https://www.occ.gov/publications/publications-by-type/occ-working-papers/2012-2009/wp2011-1.pdf.

Robertson, Jamie (2016). "How the Big Bang Changed the City of London for Ever" (Oct. 27, 2016), available at http://www.bbc.com/news/business-37751599.

Robinson, Edward, Lananh Nguyen, and Yalman Onaran (2018). "On the Eve of Brexit, U.S. Banks Are Set to Conquer Europe," *Bloomberg Law: Banking* (Dec. 13. 2018).

Roca, Rosario, et al. (2017). "Risks and Challenges of Complex Financial Instruments: An Analysis of SSM Banks" (Bank of Italy Occasional Paper No. 417, Dec. 2017), available at http://ssrn.com/abstract=3123106.

Rocha, Polo (2018). "FDIC Proposes New Community Bank Leverage Ratio of 9%," *SNL Bank and Thrift Daily* (Nov. 21, 2018), available on Westlaw at 2018 WLNR 36248912.

Rodkey, Robert G. (1935–36). "State Bank Failures in Michigan," 7 *Michigan Business Studies* 101–69 (Apr. 1935–May 1936).

Rodriguez Valladares, Mayra (2019a). "Will the Japanification of Europe Help the U.S. Dollar?," *Forbes* (Feb. 18, 2019), available at https://www.forbes.com/sites/mayrarodriguezvalladares/2019/02/18/will-the-japanification-of-europe-help-the-u-s-dollar/#11c2496e530e.

Rodriguez Valladares, Mayra (2019b). "U.S. Bank Regulatory Easing Is Negative for Investors and Taxpayers," *Forbes* (Mar. 7, 2019), available at https://www.forbes.com/sites/mayrarodriguezvalladares/2019/03/07/u-s-bank-regulatory-easing-is-negative-for-investors-and-taxpayers/#43e9fb1f9a8e.

Rodriguez Valladares, Mayra (2019c). "Big Banks Are Very Exposed to Leveraged Lending and CLO Markets," *Forbes* (Apr. 15, 2019), available at https://www.forbes.com/sites/mayrarodriguezvalladares/2019/04/15/big-banks-are-very-exposed-to-leveraged-lending-and-clo-markets/#4a29105c7309.

Rodriguez Valladares, Mayra (2019d). "Weakening Dodd-Frank's Volcker Rule Puts Depositors and Taxpayers at Risk," *Forbes* (Aug. 21, 2019), available at https://www.forbes.com/sites/mayrarodriguezvalladares/2019/08/21/weakening-dodd-franks-volcker-rule-puts-depositors-and-tax-payers-at-risk/#55e931da7ba7.

Rodriguez Valladares, Mayra (2018). "Leveraged Loan Market Warnings Have Been Ignored for Five Years," *Forbes* (Oct. 26, 2018), available at https://www.forbes.com/sites/mayrarodriguezvalladares/2018/10/26/leveragedloanmarketwarningshavebeenignoredforoverive-years/#2d8fe5753df3.

Roe, Mark J. (2014). "Structural Corporate Degradation Due to Too-Big-to-Fail Finance," 162 *University of Pennsylvania Law Review* 1419–64.

Roe, Mark J. (2011). "The Derivatives Market's Payment Priorities as Financial Crisis Accelerator," 63(3) *Stanford Law Review* 539–90.

Rogoff, Kenneth (2017). "Dealing with Monetary Paralysis at the Zero Bound," 31(3) *Journal of Economic Perspectives* 47–66.

Romei, Valentina (2019). "EU Investment Rebounds to Level Before 2008 Financial Crash," *Financial Times* (Mar. 8, 2019), available at https://www.ft.com/content/b67df8ae-40d5-11e9-b896-fe36ec32aece.

Romei, Valentina, and Martin Arnold (2019). "Draghi's ECB Tenure: Saving the Euro, Faltering on Inflation," *Financial Times* (Oct. 20, 2019), available at https://www.ft.com/content/a62b221c-eb64-11e9-a240-3b065ef5fc55.

Romer, Christina D. (1993). "The Nation in Depression," 7(2) *Journal of Economic Perspectives* 19–39 (Spring).

Romer, Christina D. (1992). "What Ended the Great Depression?," 52(4) *Journal of Economic History* 757–84.

Romer, Christina D. (1990). "The Great Crash and the Onset of the Great Depression," 105(3) *Quarterly Journal of Economics* 597–624.

Rosen, Jeffrey (2016). *Louis D. Brandeis: American Prophet.* New Haven: Yale University Press.

Rothbard, Murray N. (1975). *America's Great Depression.* Third edition. Kansas City: Sheed and Ward, Inc.

Rothkopf, David (2012). *Power, Inc.: The Epic Rivalry Between Big Business and Government— and the Reckoning That Lies Ahead.* New York: Farrar, Straus & Giroux.

Roukema, Marge (1999). "Opening Statement of Chairwoman Marge Roukema, Financial Institutions and Consumer Credit Subcommittee of the House Committee on Banking and Financial Services" (Mar. 24, 1999), available on Westlaw at 1999 WL 179223.

Rubin, Robert (1995). "Statement of Robert E. Rubin, Secretary of the Treasury, before the Committee on Banking and Financial Services, U.S. House of Representatives" (Mar. 1, 1995), available on Westlaw at 1995 WL 83809.

Rubin, Robert, Alan Greenspan, and Arthur Levitt (1998). "Joint Statement by Treasury Secretary Robert E. Rubin, Federal Reserve Chairman Alan Greenspan and Securities and Exchange Commission Chairman Arthur Levitt" (May 7, 1998), available on Westlaw at 1998 WL 240809.

Rushe, Dominic (2019). "Stampede of the Unicorns: Will a New Breed of Tech Giants Burst the Bubble?," *The Guardian* (Mar. 30, 2019), available at https://www.theguardian.com/technology/2019/mar/30/lyft-ipo-stock-market-unicorns-uber-airbnb-slack.

Sablik, Tim (2013). "Fed Credit Policy During the Great Depression" (Economic Brief No. EB 1303, Federal Reserve Bank of Richmond, VA, Mar. 2013), available at https://www.richmondfed.org/publications/research/economic_brief/2013/eb_13-03.

Sanderson, Rachel, and David Crow (2019). "Jail Terms for 13 Bankers over Monte Paschi Scandal," *Financial Times* (Nov. 8, 2019), available at https://www.ft.com/content/54ace10a-023e-11ea-b7bc-f3fa4e77dd47.

S&P 500 Index (2019). "S&P 500 Index—90 Year Historical Chart" (visited Mar. 14, 2019), available at https://www.macrotrends.net/2324/sp-500-historical-chart-data.

S&P Global (2019). "JPMorgan Tops 2018 Global I-Bank Ranking," *S&P Global Market Intelligence* (Mar. 20, 2019), available at https://www.spglobal.com/marketintelligence/en/news-insights/latest-news-headlines/50672572.

S&P Global (2018). "JPMorgan Tops Coalition's 2017 I-Bank League Table," *S&P Global Market Intelligence* (Mar. 21, 2018), available at https://www.spglobal.com/marketintelligence/en/news-insights/trending/nzdlgtxu_pyrx9ntbx2dsw2.

Santayana, George (1980 [1905]). *The Life of Reason: Volume One (Reason and Common Sense).* New York: Dover Publications (reprint of 1905 Charles Scribner's Sons edition).

Santos, João A. C. (2014). "Evidence from the Bond Market on Banks' 'Too-Big-to-Fail' Subsidy," 20(3) *Economic Review* (Federal Reserve Bank of NY, Dec. 2014) 29–39.

Santos, João A. C. (1998). "Commercial Banks in the Securities Business: A Review," 14(1) *Journal of Financial Services Research* 35–60.

Sarin, Natasha (2019). "How to Make Banks Too Safe to Fail" (Univ. of Pa. Law School Institute for Law and Economics, Research Paper 19-30, July 2019), available at http://ssrn.com/abstract=3433121.

Sastry, Parinitha (2018). "The Political Origins of Section 13(3) of the Federal Reserve Act," 24(1) *Economic Policy Review* 1–33, Federal Reserve Bank of New York (Sept.).

Saunders, Anthony, and Ingo Walter (1994). *Universal Banking in the United States: What Could We Gain? What Could We Lose?* New York: Oxford University Press.

Saunders, Anthony, and Berry Wilson (1999). "The Impact of Consolidation and Safety-Net Support on Canadian, US and UK Banks: 1893–1992," 23 *Journal of Banking and Finance* 537–71.

Sayek, Selin, and Fatma Taskin (2014). "Financial Crises: Lessons from History for Today," *Economic Policy* 447–93 (July 2014).

Scannell, Kara (2015). "Lunch with the FT: Jed Rakoff," *Financial Times* (Sept. 11, 2015), available at https://www.ft.com/content/c786a354-57cb-11e5-a28b-50226830d644.

Scannell, Kara, and Richard Milne (2017). "Who Was Convicted Because of the Global Financial Crisis?," *Financial Times* (Aug. 9, 2017), available at https://www.ft.com/content/de173cc6-7c79-11e7-ab01-a13271d1ee9c.

Scheer, Robert (1999). "Privacy Issue Bubbles Beneath the Photo Op," *Los Angeles Times* (Nov. 16, 1999), B9.

Schnabel, Isabel (2009). "The Role of Liquidity and Implicit Guarantees in the German Twin Crisis of 1931," 28 *Journal of International Money and Finance* 1–25.

Schnabel, Isabel (2004). "The German Twin Crisis of 1931," 64(3) *Journal of Economic History* 822–71.

Schneider, Howard, and Ann Saphir (2019). "Fed Cuts Interest Rates, Signals Holding Panel for Now," *Reuters* (Sept. 18, 2019), available at https://www.reuters.com/article/us-usa-fed/fed-cuts-interest-rates-signals-holding-pattern-for-now-idUSKBN1W32H7.

Schooner, Heidi Mandanis, and Michael W. Taylor (2010). *Global Bank Regulation: Principles and Policies*. Boston: Elsevier Academic Press.

Schreiber, Noam (2011). *The Escape Artists: How Obama's Team Fumbled the Recovery*. New York: Simon & Schuster.

Schroeder, Pete, and Chris Prentice (2020). "U.S. bank regulator gets tough on Wells Fargo: OCC fines eight former execs $58 million," *National Post* (Canada) (Jan. 25, 2020), available on Westlaw at 2020 WLNR 2409183.

Schuker, Stephen A. (1988). *American "Reparations" to Germany, 1919–33: Implications for the Third-World Debt Crisis*. Princeton: Princeton Studies in International Finance.

Schwarcz, Daniel, and Steven L. Schwarcz (2014). "Regulating Systemic Risk in Insurance," 81 *University of Chicago Law Review* 1569–640.

Schwarcz, Daniel, and David Zaring (2017). "Regulation by Threat: Dodd-Frank and the Nonbank Problem," 84 *University of Chicago Law Review* 1813–81.

Schwarcz, Steven L., Bruce A. Markell, and Lissa Lamkin Broome (2004). *Securitization, Structured Finance and Capital Markets*. Newark, NJ: LexisNexis.

Scism, Jack (1994). "NationsBank Chief Responsible for Bill," *Greensboro* (NC) *News and Record* (Nov. 14, 1994), 7, available on Westlaw at 1994 WLNR 4939717.

Scott, Kenneth E. (2010). "The Financial Crisis: Causes and Lessons," 22(3) *Journal of Applied Corporate Finance* 22–29 (Summer 2010).

Scott, Peter, and Lucy Newton (2007). "Jealous Monopolists? British Banks and Responses to the Macmillan Gap during the 1930s," 8(4) *Enterprise and Society* 881–919.

SEC (2011a). SEC Litigation Release No. 22008 (JPMorgan Securities), June 21, 2011, available at https://www.sec.gov/litigation/litreleases/2011/lr22008.htm.

SEC (2011b). SEC Press Release No. 2011-136, "SEC Charges Raymond James for Auction Rate Securities Sales Practices: Firm Agrees to Buy Back All Outstanding ARS from Eligible

Customers" (June 29, 2011), available at https://www.sec.gov/news/press/2011/2011-136. htm.

SEC (2011c). SEC Press Release No. 2011-214 (Citigroup), Oct. 19, 2011, available at https://www.sec.gov/news/press/2011/2011-214.htm.

SEC (2010a). SEC Litigation Release No. 21489 (Goldman Sachs), Apr. 16, 2010, available at https://www.sec.gov/litigation/litreleases/2010/lr21489.htm.

SEC (2010b). SEC Litigation Release No. 21592 (Goldman Sachs), July 15, 2010, available at https://www.sec.gov/litigation/litreleases/2010/lr21592.htm.

SEC (2010c). SEC Press Release No. 2010-197 (Angelo Mozilo), Oct. 15, 2010, available at https://www.sec.gov/news/press/2010/2010-197.htm.

SEC (2009a). SEC Press Release No. 2009-129 (Countrywide Executives), June 4, 2009, available at https://www.sec.gov/news/press/2009/2009-129.htm.

SEC (2009b). SEC Litigation Release No. 21068A (Countrywide Executives), June 4, 2009, available at https://sec.gov/litigation/litreleases/2009/lr21068a.htm.

SEC (2009c). "Excerpts of E-Mails from Angelo Mozilo," available at https://www.sec.gov/news/press/2009/2009-129-email.htm.

Seligman, Joel (2003). *The Transformation of Wall Street: A History of the Securities and Exchange Commission and Modern Corporate Finance.* Third edition. Boston: Northeastern University Press.

Sengupta, Rajdeep (2010). "Alt-A: The Forgotten Segment of the Mortgage Market," 92(1) *Review* 55–71 (Federal Reserve Bank of St. Louis, MO, Jan./Feb. 2010).

Sesit, Michael R. (1996). "Top Dogs: U.S. Financial Firms Seize Dominant Role in the World Markets—Tough Competition at Home Sharpens Their Skills, Willingness to Innovate," *Wall Street Journal*, Jan. 5, 1996, A1.

Shiller, Robert J. (2015). *Irrational Exuberance.* Revised and expanded third edition. Princeton: Princeton University Press.

Shin, Hyun Song (2012). "Global Banking Glut and Loan Risk Premium," 60(2) *IMF Economic Review* 155–92.

Shin, Hyun Song (2009). "Reflections on Northern Rock: The Bank Run That Heralded the Global Financial Crisis," 23(1) *Journal of Economic Perspectives* 101–19.

Shive, Sophie A., and Margaret M. Forster (2017). "The Revolving Door for Financial Regulators," 4 *Review of Finance* 1445–84.

Shubber, Kadhim (2017). "Small Businesses Hate Fintech Lenders More than Big Banks," *Financial Times* (Apr. 12, 2017), available at https://ftalphaville.ft.com/2017/04/12/2187388/small-businesses-hate-fintech-lenders-more-than-big-banks.

Siconolfi, Michael (1998). "Big Umbrella: Travelers and Citicorp Agree to Join Forces in $83 Billion Merger," *Wall Street Journal* (Apr. 7, 1998), at A1.

SIGTARP (2016). Office of the Special Inspector General for the Troubled Asset Relief Program, *Quarterly Report to Congress* (Oct. 26, 2016), available at https://www.sigtarp.gov/Quarterly%20Reports/October_26_2016_Report_To_Congress.pdf.

Silber, William L. (2012). *Volcker: The Triumph of Persistence.* New York: Bloomsbury Press.

Silber, William L. (2009). "Why Did FDR's Bank Holiday Succeed?," *Economic Policy Review* (Federal Reserve Bank of New York, July 2009), 19–30.

Simon, Ruth (2015). "Big Banks Cut Back on Small Business," *Wall Street Journal* (Nov. 27, 2015), A1.

Simon, Ruth, and Coulter Jones (2017). "Rural Business Owners Face Dwindling Pool of Lenders—Banks Abandon Small Towns to Focus on Booming Urban Markets," *Wall Street Journal* (Dec. 26, 2017), A1.

Sironi, Andrea (2018). "The evolution of banking regulation since the financial crisis: A critical assessment" (Baffi Carefin Centre Research Paper No. 2018-103, Nov. 2018), available at http://ssrn.com/abstract=3304672.

Sissoko, Carolyn (2017). "The Plight of Modern Markets: How Universal Banking Undermines Capital Markets," 46(1) *Economic Notes* 53–104.

Sissoko, Carolyn (2009). "The Legal Foundations of Financial Collapse" (Working paper, Oct. 6, 2009), available at http://ssrn.com/abstract=1525120.

Sitaraman, Ganesh (2018). "The Case for Glass-Steagall Act, the Depression-Era Law We Need Today," *The Guardian* (June 16, 2018), available at https://www.theguardian.com/comment-isfree/2018/jun/16/case-glass-steagall-act-ganesh-sitaraman.

Sitaraman, Ganesh (2017). *The Crisis of the Middle-Class Constitution: Why Inequality Threatens Our Republic*. New York: Alfred A. Knopf.

Skeel, David (2017). "What if a Clearinghouse Fails?" (Brookings Report, June 6, 2017), available at https://www.brookings.edu/research/what-if-a-clearinghouse-fails.

Skeel, David (2011). *The New Financial Deal: Understanding the Dodd-Frank Act and Its (Unintended) Consequences*. Hoboken, NJ: John Wiley & Sons.

Skeel, David A., Jr. (1999). "The Market Revolution in Bank and Insurance Firm Governance: Its Logic and Limits," 77 *Washington University Law Quarterly* 433–59.

Slipek, Edwin (2005). "The Tycoon: The Story of Thomas Fortune Ryan, and His Legacy in Richmond," *Style Weekly* (Jan. 19, 2005), available at http://www.styleweekly.com/rich-mond/the-tycoon/Content?oid=1378337.

Smith, Colby (2019). "Fed Averts Another Bout of Repo Turmoil Despite Cash Squeeze," *Financial Times* (Dec. 16, 2019), available at https://www.ft.com/content/6e7902e2-201d-11ea-92da-f0c92e957a96.

Smith, Colby, and Joe Rennison (2019). "Fed Plans to Double Repo Market Intervention to Avoid Cash Crunch," *Financial Times* (Dec. 12, 2019), available at https://www.ft.com/content/f9c20bde-1d23-11ea-97df-cc63de1d73f4.

Smith, Greg (2012). "Why I Am Leaving Goldman Sachs," *New York Times* (Mar. 14, 2012), A27.

Smith, Noah (2019). "The Fed Will Have to Risk More in the Next Recession," *Bloomberg* (Apr. 17, 2019), available at https://www.bloomberg.com/opinion/articles/2019-04-17/the-fed-will-have-to-risk-more-in-the-next-recession.

Smith, Randall (2009). *The Prince of Silicon Valley: Frank Quattrone and the Dot-Com Bubble*. New York: St. Martin's Press.

Smith, Rixley, and Norman Beasley (1939). *Carter Glass: A Biography*. New York: Longmans, Green & Co.

Smith, Robert (2019a). "Credit Default Swaps: How an $8tn Market Came to Blows over a Lower Case 'o'," *Financial Times* (Jan. 23, 2019), available at https://www.ft.com/content/3c4b7754-1eee-11e9-b2f7-97e4dbd3580d.

Smith, Robert (2019b). "Blackstone's €1.5bn Offer Shows Growing Threat to Wall St Banks," *Financial Times* (Mar. 12, 2019), available at https://www.ft.com/content/763a5ce4-43f3-11e9-b168-96a37d002cd3.

Smith, Robert (2018). "Banco Popular Bondholders Take Legal Fight to US," *Financial Times* (Apr. 5, 2018), available at https://www.ft.com/content/6370c752-37e6-11e8-8eee-e06bde01c544.

Smyth, Jamie (2019a). "Australian Bank Chiefs Could Face Criminal Charges After Report," *Financial Times* (Feb. 4, 2019), available at https://www.ft.com/content/148725a4-2837-11e9-a5ab-ff8ef2b976c7.

Smyth, Jamie (2019b). "Australia Banks Brace for Tighter Regulation and Weaker Economy," *Financial Times* (Nov. 10, 2019), available at https://www.ft.com/content/3670ce80-00fa-11ea-b7bc-f3fa4e77dd47.

Snowden, Kenneth A., Jr. (2010). "The Anatomy of a Residential Mortgage Crisis: A Look Back to the 1930s," in Lawrence E. Mitchell and Arthur E. Wilmarth, Jr., eds., *The Panic of 2008: Causes, Consequences and Implications for Reform* 51–74. Cheltenham, UK: Edward Elgar.

Son, Hugh (2019). "American Savers Lost an Estimated $500 billion Due to Low Interest Rates Since the Financial Crisis," *CNBC* (Apr. 10, 2019), available at https://www.cnbc.com/2019/04/10/americans-have-lost-500-billion-in-interest-after-financial-crisis.html.

Sorkin, Andrew Ross (2019). "An Enabler on Wall Street for WeWork," *New York Times* (Sept. 26, 2019), at B1.

Sorkin, Andrew Ross (2015). "Many on Wall Street Say It Remains Untamed," *New York Times* (May 19, 2015), B1.

Sorkin, Andrew Ross (2009). *Too Big to Fail: The Inside Story of How Wall Street and Washington Fought to Save the Financial System—and Themselves.* New York: Viking.

Sornette, Didier, and Peter Cauwels (2014). "1980–2008: The Illusion of the Perpetual Money Machine and What It Bodes for the Future," 2 *Risks* 103–31 (Apr. 2014).

Stabler, C. Norman (1927). "Mr. Coolidge Says, 'I Do Not Choose to Run in 1928'; Statement Puzzles Leaders, Who See Him Still in Race; Wall Street Hopes Mr. Coolidge Reconsiders," *New York Herald Tribune* (Aug. 3, 1927), at 1.

Stacey, Kiran (2019). "Fed Says It Will Hold Larger Balance Sheet in the Long Term," *Financial Times* (Feb. 22, 2019), available at https://www.ft.com/content/a9d58b5e-36bb-11e9-bd3a-8b2a211d90d5.

Stallings, Barbara (1987). *Banker to the Third World: U.S. Portfolio Investments in Latin America, 1900–1986.* Berkeley: University of California Press.

Steele, Graham (2019). "Emergency Guarantee Authority: Not Letting a Crisis Go to Waste," *CLS Blue Sky Blog* (May 15, 2019), available at http://clsbluesky.law.columbia.edu/2019/05/15/emergency-guarantee-authority-not-letting-a-crisis-go-to-waste.

Stein, Jeff (2018). "Many Lawmakers and Aides Who Crafted Financial Regulations After the 2008 Crisis Now Work for Wall Street," *Washington Post* (Sept. 7, 2018), available on Westlaw at 2018 WLNR 27450864.

Stephens, Philip (2018). "Populism Is the True Legacy of the Global Financial Crisis," *Financial Times* (Aug. 30, 2018), available at https://www.ft.com/content/687c0184-aaa6-11e8-94bd-cba20d67390c.

Sternberg, Joseph C. (2019). "Political Economics: Italy's 'Doom Loops,' Imagined and Real," *Wall Street Journal* (Jan. 4, 2019), A15.

Stevenson, Richard W. (1998). "Financial Services Heavyweights Try Do-It-Yourself Deregulation," *New York Times* (Apr. 7, 1998), A1.

Stewart, James B. (2015). "When the Buck Doesn't Stop," *New York Times* (Feb. 20, 2015), B1.

Stewart, James B. (2014). "Solvency, Lost in the Fog at the Fed," *New York Times* (Nov. 18, 2014), B1.

Stewart, James B., and Peter Eavis (2014). "Lehman Revisited: The Bailout That Never Was," *New York Times* (Sept. 30, 2014), A1.

Stiglitz, Joseph E. (2018). "Where Modern Macroeconomics Went Wrong," 34(1–2) *Oxford Review of Economic Policy* 70–106.

Stiglitz, Joseph E. (2003). *The Roaring Nineties: A New History of the World's Most Prosperous Decade.* New York: W. W. Norton & Co.

Stiroh, Kevin J. (2006a). "A Portfolio View of Banking with Interest and Noninterest Activities," 38(5) *Journal of Money, Credit, and Banking* 1351–61.

Stiroh, Kevin J. (2006b). "New Evidence on the Determinants of Bank Risk," 30 *Journal of Financial Services Research* 237–63.

Stiroh, Kevin J., and Adrienne Rumble (2006). "The Dark Side of Diversification: The Case of US Financial Holding Companies," 30 *Journal of Banking & Finance* 2131–61.

Stojanovich, Dusan, and Mark D. Vaughan (1998). "The Commercial Paper Market: Who's Minding the Shop?", *Regional Economist* (Federal Reserve Bank of St. Louis, April 1998), at 5–9.

Storbeck, Olaf (2018). "Deutsche Bank Disarray May Not End with Cryan's Ousting," *Financial Times* (Apr. 13, 2018), available at https://www.ft.com/content/618874ce-3f09-11e8-b7e0-52972418fec4.

Storbeck, Olaf, and Guy Chazan (2019). "Germany Steps Up Work on Potential Deutsche-Commerzbank Tie-up," *Financial Times* (Jan. 17, 2019), available at https://www.ft.com/content/7d145738-19b2-11e9-9e64-d150b3105d21.

Storbeck, Olaf, Stephen Morris, and Laura Noonan (2019). "The Day Deutsche Bank's Boss Decided on a Radical Solution," *Financial Times* (July 21, 2019), available at https://www.ft.com/content/2e7f3f22-a99d-11e9-984c-fac8325aaa04.

Story, Louise (2010). "House Advantage: A Secretive Banking Elite Rules Derivatives Trading," *New York Times* (Dec. 12, 2010), A1.

Stout, Lynn A. (2011). "Derivatives and the Legal Origin of the 2008 Credit Crisis," 1(1) *Harvard Business Law Review* 1–38.

Stout, Lynn A. (1999). "Why the Law Hates Speculators: Regulation and Private Ordering in the Market for OTC Derivatives," 48 *Duke Law Journal* 701–85.

Stowell, David P. (2010). *An Introduction to Investment Banks, Hedge Funds, and Private Equity: The New Paradigm*. Amsterdam: Elsevier.

Straumann, Tobias, Peter Kugler, and Florian Weber (2017). "How the German Crisis of 1931 Swept Across Europe: A Comparative View from Stockholm," 70(1) *Economic History Review* 224–47.

Stubbington, Tommy (2019). "Global Debt Surges to Highest Level in Peacetime," *Financial Times* (Sept. 24, 2019), available at https://www.ft.com/content/661f5c8a-dec9-11e9-9743-db5a370481bc.

Suarez, Sandra L., and Robin Kolodny (2010). "Paving the Road to 'Too Big to Fail': Business Interests and the Politics of Financial Deregulation in the U.S." (Working paper, 2010), available at http://ssrn.com/abstract=1642271.

Sullivan, Kristin (2006). "Corporate Accounting Scandals" (OLR Research Report No. 2006-R-0122, Feb. 16, 2006), available at https://www.cga.ct.gov/2006/rpt/2006-R-0122.htm.

Sullivan & Cromwell (2018). "Financial Services Regulatory Reform Legislation" (May 24, 2018), available at https://www.sullcrom.com/siteFiles/Publications/SC_Publication_Financial_Services_Regulatory_Reform_Legislation_05_24_18.pdf.

Summers, Lawrence H. (1998). "Treasury Deputy Secretary Lawrence H. Summers Testimony Before the Senate Committee on Agriculture, Nutrition, and Forestry on the CFTC Concept Release" (July 30, 1998), available on Westlaw at 1998 WL 459547.

Summers, Lawrence H., and Anna Stansbury (2019). "Whither Central Banking?," *Project Syndicate* (Aug. 23, 2019) (blog post), available at https://www.project-syndicate.org/commentary/central-bankers-in-jackson-hole-should-admit-impotence-by-lawrence-h-summers-and-anna-stansbury-2-2019-08.

Suskind, Ron (2011). *Confidence Men: Wall Street, Washington, and the Education of a President*. New York: HarperCollins.

Sutch, Richard C. (2015). "Financing the Great War: A Class Tax for the Wealthy, Liberty Bonds for All" (Berkeley Economic History Laboratory Working Paper No. 2015-69, Sept. 2015), available at http://ssrn.com/abstract=2665730.

Swagel, Phillip (2015). "Legal, Political, and Institutional Constraints on the Financial Crisis Policy Response," 29(2) *Journal of Economic Perspectives* 107–22.

Swagel, Phillip (2009). "The Financial Crisis: An Inside View," *Brookings Papers on Economic Activity* (Spring 2009), 1–78.

Sweet, Charles A., and Melissa R. H. Hall (2017). "Treasury Recommends Changes to Post-Financial Securitization Rules," *National Law Review* (Oct. 28, 2017), available at https://www.natlawreview.com/article/treasury-recommends-changes-to-post-financial-crisis-securitization-rules.

Sweet, Ken (2019). "Banks Announce Billions in Share Buybacks After Fed Approval," *Associated Press* (June 27, 2019), available at https://www.apnews.com/bdc1d0cf5f2546558860767d48f371e7.

Sy, Wilson (2019). "The Farce of Fake Regulation: Royal Commission Exposed Australia" (Investment Analytics Research working paper, Mar. 29, 2019), available at http://ssrn.com/abstract=3375629.

Symons, Edward L., Jr. (1983). "The Business of Banking in Historical Perspective," 51(5) *George Washington Law Review* 676–726.

Tadena, Nathalie (2012). "Financial Briefing Book: Former Sen. Gramm Retires from UBS Post," *Wall Street Journal* (Feb. 11, 2012), B13.

Taibbi, Matt (2014a). *The Divide: American Injustice in the Age of the Wealth Gap*. New York: Spiegel & Grau.

Taibbi, Matt (2014b). "The $9 Billion Witness: Meet JPMorgan Chase's Worst Nightmare," *Rolling Stone* (Nov. 6, 2014), available at https://www.rollingstone.com/politics/politics-news/the-9-billion-witness-meet-jpmorgan-chases-worst-nightmare-242414.

Tallman, Jon, and Ellis W. Moen (1990). "Lessons from the Panic of 1907," *Economic Review* (Fed. Res. Bank of Atlanta, May 1990), 2–13.

Tarullo, Daniel K. (2019). "Financial Regulation: Still Unsettled a Decade After the Crisis," 33(1) *Journal of Financial Perspectives* 61–80.

Tarullo, Daniel K. (2008). *Banking on Basel: The Future of International Financial Regulation*. Washington, DC: Peterson Institute for International Economics.

Taub, Jennifer (2014). *Other People's Houses: How Decades of Bailouts, Captive Regulators, and Toxic Bankers Made Home Mortgages a Thrilling Business*. New Haven: Yale University Press.

Tayan, Brian (2019). "The Wells Fargo Cross-Selling Scandal" (Stanford Closer Look Series, Jan. 8, 2019), available at http://ssrn.com/abstract=2879102.

Taylor, Arthur R. (1962). "Losses to the Public in the Insull Collapse, 1932–1946," 36(2) *Business History Review* 188–204.

Taylor, John B. (2018). "Alternatives for Reserve Balances and the Fed's Balance Sheet in the Future," in Michael Bordo, John Cochrane, and Amit Seru, eds., *The Structural Foundations of Monetary Policy* 16–27. Stanford, CA: Hoover Institution Press.

Taylor, John B. (2009). *Getting Off Track: How Government Actions and Interventions Caused, Prolonged, and Worsened the Financial Crisis*. Stanford, CA: Hoover Institution Press.

Tenbrunsel, Ann, and Jordan Thomas (2015). "The Street, the Bull and the Crisis: A Survey of the US and UK Financial Services Industry" (Notre Dame University, Mendoza College of Business, and Labaton Sucharow LLP, May 2015), available at https://www.secwhistleblow-eradvocate.com/pdf/Labaton-2015-Survey-report_12.pdf.

Tett, Gillian (2018a). "Have We Learnt the Lessons of the Financial Crisis?," *Financial Times* (Aug. 31, 2018), available at https://www.ft.com/content/a9b25e40-ac37-11e8-89a1-e5de165fa619.

Tett, Gillian (2018b). "Five Surprising Outcomes of the 2008 Financial Crisis," *Financial Times* (Sept. 6, 2018), available at https://www.ft.com/content/73e3ae2a-b1ca-11e8-8d14-6f049d06439c.

Tett, Gillian (2018c). "Banker Paul Volcker Sets a Challenge for the Next Generation," *Financial Times* (Oct. 25, 2018), available at https://www.ft.com/content/cf8641ac-d7ae-11e8-ab8e-6be0dcf18713.

Tett, Gillian (2009). *Fool's Gold: How the Bold Dream of a Small Tribe at J. P. Morgan Was Corrupted by Wall Street Greed and Unleashed a Catastrophe*. New York: Free Press.

Theodore, Sam, and André Fischer (2018). "Sovereign Risk Weights: The Big Missing Piece of Basel III" (Scope Ratings Commentary, June 21, 2018), available at https://www.globalbank-ingandfinance.com/sovereign-risk-weights-the-big-missing-piece-of-basel-iii.

Thomas, Hugh, and Ingo Walter (1991). "The Introduction of Universal Banking in Canada: An Event Study," 3(2) *Journal of International Financial Management and Accounting* 110–32.

Thomas, Jason (2009). "An Assessment of Fannie Mae and Freddie Mac's Contribution to the Financial Crisis of 2008" (Dec. 14, 2009), available at http://ssrn.com/abstract=1524940.

Thomas, R. G. (1933). "Concentration in Banking Control Through Interlocking Directorates as Typified by Chicago Banks," 6(1) *Journal of Business* 1–14.

Toniolo, Gianni (1995). "Italian Banking, 1919–1936," in Charles H. Feinstein, *Banking, Currency, and Finance in Europe Between the Wars* 296–314. Oxford: Clarendon Press.

Toniolo, Gianni, and Eugene N. White (2016). "The Evolution of the Financial Stability Mandate, from Its Origins to the Present Day," in Michael D. Bordo et al., eds., *Central Banks at a Crossroads: What Can We Learn From History?* 424–92. Cambridge: Cambridge University Press.

Tooze, Adam (2018). *Crashed: How a Decade of Financial Crises Changed the World.* New York: Viking.

Torres, Craig, and Lisa Lee (2019). "Wall Street Deaf to Federal Reserve Warnings on Leveraged Loans," *Bloomberg Law* (May 1, 2019).

Treanor, Jill (2016). "Why Don't Bankers Go to Jail? You Asked Google—Here's the Answer," *The Guardian* (Sept. 7, 2016), available at https://www.theguardian.com/commentisfree/2016/sep/07/why-not-imprison-bankers-google.

Treanor, Jill (2015). "Why Putting Bank Bosses Behind Bars Is Still Nigh on Impossible," *The Guardian* (May 23, 2015), available at https://www.theguardian.com/business/2015/may/23/putting-bankers-in-jail-nigh-on-impossible.

Trescott, Paul B. (1992). "The Failure of the Bank of United States, 1930: A Rejoinder to Anthony Patrick O'Brien," 24(3) *Journal of Money, Credit and Banking* 384–99.

Trigaux, Robert (1987a). "Revival of Continental's Woes Raises Doubts on New Powers," *American Banker* (Oct. 28, 1987), 1, available on Westlaw at 1987 WLNR 567921.

Trigaux, Robert (1987b). "Briefing: Playing on Glass-Steagall Fears," *American Banker* (Nov. 23, 1987), 12, available on Westlaw at 1987 WLNR 570383.

Tuch, Andrew F. (2017). "The Remaking of Wall Street," 7(2) *Harvard Business Law Review* 315–73.

Tucker, Paul (2018a). *Unelected Power: The Quest for Legitimacy in Central Banking and the Regulatory State.* Princeton: Princeton University Press.

Tucker, Paul (2018b). "Resolution Policy and Resolvability at the Center of Financial Stability Regimes?" (Feb. 1, 2018), available at https://www.bis.org/fsi/p180209_tucker.pdf.

Turner, Adair (2018). "After the Crisis, the Banks Are Safer but Debt Is a Danger," *Financial Times* (Sept. 11, 2018), available at https://www.ft.com/content/9f481d3c-b4de-11e8-a1d8-15c2dd1280ff.

Turner, Adair (2010). "What Do Banks Do? Why Do Credit Booms and Busts Occur and What Can Public Policy Do About it?," in *The Future of Finance: The LSE Report* 5–86. London: London School of Economics and Political Science.

Turner, John D. (2014). *Banking in Crisis: The Rise and Fall of British Banking Stability, 1800 to the Present.* Cambridge: Cambridge University Press.

Tuttle, Beecher (2019). "The Investment Bankers Who Won and Lost in 2018" (Jan. 7, 2019), available at https://news.efinancialcareers.com/us-en/331345/investment-bankers-won-lost-2018.

Uchitelle, Louis (2010). "Volcker, Loud and Clear: Pushing for Stronger Reforms, and Regretting Decades of Silence," *New York Times* (July 11, 2010), §BU, 1.

UNCTAD (2010). United Nations Conference on Trade and Development, *Corporate Governance in the Wake of the Financial Crisis: Selected international views* (2010), available at https://unctad.org/en/Docs/diaeed20102_en.pdf.

Upham, Cyril B., and Edwin Lamke (1934). *Closed and Distressed Banks: A Study in Public Administration*. Washington, DC: Brookings Institution.

U.S. House of Representatives (2000). "Commodity Futures Modernization Act of 2000," Report No. 106-711(III) of the Committee on Commerce, United States House of Representatives, 106th Congress, 2d Session (Sept. 6, 2000), available on Westlaw at 2000 WL 1279131 (Leg. Hist.).

U.S. House of Representatives (1933). "Banking Act of 1933," Report No. 150 of the Committee of Banking and Currency, United States House of Representatives, 73d Congress, 1st Session (May 19, 1933).

U.S. House of Representatives (1913). Report No. 1593 of the Committee Appointed Pursuant to House Resolutions 429 and 504 to Investigate the Concentration of Control of Money and Credit, 62d Congress, 3d Session (Feb. 28, 1913).

U.S. Senate (2010). "The Restoring American Financial Stability Act of 2010," Report No. 111-176 of the Committee of Banking, Housing, and Urban Affairs, United States Senate, 111th Congress, 2d Session (Apr. 30, 2010), available on Westlaw at 2010 WL 11236001.

U.S. Senate (2000). "Commodity Futures Modernization Act of 2000," Report No. 106-390 of the Committee on Agriculture, Nutrition, and Forestry, United States Senate, 106th Congress, 2d Session (Aug. 25, 2000), available on Westlaw at 2000 WL 1358765 (Leg. Hist.).

U.S. Senate (1999). "Financial Services Modernization Act of 1999," Report No. 106-44 of the Committee on Banking, Housing, and Urban Affairs, United States Senate to Accompany S. 900, 106th Congress, 1st Session (Apr. 28, 1999), available on Westlaw at 1999 WL 266803 (Leg. Hist.).

U.S. Senate (1934). "Stock Exchange Practices," Report No. 1455 of the Committee on Banking and Currency Pursuant to S. Res. 84, S. Res. 56, and S. Res. 97, United States Senate, 73d Congress, 2d Session (June).

U.S. Senate (1933a). "Stock Exchange Practices," Hearings on S. Res. 84 and S. Res. 239 Before a Subcommittee of the Committee on Banking and Currency, United States Senate, 72d Congress, 2d Session.

U.S. Senate (1933b). "Stock Exchange Practices," Hearings on S. Res. 84 and S. Res. 56 Before the Committee on Banking and Currency, United States Senate, 73d Congress, 1st Session.

U.S. Senate (1933c). "Operation of the National and Federal Reserve Banking Systems," Report No. 77 of the Committee on Banking and Currency, United States Senate, 73d Congress, 1st Session (May).

U.S. Senate (1932a). "Operation of the National and Federal Reserve Banking Systems," Hearings on S. 4115 Before the Committee on Banking and Currency, United States Senate, 72d Congress, 1st Session (Mar.).

U.S. Senate (1932b). "Operation of the National and Federal Reserve Banking Systems," Report No. 584 of the Committee on Banking and Currency, United States Senate, 72d Congress, 1st Session (Apr. 22, 1932).

U.S. Senate (1931–32). "Sale of Foreign Bonds or Securities in the United States," Hearings Before the Committee on Finance Pursuant to S. Res. 19, United States Senate, 72d Congress, 1st Session.

U.S. Senate (1931). "Operation of the National and Federal Reserve Banking Systems," Hearings Before a Subcommittee of the Committee on Banking and Currency Pursuant to S. Res. 71, United States Senate, 71st Congress, 3d Session.

U.S. Treasury (2016). *Opportunities and Challenges in Online Marketplace Lending* (U.S. Dept. of the Treasury, May 10 2016), available at https://www.treasury.gov/connect/blog/documents/opportunities_and_challenges_in_online_marketplace_lending_white_paper.pdf.

U.S. Treasury (1991). *Modernizing the Financial System: Recommendations for Safer, More Competitive Banks* (U.S. Dept. of the Treasury, Feb. 1991), available at http://heinonline.org/

HOL/Page?handle=hein.tera/modfisy0001&div=2&start_page=i&collection=tera&set_as_cursor=3&men_tab=srchresults.

U.S. Treasury (1926). *Annual Report of the Secretary of the Treasury on the State of the Finances for the Fiscal Year Ended June 30, 1926 with Appendices* (1927), available at https://fraser.stlouisfed.org/scribd/?item_id=5572&filepath=/files/docs/publications/treasar/AR_TREASURY_1926.pdf.

Valukas, Anton R. (2010). "Report of Anton R. Valukas, Examiner" (Mar. 11, 2010), *In re Lehman Brothers Holdings Inc.* (U.S. Bankruptcy Court for the Southern District of N.Y.) (No. 18-13555), Volume 1, available at http://web.stanford.edu/~jbulow/lehmandocs/VOLUME%201.pdf.

Vandevelde, Mark (2018). "How the Biggest Private Equity Firms Became the New Banks," *Financial Times* (Sept. 10, 2018), available at https://www.ft.com/content/ec43db70-ba8e-11e8-94b2-17176fbf93f5.

Vandevelde, Mark, et al. (2018). "The Story of a House: How Private Equity Swooped In After the Subprime Crisis," *Financial Times* (Sept. 5, 2018), available at https://ig.ft.com/story-of-a-house.

Van Hoof, Kat (2019). "North American Regulators Lead the Way in Fine Enforcement," *The Banker* (Mar. 28, 2019), available at https: //www.thebanker.com/Banker-Data/Banker-Database/North-American-regulators-lead-the-way-in-fine-enforcement.fo.

van Riet, Ad (2018). "Modern Financial Repression in the Euro Area Crisis: Making High Public Debt Sustainable?" (SUERF Policy Note No. 24, May 2018), available at http://ssrn.com/abstract=3123740.

Vanthemsche, Guy (1991). "State, Banks and Industry in Belgium and The Netherlands, 1919–1939," in Harold James et al., eds., *The Role of Banks in the Interwar Economy* 104–21. New York: Cambridge University Press.

Verner, Emil (2019). "Private Debt Booms and the Real Economy: Do the Benefits Outweigh the Costs?" (Working paper, Aug. 2019), available at http://ssrn.com/abstract=3441608.

Vernon, J. R. (1994). "World War II Fiscal Policies and the End of the Great Depression," 54(4) *Journal of Economic History* 850–68.

Véron, Nicholas (2018). "EU Financial Services Policy Since 2007: Crisis, Responses, and Prospects" (Peterson Institute for International Economics Working Paper 18-6, June 2018), available at http://ssrn.com/abstract=3210866.

Vickers, John (2018). "Safer But Not Safe Enough" (Keynote address at the 20th International Conference of Banking Supervisors, Nov. 29, 2018), available at https://www.bis.org/bcbs/events/icbs20/vickers.pdf.

Viscusi, Gregory (2018). "How Yellow Vest Protests Swelled into Risk for Macron," *Bloomberg* (Dec. 13, 2018), available at https://www.bloomberg.com/news/articles/2018-12-13/how-yellow-vest-protests-swelled-into-risk-for-macron-quicktake.

Voth, Hans-Joachim (2003). "With a Bang, not a Whimper: Pricking Germany's 'Stock Market Bubble' in 1927 and the Slide into Depression," 63(1) *Journal of Economic History* 65–99.

Wack, Kevin (2016a). "How Wells Fargo's Aggressive Sales Culture Took Root," *American Banker* (Dec. 19, 2016), available on Westlaw at 2016 WLNR 38826115.

Wack, Kevin (2016b). "Wells Execs Stuck to the Script as Evidence of Sales Abuses Mounted," *American Banker* (Dec. 20, 2016), available on Westlaw at 2016 WLNR 38942870.

Wack, Kevin (2012). "Weill Puts Glass-Steagall Back on Washington's Agenda," *American Banker* (July 26, 2012), available on Westlaw at 2012 WLNR 15612140.

Wagner, Wolf (2010). "Diversification at Financial Institutions and Systemic Crises," 19 *Journal of Financial Intermediation* 373–86.

Wagster, John D. (2012). "Canadian Bank Capital During the Great Depression of the 1930s: A Comparison to the Basel III Requirements," 13(2) *Journal of Banking Regulation* 89–98.

Wahl, Melissa (1999). "Bank One Chief Bows Out Under Pressure: Earnings, Stock Troubles Catch Up with CEO McCoy," *Chicago Tribune* (Dec. 22, 1999), available at http://articles. chicagotribune.com/1999-12-22/news/9912220113_1_verne-istock-bank-one-first-usa,

Wallison, Peter J. (2015). *Hidden in Plain Sight: What Really Caused the World's Worst Financial Crisis—and Why It Could Happen Again.* New York: Encounter Books.

Wallison, Peter J. (2009). "Did the 'Repeal' of Glass-Steagall Have Any Role in the Financial Crisis? Not Guilty; Not Even Close" (Networks Institute Financial Institutions Public Policy Brief 2009-PB-09), available at http://ssrn.com/abstract=1507803.

Wall Street Journal (2019). "Global Stack" (graph), *Wall Street Journal* (Jan. 2, 2019), R1.

Warren, Elizabeth (2017). Press Release: "Senators Warren, McCain, Cantwell and King Introduce 21st Century Glass-Steagall Act" (Apr. 6, 2017), available at https://www. warren.senate.gov/newsroom/press-releases/senators-warren-mccain-cantwell-and-king-introduce-21st-century-glass-steagall-act.

Washington Post (1933). "C. E. Mitchell Arrested on '29 Tax Count," *Washington Post* (Mar. 22, 1933), 1.

Wayne, Leslie (1991). "Bank Barrier Resists Foes: Glass-Steagall Walls May Just Be Replaced," *New York Times* (Sept. 18, 1991), D1.

Webb, Merryn Somerset (2019). "Negative Rates Are Tarnishing Central Bankers' Halos," *Financial Times* (Oct. 4, 2019), available at https://www.ft.com/content/07a5262c-e607-11e9-9743-db5a370481bc.

Webb, Merryn Somerset (2018a). "Payback Time for QE Looms—and It Will Be Expensive," *Financial Times* (Apr. 20, 2018), available at https://www.ft.com/content/8e131f28-431c-11e8-803a-295c97e6fd0b.

Webb, Merryn Somerset (2018b). "A Post-Crisis Cure That Has Stored Up Economic Pain," *Financial Times* (Sept. 14, 2018), available at https://www.ft.com/content/de61140c-b68b-11e8-a1d8-15c2dd1280ff.

Weber, Alexander (2019). "Deutsche Bank CEO Sewing Promises Discipline in Pursuing Growth," *Bloomberg Law* (Feb. 6, 2019).

Weber, Alexander, and Nikos Chrysoloras (2019). "A Decade After Crisis, Europe's Taxpayers Keep Bailing Out Banks," *Bloomberg Law* (Dec. 18, 2019).

Weber, Alexander (2017). "International Banking: EU Bank-Disposal Chief Keonig Renominated amid Popular Lawsuits," 109 *Bloomberg BNA's Banking Report* 1606 (Dec. 4, 2017).

Weber, Fritz (1995). "From Imperial to Regional Banking: The Austrian Banking System, 1918–1938," in Charles H. Feinstein, ed., *Banking, Currency, and Finance in Europe Between the Wars* 337–57. Oxford: Clarendon Press.

Weber, Fritz (1991). "Universal Banking in Interwar Central Europe," in Harold James et al., eds., *The Role of Banks in the Interwar Economy.* New York: Cambridge University Press.

Weinberger, Evan (2018). "Senate Confirms Kraninger to Lead Consumer Finance Bureau," *Bloomberg Law* (Dec. 6, 2018).

Weinberger, Evan, and Lydia Beyoud (2019). "CFPB Moves to Weaken Obama-Era Payday Lending Standards (2)," *Bloomberg Law* (Feb. 6, 2019).

Weise, Charles L. (2012). "Political Pressures on Monetary Policy During the US Great Inflation," 4(2) *American Economic Journal: Macroeconomics* 33–64.

Wells, Harwell (2010). "No Man Can Be Worth $1,000,000 a Year: The Fight over Executive Compensation in 1930s America," 44(2) *University of Richmond Law Review* 689–769.

Welsch, Andrew (2018). "Last-Minute Bid to save Fiduciary Duty Rule Fails," *Employee Benefit News* (May 4, 2018), available on Westlaw at 2018 WLNR 13629240.

Werner, Morris R. (1933). *Little Napoleons and Dummy Directors: Being the Narrative of the Bank of United States.* New York: Harper & Brothers.

Wessel, David (2009). *In Fed We Trust: Ben Bernanke's War on the Great Panic.* New York: Crown Business.

Westerfield, Ray B. (1933). "The Banking Act of 1933," 41(6) *Journal of Political Economy* 721–49.

White, Alan, Carolina Reid, Lei Ding, and Roberto G. Quercia (2011). "The Impact of State Anti-Predatory Lending Laws on the Foreclosure Crisis," 21(2) *Cornell Journal of Law and Public Policy* 247–90.

White, Eugene N. (2009). "Lessons from the Great American Real Estate Boom and Bust of the 1920s" (National Bureau of Economic Research Working Paper 15573), available at www.nber.org/papers/w15573.

White, Eugene N. (1990). "The Stock Market Boom and Crash of 1929 Revisited," 4(2) *Journal of Economic Perspectives* 67–83 (Spring).

White, Eugene N. (1986). "Before the Glass-Steagall Act: An analysis of the investment banking activities of national banks," 23(1) *Explorations in Economic History* 33–55.

White, Eugene N. (1983). *The Regulation and Reform of the American Banking System, 1900–1929.* Princeton: Princeton University Press.

White, Lawrence J. (2010). "The Gramm-Leach-Bliley Act: A Bridge Too Far? Or Not Far Enough?," 43(4) *Suffolk University Law Review* 937–56.

White, William (2018a). "Start Preparing for the Next Financial Crisis Now," *Financial Times* (Feb. 18, 2018), available at https://www.ft.com/content/e1dc1286-0ccb-11e8-bacb-2958fde95e5e.

White, William (2018b). "Beware the Bad Financial Moon Rising," *Japan Times* (Oct. 21, 2018), available at https://www.japantimes.co.jp/opinion/2018/10/21/commentary/world-commentary/beware-bad-financial-moon-rising/#.XNwmWMhKiUk.

Whitehouse, Mark (2018). "Maybe Big Banks Are Giving Back Too Much," *Bloomberg* (June 18, 2018), available at https://www.bloomberg.com/opinion/articles/2018-06-18/maybe-big-u-s-banks-are-giving-back-too-much.

Whitehouse, Mark (2017). "We're Still Not Ready for the Next Banking Crisis," *Bloomberg* (Aug. 14, 2017).

Wicker, Elmus (1996). *The Banking Panics of the Great Depression.* New York: Cambridge University Press.

Wicker, Elmus (2000). *Banking Panics of the Gilded Age.* New York: Cambridge University Press.

Wiggers, Tyler, and Adam B. Ashcraft (2012). "Defaults and Losses on Commercial Real Estate Bonds During the Great Depression Era" (Federal Reserve Bank of N.Y. Staff Report No. 544), available at http://ssrn.com/abstract=2002078.

Wigglesworth, Robin (2019). "Repo Risks Still Hang over Upbeat End to Year in markets," *Financial Times* (Dec. 18, 2019), available at https://www.ft.com/content/9b99ab96-20bd-11ea-b8a1-584213ee7b2b.

Wigglesworth, Robin, Adam Samson, and Michael Hunter (2018). "US Stocks Heading for Worst Month Since the Financial Crisis," *Financial Times* (Oct. 26, 2018), available at https://www.ft.com/content/3fe7d8b2-d907-11e8-a854-33d6f82e62f8.

Wigmore, Barrie A. (1987). "Was the Bank Holiday of 1933 Caused by a Run on the Dollar?", 47(3) *Journal of Economic History* 739–55.

Wigmore, Barrie A. (1985). *The Crash and Its Aftermath: A History of Securities Markets in the United States, 1929–1933.* Westport, CT: Greenwood Press.

Williamson, Stephen (2017). "Quantitative Easing: How Well Does This Tool Work?," *Regional Economist* (Federal Reserve Bank of St. Louis, Third Quarter 2017), 8–14, available at https://www.stlouisfed.org/~/media/publications/regional-economist/2017/third_quarter_2017/qe_lead.pdf.

Willis, H. Parker, and John M. Chapman (1934). *The Banking Situation: American Post-War Problems and Developments.* New York: Columbia University Press.

Willis, Lauren E. (2019). "CFPB Head Misguided in Reliance on Consumer Education," *The Hill* (Sept. 7, 2019), available at https://thehill.com/opinion/finance/460384-cpfb-head-misguided-in-reliance-on-consumer-education.

Wilmarth, Arthur E., Jr. (2018). "Raising SIFI Threshold to $250B Ignores Lessons of Past Crises," *American Banker* (Feb. 7, 2018), available on Westlaw at 2018 WLNR 3935409.

Wilmarth, Arthur E., Jr. (2017). "The Road to Repeal of the Glass-Steagall Act," 17(4) *Wake Forest Journal of Business and Intellectual Property Law* 441–548, available at http://ssrn.com/abstract=3026287.

Wilmarth, Arthur E., Jr. (2016). "Prelude to Glass-Steagall: Abusive Securities Practices by National City Bank and Chase National Bank During the 'Roaring Twenties,'" 90(5) *Tulane Law Review* 1285–329, available at http://ssrn.com/abstract=2828339.

Wilmarth, Arthur E., Jr. (2015a). "A Two-Tiered System of Regulation Is Needed to Preserve the Viability of Community Banks and Reduce the Risks of Megabanks," 2015(1) *Michigan State Law Review* 249–370, available at http://ssrn.com/abstract=2518690.

Wilmarth, Arthur E., Jr. (2015b). "The Financial Industry's Plan for Resolving Failed Megabanks Will Ensure Future Bailouts for Wall Street," 50(1) *Georgia Law Review* 43–87, available at http://ssrn.com/abstract=2648572.

Wilmarth, Arthur E., Jr. (2014). "Citigroup: A Case Study in Managerial and Regulatory Failures," 47(1) *Indiana Law Review* 69–137, available at http://ssrn.com/abstract=2370131.

Wilmarth, Arthur E., Jr. (2013). "Turning a Blind Eye: Why Washington Keeps Giving in to Wall Street," 81(4) *University of Cincinnati Law Review* 1283–446, available at http://ssrn.com/abstract=2327872.

Wilmarth, Arthur E., Jr. (2012a). "The Financial Services Industry's Misguided Quest to Undermine the Consumer Financial Protection Bureau," 31(2) *Review of Banking and Financial Law* 881–956, available at http://ssrn.com/abstract=1982149.

Wilmarth, Arthur E., Jr. (2012b). "Narrow Banking: An Overdue Reform That Could Solve the Too-Big-to-Fail Problem and Align U.S. and U.K. Regulation of Financial Conglomerates," 31 *Banking and Financial Services Policy Report* No. 3, 1–24 (Part 1) (Mar. 2012), available at http://ssrn.com/abstract=2050544.

Wilmarth, Arthur E., Jr. (2011a). "The Dodd-Frank Act: A Flawed and Inadequate Response to the Too-Big-to-Fail Problem," 89(3) *Oregon Law Review* 951–1057, available at http://ssrn.com/abstract=1719126.

Wilmarth, Arthur E., Jr. (2011b). "The Dodd-Frank Act's Expansion of State Authority to Protect Consumers of Financial Services," 36(4) *Journal of Corporation Law* 893–954 (2011), available at http://ssrn.com/abstract=1891970.

Wilmarth, Arthur E., Jr. (2010). "*Cuomo v. Clearing House*: The Supreme Court Responds to the Subprime Financial Crisis and Delivers a Major Victory for the Dual Banking System and Consumer Protection" (George Washington University Legal Studies Research Paper No. 479, 2010), available at http://ssrn.com/abstract=1499216.

Wilmarth, Arthur E., Jr. (2009). "The Dark Side of Universal Banking: Financial Conglomerates and the Origins of the Subprime Financial Crisis," 41(4) *Connecticut Law Review* 963–1050, available at http://ssrn.com/abstract=1403973.

Wilmarth, Arthur E., Jr. (2008). "Subprime Crisis Confirms Wisdom of Separating Banking and Commerce," 27(5) *Banking & Financial Services Policy Report* (May) 1–18, available at http://ssrn.com/abstract=1263453.

Wilmarth, Arthur E., Jr. (2007). "Wal-Mart and the Separation of Banking and Commerce," 39(4) *Connecticut Law Review* 1539–622, available at http://ssrn.com/abstract=984103.

Wilmarth, Arthur E., Jr. (2006). "Conflicts of Interest and Corporate Governance Failures at Universal Banks During the Stock Market Boom of the 1990s: The Cases of Enron and WorldCom" (George Washington Univ. Law School Legal Studies Research Paper No. 234, Nov. 20, 2006), available at http://ssrn.com/abstract=952486.

Wilmarth, Arthur E., Jr. (2005). "Did Universal Banks Play a Significant Role in the U.S. Economy's Boom-and-Bust Cycle of 1921–33? A Preliminary Assessment," 4 *Current Developments in Monetary and Financial Law* 559–645 (International Monetary Fund), available at http://ssrn.com/abstract=838267.

Wilmarth, Arthur E., Jr. (2004a). "Does Financial Liberalization Increase the Likelihood of a Systemic Banking Crisis? Evidence from the Past Three Decades and the Great Depression," in Benton E. Gup, ed., *Too Big to Fail: Policies and Practices in Government Bailouts* 77–106. Westport, CT: Praeger Publishers. (A working paper version of this chapter is available at http://ssrn.com/abstract=547383.)

Wilmarth, Arthur E., Jr. (2004b). "The OCC's Preemption Rules Exceed the Agency's Authority and Present a Serious Risk to the Dual Banking System and Consumer Protection," 23 *Annual Review of Banking and Financial Law* 225–364, available at http://ssrn.com/abstract=577863.

Wilmarth, Arthur E., Jr. (2002). "The Transformation of the U.S. Financial Services Industry, 1975–2000: Competition, Consolidation, and Increased Risks," 2002(2) *University of Illinois Law Review* 215–476, available at http://ssrn.com/abstract=315345.

Wilmarth, Arthur E., Jr. (1995). "Too Good to Be True? The Unfulfilled Promises Behind Big Bank Mergers," 2(1) *Stanford Journal of Law, Business and Finance* 1–88.

Wilmarth, Arthur E., Jr. (1992). "Too Big to Fail, Too Few to Serve? The Potential Risks of Nationwide Banks," 77(3) *Iowa Law Review* 957–1081.

Wilmarth, Arthur E., Jr. (1990). "The Expansion of State Bank Powers, the Federal Response, and the Case for Preserving the Dual Banking System," 58(6) *Fordham Law Review* 1133–256.

Wilson, Edmund (1936). "Sunshine Charley," in *Travels in Two Democracies* 55–63. New York: Harcourt Brace.

Winkler, Max (1933). *Foreign Bonds: An Autopsy*. Philadelphia: Roland Swain Co.

Wise, Peter (2018). "Portugal and Italy Tell Contrasting Economic Tales After Crisis," *Financial Times* (Oct. 19, 2018), available at https://www.ft.com/content/d62b03c8-d220-11e8-a9f2-7574db66bcd5.

Witkowski, Rachel (2018). "FDIC Seeks Industry Help in Effort to Revive De Novo Banks," *American Banker* (Dec. 7, 2018), available on Westlaw at 2018 WLNR 37848270.

Wolf, Martin (2019a). "Why the World Economy Feels So Fragile," *Financial Times* (Jan. 8, 2019), available at https://www.ft.com/content/eb14cacc-1298-11e9-a581-4ff78404524e.

Wolf, Martin (2019b). "Why Further Financial Crises Are Inevitable," *Financial Times* (Mar. 19, 2019), available at https://www.ft.com/content/d9d94f4a-4884-11e9-bbc9-6917dce3dc62.

Wolf, Martin (2018). "Why So Little Has Changed Since the Financial Crash," *Financial Times* (Sept. 3, 2018), available at https://www.ft.com/content/c85b9792-aad1-11e8-94bd-cba20d67390c.

Wolf, Martin (2014). *The Shifts and the Shocks: What We've Learned—and Have Still to Learn—from the Financial Crisis*. New York: Penguin Press.

Wolf, Nikolaus (2010). "Europe's Great Depression: Coordination Failure After the First World War," 26(3) *Oxford Review of Economic Policy* 339–69.

Wolff, Edward N. (2017). "Household Wealth Trends in the United States, 1962 to 2016: Has Middle Class Wealth Recovered?" (National Bureau of Economic Research Working Paper 24085, Nov. 2017), available at http://www.nber.org/paper/w24085.

Woll, Cornelia (2014). *The Power of Inaction: Bank Bailouts in Comparison*. Ithaca: Cornell University Press.

Wooten, Casey (2019). "Lots of Headlines, Limited Legislation from House Financial Services This Year," *National Journal Daily* (Jan. 3, 2019), available on Westlaw at 2019 WLNR 214783.

Xiao, Kairong (2018). "Monetary Transmission Through Shadow Banks" (Apr. 20, 2018), available at http://ssrn.com/abstract=3166114.

Zandi, Mark (2008). *Financial Shock: A 360 Degree Look at the Subprime Mortgage Implosion, and How to Avoid the Next Financial Crisis.* Upper Saddle River, NJ: FT Press.

Zandi, Mark, and Cristian deRitis (2013). *The Road to Reform* (Moody's Analytics, Sept. 2013), available at https://www.economy.com/mark-zandi/documents/2013-09-12-Road-to-Reform.pdf.

Zingales, Luigi (2015). "Does Finance Benefit Society?" 70(4) *Journal of Finance* 1327–63.

Zingales, Luigi (2012). "Why I Was Won Over by Glass-Steagall," *Financial Times* (June 10, 2012), available at http://www.ft.com/intl/cms/s/0/cb3e52be-b08d-11e1-8b36-00144feabdc0.html.

Index

For the benefit of digital users, indexed terms that span two pages (e.g., 52–53) may, on occasion, appear on only one of those pages.